Lecture Notes in Computer Science   **12495**

Advanced Research in Computing and Software Science
Subline of Lecture Notes in Computer Science

More information about this subseries at http://www.springer.com/series/7409

Xujin Chen · Nikolai Gravin ·
Martin Hoefer · Ruta Mehta (Eds.)

Web and Internet Economics

16th International Conference, WINE 2020
Beijing, China, December 7–11, 2020
Proceedings

 Springer

Editors
Xujin Chen (iD)
Academy of Mathematics
and Systems Science
Chinese Academy of Sciences
Beijing, China

Martin Hoefer (iD)
Goethe University Frankfurt
Frankfurt am Main, Germany

Nikolai Gravin
Shanghai University of Finance
and Economics
Shanghai, China

Ruta Mehta
University of Illinois at Urbana-Champaign
Urbana, IL, USA

ISSN 0302-9743 ISSN 1611-3349 (electronic)
Lecture Notes in Computer Science
ISBN 978-3-030-64945-6 ISBN 978-3-030-64946-3 (eBook)
https://doi.org/10.1007/978-3-030-64946-3

LNCS Sublibrary: SL3 – Information Systems and Applications, incl. Internet/Web, and HCI

This Springer imprint is published by the registered company Springer Nature Switzerland AG
The registered company address is: Gewerbestrasse 11, 6330 Cham, Switzerland

Preface

This volume contains all regular papers and abstracts presented at the 16th Conference on Web and Internet Economics (WINE 2020). WINE 2020 was held as an Internet event during December 7–11, 2020, organized at Peking University, Beijing, China.

Over the last 16 years, the WINE conference series has become a leading interdisciplinary forum for the exchange of ideas and scientific progress across continents on incentives and computation arising in diverse areas, such as theoretical computer science, artificial intelligence, economics, and applied mathematics. WINE 2020 built on the success of the previous editions of WINE (named Workshop on Internet and Network Economics until 2013) which were held annually from 2005 to 2019.

The Program Committee was composed of 45 active researchers from the field. They reviewed 136 submissions and decided to accept 42 papers. Each paper had at least three reviews, with additional reviews solicited as needed. We are very grateful to all members of the Program Committee for their insightful reviews and discussions. We thank EasyChair for providing a virtual platform to organize the review process. We also thank Springer for providing the proceedings and offering support for Best Paper and Best Student Paper Awards.

In addition to the contributed talks, the program included four invited talks by leading researchers in the field: Eric Budish (University of Chicago, USA), Jose Correa (Universidad de Chile, Chile), Yiling Chen (Harvard University, USA), and Constantinos Daskalakis (MIT, USA).

Our special thanks go to the general chair Xiaotie Deng and the local organization team, as well as the poster chair Umang Bhaskar.

October 2020

Xujin Chen
Nikolai Gravin
Martin Hoefer
Ruta Mehta

Organization

General Chair

Xiaotie Deng   Peking University, China

Program Committee Chairs

Xujin Chen   Chinese Academy of Sciences, China
Nikolai Gravin   Shanghai University of Finance and Economics, China
Martin Hoefer   Goethe University Frankfurt, Germany
Ruta Mehta   University of Illinois at Urbana-Champaign, USA

Steering Committee

Xiaotie Deng   Peking University, China
Paul Goldberg   Oxford University, UK
Christos Papadimitriou   Columbia University, USA
Paul Spirakis   The University of Liverpool, UK
Rakesh Vohra   University of Pennsylvania, USA
Andrew Yao   Tsinghua University, China
Yinyu Ye   Stanford University, USA

Program Committee

Bo An   Nanyang Technological University, Singapore
Siddharth Barman   Indian Institute of Science, India
Xiaohui Bei   Nanyang Technological University, Singapore
Simina Branzei   Purdue University, USA
Yang Cai   Yale University, USA
Shuchi Chawla   University of Wisconsin-Madison, USA
Jing Chen   Stony Brook University, USA
Xi Chen   Columbia University, USA
Yukun Cheng   Suzhou University of Science and Technology, China
Jose Correa   Universidad de Chile, Chile
Edith Elkind   University of Oxford, UK
Dimitris Fotakis   National Technical University of Athens, Greece
Vasilis Gkatzelis   Drexel University, USA
Kira Goldner   Columbia University, USA
Tobias Harks   University of Augsburg, Germany
Zhiyi Huang   The University of Hong Kong, China
Thomas Kesselheim   University of Bonn, Germany
Max Klimm   Humboldt University Berlin, Germany

Yuqing Kong   Peking University, China
Tie-Yan Liu   Microsoft Research Asia, China
Irene Lo   Stanford University, USA
Brendan Lucier   Microsoft Research New England, USA
Luca Moscardelli   University of Chieti-Pescara, Italy
Sigal Oren   Ben-Gurion University, Israel
Georgios Piliouras   Singapore University of Technology and Design,
                             Singapore
Qi Qi   Hong Kong University of Science and Technology,
                             China
Daniela Saban   Stanford University, USA
Rahul Savani   The University of Liverpool, UK
Marco Scarsini   LUISS Rome, Italy
Alkmini Sgouritsa   The University of Liverpool, UK
Xiaoming Sun   Chinese Academy of Sciences, China
Vasilis Syrgkanis   Microsoft Research New England, USA
Sam Taggart   Oberlin College, USA
Christos Tzamos   University of Wisconsin-Madison, USA
Adrian Vetta   McGill University, Canada
Carmine Ventre   King's College London, UK
Zihe Wang   Shanghai University of Finance and Economics, China
Matt Weinberg   Princeton University, USA
Lirong Xia   Rensselaer Polytechnic Institute, USA
Jialin Zhang   Chinese Academy of Sciences, China
Song Zuo   Google Research, China

Additional Reviewers

Andreas Abels   Yurong Chen
Mete Şeref Ahunbay   Zhihuai Chen
Michele Aleandri   Yun Kuen Cheung
Maxwell Allman   Je-Ok Choi
Siddhartha Banerjee   Avi Cohen
Umang Bhaskar   Vincent Conitzer
Davide Bilò   Andrés Cristi
Vittorio Bilò   Bart de Keijzer
Georgios Birmpas   Argyrios Deligkas
Peter Biro   Yuan Deng
Shant Boodaghians   Jack Dippel
Alexander Braun   Shahar Dobzinski
William Brown   Valerio Dose
Johannes Brustle   Alon Eden
Linda Cai   Guillaume Escamocher
Rahul Chandan   Meryem Essaidi
Wei Chen   Angelo Fanelli

Yiding Feng
Diodato Ferraioli
Matheus V. X. Ferreira
Aris Filos-Ratsikas
Rupert Freeman
Rafael Frongillo
Sai Ganesh Nagarajan
Evangelia Gergatsouli
Daniele Giachini
Yiannis Giannakopoulos
Sreedurga Gogulapati
Lukas Graf
Hadi Hosseini
Neng Huang
Jan Hazła
Zhihao Jiang
Alkis Kalavasis
Anthimos-Vardis Kandiros
Jamie Kang
Artem Kaznatcheev
Suleyman Kerimov
Pieter Kleer
Vasilis Kontonis
Anand Krishna
Stefanos Leonardos
Bo Li
Minming Li
Weian Li
Thanasis Lianeas
Shengxin Liu
Tian Liu
Tracy Liu
Yang Liu
Zhengyang Liu
Xinhang Lu
Thodoris Lykouris
Weidong Ma
Yishay Mansour
Simon Mauras
Alejandro Melo Ponce
Kaleigh Mentzer
Divyarthi Mohan
Faidra Monachou
Gianpiero Monaco
Barnabé Monnot
Ilan Morgenstern

Daniel Moroz
Rolf H. Möhring
Vishnu Narayan
Ndiamé Ndiaye
Eric Neyman
Kim Thang Nguyen
Rad Niazadeh
Argyris Oikonomou
Dario Paccagnan
Panagiotis Patsilinakos
Dominik Peters
Chara Podimata
Luciano Pomatto
Emmanouil Pountourakis
Bary Pradelski
Li Qian
Goran Radanovic
Nidhi Rathi
Bhaskar Ray Chaudhury
Rebecca Reiffenhäuser
Rojin Rezvan
Fedor Sandomirskiy
Alvaro Sandroni
Daniel Schmand
Marc Schroder
Steffen Schuldenzucker
Ariel Schvartzman
Erel Segal-Halevi
Ella Segev
Xiaohan Shan
Xinkai Shu
Sujoy Sikdar
Ryann Sim
Sahil Singla
Stratis Skoulakis
Warut Suksompong
Ranjani Sundaram
Mashbat Suzuki
Zhihao Tang
Yifeng Teng
Clayton Thomas
Artem Tsikiridis
Marc Uetz
Rohit Vaish
Grigoris Velegkas
Xavier Venel

Contents

Matching

Almost Envy-Free Repeated Matching in Two-Sided Markets. 3
  Sreenivas Gollapudi, Kostas Kollias, and Benjamin Plaut

Dynamic Weighted Matching with Heterogeneous Arrival
and Departure Rates 17
  Natalie Collina, Nicole Immorlica, Kevin Leyton-Brown,
  Brendan Lucier, and Neil Newman

A Fine-Grained View on Stable Many-To-One Matching Problems
with Lower and Upper Quotas 31
  Niclas Boehmer and Klaus Heeger

The Ad Types Problem 45
  Riccardo Colini-Baldeschi, Julián Mestre, Okke Schrijvers,
  and Christopher A. Wilkens

Multidimensional Stable Roommates with Master List 59
  Robert Bredereck, Klaus Heeger, Dušan Knop, and Rolf Niedermeier

Markets

Optimal Nash Equilibria for Bandwidth Allocation 77
  Benjamin Plaut

Counteracting Inequality in Markets via Convex Pricing 89
  Ashish Goel and Benjamin Plaut

Markets for Efficient Public Good Allocation with Social Distancing. 102
  Devansh Jalota, Marco Pavone, Qi Qi, and Yinyu Ye

Mechanism Design and Pricing

Two Strongly Truthful Mechanisms for Three Heterogeneous Agents
Answering One Question 119
  Grant Schoenebeck and Fang-Yi Yu

A Generic Truthful Mechanism for Combinatorial Auctions 133
  Hanrui Zhang

The Price of Anarchy of Two-Buyer Sequential Multiunit Auctions.   147
  Mete Şeref Ahunbay and Adrian Vetta

Revenue-Optimal Deterministic Auctions for Multiple Buyers with Ordinal
Preferences over Fixed-Price Items   162
  Will Ma

Robust Revenue Maximization Under Minimal Statistical Information   177
  *Yiannis Giannakopoulos, Diogo Poças,
  and Alexandros Tsigonias-Dimitriadis*

Revenue Monotonicity Under Misspecified Bidders.   191
  Makis Arsenis, Odysseas Drosis, and Robert Kleinberg

On the Power and Limits of Dynamic Pricing in Combinatorial Markets   206
  Ben Berger, Alon Eden, and Michal Feldman

Competitively Pricing Parking in a Tree.   220
  Max Bender, Jacob Gilbert, Aditya Krishnan, and Kirk Pruhs

Routing, Scheduling, Load Balancing

The Price of Anarchy for Instantaneous Dynamic Equilibria.   237
  Lukas Graf and Tobias Harks

Data-Driven Models of Selfish Routing: Why Price of Anarchy Does
Depend on Network Topology   252
  *Francisco Benita, Vittorio Bilò, Barnabé Monnot, Georgios Piliouras,
  and Cosimo Vinci*

Competition Alleviates Present Bias in Task Completion   266
  Aditya Saraf, Anna R. Karlin, and Jamie Morgenstern

Improving Approximate Pure Nash Equilibria in Congestion Games   280
  Vipin Ravindran Vijayalakshmi and Alexander Skopalik

The Curse of Rationality in Sequential Scheduling Games   295
  Cong Chen and Yinfeng Xu

Sequential Solutions in Machine Scheduling Games   309
  *Cong Chen, Paul Giessler, Akaki Mamageishvili, Matúš Mihalák,
  and Paolo Penna*

Nash Social Welfare in Selfish and Online Load Balancing   323
  Vittorio Bilò, Gianpiero Monaco, Luca Moscardelli, and Cosimo Vinci

Fairness

Simultaneously Achieving Ex-ante and Ex-post Fairness 341
Haris Aziz

Optimal Bounds on the Price of Fairness for Indivisible Goods. 356
Siddharth Barman, Umang Bhaskar, and Nisarg Shah

Fair Division with Binary Valuations: One Rule to Rule Them All 370
*Daniel Halpern, Ariel D. Procaccia, Alexandros Psomas,
and Nisarg Shah*

Consensus Halving for Sets of Items 384
*Paul W. Goldberg, Alexandros Hollender, Ayumi Igarashi,
Pasin Manurangsi, and Warut Suksompong*

Learning

Learning Strong Substitutes Demand via Queries 401
Paul W. Goldberg, Edwin Lock, and Francisco Marmolejo-Cossío

A Cardinal Comparison of Experts 416
Itay Kavaler and Rann Smorodinsky

Minimum-Regret Contracts for Principal-Expert Problems 430
Caspar Oesterheld and Vincent Conitzer

Bayesian Repeated Zero-Sum Games with Persistent State,
with Application to Security Games 444
Vincent Conitzer, Yuan Deng, and Shaddin Dughmi

Abstracts

Large Random Matching Markets with Localized Preference Structures Can
Exhibit Large Cores 461
Ross Rheingans-Yoo

The Influence of One Strategic Agent on the Core of Stable Matchings 463
Ron Kupfer

How Many Citizens Have Already Voted? The Effect of (Interim) Turnout
Rate Polls in Elections. 464
Akaki Mamageishvili and Oriol Tejada

Online Hypergraph Matching with Delays 465
Marco Pavone, Amin Saberi, Maximilian Schiffer, and Matthew Tsao

Market Equilibrium in Multi-tier Supply Chain Networks. 467
   Tao Jiang, Young-San Lin, and Thành Nguyen

Decision Scoring Rules 468
   Caspar Oesterheld and Vincent Conitzer

Bayesian Learning in Dynamic Nonatomic Routing Games 469
   Emilien Macault, Marco Scarsini, and Tristan Tomala

Privacy Rights and Data Security: GDPR and Personal
Data Driven Markets. 470
   T. Tony Ke and K. Sudhir

Closing the Gap: Mitigating Bias in Online Résumé-Filtering. 471
   Jad Salem and Swati Gupta

Catastrophe by Design in Population Games: Destabilizing Wasteful
Locked-In Technologies. 473
   Stefanos Leonardos, Iosif Sakos, Costas Courcoubetis,
   and Georgios Piliouras

Assortment Planning for Two-Sided Sequential Matching Markets 475
   Itai Ashlagi, Anilesh K. Krishnaswamy, Rahul Makhijani,
   Daniela Saban, and Kirankumar Shiragur

Author Index 477

Matching

Almost Envy-Free Repeated Matching in Two-Sided Markets

Sreenivas Gollapudi[1], Kostas Kollias[1], and Benjamin Plaut[2(✉)]

[1] Google Research, Mountain View, USA
sgollapu@google.com, kostaskollias@google.com
[2] Stanford University, Stanford, USA
bplaut@stanford.edu

Abstract. A two-sided market consists of two sets of agents, each of whom have preferences over the other (Airbnb, Upwork, Lyft, Uber, etc.). We propose and analyze a repeated matching problem, where some set of matches occur on each time step, and our goal is to ensure fairness with respect to the cumulative allocations over an infinite time horizon. Our main result is a polynomial-time algorithm for additive, symmetric $(v_i(j) = v_j(i))$, and binary $(v_i(j) \in \{a, 1\})$ valuations that both (1) guarantees *envy-freeness up to a single match* (EF1) and (2) selects a maximum weight matching on each time step. Thus for this class of valuations, fairness can be achieved without sacrificing economic efficiency. This result holds even for *dynamic valuations*, i.e., valuations that change over time. Although symmetry is a strong assumption, we show that this result cannot be extended to asymmetric binary valuations: (1) and (2) together are impossible even when valuations do not change over time, and for dynamic valuations, even (1) alone is impossible. To our knowledge, this is the first analysis of envy-freeness in a repeated matching setting.

1 Introduction

Recent years have seen a dramatic increase in electronic marketplaces, both in quantity and scale. Many of these are *two-sided* markets, meaning that the market makes matches between two sets of agents (homeowners and guests for Airbnb, employers and workers for Upwork, drivers and riders for Lyft and Uber, etc.), each of whom has preferences over the other. This is in contrast to traditional resource allocation (cake cutting, Fisher markets, auctions, etc.) where only one side of the market has preferences. Although envy-freeness and relaxations thereof have been studied extensively in one-sided resource allocation (this research area is typically referred to as "fair division"), we are aware of just one paper considering envy-freeness for two-sided preferences [22].[1]

There are two primary motivations for our work. The first is to simply study fair division for two-sided preferences. The second is that in some ways, two-sided electronic marketplaces like Airbnb, Upwork, Lyft, and Uber are actually

---

[1] Although [22] is conceptually similar, it is in different setting of *recommendation algorithms*, and so it is technically quite different.

© Springer Nature Switzerland AG 2020
X. Chen et al. (Eds.): WINE 2020, LNCS 12495, pp. 3–16, 2020.
https://doi.org/10.1007/978-3-030-64946-3_1

in a better position to impose fairness than one-sided marketplaces. The reason is that most one-sided markets are *decentralized*, in the sense that a seller offers different goods at different prices, buyers peruse the wares at their leisure, and make individual decisions about what they wish to purchase. On the contrary, most two-sided markets operate by way of matches mediated by a centralized platform, giving the platform the ability to affect the outcomes of the system. Indeed, on Lyft and Uber, an automated central authority has almost complete control over the matches, giving the algorithm tremendous power over the outcomes for each individual agent. The power dynamic between the platform and the participating agents makes it even more important to ensure that the matching algorithms are fair to each agent.

1.1 Repeated Matching

A crucial element of marketplaces is *repeated* matching. Agents do not receive all of their matches at once; typically, an agent can only process a few matches at a time (a driver can only fit so many riders in the car, a worker can only handle so many contracts at once). Only after an agent completes some of her current matches can she be given new matches. This motivates a model where on each time step, an irrevocable matching decision must be made, and we expect fairness with respect to the cumulative matching at each time step. We consider an infinite time horizon and a finite set of agents, so we must allow the same pair of agents to be matched multiple times; thus each agent's cumulative set of matches will be a multiset.

A vital aspect of any repeated setting is that preferences can change. In some cases, preferences may change in direct response to the matches an agent receives: if a driver is matched with a rider who wishes to go to location X, once that ride is completed, the driver will prefer riders whose pickups are close to X. In other cases, agents may desire variety among matches: Airbnb guests may not wish to vacation in the same area every time. Additionally, preferences may simply drift over time. We refer to valuations that change over time as *dynamic* valuations.

1.2 Fairness Notions

For one-sided fair division with indivisible items, full envy-freeness is impossible: for two agents and a single item, one must receive the item and the other agent will be envious. The same issue applies in our setting: if every agent on one side of the market is interested in the same agent on the other side, no algorithm can guarantee envy-freeness.

One solution is to consider relaxations of envy-freeness, such as *envy-freeness up to one good* (EF1). An outcome is EF1 if whenever agent i envies agent j, there exists a good in j's bundle such that i would not envy j after removing that good.[2] This property has been studied widely for one-sided preferences, but

---

[2] Note that this good is not actually removed: this is simply a thought experiment used in the definition of EF1.

to our knowledge has not been considered for two-sided markets. We can define EF1 equivalently for two-sided preferences: simply replace "there exists a good" with "there exists a match", etc.

The less obvious question is how to adapt EF1 to the repeated setting. In this paper, we assume time is divided into discrete steps, where on each step, some set of matches occur. Each match consists of two agents, one from each side of the market. We would like the cumulative matching after each time step to be EF1. We will also assume that each side of the market has the same number of agents (if not, add "dummy" agents to the smaller side).

We consider two different versions of this model. In the first version, each time step consists of just a single match, so we are effectively requiring the cumulative matching to be EF1 at every point in time. We call this *EF1-over-time.*

However, asking for fairness at every point in time may be too strong. Furthermore, in most real-world applications, matches would be happening in parallel anyway. Conversely, EF1-over-time poses no restrictions on how many matches agents receive. In real life, agents often have similar "capacities" (e.g., most cars have a similar number of seats) and thus should arguably receive matches at similar rates. These concerns motivate a second version of the model, where on each time step, each agent is matched exactly once (i.e., we select a perfect matching). Thus each time step represents a "round" of matches (which may happen in parallel). We still require that the cumulative matching is EF1 after time step, and we call this *EF1-over-rounds.*

1.3   Our Results

We use $v_i(j)$ to denote agent i's value for agent j, and assume valuations are additive. We say that valuations are *symmetric* if $v_i(j) = v_j(i)$ for all agents i, j, and *binary* if there exists $a \in [0, 1)$ such that $v_i(j) \in \{a, 1\}$ for all i, j.[3] It is worth noting that for symmetric valuations, negative values for $v_i(j)$ are subsumed in the following sense: if the algorithm ever says to match agents i and j where $v_i(j) < 0$, we simply ignore this and never make the match, which gives both agents value 0 for the "match".[4]

We now describe our results. Due to space constraints, all proofs are deferred to the full version of the paper [16].

EF1-Over-Rounds for Dynamic Symmetric, and Binary Valuations. Our main result is that for dynamic, symmetric, and binary valuations, we give an algorithm which both satisfies EF1-over-rounds, and selects a maximum weight matching on each time step (Theorem 3.1) This holds even when valuations are dynamic.[5] This

---

[3] If we wish to add dummy agents to one side of the market, the most natural case would be $a = 0$, in order to express that dummy agents have no value.

[4] In order for this argument to be complete when considering EF1-over-rounds, this "match" must still count as part of the perfect matching for that time step.

[5] We allow valuations to change arbitrarily between time steps. Furthermore, our algorithm does not need to know how valuations will change in response to a given match.

shows that for this class of valuations, fairness can be achieved without sacrificing economic efficiency. Our algorithm runs in time $O(n^{2.5})$ per time step.

The class of symmetric and binary valuations is somewhat restricted, but is important to keep several things in mind. First, it is often hard to elicit more complex valuations. Agents can easily answer binary questions such as "Would you be happy with this match?", but may not be able to provide a real number value for potential matches. Second, the best interpretation of our result (in our opinion) is that agents' preferences are not truly binary, but that our algorithm is guaranteeing EF1 with respect to a *binary projection of the preferences*. That is, ask each agent to label each possible match as "good" or "bad", and guarantee EF1 with respect to those preferences. This interpretation is reinforced by the fact that the cumulative matchings computed by our algorithm will be EF1 uniformly across all possible values a, and agents can even have different values of a. See Sect. 3.1 for a discussion of this.

Symmetry, however, is a significant assumption on the agents' preferences. There are reasons to believe real-world preferences are largely symmetric: a rider is likely to prefer a driver closer to her, and vice versa. However, a natural question is whether this assumption is necessary.

Counterexamples. Our next set of results shows that the symmetry assumption is in fact necessary. First, we show that for dynamic binary valuations, EF1-over-rounds alone is impossible (Theorem 4.1). Second, for non-dynamic (i.e., valuations do not change over time) binary valuations, it is impossible to satisfy EF1-over-rounds while guaranteeing a maximum weight matching for each time step (Theorem 4.2). These impossibility results suggest that EF1-over-rounds may be too much to ask for in the setting of two-sided repeated matching. However, our counterexamples do not rule out the possibility of EF1-over-time, even for general additive valuations. We leave this as our primary open question.

Beyond Symmetric Valuations. Despite this negative result, we show that it is possible to relax the symmetry assumption, at least in the context of EF1-over-time. We show that for $\{0, 1\}$ binary valuations[6] with an assumption that we call "only symmetric cycles", EF1-over-time can be guaranteed. We formally define "only symmetric cycles" in the full version of the paper [16], but this assumption is strictly weaker than full symmetry of valuations.

Beyond Binary Valuations. In a similar vein, we show that when one side of the market has two agents, the binary assumption can also be relaxed. Specifically, we give an algorithm which is EF1-over-time for any additive valuations.

1.4   Related Work

There are two primary bodies of related work: (one-sided) fair division, and matching markets.

---

[6] For this result, we assume that $v_i(j) \in \{0, 1\}$ for each agent, as opposed $v_i(j) \in \{a, 1\}$ for any $a \in [0, 1)$.

Fair Division. Fair division has a long history. In fact, the Bible documents Abraham and Lot's use of the cut-and-choose protocol to fairly divide land. The formal study of fair division was started by [27] in 1948, and envy-freeness was proposed in 1958 [15] and further developed by [13]. A full overview of the fair division literature is outside the scope of this paper (we refer the interested reader to [5,21]), and we discuss only the work most relevant to our own.

There are two main differences between our work and that of traditional fair division. First, we study two-sided preferences instead of one-sided preferences. Second, we study a repeated setting, where we must make an irrevocable decision on each time step; most fair division research considers a "one-shot" model where all the goods are allocated at once.

We briefly overview some key results in the one-sided one-shot model of fair division for indivisible items[7]. The EF1 property was proposed for this model by [6]. EF1 allocations always exist, and can be computed in polynomial time, even for general combinatorial valuations [20][8]. This sweeping positive result for the one-sided one-shot model lies in stark contrast to our negative results for the two-sided repeated model. It was later shown that for additive valuations, maximizing the product of valuations yields an allocation that is both EF1 and Pareto optimal [8].

Envy-Freeness up to Any Good (EFX). The same paper suggested a new fairness notion that is strictly stronger than EF1, which they called EFX[9]. The first formal results regarding EFX allocations were given by [23]. A major breakthrough recently proved the existence of EFX allocations for additive valuations and three agents [9], but despite ongoing effort, the question of existence remains unsolved for more than three agents (or more complex valuations). This is perhaps the most significant open problem in the fair division of indivisible items.

In many contexts (especially for additive valuations), it is common to modify the requirement to be that whenever i envies j, removing any good which i values positively from j's bundle is sufficient to eliminate the envy [8].[10] Under the latter definition, for $\{0,1\}$ binary valuations, EF1 and EFX coincide. This is because the only positively valued goods are the maximum value goods. In this sense, our positive results for $\{0,1\}$ binary valuations immediately extend to EFX as well.

Repeated Fair Division. There are a smattering of recent works studying envy-freeness for one-sided preferences in a repeated (i.e., not one-shot) setting; see [1]

---

[7] *Indivisible* items, such as cars, must each go entirely to a single agent. In contrast, *divisible* items, such as a cakes, can be split between multiple players. Fair division studies both of these settings, but the indivisible case is more relevant to our work.

[8] The algorithm of [20] was originally developed with a different property in mind.

[9] An allocation is *envy-free up to any good* (EFX) if whenever i envies j, removing *any* good from j's bundle eliminates the envy.

[10] The reason this is less common when considering non-additive valuations is that for general combinatorial valuations, it is less clear what "values positively" means.

for a short survey. One example is [2], which focuses on minimizing the maximum envy (i.e., the maximum difference between an agent's value for her own bundle and her value for another agent's bundle) at each time step. Despite the growing interest in repeated one-sided fair allocation, the literature on the analogous two-sided problem remains sparse.

Matching Markets. The other relevant field is (bipartite) matching markets[11]. In a *one-to-one* matching market, each agent receives exactly one match. Perhaps the most famous result for one-to-one matching is that of Gale and Shapley, whose algorithm finds a stable matching [14]. More relevant to us is the model of *many-to-many matching markets*, where each agent can receive multiple matches; stability has often been the primary criterion in this model as well [11,19,25,26]. There is also some work on stability in dynamic matching markets [10,18].

In contrast, fairness in many-to-many matching has received considerably less attention. In fact, Gale and Shapley's algorithm for one-to-one matching is known to compute the stable matching which is the worst possible for one side of the market, and best possible for the other.

Fair Ride-Hailing. There is a growing body of work surrounding the ethics of crowdsourced two-sided markets, especially ride-hailing (e.g., Lyft and Uber) [3,4,7,12,17]. We are aware of just two works studying fairness for two-sided markets from an algorithmic perspective: [29] and [28], both of which focus on ride-hailing. The former paper considers ride-*sharing*, where multiple passengers are matched with a single driver. The authors focus on fairness with respect to the savings achieved by each passenger. This paper is primarily theoretical, like ours, but is specific to ride-hailing, unlike ours. The latter paper studies a fairness notion based on the idea that "spread over time, all drivers should receive benefits proportional to the amount of time they are active in the platform". The model considered in this paper is more general than just ride-hailing, however the paper is primarily experimental, and the experiments are in the ride-hailing setting.

Consequently, we are not aware of any prior work studying algorithms with provable fairness guarantees for repeated two-sided matching markets. In this way, our work can be viewed as simultaneously building on the fair division literature (by considering two-sided preferences) and building on the matching market literature (by studying envy-freeness for repeated two-sided markets).

The paper proceeds as follows. Section 2 describes the formal model. Section 3 presents our main result: an algorithm for symmetric and binary valuations such that (1) the sequence of cumulative matchings is EF1-over-rounds, (2) a maximum weight matching is chosen for each time step, and (3) this holds even for dynamic valuations (Theorem 3.1). Section 4 presents our counterexamples: Theorem 3.1 cannot be extended to non-symmetric binary valuations. Specifically, without symmetry, (1) and (3) together and (1) and (2) together are both

---

[11] For a broad overview of this topic, see [24].

impossible (Theorems 4.1 and 4.2, respectively). The rest of the results (and all of the proofs) can be found in the full version of the paper [16].

2 Model

Let N and M be two sets of agents. We assume that $|N| = |M| = n$; if this is not the case, we can add "dummy" agents (i.e., agents i such that $v_i(j) = v_j(i) = 0$ for all j) to the smaller side of the market until both sides have the same number of agents. We will typically use odd numbers for the elements of N and even numbers for the elements of M, i.e., $N = \{1, 3, \ldots, 2n-1\}$ and $M = \{2, 4, \ldots, 2n\}$. A *matching* X assigns a multiset of agents in N to each agent in M, and a multiset of agents in M to each agent in N. For each $i \in N \cup M$, we will use X_i to denote agent i's *bundle*, i.e., the multiset of agents she is matched to. Throughout the paper, we will use standard set notation for operations on the multisets X_i. For example, $X_i \cup \{j\}$ increments the *multiplicity* of j in X_i, i.e., the number of times j occurs in X_i. In order for X to be a valid matching, the multiplicity of j in X_i must be equal to the multiplicity of i in X_j for each $i \in N$, $j \in M$.

Each agent i also has a *valuation function* v_i, which assigns a real number to each possible bundle she might receive. We will use **v** to denote the *valuation profile* which assigns valuation v_i to agent i. We say that v_i is *additive* if for any bundle X_i,

$$v_i(X) = \sum_{j \in X} v_i(\{j\})$$

Since X is a multiset, the sum over $j \in X$ includes each j a number of times equal to its multiplicity. For example, if $X = \{j, j\}$ and $v_i(\{j\}) = 1$, then $v_i(X) = 2$. With slight abuse of notation, we will write $v_i(\{j\}) = v_i(j)$. We say that a valuation v_i is *binary* if there exists $a \in [0, 1)$ such that $v_i(j) \in \{a, 1\}$ for all $i, j \in N$ or $i, j \in M$. We say that a valuation profile **v** is *symmetric* if $v_i(j) = v_j(i)$ for all $i \in N, j \in M$.

We say that i *envies* j under X if $v_i(X_i) < v_i(X_j)$. We only consider envy within the same side of the market: it is unclear what it would mean for some $i \in N$ to envy $j \in M$. We can express this by setting $v_i(j) = 0$ for $i, j \in N$ or $i, j \in M$.

Definition 2.1. *A matching X is* envy-free up to one match *(EF1) if whenever i envies j, there exists $k \in X_j$ such that $v_i(X_i) \geq v_i(X_j \setminus \{k\})$.*

Note that the set subtraction $X_j \setminus \{k\}$ decreases the multiplicity of k by 1; it does not remove k altogether. Also, we will say that X is EF1 with respect to N (resp., M) if the above holds for every pair $i, j \in N$ (resp., $i, j \in M$).

One important tool we will use is the *envy graph*:

Definition 2.2. *The* envy graph *of a matching X is a graph with a vertex for each agent, and a directed edge from agent i to agent j if i envies j under X.*

We will especially be interested in cycles in the envy graph, and will use the terms "cycle in the envy graph" and "envy cycle" interchangeably.

2.1   Repeated Matching

We consider a repeated setting, where on each time step t, some set of matches occur. Each "match" (alternatively, *pairing*) consists of one agent in N and one agent in M.

Let x^t denote the set of matches which occur at time t. Each agent will receive at most one match per time step. If agent i is matched to an agent j at time t, let $x_i^t = \{j\}$; otherwise, let $x_i^t = \emptyset$. For an infinite sequence $x^1, x^2, x^3 \ldots$, let X^t denote the cumulative matching up to and including time t. Formally, for each $i \in N \cup M$,

$$X_i^t = \begin{cases} \emptyset & \text{if } t = 0 \\ X_i^{t-1} \cup x_i^t & \text{if } t > 0 \end{cases}$$

In words, X_i^t is the set of matches i has received up to and including time t.

Our main result holds even when valuations are allowed to vary over time. Specifically, a *dynamic* valuation v_i will have a value $v_i^t(j)$ for each agent j on each time step t (as before, we write $v_i^t(j) = 0$ for $i, j \in N$ or $i, j \in M$). A profile of dynamic valuations is symmetric if $v_i^t(j) = v_j^t(i)$ for all i, j, t. For a pair of agents i, j (with $i = j$ allowed), $v_i(X_j^t)$ is given by

$$v_i(X_j^t) = \sum_{t'=1}^{t} v_i^{t'}(x_j^{t'})$$

where $v_i^{t'}(\emptyset) = 0$. That is, i's value for a bundle X_j is as if i had received exactly those matches at exactly those times. It is important for this definition to include both $i = j$ and $i \neq j$, so that we can evaluate envy between agents.

We make no assumptions on how valuations change between time steps: they can even change adversarially, since our algorithm will not use any knowledge about future valuations when making matching decisions.

We consider two definitions of EF1 in the repeated matching setting. In both cases, we require the cumulative matching at the end of each time step to be EF1. The difference is that for EF1-over-time, each time step consists a single match, and for EF1-over-rounds, each time step consists of a "round" of matches where all agents receive exactly one match (i.e., a perfect matching between N and M).

Definition 2.3. *The sequence* $\mathcal{X} = X^0, X^1, X^2 \ldots$ *is* EF1-over-time *if for all* $t \geq 0$, *each* x^t *contains a single match, and* X^t *is EF1.*

Definition 2.4. *The sequence* $\mathcal{X} = X^0, X^1, X^2 \ldots$ *is* EF1-over-rounds *if for all* $t \geq 0$, x^t *is a perfect matching, and* X^t *is EF1.*

Formally, these notions are incomparable: EF1-over-time has a stronger fairness requirement (the cumulative matching should be EF1 after every match, not just after every round of matches), but does not require agents to receive the same number of matches. However, EF1-over-rounds does imply EF2-over-time (where we may remove two matches in order to eliminate the envy): expand each "round" into n time steps, each containing one match, in an arbitrary order. We know that at the end of each round of n time steps, the cumulative matching is EF1. Within each round, each agent only gains one additional match, and we can always remove that match to return to an EF1 state.

Our goal will be to show the existence of (and efficiently compute) a sequence $x^1, x^2, x^3 \ldots$ such that the induced sequence $\mathcal{X}$ is EF1-over-time and/or EF1-over-rounds. For brevity, if an algorithm is guaranteed to produce a sequence $\mathcal{X}$ that is EF1-over-time (resp., EF1-over-rounds), we simply say that the algorithm is EF1-over-time (resp., EF1-over-rounds).

3   EF1 for Dynamic, Symmetric, and Binary Valuations

In this section, we consider binary and symmetric valuations that may change over time. For this class of valuations, we give a polynomial-time algorithm that produces a sequence which is EF1-over-rounds, and chooses a maximum weight matching for each time step. This leads to the following theorem:

Theorem 3.1. *For dynamic, binary, and symmetric valuations, Algorithm 1 is EF1-over-rounds, and the matching x^t for each time step t is a maximum weight matching (with respect to the valuations on that time step). Furthermore, the algorithm runs in time $O(n^{2.5})$ per time step.*

3.1   Algorithm Setup

Before we discuss the algorithm, we need the following definition, which will imply EF1 (Lemma 3.2):

Definition 3.1. *We say that a pair of agents (i, j) is c-envy-bounded if $v_i(X_j) - v_i(X_i) \leq c$, and we say a matching X is c-envy-bounded if every pair (i, j) is c-envy-bounded.*

A quick note: recall that our goal is to choose a sequence of pairings $x^1, x^2 \ldots$, and that these pairings fully specify the sequence of cumulative matchings $\mathcal{X}$. Consequently, when giving pseudocode for our algorithms (throughout the paper), we do not explicitly update $\mathcal{X}$: we assume that whenever some x^t is changed, every $X^{t'}$ for $t' \geq t$ is automatically updated. We feel that this leads to more concise and intuitive pseudocode.

Algorithm 1 is very simple. For each time step t, we initialize x^t to be an arbitrary maximum weight matching for the current valuations, and make changes to this matching until we are satisfied. Specifically, while there exist agents i, j such that (i, j) is not $(1-a)$-envy-bounded in the cumulative matching, we swap their matches in x^t. When no such pair of agents exists, we exit the while loop and confirm the matches. Throughout all of our algorithms, we will use the function MakeMatch to indicate that we are confirming the matches in x^t.

It is important to note that the algorithm is *not* going back in time and changing pairings already made: once a pairing is confirmed with MakeMatch, it

Algorithm 1. An EF1-over-rounds algorithm for agents with dynamic, symmetric, and binary valuations.

1: **function** EF1MATCHING($N, M, \mathbf{v}$)
2:     **for each** $t \in \mathbb{N}_{\geq 0}$ **do**
3:         $\{x^t\} \leftarrow$ MaxWeightMatching($N, M, \mathbf{v}$)
4:         **while** $\exists$ agents i, j s.t. $v_i(X_j^t) - v_i(X_i^t) > 1 - a$ **do**
5:             $(x_i^t, x_j^t) \leftarrow (x_j^t, x_i^t)$
6:         MakeMatch(x^t)

---

is never changed. The algorithm starts with a tentative matching, and changes *tentative* matches until it is satisfied for the current time step (see Fig. 1), at which point the matches are confirmed with MakeMatch. The algorithm then proceeds to the next time step and never changes pairings from previous time steps. Note also that the algorithm uses no information about valuations for future time steps.

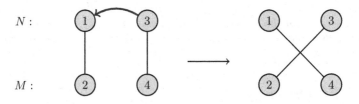

Fig. 1. A hypothetical swap performed by Algorithm 1. On the left we see a tentative perfect matching: $(\{1, 2\}, \{3, 4\})$. The blue arrow indicates that if this matching were to be chosen, the pair $(3, 1)$ would not be $(1 - a)$-envy-bounded. Thus agents 1 and 3 swap their (tentative) matches, and the new tentative matching is $(\{1, 4\}, \{3, 2\})$. The matching $(\{1, 2\}, \{3, 4\})$ is never confirmed by MakeMatch: it is merely a stepping stone in the process of computing the eventual matches to be chosen for this time step. For the case of more than four agents, this process could repeat (although not indefinitely; see the full version of the paper for this proof [16]. (Color figure online)

Our central correctness lemma will be the following:

Lemma 3.1. *Let* $t \geq 1$ *be any time step, and suppose that* X^{t-1} *is* $(1 - a)$-*envy-bounded and has no envy cycles. Then* X^t *is* $(1 - a)$-*envy-bounded and has no envy cycles. Furthermore, the chosen matching* x^t *is a maximum weight matching (with respect to the valuations on that time step).*

Before diving into the proof of Lemma 3.1 (and the runtime analysis), we briefly show that $(1 - a)$-envy-boundedness will actually give us the result we want:

Lemma 3.2. *Suppose valuations are binary, and suppose* X *is* $(1 - a)$-*envy-bounded. Then* X *is EF1.*

Proof. Suppose i envies j under X^t. If $v_i(X_j^t) = a|X_j^t|$, then $v_i(X_i^t) \geq v_i(X_j^t)$, which contradicts i envying j. Thus $v_i(X_j^t) \geq 1 + a(|X_j^t| - 1)$. Thus there exists $k \in X_j^t$ such that $v_i(X_j^t \setminus \{k\}) = v_i(X_j^t) - 1$. Therefore $v_i(X_i) - v_i(X_j^t \setminus \{k\}) \geq 1 + (a - 1) = a \geq 0$, which proves the claim.

The role of a. Before diving into the main proof, we briefly discuss the role of a. For Theorem 3.1, we assume that there exists $a \in [0, 1)$ such that $v_i(j) \in \{a, 1\}$ for all $i, j \in N$ or $i, j \in M$. For ease of notation, we assume that all agents have the same value of a, but this is in fact not necessary. In fact, Algorithm 1 will be EF1-over-rounds simultaneously for all values of a.

Lemma 3.3. *Assume (i, j) is $(1 - a)$-envy-bounded and that $|X_i^t| = |X_j^t|$. Let $a' \in [0, 1)$, and define a new valuation v_i' such that $v_i'(k) = a'$ whenever $v_i(k) = a$, and $v_i'(k) = 1$ otherwise. Then (i, j) is $(1 - a')$-envy-bounded with respect to v_i'.*

Note that the assumption of $|X_i^t| = |X_j^t|$ is always satisfied when working with EF1-over-rounds, since we will match every agent once on each time step. Therefore we can actually just choose an arbitrary value of $a \in [0, 1)$ and run Algorithm 1. Lemma 3.3 implies that the resulting sequence of matchings will be EF1-over-rounds simultaneously for all values of a, even if different agents have different values of a. That said, if we need to include dummy agents in order to equalize the sizes of N and M, $a = 0$ probably makes the most sense.

4 Counterexamples

A natural question is whether Theorem 3.1 can be extended to all dynamic binary valuations (i.e., not necessarily symmetric). The answer is unfortunately no, which we show in two different ways. First, for dynamic binary valuations, EF1-over-rounds alone is impossible (Theorem 4.1). Second, for non-dynamic binary valuations, it is impossible to guarantee both EF1-over-rounds and maximum weight matching for each time step (Theorem 4.2).

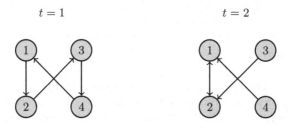

Fig. 2. An instance with dynamic and binary valuations where EF1-over-rounds is impossible.

Theorem 4.1 uses the instance in Fig. 2. Essentially, after the first round, either agents 1 and 3 form an envy cycle, or agents 2 and 4 form an envy cycle.

After the second round of matching, one of the agents in the envy cycle will become even more envious, violating EF1.

Theorem 4.1. *For dynamic and binary valuations, there is no algorithm which is EF1-over-rounds.*

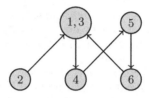

Fig. 3. An instance with binary valuations where guaranteeing both EF1-over-rounds and maximum weight matching is impossible.

Theorem 4.2 uses the instance in Fig. 3. For some intuition, note that are two cycles of desire: $(1, 4, 5, 6)$ and $(3, 4, 5, 6)$. Like in the previous counterexample, these cycles will cause problems, but here we have the additional consideration that agents 1 and 3 are competing for agent 4. We show that the frequency with which agents 4 and 5 are matched is at least the frequency with which *either* agent 1 or agent 3 is matched with agent 4. For example, if agents 1 and 3 have each been matched to agent 4 twice, then agents 4 and 5 will have been matched 4 times. This leads to agents 1 and 3 increasingly envying agent 5, until EF1 is violated.

The assumption of maximum weight is necessary only to prevent agents 2 and 5 from ever being matched: if agents 2 and 5 can be matched, the above argument can be circumvented.

Theorem 4.2. *For binary valuations, there is no algorithm which is EF1-over-rounds and also chooses a maximum weight matching for each time step, even for non-dynamic valuations.*

5   Conclusion

In this paper, we proposed a model of envy-freeness for repeated two-sided matching. For binary and symmetric valuations, we gave an algorithm that (1) satisfies EF1-over-rounds, (2) chooses a maximum weight matching for each time step, and (3) works even for dynamic valuations (Sect. 3). Furthermore, without symmetry, (1) + (2) together and (1) + (3) together are each impossible. All proofs can be found in the full version of the paper, along with several additional results [16].

Our negative results for even binary valuations suggest that EF1-over-rounds may be too much to ask for. However, our results do not rule out the possibility of EF1-over-time, even for general additive valuations. More broadly, future work could investigate other possible fairness notions for this setting.

Another possible future direction concerns more general study of two-sided preferences. Envy-freeness is an example of a topic that has been widely studied for one-sided resource allocation, but not for two-sided markets. We wonder if there are other such topics that are worthy of study for two-sided preferences.

References

1. Aleksandrov, M., Walsh, T.: Online Fair Division: A Survey. arXiv preprint arXiv:1911.09488 (2019)
2. Benade, G., Kazachkov, A.M., Procaccia, A.D., Psomas, C.A.: How to make envy vanish over time. In: Proceedings of the 2018 ACM Conference on Economics and Computation, EC 2018, pp. 593–610. ACM, New York (2018)
3. Bokányi, E., Hannák, A.: Evaluating Algorithm Fairness in an Agent-based Taxi Simulation (2018, working paper)
4. Bokányi, E., Hannák, A.: Ride-share Matching Algorithms Generate Income Inequality (2019, working paper)
5. Brandt, F., Conitzer, V., Endriss, U., Lang, J., Procaccia, A.D.: Handbook of Computational Social Choice. Cambridge University Press, Cambridge (2016)
6. Budish, E.: The combinatorial assignment problem: approximate competitive equilibrium from equal incomes. J. Polit. Econ. **119**(6), 1061–1103 (2011)
7. Calo, R., Rosenblat, A.: The taking economy: uber, information, and power. Columbia Law Rev. (2017)
8. Caragiannis, I., Kurokawa, D., Moulin, H., Procaccia, A.D., Shah, N., Wang, J.: The unreasonable fairness of maximum Nash welfare. In: Proceedings of the 2016 ACM Conference on Economics and Computation, pp. 305–322. ACM (2016)
9. Chaudhury, B.R., Garg, J., Mehlhorn, K.: EFX exists for three agents. arXiv preprint arXiv:2002.05119 (2020)
10. Damiano, E., Lam, R.: Stability in dynamic matching markets. Games Econ. Behav. **52**, 34–53 (2005)
11. Echenique, F., Oviedo, J.: A theory of stability in many-to-many matching markets. Theor. Econ. **1**(2), 233–273 (2006)
12. Fieseler, C., Bucher, E., Hoffmann, C.P.: Unfairness by design? The perceived fairness of digital labor on crowdworking platforms. J. Bus. Ethics **156**(4), 987–1005 (2019)
13. Foley, D.K.: Resource allocation and the public sector. Yale Econ. Essays **7**(1), 45–98 (1967)
14. Gale, D., Shapley, L.S.: College admissions and the stability of marriage. Am. Math. Mon. **69**(1), 9–15 (1962)
15. Gamow, G., Stern, M.: Puzzle-math. Viking Adult (1958). http://www.worldcat.org/isbn/0670583359
16. Gollapudi, S., Kollias, K., Plaut, B.: Almost Envy-free Repeated Matching in Two-sided Markets. arXiv preprint arXiv:2009.09336 (2020)
17. Hannák, A., Wagner, C., Garcia, D., Mislove, A., Strohmaier, M., Wilson, C.: Bias in online freelance marketplaces: evidence from Taskrabbit and Fiverr. In: Proceedings of the 2017 ACM Conference on Computer Supported Cooperative Work and Social Computing, CSCW 2017, pp. 1914–1933. ACM, New York (2017)

18. Haruvy, E., Ünver, M.U.: Equilibrium selection and the role of information in repeated matching markets. Econ. Lett. **94**(2), 284–289 (2007)
19. Konishi, H., Ünver, M.U.: Credible group stability in many-to-many matching problems. J. Econ. Theor. **129**(1), 57–80 (2006)
20. Lipton, R.J., Markakis, E., Mossel, E., Saberi, A.: On approximately fair allocations of indivisible goods. In: Proceedings of the 5th ACM conference on Electronic commerce, pp. 125–131. ACM (2004)
21. Moulin, H.: Fair Division and Collective Welfare. MIT Press, Cambridge (2004)
22. Patro, G.K., Biswas, A., Ganguly, N., Gummadi, K.P., Chakraborty, A.: FairRec: two-sided fairness for personalized recommendations in two-sided platforms. Proc. Web Conf. **2020**, 1194–1204 (2020)
23. Plaut, B., Roughgarden, T.: Almost envy-freeness with general valuations. In: Proceedings of the 29th Annual ACM-SIAM Symposium on Discrete Algorithms, pp. 2584–2603. Society for Industrial and Applied Mathematics (2018)
24. Roth, A.E., Sotomayor, M.: Two-Sided Matching: A Study in Game-Theoretic Modeling and Analysis. Cambridge University Press, Cambridge (1990)
25. Sotomayor, M.: Three remarks on the many-to-many stable matching problem. Math. Soc. Sci. **38**(1), 55–70 (1999)
26. Sotomayor, M.: Implementation in the many-to-many matching market. Games Econ. Behav. **46**(1), 199–212 (2004)
27. Steinhaus, H.: The problem of fair division. Econometrica **16**(1), 101–104 (1948)
28. Sühr, T., Biega, A.J., Zehlike, M., Gummadi, K.P., Chakraborty, A.: Two-sided fairness for repeated matchings in two-sided markets: a case study of a ride-hailing platform. In: Proceedings of the 25th ACM SIGKDD International Conference on Knowledge Discovery & Data Mining, KDD 2019, pp. 3082–3092. ACM, New York (2019)
29. Wolfson, O., Lin, J.: Fairness versus optimality in ridesharing. In: 2017 18th IEEE International Conference on Mobile Data Management (MDM), pp. 118–123. IEEE (2017)

Dynamic Weighted Matching
with Heterogeneous Arrival
and Departure Rates

Natalie Collina[1]([✉]), Nicole Immorlica[2], Kevin Leyton-Brown[3],
Brendan Lucier[2], and Neil Newman[3]

[1] Harvard University, Cambridge, USA
nataliecollina@gmail.com
[2] Microsoft Research, Redmond, USA
{nicimm,brlucier}@microsoft.com
[3] University of British Columbia, Vancouver, Canada
{kevinlb,newmanne}@cs.ubc.ca

Abstract. We study a dynamic non-bipartite matching problem. There is a fixed set of agent types, and agents of a given type arrive and depart according to type-specific Poisson processes. The value of a match is determined by the types of the matched agents. We present an online algorithm that is (1/8)-competitive with respect to the value of the optimal-in-hindsight policy, for arbitrary weighted graphs. This is the first result to achieve a constant competitive ratio when both arrivals and departures are random and unannounced. Our algorithm treats agents heterogeneously, interpolating between immediate and delayed matching in order to thicken the market while still matching valuable agents opportunistically.

1 Introduction

Matching markets are ubiquitous in online platforms. Sponsored search auctions like Google Adwords match ads and users, ridesharing systems like Uber and Lyft match drivers and riders, online markets like Amazon and eBay match sellers and buyers. In each case, the value of a match is a function of the types of participating agents. In sponsored search auctions, a restaurant ad is more valuable when matched to a geographically co-located user. In ridesharing systems, a driver and rider have higher utility for being matched to each other if they are nearby. In an online market, buyers might have heterogeneous preferences over service/product quality and price trade-offs which impact match quality.

The role of the platform is to find high-value matches. However, this task is significantly complicated by the fact that agents arrive and depart dynamically over time, and may fail to inform the platform of their departure. In this paper, we mitigate this complication by assuming that agents have known Poisson arrival and departure rates that are a function only of their type. This allows us to characterize the optimal expected value from matches using a linear

© Springer Nature Switzerland AG 2020
X. Chen et al. (Eds.): WINE 2020, LNCS 12495, pp. 17–30, 2020.
https://doi.org/10.1007/978-3-030-64946-3_2

program. This program bounds the rate at which each pair of types match to one-another in the optimal solution. Our algorithm uses these LP-based estimates of the optimal rates as guidelines. When an agent arrives to the market, we attempt to match it to each previous agent with a probability equal to a scaled-back version of the corresponding rate. We prove the resulting algorithm is a constant approximation to the optimal-in-hindsight policy, with competitive ratio at most 8. While we motivate our problem in the context of bipartite matchings, we note our solution holds for general non-bipartite graphs.

There is a significant body of prior literature on dynamic stochastic matching in settings where agent departures are immediate or deterministic (and hence predictable) [9,11–13,15], or where the platform is informed immediately before an agent departs [1,5,8,19]. In such settings, it is natural for the platform to delay matches until an agent is about to depart, in order to maximize the set of available options. In contrast, when the platform cannot predict departures, there is a tension between taking a guaranteed (but potentially suboptimal) match now, or pushing one's luck to see if a better match arrives later. The main technical challenge in developing an online policy is navigating this tradeoff for agents of different types.

Our LP-based approach is certainly not new in the context of stochastic matching, but we find that our result has several interesting qualitative insights, especially for settings where agent departures are random, heterogeneous, and unannounced. First, our algorithm treats matches heterogeneously. For some matches, the linear program suggests forming them at a high rate. Our algorithm treats these matches as a greedy algorithm would, matching them (almost) immediately upon arrival. For other matches, the linear program suggests forming them at a low rate. Our algorithm treats these matches more like a periodic clearing algorithm would, allowing the market to thicken before attempting the matches.

This heterogeneous treatment is important for good approximations in our setting. Consider, for example, an environment with two types of buyers, low and high, and one type of seller. The low buyers arrive frequently to the market and depart at a constant rate, whereas the sellers arrive less often. The high buyers arrive much less frequently than the sellers, and depart immediately after they arrive, but matches involving these high buyers account for almost all the value of the optimal policy. In this case, it is important to greedily match the high buyers and delay matches with the low buyers to thicken the market. A uniformly greedy policy, that immediately matches all agents, will likely have no sellers in the market when high buyers arrive, as there are always low buyers available to match with them. A periodic clearing algorithm that attempts to thicken the market by delaying all matches for a fixed period of time will likely have no access to high buyers at match time, since high buyers depart immediately after they arrive. See the full version of the paper for a more detailed description of such an example.

Another qualitative insight of our result is the importance of being conservative in matching attempts. Our algorithm scales back the match-rate estimates of the linear program by 50%. At first blush, this might seem incredibly wasteful.

However, this scaling is provably necessary: we show in the full version of the paper that if the algorithm does not perform this scaling then it cannot achieve any bounded approximation to the optimal matching. Intuitively, the issue is that the matching policy must leave some slack in the system—by leaving a certain fraction of agents unmatched—in order to take advantage of unexpected fortuitous events where a very valuable match becomes possible. Since an optimal LP solution typically would leave no such slack, one can instead guarantee it by being conservative when matching.

As is common in the dynamic stochastic matching literature, our approach is to solve an LP relaxation of the offline optimal matching problem, then use this solution as guidance for our online matching policy. We prove that the resulting policy obtains a constant approximation to the LP benchmark, which is only stronger than the offline optimal match value (and hence the optimal online policy). The main technical hurdle is that the outcome of matching attempts is determined by the state of which types of agents are present in the market, and this introduces correlations across time. For instance, whether a certain type of agent is present in the market is (negatively) correlated with the presence of other agents that generate high value from matches with it. In principle, such correlations could result in scenarios where a certain type is either not present at all or is overabundant, impeding our ability to match the LP relaxation which assumes smoothness across time. We address this issue by bounding the impact of such correlations, by coupling the availability of agents in the system with Poisson processes that dominate (or are dominated by) them.

1.1 Related Literature

There is a vast recent literature on algorithms for online matching (sometimes called online task arrival). In a seminal paper, Karp et al. [14] consider an (unweighted) online bipartite matching problem where one side of the graph is static and the vertices of the other side arrive online. They show that a randomized greedy matching method obtains a $(1 - 1/e)$ approximation and that this is tight. This was later extended by Mehta et al. [17] to a generalized weighted matching environment motivated by ad auctions, with budget constraints on the static side of the market. Both of these results assume adversarial types.

Stochastic variants of the online bipartite matching problem have been studied as well. Feldman et al. [9] consider a stochastic variant in which vertex types on the online side of the market are drawn i.i.d. from a fixed distribution. They showed how to beat the adversarial bound of $(1 - 1/e)$ in this stochastic setting, using an LP-based approach that solves for a fractional (expected) matching, then rounds online using a flow decomposition. This led to a sequence of papers that improved the approximation factors for both the weighted and unweighted versions of the stochastic problem [11,15], including variants with stochastic rewards [16,18] and with capacities on the fixed side [2]. Gravin and Wang [10] obtain a constant approximation for a related variant inspired by prophet inequalities, where edges (rather than nodes) arrive online and must be matched immediately or lost.

Our model is closer in spirit to the literature on dynamic matching, where agents on both sides of the market arrive and depart over time. An algorithm proposes matches online between agents that are simultaneously present. Huang et al. [12] study an unweighted model in which node arrivals and departures are adversarial, but nodes announce when they are about to depart. They derive constant competitive online algorithms; in a later paper, Huang et al. [13] find tight competitive ratios. Akbarpour et al. [1] similarly consider an unweighted version in which agents depart at arbitrary times and inform the market when they are about to depart, but arrivals are stochastic. In this case, it is approximately optimal to match agents as they go critical. On the other hand, they show that without departure warnings, greedily matching agents as they arrive is nearly optimal. As the graph is unweighted in their model and agents are homogenous, analysis can proceed by studying the limiting distribution of the number of agents in the market.

The case of weighted matching with departure warnings was studied by Ashlagi et al. [5], and they obtain a constant approximation to the optimal weighted matching. When agents on both sides arrive according to a known IID random process, Dickerson et al. [8] provide constant competitive algorithms under the assumption that one side (say workers) never depart until they are assigned, and the other side (say tasks) depart immediately after arrival if unassigned. Truong and Wang [19] consider a related weighted bipartite matching model where agents arrive according to a general stochastic process, agents on one side depart after a fixed deterministic amount of time, agents on the other side depart immediately after arrival if unassigned, and they likewise obtain constant competitive algorithms. Importantly, in all of these works it is assumed that the platform knows when an agent is about to leave the system, either because this can be perfectly predicted or because the platform is explicitly notified, and the platform can therefore wait until an agent "goes critical" before attempting a match. In contrast to these works, we assume the platform is not notified of (and cannot predict) impending departures.

Independently and concurrently with our work, Aouad and Saritac [4] studied a similar model of dynamic matching with unannounced departures. They likewise find that there is a tension between greedy matching and batching. They develop an online algorithm guided by a quadratic program, and show that it is $(4e/(e-1))$-competitive for arbitrary compatibility graphs. In contrast, our method is based on linear programming (rather than quadratic programming), and our competitive ratio bound is weaker (8 versus $4e/(e-1)$). They also study a cost-minimization version of the problem, for which they develop an online algorithm that they analyze theoretically and evaluate on empirical data. We leave open the question of whether a combination of the ideas in these works could be used to develop algorithms with improved competitive ratio.

Other papers consider the related problem of minimizing average waiting time. Anderson et al. [3] find that matching agents as they arrive is nearly optimal even with departure warnings. Ashlagi et al. [6] consider a model with two agent types – hard-to-match and easy-to-match – and derive structural insights about policies that miminize average waiting time. Baccara et al. [7] consider a hybrid model with two agent types in which agents have varying match values and also incur waiting costs (but never leave the system).

2   Preliminaries

We consider a model with agents that arrive and depart over time. The type space of agents is X. Agents of type $x \in X$ arrive according to a Poisson point process of rate λ_x.[1] Each agent of type x that arrives then departs at Poisson rate μ_x. For an agent i of type x, we will write a_i and d_i for its realized arrival and departure times, respectively. Throughout, we refer to types of agents with letters x and y, and to specific agents with letters i and j.

A *matching* is a set τ of times and a pair of matched agents for each time $t \in \tau$. A matching is *feasible* if, for all matching times $t \in \tau$, the agents matched at t a) have already arrived and not yet departed, and b) have not been matched to anyone else at or before time t. The value of matching an agent of type $x \in X$ to an agent of type $y \in X$ is v_{xy}. For convenience, we sometimes denote the total value of all matches made at time t by v_t.

A *matching policy* chooses, at each time t, based only on the history up until time t, whether to match a pair of agents or to make no match. A *policy with hindsight* can revise past decisions, whereas for an *online policy*, all decisions are irrevocable. For any policy and time T, let $\tau(T)$ be all times $t \leq T$ at which it made a match,[2] and v_t be the value of the matches made at time t, if any. Then the value of the policy is:

$$\liminf_{T \to \infty} \frac{1}{T} \cdot E \left[\sum_{t \in \tau(T)} v_t \right]$$

where the expectation is over the randomness in the arrival/departure process as well as any randomness in the policy. That is, the policy's value is the long-run average value of matches made per unit of time.

2.1   Poisson Processes

We now describe Poisson processes more formally. A point process is a random countable set of points $Z = \{z_1, z_2, \dots\}$. We restrict attention to the case $Z \subset R_{\geq 0}$, where we can interpret Z as a collection of event times. We refer to a point process by its set of points Z, which we think of as a random variable.

For any $T \geq 0$, we'll write $n_Z(T)$ for the number of points in $Z \cap [0, T]$; we think of this as the (random) number of events that occur before time T. Given two point processes Z and Y, we'll say that Z stochastically dominates Y if there is a coupling between Z and Y such that, for each $T > 0$, $\Pr[Y \subseteq Z] = 1$.

A static Poisson point process of rate $\lambda > 0$ is a point process such that

---

[1] We discuss Poisson processes more formally in Sect. 2.1.

[2] Note for an online policy, $\tau(T) \subseteq \tau(T')$ whenever $T \leq T'$; however this need not hold for a policy with hindsight.

1. the set of points in any two disjoint intervals are independent, and
2. the number of points in any given interval of length T follows a Poisson random variable with parameter (mean) λT.

From this point onward we'll refer to static Poisson point processes as just Poisson processes, for convenience. The following standard facts about Poisson processes will be helpful in our analysis.

Fact 1. *Given a Poisson process Z of rate λ, write $n_Z(T)$ for the number of events that occur before time T. Then $E[n_Z(T)] = T\lambda$. Moreover, $\lim_{T\to\infty} n_Z(T)/T$ exists and equals λ with probability 1.*

Fact 2. *Suppose we have Poisson processes $Z_1, \ldots, Z_n$ of rates $\lambda_1, \ldots, \lambda_n$ respectively. Then the probability that the earliest event (i.e., minimum point) in $\cup Z_i$ lies in Z_i is $\lambda_i/(\sum_k \lambda_k)$.*

Fact 3. *Suppose Z is a Poisson process of rate λ, and Z' is a random set generated by adding each $z \in Z$ to Z' independently with probability p. Then Z' is a Poisson process of rate λp.*

A corollary of Fact 3 is that if Z is a Poisson process of rate λ and Z' is a Poisson process of rate $\lambda' < \lambda$, then Z stochastically dominates Z'. This is because we can couple Z and Z' by first realizing Z, then adding each element of Z to Z' independently with probability λ'/λ.

3   An Upper Bound

We construct an online policy whose value is a constant fraction of the optimal-in-hindsight policy. To do so, we develop a linear-programming upper bound on the value of the optimal-in-hindsight policy for large time horizons.[3] The value of the optimal solution is the expectation over the randomness in arrivals and departures of instance-optimal solutions, and so can be written as the expectation of the sum of match values.

In the following LP, the variable α_{xy} is the fraction of nodes of type y which match to preexisting nodes of type x, when considered over all arrivals of agents of type y.

$$\textbf{LP} - \textbf{UB}: \quad \text{maximize} \quad \sum_{x,y\in X} v_{xy}\alpha_{xy}\lambda_y$$

$$\text{subject to} \quad \alpha_{xy} \le \frac{\lambda_x}{\mu_x} \qquad\qquad \forall x,y \in X \quad (1)$$

$$\sum_{y\in X} \alpha_{xy}\lambda_y + \sum_{y\in X} \alpha_{yx}\lambda_x \le \lambda_x \quad \forall x \in X \quad (2)$$

$$\alpha_{xy} \in [0,1], \qquad\qquad\qquad \forall x,y \in X \quad (3)$$

---

[3] Taking the limit as the time horizon grows allows us to ignore lower-order terms.

Constraint (1) bounds the fraction of the time that some node of type y matches to some previously arrived node of type x by the probability that a node of type x is present in the system at any given time. Constraint (2) bounds the total rate at which a type can match by the total rate at which the type arrives. On the left-hand-side, the first sum captures the rate at which a type matches to those arriving after it; the second sum captures the rate at which a type matches to those who arrived before it. Note that constraints (2) and (3) together imply that $\sum_{x \in X} \alpha_{xy} \leq 1$ for all y. This makes intuitive sense: the total fraction of the time that a node matches to any preexisting type cannot be greater than 1.

We will first demonstrate that the value of LP-UB represents an upper bound on the expected value of the max-weight offline matching. Then in Sect. 4 we will provide a policy that garners a constant approximation of the LP value in expectation, and thus of the max-weight offline expectation.

Lemma 1. *Let v^* be the optimal value of LP-UB. Then the value of any matching policy, including policies with hindsight, is at most v^*.*

The proof of Lemma 1 is omitted due to space constraints and appears in the full version of the paper. The idea of the proof is to consider the set of agents who arrive up to some time T, and interpret the constraints of LP-UB as conditions on matchings in the induced graph of potential matches. These finite conditions include lower order terms, but these disappear when taking the limit as T grows large.

4   Online Matching Policy

We now present our online matching policy, ONLINEMATCH. Our policy first solves LP-UB in advance of any arrivals, and then uses the solution to guide its matching decisions. As demonstrated in the previous section, the solution to the LP-UB should be thought of as describing the optimal matching rates between types, subject to constraints that hold as time approaches infinity. Our goal is to create a policy that approximately matches the value of this LP, which we will achieve by obtaining a constant approximation to these matching rates.

Suppose that an agent, say agent i of type y, arrives at time t. The algorithm will then iterate through all potential types (including y) in a random order (line 3). For each considered type x, if there are any agents of type x present and unmatched in the market, the algorithm will select one of them arbitrarily and attempt to match it with agent i. With probability $\gamma \cdot \alpha_{xy} \cdot \max\left(1, \frac{\mu_x}{\lambda_x}\right)$ the match occurs, in which case the algorithm completes and awaits the next agent arrival. Otherwise, the algorithm moves on to the next type in X. If agent i is not matched after every $x \in X$ has been considered, then we leave agent i in the market unmatched and await the next arrival.

ALGORITHM 1: Algorithm ONLINEMATCH

---

require: scaling parameter $\gamma \in (0, 1]$
input   : Online arrivals of agents

1 $(\alpha_{xy}) :=$ Solution to LP-UB;
2 **for** *each agent i arriving at time t, say of type* $y \in X$ **do**
3   **for** *each type* $x \in X$ *in a uniformly random order* **do**
4   **if** *there is at least one unmatched agent j of type x in the market* **then**
5   match i and j with probability $\gamma \cdot \alpha_{xy} \cdot \max\left(1, \frac{\mu_x}{\lambda_x}\right)$
6   **end**
7 **end**

The match probability on line 5 deserves some discussion. This probability depends on the solution to LP-UB, and is the mechanism by which the algorithm attempts to follow the matching rates proposed by the LP. One might be tempted to simply use α_{xy} as the match probability. However, when constructing an online policy we must consider the difference between unconditional match rates and matching rates conditional on agent types being present in the market. It may be that a particular type is extremely unlikely to be present to match during a given attempt. Consider a problem instance that includes a type x with arrival rate 1 and departure rate $1/\epsilon$, and a corresponding LP solution where $\alpha_{xy} = \epsilon$ for some y (note that this does not immediately violate any constraints, as the upper bound on α_{xy} could be as high as ϵ). The probability that any agent of type x will be present when an agent of type y arrives is at most ϵ (see Lemma 2). Thus an online policy that attempts to match agents of type x to agents of type y with probability ϵ will actually generate such a match with probability no greater than ϵ^2. In order to actually achieve the ϵ fraction that we desire, we must scale α_{xy} by $1/\epsilon$, or $\frac{\mu_x}{\lambda_x}$. Intuitively, we have scaled up the match probability according to the probability that x is present, in order to achieve the rate recommended by LP-UB. This motivates our choice of scaling factor on line 5.

The algorithm actually scales the probability by an additional factor of γ, which is a tunable parameter of the algorithm; this is to ensure that each agent has a constant probability of being available in the system unmatched when its ideal match arrives. We will optimize γ as part of our analysis of the algorithm.

Theorem 4. *Algorithm 1 is an 8-approximation to the value of LP-UB.*

4.1 Analysis

One challenge in the analysis of ONLINEMATCH is correlations across time: whether a certain type of agent is available in the market to be matched at time t depends on the types of other agents present in the market, as this influences matching probability. Thus, the availability of different types of agents are correlated through the pool of agents waiting to be matched at any given time. This correlation complicates the intuition that ONLINEMATCH will approximately mirror the aggregate match probabilities from LP-UB at every moment in time.

We address this difficulty by showing that while the evolution of which agent types are available in the market is dependent on the overall market state and correlated across types, they can be coupled with independent Poisson processes that are related via first-order stochastic dominance. That is, while agents in the market are matched at rates that vary over time with the composition of available agents, these rates are subject to uniform upper and lower bounds that reflect maximum and minimum possible matching rates. By relating to these extreme matching scenarios, we can derive uniform bounds on the success rate of matching attempts under arbitrary market conditions.

We begin by introducing the notion of an agent being *present* in the market, and bounding the probability that a node of a given type is present at any given time. We will say an agent i is present at time t if it has arrived but not yet departed; that is, if $a_i \leq t < d_i$. We'll say the node is *available* at time t if it is present and has not yet been matched to another node.

Importantly, an agent can be present but not available: even after an agent has been matched, one could simulate the departure process for that agent as though they had not matched, and we view the agent as being present until they leave under that simulated process. The advantage of considering presence, rather than availability, is that whether an agent is present at a given time depends only on their arrival and departure times, and is independent of all other agents in the market.

Lemma 2. *Choose a type $x \in X$ and any time $t \geq 0$. Then over all randomness in arrivals and departures, the probability that at least one agent of type x is present at time t is at most $\min\{\lambda_x/\mu_x, 1\}$.*

Proof. Choose some interval of time of length T, and consider all agents of type x that arrive during interval T. In expectation $\lambda_x T$ agents arrive, and each stays for an expected length of $1/\mu_x$, independently. The sum of times in market for all such agents is therefore $\lambda_x T/\mu_x$. By a union bound, the total fraction of time during which such an agent is present in the market is at most $\frac{1}{T}(\lambda_x T/\mu_x) = \lambda_x/\mu_x$. As this fraction is also at most 1, we have that the probability that such an agent is present at a given time is at most $\min(1, \lambda_x/\mu_x)$ as required.

We now wish to bound the probability that agents of a given type are present in the market, but not available. A present agent becomes unavailable in two ways: either they were matched immediately upon arriving to the market, or they are matched to another agent who arrives later. We begin by bounding the probability of the former, by showing that the occurrences of agents arriving and not being immediately matched stochastically dominate a Poisson arrival process with a reduced arrival rate.[4]

Lemma 3. *In an execution of algorithm* ONLINEMATCH, *consider the set of events that a node of type x arrives and is not immediately matched. The occurrence of such events stochastically dominates a Poisson arrival process of rate $\lambda_x(1 - \gamma \sum_{y \in X} \alpha_{yx})$.*

---

[4] Recall that if Z and Z' are two (random) point processes, then Z stochastically dominates Z' if there is a coupling of Z and Z' such that $\Pr[Z' \subseteq Z] = 1$.

Proof. Agents of type x arrive at rate λ_x. Suppose agent i of type x arrives at time t. By Lemma 2, for each $y \in X$ a node of type y is present at time t with probability at most $\min\{\lambda_y/\mu_y, 1\}$. Thus, given that Algorithm ONLINEMATCH considers a match with type y, this match will be successful with probability at least

$$\gamma \alpha_{yx} \max\{1, \mu_y/\lambda_y\} \cdot \min\{\lambda_y/\mu_y, 1\} = \gamma \alpha_{yx}.$$

The total probability that agent i matches to any other agent at time t is therefore at most

$$\gamma \sum_{y \in X} \alpha_{yx}$$

and hence the probability that agent i is not immediately matched is at least

$$1 - \gamma \sum_{y \in X} \alpha_{yx}.$$

We have argued that the event that a node of type x arrives and is not immediately matched is determined by an arrival process of rate λ_x, followed by a (state-dependent) random event of probability at least $1 - \gamma \sum_{y \in X} \alpha_{yx}$. This stochastically dominates an alternative event that simply takes this probability to be exactly $1 - \gamma \sum_{y \in X} \alpha_{yx}$ in all cases. But, by Fact 3, this latter process is equivalent to a Poisson arrival process of rate $\lambda_x(1 - \gamma \sum_{y \in X} \alpha_{yx})$, as required.

We next consider the occurrence of events in which an agent that is currently available[5] in the market is matched to some other agent who arrives. We again connect this with a Poisson arrival process with a reduced rate.

Lemma 4. *In an execution of algorithm* ONLINEMATCH, *consider the event that an agent of any type arrives to the market and would match to an agent of type x if any such agent is available. The occurrence of such events is stochastically dominated by a Poisson arrival process of rate* $\gamma \sum_{y \in X} \lambda_y \alpha_{xy} \max(1, \mu_x/\lambda_x)$.

Proof. Suppose that an agent of type x is present in the market. Agents of type y arrive at rate λ_y. Consider an agent i of type y that arrives at time t. The probability that agent i matches to a node of type x is dependent on which other agents are available in the market, but is maximized when no other agents of other types are available. In the event that no other types are available, agent i will certainly consider matching to type x, in which case the match occurs with probability $\gamma \alpha_{xy} \max(1, \mu_x/\lambda_x)$.

We have argued that a node of type y arrives at rate λ_y, and then matches to an agent of type x with a state-dependent probability that is at most $\gamma \alpha_{xy} \max(1, \mu_x/\lambda_x)$. This process is stochastically dominated by one in which the match occurs with probability exactly $\gamma \alpha_{xy} \max(1, \mu_x/\lambda_x)$ upon each arrival. But, by Fact 3, this is equivalent to a Poisson arrival process of rate $\lambda_y \gamma \alpha_{xy} \max(1, \mu_x/\lambda_x)$. Summing over all types $y \in X$ completes the proof.

---

[5] Recall by the definition of available, such an agent is also present.

Having related availability events to independent Poisson processes, we are now ready to bound the match probabilities of ONLINEMATCH.

Lemma 5. *Choose any $x, y \in X$, and suppose that an agent i of type $y \in X$ arrives at time t. Then* ONLINEMATCH *will match i to a node of type x at time t with probability at least $\gamma(1 - \gamma/2)\frac{1-\gamma}{2-\gamma}\alpha_{xy}$, where the probability is over any randomness in the algorithm and in the arrivals and departures of all other agents.*

Proof. Fix some $x, y \in X$. Suppose an agent i of type y arrives at time t, and consider the evaluation of ONLINEMATCH on this agent i. Some terminology: we'll say that agent i *considers* matching to an agent of type x if we enter an iteration of the loop on line 3 with type x chosen. We'll say that the agent *attempts* to match to an agent of type x if, in addition, the probabilistic match on line 5 *would* occur (regardless of whether or not the condition on line 4 evaluates to true). In other word, we can imagine pre-evaluating the probabilistic check on line 5 before checking the condition on line 4, and an attempted match corresponds to iterations in which the probabilistic check passes.

We will first bound the probability that agent i considers matching to an agent of type x. By Lemma 2, for each $z \in X$ a node of type z is present at time t with probability at most $\min\{\lambda_z/\mu_z, 1\}$. Thus, given that our algorithm considers a match with type z, this match will be successful with probability at most

$$\gamma\alpha_{zy} \max\{1, \mu_z/\lambda_z\} \cdot \min\{\lambda_z/\mu_z, 1\} = \gamma\alpha_{zy}.$$

The total probability that agent i matches to any other agent at time t is therefore at most

$$\sum_{z \in X} \gamma\alpha_{zy} \leq \gamma$$

where we used (2) from LP-UB. If we consider only half of the types $z \in X$ uniformly at random, the probability of a match is then at most $\gamma/2$ (where the expectation is over randomness in algorithm and over which types are chosen). This is a bound on the probability that the algorithm matches to some other type before type x is considered. So a match to type x will be considered by the algorithm with probability at least $(1 - \gamma/2)$.

Assuming it is considered, the match will be attempted with probability $\gamma \cdot \alpha_{xy} \cdot \max(1, \mu_x/\lambda_x)$. Note that the conditional attempt probability is independent of whether the match is considered. Thus the unconditional probability that the match is attempted is at least

$$\gamma(1 - \gamma/2)\alpha_{xy} \cdot \max(1, \mu_x/\lambda_x).$$

We now want to bound the probability that the attempted match to an agent of type x is successful, given that one was attempted. Consider three different events, which will occur repeatedly over time:

– Event E_1: An agent of type x arrives and is not immediately matched.

– Event E_2: An agent of any type arrives and attempts to match to an agent of type x.
– Event E_3: There is exactly one agent of type x, and that agent departs.

Suppose that the agent i of type y attempts to match to an agent of type x at time t. That match will be successful if the most recent event that occurred before t, from among events of type E_1, E_2, and E_3, is an event of type E_1.

We now consider two cases, based on the relationship between μ_x and λ_x.

Case 1: $\mu_x \leq \lambda_x$. Then $\max\{1, \mu_x/\lambda_x\} = 1$. By Lemma 3, the occurrences of event E_1 stochastically dominate a Poisson arrival process of rate $\lambda_1 := \lambda_x(1 - \gamma \sum_{y \in X} \alpha_{yx})$. By Lemma 4, the occurrences of event E_2 are stochastically dominated by a Poisson arrival process of rate $\lambda_2 := \gamma \sum_y \alpha_{xy} \lambda_y$. And finally, occurrences of event E_3 are stochastically dominated by a Poisson arrival process of rate $\lambda_3 := \mu_x$, as this is the rate of the event when there is exactly one agent of type x present in the market (and otherwise the event cannot occur). Thus, by Fact 2, the probability that the most recent event before time t was an event of type E_1 is at least

$$\frac{\lambda_1}{\lambda_1 + \lambda_2 + \lambda_3} = \frac{\lambda_x \left(1 - \gamma \sum_{y \in X} \alpha_{yx}\right)}{\gamma \sum_{y \in X} \alpha_{xy} \lambda_y + \lambda_x \left(1 - \gamma \sum_{y \in X} \alpha_{yx}\right) + \mu_x}. \tag{4}$$

Write $q = \sum_{y \in X} \alpha_{yx}$. By constraint (3) of LP-UB, we have that $\sum_{y \in X} \alpha_{xy} \lambda_y + q\lambda_x \leq \lambda_x$, which implies $\sum_{y \in X} \alpha_{xy} \lambda_y \leq \lambda_x(1 - q)$, so in particular $q \in [0, 1]$. We also have $\mu_x \leq \lambda_x$ by assumption for this case analysis. The probability (4) is therefore at least

$$\min_{q \in [0,1]} \frac{1 - \gamma q}{\gamma(1 - q) + (1 - \gamma q) + 1} = \min_{q \in [0,1]} \frac{1 - \gamma q}{2 - 2\gamma q + \gamma}. \tag{5}$$

The expression in (5) is weakly decreasing in q for all $\gamma \in (0, 1)$, so it achieves its minimum at $q = 1$, which is $(1 - \gamma)/(2 - \gamma)$. Moreover, recall that this probability is a uniform bound independent of which agents are available in the market. Thus, recalling the probability that agent i attempts to match to an agent of type x, the total unconditional probability that node i successfully matches to an agent of type x is at least

$$\gamma(1 - \gamma/2)\alpha_{xy} \max(1, \mu_x/\lambda_x)\frac{1 - \gamma}{2 - \gamma} = \gamma(1 - \gamma/2)\frac{1 - \gamma}{2 - \gamma}\alpha_{xy}.$$

Case 2: $\mu_x > \lambda_x$. Then $\max\{1, \mu_x/\lambda_x\} = \mu_x/\lambda_x$. As in case 1, Lemma 3 implies that the occurrences of event E_1 stochastically dominate a Poisson arrival process of rate $\lambda_x(1 - \gamma \sum_{y \in X} \alpha_{yx})$. And occurrences of event E_3 are still stochastically dominated by a Poisson arrival process of rate μ_x. By Lemma 4, the occurrences of event E_2 are stochastically dominated by a Poisson arrival process of rate $\gamma \sum_y \alpha_{xy} \lambda_y (\mu_x/\lambda_x)$. Thus the probability that the most recent event before time

t was an event of type E_1 is at least

$$\frac{\lambda_x \left(1 - \gamma \sum_{y \in X} \alpha_{yx}\right)}{\gamma \sum_{y \in X} \alpha_{xy} \lambda_y (\mu_x/\lambda_x) + \lambda_x \left(1 - \gamma \sum_{y \in X} \alpha_{yx}\right) + \mu_x}. \tag{6}$$

As in case 1, write $q = \sum_{y \in X} \alpha_{xy}$, so that $\sum_{y \in X} \alpha_{xy} \lambda_y \leq \lambda_x(1 - q)$. Then $\sum_{y \in X} \alpha_{xy} \lambda_y (\mu_x/\lambda_x) \leq \mu_x(1 - q)$. Also, since $\lambda_x < \mu_x$ by assumption for this case analysis, $\lambda_x \left(1 - \gamma \sum_{y \in X} \alpha_{yx}\right) < \mu_x(1 - \gamma q)$. The probability (6) is therefore at most

$$\min_{q \in [0,1]} \frac{\lambda_x(1 - \gamma q)}{\mu_x \gamma (1 - q) + \mu_x(1 - \gamma q) + \mu_x} = \min_{q \in [0,1]} \frac{\lambda_x}{\mu_x} \cdot \frac{1 - \gamma q}{2 - 2\gamma q + \gamma}. \tag{7}$$

As in case 1, the expression in (7) achieves its minimum when $q = 1$, which is $\frac{\lambda_x}{\mu_x} \cdot \frac{1-\gamma}{2-\gamma}$. Thus the total unconditional probability that node i successfully matches to an agent of type x is at least

$$\gamma(1 - \gamma/2)\alpha_{xy} \max(1, \mu_x/\lambda_x) \frac{\lambda_x}{\mu_x} \frac{1 - \gamma}{2 - \gamma} = \gamma(1 - \gamma/2)\frac{1 - \gamma}{2 - \gamma}\alpha_{xy}.$$

Optimizing over the choice of γ, we have that $\gamma(1 - \gamma/2)\frac{1-\gamma}{2-\gamma}$ takes on its maximum value at $\gamma = 1/2$, in which case $\gamma(1 - \gamma/2)\frac{1-\gamma}{2-\gamma} = 1/8$. Thus, by setting $\gamma = 1/2$ in ONLINEMATCH, Lemma 5 implies that agents of type y arrive and match to agents of type x at rate at least $\alpha_{xy}\lambda_y/8$. The total value obtained by ONLINEMATCH is therefore at least $\frac{1}{8}\sum_{x,y \in X} v_{xy}\alpha_{xy}\lambda_y$, which is 1/8 of the value of LP-UB. We conclude that ONLINEMATCH is an 8-approximation, as required.

References

1. Akbarpour, M., Li, S., Gharan, S.O.: Thickness and information in dynamic matching markets. J. Polit. Econ. **128**(3), 783–815 (2020)
2. Alaei, S., Hajiaghayi, M., Liaghat, V.: Online prophet-inequality matching with applications to Ad allocation. In: Proceedings of the 13th ACM Conference on Electronic Commerce, EC 2012, pp. 18–35. Association for Computing Machinery, New York (2012). https://doi.org/10.1145/2229012.2229018
3. Anderson, R., Ashlagi, I., Gamarnik, D., Kanoria, Y.: Efficient dynamic barter exchange. Oper. Res. **65**(6), 1446–1459 (2017). https://doi.org/10.1287/opre.2017.1644
4. Aouad, A., Saritaç, O.: Dynamic stochastic matching under limited time. In: Proceedings of the 21st ACM Conference on Economics and Computation, EC 2020, pp. 789–790. Association for Computing Machinery, New York (2020). https://doi.org/10.1145/3391403.3399524
5. Ashlagi, I., Burq, M., Dutta, C., Jaillet, P., Saberi, A., Sholley, C.: Edge weighted online windowed matching. In: Proceedings of the 2019 ACM Conference on Economics and Computation, EC 2019, pp. 729–742. ACM, New York (2019). https://doi.org/10.1145/3328526.3329573

6. Ashlagi, I., Burq, M., Jaillet, P., Manshadi, V.: On matching and thickness in heterogeneous dynamic markets. Oper. Res. **67**(4), 927–949 (2019)
7. Baccara, M., Lee, S., Yariv, L.: Optimal dynamic matching. CEPR Discussion Paper No. DP12986 (2018)
8. Dickerson, J.P., Sankararaman, K.A., Srinivasan, A., Xu, P.: Assigning tasks to workers based on historical data: online task assignment with two-sided arrivals. In: Proceedings of the 17th International Conference on Autonomous Agents and MultiAgent Systems, pp. 318–326. International Foundation for Autonomous Agents and Multiagent Systems (2018)
9. Feldman, J., Mehta, A., Mirrokni, V., Muthukrishnan, S.: Online stochastic matching: Beating 1–1/e. In: 2009 50th Annual IEEE Symposium on Foundations of Computer Science, pp. 117–126. IEEE (2009)
10. Gravin, N., Wang, H.: Prophet inequality for bipartite matching: merits of being simple and non adaptive. In: Proceedings of the 2019 ACM Conference on Economics and Computation, EC 2019, pp. 93–109. Association for Computing Machinery, New York (2019). https://doi.org/10.1145/3328526.3329604
11. Haeupler, B., Mirrokni, V.S., Zadimoghaddam, M.: Online stochastic weighted matching: improved approximation algorithms. In: Chen, N., Elkind, E., Koutsoupias, E. (eds.) WINE 2011. LNCS, vol. 7090, pp. 170–181. Springer, Heidelberg (2011). https://doi.org/10.1007/978-3-642-25510-6_15
12. Huang, Z., Kang, N., Tang, Z.G., Wu, X., Zhang, Y., Zhu, X.: How to match when all vertices arrive online. In: Proceedings of the 50th Annual ACM SIGACT Symposium on Theory of Computing, pp. 17–29 (2018)
13. Huang, Z., Peng, B., Tang, Z.G., Tao, R., Wu, X., Zhang, Y.: Tight competitive ratios of classic matching algorithms in the fully online model. In: Proceedings of the 13th Annual ACM-SIAM Symposium on Discrete Algorithms, pp. 2875–2886. SIAM (2019)
14. Karp, R.M., Vazirani, U.V., Vazirani, V.V.: An optimal algorithm for on-line bipartite matching. In: Proceedings of the 22nd Annual ACM Symposium on Theory of Computing (1990)
15. Mahdian, M., Yan, Q.: Online bipartite matching with random arrivals: an approach based on strongly factor-revealing LPs. In: Proceedings of the 43rd Annual ACM Symposium on Theory of Computing, STOC 2011, pp. 597–606. ACM, New York (2011). https://doi.org/10.1145/1993636.1993716
16. Mehta, A., Panigrahi, D.: Online matching with stochastic rewards. In: Proceedings of the 2012 IEEE 53rd Annual Symposium on Foundations of Computer Science, FOCS 2012, pp. 728–737. IEEE Computer Society, Washington (2012). https://doi.org/10.1109/FOCS.2012.65
17. Mehta, A., Saberi, A., Vazirani, U.V., Vazirani, V.V.: Adwords and generalized on-line matching. In: 46th Annual IEEE Symposium on Foundations of Computer Science (2005)
18. Mehta, A., Waggoner, B., Zadimoghaddam, M.: Online stochastic matching with unequal probabilities. In: Proceedings of the 26th Annual ACM-SIAM Symposium on Discrete Algorithms, SODA 2015, pp. 1388–1404. Society for Industrial and Applied Mathematics, Philadelphia (2015). http://dl.acm.org/citation.cfm?id=2722129.2722221
19. Truong, V.A., Wang, X.: Prophet inequality with correlated arrival probabilities, with application to two sided matchings (2019)

A Fine-Grained View on Stable Many-To-One Matching Problems with Lower and Upper Quotas

Niclas Boehmer[✉] and Klaus Heeger

Algorithmics and Computational Complexity, TU Berlin, Berlin, Germany
{niclas.boehmer,heeger}@tu-berlin.de

Abstract. In the Hospital Residents problem with lower and upper quotas ($HR\text{-}Q_L^U$), the goal is to find a stable matching of residents to hospitals where the number of residents matched to a hospital is either between its lower and upper quota or zero [Biró et al., TCS 2010]. We analyze this problem from a parameterized perspective using several natural parameters such as the number of hospitals and the number of residents. Moreover, we present a polynomial-time algorithm that finds a stable matching if it exists on instances with maximum lower quota two. Alongside $HR\text{-}Q_L^U$, we also consider two closely related models of independent interest, namely, the special case of $HR\text{-}Q_L^U$ where each hospital has only a lower quota but no upper quota and the variation of $HR\text{-}Q_L^U$ where hospitals do not have preferences over residents, which is also known as the House Allocation problem with lower and upper quotas.

1 Introduction

Since its introduction by Gale and Shapely [10], the Hospital Residents problem, which is also known as the College Admission problem, has attracted a lot of attention. Besides a rich body of theoretical work [15], also many practical applications have been identified [22]. In the classical Hospital Residents problem ($HR\text{-}Q^U$), we are given a set of residents, each with strict preferences over hospitals, and a set of hospitals, each with an upper quota and strict preferences over residents. In a feasible matching of residents to hospitals, the number of residents assigned to a hospital is at most its upper quota. A hospital-resident pair (h, r) blocks a matching if resident r prefers hospital h to the hospital to which r is currently matched and the number of residents matched to h is either below its upper quota or h prefers r to one of the residents matched to it. The task in the Hospital Residents problem is to find a stable matching, i.e., a feasible matching that does not admit a blocking pair. Gale and Shapely [10] presented a linear-time algorithm that always finds a stable matching in a Hospital Residents instance.

We thank Robert Bredereck and Rolf Niedermeier for useful discussions.

N. Boehmer—supported by the DFG project MaMu (NI 369/19).

K. Heeger—supported by DFG Research Training Group 2434 "Facets of Complexity".

© Springer Nature Switzerland AG 2020

X. Chen et al. (Eds.): WINE 2020, LNCS 12495, pp. 31–44, 2020.

https://doi.org/10.1007/978-3-030-64946-3_3

In practice, some hospitals may also have a lower quota, i.e., a minimum number of assigned residents such that the hospital can open and accommodate them. For example, at a university, courses of study might have a lower quota out of economical or political reasons or because all students in a course need to perform certain task together which require at least a given number of participants. Biró et al. [5] captured these considerations by extending the Hospital Residents problem such that each hospital has a lower and upper quota (HR-Q_L^U). Here, feasibility additionally requires that the number of residents assigned to a hospital is either zero or at least its lower quota, while stability additionally requires that there does not exist a blocking coalition, i.e., a sufficiently large subset of residents that want to open a currently closed hospital together. Biró et al. [5] proved that deciding the existence of a stable matching in an HR-Q_L^U instance is NP-complete. We complement their work with a thorough parameterized complexity analysis of HR-Q_L^U. Moreover, we study the Hospital Residents problem where hospitals have only a lower quota (HR-Q_L), which has not been considered before. Lower and upper quotas have also been applied to the House Allocation problem (HA-Q_L^U) where the goal is to match a set of applicants to a set of houses [8,19]. In HA-Q_L^U, houses have a lower and upper quota but no preferences over applicants, while applicants have preferences over houses. One possible application of this model is the assignment of kids to different activities, where lower quotas could arise due to economical or practical constraints, for instance, playing soccer with only three kids is less fun. So far, literature on HA-Q_L^U mainly focused on finding Pareto optimal matchings. However, in contrast to the classical House Allocation problem, Pareto optimality in HA-Q_L^U does not imply stability. Thus, finding stable matchings is an interesting problem on its own.

Our Contributions. We provide an extensive complexity analysis of the Hospital Residents problem with lower and upper quotas (HR-Q_L^U) and of the two closely related problems HR-Q_L and HA-Q_L^U. By applying the framework of parameterized complexity, we analyze the influence of various problem-specific parameters on the complexity of these problems, i.e., the maximum lower quota q_l of a hospital, the number n of residents, the number m of hospitals, and the number m_{quota} of hospitals with non-unit lower quota. Motivated by the observation that there might exist stable matchings opening a different set of hospitals (of possibly different size) [5], we also consider the problem of deciding whether there exists a stable matching where exactly a given set of hospitals H_{open} is open. In addition, in the full version [7], we also examine the problem of deciding whether there exists a stable matching with exactly m_{open} (m_{closed}) open (closed) hospitals parameterized by m_{open} (m_{closed}).

We present an overview of our results in Table 1. Our most important technical contribution is the design of a polynomial-time algorithm for HR-Q_L^U (and therefore also for HR-Q_L) instances where all hospitals have lower quota at most two. This answers an open question raised by Biró et al. [5] and Manlove [15, p. 231]. Such HR-Q_L^U instances are of special theoretical interest, as they, for example, subsume a variant of three-dimensional STABLE MARRIAGE, where,

Table 1. Overview of our results. All stated W[1]-hardness results also imply NP-hardness. Note that most hardness results even hold in cases where the quota of hospitals and the maximum length of a preference list are small constants.

	$q_l \leq 2$	$q_l \leq 3$	H_{open}	n	m	m_{quota}	m_{open}	m_{closed}
$HR\text{-}Q_L^U$	P (T. 4)	NP-c. (T. 1)	P (P. 1)	W[1]-h. (T. 2)	FPT (C. 1)		W[1]-h.	W[1]-h.
$HR\text{-}Q_L$								
$HA\text{-}Q_L^U$	NP-c. (P. 2)		NP-c. (T. 3)		FPT (P. 2)	paraNP-h. (P. 2)	paraNP-h.	W[1]-h.

given two sets of agents each with preferences over the agents from the other set, the goal is to find a stable set of triples, each consisting of two agents from the first and one agent from the second set. Moreover, there also exist several applications where a lower quota of two is of particular interest, for example, assuming that hospitals correspond to (tennis) coaches and residents to (tennis) players, a coach may require that at least two players are assigned to her (as she does not always want to play herself).

Our rich set of tractability and intractability results highlight the differences between the three considered models from a computational perspective: While $HR\text{-}Q_L$ is very similar to $HR\text{-}Q_L^U$, $HA\text{-}Q_L^U$ is computationally more demanding than $HR\text{-}Q_L^U$. The first observation suggests that the complexity of $HR\text{-}Q_L^U$ comes solely from the lower quotas of hospitals. The second observation indicates that the hospitals' preferences in the lower and upper quotas setting make the problem easier, as they may act as a "tie-breaker" to decide which resident deserves a better spot in a stable matching.

Due to space constraints, proofs are deferred to the full version [7].

Related Work. After the work of Biró et al. [5], only few papers revisited computational problems related to the Hospital Residents problem with lower and upper quotas. A notable exception is the work of Agoston et al. [1] who proposed an ILP formulation to find stable matchings and several preprocessing rules to decide which hospitals must be open. Apart from this, most of the follow-up work applied the idea of lower and upper quotas to other settings, such as the House Allocation problem [8,19] or maximum-weight many-to-one matchings in bipartite graphs [2], or interpreted it differently.

Hamada et al. [11] introduced an alternative version of the Hospital Residents problem with lower and upper quotas. In their model, hospitals have lower and upper quotas, but are not allowed to be closed. Thus, in a feasible matching, the lower and upper quota of each hospital needs to be respected. As deciding whether a stable matching exists is polynomial-time solvable in this model, their main focus lied on finding a feasible matching minimizing the number of blocking pairs. Mnich et al. [18] studied the STABLE MARRIAGE WITH COVERING CONSTRAINTS problem, which corresponds to the special case of Hamada et al.'s model where each hospital has unit upper quota, from a parameterized perspective considering parameters such as the number of blocking pairs and the number of hospitals with non-zero lower quota. To capture sta-

ble matching problems with diversity or distributional constraints, the model of
Hamada et al. [11] has been adapted and further developed in various directions, for example, by assuming that residents belong to different types and each
hospital has type-specific lower and upper quotas [3,9,13].

Another popular stable matching problem is the Hospital Residents problem
with couples (HRC) [6,17], where some of the residents are grouped in pairs and
submit their preferences together. The HR-Q_L^U problem where all hospitals have
upper quota at most two is closely related to the special case of HRC where all
hospitals have upper quota one: Switching the roles of residents and hospitals
and interpreting couples as hospitals with lower quota two, the only difference
between the two problems is that the preferences of couples are over pairs of
hospitals, while the preferences of quota-two hospitals are over single residents.

From a technical perspective, our work falls in line with previous work on
the parameterized complexity of stable matching problems [16–18].

2   Preliminaries

We consider different models of stable bipartite many-to-one matchings. For the
sake of readability, we refer to all of them as different variants of the Hospital
Residents problem with lower and upper quotas (HR-Q_L^U). In HR-Q_L^U, we are
given a set $R = \{r_1, \ldots, r_n\}$ of *residents* and a set $H = \{h_1, \ldots, h_m\}$ of *hospitals*,
each with a lower and upper quota. Throughout the paper, n denotes the number
of residents and m the number of hospitals. We refer to the joint set of residents
and hospitals as *agents*. Each resident $r \in R$ *accepts* a subset of hospitals $A(r) \subseteq$
H and each hospital $h \in H$ *accepts* a subset of residents $A(h) \subseteq R$. Each
agent $a \in R \cup H$ has a preference list in which all agents from $A(a)$ are ranked
in strict order. For three agents a, a_1, and a_2, we say that a *prefers* a_1 to a_2 and
write $a_1 \succ_a a_2$ if $a_1, a_2 \in A(a)$ and a ranks a_1 above a_2.

A *matching* M is a subset of $R \times H$ where each resident is contained in at
most one pair and for each pair $(r, h) \in M$, agents r and h accept each other. For
a matching M and a resident $r \in R$, we denote by $M(r)$ the hospital to which
r is matched to in M, i.e., $M(r) = h$ if $(r, h) \in M$, and we set $M(r) := \square$ if r is
not assigned. All residents r prefer each hospital $h \in A(r)$ to being unmatched,
i.e., $M(r) = \square$. Further, for a hospital $h \in H$, we denote by $M(h)$ the set of
residents that are matched to h, i.e., $r \in M(h)$ if $(r, h) \in M$. We sometimes
write M as a set of pairs of the form $(h, \{r_1, \ldots, r_k\})$, which denotes that the
residents $r_1, \ldots, r_k$ are matched to hospital h in M.

In HR-Q_L^U, each hospital $h \in H$ has an upper quota $u(h)$ and a lower
quota $l(h)$ with $1 \leq l(h) \leq u(h)$. We call a matching M *feasible* if, for all
hospitals $h \in H$, it either holds that $|M(h)| = 0$ or $l(h) \leq |M(h)| \leq u(h)$. We
say that a hospital $h \in H$ is *closed* in M if $|M(h)| = 0$ and we say that it is *open*
otherwise. Moreover, we call an open hospital $h \in H$ *full* if $|M(h)| = u(h)$ and
an open hospital $h \in H$ *undersubscribed* if $|M(h)| < u(h)$. In a matching M,
a hospital-resident pair $(r, h) \in R \times H$ is a *blocking pair* if h is open in M,
both r and h find each other acceptable, r prefers h to $M(r)$, and h is either
undersubscribed or prefers r to at least one resident from $M(h)$. Moreover, we

call $(h, \{r_1, \ldots, r_k\})$ with $k = l(h)$ a *blocking coalition* if h is closed in M and, for all $i \in [k]$, resident r_i prefers h to $M(r_i)$. In this case, we also write that $\{r_1, \ldots, r_k\}$ forms a blocking coalition to open h. A feasible matching is called *stable* if it neither admits a blocking pair nor a blocking coalition.

We now describe how the other two models considered in this paper can be formulated as variants of $HR\text{-}Q_L^U$.

House Allocation Problem with Lower and Upper Quotas. $HA\text{-}Q_L^U$ corresponds to $HR\text{-}Q_L^U$ with one-sided preferences, i.e., all hospitals are indifferent among all residents and residents have strict preferences over hospitals. While the definition of a blocking coalition still applies in this setting, a hospital-resident pair $(r, h) \in R \times H$ is only *blocking* if h is open in M, resident r accepts h, resident r prefers h to $M(r)$, and h is undersubscribed. Note that $HR\text{-}Q_L^U$ does not subsume $HA\text{-}Q_L^U$, as, in $HR\text{-}Q_L^U$, no ties in the preferences are allowed.

Hospital Residents Problem with Lower Quotas. $HR\text{-}Q_L$ is the special case of $HR\text{-}Q_L^U$ where each hospital has upper quota $n + 1$. Thereby, no hospital can be full in a matching. Consequently, in a matching M, a resident r forms a blocking pair with each hospital h she prefers to $M(r)$. Thus, in every stable matching, all residents need to be matched to their most preferred open hospital. This in turn implies that the preferences of hospitals over residents can be omitted, as they have no influence on the stability of a matching. Hence, $HR\text{-}Q_L$ is equivalent to the House Allocation problem with lower quotas ($= HA\text{-}Q_L$) and thus lies in the "intersection" of $HR\text{-}Q_L^U$ and $HA\text{-}Q_L^U$.

First Observations. As already observed, $HR\text{-}Q_L$ instances can be expressed both as $HR\text{-}Q_L^U$ and $HA\text{-}Q_L^U$ instances. Notably, most instances constructed in our reductions fulfill an additional property which directly transfers the hardness results to a variant of $HR\text{-}Q_L$ where only blocking coalitions may make a matching unstable.

Observation 1. *In $HR\text{-}Q_L$ instances where for each hospital $h \in H$, the number of residents accepting h is equal to its lower quota $l(h)$, no blocking pairs can exist, while blocking coalitions can still exist.*

Unfortunately, a stable matching may fail to exist in $HR\text{-}Q_L$ instances (and therefore also in $HR\text{-}Q_L^U$ and $HA\text{-}Q_L^U$ instances), even if all hospitals have lower quota at most two. Consider as an example a $HR\text{-}Q_L$ instance consisting of three hospitals h_1, h_2, and h_3 each with lower quota two and three residents with the following preferences $r_1 : h_1 \succ h_2$; $r_2 : h_2 \succ h_3$; $r_3 : h_3 \succ h_1$. Note that this example resembles the Condorcet paradox.

3   Parameterized Complexity

We analyze the parameterized computational complexity of $HR\text{-}Q_L$, $HR\text{-}Q_L^U$, and $HA\text{-}Q_L^U$. We start by proving that all three problems are NP-complete. Then, we consider the influence of several problem-specific parameters including the number of residents and the number of hospitals.

An NP-Completeness Result. Biró et al. [5] proved that $HR\text{-}Q_L^U$ is NP-complete, even if each hospital has upper quota at most three. However, their reduction does not settle the computational complexity of $HR\text{-}Q_L$ or $HA\text{-}Q_L^U$. To answer this question, note that all three models subsume hedonic games (see [4] for definitions): We introduce a resident for each agent in the given hedonic game and a hospital for each possible coalition with lower quota equal to the size of the coalition. We replace the coalitions in the agents' preferences by the corresponding hospitals. Core stable outcomes in the hedonic game then correspond to stable matchings in the constructed $HR\text{-}Q_L$ instance, which notably falls under Observation 1. As deciding the existence of a core stable outcome is NP-complete, even if all coalitions have size three [20], this implies that all three problems are NP-complete, even if each hospital has lower quota (and upper quota) at most three. By slightly adopting the reduction from [20], one can also bound the number of residents acceptable to a hospital and the number of hospitals acceptable to a resident:

Theorem 1. $HR\text{-}Q_L$, $HR\text{-}Q_L^U$, and $HA\text{-}Q_L^U$ are NP-complete, even if each resident accepts at most four hospitals, each hospital accepts at most three residents, and the lower (and upper) quota of every hospital is at most three.

Parameterization by Number of Residents. After establishing the NP-hardness of all three problems, we now analyze their computational complexity parameterized by the number of residents. While there exists a straightforward XP algorithm for this parameter that guesses for each resident the hospital she is assigned to, all three problems are W[1]-hard.

Theorem 2. Parameterized by the number n of residents, $HR\text{-}Q_L$, $HR\text{-}Q_L^U$, and $HA\text{-}Q_L^U$ are W[1]-hard, even if every hospital has lower (and upper) quota at most four and accepts at most four residents.

Compared to Theorem 1, the hardness statement from Theorem 2 does not bound the number of hospitals accepted by each resident. In fact, combining these two parameters, all three problems become fixed-parameter tractable, as the size of the instance (ignoring hospitals which no resident accepts) can be bounded in a function of the two parameters.

Influence of Hospitals. After studying the parameterization by the number of residents, we turn to the number of hospitals and several closely related parameters. We start by considering the problem of finding a stable matching opening exactly a given set of hospitals.

Which Hospitals Should be Open? It is possible to think of finding a stable matching as a two-step process. First, decide which hospitals are open and second, compute a stable matching between the residents and the selected set of open hospitals respecting all quotas. This observation leads to the question what happens if the first step has been already done, e.g., by an oracle or by some authority, and we are left with the task of finding a stable matching where exactly a given set of hospitals is open. We show that while for $HR\text{-}Q_L$ and $HR\text{-}Q_L^U$ this problem is solvable in polynomial-time, it is NP-hard for $HA\text{-}Q_L^U$.

As already observed in Sect. 2, in an $HR\text{-}Q_L$ instance (H, R), all residents are assigned to their most preferred open hospital in a stable matching. Thereby, checking whether there exists a stable matching where exactly a given set $H_{\text{open}} \subseteq H$ of hospitals is open reduces to assigning each resident to her most preferred hospital in H_{open} and checking whether the resulting matching is stable in (H, R). For $HR\text{-}Q_L^U$, a slightly more involved reasoning is needed, which utilizes the famous Rural Hospitals Theorem [21]:

Proposition 1. *Given a subset of hospitals $H_{\text{open}} \subseteq H$, deciding whether there exists a stable matching in an $HR\text{-}Q_L$ or $HR\text{-}Q_L^U$ instance (H, R) in which exactly the hospitals from H_{open} are open is solvable in $\mathcal{O}(nm)$ time.*

This result suggests that the complexity of $HR\text{-}Q_L$ and $HR\text{-}Q_L^U$ comes purely from deciding which hospitals are open and not from the task of assigning residents to hospitals. This finding is also strengthened by the general observation that most of our hardness reductions also work if we ignore blocking pairs.

In sharp contrast to the preceding positive results for $HR\text{-}Q_L$ and $HR\text{-}Q_L^U$, $HA\text{-}Q_L^U$ remains NP-complete even if we know which hospitals are open in a stable matching.

Theorem 3. *Given a subset of hospitals $H_{\text{open}} \subseteq H$, deciding whether there exists a stable matching in an $HA\text{-}Q_L^U$ instance (H, R) in which exactly the hospitals from H_{open} are open is NP-complete, even if all hospitals have lower quota at most two.*

Parameterization by the Number of Hospitals (with Non-Unit Lower Quota). Together with the number n of residents, the number m of hospitals is an important and straightforward structural parameter of the studied problems. For both $HR\text{-}Q_L$ and $HR\text{-}Q_L^U$, it is possible to iterate over all possible subsets of hospitals $H_{\text{open}} \subseteq H$ and use Proposition 1 to decide whether there exists a stable matching in which exactly the hospitals from H_{open} are open. Let $H^{\text{quota}} \subseteq H$ denote the set of hospitals with non-unit lower quota. In fact, it is only necessary to iterate over all possible subsets $H_{\text{open}} \subseteq H^{\text{quota}}$ with non-unit lower quota. Subsequently, we can add all hospitals with lower quota one to H_{open} and apply again Proposition 1 to compute a matching which we then check for stability and feasibility.

Corollary 1. *$HR\text{-}Q_L$ and $HR\text{-}Q_L^U$ are solvable in $\mathcal{O}(nm \cdot 2^{m_{\text{quota}}})$ time, where m_{quota} is the number of hospitals with non-unit lower quota.*

Turning to $HA\text{-}Q_L^U$, despite the fact that it is NP-complete to decide whether there exists a stable matching even if the set of open hospitals is given, $HA\text{-}Q_L^U$ parameterized by the number m of hospitals turns out to be fixed-parameter tractable. The algorithm utilizes that the number of different resident types in

---

Algorithm 1. Algorithm for $HR\text{-}Q_{L\leq2}^U$ (high-level description)

Input: An $HR\text{-}Q_{L\leq2}^U$ instance $\mathcal{I}$
Output: A stable matching in $\mathcal{I}$ or NO if $\mathcal{I}$ does not admit a stable matching.
1: Apply **Phase 1a - Propose&Reject**
2: $S \leftarrow$ {residents with non-empty preferences}   ▷ Initialization
3: **while** there exists a resident r with at least two hospitals on her preferences **do**
4:     Apply **Phase 1a - Propose&Reject**
5:     **while** a hospital holding at least two proposals exists **do**
6:         **for each** hospital h holding at least two proposals **do**
7:             Split h into $u(h)$ hospitals $h^1, \ldots, h^{u(h)}$ ▷ Phase 1b
8:         Apply **Phase 1a - Propose&Reject**
9:     **if** there exists a resident r with at least two hospitals on her preferences **then**
10:        Find a generalized rotation R.   ▷ Phase 2
11:        Eliminate R.
12: **if** all residents from S have exactly one hospital on their preferences left **then**
13:     **return** matching M that matches every resident r with non-empty preferences
       to the hospital from $\mathcal{I}$ corresponding to the remaining hospital on her preferences.
14: **return** NO

---

a $HA\text{-}Q_L^U$ instance can be bounded in a function of m, as a resident is fully characterized by her preferences over hospitals. This observation can be used to construct an ILP where the number of variables is bounded in a function of m. Employing Lenstra's algorithm [14] shows that the problem is fixed-parameter tractable parameterized by the number of hospitals. However, it is not possible to follow a similar approach to construct a fixed-parameter tractable algorithm for the the number m_{quota} of hospitals with non-unit lower quota. In fact, $HA\text{-}Q_L^U$ is NP-complete even for only three hospitals with non-unit lower quota.

Proposition 2. *Parameterized by the number of hospitals, $HA\text{-}Q_L^U$ is fixed-parameter tractable. $HA\text{-}Q_L^U$ is NP-complete, even if only three hospitals have lower and upper quota two and all other hospitals have upper quota one.*

4   A Restricted Case: Quota Two

In this section, we consider the special case of $HR\text{-}Q_L^U$ where all hospitals have lower quota at most two. We denote this problem by $HR\text{-}Q_{L\leq2}^U$. We present a polynomial-time algorithm for $HR\text{-}Q_{L\leq2}^U$, which constructs a stable matching if it exists. As $HR\text{-}Q_L$ is a special case of $HR\text{-}Q_L^U$, this algorithm also applies to $HR\text{-}Q_L$ instances where all lower quotas are at most two. In the following, we refer to all hospitals with lower quota one as *quota-one hospitals* and to all hospitals with lower quota two as *quota-two hospitals*.

High-Level Description of the Algorithm. Algorithm 1 gives a high-level description of our algorithm. The algorithm consists of two phases (Phase 1 and Phase 2), where the first phase is again split into Phase 1a and Phase 1b. Phase 1a identifies hospital-resident pairs which cannot be part of a stable matching using a propose-and-reject approach. Subsequently, for each such hospital-resident pair (r, h), hospital h is deleted from the preferences of r and vice versa. Furthermore, Phase 1a identifies some quota-two hospitals which are open in every stable matching. Phase 1b further simplifies the instance by replacing quota-two hospitals that are open in every stable matching by multiple copies of this hospital with lower quota one. Phase 1a and Phase 1b are applied repeatedly until no hospital from which we know that it is open in every stable matching exists. After that, in Phase 2, we identify substructures which we call "generalized rotations" and subsequently eliminate them by deleting the acceptability of some hospital-resident pairs. While Phase 1 keeps the number of stable matchings identical, Phase 2 may reduce the number of stable matchings in the instance, but still guarantees that at least one stable matching survives (if there exists one in the original instance).

The algorithm applies Phase 1 and Phase 2 alternately until every resident has at most one hospital on her preferences. The algorithm returns NO if, after the initialization, the preferences of a resident got empty, as one can show that all residents with non-empty preferences are matched in every stable matching. Otherwise, the algorithm constructs a stable matching where all residents with empty preferences are unmatched and all residents with non-empty preferences are matched to the hospital on their preference list (if this hospital was created by splitting a hospital h, then the resident is matched to h).

Theorem 4. *If the lower quota of each hospital is at most two, then HR-Q_L^U (and thereby also HR-Q_L) is solvable in $\mathcal{O}(n^3 m)$ time.*

Our algorithm is inspired by Irving's algorithm for STABLE ROOMMATES [12]. While the general structure of the two algorithms is similar (two phases, where the first one is based on a propose-and-reject approach and the second one on a substructure called "(generalized) rotation"), the Propose&Reject-Phase and especially the definition of a rotation needs to be significantly extended and fundamentally reworked for HR-$Q_{L \leq 2}^U$. The main reason for this is the presence of quota-two hospitals for which we do not know whether they are open in a stable matching, even if they receive a proposal.

We now describe Phases 1a, 1b, and 2 in more detail. We start by observing that we may assume that quota-one hospitals have upper quota one: It is possible to replace every quota-one hospital $h \in H$ by $u(h)$ copies $h^1, \ldots, h^{u(h)}$ each with lower and upper quota one and with the same preferences as h. In the preferences of residents, h is replaced by $h^1 \succ \cdots \succ h^{u(h)}$.

Phase 1a - Propose and Reject. In Phase 1a, residents and hospitals propose to one another. Residents always propose to hospitals and hospitals always to residents. If a resident $r \in R$ proposes to a hospital $h \in H$, then the receiver h of the proposal can either *accept* or *reject* the proposal from r. We say that a hospital h *holds* a proposal r if r proposed to h and h did not reject the proposal (until now). We say that a resident r (currently) *issues* a proposal if there exists a hospital h that holds the proposal r. The notation also applies if the roles of residents and hospitals are swapped. Considering quota-two hospitals, we distinguish between *activated* and *deactivated* hospitals. Initially, all quota-two hospitals are deactivated.

Algorithm (Phase 1a). We proceed in multiple rounds. In each round, an arbitrary resident or quota-one hospital with non-empty preferences that does not currently issue a proposal or an activated quota-two hospital is selected. If a resident or quota-one hospital is selected, then it proposes to the first hospital or resident on its preference list. If an activated quota-two hospital h is selected, then the hospital proposes to the first $u(h)$ residents on its preference list unless h received exactly one proposal from a resident r which is among the first $u(h)$ residents in h's preferences: In this case, h only proposes to the first $u(h) - 1$ residents that are not r.

If a resident or a quota-one hospital receives a proposal, then it *accepts* the proposal if it does not hold a proposal or if it prefers its new proposal to the one it currently holds. Similarly, it *rejects* a proposal if it either already holds or later receives a better proposal. A quota-two hospital h *accepts* a proposal r if it does not hold $u(h)$ proposals it prefers to r. It *rejects* a proposal r if it holds or at some point receives $u(h)$ proposals it prefers to r, or if the hospital has been rejected by all but one resident on its preference list. If an agent a proposes to an agent a' and a' rejects the proposal, then we delete a' from the preference list of a and a from the preference list of a'.

A quota-two hospital h gets activated if it receives a proposal or if one of its proposals gets rejected. If h currently holds exactly one proposal by one of its $u(h)$ most preferred residents r, then it gets deactivated if it currently issues $u(h) - 1$ proposals or has proposed to all residents on its preference list except r. Otherwise, it gets deactivated if it currently issues $u(h)$ proposals or has proposed to all residents on its preference list.

At the end of Phase 1a, we delete from the preferences of all quota-one hospitals and residents holding a proposal all agents to which they prefer the held proposal. Subsequently, we restore the mutual acceptability of agents by deleting for each agent a an agent a' from its preference list if a does not appear on the preference list of a'. Finally, we delete all quota-two hospitals with at most one resident on their preference list.

The intuitive reasoning behind Phase 1a is the following. If an agent rejects the proposal of another agent, then the two can never be matched to each other in a stable matching. Thereby, no agent can be matched better than the agent it proposes to. Thus, any agent receiving a proposal can be sure that it does not end up worse than the proposal it currently holds in a stable matching, since it forms a blocking pair with the agent issuing its proposal otherwise. After Phase 1a, each resident and quota-one hospital issues a proposal to the first agent on its preference list and holds a proposal from the last agent on its preference list.

I $h_1 : r_3 \succ r_1$ $r_1 : h_1 \succ h_2$ **II** $h_1 : r_3 \succ r_1$ $r_1 : h_1 \succ h_2$

$h_2 : r_1 \succ r_2$ $r_2 : h_4 \succ h_2 \succ h_3$ $h_2 : r_1 \succ r_2$ $r_2 : h_2 \succ h_3$

$h_3 : r_2 \succ r_3$ $r_3 : h_3 \succ h_1 \succ h_4$ $h_3 : r_2 \succ r_3$ $r_3 : h_3 \succ h_1$

$h_4 : r_2 \succ r_3$ $h_4 :$

Fig. 1. An example for Phase 1. Hospital h_1 is a quota-one hospital, while the other three hospitals are quota-two hospitals. In the beginning (see instance **I**), each resident and h_1 propose to their top-choice, which all accept their received proposal. Thereby, both h_3 and h_4 get activated and propose to r_2 respectively r_3. Resident r_3 rejects the proposal from h_4, while r_2 accepts the proposal of h_3. Then, the preferences of h_4 contain only one resident, and thus h_4 rejects the proposal from r_2. Consequently, r_2 proposes to h_2, which activates h_2. Subsequently, h_2 proposes to r_1, who accepts the proposal. As no quota-two hospital received two proposals, no hospital gets split and Phase 1 ends (see instance **II**).

Phase 1b - Split Hospitals. In this phase, we identify quota-two hospitals that are open in every stable matching and replace them by quota-one hospitals:

Algorithm (Phase 1b). We replace each quota-two hospital h holding at least two proposals by $u(h)$ hospitals $h^1, \ldots, h^{u(h)}$ with lower and upper quota one with the same preferences as h. In the preferences of all residents, h is replaced by $h^1 \succ \cdots \succ h^{u(h)}$.

To summarize, Phase 1 consists of applying Phase 1a and Phase 1b as long as at least one hospital was split in the last execution of Phase 1b. An example for the execution of Phase 1 can be found in Fig. 1.

Phase 2 - Eliminate Generalized Rotations. We introduce some notation for the definition of a generalized rotation. We call a quota-two hospital with more than two residents on its preferences *flexible* and all other quota-two hospitals *inflexible*. Note that while we already know which residents will be assigned to an open inflexible hospital (as the number of residents on its preferences is equal to its lower quota), this is not clear for open flexible hospitals. Given a resident r, we denote by $h(r)$ the first hospital on r's preferences. If $h(r)$ is flexible, then we define $g(r) := h(r)$. Otherwise, we define $g(r)$ to be the second hospital on r's preference list.

A *generalized rotation* is a sequence $(a_1, b_1), \ldots, (a_k, b_k)$ consisting of residents and quota-one hospitals with $a_i \neq a_j$ for all $i \neq j$ such that (all following indices are taken modulo k):

Relationship Between a_i and b_{i+1}:

AB$^+$−1 If a_i is a quota-one hospital, then b_{i+1} is the second resident on a_i's preferences.

AB$^+$−2 If a_i is a resident and $h(a_i)$ is a flexible hospital, then b_{i+1} is the second-most preferred resident on $h(a_i)$'s preferences who is not a_i.

I	$h_1 : r_3 \succ r_1$	$r_1 : h_1 \succ h_2$	**II**	$h_1 : r_3$	$r_1 : h_2$
	$h_2 : r_1 \succ r_2$	$r_2 : h_2 \succ h_3$		$h_2 : r_1 \succ r_2$	$r_2 : h_2$
	$h_3 : r_2 \succ r_3$	$r_3 : h_3 \succ h_1$		$h_3 : r_3$	$r_3 : h_3 \succ h_1$

Fig. 2. An example for Phase 2. Hospital h_1 is a quota-one hospital, while the other two hospitals are quota-two hospitals. Initially (see instance **I**), h_1 holds the proposal of r_1, hospital h_2 the proposal of r_2, and h_3 the proposal of r_3. The instance admits the following generalized rotation: $(r_1, h_1), (r_3, r_2)$. Note that for $b_1 = h_1$ case BA-1 applies, for $a_1 = r_1$ case AB$^+$-3b(i) applies, for $b_2 = r_2$ case BA-3 applies, and for $a_2 = r_3$ case AB$^+$-3a applies. Eliminating this generalized rotation results in instance **II**.

If a_i is a resident and $h(a_i)$ is an inflexible hospital or a quota-one hospital and

AB$^+$−3a   if $g(a_i)$ is a quota-one hospital, then $b_{i+1} := g(a_i)$.
AB$^+$−3b(i)   if $g(a_i)$ is a quota-two hospital holding proposal r, then $b_{i+1} := r$.
AB$^+$−3b(ii) if $g(a_i)$ is a quota-two hospital which does not hold a proposal, then b_{i+1} is $g(a_i)$'s most preferred resident who is not a_i.

Relationship Between b_i and a_i:

BA−1 If b_i is a quota-one hospital, then a_i is the last resident on b_i's preferences.
BA−2 If b_i is a resident and the last hospital h on b_i's preferences is of quota one, then $a_i := h$.
BA−3 If b_i is a resident and the last hospital h on b_i's preferences is of quota two, then a_i is the resident with h as top-choice, i.e., the resident proposing to h.

Algorithm (Phase 2). Phase 2 computes a generalized rotation by starting with an arbitrary resident whose preference list has length at least two as a_1 and subsequently applying the relationships depicted above to find $b_2, a_2, \ldots$ until this procedure cycles and a generalized rotation has been found. It is possible to prove that this procedure always finds a generalized rotation. Subsequently, we *eliminate* the found rotation by deleting, for all $i \in [k]$, the mutual acceptability of a_i and b_i if one of them is a hospital, and otherwise the mutual acceptability of hospital $h(a_i)$ and b_i. After that, Phase 1 is applied again to the resulting instance. An example for Phase 2 can be found in Fig. 2.

In a "classical" rotation $(a_1, b_1), \ldots, (a_k, b_k)$ for STABLE ROOMMATES [12], for all $i \in [k]$, agent b_{i+1} is the second agent on the preference list of a_i and a_i is the last agent on the preference list of b_i, which implies that b_i is the top-choice of a_i. Here, eliminating a rotation consists of deleting the mutual acceptability of a_i and b_i for all $i \in [k]$ and results in an instance that admits a stable matching if the original instance admits one. Part of the reason for this is that if we assume that there exists a stable matching M which contains the pairs (a_i, b_i) for all $i \in [k]$, then the matching M' arising by replacing these pairs by the pairs (a_i, b_{i+1}) is also stable: Each agent b_i prefers M' over M, and agent a_i can only form a blocking pair with b_i, implying that no blocking pair has been introduced.

However, applying this classical definition to $HR\text{-}Q^U_{L\leq 2}$, the observation from above does not longer hold. Therefore, we generalize the definition of a rotation in a way such that no quota-two hospital appears in a generalized rotation, while keeping the intuition: For $BA-1$ and $BA-2$, a_i is still b_i's least preferred agent, while for $BA-3$ following the classical definition, it would be necessary to set a_i to a quota-two hospital h. Instead, we set a_i to be the resident proposing to h, which can be interpreted as matching b_i to h together with a_i. For the relationship between a_i and b_{i+1}, for AB^+-1, b_{i+1} is still the second agent in the preferences of a_i. For AB^+-2, it is necessary to recall that for a flexible hospital h there exist multiple possibilities which residents are matched to h in a stable matching. The "most preferred option" of a resident r is to be matched to $h(r)$ together with $h(r)$'s most preferred remaining resident, while her second-most preferred option is to be matched to $h(r)$ with $h(r)$'s second-most preferred remaining resident. If $h(r)$ is inflexible, then there exists only one possibility for a resident r to be matched to $h(r)$ so her second-most preferred alternative is to be matched to $g(r)$ with the necessary case distinctions made in AB^+-3a, $AB^+-3b(i)$, and $AB^+-3b(ii)$.

5 Conclusion

We conducted a thorough parameterized complexity analysis of the Hospital Residents problem with lower and upper quotas. We have shown that the hardness of this problem arises from choosing the set of open hospitals such that no blocking coalition exists, as the problem remains hard even if all hospitals have only lower quotas and pairs cannot block an outcome, but it becomes easy as soon as the set of open hospitals is given. We have also analyzed two variants of this problem.

One direction for future work is to analyze what happens if the preferences may contain ties. Using the ILP approach sketched in Proposition 2, parameterized by the number of hospitals, $HR\text{-}Q_L$ and $HA\text{-}Q^U_L$ should remain fixed-parameter tractable parameterized by the number of hospitals, while for $HR\text{-}Q^U_L$ the situation is unclear. Notably, in this setting, $HR\text{-}Q^U_L$ subsumes the two other models. Moreover, it would be also interesting to analyze other stable many-to-one matching problems using a similar fine-grained parameterized approach as taken in this paper to enrich our understanding of the complexity of these problems. Finally, our polynomial-time algorithm for lower quota two might be adaptable to also work for other problems such as special variants of the three-dimensional STABLE ROOMMATES problem.

References

1. Ágoston, K.C., Biró, P., McBride, I.: Integer programming methods for special college admissions problems. J. Comb. Optim. **32**(4), 1371–1399 (2016). https://doi.org/10.1007/s10878-016-0085-x

2. Arulselvan, A., Cseh, Á., Groß, M., Manlove, D.F., Matuschke, J.: Matchings with lower quotas: algorithms and complexity. Algorithmica **80**(1), 185–208 (2018)
3. Aziz, H., Gaspers, S., Sun, Z., Walsh, T.: From matching with diversity constraints to matching with regional quotas. In: AAMAS 2019, pp. 377–385 (2019)
4. Aziz, H., Savani, R.: Hedonic games. In: Handbook of Computational Social Choice, pp. 356–376 (2016)
5. Biró, P., Fleiner, T., Irving, R.W., Manlove, D.: The college admissions problem with lower and common quotas. Theor. Comput. Sci. **411**(34–36), 3136–3153 (2010)
6. Biró, P., Manlove, D.F., McBride, I.: The hospitals/residents problem with couples: complexity and integer programming models. In: Gudmundsson, J., Katajainen, J. (eds.) SEA 2014. LNCS, vol. 8504, pp. 10–21. Springer, Cham (2014). https://doi.org/10.1007/978-3-319-07959-2_2
7. Boehmer, N., Heeger, K.: A fine-grained view on stable many-to-one matching problems with lower and upper quotas. CoRR abs/2009.14171 (2020)
8. Cechlárová, K., Fleiner, T.: Pareto optimal matchings with lower quotas. Math. Soc. Sci. **88**, 3–10 (2017)
9. Ehlers, L., Hafalir, I.E., Yenmez, M.B., Yildirim, M.A.: School choice with controlled choice constraints: hard bounds versus soft bounds. J. Econ. Theor. **153**, 648–683 (2014)
10. Gale, D., Shapley, L.S.: College admissions and the stability of marriage. Am. Math. Mon. **69**(1), 9–15 (1962)
11. Hamada, K., Iwama, K., Miyazaki, S.: The hospitals/residents problem with lower quotas. Algorithmica **74**(1), 440–465 (2016)
12. Irving, R.W.: An efficient algorithm for the "stable roommates" problem. J. Algorithms **6**(4), 577–595 (1985)
13. Kurata, R., Hamada, N., Iwasaki, A., Yokoo, M.: Controlled school choice with soft bounds and overlapping types. J. Artif. Intell. Res. **58**, 153–184 (2017)
14. Lenstra, H.W.: Integer programming with a fixed number of variables. Math. Oper. Res. **8**(4), 538–548 (1983)
15. Manlove, D.F.: Algorithmics of Matching Under Preferences. Series on Theoretical Computer Science, vol. 2. World Scientific, Singapore (2013)
16. Marx, D., Schlotter, I.: Parameterized complexity and local search approaches for the stable marriage problem with ties. Algorithmica **58**(1), 170–187 (2010)
17. Marx, D., Schlotter, I.: Stable assignment with couples: parameterized complexity and local search. Discret. Optim. **8**(1), 25–40 (2011)
18. Mnich, M., Schlotter, I.: Stable matchings with covering constraints: a complete computational trichotomy. Algorithmica **82**(5), 1136–1188 (2020)
19. Monte, D., Tumennasan, N.: Matching with quorums. Econ. Lett. **120**(1), 14–17 (2013)
20. Ng, C., Hirschberg, D.S.: Three-dimensional stable matching problems. SIAM J. Discret. Math. **4**(2), 245–252 (1991)
21. Roth, A.E.: The evolution of the labor market for medical interns and residents: a case study in game theory. J. Polit. Econ. **92**(6), 991–1016 (1984)
22. Roth, A.E.: Deferred acceptance algorithms: history, theory, practice, and open questions. Int. J. Game Theor. **36**(3–4), 537–569 (2008)

The Ad Types Problem

Riccardo Colini-Baldeschi[1], Julián Mestre[2]([📧]), Okke Schrijvers[1], and Christopher A. Wilkens[3]

[1] Core Data Science, Facebook Inc., Cambridge, USA
[2] School of Computer Science, University of Sydney, Camperdown, Australia
julian.mestre@sydney.edu.au
[3] Tremor Technologies, Boston, USA

Abstract. In this paper we introduce the *Ad Types Problem*, a generalization of the traditional positional auction model for ad allocation that better captures some of the challenges that arise when ads of different types need to be interspersed within a user feed of organic content.

The Ad Types problem (without gap rules) is a special case of the assignment problem in which there are k types of nodes on one side (the ads), and an ordered set of nodes on the other side (the slots). The edge weight of an ad i of type θ to slot j is $v_i \cdot \alpha_j^\theta$ where v_i is an advertiser-specific value and each ad type θ has a discount curve $\alpha_1^{(\theta)} \geq \alpha_2^{(\theta)} \geq \ldots \geq 0$ over the slots that is common for ads of type θ. We present two contributions for this problem: 1) we give an algorithm that finds the maximum weight matching that runs in $O(n^2(k + \log n))$ time for n slots and n ads of each type—cf. $O(kn^3)$ when using the Hungarian algorithm—, and 2) we show how to apply reserve prices in total time $O(n^3(k + \log n))$.

The Ad Types Problem (with gap rules) includes a matrix G such that after we show an ad of type θ_i, the next G_{ij} slots cannot show an ad of type θ_j. We show that the problem is hard to approximate within $k^{1-\epsilon}$ for any $\epsilon > 0$ (even without discount curves) by reduction from Maximum Independent Set. On the positive side, we show a Dynamic Program formulation that solves the problem (including discount curves) optimally and runs in $O(k \cdot n^{2k+1})$ time.

1 Introduction

Feeds aggregate a variety of content into a one-stop source of information. In order to present content in a way that maximizes engagement, state-of-the-art feeds like Facebook's News Feed, Reddit, and Apple News must consider not only the user's independent interest in each item but also the position in the feed and the relative order of items. Optimizing ad placement in these platforms presents similar challenges; to capture some of them, we introduce a generalization of the canonical position auction known as the *Ad Types Problem*.

Position auction [11,39] is the default mechanism for simultaneously selecting multiple ads. A standard position auction is simple: rank ads according to their expected advertising value and rank slots according to their prominence (position

© Springer Nature Switzerland AG 2020
X. Chen et al. (Eds.): WINE 2020, LNCS 12495, pp. 45–58, 2020.
https://doi.org/10.1007/978-3-030-64946-3_4

in the feed); the highest-value ad then appears in the most prominent slot and so on until all slots are filled. Formally, the auction maximizes value using a separable value model that combines baseline value for each ad with a position discount for each slot $1 \geq \alpha_1 \geq \ldots \geq 0$ capturing the decay in value associated with lower-prominence.

Content feeds bring two important complexities that violate the simple separable model: ads are not homogeneous, and spacing matters. Firstly, in the same way that a feed aggregates many types of content, a feed may simultaneously include ads in many formats, including text, images, and video. Advertisers may also have different objectives – some advertisers only want users to see a static image, while other advertisers want users to finish a video or visit their site and make a purchase. Prominence impacts every type differently – for example, a user who has already scrolled deep into a content feed will still see an image ad but may be less likely to watch a video ad to completion. Secondly, spacing matters, since a user who (say) sees two video ads in a row may be less likely to view the second video ad (or simply be annoyed).

Given these complexities, naïvely implementing a position auction using a traditional separable model will be suboptimal. The following example illustrates the problem when the probability of a user watching a video ad decays differently than a link-click ad:

Example 1. Suppose we have a setting with 2 ad types, link-click ads and video ads, two ad slots, and we have discount curve $\alpha_1 = \frac{1}{2}, \alpha_2 = \frac{1}{4}$. These discounts are accurate for link-click ads (i.e. $\alpha_1^{(\text{link})} = \frac{1}{2}, \alpha_2^{(\text{link})} = \frac{1}{4}$), but for video ads, the user is more likely to watch the video in the second slot than they are to click a link in that slot: $\alpha_1^{(\text{video})} = \frac{1}{2}, \alpha_2^{(\text{video})} = \frac{1}{3}$.

Consider a video ad with bid \$12 and a link-click ad with bid \$10. The optimal allocation assuming that discount curve α is accurate for both ads would assign the video ad to slot 1 and the link-click ad to slot 2 for total (reported) value $\frac{1}{2} \cdot \$12 + \frac{1}{4} \cdot \$10 = \$8.50$. However, switching the ads yields total (reported) value $\frac{1}{2} \cdot \$10 + \frac{1}{3} \cdot \$12 = \$9 > \$8.50$.[1]

In this paper we propose a new theoretical model for online advertising that addresses these issues. It captures the position auction as a special case, but can handle discount curves for multiple types and intersperse advertising with organic content in a dynamic manner.[2] An *Ad Types Problem* instance has k ad

---

[1] Note that this example also implies that VCG prices w.r.t. α would not be incentive compatible.

[2] While our motivation for studying this problem comes from online advertising in content streams, it captures many other interesting settings that are unrelated to online advertising. For example, the setting without gap rules can model a worker with different time slots and jobs of different types that need to be done; jobs are most valuable when completed early and delays for jobs of the same type are discounted similarly. Adding gap rules can model the cost of moving between locations (in the physical world) or context-switching (in the digital world).

types[3], that each have their own discount curve over n slots, i.e. all ads of type θ have discount curve $\alpha_1^{(\theta)} \geq \alpha_2^{(\theta)} \geq \ldots \geq \alpha_n^{(\theta)} \geq 0$ that represents the slot-specific action-rates. All ad types agree on the order of the slots. Gap rules are modeled by a $k \times k$ matrix G, which indicates for each pair of ad types (θ_i, θ_j), that after showing an ad of type θ_i, the next G_{ij} stories cannot be of type θ_j.

We first focus on the special case where $G = \mathbf{0}$, i.e. different ad types have different discount curves but there are no constraints on the gaps between ads. In this setting, the Ad Types Problem is a special case of the maximum-weight bipartite matching problem (also known as the assignment problem), so we could find an optimal allocation using the Hungarian algorithm in $O(kn^3)$ time [36] (where k is the number of types, n the number of slots, and we have n ads per type). Our first result is an algorithm that finds the optimal allocation in $O(n^2(k + \log n))$ time, saving a linear factor. We also show that we can compute incentive-compatible prices with advertiser-specific reserve prices for all ads in $O(n^3(k + \log n))$ time.

Next we consider the more general Ad Types problem with both discount curves and gap rules (where $G \neq \mathbf{0}$). We show that the problem is hard to approximate within $k^{1-\epsilon}$ for any $\epsilon > 0$ (even without discount curves) by reduction from Maximum Independent Set. On the positive side, we show a Dynamic Program formulation that solves the problem (including discount curves) optimally and runs in $O(k \cdot n^{2k+1})$ time, which is a significant improvement over the brute-force running time of $O(k^n)$ since typically $k \ll n$.

1.1 Related Work

Assignment Problem. The maximum-weight bipartite matching problem, also known as the assignment problem, is a classical problem in operations research. Let (A, B, E) be a complete bipartite graph with edge weights $v : E \to \mathbb{R}^+$, and $V = A \cup B$ the set of nodes; the goal is to find a matching M of maximal total weight $\sum_{e \in M} v(e)$. Kuhn [28] proposed an algorithm for this problem—which he called the Hungarian algorithm—based on ideas by Kőnig and Egerváry, though he only proved that the algorithm would terminate, not what the time complexity is. Munkres [31] showed that the time complexity of the Hungarian algorithm is $O(|V|^4)$. Edmonds and Karp [12] gave an $O(|V|^3)$ time algorithm for balanced graphs, and Ramshaw and Tarjan [36] more recently gave an algorithm for unbalanced graphs (without loss of generality, assume $|A| < |B|$) that runs in $O(|E||A| + |A|^2 \log |A|)$. Since the seminal work on the assignment problem, there has been active research into relevant special cases. In particular there is a line of work on *convex bipartite graphs*, where the right side of the graph is ordered, and nodes on the left can only be connected to a single contiguous block of nodes on the right. For the unweighted case, a line of work starting with Glover [16,21,29] shows that the problem can be solved in time linear in the number of nodes

---

[3] In economics literature, "type" sometimes refers to private information. That's not the case here: type represents the content type, e.g. video or link-click, and is publicly known.

$O(|V|)$. General weights are not considered, though early work on *vertex-weighted* bipartite graphs (where each node i has an associated weight w_i and the weight of an edge from i to j is $w_{ij} = w_i + w_j$) yield an $O(|E| + |B| \log |A|)$ time algorithm [25]. More recently, Plaxton [34,35] showed that Two-Directional Orthogonal Ray Graphs (a generalization of convex graphs) admit an $O(|V| \log |V|)$ time algorithm.

Sharathkumar and Agarwal [38] consider a more general set of edge weights, where nodes are embedded in d-dimensional space, and the weights of the complete bipartite graph are all either the L_1 or L_∞ metric. They give an algorithm to solve maximum weight bipartite matching in $O(|V|^{3/2} \log^{d+O(1)}(|V|) \log \Delta)$, where Δ is the diameter of the space that contains the points.

None of the results on specializations cover The Ad Types Problem setting (even without gap rules).

Ad Auctions. The simple separable model for position auctions appears in Varian [39] and Edelman et al. [11]. One body of related work relaxes the assumption that action rates are separable. One common theme is to model externalities between ads (also related to our gap rules) [2,3,14,17–20,22,26]. Of note, [2,13, 18,26] study algorithms for computing allocations in models where the user's attention cascades and prove hardness results. A different generalization is to allow arbitrary action rates that are still independent between ads [1,5,6], which corresponds to the Ad Type Problem (without gap rules) where each ad has a unique type.

Another generalization of the basic position auction allows ads to be placed in complex ways. A few papers study mechanisms that permit presentation constraints and/or ads with variable presentation [4,8,23,24,32]. Mahdian *et al.* [30] study auctions for ads displayed on maps along with organic results (since places of interest are connected to a physical location, this imposes constraints on where ads can be placed).

Finally, the connections between ad auctions and max-weight matching (and the Hungarian algorithm) have been studied before as well [5,9,10,27].

1.2 Contributions

This paper presents three main contributions:

- **Optimal Allocation.** Firstly, we give an algorithm to optimally solve the Ad Types problem *without* gap rules. This setting is a special case of the assignment problem with applications beyond ad auctions. Our algorithm is a specialization of the Hungarian algorithm to find the maximum-weight matching in the bipartite graph that uses the structure of the Ad Types Problem to run in $O(n^2(k + \log n))$ time (compared to $O(kn^3)$ for running the Hungarian algorithm on the instance; Theorem 1).
- **Pricing.** Secondly, we show that we can do incentive-compatible pricing in this setting with minimal overhead. First, we show that we can apply reserve prices (and in fact in all single-parameter environments) without a change-point algorithm [33,37]. For our case, this yields an $O(n^3(k + \log n))$ time

algorithm. We also confirm that—similar to the general bipartite matching case—the dual variables in our algorithm for the Ad Types setting (without reserves) can be used to recover VCG prices without increasing the asymptotic running time. This yields VCG prices in $O(n^2(k + \log n))$. Due to lack of space these results appear in the full version of this paper [7].

- **Gap Rules.** Finally, we consider the more general Ad Types problem with both discount curves and gap rules (where $G \neq \mathbf{0}$). We show that the problem is hard to approximate within $k^{1-\epsilon}$ for any $\epsilon > 0$ (even without discount curves) by reduction from Maximum Independent Set (Theorem 2). On the positive side, we give a Dynamic Program formulation that solves the problem (including discount curves) optimally and runs in $O(k \cdot n^{2k+1})$ time (Theorem 3) which is a significant improvement over the brute-force running time of $O(k^n)$ since typically $k \ll n$.

2   Preliminaries

In this section we give a formal definition of the Ad Types problems and with it, the notation that we will be using throughout the paper. Our results build on the known results from Auction Theory and the Hungarian Algorithm for solving the assignment problem.

The Ad Types Problem involves computing an allocation of a set of N ads to $n \leq N$ slots. Ads come in one of k different ad types θ_l, for $l \in \{1, \ldots, k\}$. We let the ads of type θ_l be $a_i^{(\theta_l)}$ for $i \in 1, \ldots, n_l$, where n_l represents the number of ads of type θ_l. There are three main components to the definition of the problem:

- **Valuations.** Ad i of type θ has a value-per-conversion (a.k.a. value-per-action) $v_i^{(\theta)}$. Ads of different types have different conversion events, e.g. for a display ad the conversion event is a view, for a link ad the conversion event is a link click, and for a video ad the conversion event is the user watching video ad. For each ad type θ, we index the ads in non-increasing order of valuation, i.e. $v_1^{(\theta)} \geq v_2^{(\theta)} \geq \ldots \geq v_{n_l}^{(\theta)} \geq 0$.
- **Discount Curves.** We assume a separable model for discount curves where we can write

$$\Pr[\text{conversion on ad } i \text{ (of type } \theta) \text{ in slot } j] = \alpha_j^\theta \cdot \beta_i$$

where α_j^θ is the slot effect for a particular ad type θ (e.g., the probability that a user will watch a video ad if it is shown in the jth slot) and β_i is the advertiser quality (this separable model is also standard in position auctions [11,39]). In the remainder of the paper we assume without loss of generality that the advertiser effect has already been included in the advertiser's value, i.e., if the value-per-conversion of the advertiser is v_i', then $v_i = \beta_i \cdot v_i'$. We further abuse notation to let $v_{ij} = \alpha_j^\theta \cdot v_i$ for ad i of type θ in slot j.

Discounts are monotonically non-increasing, and all ad types agree on the order of slots, i.e. for each ad type θ, we have $\alpha_1^{(\theta)} \geq \alpha_2^{(\theta)} \geq \ldots \geq \alpha_n^{(\theta)} \geq 0$.

- **Gap Rules.** When ads are interspersed with organic content, there must be some way to control how many ads are shown. In the simplest case, where there's only one type of ad, this can be implemented by a gap rule g, which states that two ads must be at least g slots apart from each other. When there are multiple ad types, there is a $k \times k$ matrix G, which indicates for each pair of ad types (θ_i, θ_j), that after showing an ad of type θ_i, the next G_{ij} stories cannot be of type θ_j.

The Ad Types Problem is to find a social welfare maximizing allocation that obeys the gap rules.

2.1   The Hungarian Algorithm

The Hungarian Algorithm [28,31] is a classical algorithm for computing a maximum weight matching in a bipartite graph. Starting from a trivial primal solution (empty matching) and a trivial dual solution, the algorithm iteratively increases the cardinality of the matching while improving the value of the dual solution until the value of the primal solution equals that of the dual.

Let (U, V, E) be a complete bipartite graph with edge weights $v : E \to \mathbb{R}^+$. The primal/dual pair of linear programs capturing the problem are as follows.

$$\text{maximize } \sum_{(i,j) \in E} v_{ij} x_{ij}$$

$$\begin{aligned} \text{subject to } \quad & \sum_j x_{ij} \leq 1 & & \forall i \in U \\ & \sum_i x_{ij} \leq 1 & & \forall j \in V \\ & x_{ij} \geq 0 & & \forall (i,j) \in E \end{aligned}$$

$$\text{minimize } \sum_{i \in U} u_i + \sum_{j \in V} p_j$$

$$\begin{aligned} \text{subject to } \quad & u_i + p_j \geq v_{ij} & & \forall (i,j) \in E \\ & u_i \geq 0 & & \forall i \in U \\ & p_j \geq 0 & & \forall j \in V \end{aligned}$$

The algorithm starts from an empty primal solution $M = \emptyset$, and a trivial feasible dual solution $u_i = 0$ for all $i \in U$ and $p_j = \max_{(i,j) \in E} v_{ij}$ for all $j \in V$. In each iteration, the algorithm identifies the set of tight edges $T = \{(i,j) \in E : u_i + p_j = v_{ij}\}$ and builds an alternating BFS tree B (also known as Hungarian tree) in (U, V, T) out of the free vertices in V. If the alternating tree contains an augmenting path A, we augment M with A thus increasing its cardinality; if no such path is available, we can update the dual solution by reducing the dual value of $V \cap B$ and increasing the dual value of $U \cap B$ by the same amount until a new edge becomes tight. This update maintains feasibility while reducing the value of the dual solution and makes at least one new edge tight, which in turn allows us to grow the alternating tree further.

Throughout the execution of the algorithm we maintain the invariants that the dual solution is feasible and that the edges in the matching M are tight. As a result, at the end of the algorithm we have a matching whose weight equals the value of the dual feasible solution, which acts as a certificate of its optimality.

Using the right data structures, it is possible to implement the algorithm so that the amount of work done between each update to M is $O(|E| + |U| \log |U|)$. Therefore, if we let M^* be a maximum weight matching, then the Hungarian algorithm can be implemented to run in $O(|M^*|(|E| + |U| \log |U|))$ time [15].

Algorithm 1 provides the full pseudo-code of the Hungarian Algorithm applied to the Ad Types problems.

Algorithm 1. Hungarian algorithm for the Ad Types problem.

Input: Values $v_1^{(\theta)} > v_2^{(\theta)} > \ldots > 0$, and
   discounts $\alpha_1^{(\theta)} > \alpha_2^{(\theta)} > \ldots > 0$ for each ad type θ.
Output: Matching M that maximizes $\sum_{(i,j) \in M} v_{ij}$.
1: Initialize the dual solution so that
      ◦ $u_i \leftarrow 0$ for all ads i,
      ◦ $p_j \leftarrow \max v_{i',j'}$ for all slots j.
2: Let $M \leftarrow \emptyset$ be the matching.
3: **for** slot j in descending order **do**
4:    Let $B \leftarrow \{j\}$ be an alternating BFS tree
5:    Let P be an empty priority queue
6:    $P \leftarrow \text{UPDATEPOSSIBLENEWEDGES}(P, v, \alpha, M, j)$
7:    **while** B does not contain an augmenting path **do**
8:       $(i', j') \leftarrow$ remove from P next tight edge
9:       $\Delta \leftarrow v_{i'j'} - u_{i'} - p_{j'}$ // note that Δ could be 0
10:      Implicitly update the dual solution so that
            ◦ $u_{i''} \leftarrow u_{i''} + \Delta$ for all ads $i'' \in B$,
            ◦ $p_{j''} \leftarrow p_{j''} - \Delta$ for all slots $j'' \in B$.
11:      **if** i' is matched in M **then**
12:         $B \leftarrow B \cup \{(i', j'), (i', M(i'))\}$
13:         $\text{UPDATEPOSSIBLENEWEDGES}(P, v, \alpha, M(i'))$
14:      **else**
15:         $B \leftarrow B \cup \{(i', j')\}$ // now an augmenting path exits
16:      **end if**
17:   **end while**
18:   $A \leftarrow$ augmenting path in B
19:   $M \leftarrow \text{AUGMENTMATCHING}(M, A)$.
20:   explicitly update the dual solution (u, p)
21: **end for**

---

3 Ad Types Problem Without Gap Rules

In this section we consider the ad types problem with discount curves but no gap rules. In this model we have k ad types, and each ad type has its own monotonically decreasing discount curve $\alpha_j^{(\theta_l)}$ for $l \in 1, 2, \ldots, k$. Without gap rules, the problem becomes a simple maximum weight bipartite assignment on a complete graph with N vertices (ads) on one side of the bipartition and n

vertices (slots) on the other side of the bipartition, with $n < N$. Therefore, the Hungarian algorithm can solve this problem in $O(Nn^2)$ time. We will assume throughout there are exactly n ads of each type[4], hence the Hungarian algorithm runs in $O(kn^3)$ time.

In this section we start by giving an algorithm that finds the maximum-weight bipartite matching in $O(n^2(k + \log n))$ time (Sect. 3.1). We show that in some sense the dependency on k unavoidable: namely if $k = n$, we show that the Ad Types problem reduces to the assignment problem (i.e. monotonicity and a common order of the slots does not improve the running time; see Sect. 3.2).

3.1   Finding the Optimal Allocation

We present an adaptation of the Hungarian algorithm [28,31] that exploits the special structure of the Ad Types problem. In the following we use the language of markets to describe the Hungarian algorithm: the dual variable of a slot j corresponds to a price p_j, while a dual variable of an advertiser i corresponds to the utility u_i of the advertiser if they get an item out of their demand set (given the prices) [10]. Moreover, the instance is a complete bipartite graph with ads on one side and slots on the other side where the weight of the edge (i, j) is v_{ij}. The maximum-weight matching in the bipartite graph corresponds to the social-welfare maximizing allocation of ads to slots. For ease of exposition, we assume that values and discounts are monotonically *strictly* decreasing, this restriction can be lifted by consistent tie-breaking.

Algorithm 1 in the preliminaries shows how to compute the optimal allocation in an Ad Types instance using the Hungarian Algorithm. Our approach is to implement more efficiently how we maintain the set of possible new edges in Lines 6 and 13. The algorithm initializes the dual solution (u, p) to be feasible, and starts with an empty matching M. Algorithm considers slots in descending order in each iteration of the for loop in Line 3; we call each such iteration a *phase*.

During each phase we iteratively update the dual variables until we find an augmenting path to increase the size of the matching M by one. In each of these iterations within a phase we explore a tight edge leading to a matched edge and both edges are added to our alternating tree. Every time we add a new matched slot j' to the alternating tree we explore the edges incident on j' using the routine UPDATEPOSSIBLENEWEDGES, which scans the edges incident on j' and works out which edges are tight and when the remaining edges will become tight. All these new edges are stored in a priority queue for later retrieval.

High-Level Analysis Approach. Even though the algorithm is not fully defined yet (the implement of UPDATEPOSSIBLENEWEDGES is given in the next subsection), still we can say something about the running time of the algorithm.

---

[4] If an ad type has fewer than n ads, we can append ads with value 0, if there are more than n ads of a type, with loss of generality we can restrict attention to the n highest-value ads.

Each phase is implemented using a priority queue P over some of the ads not in B. For each ad i' in P we keep track of the next edge (i', j') that would become tight given the current structure of B. The priority of i' captures *when* this next edge becomes tight, the smaller the priority the sooner it becomes tight; similarly, if i' already has a tight edge incident on itself then it should have the smallest priority in the queue.

In the normal implementation of the Hungarian Algorithm, the procedure UPDATEPOSSIBLENEWEDGES(P, v, α, j') iterates over all edges (i', j') incident on j'. If $i' \in B$ we can ignore the edge as i' has already been discovered and its slack $v_{i',j'} - p_{j'} - u_{i'}$ will not change with future updates (since now both i' and j' belong to B). If $i' \notin B$ then we compute its current slack $v_{i',j'} - p_{j'} - u_{i'}$ to work out when it will become tight and compare this against the time of the current next tight edge incident on i', which we may need to update.

Without making any assumptions on the structure of the valuations, in the worst case in each iteration of the while loop in Line 7 we perform $O(nk + \log nk) = O(nk)$ work (assuming a Fibonacci heap implementation for P) since there are kn ads in total and kn edges incident on j' (one per ad). In each iteration be grow B by adding one new matched edge, so we have at most j iterations of the while loop. Therefore, the overall running time is $O(\sum_{j=1}^{n} jnk) = O(n^3 k)$.

However, as we shall see shortly, we can come up with a more efficient implementation of UPDATEPOSSIBLENEWEDGES(P, v, α, j') that exploits the special structure of our valuation function so that P holds at most $n + k$ ads and only $O(k)$ edges incident on j' need to be scanned without sacrificing the overall correctness of the algorithm. With this improvement in performance, each iteration of the while loop in Line 7 takes at most $O(\log n + k)$ work. Again, since in each iteration be grow B by adding one new matched edge, we have at most j iterations of the while loop. Therefore, the overall running time is $O(\sum_{j=1}^{n} j(k + \log n)) = O(n^2(k + \log n))$.

Theorem 1. *Given an input with k ad types and n slots, Algorithm 1 can be implemented to run in time $O(n^2(k + \log n))$.*

Our goal for the rest of this section is to provide an efficient implementation of UPDATEPOSSIBLENEWEDGES(P, v, α, j') where the size of P is always at most $n + k$ and only $O(k)$ edges are considered in each invocation of the routine. Key to our analysis is the observation that tight edges cannot cross is the following sense: Given two ads $i < i'$ of the same type θ, and two slots $j < j'$, then we cannot have the edge from ad i to slot j' be tight, and simultaneously have the edge from ad i' to j be tight.

Lemma 1 (Non-crossing lemma). *Given two ads $i < i'$ of the same type θ, and two slots $j < j'$, if $v_i > v_{i'}$ and $\alpha_j^{(\theta)} > \alpha_{j'}^{(\theta)}$ then in any feasible dual solution we cannot have the edge from ad i to slot j' be tight, and simultaneously have the edge from ad i' to j be tight.*

Proof. We prove by contradiction. If the edges between i and j' and i' and j are both tight, then we must have dual variables $u_i, u_{i'}, p_j, p_{j'}$ such that

$$\alpha_{j'}^{(\theta)} \cdot v_i = u_i + p_{j'} \quad \text{and} \quad \alpha_j^{(\theta)} \cdot v_{i'} = u_{i'} + p_j.$$

At the same time, due to the slackness constraints, we must have that

$$\alpha_j^{(\theta)} \cdot v_i \leq u_i + p_j \quad \text{and} \quad \alpha_{j'}^{(\theta)} \cdot v_{i'} \leq u_{i'} + p_{j'}.$$

We can combine these and obtain

$$\alpha_{j'}^{(\theta)} \cdot v_i + \alpha_j^{(\theta)} \cdot v_{i'} = u_i + p_{j'} + u_{i'} + p_j \geq \alpha_j^{(\theta)} \cdot v_i + \alpha_{j'}^{(\theta)} \cdot v_{i'}.$$

Which is false due to the standard exchange argument. We give the argument for completeness: Rearranging we have $(\alpha_j^{(\theta)} - \alpha_{j'}^{(\theta)}) \cdot (v_i - v_{i'}) \leq 0$; however, due to strict monotonicity $\alpha_j^{(\theta)} > \alpha_{j'}^{(\theta)}$ and $v_i > v_{i'}$, so have reached a contradiction. $\square$

UpdatePossibleNewEdges. The goal of UPDATEPOSSIBLENEWEDGES(P, v, α, j') is to iterate over the edges incident on j' that are tight or that can potentially become tight later in the execution of the current phase. For each such edge (i', j') we compare its slack with the priority associated with i' and update the entry for i' in P accordingly if needed.

The exact definition of the edges inspected is given by Algorithm 2. Before we describe how this works, let us make some observations about the set of edges that can potentially become tight, and then we shall see that the Algorithm indeed considers all these edges.

For each ad type θ we first consider the edges of the form $(a_i^{(\theta)}, j')$ where $a_i^{(\theta)}$ is matched and $M(a_i^{(\theta)}) < j'$. We claim that we only need to consider the largest such i. Recall that all the edges in M are tight and remain tight throughout the execution of the phase; in particular, $(a_i^{(\theta)}, M(a_i^{(\theta)}))$ is tight and remains tight. Thus, any edge $(a_{i'}^{(\theta)}, j')$ with $i' < i$ is not tight and will never become tight due the Non-crossing Lemma 1 and the fact that $i' < i$ and $M(a_i^{(\theta)}) < j'$.

Now consider the edges of the form $(a_i^{(\theta)}, j')$ where $a_i^{(\theta)}$ is matched and $M(a_i^{(\theta)}) > j'$. We claim that we only need to consider the smallest such i. Recall that all the edges in M are tight and remain tight throughout the execution of the phase; in particular, $(a_i^{(\theta)}, M(a_i^{(\theta)}))$ is tight and remains tight. Thus, any edge $(a_{i'}^{(\theta)}, j')$ with $i' > i$ is not tight and will never become tight due the Non-crossing Lemma 1 and the fact that $i' > i$ and $M(a_i^{(\theta)}) > j'$.

Finally, we need to consider edges of the form $(a_i^{(\theta)}, j')$ where $a_i^{(\theta)}$ is unmatched. We claim that we only need to consider the smallest such i available[5]. Indeed, for any other $i' > i$ note that $v_i^{(\theta)} > v_{i'}^{(\theta)}$ and since the u variable

---

[5] It is worth noting that even this case can be ignored if there exists a matched $a_i^{(\theta)}$ such that $M(a_i^{(\theta)}) > j'$; however, for ease of presentation we add the slot to X even if such $a_i^{(\theta)}$ exists.

of both ads is 0 (only slots that are part of an alternating tree get their dual variables increased and those are always matched) the slack of $(a_i^{(\theta)}, j')$ will always be smaller than the slack of $(a_{i'}^{(\theta)}, j')$ since $v_i^{(\theta)} \alpha_{j'}^{(\theta)} - p_{j'} < v_{i'}^{(\theta)} \alpha_{j'}^{(\theta)} - p_{j'}$. Furthermore, notice that if the edge $(a_i^{(\theta)}, j')$ become tight, then we immediately have an augmenting path in B, which concludes the phase.

These three cases are precisely those covered by Algorithm 2.

Algorithm 2. UPDATEPOSSIBLENEWEDGES

Input: P, v, α, M, j'
1: $X \leftarrow \emptyset$
2: **for** ad type θ **do**
3:    let $a_i^{(\theta)}$ be the unmatched ad of type θ with smallest i
4:    add $a_i^{(\theta)}$ to X
5:    **if** exists matched ad $a_i^{(\theta)}$ such that $M(a_i^{(\theta)}) < j'$ **then**
6:       let $a_i^{(\theta)}$ be such an ad with largest i
7:       add $a_i^{(\theta)}$ to X
8:    **end if**
9:    **if** exists matched ad $a_i^{(\theta)}$ such that $M(a_i^{(\theta)}) > j'$ **then**
10:      let $a_i^{(\theta)}$ be such an ad with smallest i
11:      add $a_i^{(\theta)}$ to X
12:   **end if**
13: **end for**
14: **for** $i' \in X$ **do**
15:   **if** $i' \notin B$ and either $i' \notin P$ or i'' current slack in P is $> (v_{i',j'} - u_{i'} - p_{j'})$ **then**
16:      update the priority of i' using (i', j') or set if $i' \notin P$
17:   **end if**
18: **end for**

Lemma 2. *There can be at most $n + k$ ads in P at any given point in time.*

Proof. Notice that the only edges (i', j') that we consider in Line 16 are either to a matched node in M or to the highest unmatched ad of each type. There are exactly $j < n$ matched ads in phase j and there are k ad types, so the lemma follows. $\square$

Lemma 3. UPDATEPOSSIBLENEWEDGES *considers only $O(k)$ edges when updating P and these are the only edges we need to look at. Furthermore, these edges can be identified in $O(k)$ time provided we carry out $O(nk)$ pre-processing every time the matching M is augmented in Line 19 of Algorithm 1.*

Proof. For each ad type we need to consider at most three edges incident on j' (namely, those consider the for loop in Line 14) so the algorithm inspects at most $3k$ edges. The reason why we can focus just on these edges has already been explained in the description of the algorithm UPDATEPOSSIBLENEWEDGES.

In order to identify these edges efficiently, we maintain an array of length k where for each ad type θ we store the smallest index i such that $a_i^{(\theta)}$ is unmatched. In addition to this, we maintain a $k \times n$ array where for each ad type θ and position j' we store the largest index i such that $M(a_i^{(\theta)}) < j'$ and the smallest index i such that $M(a_i^{(\theta)}) > j'$.

It is easy to see that constructing these data structures can be done in $O(kn)$ time given M and that given these data structures we can execute Algorithm 2 in $O(k)$ time.   □

Notice that the pre-processing needed for executing Algorithm 2 efficiently, does not add to the time complexity of the algorithm since the matching is updated at most n times, so the overall time spent on the pre-processing step alluded in Lemma 3 is $O(kn^2)$.

Similar to the general bipartite matching case, the dual variables in our algorithm for the Ad Types setting can be used to recover VCG prices without increasing the asymptotic running time. This yields VCG prices in $O(n^2(k + \log n))$ time.

3.2   Large Number of Ad Types

When each ad has its own type (so $k = n$) the running time from Theorem 1 becomes $O(n^3)$, meaning that it is no faster than running the standard Hungarian algorithm. The following lemma shows that this is to be expected as any instance of the assignment problem can be reduced to an instance where all ads agree on the order of the slots.

Lemma 4. *With $k = n$ ad types, the Ad Types problem is no easier to solve than the assignment problem, even with monotone discount curves.*

Due to lack of space, this proof is deferred to the full version of the paper [7].

4   The Ad Types Problem with Gap Rules

In this section we switch our attention to the full version of the Ad Types problem where we do have gap rules. This problem is much harder if we do not place any restriction on the instances.

Theorem 2. *The Ad Types problem with Gap Rules is hard to approximate better than $k^{1-\epsilon}$ for any $\epsilon > 0$, unless $P = NP$, even when the discount curves of all the ad types are identically equal to 1.*

On the positive side, we show that the problem is tractable if the number of ad types is very small. Note that this running time still represents a significant improvement over the brute-force approach yielding a $O(k^n)$ running time.

Theorem 3. *The Ad Types Problem with Gap Rules can solved optimally in $O(k \cdot n^{2k+1})$ time.*

Due to lack of space, the proofs in this section are given in the full version [7].

References

1. Abrams, Z., Ghosh, A., Vee, E.: Cost of conciseness in sponsored search auctions. In: Proceedings of 3rd WINE, pp. 326–334, 2007
2. Aggarwal, G., Feldman, J., Muthukrishnan, S., Pal, M.: Sponsored search auctions with Markovian users. In: Proceedings of 4th WINE, pp. 621–628 (2008)
3. Athey, S., Ellison, G.: Position auctions with consumer search. Q. J. Econ. **126**(3), 1213–1270 (2011)
4. Cavallo, R., Krishnamurthy, P., Sviridenko, M., Wilkens, C.A.: Sponsored search auctions with rich ads. In: Proceedings of the 26th WWW, pp. 43–51 (2017)
5. Cavallo, R., Sviridenko, M., Wilkens, C.A.: Matching auctions for search and native ads. In: Proceedings of the 19th EC, pp. 663–680 (2018)
6. Cavallo, R., Wilkens, C.A.: GSP with general independent click-through-rates. In: Liu, T.-Y., Qi, Q., Ye, Y. (eds.) WINE 2014. LNCS, vol. 8877, pp. 400–416. Springer, Cham (2014). https://doi.org/10.1007/978-3-319-13129-0_32
7. Colini-Baldeschi, R., Mestre, J., Schrijvers, O., Wilkens, C.A.: The ad types problem. CoRR, abs/1907.04400 (2019)
8. Deng, X., Sun, Y., Yin, M., Zhou, Y.: Mechanism design for multi-slot ads auction in sponsored search markets. In: Lee, D.-T., Chen, D.Z., Ying, S. (eds.) FAW 2010. LNCS, vol. 6213, pp. 11–22. Springer, Heidelberg (2010). https://doi.org/10.1007/978-3-642-14553-7_4
9. Dütting, P., Henzinger, M., Weber, I.: Sponsored search, market equilibria, and the Hungarian method. Inf. Process. Lett. **113**(3), 67–73 (2013)
10. Easley, D., Kleinberg, J., et al.: Networks, Crowds, and Markets, vol. 8. Cambridge University Press, Cambridge (2010)
11. Edelman, B., Ostrovsky, M., Schwarz, M.: Internet advertising and the generalized second-price auction: selling billions of dollars worth of keywords. Am. Econ. Rev. **97**(1), 242–259 (2007)
12. Edmonds, J., Karp, R.M.: Theoretical improvements in algorithmic efficiency for network flow problems. J. ACM **19**(2), 248–264 (1972)
13. Farina, G., Gatti, N.: Ad auctions and cascade model: GSP inefficiency and algorithms. In: Proceedings of the 13th AAAI, pp. 489–495 (2016)
14. Fotakis, D., Krysta, P., Telelis, O.: Externalities among advertisers in sponsored search. In: Persiano, G. (ed.) SAGT 2011. LNCS, vol. 6982, pp. 105–116. Springer, Heidelberg (2011). https://doi.org/10.1007/978-3-642-24829-0_11
15. Fredman, M.L., Tarjan, R.E.: Fibonacci heaps and their uses in improved network optimization algorithms. J. ACM **34**(3), 596–615 (1987)
16. Gabow, H.N., Tarjan, R.E.: A linear-time algorithm for a special case of disjoint set union. J. Comput. Syst. Sci. **30**(2), 209–221 (1985)
17. Gatti, N., Rocco, M., Serafino, P., Ventre, C.: Towards better models of externalities in sponsored search auctions. Theor. Comput. Sci. **745**, 150–162 (2018)
18. Ghosh, A., Mahdian, M.: Externalities in online advertising. In: Proceedings of the 17th WINE, pp. 161–168 (2008)
19. Ghosh, A., Sayedi, A.: Expressive auctions for externalities in online advertising. In: Proceedings of the 19th WINE, pp. 371–380 (2010)
20. Giotis, I., Karlin, A.R.: On the equilibria and efficiency of the GSP mechanism in keyword auctions with externalities. In Proceedings of the 4th WINE, pp. 629–638 (2008)
21. Glover, F.: Maximum matching in a convex bipartite graph. Nav. Res. Logist. Q. **14**(3), 313–316 (1967)

22. Gomes, R., Immorlica, N., Markakis, E.: Externalities in keyword auctions: an empirical and theoretical assessment. In: Leonardi, S. (ed.) WINE 2009. LNCS, vol. 5929, pp. 172–183. Springer, Heidelberg (2009). https://doi.org/10.1007/978-3-642-10841-9_17

23. Hartline, J., Immorlica, N., Khani, M.R., Lucier, B., Niazadeh, R.: Fast core pricing for rich advertising auctions. In: Proceedings of the 19th EC, pp. 111–112 (2018)

24. Hummel, P.: Position auctions with dynamic resizing. Int. J. Ind. Organ. **45**, 38–46 (2016)

25. Katriel, I.: Matchings in node-weighted convex bipartite graphs. INFORMS J. Comput. **20**(2), 205–211 (2008)

26. Kempe, D., Mahdian, M.: A cascade model for externalities in sponsored search. In: Papadimitriou, C., Zhang, S. (eds.) WINE 2008. LNCS, vol. 5385, pp. 585–596. Springer, Heidelberg (2008). https://doi.org/10.1007/978-3-540-92185-1_65

27. Kern, W., Manthey, B., Uetz, M.: Note on VCG vs. price raising for matching markets. CoRR, abs/1604.04157 (2016)

28. Kuhn, H.W.: The Hungarian method for the assignment problem. Nav. Res. Logist. Q. **2**(1–2), 83–97 (1955)

29. Lipski, W., Preparata, F.P.: Efficient algorithms for finding maximum matchings in convex bipartite graphs and related problems. Acta Informatica **15**(4), 329–346 (1981)

30. Mahdian, M., Schrijvers, O., Vassilvitskii, S.: Algorithmic cartography: placing points of interest and ads on maps. In: Proceedings of the 21st KDD, pp. 755–764 (2015)

31. Munkres, J.: Algorithms for the assignment and transportation problems. J. SIAM **5**(1), 32–38 (1957)

32. Muthukrishnan, S.: Bidding on configurations in internet ad auctions. In: Ngo, H.Q. (ed.) COCOON 2009. LNCS, vol. 5609, pp. 1–6. Springer, Heidelberg (2009). https://doi.org/10.1007/978-3-642-02882-3_1

33. Myerson, R.B.: Optimal auction design. Math. Oper. Res. **6**(1), 58–73 (1981)

34. Plaxton, C.G.: Fast scheduling of weighted unit jobs with release times and deadlines. In: Aceto, L., Damgård, I., Goldberg, L.A., Halldórsson, M.M., Ingólfsdóttir, A., Walukiewicz, I. (eds.) ICALP 2008. LNCS, vol. 5125, pp. 222–233. Springer, Heidelberg (2008). https://doi.org/10.1007/978-3-540-70575-8_19

35. Plaxton, C.G.: Vertex-weighted matching in two-directional orthogonal ray graphs. In: Cai, L., Cheng, S.-W., Lam, T.-W. (eds.) ISAAC 2013. LNCS, vol. 8283, pp. 524–534. Springer, Heidelberg (2013). https://doi.org/10.1007/978-3-642-45030-3_49

36. Ramshaw, L., Tarjan, R.E.: On minimum-cost assignments in unbalanced bipartite graphs. HP Labs, Palo Alto, CA, USA, Technical report, HPL-2012-40R1 (2012)

37. Roughgarden, T.: Revenue-maximizing auctions. In: Twenty Lectures on Algorithmic Game Theory (2016)

38. Sharathkumar, R., Agarwal, P.K.: Algorithms for the transportation problem in geometric settings. In: Proceedings of the 23rd SODA, pp. 306–317 (2012)

39. Varian, H.R.: Position auctions. Int. J. Ind. Organ. **25**(6), 1163–1178 (2007)

Multidimensional Stable Roommates
with Master List

Robert Bredereck[1,3], Klaus Heeger[1(✉)], Dušan Knop[2],
and Rolf Niedermeier[1]

[1] Algorithmics and Computational Complexity, TU Berlin, Berlin, Germany
{robert.bredereck,heeger,rolf.niedermeier}@tu-berlin.de
[2] Czech Technical University in Prague, Prague, Czech Republic
dusan.knop@fit.cvut.cz
[3] Insitut für Informatik, Algorithm Engineering, Humboldt-Universität Berlin,
Berlin, Germany
robert.bredereck@hu-berlin.de

Abstract. Since the early days of research in algorithms and complexity, the computation of stable matchings is a core topic. While in the classic setting the goal is to match up two agents (either from different "gender" (this is STABLE MARRIAGE) or "unrestricted" (this is STABLE ROOMMATES)), Knuth [1976] triggered the study of three- or multidimensional cases. Here, we focus on the study of MULTIDIMENSIONAL STABLE ROOMMATES, known to be NP-hard since the early 1990's. Many NP-hardness results, however, rely on very general input instances that do not occur in at least some of the specific application scenarios. With the quest for identifying islands of tractability, we look at the case of master lists. Here, as natural in applications where agents express their preferences based on "objective" scores, one roughly speaking assumes that all agent preferences are "derived from" a central master list, implying that the individual agent preferences shall be similar. Master lists have been frequently studied in the two-dimensional (classic) stable matching case, but seemingly almost never for the multidimensional case. This work, also relying on methods from parameterized algorithm design and complexity analysis, performs a first systematic study of MULTIDIMENSIONAL STABLE ROOMMATES under the assumption of master lists.

1 Introduction

Computing stable matchings is a core topic in the intersection of algorithm design, algorithmic game theory, and computational social choice. It has numerous applications such as higher education admission in several countries [2,4], kidney exchange [31], assignment of dormitories [28], P2P-networks [13], and wireless three-sided networks [8]. The research started in the 1960's with the seminal work of Gale and Shapley [14], introducing the STABLE MARRIAGE problem: given two different types of agents, called "men" and "women", each agent of one gender has preferences (i.e., linear orders aka rankings) over the

---

Main work done while all authors were with TU Berlin.

© Springer Nature Switzerland AG 2020
X. Chen et al. (Eds.): WINE 2020, LNCS 12495, pp. 59–73, 2020.
https://doi.org/10.1007/978-3-030-64946-3_5

agents of the opposite gender. Then, the task is to find a matching which is stable. Informally, a matching is *stable* if no pair of agents can improve by breaking up with their currently assigned partners and instead matching to each other.

Many variations of this problem have been studied; STABLE ROOMMATES, with only one type of agents, is among the most prominent ones. Knuth [22] asked for generalizing STABLE MARRIAGE to dimension three, i.e., having three types of agents and having to match the agents to groups of size three, where any such group contains exactly one agent of each type. Here, a matching is called *stable* if there is no group of three agents which would improve by being matched together. We focus on the MULTIDIMENSIONAL STABLE ROOMMATES PROBLEM. Here again, there is only one type of agents, now having preferences over $(d-1)$-*sets* (that is, sets of size $d-1$) of (the other) agents. As this problem is NP-hard in general [25], we focus on the case where the preferences of all agents are derived from a master list. For instance, master lists naturally arise when the agent preferences are based on scores, e.g., when assigning junior doctors to medical posts in the UK [18] or when allocating students to dormitories [28]. Master lists have been frequently used in the context of (two-dimensional) stable matchings [3,18,26,28] or the related POPULAR MATCHING problem [21]. We generalize master lists to the multidimensional setting in two natural ways. First, following the above spirit of preference orders, we assume that the master list consists of sets of size $d-1$. Each agent then derives its preferences from the master list by just deleting all $(d-1)$-sets containing the agent itself. Second, the master list orders all agents. In this case, any agent a shall prefer a $(d-1)$-set t over a $(d-1)$-set t' if t is "better" than t' according to the master list, where "better" means that a does not prefer the kth best agent of t' over the kth best agent from t (according to the master list). For any tuples t, t' for which neither t is "better" than t' nor t' is "better" than t, an agent may prefer t over t' or t' over t independently of the other agents. More formally, we require that any agent prefers a set of $d-1$ agents t over any set of $d-1$ agents t' dominated by $\{a_1, \ldots, a_{d-1}\}$, where we say that $t = \{a_1, \ldots, a_{d-1}\}$ dominates $t' = \{b_1, \ldots, b_{d-1}\}$ if the master list does not prefer b_i over a_i for all $i \in [d-1]$. The agent preferences of any agent must then fulfill for any two sets $\{a_1, \ldots, a_{d-1}\}$ and $\{b_1, \ldots, b_{d-1}\}$ of $d-1$ agents with b_i not being before a_i that in the master list the set $\{b_1, \ldots, b_{d-1}\}$ is not before $\{a_1, \ldots, a_{d-1}\}$. In this case, we also relax the condition that the master list is a strict order by the condition that the master list is a partially ordered set (poset), and consider the parameterized complexity with respect to parameters measuring the similarity to a strict order. Preferences where such a parameter is small might arise if there are few similar rankings, and each agent derives its ranking from these orders, or if the objective score consists of several attributes and each agent weights these attributes slightly differently. Two agents are then incomparable in the master poset if they are ranked in different order by some agents.

Related Work. STABLE ROOMMATES can be solved in linear time [17]. If the preferences are incomplete and derived from a master list, then both STABLE MARRIAGE and STABLE ROOMMATES admit a unique stable matching [18]. If the preferences are complete but contain ties, then finding a weakly stable matching in a STABLE ROOMMATES instance becomes NP-hard [30]. However, if the preferences are complete and derived from a master list, then one can decide whether an edge of a STABLE MARRIAGE instance is contained in a stable matching in linear time [18], and a stable matching in a STABLE ROOMMATES instance always exists and can be found in linear time. For incomplete preferences with ties derived from a master list, an $O(\sqrt{n}m)$-time algorithm for finding a strongly stable matching is known [26] (where n is the number of agents and m is the number of acceptable pairs), while for general preferences, only an $O(mn)$-time algorithm is known [23].

Several STABLE MARRIAGE problems become easier for complete preferences derived from a master list [33, Chapter 8]. STABLE ROOMMATES, however, is NP-hard if the preferences contain ties, are incomplete, and are derived from a master list [18]. There is quite some work for 3-DIMENSIONAL STABLE MARRIAGE [9, 27,35,36], but less so for 3-DIMENSIONAL STABLE ROOMMATES.

While master lists are a standard setting for finding 2-dimensional stable matchings [3,18,20,26,28], we are only aware of few works combining multidimensional stable matchings with master lists. Escamocher and O'Sullivan [12] gave a recursive formula for the number of 3-dimensional stable matchings for cyclic preferences (i.e., the agents are partitioned into three sets V_1, V_2, and V_3, and each agent from V_i only cares about the agent from V_{i+1} it is matched to) derived from master lists. Cui and Jia [8] showed that if the preferences are cyclic and the preferences of the agents from V_1 are derived from a master list, while each agent from V_3 is indifferent between all agents from V_1, then a stable matching always exists and can be found in polynomial time, but it is NP-complete to find a maximum-cardinality stable matching. There is some work on d-dimensional stable matchings and cyclic preferences (without master lists) [16,24].

Deineko and Woeginger [10] showed that 3-DIMENSIONAL STABLE ROOMMATES is NP-complete for preferences derived from a metric space. For the special case of the Euclidean plane, Arkin et al. [1] showed that a stable matching does not always exist, but left the complexity of deciding existence open.

Iwama et al. [19] introduced the NP-hard STABLE ROOMMATES WITH TRIPLE ROOMS, where each agent has preferences over all other agents, and prefers a 2-set p of agents over a 2-set p' if it prefers the best-ranked agent of p over the best-ranked agent of p', and the second-best agent of p over the second-best agent of p'.

Our scenario of MULTIDIMENSIONAL STABLE ROOMMATES can be seen as a special case of finding core-stable outcomes for hedonic games where each agent prefers size-d coalitions over singleton-coalitions which are then preferred over all other coalitions [32,34]. Notably, there are fixed-parameter tractability results for hedonic games (without fixed "coalition" size as we request) with respect to treewidth (MSO-based) [15,29]. Other research considers hedonic games with fixed coalition size [7], but aims for Pareto optimal outcomes instead of core stability which we consider.

To the best of our knowledge, the parameterized complexity of multidimensional stable matching problems has not yet been investigated.

Table 1. Results overview: six variations of MULTIDIMENSIONAL STABLE ROOMMATES.

Setting/Parameter	Complexity
Master list of 2-sets	NP-complete for $d = 3$ (Theorem 2)
Strict master list of agents	Linear time (Proposition 1)
κ (max. # of incomparable agents)	$O(n^2) + (\kappa^2 2^{12\kappa})^{O(\kappa^2 2^{12\kappa})} n$ (Theorem 3)
Width of poset	W[1]-hard for $d = 3$ (Theorem 4)
Incomplete preferences, strict master list	NP-complete for $d \geq 3$ (Theorem 5)
Deletion distance to strict master list	W[1]-hard for $d = 3$ (Theorem 6)

Our Contributions. For an overview of our results, we refer to Table 1. To our surprise, even if the preferences are derived from a master list of 2-sets of agents (in this case, dimension $d = 3$), a stable matching is not guaranteed to exist (Sect. 3). We use such an instance not admitting a stable matching to show that THREE-DIMENSIONAL STABLE ROOMMATES is NP-complete also when restricted to preferences derived from a master list of 2-sets (Theorem 2).

If the preferences are derived from a strict master list of agents, then a unique stable matching always exists and can be found by a straightforward algorithm (Proposition 1). When relaxing the condition that the master list is strict to being a poset, then the problem clearly is NP-complete, as a master list which ties all agents does not impose any condition on the preferences of the agents, and THREE-DIMENSIONAL STABLE ROOMMATES is NP-complete. Consequently, in the spirit of "distance from tractability"-parameterization, we investigate the parameterized complexity with respect to several parameters measuring the distance of the poset to a strict order. For the parameter maximum number of agents incomparable to a single agent, we show that MULTIDIMENSIONAL STABLE ROOMMATES is fixed-parameter tractable (FPT)[1] (even when d is part of the input) (Theorem 3). If this parameter is bounded, then this results in one of the rare special cases of 3-dimensional stable matching problems which can be solved by an "efficient" nontrivial algorithm. Considering the stronger parameter width of the master poset, we show THREE-DIMENSIONAL STABLE ROOMMATES to be W[1]-hard[2], and this is true also for the orthogonal parameter deletion (of agents) distance to a linear master list (Theorem 6). We also show that MULTIDIMENSIONAL STABLE ROOMMATES is NP-complete even with a linear order of the agents as a master list if each agent is allowed to declare an arbitrary set of 2-sets unacceptable (Theorem 5).

Proofs omitted due to space restrictions are marked by a star ($\star$) and can be found in the full version [5].

---

[1] FPT with respect to a parameter k means that the problem can be solved in $f(k) \operatorname{poly}(|\mathcal{I}|)$ time, where f is an arbitrary computable function and $|\mathcal{I}|$ denotes the size of the input instance.

[2] Informally, W[1]-hardness with respect to a specific parameter indicates that it is very unlikely to show fixed-parameter tractability.

2   Preliminaries

Let $[n] := \{1, 2, 3, \ldots, n\}$ and $[n, m] := \{n, n+1, \ldots, m\}$. For a set X and an integer d, we denote by $\binom{X}{d}$ the set of size-d subsets of X. A *preference list* $\succ$ over a set X is a strict order of X. We call a set of pairwise disjoint d-subsets of V a d-*dimensional matching*. If it is clear from the context that it is a d-dimensional matching, then we may only write matching. We say that an agent v *prefers* a $(d-1)$-set A over a $(d-1)$-set B if $A \succ_v B$ where $\succ_v$ is the preference list of v. Any agent prefers any $(d-1)$-set not containing itself over being unmatched. A *blocking* d-*set* for a d-dimensional matching M is a set of d agents $\{v_1, v_2, \ldots, v_d\}$ such that for all $i \in [d]$, either v_i is unmatched in M or $\{v_1, v_2, \ldots, v_d\} \backslash \{v_i\} \succ_{v_i} \{w_1^i, w_2^i, \ldots, w_{d-1}^i\}$, where $\{w_j^i : j \in [d-1]\} \cup \{v_i\} \in M$. A matching is called *stable* if it does not admit a blocking d-set.

> MULTIDIMENSIONAL STABLE ROOMMATES (MDSR)
>
> *Input:*   An integer d, a set V of agents together with a preference list $\succ_v$
> over $\binom{V \backslash \{v\}}{d-1}$ for each agent $v \in V$.
> *Task:*   Decide whether a stable matching exists.

Note that we require each agent to list each size-$(d-1)$ set of other agents. We denote by ℓ-DSR the restriction of MDSR to instances with $d = \ell$. We set $n := |V|$. A 3-dimensional stable matching does not always exist, and 3-DSR is NP-complete [25].

A *master list* ML is a preference list over $\binom{V}{d-1}$. A preference list $\succ_v$ for an agent v is *derived from a master list* ML by deleting all $(d-1)$-sets containing v.

Example 1. Let $V = \{v_1, v_2, v_3, v_4\}$ be a set of agents, $d = 3$, and let $\{v_1, v_2\} \succ \{v_2, v_4\} \succ \{v_1, v_3\} \succ \{v_3, v_4\} \succ \{v_2, v_3\} \succ \{v_1, v_4\}$ be the master list.

Then the preferences of v_1 are $\{v_2, v_4\} \succ_{v_1} \{v_3, v_4\} \succ_{v_1} \{v_2, v_3\}$, the preferences of v_2 are $\{v_1, v_3\} \succ_{v_2} \{v_3, v_4\} \succ_{v_2} \{v_1, v_4\}$, the preferences of v_3 are $\{v_1, v_2\} \succ_{v_3} \{v_2, v_4\} \succ_{v_3} \{v_1, v_4\}$, and the preferences of v_4 are $\{v_1, v_2\} \succ_{v_4} \{v_1, v_3\} \succ_{v_4} \{v_2, v_3\}$.

We now define the MULTIDIMENSIONAL STABLE ROOMMATES WITH MASTER LIST OF $(d-1)$-SETS problem (MDSR-ML-SETS).

> MDSR-ML-SETS
>
> *Input:*   An integer d, a set V of agents, and a master list $\succ_{\text{ML}}$ over $\binom{V}{d-1}$,
> from which the preference list of each agent is derived.
> *Task:*   Decide whether a stable matching exists.

Again, we denote by ℓ-DSR-ML-SETS the problem MDSR-ML-SETS restricted to instances with $d = \ell$.

We now turn to the case that the master list orders single agents instead of $(d-1)$-sets of agents. We first need the definition of a partially ordered set.

A *partially ordered set (poset)* is a pair $(V, \succeq)$, where $\succeq$ is a binary relation over the set V such that (i) $v \succeq v$ for all $v \in V$, (ii) $v \succeq w$ and $w \succeq v$ if and only if $v = w$, and (iii) if $u \succeq v$ and $v \succeq w$, then $u \succeq w$.

If $v \succeq w$ and $v \neq w$, then we write $v \succ w$. If neither $v \succeq w$ nor $w \succeq v$, then we say that v and w are *incomparable*, and write $v \sim w$. Instead of $v \succeq w$ or $v \succ w$, we may also write $w \preceq v$ or $w \prec v$.

A *chain* is a subset $X = \{x_1, x_2, \ldots, x_k\} \subseteq V$ such that $x_i \succ x_{i+1}$ for all $i \in [k-1]$. An *antichain* is a subset $X \subseteq V$ such that for all $v, w \in X$ with $v \neq w$, we have $v \sim w$. The *width* of a poset is the size of a maximum antichain.

For a poset $\succ$ over a set V, we define $\kappa_\succ(v) := |\{w \in V : v \sim w\}|$ to be the number of elements incomparable with v. We define $\kappa(\succ) := \max_{v \in V} \kappa_\succ(v)$.

Note that if $\bar{G}_\succ$ is the incomparability graph of the poset $(V, \succ)$ (i.e., the graph whose vertex set is the set V, and there is an edge between $v, w \in V$ if and only if $v \sim w$), then $\Delta(\bar{G}_\succ) = \kappa(\succ)$, where $\Delta(\bar{G}_\succ)$ is the maximum degree of a vertex in $\bar{G}_\succ$. If $\succ$ is a weak order (i.e., a linear order with ties), the parameter $\kappa(\succ)$ is equal to the maximum size of a ti.e.

Dilworth's Theorem [11] states that the width of a poset is the minimum number of chains such that each element of the poset is contained in one of these chains.

Having defined posets, we now show the connection to MULTIDIMENSIONAL STABLE ROOMMATES by defining preferences derived from a poset of agents.

Definition 1. *Given a set of agents V, a poset $(V, \succ_{ML})$ (which we call the master poset), and an integer d, we say that a preference list $\succ_v$ on $\binom{V \setminus \{v\}}{d-1}$ is derived from $\succ_{ML}$ if whenever $a_1, \ldots, a_{d-1}$ and $b_1, \ldots, b_{d-1}$ with $a_i \succeq_{ML} b_i$ for all $i \in [d-1]$, then we have $\{a_1, \ldots, a_{d-1}\} \succeq_v \{b_1, \ldots, b_{d-1}\}$.*

Example 2. Let $v_1 \succ v_2 \succ v_3 \succ v_4 \succ v_5$ be a master poset. Then v_1 has one of the two preferences: $\{v_2, v_3\} \succ_{v_1} \{v_2, v_4\} \succ_{v_1} \{v_2, v_5\} \succ_{v_1} \{v_3, v_4\} \succ_{v_1} \{v_3, v_5\} \succ_{v_1} \{v_4, v_5\}$ or $\{v_2, v_3\} \succ_{v_1} \{v_2, v_4\} \succ_{v_1} \{v_3, v_4\} \succ_{v_1} \{v_2, v_5\} \succ_{v_1} \{v_3, v_5\} \succ_{v_1} \{v_4, v_5\}$.

For the master poset $v_2 \succ v_3 \sim v_4 \succ v_1$, agent v_1 has one of the following preferences: $\{v_2, v_3\} \succ_{v_1} \{v_2, v_4\} \succ_{v_1} \{v_3, v_4\}$ or $\{v_2, v_4\} \succ_{v_1} \{v_2, v_3\} \succ_{v_1} \{v_3, v_4\}$.

We are now ready to formally define MDSR-POSET.

MDSR-POSET

Input: An MDSR instance $\mathcal{I} = (V, (\succ_v)_{v \in V}, d)$ and a master poset $\succeq_{ML}$ such that the preferences $\succ_v$ of each agent v are derived from $\succeq_{ML}$.

Task: Decide whether there exists a stable matching in $\mathcal{I}$.

---

3 Three-Dimensional Stable Roommates with Master List of 2-sets

In this section, we consider the case that the preferences are complete and derived from a master list of $(d-1)$-sets. First, we give a small instance with six agents

Table 2. A blocking 3-set for each matching in instance $\mathcal{I}_{\text{instable}}$ from Observation 1.

Matching	Blocking 3-set	Matching	Blocking 3-set
$\{a,b,c\}, \{d,e,f\}$	$\{a,d,e\}$	$\{a,c,e\}, \{b,d,f\}$	$\{a,b,e\}$
$\{a,b,d\}, \{c,e,f\}$	$\{a,c,e\}$	$\{a,c,f\}, \{b,d,e\}$	$\{a,b,e\}$
$\{a,b,e\}, \{c,d,f\}$	$\{b,c,d\}$	$\{a,d,e\}, \{b,c,f\}$	$\{a,b,e\}$
$\{a,b,f\}, \{c,d,e\}$	$\{a,c,d\}$	$\{a,d,f\}, \{b,c,e\}$	$\{a,b,e\}$
$\{a,c,d\}, \{b,e,f\}$	$\{a,b,e\}$	$\{a,e,f\}, \{b,c,d\}$	$\{a,c,d\}$

not admitting a stable matching, and use this to show that already for $d = 3$ and preferences derived from a master list of 2-sets, deciding whether an instance admits a stable matching is NP-complete.

We first present a 3DSR-ML-SETS instance $\mathcal{I}_{\text{instable}}$ with six agents not admitting a stable matching, showing that stable matchings do not have to exist even in the presence of master lists.

The instance $\mathcal{I}_{\text{instable}}$ has six agents a, b, c, d, e, and f. The master list is:
$\{a,b\} \succ \{a,c\} \succ \{a,d\} \succ \{a,f\} \succ \{b,e\} \succ \{c,d\} \succ \{a,e\} \succ \{b,f\} \succ \{c,e\} \succ \{b,d\} \succ \{d,e\} \succ \{b,c\} \succ \{c,f\} \succ \{d,f\} \succ \{e,f\}$.

Observation 1. *The instance $\mathcal{I}_{\text{instable}}$ does not admit a stable matching.*

Proof. Table 2 presents for each of the $\frac{\binom{6}{3}}{2} = 10$ matchings a blocking 3-set. □

Using the instance $\mathcal{I}_{\text{instable}}$, we show NP-completeness of 3DSR-ML-SETS, reducing from 1-IN-3 POSITIVE 3-OCCURRENCE-SAT.

Note that MDSR is in NP as the size of the input is $\Omega(\binom{n}{d-1})$, where n is the number of agents, as the master preference list contains $\binom{n}{d-1}$ sets of size $d - 1$, and, thus, stability can be checked in polynomial time in the input by just checking for each d-set whether it is blocking. We arrive at the following theorem.

Theorem 2 ($\star$). 3-DSR-ML *is* NP-*complete*.

4 Master Lists of Agents

We now consider the case when there does not exist a master list of $(d - 1)$-sets of agents, but a master list $\succ_{\text{ML}}$ of single agents. Each agent can derive its preferences from this master list, meaning that if for two $(d - 1)$-sets t and t', one can find a bijection σ from the elements of t to the elements of t' such that $v \succeq_{\text{ML}} \sigma(v)$ for all $v \in t$, then any agent (not occurring in t or t') shall prefer t over t'. If the master list is an arbitrary poset, then MDSR-POSET clearly is NP-complete, as the preferences of any instance of 3-DSR are derived from the poset in which no two different agents are comparable, and 3-DIMENSIONAL STABLE MATCHING is NP-complete. We show that this problem is polynomial-time solvable if the master list is a strict order. Afterwards, we generalize this result by showing fixed-parameter tractability for the parameter κ, the "maximum number of agents incomparable to a single agent". On the contrary, for the stronger parameter width of the poset, we show W[1]-hardness, leaving open whether it can be solved in polynomial time for constant width (in parameterized complexity known as the question for containment in XP).

4.1 Strict Orders

We first consider the case that the master list is a strict order. In this case, an easy algorithm solves the problem: Just match the first d agents from the master list together, delete them, and recurse. Note that the preferences of any agent cannot be directly derived from the master list, as e.g. an agent may prefer either $\{v_1, v_4\}$ over $\{v_2, v_3\}$ or $\{v_2, v_3\}$ over $\{v_1, v_4\}$. Thus, the input contains the complete preferences of all agents, and the input size is $\Theta(d\binom{n}{d-1})$. Hence, the running time subsequent algorithm is sublinear.

Proposition 1 ($\star$). *If $\succeq_{\mathrm{ML}}$ is a strict order, then any* MDSR-POSET *instance admits a unique stable matching that can be found in $O(n)$ time.*

4.2 Posets

In two-dimensional stable (or popular) matching problems with master lists, the master list usually contains ties [3, 18, 21, 26, 28]. We allow the master list not only to contain ties, but to be an arbitrary poset. In this case, the problem clearly is NP-complete, as the poset where each agent is incomparable to each other agent does not pose any restrictions on the preferences of the agents. Therefore, we consider several parameters measuring the similarity of the poset to a strict order. For the parameter "maximum number of agents incomparable to a single agent", we show fixed-parameter tractability, and for the stronger parameter width of the poset, we show W[1]-hardness.

Maximum Number of Agents Incomparable to a Single Agent. In this section, we show that MDSR-POSET is fixed-parameter tractable when parameterized by $\kappa(\succ_{\mathrm{ML}})$. As a first step of the algorithm, we show how to derive a strict order from the given poset, which guarantees that for any two elements v and w with v being "much earlier" in the strict order than w, we have that $v \succ_{\mathrm{ML}} w$.

Lemma 1 ($\star$). *For any poset $(V, \succeq)$, there is an order $v_1, v_2, \ldots, v_n$ of V such that (i) for all $i < j$, we have that $v_i \succ v_j$ or $v_i \sim v_j$, and (ii) for all $j > i + 2\kappa(\succeq)$, we have $v_i \succ v_j$. Moreover, such an order can be found in $O(|V|^2)$ time.*

For the rest of Sect. 4.2, we fix an instance $\mathcal{I} = (V, (\succeq_v)_{v \in V}, \succeq_{\mathrm{ML}})$ of MDSR-POSET, and an order $V = \{v_1, \ldots, v_n\}$ of V fulfilling the conditions of Lemma 1 for the poset $(V, \succeq_{\mathrm{ML}})$. We set $\kappa := \kappa(\succeq_{\mathrm{ML}})$. Furthermore, we denote by $V^{\leq i} = \{v_1, \ldots, v_i\}$, by $V^{[i,j]} = \{v_i, v_{i+1}, \ldots, v_j\}$, and by $V^{\geq i} = \{v_i, v_{i+1}, \ldots, v_n\}$.

We now show that the agents contained in a d-set of a stable matching are close to each other in the strict order derived from the master poset by Lemma 1.

Lemma 2. *Let $\mathcal{I} = (V, (\succeq_v)_{v \in V}, \succeq_{ML})$ be an* MDSR-POSET-*instance and let $V = \{v_1, v_2, \ldots, v_n\}$ such that this order fulfills Lemma 1 for the poset $(V, \succeq_{ML})$.*

For any stable matching M and any d-set $\{v_{i_1}, v_{i_2}, \ldots, v_{i_d}\} \in M$ with $i_1 < i_2 < \cdots < i_d$, we have that $i_{j+1} - i_j \leq 2\kappa d^2 + 4\kappa + 3d + 1$ for all $j \in [d-1]$.

Proof. Let M be a stable matching, and $\{v_{i_1}, v_{i_2}, \ldots, v_{i_d}\} \in M$ be a d-set contained in M. We assume $i_1 < i_2 < \cdots < i_d$, and fix some $j \in [d-1]$.

Let $\mathcal{T}^+$ be the set of d-sets in M containing an agent from $V^{[i_j + 2\kappa + 1, i_{j+1} - 2\kappa - 1]}$, and an agent from $V^{\geq i_{j+1} - 2\kappa}$, and let $\mathcal{T}^-$ be the set of d-sets in M containing an agent from $V^{[i_j + 2\kappa + 1, i_{j+1} - 2\kappa - 1]}$, and an agent from $V^{\leq i_j + 2\kappa}$. We now give an example for the definitions of $\mathcal{T}^+$ and $\mathcal{T}^-$.

Example 3. Let $d = 4$, $\kappa = 5$, and M be a stable matching. Assume that M contains the 4-set $\{v_3, v_{14}, v_{50}, v_{157}\}$. Thus, it holds that $i_1 = 3$, $i_2 = 14$, $i_3 = 50$, and $i_4 = 157$. Taking $j = 3$ as an example, the set $\mathcal{T}^+$ contains all 4-sets containing an agent from $\{v_{61}, v_{62}, \ldots, v_{146}\}$, an agent from $\{v_{147}, v_{148}, \ldots, v_n\}$, and two more arbitrary agents. The set $\mathcal{T}^-$ contains all 4-sets containing an agent from $\{v_1, v_2, \ldots, v_{60}\}$, an agent from $\{v_{61}, v_{62}, \ldots, v_{146}\}$, and two more arbitrary agents.

Let t be a d-set from $\mathcal{T}^+$. We claim that for every d-set $t' \in \mathcal{T}^+$ other than t, there exist agents $a \in t$ and $a' \in t'$ with $a \sim_{ML} a'$. Assume that there are two d-sets t and t' such that there do not exist $a \in t$ and $a' \in t'$ with $a \sim_{ML} a'$. Let t^* contain the d agents with minimum index from $t \cup t'$. By the definition of $\mathcal{T}^+$, any d-set from $\mathcal{T}^+$ contains an agent from $V^{\leq i_{j+1} - 2\kappa - 1}$ and one agent from $V^{\geq i_{j+1} - 2\kappa}$. Therefore, at least one agent of t^* is contained in t, and at least one agent is contained in t'. For any agent $v_p \in t \setminus t^*$ and any $v_q \in t' \cap t^*$, it holds by the definition of t^* that $q < p$. By Lemma 1, it follows that $v_q \succ_{ML} v_p$ or $v_q \sim_{ML} v_p$. However, the latter is not possible, since we assumed that there are no two agents $a \in t$ and $a' \in t'$ with $a \sim_{ML} a'$. Thus, we have that each $a \in t$ prefers t^* over t, and by symmetry, also each $a' \in t'$ prefers t^* over t'. It follows that the d-set t^* is blocking, contradicting the assumption that M is stable.

As any agent is incomparable to at most κ other agents, it follows that $|\mathcal{T}^+| \leq \kappa d + 1$. By analogous arguments, one can show that $|\mathcal{T}^-| \leq \kappa d + 1$.

Any d-set $s \in M$ consisting solely of agents from $V^{[i_j + 2\kappa + 1, i_{j+1} - 2\kappa - 1]}$ directly implies a blocking d-set $\{v_{i_1}, \ldots, v_{i_j}\} \cup S_{d-j}$, where S_{d-j} contains $d - j$ arbitrary agents from s.

It follows that M contains at most $2(\kappa d + 1)$ sets containing an agent from $V^{[i_j + 2\kappa + 1, i_{j+1} - 2\kappa - 1]}$, implying that $(i_{j+1} - 2\kappa - 1) - (i_j + 2\kappa + 1) \leq d \cdot 2(\kappa d + 1) + d - 1$, where $d - 1$ is added since there can be at most $d - 1$ unmatched agents. It follows that $i_{j+1} - i_j \leq 2\kappa d^2 + 4\kappa + 3d + 1$. □

We call a matching M *local* if for all $t \in M$ and any two agents $v_j, v_{j'} \in t$ it holds that $|j - j'| \leq (d-1)(2\kappa d^2 + 4\kappa + 3d + 1)$. Note that any stable matching is local due to Lemma 2. Using a dynamic program on the local matchings, we derive an FPT-algorithm for the combined parameter $\kappa + d$. This will lead to an FPT-algorithm for the parameter κ as we will later show that if κ is much smaller than d, then a stable matching always exists.

Proposition 2. $(\star)$. MDSR-POSET *can be solved in* $O(n^2)+(\kappa d^4)^{O(\kappa d^4)}n$ *time, where* κ *is the maximum number of agents incomparable to a single agent,* d *is the dimension (i.e., the group size), and* n *is the number of agents.*

Proof (Sketch). We first apply Lemma 1 to the poset $(V, \succeq_{\mathrm{ML}})$ to get an order $v_1, \ldots, v_n$ of the agents in $O(n^2)$ time. Let $k := 2(d-1)d(2\kappa d^2 + 4\kappa + 3d + 1)$.

We store an entry $\tau[i, M]$ for each $i \in [n]$ and each local matching M such that any d-set $t \in M$ contains at least one agent of $v_i, \ldots, v_{i+k}$. This entry shall be true if and only if M can be extended to a local matching M^* not admitting a blocking d-set consisting solely of agents from $v_1, \ldots, v_{i+k}$.

By Lemma 2, there exists a stable matching if and only if $\tau[n-k, M] = \mathsf{true}$ for some local matching M. It remains to show how to compute these values.

For $i = 1$, we set $\tau[1, M] := \mathsf{true}$ if and only if M does not contain a blocking d-set inside $v_1, \ldots, v_{k+1}$. For $i > 1$, given a local matching M_i fulfilling that every d-set of M_i contains an agent from $v_i, \ldots, v_{i+k}$, we look up whether there exists a local matching M_{i-1} of $v_{i-1}, \ldots, v_{i+k-1}$ such that for any $j \in [i, i+k-1]$, we have $M_i(v_j) = M_{i-1}(v_j)$, and such that $M_{i-1} \cup M_i$ does not admit a blocking d-set consisting of agents from $v_{i-1}, \ldots, v_{i+k}$. If this is the case, then we set $\tau[i, M_i] = \mathsf{true}$, and otherwise we set $\tau[i, M_i] = \mathsf{false}$.

Since there are at most $k^{O(k)}$ partitions of a k-elementary set [6], the table τ contains at most $nk^{O(k)}$ entries. Each entry can be computed in $k^{O(k)}$ time, resulting in an overall running time of $k^{O(k)}n = (\kappa d^3)^{O(\kappa d^3)}n$.

We defer the correctness proof to the full version [5]. $\square$

We now extend Proposition 2 to an FPT-algorithm for the single parameter κ. To do so, we show that if κ is much smaller than d, then there always exists a stable matching. Due to space constraints, we only sketch the proof here.

Lemma 3 $(\star)$. *If* $4\kappa 2^{4\kappa} \leq d$, *then there exists a stable matching.*

Proof (Sketch). Start with an empty matching $M = \emptyset$. Construct a d-set t^* such that in any matching containing t^*, no agent of t^* can be contained in a blocking d-set. Add t^* to M, delete the agents from t^* from the instance. Repeat this as long as there are at least d unmatched agents. Construct t^* as follows: For any agent $a \in V^{\leq d-2\kappa}$ and the first $(d-1)$-set t_a in its preferences, it holds that $\{a\} \cup t_a$ contains $V^{\leq d-2\kappa}$ and 2κ agents from $V^{[d-2\kappa+1, d+2\kappa]}$. Since $d \gg \kappa$, it follows that there exists a d-set t such that $t = \{a\} \cup t_a$ for at least 4κ agents. We set $t^* := t$. $\square$

Theorem 3. MDSR-POSET *can be solved in* $O(n^2) + (\kappa^5 2^{16\kappa})^{O(\kappa^5 2^{16\kappa})}n$ *time, where* κ *is the maximum number of agents an agent is incomparable to, and* n *is the number of agents.*

Proof. If $4\kappa 2^{4\kappa} \leq d$, then we can safely answer yes by Lemma 3. Otherwise we have $d \leq 4\kappa 2^{4\kappa}$ and thus, Proposition 2 yields an algorithm running in $h(\kappa)n$ time with $h(\kappa) = f(\kappa, 4\kappa 2^{4\kappa})$ where $f(\kappa, d) = (\kappa d^4)^{O(\kappa d^4)}$. $\square$

In the natural generalization of STABLE MARRIAGE to dimension d, the set V of agents is partitioned into d sets $V^1, \ldots, V^d$ of agents, and each agent of V^i has preferences over all $(d-1)$-sets containing exactly one agent from V^j for all $j \in [d] \setminus \{i\}$. This problem is also fixed-parameter tractable parameterized by $\kappa + d$: The master list of agents can then be decomposed into d master lists of agents, one for each set V^i. Then, one can apply Lemma 1 to each of these d master lists to get a strict order for the agents from $V^i = \{v_1^i, \ldots, v_n^i\}$. Similarly to Lemma 2, one can show that for any stable matching M and any d-set $\{v_{i_1}^1, \ldots, v_{i_d}^d\}$ (w.l.o.g. we have $i_j \leq i_{j+1}$), it holds that $i_{j+1} \leq i_j + O(\kappa d^2)$. Now one can apply an algorithm similar to Proposition 2 (sweeping over the sets $V^1, \ldots, V^d$ from top to bottom, considering any matching on $k = f(\kappa, d)$ consecutive agents) to get an FPT-algorithm parameterized by $\kappa + d$. However, Lemma 3 does not seem to generalize to this case: for $d = 3$, there exists a small instance with $|V_1| = |V_2| = |V_3| = 3$ without a stable matching. "Cloning" the agents from one of the sets, say V_3, an arbitrary number of times will result in an instance of unbounded d but $\kappa = 3$. It is therefore unclear whether Theorem 3 generalizes to the d-partite version of MDSR-POSET.

Remark 1. Until now, we assumed that the input is encoded naively, i.e., for each agent, its complete preference list is given as part of the input. However, this list is of length $\Omega(n^{d-1})$, which would result in a total input size of $\Omega(n^d)$. Thus, it may be more reasonable to assume that the input is given by an oracle, which can answer queries about the preferences. In fact, the FPT-algorithm parameterized by $\kappa + d$ only needs one type of queries, namely given two $(d-1)$-sets t and t' and an agent a, the oracle tells whether a prefers t over t'. Thus, our FPT-algorithm parameterized only by κ also works when only using this query; however, in the case that κ is much smaller than d, it cannot compute a stable matching, but only state its existence. In order to also compute a stable matching efficiently, the algorithm would also need to be able to query what, given an agent a and a set X of agents, the first $(d-1)$-set in a's preference list not containing an agent from X.

Having shown that MDSR-POSET is fixed-parameter tractable for the parameter κ, we turn to a weaker parameter, the width of the master poset.

Width of the Poset. Reducing from MULTICOLORED INDEPENDENT SET, we show that MDSR-POSET is W[1]-hard parameterized by the width of the poset.

Theorem 4 (⋆). *MDSR-POSET is* W[1]-*hard parameterized by the poset width.*

4.3 Incomplete Preferences Derived from a Strict Master List

Let MDSRI be the MDSR problem with incomplete preference lists, i.e., $\succ_v$ is not a total order of $\binom{V \setminus \{v\}}{d-1}$, but a total order of a subset $X_v \subseteq \binom{V \setminus \{v\}}{d-1}$ for each $v \in V$. In this case, we define a *matching* M to be a set of disjoint d-sets such that for all $\{v_1, v_2, \ldots, v_d\} \in M$, we have $\{v_1, v_2, \ldots, v_d\} \setminus \{v_i\} \in X_{v_i}$ for all $i \in [d]$. Similarly, MDSRI-ML is the MDSRI problem restricted to instances where the preferences are derived from a master list, and ℓ-DSRI is MDSRI for the special case $d = \ell$. We refer to the full version [5] for formal problem definitions.

In this section, we show that 3-DSRI-ML, the restriction of MDSRI-ML to $d = 3$, is NP-complete, even if the master list is strict. In order to do so, we reduce from PERFECT-SMTI-ML. The input of this problem is an instance of MAXIMUM STABLE MARRIAGE WITH TIES AND INCOMPLETE PREFERENCES such that the preferences of the women are derived from a strict master list, while the preference list of men is derived from a master list which may contain ties of size two. The problem asks whether there exists a perfect weakly stable matching. PERFECT-SMTI-ML is known to be NP-complete [18].

Theorem 5 (⋆). 3-DSRI-ML *is* NP-*complete, even if the master list is derived from a master list of agents.*

Theorem 5 also shows NP-completeness for the tripartite version of 3-DSRI-ML. By "cloning" each agent corresponding to a man $d - 3$ times (and for each "acceptable 3-set", add the cloned men to this 3-set, and add all $d - 1$-subsets of the resulting d-set at their corresponding place in the preferences), one can derive NP-completeness of d-DSRI-ML for any fixed $d \geq 3$.

4.4 Deletion Distance to a Strict Master List

We saw that MDSR-POSET is FPT for the maximum number of agents incomparable to a single agent but is W[1]-hard parameterized by the width of the poset. We now consider another parameter measuring the similarity to a strict order, namely the deletion distance to a strict order, i.e., the minimum number of agents which need to be deleted such that the resulting preferences are derived from a strict order. Note that this parameter is orthogonal to the two parameters investigated before: If the master list is the weak order $a_1 \sim_{ML} a_2 \succ_{ML} a_3 \sim_{ML} a_4 \succ_{ML} a_5 \sim_{ML} a_6 \succ_{ML} \cdots \succ_{ML} a_{n-1} \sim_{ML} a_n$, then $\kappa(ML) = 2$, while one has to delete $\frac{n}{2}$ agents in order to arrive at a strict order. If the preferences of all but one agent are derived from a strict order, and the last agent's preferences are derived from the inverse of this strict order, then the deletion distance is one while any master poset from which this preferences are derived from is only a single tie and thus has width n. In this section, reducing from MULTICOLORED CLIQUE we show that MDSR-POSET is W[1]-hard parameterized by the deletion distance to a strict master list.

Theorem 6 (⋆). 3-DSR *parameterized by* $\lambda(\mathcal{I})$ *is* W[1]-*hard, where* $\lambda(\mathcal{I})$ *denotes the minimum number of agents such that the preferences of the instance arising through the deletion of these agents are derived from a strict master list.*

5   Conclusion

Being a fundamental problem within the field of stable matching and the analysis of hedonic games, our work provides a seemingly first systematic study on the parameterized complexity of MULTIDIMENSIONAL STABLE ROOMMATES. Focusing on the concept of master lists with the goal to identify efficiently solvable special cases, we could only report partial success. While we have one main algorithmically positive result, namely fixed-parameter tractability for the parameter "maximum number of agents incomparable to a single agent", all other (single) parameterizations led again to (often surprising) hardness results (see Table 1).

As to challenges for future research, first, it remained open whether our fixed-parameter tractability result mentioned above also transfers to the setting of MULTIDIMENSIONAL STABLE MARRIAGE. Second, further following the quest for identifying islands of tractability, the study of further, perhaps also combined parameters might be a worth-while goal.

Acknowledgements. KH was supported by DFG Research Training Group 2434 "Facets of Complexity". DK was partially supported by DFG project NI 369/19 while at TU Berlin.

References

1. Arkin, E.M., Bae, S.W., Efrat, A., Okamoto, K., Mitchell, J.S.B., Polishchuk, V.: Geometric stable roommates. Inf. Process. Lett. **109**(4), 219–224 (2009)
2. Balinski, M., Sönmez, T.: A tale of two mechanisms: student placement. J. Econ. Theor. **84**(1), 73–94 (1999)
3. Biró, P., Irving, R.W., Schlotter, I.: Stable matching with couples: an empirical study. ACM J. Exp. Algorithmics **16**, 1–27 (2011)
4. Braun, S., Dwenger, N., Kübler, D.: Telling the truth may not pay off: an empirical study of centralized university admissions in Germany. B. E. J. Econ. Anal. Policy **10**(1), 22 (2010)
5. Bredereck, R., Heeger, K., Knop, D., Niedermeier, R.: Multidimensional stable roommates with master list. arXiv:2009.14191 (2020)
6. de Bruijn, N.G.: Asymptotic Methods in Analysis. Bibliotheca Mathematica, vol. 4. Interscience Publishers Inc., New York (1958). North-Holland Publishing Co., Amsterdam; P. Noordhoff Ltd., Groningen
7. Cseh, Á., Fleiner, T., Harján, P.: Pareto optimal coalitions of fixed size. arXiv:1901.06737 (2019)
8. Cui, L., Jia, W.: Cyclic stable matching for three-sided networking services. Comput. Netw. **57**(1), 351–363 (2013)
9. Danilov, V.I.: Existence of stable matchings in some three-sided systems. Math. Soc. Sci. **46**(2), 145–148 (2003)
10. Deineko, V.G., Woeginger, G.J.: Two hardness results for core stability in hedonic coalition formation games. Discret. Appl. Math. **161**(13–14), 1837–1842 (2013)
11. Dilworth, R.P.: A decomposition theorem for partially ordered sets. Ann. Math. **2**(51), 161–166 (1950)
12. Escamocher, G., O'Sullivan, B.: Three-dimensional matching instances are rich in stable matchings. In: van Hoeve, W.-J. (ed.) CPAIOR 2018. LNCS, vol. 10848, pp. 182–197. Springer, Cham (2018). https://doi.org/10.1007/978-3-319-93031-2_13

13. Gai, A.-T., Lebedev, D., Mathieu, F., de Montgolfier, F., Reynier, J., Viennot, L.: Acyclic preference systems in P2P networks. In: Kermarrec, A.-M., Bougé, L., Priol, T. (eds.) Euro-Par 2007. LNCS, vol. 4641, pp. 825–834. Springer, Heidelberg (2007). https://doi.org/10.1007/978-3-540-74466-5_88
14. Gale, D., Shapley, L.S.: College admissions and the stability of marriage. Am. Math. Mon. **69**(1), 9–15 (1962)
15. Hanaka, T., Kiya, H., Maei, Y., Ono, H.: Computational complexity of hedonic games on sparse graphs. In: Baldoni, M., Dastani, M., Liao, B., Sakurai, Y., Zalila Wenkstern, R. (eds.) PRIMA 2019. LNCS (LNAI), vol. 11873, pp. 576–584. Springer, Cham (2019). https://doi.org/10.1007/978-3-030-33792-6_43
16. Hofbauer, J.: *d*-dimensional stable matching with cyclic preferences. Math. Soc. Sci. **82**, 72–76 (2016)
17. Irving, R.W.: An efficient algorithm for the "Stable Roommates" problem. J. Algorithms **6**(4), 577–595 (1985)
18. Irving, R.W., Manlove, D., Scott, S.: The stable marriage problem with master preference lists. Discret. Appl. Math. **156**(15), 2959–2977 (2008)
19. Iwama, K., Miyazaki, S., Okamoto, K.: Stable roommates problem with triple rooms. In: Proceedings of WAAC 2007, pp. 105–112 (2007)
20. Kamiyama, N.: Many-to-many stable matchings with ties, master preference lists, and matroid constraints. Proceedings of AAMAS 2019, pp. 583–591 (2019)
21. Kavitha, T., Nasre, M., Nimbhorkar, P.: Popularity at minimum cost. J. Comb. Optim. **27**(3), 574–596 (2012). https://doi.org/10.1007/s10878-012-9537-0
22. Knuth, D.E.: Mariages stables et leurs relations avec d'autres problèmes combinatoires. Les Presses de l'Université de Montréal, Montreal, Que (1976)
23. Kunysz, A.: The strongly stable roommates problem. In: Proceedings of ESA, pp. 60:1–60:15 (2016)
24. Lam, C.-K., Plaxton, C.G.: On the existence of three-dimensional stable matchings with cyclic preferences. In: Fotakis, D., Markakis, E. (eds.) SAGT 2019. LNCS, vol. 11801, pp. 329–342. Springer, Cham (2019). https://doi.org/10.1007/978-3-030-30473-7_22
25. Ng, C., Hirschberg, D.S.: Three-dimensional stable matching problems. SIAM J. Discret. Math. **4**(2), 245–252 (1991)
26. O'Malley, G.: Algorithmic Aspects of Stable Matching Problems. Ph.D. thesis, University of Glasgow, Department of Computing Sciences (2007)
27. Ostrovsky, R., Rosenbaum, W.: It's not easy being three: The approximability of three-dimensional stable matching problems. arXiv:1412.1130 (2014)
28. Perach, N., Polak, J., Rothblum, U.G.: A stable matching model with an entrance criterion applied to the assignment of students to dormitories at the Technion. Int. J. Game Theor. **36**, 519–535 (2008). https://doi.org/10.1007/s00182-007-0083-4
29. Peters, D.: Graphical hedonic games of bounded treewidth. Proceedings of AAAI 2016, pp. 586–593 (2016)
30. Ronn, E.: NP-complete stable matching problems. J. Algorithms **11**(2), 285–304 (1990)
31. Roth, A.E., Sönmez, T., Ünver, M.U.: Kidney exchange. Q. J. Econ. **119**(2), 457–488 (2004)
32. Rothe, J. (ed.): Economics and Computation. STBE. Springer, Heidelberg (2016). https://doi.org/10.1007/978-3-662-47904-9
33. Scott, S.: A Study of Stable Marriage Problems with Ties. Ph.D. thesis, University of Glasgow, Department of Computing Sciences (2005)

34. Woeginger, G.J.: Core stability in hedonic coalition formation. In: van Emde Boas, P., Groen, F.C.A., Italiano, G.F., Nawrocki, J., Sack, H. (eds.) SOFSEM 2013. LNCS, vol. 7741, pp. 33–50. Springer, Heidelberg (2013). https://doi.org/10.1007/978-3-642-35843-2_4
35. Wu, J.: Stable matching beyond bipartite graphs. In: IPDPS Workshops 2016, pp. 480–488. IEEE Computer Society (2016)
36. Zhong, L., Bai, Y.: Three-sided stable matching problem with two of them as cooperative partners. J. Comb. Optim **37**(1), 286–292 (2017). https://doi.org/10.1007/s10878-017-0224-z

Markets

Optimal Nash Equilibria for Bandwidth Allocation

Benjamin Plaut[(⊠)]

Stanford University, Stanford, USA
bplaut@stanford.edu

Abstract. In bandwidth allocation, competing agents wish to transmit data along paths of links in a network, and each agent's utility is equal to the minimum bandwidth she receives among all links in her desired path. Recent market mechanisms for this problem have either focused on only Nash welfare [9], or ignored strategic behavior [21]. We propose a nonlinear variant of the classic trading post mechanism, and show that for almost the entire family of CES welfare functions (which includes maxmin welfare, Nash welfare, and utilitarian welfare), every Nash equilibrium of our mechanism is optimal. We also prove that fully strategyproof mechanisms for this problem are impossible in general, with the exception of maxmin welfare. More broadly, our work shows that even small modifications (such as allowing nonlinear constraints) can dramatically increase the power of market mechanisms like trading post.

1 Introduction

Bandwidth allocation is a classic resource allocation problem where competing agents wish to transmit data across paths in a network. Each link has a fixed capacity, and each agent's utility is equal to the minimum bandwidth she receives among all links in her desired path, i.e., the rate at which she is able to transmit data. We follow the standard model of Kelly et al. [24], where each agent's path is fixed in advance. We also assume that there are no monetary payments (i.e., no "real money").

Although one could consider a model where bandwidth allocation and routing are handled simultaneously (i.e., by allowing agents to choose their paths), that would be less accurate in terms of how the internet actually works: routing (which is handled by IP) and bandwidth allocation (which is handled by TCP) are generally separate problems. This paper is about bandwidth allocation, where pricing-based schemes (like trading post) naturally correspond to signaling mechanisms that indicate which links are congested, and an end-point protocol like TCP [11] can be thought of as agent responses. One of the foundational works in the area of bandwidth allocation is Kelly et al. [24], whose pricing scheme results in the allocation maximizing Nash welfare (the product of utilities).

© Springer Nature Switzerland AG 2020
X. Chen et al. (Eds.): WINE 2020, LNCS 12495, pp. 77–88, 2020.
https://doi.org/10.1007/978-3-030-64946-3_6

In this paper, we take the role of a social planner, whose goal is to design a mechanism that leads to a "desirable" outcome (for some definition of "desirable"). We study this through the lens of *implementation theory*. A mechanism is said to Nash-implement a social choice rule Ψ (for example, Ψ could denote Nash welfare maximization) if every problem instance has least one Nash equilibrium, and every Nash equilibrium outcome is optimal with respect to Ψ. This is similar to saying that the price of anarchy – the ratio of the optimum and the "worst" Nash equilibrium – of the mechanism is 1.[1] In this paper, we focus on pure Nash equilibria, i.e., we do not consider randomized strategies.

The result of Kelly et al. [24] assumes that agents are not strategic, and thus the Nash equilibria of their mechanism may be poor. In contrast, our augmented trading post mechanism will lead to optimal Nash equilibria, not just for Nash welfare, but for an entire family of welfare functions.

1.1   Trading Post

Our main tool will be an augmented version of the *trading post* mechanism. In the standard trading post mechanism, each agent i submits a bid $b_{ij} \in \mathbb{R}_{\geq 0}$ on each good j, with the constraint that $\sum_j b_{ij} \leq 1$ for each agent i. Let x_{ij} be the fraction of good j that agent i receives: then trading post's allocation rule is $x_{ij} = \frac{b_{ij}}{\sum_k b_{kj}}$. In words, each agent receives a share of the good proportional to her share of the aggregate bid on that good. The bids consist of "fake money": agents have no value for leftover money.

Trading post has the desirable property that the information requirements are quite light. Each agent's best response only depends on the aggregate bid of the other agents (i.e., $\sum_{k \neq i} b_{kj}$), not on their individual bids. Furthermore, the allocation rule is decentralized in the sense that there is no centralized price computation, and each link j only needs to know the bids $b_{1j}, b_{2j}, \ldots b_{nj}$.

However, the vanilla version of trading post also has limitations. First of all, it is not even guaranteed to have a Nash equilibrium for every problem instance.[2] A partial solution to this was proposed by [9]. For every $\varepsilon > 0$, they gave a modified version of trading post (parameterized by ε) that always has a Nash equilibrium, and where every Nash equilibrium attains at least $1 - \varepsilon$ of the maximum possible Nash welfare.[3] In the language of implementation theory, this mechanism Nash-implements a $1 - \varepsilon$ approximation of Nash welfare. In the course of our main result, we will strengthen this to full Nash implementation. It is important to note that their mechanism still uses the linear constraint of

---

[1] The price of anarchy [25] concept applies only when Ψ can be written as the maximization of some cardinal function. This is true when Ψ denotes Nash welfare maximization, but is not true in general.

[2] This happens when there is a good that has large enough supply that is not the "rate limiting factor" for any agent; see Sect. 3 and the full version of the paper [35] for additional discussion.

[3] They study *Leontief utilities*, which is a generalization of bandwidth allocation to the setting where agents may desire goods in different proportions.

$\sum_j b_{ij} \leq 1$; their modification has to do with a minimum allowable bid (see Sect. 3 for additional discussion).

In this paper, we augment the trading post mechanism by allowing nonlinear bid constraints: instead of $\sum_j b_{ij} \leq 1$, we require $\sum_j f_j(b_{ij}) \leq 1$ for each agent i, where each f_j is a nondecreasing function chosen by us ahead of time. Importantly, all agents are still subject to the same bid constraint, and we use the same allocation rule of $x_{ij} = \frac{b_{ij}}{\sum_k b_{kj}}$. This novel augmentation allows us to Nash-implement a wide range welfare functions, as opposed to just Nash welfare. Specifically, we will Nash-implement almost the entire family of CES welfare functions (see Sect. 2 for more details). This is our main result.

1.2   CES Welfare Functions

A welfare function [4,37] assigns a real number to each possible outcome, with higher numbers (i.e, higher welfare) indicating outcomes that are more desirable to the social planner. Different welfare functions represent different priorities: in particular the tradeoff of overall efficiency and individual equality. For any constant $\rho \in (-\infty, 0) \cup (0, 1]$, the *constant elasticity of substitution* (CES) welfare of outcome $\mathbf{x}$ is defined by

$$\Phi_\rho(\mathbf{x}) = \Big(\sum_{\text{agents } i} u_i(\mathbf{x})^\rho \Big)^{1/\rho}$$

where $u_i(\mathbf{x})$ is agent i's utility for $\mathbf{x}$. In general, different values of ρ lead to different optimal allocations, so whenever we say "maximum CES welfare", we always mean with respect to a specific value of ρ.

When $\rho = 1$, CES welfare is just utilitarian welfare, i.e., the sum of utilities. The limit as $\rho \to -\infty$ yields maxmin welfare (the minimum utility) [36,38,39], whereas $\rho \to 0$ yields Nash welfare (the product of utilities) [23,31]. This class of welfare functions was first proposed by Atkinson [3], and further developed by [5]. See [30] for a modern introduction to this class of welfare functions.

The closer ρ gets to $-\infty$, the more the social planner cares about individual equality (maxmin welfare being the extreme case of this), and the closer ρ gets to 1, the more the social planner cares about overall societal good (utilitarian welfare being the extreme case of this). For this reason, ρ is called the *inequality aversion* parameter. The CES welfare function (as opposed to the CES agent utility function) has received almost no attention in the computational economics community, despite being extremely influential in the traditional economics literature.

These welfare functions also admit an axiomatic characterization [30]:

1. Monotonicity: if one agent's utility increases while all others are unchanged, the welfare function should prefer the new allocation.
2. Symmetry: the welfare function should treat all agents the same.

3. Continuity: the welfare function should be continuous.[4]
4. Independence of common scale: scaling all agent utilities by the same factor should not affect which allocations have better welfare than others.
5. Independence of unconcerned agents: when comparing the welfare of two allocations, the comparison should not depend on agents who have the same utility in both allocations.
6. The Pigou-Dalton principle: all things being equal, the welfare function should prefer more equitable allocations [13,34].

Ignoring monotonic transformations of the welfare function (which of course do not affect which allocations have better welfare than others), the set of welfare functions satisfying these axioms is exactly the set of CES welfare functions with $\rho \in (-\infty, 0) \cup (0, 1]$[5], including Nash welfare [30].[6] This axiomatic characterization shows that we are not just focusing on an arbitrary class of welfare functions: CES welfare functions are arguably the most reasonable welfare functions.

Recently, [21] showed that in the bandwidth allocation setting, for any CES welfare function except $\rho = 1$, nonlinear pricing can be used to obtain market equilibria with optimal CES welfare. Specifically, each good j is assigned a weakly increasing (potentially nonlinear) function g_j, and the cost of buying a bundle $x_i = (x_{i1}, x_{i2}, \ldots x_{im})$ is $\sum_j g_j(x_{ij})$. Subject to these prices, each agent purchases her favorite affordable bundle x_i, and if the allocation $\mathbf{x} = (x_1 \ldots x_n)$ clears the market, $(\mathbf{x}, \mathbf{g})$ is called a *price curve equilibrium*. It was shown by [21] that for any $\rho \in (-\infty, 1)$, there exists a choice of price curves $\mathbf{g} = g_1 \ldots g_m$ such that $(\mathbf{x}, \mathbf{g})$ is a price curve equilibrium if and only if $\mathbf{x}$ maximizes CES welfare.

However, their result assumes that agents are not strategic. In this paper, we present a market mechanism with the same guarantee of optimal CES welfare, while also handling strategic behavior.

2 Our Results

Our results fall into two categories, both summarized by Table 1. Due to space constraints, all proofs are deferred to the full version of the paper [35].

Nash-Implementing CES Welfare Functions. We view the Nash implementation of CES welfare functions by trading post as our main result. For each

---

[4] A slightly weaker version of continuity is often used: given an allocation $\mathbf{x}$, the sets $\{\mathbf{y} : \Phi(\mathbf{x}) \geq \Phi(\mathbf{y})\}$ and $\{\mathbf{y} : \Phi(\mathbf{x}) \leq \Phi(\mathbf{y})\}$ should be closed. This weaker version only requires a welfare *ordering* and does not require that this ordering be expressed by a function. However, any such ordering which also satisfies the rest of our axioms is indeed representable by a welfare function [30], and so both sets of axioms end up specifying the same set of welfare functions/orderings.

[5] Without the Pigou-Dalton principle, $\rho > 1$ is also allowed. This can result in unnatural cases where it is optimal to give one agent everything and the rest none, even when this does not maximize the sum of utilities.

[6] This actually does not include maxmin welfare, which obeys weak monotonicity but not strict monotonicity.

Table 1. A summary of our main implementation results. Here $\rho = -\infty$ denotes maxmin welfare, $\rho \in (-\infty, 1)$ includes Nash welfare as $\rho = 0$, and $\rho = 1$ denotes utilitarian welfare. DSE stands for "dominant strategy equilibrium". "✓" indicates that the type of implementation specified by the row is possible for the social choice rule specified by the column, while "✗" indicates that we give a counterexample, and "?" indicates an open question.

	$\rho = -\infty$	$\rho \in (-\infty, 1)$	$\rho = 1$
Nash-implementable?	✓	✓	?
DSE-implementable?	✓	✗	✗

$\rho \in (-\infty, 1)$, we define an augmented trading post mechanism with a nonlinear bid constraint of $\sum_j b_{ij}^{1-\rho} \leq 1$ for each agent i.[7] We denote this mechanism by $\mathcal{ATP}(\rho)$. We show that $\mathcal{ATP}(\rho)$ has at least one Nash equilibrium, and that all of its Nash equilibria maximize CES welfare.

Our result improves that of [21] by strengthening their price curve equilibrium (which assumes agents are not strategic) to a strategic equilibrium, and improves that of [9] by generalizing from just Nash welfare to all CES welfare functions (except $\rho = 1$) and strengthening their $1 - \varepsilon$ approximation to exact implementation.[8] Furthermore, because the price curve equilibria can be computed in polynomial time [21], our Nash equilibria can also be computed in polynomial time.

Our proof makes use of the following results (stated informally):

1. Any Nash equilibrium of $\mathcal{ATP}$ can be converted into an "equivalent" price curve equilibrium (full version of this paper: [35]).
2. Any price curve equilibrium can be converted into an "equivalent" Nash equilibrium of $\mathcal{ATP}$ (full version of this paper: [35]).
3. If $\mathbf{x}$ is a maximum CES welfare allocation, then there exist price curves $\mathbf{g}$ of the form $g_j(x) = q_j x^{1-\rho}$ such that $(\mathbf{x}, \mathbf{g})$ is a price curve equilibrium [21].
4. If $(\mathbf{x}, \mathbf{g})$ is a price curve equilibrium and each g_j has the form $g_j(x) = q_j x^{1-\rho}$, then $\mathbf{x}$ is a maximum CES welfare allocation [21].

Results 3 and 4 together imply that $\mathbf{x}$ is a maximum CES welfare allocation if and only if it is a price curve equilibrium with respect to some price curves $\mathbf{g}$ of the form $g_j(x) = q_j x^{1-\rho}$ (where $q_1 \ldots q_m$ are nonnegative constants). Results 1 and 2 allow us to convert between price curve equilibria and Nash equilibria of $\mathcal{ATP}$, and thus enable us to apply results 1 and 2 to the Nash equilibria of $\mathcal{ATP}(\rho)$. This will show that $\mathcal{ATP}(\rho)$ is guaranteed to have at least one Nash

---

[7] The reader may notice that for $\rho = 0$ – which corresponds to Nash welfare – this constraint reduces to the standard linear constraint of $\sum_j b_{ij} \leq 1$, which is what we should expect: we know from [9] that trading post with the linear constraint leads to good Nash welfare.

[8] It is worth noting that the result of [9] holds for Leontief utilities, a generalization of bandwidth allocation utilities.

equilibrium, and every Nash equilibrium maximizes CES welfare (with respect to ρ).

Our trading post approach breaks down for $\rho = -\infty$ and $\rho = 1$. We are able to Nash-implement $\rho = -\infty$ by a different mechanism (see below), but we were not able to resolve whether $\rho = 1$ is Nash-implementable. We leave this as an open question.

Results for Dominant Strategy Implementation and Maxmin Welfare. A natural question is whether these results can be improved from Nash implementation to implementation in dominant strategy equilibrium (DSE). We show that the answer is mostly no: for any $\rho \in (-\infty, 1]$, there is no mechanism which DSE-implements CES welfare maximization.

On the positive side, we show that maxmin welfare ($\rho = -\infty$) can in fact be DSE-implemented by a simple revelation mechanism. This is actually stronger than strategyproofness: strategyproofness requires truth-telling to be *a* DSE, but does not rule out the possibility of additional dominant strategy equilibria that are not optimal. In contrast, DSE implementation requires *every* DSE to be optimal.

Although every DSE is also a Nash equilibrium, DSE-implementability does *not* imply Nash-implementability [14]. A DSE implementation requires every DSE to be optimal, but there could be Nash equilibria (which are not dominant strategy equilibria) that are not optimal. This means that our above result does not imply Nash-implementability of maxmin welfare. In fact, our revelation mechanism which DSE-implements maxmin welfare is not a Nash implementation: there exist Nash equilibria which are not optimal (see the full version of this paper for the counterexample). Our last result is that there is a different mechanism which does Nash-implement maxmin welfare.[9]

All proofs, along with the formal mathematical model, can be found in the full version of the paper [35].

3   Related Work

Trading Post and Market Games. The trading post mechanism – first proposed by Shapley and Shubik [40], and sometimes called the "Shapley-Shubik game"[10] – is an example of a *strategic market game* (for an overview of strategic market games, see [20]). The study of markets has a long history in the economics literature [2,7,41,43][11], but most of this work assumes that agents are

---

[9] The mechanism for this result is unrelated to trading post: our trading post approach breaks down for both maxmin welfare and utilitarian welfare. This is because $g_j(x) = q_j x^{1-\rho}$ is not a valid price curve when $\rho \to -\infty$ or when $\rho = 1$.

[10] A plethora of other names have been applied to this mechanism as well, including the proportional share mechanism [18], the Chinese auction [28], and the Tullock contest in rent seeking [10].

[11] Recently, this topic has garnered significant attention in the computer science community as well (see [42] for an algorithmic exposition).

price-taking, meaning that they treat the market prices are fixed, and do not behave strategically to affect these prices.[12] A market game, however, treats the agents as strategic players who wish to selfishly maximize their own utility. Trading post does not have explicit prices set by a centralized authority: instead, prices arise implicitly from agents' strategic behavior. In particular, $\sum_k b_{kj}$ – the aggregate bid on good j – functions as the implicit price of good j. Although the trading post mechanism is well-defined for any utility functions, the Nash equilibria are not guaranteed to have many nice properties in general, except in the limit as the number of agents goes to infinity [15] (in this case, the trading post Nash equilibria converge to the price-taking market equilibria).

The paper most relevant to ours is [9], which analyzed the performance of trading post (with a linear bid constraint) with respect to Nash welfare. They showed that for Leontief utilities (which generalize bandwidth allocation), a modified trading post mechanism approximates the Nash welfare arbitrarily well. Specifically, for any $\varepsilon > 0$, they gave a mechanism (parameterized by ε) which achieves a $1 - \varepsilon$ Nash welfare approximation: there is at least one Nash equilibrium, and every Nash equilibrium has Nash welfare at least $1 - \varepsilon$ times the optimal Nash welfare. Thus the price of anarchy is at most $\frac{1}{1-\varepsilon}$; equivalently, this mechanism Nash-implements a $1 - \varepsilon$ approximation of Nash welfare. The reason that they were unable to perfectly implement Nash welfare is because when there is a good that should have price zero, vanilla trading post may not even have a Nash equilibrium. To fix this, they added a minimum allowable bid, and showed that for any $\varepsilon > 0$, there is a minimum bid that gives them a $1 - \varepsilon$ Nash implementation. Instead of restricting the bid space with a minimum bid, our mechanism enhances the bid space by adding a special bid β. This which will allow us to strengthen the result to full Nash implementation.

It is worth noting that [9] also considers a broader class of utility functions than Leontief (general concave utility functions), but for this broader class, only a 1/2 approximation is achieved. Another paper gave a strategyproof mechanism achieving a $1/e \approx .368$ approximation of the optimal Nash welfare when utility functions are homogeneous of degree one (this also generalizes Leontief) [12]. Their $1/e$ approximation guarantee is weaker than the 1/2 guarantee of [9] (and the $1 - \varepsilon$ guarantee for Leontief), but strategyproofness is sometimes more desirable that Nash implementation. Unfortunately, strategyproofness in the bandwidth allocation setting is generally impossible (see the full version of the paper: [35]).

Price-Taking Markets. The simplest mathematical model of a price-taking market is a *Fisher market*, due to Irving Fisher [7]. In a Fisher market, there is a set of goods for sale, and each buyer enters the market with a budget she wishes to spend. Each good has a price, and each buyer purchases her favorite bundle among those that are affordable under her budget constraint. Prices are linear, meaning that the cost of a good is proportional to the quantity purchased, and buyers are assumed to have no value for leftover money, so they will

---

[12] There is some work treating price-taking market models as strategic games; see e.g., [1,8,9].

always exhaust their entire budgets. A market equilibrium assigns a price to each good so that the demand exactly equals the supply. For a wide class of agent utilities, including bandwidth allocation utilities, an equilibrium is guaranteed to exist [2].[13] The seminal work of Eisenberg and Gale showed that for linear prices and a large class of agent utilities (including bandwidth allocation), the market equilibria correspond exactly to the allocations maximizing Nash welfare [16,17].[14] Furthermore, the prices are equal to the optimal Lagrange multipliers in the convex program for maximizing Nash welfare (the Eisenberg-Gale convex program).

Recently, [21] extended this model to allow nonlinear prices, where the cost of a good may be any nondecreasing function of the quantity purchased. These functions are called *price curves*. They showed that for bandwidth allocation, for any $\rho \in (-\infty, 1)$, there exist price curves such that the set of market equilibria are exactly the set of maximum CES welfare allocations. Furthermore, these prices take a natural form: the cost of purchasing $x \in \mathbb{R}_{\geq 0}$ of good j is $g_j(x) = q_j x^{1-\rho}$, for some nonnegative constants $q_1 \ldots q_m$. Interestingly, for $\rho = 0$ – which denotes Nash welfare – this function form reduces to a linear price q_j, and we know that linear pricing maximizes Nash welfare. Furthermore, $q_1 \ldots q_m$ are the optimal Lagrange multipliers in the convex program for maximizing CES welfare.

Trading post with linear bid constraints ($\sum_j b_{ij} \leq 1$) can be thought of as a market game equivalent of the Fisher market model: it implements Nash welfare ([9] proved a $1 - \varepsilon$ approximation, but we will strengthen this to exact implementation), and the implicit trading post prices (the aggregate bids) are equal to the Fisher market equilibrium prices. Our augmented trading post, with bid constraint $\sum_j f_j(b_{ij}) \leq 1$, can be thought of as a market game equivalent of the price curves model. The augmented trading post mechanism we use to implement CES welfare will use $f_j(b) = b^{1-\rho}$ for each good j, further strengthening this analogy.

Bandwidth Allocation. Bandwidth allocation has been studied both with and without monetary payments; we focus on the latter setting, following the model of Kelly et al. [24]. It has been known that different marking schemes (such as RED and CHOKe [19,33]) and versions of TCP lead to different objective functions [32], with CES welfare (also known as "α-fairness") being one such objective [6,29]. However, a market-based understanding was developed only for Nash Welfare (also known as "proportional fairness"), starting with the pioneering work of Kelly et al. [24]. Furthermore, the market scheme of Kelly et al. is in the price-taking setting; the only strategic market analysis of bandwidth

---

[13] Specifically, an equilibrium is guaranteed to exist as long agent utilities are continuous, quasi-concave, and non-satiated. The full Arrow-Debreu model also allows for agents to enter to market with goods themselves and not only money; the necessary conditions on utilities are slightly more complex in that setting.

[14] The conditions for the correspondence between Fisher market equilibria and Nash welfare are slightly stricter than those for market equilibrium existence, but are still quite general. Sufficient criteria were given in [16] and generalized slightly by [22].

allocation that we are aware of is the $1 - \varepsilon$ approximation of Nash welfare due to [9].

Implementation Theory. Implementation theory is the study of designing mechanisms whose outcomes coincide with some desirable social choice rule. A social choice rule could be the maximization of a cardinal function, such as a CES welfare function, or something else, such as the set of Pareto optimal allocations. A full survey is outside the scope of this paper; we direct the interested reader to [27].

The "outcome" of a mechanism is not really well-defined; we need to specify a *solution concept*. The solution concept that we focus on for most of this paper is Nash equilibrium. Possibly the most crucial result regarding implementation in Nash equilibrium (Nash implementation, for short) is due to Maskin [26], who identified a necessary condition for Nash implementation, and a partial converse. He showed that in a very general environment (much broader than bandwidth allocation), any Nash-implementable social choice rule must satisfy what he calls *monotonicity*. Monotonicity, in combination with a property called *no veto power*, is sufficient for Nash implementation. In the full version of this paper, we show that CES welfare functions do not satisfy no veto power, and so cannot be Nash-implemented by Maskin's approach [35].

4   Conclusion and Future Work

In this paper, we presented an augmented trading post mechanism which can Nash-implement any CES welfare function except $\rho = 1$. This strengthened previous results which only handled Nash welfare [9] or assumed agents did not behave strategically [21]. In the full version of the paper [35], we show that DSE implementation for this problem is generally impossible, with the exception of maxmin welfare, where a simple revelation mechanism does indeed DSE-implement maxmin welfare. Although this revelation mechanism does not Nash-implement maxmin welfare, we are able to Nash-implement maxmin welfare with a different mechanism.

We were not able to resolve whether utilitarian welfare is Nash-implementable for bandwidth allocation. Our trading post mechanism breaks down in this setting, since $f_j(b) = b^{1-1} = 1$ is not a valid constraint curve. Maskin's monotonicity approach is not viable either, since utilitarian welfare does not satisfy no veto power. We leave this as an open question.

Another interesting direction would be to extend these results to a wider range of utility functions. Our reduction between price curves and trading post means that if price curve equilibria maximizing CES welfare were shown to exist for a wider range of utility functions, it seems likely that our Nash implementation results would carry over as well (depending on the form of the price curves).

It would also be interesting to consider another dimension of strategic behavior by allowing agents to choose which path in the network to use. In this case, we could write each agent's utility function as $u_i(x_i) = \max_{p \in P_i} \min_{j \in p} x_{ij}$, where P_i is the set of paths from agent i's desired source to desired destination. This is reminiscent of routing games, in that agents are strategically choosing their paths, but still distinct, in that each agent may use the same link in different quantities (i.e., receive different amounts of bandwidth). Although this model is less accurate in terms of how the internet actually works (see Sect. 1), it may be an appropriate model for other situations.

More broadly, we feel that trading post is a powerful mechanism that is able to simulate a price-taking market while also handling strategic behavior. We wonder if trading post, or variants thereof, may be useful in designing mechanisms for other resource allocation problems as well.

Acknowledgements. This work would not have been possible without my advisor Ashish Goel, who I would like to thank for continued guidance and feedback. This research was supported by NSF Graduate Research Fellowship under grant DGE-1656518.

References

1. Adsul, B., Babu, C.S., Garg, J., Mehta, R., Sohoni, M.: Nash equilibria in fisher market. In: Kontogiannis, S., Koutsoupias, E., Spirakis, P.G. (eds.) SAGT 2010. LNCS, vol. 6386, pp. 30–41. Springer, Heidelberg (2010). https://doi.org/10.1007/978-3-642-16170-4_4

2. Arrow, K.J., Debreu, G.: Existence of an equilibrium for a competitive economy. Econometrica **22**(3), 265–290 (1954)

3. Atkinson, A.B.: On the measurement of inequality. J. Econ. Theor. **2**(3), 244–263 (1970)

4. Bergson, A.: A reformulation of certain aspects of welfare economics. Quart. J. Econ. **52**(2), 310–334 (1938)

5. Blackorby, C., Donaldson, D.: Measures of relative equality and their meaning in terms of social welfare. J. Econ. Theor. **18**(1), 59–80 (1978)

6. Bonald, T., Massoulié, L.: Impact of fairness on internet performance. SIGMETRICS Perform. Eval. Rev. **29**(1), 82–91 (2001)

7. Brainard, W.C., Scarf, H.E.: How to compute equilibrium prices in 1891. Am. J. Econ. Sociol. **64**(1), 57–83 (2005)

8. Brânzei, S., Chen, Y., Deng, X., Filos-Ratsikas, A., Frederiksen, S.K.S., Zhang, J.: The fisher market game: equilibrium and welfare. In: Proceedings of the Twenty-Eighth AAAI Conference on Artificial Intelligence, AAAI 2014, pp. 587–593. AAAI Press (2014)

9. Branzei, S., Gkatzelis, V., Mehta, R.: Nash social welfare approximation for strategic agents. In: Proceedings of the 2017 ACM Conference on Economics and Computation, EC 2017, pp. 611–628. ACM, New York (2017)

10. Buchanan, J.M., Tollison, R.D., Tullock, G.: Toward a Theory of the Rent-Seeking Society. vol. 4. Texas A & M University Press, College Station (1980)

11. Cerf, V., Kahn, R.: A protocol for packet network intercommunication. IEEE Trans. Commun. **22**(5), 637–648 (1974)

12. Cole, R., Gkatzelis, V., Goel, G.: Mechanism design for fair division: allocating divisible items without payments. In: EC 2013 (2013)

13. Dalton, H.: The measurement of the inequality of incomes. Econ. J. **30**(119), 348–361 (1920)

14. Dasgupta, P., Hammond, P., Maskin, E.: The implementation of social choice rules: some general results on incentive compatibility. Rev. Econ. Stud. **46**(2), 185–216 (1979)
15. Dubey, P., Shubik, M.: A theory of money and financial institutions. 28. the noncooperative equilibria of a closed trading economy with market supply and bidding strategies. J. Econ. Theor. **17**(1), 1–20 (1978)
16. Eisenberg, E.: Aggregation of utility functions. Manage. Sci. **7**(4), 337–350 (1961)
17. Eisenberg, E., Gale, D.: Consensus of subjective probabilities: the pari-mutuel method. Ann. Math. Stat. **30**(1), 165–168 (1959)
18. Feldman, M., Lai, K., Zhang, L.: The proportional-share allocation market for computational resources. Trans. Parallel Distrib. Syst. **20**(8), 1075–1088 (2009)
19. Floyd, S., Jacobson, V.: Random early detection gateways for congestion avoidance. IEEE/ACM Trans. Netw. **1**(4), 397–413 (1993)
20. Giraud, G.: Strategic market games: an introduction. J. Math. Econ. **39**(5), 355–375 (2003)
21. Goel, A., Hulett, R., Plaut, B.: Markets beyond nash welfare for leontief utilities. CoRR abs/1807.05293 (2018)
22. Jain, K., Vazirani, V.V.: Eisenberg–gale markets: algorithms and game-theoretic properties. Games Econ. Behav. **70**(1), 84–106 (2010)
23. Kaneko, M., Nakamura, K.: The nash social welfare function. Econometrica **47**(2), 423–35 (1979)
24. Kelly, F.P., Maulloo, A.K., Tan, D.K.H.: Rate control for communication networks: shadow prices, proportional fairness and stability. J. Oper. Res. Soc. **49**(3), 237–252 (1998)
25. Koutsoupias, E., Papadimitriou, C.: Worst-case equilibria. In: Meinel, C., Tison, S. (eds.) STACS 1999. LNCS, vol. 1563, pp. 404–413. Springer, Heidelberg (1999). https://doi.org/10.1007/3-540-49116-3_38
26. Maskin, E.: Nash equilibrium and welfare optimality. Rev. Econ. Stud. **66**(1), 23–38 (1999)
27. Maskin, E., Sjöström, T.: Implementation Theory, pp. 237–288. North Holland, Amsterdam (2002)
28. Matros, A.: Chinese auctions. In: Petrosyan, L.A., Zenkevich, N.A. (eds.) GAME THEORY AND MANAGEMENT. Collected abstracts of papers presented on the Fifth International Conference Game Theory and Management. SPb.: Graduate School of Management SPbU, 2011, 268 p. The collection contains abstracts of papers accepted for the Fifth International, p. 153 (2011)
29. Mo, J., Walrand, J.: Fair end-to-end window-based congestion control. IEEE/ACM Trans. Netw. **8**(5) (2000)
30. Moulin, H.: Fair Division and Collective Welfare, Chap. 3. MIT Press, Cambridge (2003)
31. Nash, J.: The bargaining problem. Econometrica **18**(2), 155–162 (1950)
32. Padhye, J., Firoiu, V., Towsley, D., Kurose, J.: Modeling TCP throughput: a simple model and its empirical validation. SIGCOMM Comput. Commun. Rev. **28**(4), 303–314 (1998)
33. Pan, R., Prabhakar, B., Psounis, K.: Choke - a stateless active queue management scheme for approximating fair bandwidth allocation. In: Proceedings IEEE INFOCOM 2000. Conference on Computer Communications. Nineteenth Annual Joint Conference of the IEEE Computer and Communications Societies (Cat. No. 00CH37064), vol. 2, pp. 942–951 (2000)
34. Pigou, A.: Wealth and Welfare. Macmillan and Company, limited, PCMI collection (1912)

35. Plaut, B.: Optimal nash equilibria for bandwidth allocation. arXiv preprint arXiv:1904.03322 (2019)
36. Rawls, J.: A Theory of Justice, 1st edn. Belknap Press of Harvard University Press, Cambridge (1971)
37. Samuelson, P.A.: Foundations of economic analysis (1947)
38. Sen, A.: Welfare inequalities and rawlsian axiomatics. Theor. Decis. **7**(4), 243–262 (1976)
39. Sen, A.: Social choice theory: a re-examination. Econometrica **45**(1), 53–89 (1977)
40. Shapley, L., Shubik, M.: Trade using one commodity as a means of payment. J. Polit. Econ. **85**(5), 937–68 (1977)
41. Varian, H.: Equity, envy, and efficiency. J. Econ. Theor. **9**(1), 63–91 (1974)
42. Vazirani, V.V.: Combinatorial algorithms for market equilibria. In: Algorithmic Game Theory, pp. 103–134 (2007)
43. Walras, L.: Éléments d'économie politique pure; ou, Théorie de la richesse sociale. No. vol. 1–2, Corbaz (1874)

Counteracting Inequality in Markets via Convex Pricing

Ashish Goel and Benjamin Plaut[✉]

Stanford University, Stanford, USA
{ashishg,bplaut}@stanford.edu

Abstract. We study market mechanisms for allocating divisible goods to competing agents with quasilinear utilities. For *linear* pricing (i.e., the cost of a good is proportional to the quantity purchased), the First Welfare Theorem states that Walrasian equilibria maximize the sum of agent valuations. This ensures efficiency, but can lead to extreme inequality across individuals. Many real-world markets – especially for water – use *convex* pricing instead, often known as increasing block tariffs (IBTs). IBTs are thought to promote equality, but there is a dearth of theoretical support for this claim.

In this paper, we study a simple convex pricing rule and show that the resulting equilibria are guaranteed to maximize a CES welfare function. Furthermore, a parameter of the pricing rule directly determines which CES welfare function is implemented; by tweaking this parameter, the social planner can precisely control the tradeoff between equality and efficiency. Our result holds for any valuations that are homogeneous, differentiable, and concave. We also give an iterative algorithm for computing these pricing rules, derive a truthful mechanism for the case of a single good, and discuss Sybil attacks.

Keywords: Walrasian equilibrium · Convex pricing · First Welfare Theorem

1 Introduction

Markets are one of the oldest mechanisms for distributing resources; indeed, commodity prices were meticulously recorded in ancient Babylon for over 300 years [36,37]. In a market, buyers and sellers exchange goods according to some sort of pricing system, and *Walrasian equilibrium*[1] occurs when the demand of the buyers exactly equals the supply of the sellers. This concept was first studied by Walras in the 1870's [41]. In 1954, Arrow and Debreu showed that

A. Goel—Supported by NSF grant CCF-1637418 and ONR grant N00014-15-1-2786.
B. Plaut—Supported by a NSF Graduate Research Fellowship under grant DGE-1656518.

[1] This is also known as market equilibrium, competitive equilibrium, and general equilibrium, depending on the context.

© Springer Nature Switzerland AG 2020
X. Chen et al. (Eds.): WINE 2020, LNCS 12495, pp. 89–101, 2020.
https://doi.org/10.1007/978-3-030-64946-3_7

under some conditions, a Walrasian equilibrium is guaranteed to exist [1]. Most of the literature on Walrasian equilibrium only considers *linear* pricing, meaning the cost of a good is proportional to the quantity purchased.

In this paper, we consider the problem of allocating divisible goods to competing agents via a market mechanism. We assume each agent has quasilinear utility: an agent's utility is her value for the resources she obtains (her *valuation*), minus the money she spends (her *payment*). The First Welfare Theorem states that in this setting, the linear-pricing Walrasian equilibria are exactly the allocations maximizing utilitarian welfare, i.e., the sum of agent valuations. Thus linear pricing *implements* utilitarian welfare in Walrasian equilibrium (sometimes abbreviated "WE").

The result is powerful, but also limiting. Maximizing utilitarian welfare yields the most efficient outcome, but may also cause maximal inequality (see Fig. 1).

One common alternative is *convex* pricing. In this paper, we study convex pricing rules p of the form

$$p(x_i) = \Big(\sum_j q_j x_{ij} \Big)^{1/\rho}$$

where x_i is *bundle* agent i receives, $x_{ij} \in \mathbb{R}_{\geq 0}$ is the fraction of good j she receives, $q_1, \ldots, q_m$ are constants, and $\rho \in (0,1]$ determines the curvature of the pricing rule. Like linear pricing, p is still *anonymous*, meaning that agents' payments depend only on their purchases (and not on their preferences, for example).

When $\rho = 1$, p reduces to linear pricing. When $\rho < 1$, p is strictly convex, meaning that doubling one's consumption will more than double the price. This will make it easy to buy a small amount, but hard to buy a large amount, which intuitively should lead to a more equal distribution of resources. As the curvature of the pricing rule grows, this effect should be amplified, leading to a different equality/efficiency tradeoff.

Our work seeks to formalize that claim. We will show that the Walrasian equilibria of these convex pricing rules are guaranteed to maximize a *constant elasticity of substitution* (CES) welfare function, where the choice of ρ determines the specific welfare function and thus the precise equality/efficiency tradeoff (Theorem 2.1). Our result holds for a wide range of agent valuations.

Convex Pricing in the Real World. Convex pricing is especially pervasive in the water sector, where such pricing rules are known as *increasing block tariffs* (IBTs) [42], typically implemented with discrete blocks of water (hence the name). IBTs have been implemented and empirically studied in Israel [4], South Africa [9], Spain [17], Jordan [22], and the United States [32], among many other countries.

IBTs are often claimed to promote equality in water access [42], but there has been limited theoretical evidence supporting this (see [25] for one of the only examples). On the other hand, a common concern is that IBTs may lead to poor "economic efficiency" [7,25]. Our work shows that at least on a theoretical level, convexity of pricing does not necessarily lead to inefficiency: it simply maximizes

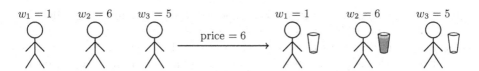

Fig. 1. An example of how linear pricing can lead to maximal inequality. Consider the three agents above and a single good (say, water), where each agent i's value for x units of the good is $w_i \cdot x$. The unique linear-pricing Walrasian equilibrium sets a price of 6 per unit, which results in agent 2 buying all of the good and the other two agents receiving nothing. More generally, the equilibrium price reflects the maximum anyone is willing to pay, and anyone who is not willing to pay that much is priced out of the market and receives nothing. In contrast, our nonlinear pricing rule always ensures that everyone receives a nonzero amount; see Sect. 2.

a different welfare function than the traditional utilitarian one. In particular, it maximizes a CES welfare function.

The Second Welfare Theorem and Personalized Pricing. The Second Welfare Theorem is perhaps the most famous theoretical result regarding implementation in Walrasian equilibrium. It states any Pareto optimum can be a WE when an arbitrary redistribution of initial wealth is allowed.[2] Another method that achieves the same goal is *personalized pricing*, where different agents can be charged different (linear) prices. In contrast, convex pricing is anonymous: agents purchasing the same bundle always pay the same price.

Each of these approaches certainly has its own pros and cons. In this paper, our goal is not to claim that convex pricing is "better" than other approaches (or vice versa). Regardless of which is "better" in any given situation, convex pricing *is* widely used in practice, and is often claimed to promote equality. Our goal in this paper is to formally quantify that claim.

1.1 CES Welfare Functions

A welfare function [5,33] assigns a real number to each possible outcome, with higher numbers (i.e, higher welfare) indicating outcomes that are more desirable to the social planner. Different welfare functions represent different priorities; our focus will be the tradeoff between overall efficiency and individual equality. For a fixed constant $\rho \in (-\infty, 0) \cup (0, 1]$, the constant elasticity of substitution (CES) welfare of outcome $\mathbf{x}$ is

$$\Phi(\rho, \mathbf{x}) = \left(\sum_{\text{agents } i} v_i(\mathbf{x})^\rho \right)^{1/\rho}$$

---

[2] Specifically, for any Pareto optimal allocation, there exists a redistribution of initial wealth which makes that allocation a WE. However, our quasilinear utility model does not have a concept of initial wealth (alternatively, initial wealth is simply an additive constant in agents' utilities which does not affect their behavior), so this result is not as mathematically relevant. See Sect. 3 for additional discussion.

where $v_i(\mathbf{x})$ is agent i's value for $\mathbf{x}$. In general, different values of ρ will lead to different optimal allocations, so whenever we say "maximum CES welfare allocation", we mean with respect to a fixed value of ρ.

For $\rho = 1$, this is utilitarian welfare, i.e., the sum of valuations. The limit as $\rho \to -\infty$ yields max-min welfare (the minimum valuation) [31,34,35], whereas $\rho \to 0$ yields Nash welfare (the product of valuations) [20,27]. The closer ρ gets to $-\infty$, the more the social planner cares about individual equality (max-min welfare being the extreme case of this), and the closer ρ gets to 1, the more the social planner cares about overall societal good (utilitarian welfare being the extreme case of this). For this reason, ρ is called the *inequality aversion* parameter, and this family of welfare functions is thought to exhibit an *equality/efficiency* tradeoff.

These welfare functions were originally proposed by Atkinson [3]; indeed, his motivation was to measure the level of inequality in a society. Despite being extremely influential in the traditional economics literature (see [10] for a survey), the CES welfare function has received almost no attention in the computational economics community.[3]

Finally, note that $\Phi(\rho, \mathbf{x})$ is defined with respect to the each agent's valuation v_i and *not* her overall quasilinear utility u_i. We acknowledge that it is standard to define welfare with respect to the overall utility u_i, and we have two reasons for not doing so. First, in the case of scarce resources, a social planner may be interested in equality in *consumption* (e.g., equality in water access), not just equality in utility derived. Second, it turns out mathematically that this is the welfare function maximized by convex pricing WE in our model; the version where $\Phi(\rho, \mathbf{x})$ considers u_i may be not be maximized by the resulting WE. This may yield valuable qualitative insights about convex pricing; for example, does convex pricing lead to equality with respect to consumption but not necessarily with respect to underlying utility?

CES Welfare in Healthcare. These welfare functions have also seen substantial use in healthcare under the name of *isoelastic welfare functions*. This began with [40], largely motivated by concerns about purely utilitarian approaches to healthcare (i.e., allocating resources to maximize total health in a community, without concern for equality). Since these decisions can affect who lives and who dies, significant effort has been invested into understanding the equality/efficiency tradeoff, with this class of welfare functions serving as a theoretical tool [11,29,40]; see Sect. 3 for additional discussion. Despite the ongoing interest in this tradeoff, the healthcare literature has not (to our knowledge) considered convex pricing as a mechanism for balancing equality and efficiency.

More broadly, our work can be thought of as weaving together the previously disjoint threads of CES welfare and convex pricing to provide theoretical support for the oft-cited but rarely quantified claim that IBTs promote equality.

---

[3] To our knowledge, only three other computational economics papers have studied CES welfare in any context: [2,18,30].

2 Results

2.1 Main Result: Convex Pricing Implements CES Welfare Maximization in Walrasian Equilibrium

Our main result is that for convex pricing of the form $p(x_i) = (\sum_j q_j x_{ij})^{1/\rho}$ for any $\rho \in (0,1]^4$, a Walrasian equilibrium is guaranteed to exist, and every WE maximizes CES welfare with respect to ρ. This holds for a wide range of agent valuations.

Theorem 2.1. *Assume each valuation is homogeneous of degree r,[5] differentiable, and concave, and fix $\rho \in (0,1]$. Then an allocation $\mathbf{x} = (x_1, \ldots, x_n)$ maximizes CES welfare if and only if there exist constants $q_1, \ldots, q_m \in \mathbb{R}_{\geq 0}$ such that for the pricing rule*

$$p(x_i) = \Big(\sum_j q_j x_{ij} \Big)^{1/\rho},$$

$\mathbf{x}$ *and p form a WE.*

Note that the ρ in $p(x_i)$ is the same ρ for which CES welfare is maximized.

We call the reader's attention to two important aspects of this result. Perhaps most importantly, our result is not simply a reformulation of the First Welfare Theorem: although maximizing CES welfare for valuations $v_1, \ldots, v_n$ is equivalent to maximizing utilitarian welfare for valuations $v_1^\rho, \ldots, v_n^\rho$, the First Welfare Theorem does not say anything about the agent demands in response to this convex pricing rule. The First Welfare Theorem also does not help with identifying the exact conditions under which Theorem 2.1 holds, e.g., homogeneity of valuations.[6]

Secondly, the class of homogeneous, differentiable, and concave valuations is quite large: it generalizes most of the commonly studied valuations, e.g., linear, Cobb-Douglas, and CES (note that here we are referring to CES agent valuations, not CES welfare functions). Although Leontief valuations are not differentiable, we handle them as a special case and show that the same result holds.

The following additional properties are of note:

1. For this class of utilities, Theorem 2.1 generalizes the First Welfare Theorem: when $\rho = 1$, $p(x_i)$ yields linear pricing and CES welfare yields utilitarian welfare.

---

[4] The case of $\rho < 0$ is slightly unintuitive, as it can result in agents who care more receiving *less* of the good. Consequently, implementation in WE is impossible (Theorem 2.6).

[5] A valuation is homogeneous of degree r if scaling any bundle by a constant c scales the resulting value by c^r.

[6] In fact, not only is homogeneity necessary, but homogeneity of the same degree is necessary: if we allow the degree of homogeneity to differ across agents, the result no longer holds (Theorem 2.5).

2. The constants $q_1, \ldots, q_m$ will be the optimal Lagrange multipliers for a convex program maximizing CES welfare.
3. Our pricing rule is strictly convex for $\rho < 1$, with the curvature growing as ρ goes to 0. The smaller ρ gets, the easier it is to buy a small amount, but the harder it is to buy a large amount. Intuitively, this should prevent any single individual from dominating the market and lead to a more equitable outcome. Furthermore, the marginal price at $x_i = \mathbf{0}$ is zero, which ensures that everyone ends up with a nonempty bundle (in contrast to linear pricing: see Fig. 1). Theorem 2.1 provides a tight relationship between the curvature of the pricing rule and the exact equality/efficiency tradeoff.

Due to space constraints, all proofs are deferred to the full version of the paper [19].

Towards an Implementation. We also prove several supporting results: in particular, regarding implementation. The WE from Theorem 2.1 can always be computed by asking each agent for her entire utility function, and then solving a convex program for maximizing CES welfare maximization to obtain the optimal Lagrange multipliers $q_1, \ldots, q_m$. However, this is not very practical: people are generally not able to articulate a full cardinal utility function, and even if they are, doing so could require transmitting an enormous amount of information. Our first supporting result is an iterative algorithm for computing the WE, where in each step, each agent only needs to report the gradient of her valuation at the current point. Our algorithm is based on the ellipsoid method, and inherits its polynomial-time convergence properties. We recognize that even valuation gradient queries may be difficult for agents to answer, and we leave the possibility of an improved implementation – in particular, a *tâtonnement*[7] – as an open question.

2.2 Truthfulness

Our second supporting result considers a different approach to implementation: *truthful* mechanisms. Walrasian equilibria are generally not truthful: agents can lie about their preferences to affect the equilibrium prices for their personal gain.[8] For $\rho = 1$, the Vickrey-Clarke-Groves (VCG) mechanism is known to truthfully maximize utilitarian welfare [28]. For the case of a single good and any $\rho \in (0,1)$, we give a mechanism which truthfully maximizes CES welfare:

Theorem 2.2. *Assume $m = 1$, and that each v_i is homogenous of degree r (with r publicly known), concave, and differentiable. Then for all $\rho \in (0,1)$, there is a truthful mechanism which outputs an allocation $\mathbf{x}$ maximizing $\Phi(\rho, \mathbf{x})$.*

---

[7] A tâtonnement is an iterative algorithm which only asks *demand queries*, i.e., what would each agent purchase given the current prices. Demand queries may be easier to answer than the valuation gradient queries in our algorithm.

[8] Another interpretation is that WE assumes agents are *price-taking* (i.e., treat the prices are given and do not lie about their preferences to affect the equilibrium prices) and breaks down when agents are *price-anticipating*.

We also show that our mechanism is the unique truthful mechanism up to an additive constant in the payment rule The proof of Theorem 2.3 is quite involved, and requires techniques from real analysis such as Kirszbraun's Theorem for Lipschitz extensions and the Fundamental Theorem of Lebesgue Calculus.

Theorem 2.3. *Assume $m = 1$, and that each v_i is homogenous of degree r (with r publicly known), concave, and differentiable. Fix $\rho \in (0,1)$, and let Γ be a truthful mechanism which outputs an allocation $\mathbf{x} \in \Psi(\rho)$. Then the allocation rule is the same as the mechanism for Theorem 2.2, and the payment rule $p_i(\mathbf{b})$ is the same up to an additive constant.*

2.3   Negative Results

We prove the following negative results. Most importantly, we show that for any $\rho \neq 1$, linear-pricing WE can have arbitrarily poor CES welfare; were this not the case, perhaps it would suffice to simply use linear pricing and accept an approximation of CES welfare.

Theorem 2.4. *Let $m = 1$, $\rho \in (0,1]$, $v_1(x) = (1 + \varepsilon)x$ for some $\varepsilon > 0$, and $v_i(x) = x$ for all $i \neq 1$. Suppose $(\mathbf{x}, p)$ is a WE where p is linear. Then*

$$\frac{\Phi(\rho, \mathbf{x})}{\max_{\mathbf{y}} \Phi(\rho, \mathbf{y})} \leq \frac{1 + \varepsilon}{n^{\frac{1}{\rho} - 1}}$$

Next, note that Theorem 2.1 requires each agent's valuation to be homogeneous with the same degree r. We show that when agents' valuations have different homogeneity degrees, there exist instances where no pricing rule can implement CES welfare maximization in WE, and thus our assumption is necessary.

Theorem 2.5. *Let $n = 2$ and $m = 1$, and for $x \in \mathbb{R}_{\geq 0}$, let $v_1(x) = x$ and $v_2(x) = \sqrt{2x}$. Then for all $\rho \in (0,1)$, there exists no allocation $\mathbf{x} \in \Psi(\rho)$ and pricing rule $p : \mathbb{R}_{\geq 0} \to \mathbb{R}_{\geq 0}$ such that $(\mathbf{x}, p)$ is a WE.*

We also show that CES welfare maximization cannot be implemented in WE for $\rho < 0$:

Theorem 2.6. *Consider the instance with $n = 2$, $m = 1$, $v_1(x) = x$ and $v_2(x) = 2x$. Then for every $\rho < 0$, there is no pricing rule p and allocation $\mathbf{x} \in \Psi(\rho)$ such that $(\mathbf{x}, p)$ is a WE.*

There is an additional crucial issue which any practical implementation of Theorem 2.1 would need to address: *Sybil attacks*. A Sybil attack is when a selfish agent attempts to gain an advantage in a system by creating fake identities [13]. Since the pricing rule from Theorem 2.1 is strictly convex for $\rho < 1$, an agent can decrease her payment by masquerading as multiple individuals and splitting her purchase across those identities.[9] We propose a model for analyzing Sybil attacks

---

[9] In contrast, for $\rho = 1$, there is nothing to be gained by creating fake identities.

in markets, and show that if these attacks are possible, there exist instances where no pricing rule can implement CES welfare maximization in WE:[10]

Theorem 2.7. *Assume each v_i is concave, differentiable, and homogeneous of degree 1. Let $\rho \in (0,1]$, and define p as in Theorem 2.1. Then for any allocation $\mathbf{x}$ and multiplicities $\boldsymbol{\eta}$ such that $(\mathbf{x}, p, \boldsymbol{\eta})$ is a SWE, we have*

$$v_i(x_i) \leq \frac{\kappa}{1 - \rho}$$

3   Related Work

The study of markets has a long history in economics [1,8,16,38,41]. Recently, this topic has received substantial attention in the computer science community as well (see [39] for an algorithmic introduction). We first provide some important background on different market models and the First and Second Welfare Theorems, and then move on to more recent related work.

Quasilinear Markets and Fisher Markets. There are two primary market models for divisible goods. This paper considers the quasilinear utility model, where each agent can spend as much as she wants, and the amount spent is incorporated into her utility function. The other predominant model is the *Fisher market* model [8,16], where each agent has a fixed budget constraint, and the amount spent does not affect her resulting utility (as a result, each agent always spends exactly her budget). Although these two models share many of the same conceptual messages, some of the technical results vary. See the full version of the paper [19] for the precise technical relationship between the two models with respect to WE and CES welfare maximization.

Since agents in Fisher markets always spend exactly their budgets, there is no way to elicit the absolute scale of agent valuations. Nash welfare maximization is invariant to this type of scaling, but no other CES welfare function is [26]. For this reason, the Fisher market model is not well suited to reason about other welfare functions. In contrast, the quasilinear model *does* allow agents to express the absolute scale of their valuation: specifically, by choosing how much to spend. That is one reason that we focus on the quasilinear model for this paper. The other is that convex pricing is most easily applied to a small submarket of the broader economy (e.g., water pricing), and quasilinear utility captures the fact that agents may wish to spend money on other goods outside of this submarket. In contrast, Arrow and Debreu's model (see below) can arguably capture the entire economy, so there is nothing outside of the market to spend money on.

---

[10] There are combinations of parameters, however, where our pricing rule is naturally robust to Sybil attacks: in particular, when $v_i(\mathbf{x})(1 - \rho) \leq \kappa$ (where $v_i(\mathbf{x})$ is agent i's value for the maximum CES welfare allocation and κ is the identity creation cost). This suggests a natural way for an equality-focused social planner to choose a specific value for ρ: estimate the identity creation cost and scale of valuations in the system of interest, and pick ρ to be as small as possible without incentivizing Sybil attacks.

The First and Second Welfare Theorems. Conceptually, the First Welfare Theorem establishes an efficiency property that any WE must satisfy, and the Second Welfare Theorem deals with implementing a wide range of allocations as WE. The two welfare theorems originate in the context of *Arrow-Debreu* markets [1], which generalize Fisher markets to allow for (1) agents to enter the market with goods (as opposed to just money)[11] and (2) production of goods. The statements of the First and Second Welfare Theorems in that model are, respectively, "Any (linear pricing) WE is Pareto optimal" and "Any Pareto optimal allocation can be a (linear pricing) WE with *transfers*, i.e., under a suitable redistribution of initial wealth".

In the Fisher market and quasilinear utility models, the First Welfare Theorem can be strengthened to "Any (linear pricing) WE maximizes budget-weighted Nash welfare" [14,15,39] and "Any (linear pricing) WE maximizes utilitarian welfare", respectively. The version of the Second Welfare Theorem stated above is appropriate for Fisher markets, since agents' budgets constitute the "initial wealth". However, for quasilinear utilities, there is no notion of initial wealth (alternatively, initial wealth is an additive constant in agents' utilities which does not affect their behavior). Thus for quasilinear utilities, allowing transfers actually does not affect the set of WE. This may seem counterintuitive, since the Second Welfare Theorem (which still holds in this setting) states that any Pareto optimum can be a WE. However, Pareto optimality here is referring to agents' overall quasilinear utilities, *not* the agents' valuations. It can be shown that the only allocations which are Pareto optimal with respect to the quasilinear utilities are allocations maximizing utilitarian welfare, which are already covered by the First Welfare Theorem (without transfers).

Thus on a technical level, the Second Welfare Theorem is not helpful in the world of quasilinear utilities. However, even when the Second Welfare Theorem is mathematically relevant, a centrally mandated redistribution of wealth is often out of the question in practice.

The Equality/Efficiency Tradeoff in Healthcare. In Sect. 1.1, we discussed how CES welfare has been studied from a theoretical perspective in healthcare [11,29,40]. There have also been several empirical studies aiming to understand the general population's view of the equality/efficiency tradeoff, with results generally indicating a disapproval of purely utilitarian approaches to healthcare [12,43]. For example, a survey of 449 Swedish politicians found widespread rejection of purely utilitarian decision-making in healthcare, and under some conditions, the respondents were willing to sacrifice up to 15 of 100 preventable deaths in order to ensure equality across subgroups [23].

CES Welfare and α-Fairness in Networking. CES welfare functions have also enjoyed considerable attention from the field of networking, under the name of α-*fairness* (the parameter α corresponds to $1 - \rho$ in our definition). The α-fairness notion was proposed by [24], motivated in part as a generalization of the prominent *proportional fairness* objective (which is equivalent to Nash

---

[11] These are known as "exchange markets" or "exchange economies".

welfare) [21]. See [6] and references therein for further background on α-fairness in networking. To our knowledge, a market-based understanding was developed only for proportional fairness, starting with the seminal work of Kelly et al. [21].

Nonlinear Market Mechanisms and CES Welfare Maximization. We are aware of just two papers studying market mechanisms for CES welfare functions: [18,30]. Like our work, both of these papers explore nonlinear pricing rules, but unlike our work, only consider Leontief valuations. Furthermore, both of those papers are in the Fisher market model and only achieve CES welfare maximization under strong assumptions on the absolute scale of the agents' valuations.[12] In contrast, our main result holds for any valuations that are homogeneous of degree r, differentiable, and concave, a much larger range of valuations. (Leontief valuations are not differentiable, but we handle them as a special case in the full version of the paper and show that our result still holds [19].) It is worth noting that [18] focuses on the WE model, whereas [30] considers strategic agents and Nash equilibria. On a related note, we are not aware of any broader results regarding general nonlinear pricing, i.e., what set of allocations can be implemented if we allow $p(x_i)$ to be any nondecreasing function of x_i (but still require anonymity)? This could be an interesting direction for future work.

4 Conclusion

In this paper, we studied a simple family of convex pricing rules, motivated by the widespread use of convex pricing in the real world, especially for water. We proved that these pricing rules implement CES welfare maximization in Walrasian equilibrium, providing a formal quantitative interpretation of the frequent informal claim that convex pricing promotes equality. Furthermore, by tweaking the exponent of the pricing rule, the social planner can precisely control the tradeoff between equality and efficiency. This result also shows that convex pricing is not necessarily economically inefficient, as often claimed; it simply maximizes a different welfare function than the traditional utilitarian one. All proofs can be found in the full version of the paper [19].

Improved implementation is perhaps the most important of the future directions we propose. One concrete possibility is a *tâtonnement*: an iterative algorithm where on each step, each agent reports her demand for the current pricing rule, and the pricing rule is adjusted accordingly. Demand queries are arguably easier for agents to answer than valuation gradient queries. Some implementation questions – in particular, how to deal with Sybil attacks – would likely need to be handled on a case-by-case basis.

Aside from the implementation itself, there is the additional challenge of convincing market designers to consider using this type of convex pricing. Equality is generally thought to be desirable, but sellers may be concerned that this will

---

[12] In particular, that each agent's weight for each good is either 0 or 1. This subclass of Leontief valuations is known as "bandwidth allocation" valuations, where each good is a link in a network, and agents transmit data over fixed paths.

decrease their revenue. In future work, we hope to show that our pricing rule guarantees a good approximation of the optimal revenue for sellers.

Another possible direction would be CES welfare maximization for indivisible goods. The analogous pricing rule would be $p(S) = (\sum_{j \in S} q_j)^{1/\rho}$, where S is a set of indivisible goods. It seems like very different theoretical techniques would be needed in this setting (along with perhaps a gross substitutes assumption), but we suspect that the same intuition of convex pricing improving equality would hold.

References

1. Arrow, K.J., Debreu, G.: Existence of an equilibrium for a competitive economy. Econ. J. Econ. Soc. **22**(3), 265–290 (1954)
2. Arunachaleswaran, E.R., Barman, S., Kumar, R., Rathi, N.: Fair and efficient cake division with connected pieces. In: Caragiannis, I., Mirrokni, V., Nikolova, E. (eds.) WINE 2019. LNCS, vol. 11920, pp. 57–70. Springer, Cham (2019). https://doi.org/10.1007/978-3-030-35389-6_5
3. Atkinson, A.B.: On the measurement of inequality. J. Econ. Theor. **2**(3), 244–263 (1970)
4. Becker, N.: Water pricing in Israel: various waters, various neighbors. In: Dinar, A., Pochat, V., Albiac-Murillo, J. (eds.) Water Pricing Experiences and Innovations. GIWP, vol. 9, pp. 181–199. Springer, Cham (2015). https://doi.org/10.1007/978-3-319-16465-6_10
5. Bergson, A.: A reformulation of certain aspects of welfare economics. Quart. J. Econ. **52**(2), 310–334 (1938)
6. Bertsimas, D., Farias, V.F., Trichakis, N.: On the efficiency-fairness trade-off. Manage. Sci. **58**(12), 2234–2250 (2012)
7. Boland, J.J., Whittington, D.: Water tariff design in developing countries: disadvantages of increasing block tariffs (IBTs) and advantages of uniform price with rebate (UPR) Designs. World Bank Water and Sanitation Program, Washington, DC, p. 37 (2000)
8. Brainard, W.C., Scarf, H.E.: How to compute equilibrium prices in 1891. Am. J. Econ. Sociol. **64**(1), 57–83 (2005)
9. Burger, C., Jansen, A.: Increasing block tariff structures as a water subsidy mechanism in South Africa: an exploratory analysis. Dev. South. Africa **31**(4), 553–562 (2014)
10. Cowell, F.: Measuring Inequality. Oxford University Press, Oxford (2011)
11. Dolan, P.: The measurement of individual utility and social welfare. J. Health Econ. **17**(1), 39–52 (1998)
12. Dolan, P., Cookson, R.: A qualitative study of the extent to which health gain matters when choosing between groups of patients. Health Policy **51**(1), 19–30 (2000)
13. Douceur, J.: The sybil attack. In: Proceedings of the International Workshop on Peer-to-Peer Systems (2002)
14. Eisenberg, E.: Aggregation of utility functions. Manage. Sci. **7**(4), 337–350 (1961)
15. Eisenberg, E., Gale, D.: Consensus of subjective probabilities: the pari-mutuel method. Ann. Math. Stat. **30**(1), 165–168 (1959)
16. Fisher, I.: Mathematical Investigations in the Theory of Value and Prices. Connecticut Academy of Arts and Sciences (1892)

17. García-Rubio, M.A., Ruiz-Villaverde, A., González-Gómez, F.: Urban water tariffs in Spain: what needs to be done? Water **7**(4), 1456–1479 (2015)
18. Goel, A., Hulett, R., Plaut, B.: Markets beyond nash welfare for Leontief utilities. In: Proceedings of the 15th Conference on Web and Internet Economics (WINE 2019) (2019)
19. Goel, A., Plaut, B.: Counteracting inequality in markets via convex pricing. arXiv preprint arXiv:2009.09351 (2020)
20. Kaneko, M., Nakamura, K.: The nash social welfare function. Econometrica **47**(2), 423–435 (1979)
21. Kelly, F.P., Maulloo, A.K., Tan, D.K.: Rate control for communication networks: shadow prices, proportional fairness and stability. J. Oper. Res. Soc. **49**(3), 237–252 (1998)
22. Klassert, C., Sigel, K., Klauer, B., Gawel, E.: increasing block tariffs in an arid developing Country: a discrete/continuous choice model of residential water demand in Jordan. Water **10**(3), 248 (2018)
23. Lindholm, L., Rosén, M., Emmelin, M.: How many lives is equity worth? a proposal for equity adjusted years of life saved. J. Epidemiol. Commun. Health **52**(12), 808–811 (1998)
24. Mo, J., Walrand, J.: Fair end-to-end window-based congestion control. IEEE/ACM Trans. Netw. **8**(5), 556–567 (2000)
25. Monteiro, H., Roseta-Palma, C.: Pricing for scarcity? an efficiency analysis of increasing block tariffs. Water Resour. Res. **47**(6) (2011)
26. Moulin, H.: Fair Division and Collective Welfare, Chap. 3. MIT Press, Cambridge (2003)
27. Nash, J.: The Bargaining problem. Econometrica **18**(2), 155–162 (1950)
28. Nisan, N.: Introduction to mechanism design (for computer scientists). In: Nisan, N., Roughgarden, T., Tardos, E., Vazirani, V.V. (eds.) Algorithmic Game Theory, Chap. 9, pp. 209–242. Cambridge University Press (2007)
29. Ortún, V.: Contradictions and trade-offs between efficiency and equity. Institut Borja de Bioetica, Allocation of Resources in Health Care. Barcelona: Fundación MAPFRE Medicina, pp. 113–124 (1996)
30. Plaut, B.: Optimal nash equilibria for bandwidth allocation. CoRR abs/1904.03322 (2019)
31. Rawls, J.: A Theory of Justice. Harvard University Press, Cambridge (2009)
32. Renwick, M.E., Green, R.D.: Do residential water demand side management policies measure up? An analysis of eight California water agencies. J. Env. Econ. Manage. **40**(1), 37–55 (2000)
33. Samuelson, P.A.: Foundations of Economic Analysis. Harvard University Press, Cambridge (1947)
34. Sen, A.: Welfare inequalities and Rawlsian Axiomatics. Theor. Decis. **7**(4), 243–262 (1976)
35. Sen, A.: Social choice theory: a re-examination. Econ. J. Econ. Soc. **45**(1), 53–89 (1977)
36. van der Spek, R.J.: Commodity Prices in Babylon 385–61 BC (2005). http://www.iisg.nl/hpw/babylon.php. Accessed 14 Dec 2019
37. van der Spek, R.J., Mandemakers, C.: Sense and nonsense in the statistical approach of babylonian prices. Bibl. Orient. **60**(5), 521–537 (2003)
38. Varian, H.: Equity, envy, and efficiency. J. Econ. Theor. **9**(1), 63–91 (1974)
39. Vazirani, V.V.: Combinatorial algorithms for market equilibria. In: Nisan, N., Roughgarden, T., Tardos, E., Vazirani, V.V. (eds.) Algorithmic Game Theory, Chap. 5, pp. 103–134. Cambridge University Press (2007)

40. Wagstaff, A.: Qalys and the equity-efficiency trade-off. J. Health Econ. **10**(1), 21–41 (1991)
41. Walras, L.: Elements of Pure Economics: Or, the Theory of Social Wealth. Published for the American Economic Association and the Royal Economic Society, Translated by William Jaffé (1954)
42. Whittington, D.: Possible adverse effects of increasing block water tariffs in developing Countries. Econ. Dev. Cult. Change **41**(1), 75–87 (1992)
43. Wittrup-Jensen, K.U., Pedersen, K.M.: An empirical assessment of the person trade-off: valuation of health, framing effects, and estimation of weights for fairness. Syddansk Universitet (2008)

Markets for Efficient Public Good Allocation with Social Distancing

Devansh Jalota[1], Marco Pavone[1], Qi Qi[2(✉)], and Yinyu Ye[1]

[1] Stanford University, Stanford, CA 94305, USA
{djalota,pavone,yyye}@stanford.edu
[2] The Hong Kong University of Science and Technology, Hong Kong, China
kaylaqi@ust.hk

Abstract. Public goods are often either over-consumed in the absence of regulatory mechanisms, or remain completely unused, as in the Covid-19 pandemic, where social distance constraints are enforced to limit the number of people who can share public spaces. In this work, we plug this gap through market mechanisms designed to efficiently allocate capacity constrained public goods. To design these mechanisms, we leverage the theory of Fisher markets, wherein each agent is endowed with an artificial currency budget that they can spend to avail public goods. While Fisher markets provide a strong methodological backbone to model resource allocation problems, their applicability is limited to settings involving two types of constraints - budgets of individual buyers and capacities of goods. Thus, we introduce a modified Fisher market, where each individual may have additional physical constraints, characterize its solution properties and establish the existence of a market equilibrium. Furthermore, to account for additional constraints we introduce a social convex optimization problem where we perturb the budgets of agents such that the KKT conditions of the perturbed social problem establishes equilibrium prices. Finally, to compute the budget perturbations we present a fixed point scheme and illustrate convergence guarantees through numerical experiments. Thus, our mechanism, both theoretically and computationally, overcomes a fundamental limitation of classical Fisher markets, which only consider capacity and budget constraints.

1 Introduction

A public good is a product that an individual can consume without reducing its availability to others and of which no one is deprived. In reality, almost no good can satisfy the precise definitions of both non-rivalry and non-excludability [6], as these goods often suffer from over consumption [22], which leads to a decreased utility for consumers. This phenomena becomes more so during the Covid-19

This work is partly supported by the Research Grant Council of Hong Kong (GRF Project no. 16215717 and 16243516), National Science Foundation (NSF) under CAREER Award CMMI1454737 and Toyota Research Institute (TRI). This article solely reflects the opinions of its authors and not NSF, TRI, or any other entity.

X. Chen et al. (Eds.): WINE 2020, LNCS 12495, pp. 102–116, 2020.
https://doi.org/10.1007/978-3-030-64946-3_8

pandemic, where social distance constraints are enforced so that only a limited number of people can share public spaces [16]. A consequence of such constraints is that it results in completely closing parks or beaches [1], which leads to goods becoming non-public. These contrasting outcomes of overused and underused public resources in society, illustrated in Fig. 1, highlight the need for regulatory mechanisms that impose restrictions on the use of shared resources.

Fig. 1. The current scenario involving either an overcrowded beach (left) or a completely unused beach (right) generating no value to society.

In this paper, we attempt to design market mechanisms to efficiently allocate shared resources and thereby achieve an intermediate between these opposing and undesirable outcomes. To achieve such a balance, we study capacity constrained public resources and distribute consumer load over public good alternatives. As demand often outweighs supply of public goods, we need to make decisions on who gets preference to use capacity constrained public spaces. These allocation decisions are facilitated through a pricing mechanism that ensures the formation of a *market equilibrium*, i.e., each agent purchases their most preferred bundle of goods affordable under the set prices. The pricing decisions must be made with fairness considerations, as public goods are by design available to all individuals and of which no person is deprived. We ensure fairness of our mechanism through two methods. First, we use artificial currencies to ensure that allocations are not biased towards those with higher incomes. Second, when setting prices we simultaneously take into account individual consumer preferences, i.e., each agent's utility, while ensuring that resulting allocations are beneficial for society.

To study our resource allocation problem under capacity constraints while considering both individual preferences and societal benefit, we resort to the canonical model of Fisher markets. In a Fisher market, consumers spend their budget of money (or artificial currency) to buy goods that maximize their utilities, while producers sell capacity constrained goods in exchange for currency. A key property of interest is the formation of an equilibrium when the *market clears*, i.e. all budgets are spent and all goods are sold. At this equilibrium, buyers get their most preferred bundle of goods, while a social objective is maximized.

We first describe each agent's individual optimization problem in Fisher markets. In this framework, the decision variable for agent i is the quantity of each good j they wish to purchase and is represented by x_{ij}. We denote the allocation vector for agent i as $\mathbf{x}_i \in \mathbb{R}^m$, when there are m goods in the market.

A key assumption of Fisher markets is that goods are divisible and so fractional allocations are possible. Thus, we interpret x_{ij} as the probability that agent i is allocated to good j. Finally, denoting w_i as the budget of agent i, $u_i(\mathbf{x}_i)$ as the utility of agent i as a concave function of their allocation and $\mathbf{p} \in \mathbb{R}_{\geq 0}^m$ as the vector of prices for the goods, individual decision making in Fisher markets can be modelled as the following optimization problem:

$$\max_{\mathbf{x}_i \in \mathbb{R}^m} \quad u_i(\mathbf{x}_i) \tag{1a}$$

$$\text{s.t.} \quad \mathbf{p}^T \mathbf{x}_i \leq w_i \tag{1b}$$

$$\mathbf{x}_i \geq \mathbf{0} \tag{1c}$$

where (1b) is a budget constraint and (1c) is a non-negativity constraint.

The vector of prices $\mathbf{p} \in \mathbb{R}_{\geq 0}^m$ that each agent observes are computed through the solution of a social optimization problem that aggregates the utilities of all agents. The choice of the social objective is such that under certain conditions on the utility function, there exists an equilibrium price vector defined as:

Definition 1. *A vector $\mathbf{p} \in \mathbb{R}_{\geq 0}^m$ is an equilibrium price vector if $\sum_{i=1}^{n} x_{ij}^*(\mathbf{p}) = \bar{s}_j, \forall j$, i.e., all the goods are sold, where each resource j has a price p_j and has a strict capacity constraint of $\bar{s}_j \geq 0$, and $\sum_{j=1}^{m} p_j x_{ij}^*(\mathbf{p}) = w_i, \forall i$, i.e., budgets of all agents are completely used. Furthermore, $x^*(\mathbf{p})_i \in \mathbb{R}^m$ is an optimal solution of the individual optimization problem (1a)-(1c) for all agents i.*

When the utilities are homogeneous functions, e.g., linear utilities, the price vector is computed as the dual variables of the capacity constraint (2b) in the following social optimization problem:

$$\max_{\mathbf{x}_i \in \mathbb{R}^m, \forall i \in [n]} \quad u(\mathbf{x}_1, ..., \mathbf{x}_n) = \sum_{i=1}^{n} w_i \log(u_i(\mathbf{x}_i)) \tag{2a}$$

$$\text{s.t.} \quad \sum_{i=1}^{n} x_{ij} = \bar{s}_j, \forall j \in [m] \tag{2b}$$

$$x_{ij} \geq 0, \forall i, j \tag{2c}$$

where there are n agents and m shared resources. We denote $[a] = \{1, 2, ..., a\}$.

Since both the individual and social problems are convex optimization problems, the equivalence of their first order KKT conditions is necessary and sufficient at the equilibrium price condition. This establishes that under the prices set through the solution of the social optimization problem each agent receives their most favourable bundle of goods [12].

These appealing properties of Fisher markets have been leveraged in applications including online advertising [20] and revenue optimization [15]; however, the consideration of only two types of constraints - budgets of buyers and capacities of goods - in Fisher markets limits its use in public good allocation settings. This is because the availability of public good substitutes imposes additional physical constraints that are necessary to consider for the allocation to be meaningful. To model the availability of public good alternatives, we pool together public goods serving similar functionality, e.g., beaches or parks, into their own resource *types*. These additional constraints (described in detail in Sect. 2.1) raise the question of whether we can still find equilibrium prices, which leads to the main focus of this paper which is to:

Design a market based mechanism that achieves the same properties as Fisher markets while also supporting additional physical constraints.

1.1 Our Contributions

In our pursuit of such a mechanism, we start by defining each agent's individual optimization problem (**IOP**) with the addition of physical constraints. The properties of the **IOP** are fundamentally different from traditional Fisher markets with linear utilities, as there are no guarantees on the existence and uniqueness of an equilibrium. However, we derive a technical condition to overcome the question of existence and provide a characterization of **IOP**s optimal solution.

Having established the existence of a market equilibrium, we then turn to deriving market clearing prices with physical constraints. We first show that market clearing conditions fail to hold when we add physical constraints to the social optimization problem (2a)–(2c) and derive prices using this constraint augmented problem. This negative result is overcome through a new social optimization problem (**BP-SOP**) wherein we perturb the budgets of agents by constants that depend on the dual variables of the physical constraints. We then show that the *market clears* under the prices set based on the dual variables of **BP-SOP**s capacity constraints. Finally, we present a fixed point scheme to determine the perturbation constants and establish its convergence through experiments.

We note that the physical constraints we consider extend beyond public goods allocation, as such constraints arise in retail, e-commerce and the AdWords market, as buyers have restrictions on the amount of goods they can purchase and advertisers on the number of people in each demographic class they can target. In addition, such constraints help in achieving fairness by restricting the purchase of certain goods by individual agents to enable wider access.

1.2 Related Work

Setting market clearing prices has been a prominent topic of research at the intersection of economic and optimization theory. While Walras [21] was the first to question whether goods could be priced in a n buyer m good market such that each person receives a bundle of goods to maximize their utilities, it was Arrow and Debreu who established the existence of such a market equilibrium under mild conditions on the utility function of buyers [2]. However, it was not until Fisher that there was an algorithm to compute equilibrium prices [7]. Later Eisenberg and Gale formulated Fisher's original problem with linear utilities as a convex optimization problem that could be solved in polynomial time [13,14].

While Fisher markets have since been studied extensively in the computer science and algorithmic game theory communities, there has been recent interest in considering additional constraints in the Fisher market framework. For instance, Bei et al. [3] impose limits on sellers' earnings and question the assumption that utilities of buyers strictly increase in the amount of good allocated. A different generalization is considered by Vazirani [20], Devanur [10] and Birnbaum et al. [4], wherein utilities of buyers depend on prices of goods through spending constraints. Yet another generalization has been considered by Devanur et al. [11] in which goods can be left unsold as sellers declare an upper bound on their earnings and budgets can be left unused as buyers declare an upper bound on their utilities. Along similar lines Chen et al. [9] study equilibrium properties when agents keep unused budget for future use. These generalizations of Fisher markets are primarily associated with spending constraints of buyers and earning constraints of sellers; however, to the best of our knowledge there has been no generalization of Fisher markets to the case of additional physical constraints.

While such physical constraints have not been studied in the Fisher market literature, there have been other market equilibrium characterizations that take into account such constraints. One notable such work is that on the Combinatorial Assignment problem by Budish [8] wherein a market mechanism is used to assign students to courses while respecting student's schedule constraints. In Budish's framework, courses have capacity constraints and students are endowed with budgets and must submit their preferences to a centralized mechanism that provides approximately efficient allocations. In contrast to Budish's approach, we study the public goods allocation problem from the standpoint of setting equilibrium prices through the maximization of a societal objective.

Finally, since we are allocating public goods we must take fairness considerations into account. A popular method to achieve an equal playing ground for all agents is the use of artificial currencies. For instance, Gorokh et al. established how artificial currencies can be equally distributed to agents to achieve fairness [17]. We follow a similar idea in our work by endowing agents with (artificial) budgets that they can spend, to help overcome concerns of priced mechanisms, e.g., congestion pricing, in regulating the use of public resources.

The rest of this paper is organized as follows. We first present the individual optimization problem **IOP** and study properties of the corresponding market equilibrium in Sect. 2. Then, in Sect. 3, we provide a motivation for why modifying Fisher markets is necessary to guarantee market clearing properties with the addition of physical constraints and propose a new budget perturbed social optimization problem that guarantees a market equilibrium. As the budget perturbed problem involves setting the perturbation constants as the dual variables of the added constraints, we present a fixed point procedure to compute these constants in Sect. 4. Finally, we conclude the paper in Sect. 5.

All details omitted due to space constraints can be found in [18].

2   Properties of the Individual Optimization Problem

In this section, we study the individual optimization problem with physical constraints that are not considered in Fisher markets. We start by defining a new individual optimization problem **IOP** in Sect.,2.1 and study the existence and non-uniqueness of an equilibrium in Sects. 2.2–2.4. Finally, we close this section through a characterization of the optimal solution of **IOP** in Sect. 2.5.

2.1   Modelling Framework for Individual Optimization Problem

As in Fisher markets, we model agents as utility maximizers and in this work, each agent's utility function is assumed to be linear in the allocations, which is a common utility function used in the Fisher market literature [5,13]. We model the preference of an agent i for one unit of good j through the utility u_{ij}. Furthermore, we extend the Fisher market framework through the consideration of each agent's physical constraints. To model this physical constraint we consider each public good j as belonging to at most one resource *type*, with the set of all resource *types* denoted as T. Goods not belonging to any resource *type* do not have any physical constraints. We further let $T_i \subseteq T$ denote the resource *types* for which agent i has physical constraints and assume that agent i would like to obtain at most $b_{it} \geq 0$ unit of goods in each resource *type* t, i.e., $\sum_{j \in t} x_{ij} \leq b_{it}$, where we take the sum over all goods j belonging to *type* t. These physical constraints can be specified by a 0–1 matrix $A^{(i)} \in \mathbb{R}^{l_i \times m}$, where $l_i = |T_i|$. Furthermore, the row corresponding to resource *type* $t \in T_i$ is represented as a row vector $A_t^{(i)}$. Using our notation for budgets and prices, we have the following individual optimization problem (**IOP**):

$$\max_{\mathbf{x}_i \in \mathbb{R}^m} u_i(\mathbf{x}_i) = \sum_{j=1}^{m} u_{ij} x_{ij} \tag{3a}$$

$$\text{s.t.} \mathbf{p}^T \mathbf{x}_i \leq w_i \tag{3b}$$

$$A_t^{(i)} \mathbf{x}_i \leq b_{it}, \forall t \in T_i \tag{3c}$$

$$\mathbf{x}_i \geq \mathbf{0} \tag{3d}$$

with budget (3b), physical (3c) and non-negativity constraints (3d). We further note that $A_t^{(i)} \mathbf{x}_i \leq b_{it}$ is identical to $\sum_{j \in t} x_{ij} \leq b_{it}$, as remarked above.

2.2   Market Equilibrium May Not Exist

In the traditional Fisher market framework with linear utilities, there exists a unique market equilibrium under mild assumptions [19]. However, with additional physical constraints an equilibrium price is not guaranteed to exist.

Proposition 1. *There exists a market wherein each good $j \in [m]$ has a potential buyer $i \in [n]$, i.e., $u_{ij} > 0$, but no equilibrium for **IOP** exists.*

2.3   Condition to Guarantee Existence of Market Equilibrium

While Proposition 1 indicates that a market equilibrium may not exist for the **IOP**, we now show that under a mild condition it is guaranteed to exist.

Theorem 1. *There exists a market equilibrium if for any agent i, there exists a good j, such that j does not belong to any type, i.e., it is not associated with any physical constraints, and i has positive utility for all goods, i.e., $u_{ij} > 0$, $\forall j$.*

Proof (Sketch). We normalize the capacities of each good and the total budget of all agents to 1, and consider an excess demand function $f_j(\mathbf{p}) = \sum_{i=1}^{n} x_{ij}(\mathbf{p}) - 1$ for $\mathbf{p} \in \Delta_m$, where Δ_m is a standard simplex. Next, we define a coloring function $c : \mathbf{p} \mapsto \{1, ..., m\}$, such that $c(\mathbf{p}) = j$ if $f_j(\mathbf{p}) \le 0$ and $p_j \ne 0$. Such a coloring function on the standard simplex satisfies Sperner's lemma, which implies that we can find a $\mathbf{p}^*$, such that $f_j(\mathbf{p}^*) \le 0$, $\forall j$, showing $\forall j$ that $\sum_{i=1}^{n} x_{ij}(\mathbf{p}^*) \le 1$.
    To prove that the above inequality is an equality, we suppose that $\exists j$, such that $\sum_{i=1}^{n} x_{ij}(\mathbf{p}^*) < 1$. Then we consider two cases: i) $p_j > 0$ and ii) $p_j = 0$. For both cases we find contradictions and prove the strict inequality is impossible under the condition that there exists a good j without any physical constraints. This establishes our claim that $\mathbf{p}^*$ is the equilibrium price vector.

The condition to guarantee existence of a market equilibrium arises as there may be instances when agents cannot spend all of their budget. Thus, we must ensure that there is a good not restrained by physical constraints so that agents can purchase more units of it to spend their budget. We also note the technical assumption is not very demanding. This is because we can allow agents to keep unused budget for future use, in which case we can treat budget as a good, which has been considered and analyzed in [9].

2.4   Market Equilibrium May Not Be Unique

We show that even if the market equilibrium exists, it may not be unique. This further establishes that the problem of determining a market equilibrium with physical constraints is fundamentally different from traditional Fisher markets.

Proposition 2. *The market equilibrium for **IOP** may not be unique.*

2.5   Characterizing Optimal Solution of IOP

In this section, we characterize the optimal solution of the **IOP**. In traditional linear Fisher markets, each agent purchases goods j^* corresponding to the highest *bang-per-buck* ratio, i.e., $j^* = \arg\max_j \left\{ \frac{u_{ij}}{p_j} \right\}$. However, with physical constraints, when a buyer observes a price $\mathbf{p}$, which goods will they purchase in each resource *type* and how many different goods will they purchase in each *type*?
    To answer these questions, we study the influence of physical constraints through a feasible solution set for buyer i and resource *type* $t \in T_i$ as follows:

Definition 2. *(Feasible Set). Given a price vector* $\mathbf{p} \in \mathbb{R}^m_{\geq 0}$, *a feasible solution set for buyer* i *and resource type* t *when* $b_{it} > 0$ *is given by:*

$$S_t = \left\{ (u_t, w_t) | \exists \{x_{ij}\}_{j \in t}, \sum_{j \in t} x_{ij} \leq 1, x_{ij} \geq 0, \forall j \in t, u_t = \sum_{j \in t} u_{ij} x_{ij}, w_t = \sum_{j \in t} x_{ij} p_j \right\}$$

Definition 2 specifies agent i's utility and budget when consuming *type* t. When $b_{it} = 0$, S_t is $\{(0,0)\}$, i.e., no good is purchased in type t by agent i. However, when $b_{it} > 0$, each agent's physical constraints can be normalized to $b_{it} = 1$, as in Definition 2. Next, we observe that the solution set S_t can be viewed as lying in the convex hull of the points defined by (u_{ij}, p_{ij}), $j \in t$ and the origin in the price-utility plane, as shown by the enclosed region in Fig. 2. The lower frontier of this convex hull, as shown in bold, from the origin to $(u_{ij_{\max}}, p_{j_{\max}})$, where $j_{\max} = \arg\max_{j \in t} \{u_{ij}\}$, is piece-wise linear and is characterised by slopes $\theta^t = (\theta^t_1, \theta^t_2, ..., \theta^t_{k_t})$, where $k_t = |j : j \in t|$. As shown on the right in Fig. 2, given a fixed budget w_t for *type* t, the maximal utility that can be obtained from *type* t must be the intersection of the line $p = w_t$ and the lower frontier of the convex hull when $w_t \leq p_{j_{\max}}$. Otherwise the maximal utility is $u_{ij_{\max}}$. Therefore, an optimal solution of **IOP** must lie on the lower frontier, with endpoints of the line segments corresponding to goods and line segments corresponding to *virtual products*, defined as:

Definition 3. *(Virtual Product). A virtual product is characterized by its two endpoints* $A = (u_{ij_1}, p_{j_1})$ *and* $B = (u_{ij_2}, p_{j_2})$ *with a slope* $\theta_{j_1 j_2} = \frac{p_{j_2} - p_{j_1}}{u_{ij_2} - u_{ij_1}}$. *Then its bang-per-buck* $= \frac{1}{\theta_{j_1 j_2}} = \frac{u_{ij_2} - u_{ij_1}}{p_{j_2} - p_{j_1}}$.

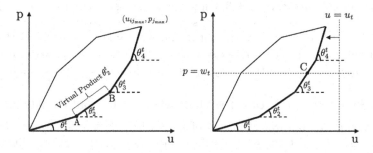

Fig. 2. The enclosed region represents the convex hull corresponding to the solution set S_t. The vertices on the lower frontier (in bold) correspond to the goods and the segments correspond to *virtual products*. The figure on the right shows that any optimal solution must lie on the lower frontier of the convex hull, as indicated by the point C.

We now show that with physical constraints agents purchase goods in the descending order of the *virtual products' bang-per-buck* ratios.

Theorem 2. *Given a price vector* $\mathbf{p} \in \mathbb{R}^m_{\geq 0}$, *agent* i *can obtain an optimal solution* $\mathbf{x}^*_i \in \mathbb{R}^m$ *of **IOP** by mixing all virtual products from different types and* *spending their budget in the descending order of virtual products' bang-per-buck. Furthermore, each agent i can purchase at most one unit of each virtual product.*

Note that when two *virtual products* have the same slope ties can be broken arbitrarily. Further, an immediate corollary follows, which answers the question of how many different goods an agent will purchase in each *type*.

Corollary 1. *For any agent i, there exists an optimal solution* $\mathbf{x}_i^* \in \mathbb{R}^m$, *such that i purchases two different goods in at most one resource type. For all other resource types, agent i buys at most one good.*

We note that $\mathbf{x}_i^*$ is the optimal solution for **IOP** given any price vector $\mathbf{p}$ and may not be unique. Corollary 1 states there exists such an optimal solution but this does not imply all solutions must satisfy these conditions. Furthermore, these results can easily be extended to the case when there is a product without physical constraints. We now turn to the problem of deriving equilibrium prices.

3   Generalizing the Fisher Social Optimization Problem to Accommodate Physical Constraints

A desirable property of Fisher markets is that the equilibrium outcome maximizes a social objective while individuals receive their most favoured bundle of goods given the prices. We now study whether we can still achieve this property with physical constraints (3c). We start by showing that with these constraints and no further modifications to Fisher markets, an equilibrium fails to hold. To do this we define a social optimization problem with additional constraints in Sect. 3.1 and compare its KKT conditions to that of **IOP** in Sect. 3.2.

We then address this negative result by defining a perturbed social optimization problem (**BP-SOP**) in Sect. 3.3 in which we adjust budgets of agents. Then, in Sect. 3.4, we show how to choose these perturbations to guarantee the equivalence of its KKT conditions with that of the **IOP** when prices are set through the dual variables of **BP-SOP**s capacity constraints. Finally, we provide an economic interpretation of the budget perturbed formulation in Sect. 3.5.

3.1   A Social Optimization Problem with Additional Constraints

We first define the natural extension of the Fisher market social optimization problem (2a)–(2c) with physical constraints (3c), giving the problem **SOP1**:

$$\max_{\mathbf{x}_i \in \mathbb{R}^m, \forall i \in [n]} u(\mathbf{x}_1, ..., \mathbf{x}_n) = \sum_{i=1}^{n} w_i \log \left(\sum_{j=1}^{m} u_{ij} x_{ij} \right) \tag{4a}$$

$$\text{s.t.} \quad \sum_{i=1}^{n} x_{ij} = \bar{s}_j, \forall j \in [m] \tag{4b}$$

$$A_t^{(i)} \mathbf{x}_i \le b_{it}, \forall t \in T_i, \forall i \in [n] \tag{4c}$$

$$x_{ij} \ge 0, \forall i, j \tag{4d}$$

3.2   A KKT Comparison of IOP and SOP1

In classical Fisher Markets, the equilibrium price corresponds to the dual variables of the capacity constraints of the social optimization problem, and at this equilibrium, the KKT conditions of the individual and social optimization problems are equivalent [12]. We follow a similar approach with **IOP** and **SOP1** and show that market clearing conditions may fail to exist through the following result.

Theorem 3. *The price vector* $\mathbf{p} \in \mathbb{R}^m_{\geq 0}$ *corresponding to the optimal dual variables of the capacity constraint (4b) of* **SOP1** *may not be an equilibrium price, i.e., the market clearing KKT conditions of* **IOP** *and* **SOP1** *may not be equivalent. However, they are equivalent if* $b_{it} = 0$ *for all* i, t, *i.e, the feasible constraints for each individual are homogeneous.*

Proof (Sketch). We derive the first order necessary and sufficient KKT conditions of **SOP1** and show that under the optimal price vector corresponding to the dual variables of the capacity constraint, the budgets of the agents will not be completely used up. As a result, a market clearing equilibrium cannot hold.

3.3   A Budget Perturbed Social Optimization Problem

We now address this negative result through a reformulated social optimization problem in which we modify the budget of agents through a variable λ_i for each agent i. This variable is introduced because of the additional constraints not present in Fisher markets and its exact value is derived in the KKT analysis in Sect. 3.4. The Budget Perturbed Social Optimization Problem (**BP-SOP**) is:

$$\max_{\mathbf{x}_i \in \mathbb{R}^m, \forall i \in [n]} u(\mathbf{x}_1, ..., \mathbf{x}_n) = \sum_{i=1}^{n} (w_i + \lambda_i) \log \left(\sum_{j=1}^{m} u_{ij} x_{ij} \right) \tag{5a}$$

$$\text{s.t.} \qquad \sum_{i=1}^{n} x_{ij} = \bar{s}_j, \forall j \tag{5b}$$

$$A_t^{(i)} \mathbf{x}_i \leq b_{it}, \forall t \in T_i, \forall i \in [n] \tag{5c}$$

$$x_{ij} \geq 0, \forall i, j \tag{5d}$$

with capacity (5b), physical (5c) and non-negativity constraints (5d).

3.4   Deriving Perturbation Constants Using KKT Conditions

We now show that under an appropriate choice of the λ_i perturbations for all agents i, the KKT conditions of **BP-SOP** and **IOP** are equivalent when prices are set through the dual variables of the capacity constraints (5b). Observing that for any choice of $\lambda = (\lambda_1, ..., \lambda_n)$, **BP-SOP** remains a convex optimization problem, it is necessary and sufficient to verify the first order KKT conditions for

BP-SOP and **IOP**. To establish the first order KKT equivalence between the two problems, we define r_{it} as the dual variable associated with the allocation constraint (5c) associated with agent i and good *type t*. Further, we define a *fixed point* of the problem **BP-SOP** as one when $\lambda_i = \sum_{t=1}^{l_i} r_{it} b_{it}$, where $l_i = |T_i|$. The reasons for this choice of a *fixed point* is to establish the following theorem:

Theorem 4. *There is a one-to-one correspondence of the equilibrium price vector* $\mathbf{p} \in \mathbb{R}_{\geq 0}^m$ *and a fixed point solution of **BP-SOP**, i.e.,* $\lambda_i = \sum_{t=1}^{l_i} r_{it} b_{it}$, $\forall i$, *where* r_{it} *is the optimal dual multiplier of the constraint* $A_t^{(i)} \mathbf{x}_i \leq b_{it}$ *in **BP-SOP**.*

Proof (Sketch). We first derive the necessary and sufficient first order KKT conditions for the **BP-SOP** and **IOP**. The forward direction of our claim follows from considering a market equilibrium of the **IOP** and using this to show that $\lambda_i = \sum_{t=1}^{l_i} r_{it} b_{it}$, $\forall i$ is the *fixed point* of **BP-SOP**. For the converse, we can show that if we set $\lambda_i = \sum_{t=1}^{l_i} r_{it} b_{it}$, $\forall i$, then each agent completely uses up their budget, while all the goods are sold to capacity.

The above theorem states in one direction that the market clearing KKT conditions of **BP-SOP** are equivalent to that of the **IOP** if $\lambda_i = \sum_{t=1}^{l_i} r_{it} b_{it}$. Furthermore, it also states the converse that any equilibrium price in the market for **BP-SOP** must correspond to a *fixed point*, i.e., $\lambda_i = \sum_{t=1}^{l_i} r_{it} b_{it}$.

3.5   Economic Relevance of Solution of BP-SOP

We now show the economic relevance of the allocations under the appropriately chosen budget perturbations. We first observe that due to the KKT equivalence of **BP-SOP** and **IOP** at the equilibrium price and the corresponding *fixed point*, each agent obtains their most preferred bundle of goods given the prices.

We now interpret the dual variable r_{it} of the physical constraint as the price that agent i must pay to purchase one unit of good type t. Hence, the total price that a buyer must pay to purchase goods j belonging to type t is $\sum_{j \in t} p_j x_{ij} + r_{it} b_{it}$; however, the buyer only observes the price p_j for good j in the **IOP**. Thus, to reconcile the price difference the buyer observes and that in **BP-SOP**, we need to pay the additional price $\sum_t r_{it} b_{it}$ for buying goods in the different *types* by augmenting agents' budgets. Further, buyers are no longer purchasing goods with the highest *bang-per-buck*, and under the adjusted price set $p_j' = p_j + r_{it} b_{it}$, where one unit of good j is purchased and $j \in t$, agents are purchasing goods with the highest "adjusted" *bang-per-buck*. Finally, we observe that more constrained agents, e.g., healthcare workers in a pandemic environment, have larger weights λ_i than less constrained agents, ensuring more constrained agents have "higher priorities" and thus an allocation that lies within their feasible constraint set.

4   Fixed Point Scheme to Determine Perturbations

In **BP-SOP**, we required that $\lambda_i = \sum_{t=1}^{l_i} r_{it} b_{it}$, i.e., λ_i depends on the dual variables of the problem, which we have no knowledge of apriori. In this section, we show how to compute the appropriate value of λ_i through a fixed point iteration in Sect. 4.1 and numerically establish its convergence in Sect. 4.2.

4.1 Fixed Point Iteration Algorithm

To determine the true value of the perturbation parameters specified by the vector $\lambda \in \mathbb{R}^n_{\geq 0}$, we consider an iterative scheme of the form $G\left(\lambda_1^{(k)}, ..., \lambda_n^{(k)}\right) = \left(\mathbf{r}_1^{(k)}, ..., \mathbf{r}_n^{(k)}\right)$, where we update the perturbations as: $\left(\lambda_1^{(k+1)}, ..., \lambda_n^{(k+1)}\right) = \left(\sum_{t=1}^{l_1} r_{1t}^{(k)} b_{1t}, ..., \sum_{t=1}^{l_n} r_{nt}^{(k)} b_{nt}\right)$. Here G is a function that takes in the kth iterate $\lambda_i^{(k)}$ for all agents i, solves the corresponding social optimization problem **BP-SOP** and returns the dual variables, $\mathbf{r}_i^{(k)} \in \mathbb{R}^{l_i}_{\geq 0}$ of the physical constraints.

Algorithm 1 depicts the fixed point scheme, where $\lambda = (\lambda_1, ..., \lambda_n)$, and $\mathbf{R} = (\mathbf{r}_1, ..., \mathbf{r}_n)$, the dual variables of **BP-SOP**s physical constraints.

Algorithm 1: Fixed Point Scheme

Input   : Tolerance ϵ, Function $G(\cdot)$ to calculate dual variables of physical constraints of **BP-SOP**

Output: Budget Perturbation Parameters λ

$\lambda \leftarrow \mathbf{0}$; $\mathbf{R} \leftarrow G(\lambda)$; $q_i \leftarrow \sum_{t=1}^{l_i} r_{it} b_{it}$, $\forall i$;

while $\|\lambda - \mathbf{q}\|_2 > \epsilon$ do

$\quad \mid \quad \lambda_i \leftarrow \sum_{t=1}^{l_i} r_{it} b_{it}$, $\forall i$; $\mathbf{R} \leftarrow G(\lambda)$; $q_i \leftarrow \sum_{t=1}^{l_i} r_{it} b_{it}$, $\forall i$;

end

4.2 Numerical Experiments with Iterative Scheme

We now numerically evaluate the convergence of Algorithm 1 to the allocate agents to public spaces. We consider a neighborhood with $n = 200$ people and $m = 6$ public spaces, with three resource *types* including two grocery stores, two parks, and two beaches. The capacities of the public spaces are $\bar{s}_j = 100$, $\forall j \in [m]$ and the physical constraint is that each individual would not want to go to more than one of the public spaces within the same resource *type* over the course of a day, defining three identical physical constraints for each person. Furthermore, in this experiment each person i is endowed with a random budget w_i and their preferences are captured through randomly generated utilities.

On the above problem instance, we run Algorithm 1, wherein we terminate when $\left\|\lambda^{(k)} - \sum_{t=1}^{3} \mathbf{r}_t^{(k)}\right\| \leq \epsilon$, since $b_{it} = 1$ for all i, t. Here $\lambda^{(k)} = \left(\lambda_1^{(k)}, ..., \lambda_n^{(k)}\right)$ and $\mathbf{r}_t^{(k)} = \left(r_{1t}^{(k)}, ..., r_{nt}^{(k)}\right)$, where $r_{it}^{(k)}$ is the dual variable of the optimization problem at iteration k, and n is the number of people. The experiment confirmed that the iterative scheme converges quickly to a fixed point on this and other problem instances. Convergence in fewer than 40 iterations can be observed in Fig. 3, highlighting the computational feasibility of our mechanism. We note that the experiments confirmed feasibility of allocations with respect to physical constraints, which may have been violated with classical Fisher markets.

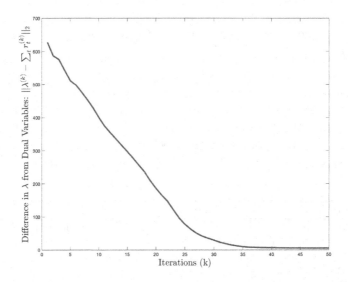

Fig. 3. Numerical Convergence of fixed point scheme with 200 people, 6 goods and 3 good *types*. The budgets and utilities were assigned randomly to agents.

5   Conclusions and Future Work

In this work, we have developed market based mechanisms to more efficiently allocate capacity constrained public goods that are priced in non-monetary units. We defined a new individual optimization problem **IOP** in the presence of physical constraints and established market equilibrium properties of this problem, including existence, non-uniqueness and thoroughly characterized its optimal solution. Even though the properties of **IOP** are fundamentally different from that of the individual optimization problem in Fisher markets, we proposed a mechanism to derive a market equilibrium in the presence of physical constraints, thereby generalizing the Fisher market framework. In particular, we reformulated the Fisher market setup to account for additional physical constraints by perturbing the budgets of agents and defining a new social optimization problem **BP-SOP**. We then showed a one-to-one correspondence between the equilibrium price vector and a *fixed point* solution of **BP-SOP** through the verification of KKT conditions. Next, we established the significance of the budget perturbation constants and that under the appropriate choice of these constants, a market equilibrium is attained such that under the set prices each agent's individual utilities are maximized. To obtain the right budget perturbation parameters, we used a fixed point iteration scheme for the reformulated social optimization problem and numerically showed the convergence of this iterative procedure indicating the applicability of our mechanism for real world problem instances.

There are various interesting directions for future research that warrant more study. First, the allocations provided by our market mechanism are fractional, and as we would like to make discrete allocations, it would be interesting to investigate the loss in social efficiency under integral constraints. Furthermore, while we have numerically shown convergence guarantees of our iterative scheme, it would be beneficial to theoretically understand the convergence to the fixed point as well as the rate of convergence of our procedure. Next, we believe that a stronger characterization of the computational complexity of this problem would provide a more nuanced appreciation of whether computing the exact fixed point is feasible in polynomial time. Finally, an interesting area of research is generalizing this framework to an online setting in which customers arrive in the market platform sequentially and an irrevocable decision needs to be made about the prices in the market while still achieving a socially efficient allocation.

References

1. Coronavirus disease (COVID-19) (2020). https://www.who.int/emergencies/diseases/novel-coronavirus-2019/advice-for-public. Accessed 8 Jul 2020
2. Arrow, K.J., Debreu, G.: Existence of an equilibrium for a competitive economy. Econometrica **22**(3), 265–290 (1954)
3. Bei, X., Garg, J., Hoefer, M., Mehlhorn, K.: Earning limits in fisher markets with spending-constraint utilities. In: Bilò, V., Flammini, M. (eds.) SAGT 2017. LNCS, vol. 10504, pp. 67–79. Springer, Cham (2017). https://doi.org/10.1007/978-3-319-66700-3_6
4. Birnbaum, B., Devanur, N.R., Xiao, L.: New convex programs and distributed algorithms for fisher markets with linear and spending constraint utilities (2010). Unpublished Manuscript
5. Birnbaum, B., Devanur, N.R., Xiao, L.: Distributed algorithms via gradient descent for fisher markets. In: Proceedings of the 12th ACM Conference on Electronic Commerce, pp. 127–136 (2011)
6. Blümel, W., Pethig, R., von dem Hagen, O.: The theory of public goods: a survey of recent issues. J. Inst. Theoret. Econ. (JITE)/Zeitschrift für die gesamte Staatswissenschaft **142**(2), 241–309 (1986)
7. Brainard, W.C., Scarf, H.E.: How to compute equilibrium prices in 1891. Am. J. Econ. Sociol. **64**(1), 57–83 (2005)
8. Budish, E.: The combinatorial assignment problem: approximate competitive equilibrium from equal incomes. J. Polit. Econ. **119**(6), 1061–1103 (2011)
9. Chen, L., Ye, Y., Zhang, J.: A note on equilibrium pricing as convex optimization. In: International Workshop on Web and Internet Economics (2007)
10. Devanur, N.R.: The spending constraint model for market equilibrium: algorithmic, existence and uniqueness results. In: Proceedings of the Thirty-Sixth Annual ACM Symposium on Theory of Computing, STOC 2004, pp. 519–528. Association for Computing Machinery, New York (2004). https://doi.org/10.1145/1007352.1007431

11. Devanur, N.R., Jain, K., Mai, T., Vazirani, V.V., Yazdanbod, S.: New convex programs for fisher's market model and its generalizations. CoRR (2016). http://arxiv.org/abs/1603.01257

12. Devanur, N.R., Papadimitriou, C., Saberi, A., Vazirani, V.V.: Market equilibrium via a primal-dual algorithm for a convex program. J. ACM **55**(5) (2008)

13. Eisenberg, E., Gale, D.: Consensus of subjective probabilities: the pari-mutuel method. Ann. Math. Stat. **30**(1), 165–168 (1959)

14. Gale, D.: The Theory of Linear Economic Models. The University of Chicago Press, Chicago (1960)

15. Garg, J., Hoefer, M., Mehlhorn, K.: Approximating the nash social welfare with budget-additive valuations. In: Proceedings of the Twenty-Ninth Annual ACM-SIAM Symposium on Discrete Algorithms, SODA 2018, pp. 2326–2340. Society for Industrial and Applied Mathematics, USA (2018)

16. Goldfarb, A.: How to navigate public spaces and more (2020). https://www.nytimes.com/2020/04/03/style/etiquette-coronavirus.html. Accessed 10 Jul 2020

17. Gorokh, A., Banerjee, S., Iyer, K.: Near-efficient allocation using artificial currency in repeated settings. Social Science Research Network (2016)

18. Jalota, D., Qi, Q., Pavone, M., Ye, Y.: Markets for efficient public good allocation with social distancing. CoRR (2020). https://arxiv.org/abs/2005.10765

19. Vazirani, V.V.: Combinatorial algorithms for market equilibria. In: Nisan, N., Roughgarden, T., Tardos, E., Vazirani, V.V. (eds.) Algorithmic Game Theory, pp. 103–134. Cambridge University Press (2007)

20. Vazirani, V.V.: Spending constraint utilities with applications to the adwords market. Math. Oper. Res. **35**(2), 458–478 (2010)

21. Walras, L.: Elements of Pure Economics: Or, The Theory of Social Wealth. American Economic Association. Translation series, American Economic Association (1954)

22. Yamagishi, T., Sato, K.: Motivational bases of the public goods problem. J. Pers. Soc. Psychol. **50**(1), 67–73 (1986)

Mechanism Design and Pricing

Two Strongly Truthful Mechanisms
for Three Heterogeneous Agents
Answering One Question

Grant Schoenebeck[1] and Fang-Yi Yu[2]($\boxtimes$)

[1] University of Michigan, Ann Arbor, USA
schoeneb@umich.edu
[2] Harvard University, Cambridge, USA
fayu@umich.edu

Abstract. Peer prediction mechanisms incentivize self-interested agents to truthfully report their signals even in the absence of verification, by comparing agents' reports with their peers. We propose two new mechanisms, Source and Target Differential Peer Prediction, and prove very strong guarantees for a very general setting.

Our Differential Peer Prediction mechanisms are *strongly truthful*: Truth-telling a strict Bayesian Nash equilibrium. Also, truth-telling pays strictly higher than any other equilibria, excluding permutation equilibria, which pays the same amount as truth-telling.

The guarantees hold for *asymmetric priors* which the mechanisms need not know (*prior-free*) in the *signal question setting*. Moreover, they only require *three agents*, each of which submits a *signal item report*: one reports her forecast and the others their signals.

Our proof technique is straightforward, conceptually motivated, and turns on the logarithmic scoring rule's special properties.

Moreover, we can recast the Bayesian Truth Serum mechanism [11] into our framework. We can also extend our results to the setting of *continuous signals* with a slightly weaker guarantee on the optimality of the truthful equilibrium.

Keywords: Peer prediction · Log scoring rule · Prediction market

1 Introduction

Crowd-sourcing relies on eliciting truthful information from agents. Peer prediction is the problem of information elicitation without verification. Incentivizing agents is important so that they not only participate, but provide thoughtful and accurate information. This has a multitude of applications including peer-grading, reviews, and labeling data (for machine learning or research). In the

Grant Schoenebeck and Fang-Yi Yu are pleased to acknowledge the support of the National Science Foundation grants 1618187 and 2007256. Fang-Yi Yu is pleased to acknowledge the support of the National Science Foundation grants 2007887.

ⓒ Springer Nature Switzerland AG 2020
X. Chen et al. (Eds.): WINE 2020, LNCS 12495, pp. 119–132, 2020.
https://doi.org/10.1007/978-3-030-64946-3_9

single-question setting agents are only asked one question. Our goal is to elicit truthful information from agents with minimal requirements.

For example, say three friends watch a political debate on television. We would like to ask each of them who won the debate and pay them to incentivize truthful answers. This situation will be modeled as each agent receiving some information from the debate about which candidate won. Moreover, prior to the debate, there is a joint prior distribution over the signals of the different agents which is common knowledge among the agents. Thus, one friend's belief on who won yields some insights about the perceived winners of the other friends.

We will design mechanisms to compensate the agents for their information. We would like our mechanisms to have the following desirable properties:

Strongly Truthful [8]. Providing truthful answers is a Bayesian Nash equilibrium (BNE) and also guarantees the maximum agents' welfare among any equilibrium. This maximum is "strict" with the exception of a few unnatural permutation equilibria where agents report according to a relabeling of the signals (defined more formally in Sect. 2).[1] This will incentivize the agents to tell the truth–even if they believe the other agents will disagree with them. Moreover, they have no incentive to coordinate on an equilibrium where they do not report truthfully. In particular, note that playing a permutation equilibrium still requires as much effort from the agents as playing truth-telling.

General Signals. The mechanism should work for *heterogeneous* agents who may even have *continuous* signals (with a weaker truthfulness guarantee). In our above example, the friends may not have the same political leanings, and the mechanism should be robust to that. Furthermore, instead of a single winner, we may want to elicit the magnitude of their (perceived) victory.

Detail-Free. The mechanism is not required to know the specifics about the different agents (e.g. the aforementioned joint prior). In the above example, the mechanism should not be required to know the a priori political leanings of the different agents.

On Few Agents. We would like our mechanisms to work using as few agents as possible, in our case, three.

Single-Item Reports. We would like to make it easy for agents so that they provide very little information: only one item, either their signal or a prediction. In our case, two agents will need to provide their signals (e.g. whom they believe won the debate). The remaining agent will need to provide a prediction on one outcome—a single real value. (e.g. their forecast for how likely a particular other agent was to choose a particular candidate as the victor).

1.1 Related Work

Single Task Setting. In this setting, each agent receives a single signal from a common prior. Miller et al. [10] introduce the first mechanism for single task signal elicitation that has truth-telling as a strict Bayesian Nash equilibrium and

---

[1] Kong and Schoenebeck [8] show that it is not possible for truth-telling to pay strictly more than permutation equilibrium in detail-free mechanisms.

does not need verification. However, their mechanism requires full knowledge of the common prior and there exist some equilibria that agents get paid more than truth-telling. At a high level, the agents can all simply submit the reports with the highest expected payment and this will typically yield a payment much higher than that of truth-telling. Note that this is both natural to coordinate on (in fact, Gao et al. [3] found that in an online experiment, agents did exactly this) and does not require any effort toward the task from the agents. Kong et al. [5] modify the above mechanism such that truth-telling pays strictly better than any other equilibrium but still requires the full knowledge of the common prior.

Prelec [11] designs the first detail-free peer prediction mechanism—Bayesian truth serum (BTS). Moreover, BTS is strongly truthful and can easily be made to have one-item reports. However, BTS requires an infinite number of participants, does not work for heterogeneous agents, and requires the signal space to be finite. The analysis, while rather short, is equally opaque. A key insight of this work is to ask agents not only about their own signals, but forecasts (prediction) of the other agents' reports.

A series of works [12,13,17–19] relax the large population requirement of BTS but lose the strongly truthful property. Zhang and Chen [19] is unique among prior work in the single question setting in that it works for heterogeneous agents whereas other previous detail-free mechanisms require homogeneous agents with conditionally independent signals.

Kong and Schoenebeck [6] introduce the Disagreement Mechanism which is detail-free, strongly truthful (for symmetric equilibrium), and works for six agents. Thus it generalizes BTS to the finite agent setting while retaining strong truthfulness. However, it requires symmetric agents, cannot handle continuous signals, and fundamentally requires that each agent reports both a signal and a prediction. Moreover, its analysis is quite involved. However, it is within the BTS framework, in that it only asks for agents' signals and predictions, whereas our mechanism typically asks at least one agent for a prediction after seeing the signal of another agent.

	Truthful	# Agents	Strongly truthful	General signals
BTS [11]	✓	∞	✓	
Robust BTS [17]	✓	3		
Disagreement [6]	✓	6	✓	
Knowledge-free peer prediction [19]	✓	3		✓
Differential peer prediction	✓	3	✓	✓

Continuous Single Task Setting. Kong et al. [9] shows how to generalize both BTS and the Disagreement Mechanism (with similar properties including homogeneous agents), into a restricted continuous setting where signals are Gaussians related in a simple manner. The generalization of the Disagreement Mechanism requires the number of agents to increase with the dimension of the continuous space.

The aforementioned Radanovic and Faltings [13] considers continuous singles. However, it uses a discretization approach which yields exceedingly complex reports. Additionally, it requires homogeneous agents.

In a slightly different setting, Kong and Schoenebeck [7] study eliciting agents' forecasts for some (possibly unverifiable) event, which are continuous values between 0 and 1. However, here we are concerned with eliciting signals which can be from a much richer space.

Multi-task Setting. In the multitask setting, introduced in Dasgupta and Ghosh [2], agents are assigned a batch of a priori similar tasks which require each agents' private information to be a binary signal. Several works extend this to multiple-choice questions [2,4,8,14]. The multi-task setting is easier to work in than the single-task setting because the mechanism can better deduce the strategy of any particular agent by comparing reports across questions. However, this setting is substantially more restrictive than the single-question setting of the present paper in that it is important the questions are all similar and gives no guarantees when questions have different priors. An example of when this requirement holds is asking agents to label images as "cat" or "no cat".

1.2   Our Contributions

- We define two Differential Peer Prediction mechanisms (Mechanism 1 and 2) which are strongly-truthful and detail-free for the single question setting and only require a single item report from three agents. Moreover, the agents need not be homogeneous and their signals may be continuous.
- We provide a simple, conceptually motivated proof for the guarantees of Differential Peer Prediction mechanisms. Especially in contrast to the most closely related work [6] our proof is very simple.
- We show special properties of the logarithmic scoring rules (see Techniques below for details). This allows the construction of *target* incentives where an agent is rewarded when is signal is predicted well, and we believe will also be of independent interest.
- We recast the Bayesian Truth Serum mechanism into our framework, showing that it is a *target* incentive mechanism (Sect. 4). This gives added intuition for its guarantees.

1.3   Summary of Our Techniques

Target Incentive Mechanisms. Many of the mechanisms for the single question use what we call *source* incentives: they pay agents for reporting a signal that improves the prediction of another agent's signal. The original peer prediction mechanism [10] does exactly this. To apply this idea to the detail-free setting [17,19], mechanisms take a two-step approach: they first elicit an agent's prediction of some target agent's report, and then measure how much that prediction improves given a report from a source agent.

In Sect. 3.2, we explicitly develop a technique, which we call *target* incentives, for rewarding certain agents for signal reports that agree with a prediction about them. In particular, we show that log scoring rules can elicit signals as well as forecasts. This may be of independent interest, and is also the foundation for the results in Sects. 3.2 and 4.

Information Monotonicity. We use information monotonicity, a tool from information theory, to obtain strong truthfulness. Like the present paper, the core of the argument that the Disagreement Mechanism [6] is strongly truthful (for symmetric equilibrium) is based on information monotonicity. However, because it is hard to characterize the equilibria in the Disagreement Mechanism, the analysis ends up being quite complex. A framework for deriving strongly truthful mechanisms from information monotonicity, which we implicitly employ, is distilled in Kong and Schoenebeck [8].

In Sect. 3, we use the above techniques to develop strongly truthful mechanisms, source-Differential Peer Prediction and target-Differential Peer Prediction, for the single question setting. Source-Differential Peer Prediction is quite similar to the Knowledge-Free Peer Prediction Mechanism[19], however, it is strongly truthful. Target-Differential Peer Prediction also uses the target incentive techniques above.

2 Preliminaries

2.1 Peer Prediction Mechanism

There are three characters, Alice, Bob and Chloe in our mechanisms. Alice (and respectively Bob, Chloe) has a privately observed signal a (respectively b, c) from a set $\mathcal{A}$ (respectively $\mathcal{B}$, $\mathcal{C}$). They all share a common belief that their signals (a, b, c) are generated from a random variable (A, B, C) which takes values from $\mathcal{A} \times \mathcal{B} \times \mathcal{C}$ with a probability measure P called *common prior*. P describes how agents' private signals relate to each other's.

Agents are Bayesian. For instance, after Alice receives $A = a$, she updates her belief to the *posterior* $P((B, C) = (\cdot, \cdot) \mid A = a)$ which is a distribution over the remaining signals. We will use $P_{B,C|A}(\cdot \mid a)$ instead to simplify the notion. Similarly Alice's posterior of Bob's signal is denoted by $P_{B|A}(\cdot \mid a)$, which is a distribution on $\mathcal{B}$.

A peer prediction mechanism on Alice, Bob, and Chloe has three payment functions (U_A, U_B, U_C). The mechanism first collects reports $\mathbf{r} := (r_A, r_B, r_C)$ from agents. We pay Alice with $U_A(\mathbf{r})$ (and Bob and Chloe analogously). Alice's strategy θ_A is a (random) function from her signal to a report. All agents are rational and risk-neutral that are only interested in maximizing their (expected) payment. Thus, given a strategy profile $\boldsymbol{\theta} := (\theta_A, \theta_B, \theta_C)$, Alice, for example, wants to maximize her expected *ex-ante payment* under common prior P which is $u_A(\boldsymbol{\theta}; P) := \mathbb{E}_{P,\boldsymbol{\theta}} [U_A(\mathbf{r})]$. Let ex-ante *agents' welfare* denote the sum of ex-ante payment to all agents, $u_A(\boldsymbol{\theta}; P) + u_B(\boldsymbol{\theta}; P) + u_C(\boldsymbol{\theta}; P)$. A strategy profile $\boldsymbol{\theta}$ is a *Bayesian Nash equilibrium* under common prior P if by changing the strategy unilaterally, an agent's payment can only weakly decrease. It is a *strict Bayesian Nash equilibrium* if an agent's payment strictly decreases as her strategy changes.

We want to design peer prediction mechanisms to "elicit" all agents to report their information truthfully without verification. We say Alice's strategy τ_A is *truthful* for a mechanism $\mathcal{M}$ if Alice truthfully reports the information requested by the mechanism.[2] We call the strategy profile τ truth-telling if each agent reports truthfully. Moreover, we want to design *detail-free* mechanisms which have no knowledge about the common prior P except agents' (possible non-truthful) reports. However, agents can always relabel their signals and detail-free mechanisms cannot distinguish such a strategy profile from the truth-telling strategy profile. We call these strategy profiles *permutation strategy profiles*. They can be translated back to truth-telling reports by some permutations applied to each component of $\mathcal{A} \times \mathcal{B} \times \mathcal{C}$—that is, the agents report according to a relabeling of the signals.

We now define some goals for our mechanism that differ in how unique the high payoff of truth-telling is. We call a mechanism **truthful** if the truth-telling strategy profile τ is a strict Bayesian Nash equilibrium. However, in a truthful mechanism, often non-truth-telling equilibria may yield a higher ex-ante payment for each agent. In this paper, we aim for **strongly truthful mechanisms** [8] which are not only truthful but also ensure the ex-ante agents' welfare in truth-telling strategy profile τ is strictly better than all non-permutation equilibria. Note that in a symmetric game, this ensures that each agent's individual expected ex-ante payment is maximized by truth-telling compared to any other symmetric equilibrium.

Now, we define the set of common priors that our detail-free mechanisms can work on. Note peer's reports are not useful when every agent's signal are independent of each other. Thus, a peer prediction mechanism needs to exploit some interdependence between agents' signals.

Definition 1 (Zhang and Chen [19]). *A common prior P is $\langle A, B, C \rangle$-second order stochastic relevant if for any distinct signals $b, b' \in \mathcal{B}$, there is $a \in \mathcal{A}$, such that $P_{C|A,B}(\cdot \mid a, b) \neq P_{C|A,B}(\cdot \mid a, b')$. Thus, when Alice with a is making a prediction to Chloe's signal, Bob's signal is relevant so that his signal induces different predictions when $B = b$ or $B = b'$.*

*We call P **second order stochastic relevant** if the above statement holds for any permutation of $\{A, B, C\}$.[3]*

To avoid measure theoretic concerns, we initially require that P has full support, and the joint signal space $\mathcal{A} \times \mathcal{B} \times \mathcal{C}$ to be finite. In the full version, we will show how to extend our results to general measurable spaces.

---

[2] Here we do not define the notion of truthful reports formally, because it is intuitive in our mechanisms. For general setting, we can use query models to formalize it [15].

[3] Our definition has some minor differences from Zhang and Chen [19]'s, for ease of exposition. For instance, they only require the statement holds for one permutation of $\{A, B, C\}$ instead of all the permutations.

2.2 Proper Scoring Rules

Scoring rules are powerful tools to design mechanisms for eliciting predictions. Consider a finite set of possible outcomes Ω, e.g., $\Omega = \{\text{sunny}, \text{rainy}\}$. An expert, Alice, first reports a distribution $\hat{P} \in \mathcal{P}(\Omega)$ as her prediction of the outcome, where $\mathcal{P}(\Omega)$ denotes the set of all probability measures on Ω. Then, the mechanism and Alice observe the outcome ω. The mechanism gives Alice a score $\mathrm{PS}[\omega, \hat{P}]$. To the end, if Alice believes the distribution of ω to be P, she maximizes her expected score by reporting P truthfully. We call such scoring function proper defined as follow:

Definition 2. *A **scoring rule** $\mathrm{PS} : \Omega \times \mathcal{P}(\Omega) \mapsto \mathbb{R}$ is **proper** if for any distributions $P, \hat{P} \in \mathcal{P}(\Omega)$ we have $\mathbb{E}_{\omega \sim P}[\mathrm{PS}[\omega, P]] \geq \mathbb{E}_{\omega \sim P}\left[\mathrm{PS}[\omega, \hat{P}]\right]$. A scoring rule PS is **strictly proper** when the equality holds only if $\hat{P} = P$.*

Given any convex function f, one can define a new proper scoring rule PS^f [8]. In this paper, we consider a special scoring rule called the **logarithmic scoring rule** [16], defined as

$$\mathrm{LSR}[\omega, P] := \log\left(p(\omega)\right), \tag{1}$$

where $p : \Omega \to \mathbb{R}$ is the probability density function of P.

2.3 Information Theory

Peer prediction mechanisms and prediction markets incentivize agents to truthfully report their signals even in the absence of verification . One key idea these mechanisms use is that agents' signals are interdependent and strategic manipulation can only dismantle this structure. Here we introduce several basic notions from information theory [1].

The *KL-divergence* is a measure of the dissimilarity between two distributions: Let P and Q be probability measures on a finite set Ω with density functions p and q respectively. The **KL divergence** (also called relative entropy) from Q to P is $D_{KL}(P\|Q) := \sum_{\omega \in \Omega} -p(\omega) \log\left(q(\omega)/p(\omega)\right)$.

We now introduce mutual information, which measures the amount of information between two random variables: Given a random variable (X, Y) on a finite set $\mathcal{X} \times \mathcal{Y}$, let $p_{X,Y}(x, y)$ be the probability density of the random variable (X, Y), and let $p_X(x)$ and $p_Y(y)$ be the marginal probability density of X and Y respectively. The **mutual information** $I(X; Y)$ is the KL-divergence from the joint distribution to the product of marginals:

$$I(X; Y) := \sum_{x \in \mathcal{X}, y \in \mathcal{Y}} p_{X,Y}(x, y) \log \frac{p_{X,Y}(x, y)}{p_X(x) p_Y(y)} = D_{KL}(P_{X,Y} \| P_X \otimes P_Y)$$

where $\otimes$ denotes the tensor product between distributions. Moreover, if (X, Y, Z) is a random variable, the *mutual information between X and Y conditional on Z* is

$$I(X; Y \mid Z) := \mathbb{E}_Z[D_{KL}(P_{(X,Y)|Z} \| P_{X|Z} \otimes P_{Y|Z})].$$

The data-processing inequality shows no manipulation of the signals can improve mutual information between two random variables, and the inequality if of fundamental importance in information theory.

Theorem 1 (Data processing inequality). *If $X \to Y \to Z$ form a Markov chain,*[4]

$$I(X;Y) \geq I(X;Z).$$

By basic algebraic manipulations, Kong and Schoenebeck [8] relate proper scoring rules to mutual information as follows: For two random variables X and Y,

$$\mathbb{E}_{x,y}\left[\text{LSR}[y, P(Y \mid x)] - \text{LSR}[y, P(Y)]\right] = I(X;Y). \tag{2}$$

We can generalize the mutual information in two ways [8]. The first is to define $f - MI$ using the f-divergence, where f is a convex function, to measure the distance between the joint distribution and the product of the marginal distributions. The KL-divergence is just a special case of the f-divergence. This retains the symmetry between the inputs.

The second way is to us a different proper scoring rule. As mentioned, any convex function f gives rise to a proper scoring rule PS^f. Then the Bregman Mutual information can be defined as in Eq. (2): $BMI^f(X,Y) := \mathbb{E}_{x,y}[\text{PS}^f(y, P_{Y|X}(\cdot \mid x)] - \text{PS}^f(y, P_Y(\cdot)]$. Note that by the properties of proper scoring rules BMI is information monotone in the first coordinate; however, in general it is not information monotone in the second.

Thus, by Eq. (2), mutual information is the unique measure that is both a Bregman mutual information and an f-MI. This observation is one key for designing our strongly truthful mechanisms.

3   Experts, Targets and Sources: Strongly Truthful Peer Prediction Mechanisms

In this section, we show how to design strongly truthful mechanisms to elicit agents' *signals* by implicitly running a prediction market.

Our mechanisms have three characters, Alice, Bob, and Chloe, and there are three roles: expert, target, and source:

- An expert makes predictions on a target's report,
- a target is asked to report his signal, and
- a source provides her information to an expert to improve the expert's prediction.

By asking agents to play these three roles, we design two strongly truthful mechanisms based on two different ideas.

The first mechanism is *source differential peer prediction* (S-DPP). This mechanism is based on the *knowledge-free peer prediction* mechanism by Zhang

---

[4] Random variables X, Y and Z form a Markov chain if the conditional distribution of Z depends only on Y and is conditionally independent of X.

and Chen [19], which rewards a *source* by how useful her signal is for an expert to predict a target's report. Their mechanism is only truthful but not strongly truthful. We carefully shift the payment functions and employ Eq. (2) and the data-processing inequality on log scoring rule to achieve the strongly truthful guarantee.

We further propose a second mechanism, *target differential peer prediction* (T-DPP). Instead of rewarding a source, the T-DPP mechanism rewards a *target* by the difference of the logarithmic scoring rule on her signal between an initial prediction and an improved prediction. Later in Sect. 4 we show Bayesian truth serum can be seen as a special case of our T-DPP mechanism.

Then we discuss how to remove the temporal separation between agents making reports in Sect. 3.3 where agents only need to report once, and their reports do not depend on other agents' reports.

3.1   The Source Differential Peer Prediction Mechanism

The main idea of the S-DPP mechanism is that it rewards a source by the usefulness of her signal for predictions. Specifically, suppose Alice acts as an expert, Bob as the target, and Chloe as the source. Our mechanism first asks Alice to make an *initial prediction* $\hat{Q}$ on Bob's report. Then after Chloe's reporting her signal, we collect Alice's *improved prediction* $\hat{Q}^+$ after seeing Chloe's additional information. In each case, Alice maximizes her utility by reporting her Bayesian posterior conditioned on her information.

The payments for Alice and Bob are simple. S-DPP pays Alice by the sum of the logarithmic scoring rule on those two predictions. And S-DPP pays Bob 0. Chloe's payment consists of two parts: First, we pay her the prediction score of the improved prediction $\hat{Q}^+$. By the definition of proper scoring rule (Definition 2), Chloe will report truthfully to maximize it. For the second part, we subtract Chloe's payment by three times the score of the initial prediction $\hat{Q}$. This ensures the ex-ante agent welfare equals the mutual information, which is maximized at the truth-telling strategy profile. To ensure Bob also reports his signal truthfully, we randomly permute Bob and Chloe's roles in the mechanism.

Theorem 2. *If the common prior P is second order stochastic relevant on a finite set with full support, Mechanism 1 is strongly truthful:*

1. *The truth-telling strategy profile τ is a strict Bayesian Nash equilibrium.*
2. *The ex-ante agents' welfare in the truth-telling strategy profile τ is strictly better than all non-permutation strategy profiles.*

We defer the proof to the full version. Intuitively, because the logarithmic scoring rule is proper, Alice (the expert) will make the truthful predictions when Bob and Chloe report their signals truthfully. Similarly, the source is willing to report her signal truthfully to maximize the improved prediction score. This shows Mechanism 1 is truthful.

Note that if the agents' common prior P is symmetric, we can randomize the roles among Alice, Bob, and Chloe to create a symmetric game where

---

Mechanism 1. Two-round Source Differential Peer Prediction

Require: Alice, Bob, and Chloe have private signals $a \in \mathcal{A}$, $b \in \mathcal{B}$, and $c \in \mathcal{C}$ drawn from second order stochastic relevant common prior P known to all three agents. LSR is the logarithmic scoring rule (1).

1: Bob and Chloe report their signals, $\hat{b}$ and $\hat{c}$.
2: Set Alice as the expert. Randomly set Bob or Chloe as the *target* and the other as the *source*. We use t to denote the target's report, and use s to denote the source's report.
3: Alice is informed who is the target and predicts the target's report t with $\hat{Q}$.
4: Given the source's report s, the expert makes another prediction $\hat{Q}^+$.
5: The payment to the expert is $\mathrm{LSR}[t, \hat{Q}] + \mathrm{LSR}[t, \hat{Q}^+]$.
6: The payment to the target is 0.
7: The payment to the source is $\mathrm{LSR}[t, \hat{Q}^+] - 3\mathrm{LSR}[t, \hat{Q}]$.

---

each agent's expected payment at the truth-telling strategy profile is both non-negative and maximized among all symmetric equilibria.

3.2 Target Differential Peer Prediction Mechanism

The target differential peer prediction mechanism (T-DPP) is identical to the S-DPP except for the payment functions. In contrast to the S-DPP mechanism, T-DPP rewards a target. We show that paying the difference between initial prediction and an improved prediction on a target's signal can incentivize the target to report truthfully. (Lemma 1).

Our mechanism pays Alice by the sum of log scoring on those two predictions. And the mechanism pays Bob by the improvement from the initial prediction $\hat{Q}$ to the improved prediction $\hat{Q}^+$. Finally, Chloe's payment depends on Alice's first initial prediction $\hat{Q}$, which is independent of Chloe's action. To ensure Chloe also reports her signal truthfully, we permute the roles of Bob and Chloe randomly in the mechanism as well.

Mechanism 2. Two-round Target Differential Peer Prediction

Require: Alice, Bob, and Chloe have private signals $a \in \mathcal{A}$, $b \in \mathcal{B}$, and $c \in \mathcal{C}$ drawn from second order stochastic relevant common prior P known to all three agents. LSR is the logarithmic scoring rule (1).

1: Bob and Chloe report their signals, $\hat{b}$ and $\hat{c}$.
2: Set Alice as the expert. Randomly set Bob or Chloe as the *target* and the other as the *source*. We use t to denote the target's report, and use s to denote the source's report.
3: Alice is informed who is the target and predicts the target's report t with $\hat{Q}$.
4: Given the source's report s, the expert makes another prediction $\hat{Q}^+$.
5: The payment to the expert is $\mathrm{LSR}[t, \hat{Q}] + \mathrm{LSR}[t, \hat{Q}^+]$.
6: The payment to the target is $\mathrm{LSR}[t, \hat{Q}^+] - \mathrm{LSR}[t, \hat{Q}]$.
7: The payment to the source is $-2\mathrm{LSR}[t, \hat{Q}]$.

Theorem 3. *If the common prior P is second order stochastic relevant on a finite set with full support, Mechanism 2 is strongly truthful*

We defer the proof to the full version, and provide a sketc.h here. We first show Mechanism 2 is truthful. Because the log scoring rule is proper, Alice (the expert) will make the truthful predictions *when Bob and Chloe report their signals truthfully*. Thus, the difficult part is to show the target is willing to report his signal truthfully, if the expert and the source are truthful. Because the roles of Bob and Chloe are symmetric in the mechanism, we can assume Bob is the target and Chloe is the source from now on.

Lemma 1 (Logarithmic proper scoring rule reversed). *Suppose Alice and Chloe are truthful, and the common prior is $\langle A, B, C \rangle$-second order stochastic relevant. As the target, Bob's best response is to report his signal truthfully.*

This is a generalization of a lemma in Prelec [11] and Kong and Schoenebeck [8], and extends to non-symmetric prior and finite agent setting. The main idea is that to maximize Bob's expected payment, we show that equivalently Bob wants to maximize a proper scoring rule with prediction $P(C \mid \theta(b))$ on predicting Chloe's report. Therefore, by the property of proper scoring rules, Bob is incentivized to tell the truth. We defer the proof to the full version. With Lemma 1, the rest of the proof is very similar to the proof of Theorem 2.

3.3 Single-Round DPP Mechanism for Finite Signal Spaces

When the signal spaces are finite, the above two-round mechanisms (Mechanisms 1 and 2) can be reduced to single-round mechanisms by using virtual signal w. That is for Alice's improved prediction we provide Alice with a random virtual signal w instead of the actual report from the source, and pay her the prediction score when the source's report is equal to the virtual signal $s = w$. We defer the formal mechanism to the full version.

4   Bayesian Truth Serum as a Prediction Market

In this section, we revisit the original Bayesian Truth Serum (BTS) by Prelec [11] from the perspective of prediction markets. We first define the setting, which is a special case of ours (Mechanism 2), and use the idea of prediction markets to understand BTS.

4.1   Setting of BTS

There are n agents. They all share a common prior P. We call P is *admissible* if it consists of two main elements: states and signals. The *state* T is a random variable in $\{1, \ldots, m\}$, $m \geq 2$ which represents the true state of the world. Each agent i observes a *signal* X_i from a finite set Ω. The agents have a common prior consisting of $P_T(t)$ and $P_{X|T}(\cdot \mid t)$ such that the prior joint distribution of $x_1, \ldots, x_n$ is $\Pr(X_1 = x_1, \ldots, X_n = x_n) = \prod_{t \in [m]} P_T(t) \prod_{i \in [n]} P_{X|T}(x_i \mid t)$.

Now we restate the main theorem concerning Bayesian Truth Serum:

Mechanism 3. The original BTS

Require: $\alpha > 1$

Ensure: The common prior is admissible

1: Agent i reports $\hat{x}_i \in \Omega$ and $\hat{Q}_i \in \mathcal{P}(\Omega)$.

2: For each agent i, choose a reference agent $j \neq i$ uniformly at random. Compute $Q_{-ij}^{(n)} \in \mathcal{P}(\Omega)$ such that for all $x \in \Omega$

$$Q_{-ij}^{(n)}(x) = \frac{1}{n-2} \sum_{k \neq i,j} \mathbf{1}[\hat{x}_k = x] \tag{3}$$

which is the empirical distribution of the other $n-2$ agents' reports.

3: The prediction score and information score of i are

$$S_{\text{Pre}} = \text{LSR}\left[\hat{x}_j, \hat{Q}_i\right] - \text{LSR}\left[\hat{x}_j, Q_{-ij}^{(n)}\right] \text{ and } S_{\text{Im}} = \text{LSR}\left[\hat{x}_i, Q_{-ij}^{(n)}\right] - \text{LSR}\left[\hat{x}_i, \hat{Q}_j\right].$$

And the payment to i is $S_{\text{Pre}} + \alpha \, S_{\text{Im}}$.

Theorem 4 [11]. *For all $\alpha > 1$, if the common prior P is admissible and $n \to \infty$, Mechanism 3 is strongly truthful.*

4.2   Information Score and Prediction Market

Prelec [11] uses clever algebraic calculation to prove this main results. Kong and Schoenebeck [8] use information theory to show that for BTS the ex-ante agents' welfare for the truth-telling strategy profile is strictly better than for all other non-permutation equilibria. Here we use prediction markets to show BTS is a truthful mechanism, and use Mechanism 2 to reproduce BTS.

The payment from BTS consists of two parts, the *information score*, S_{Im}, and the *prediction score*, S_{Pre}. The prediction score is exactly the log scoring rule and is well-studied in the previous literature. However, the role of information score is more complicated. Here we provide an interpretation based on Mechanism 2.

We consider $i = 2$ and $j = 1$ in BTS and call them Bob and Alice respectively. We let Chloe be the collection of other agent $\{3, 4, \ldots, n\}$. Let's run Mechanism 2 on this information structure. Bob is the target. Alice's initial prediction is $Q = P_{X_2|X_1}(\cdot \mid x_1)$. When Chloe's signal is $x_3, x_4, \ldots, x_n$, Alice's improved prediction is $Q^+ = P_{X_2|X_{-2}}(\cdot \mid x_{-2})$ where $x_{-2} = (x_1, x_3, \ldots, x_n)$ is the collection of all agents' reports expect Bob's. By Lemma 1, Bob is still incentivized to report his private signal x_2 which maximizes the expectation, $\text{LSR}[\hat{x}_2, Q^+] - \text{LSR}[\hat{x}_2, Q]$ that equals to

$$\text{LSR}[\hat{x}_2, P_{X_2|X_{-2}}(\cdot \mid x_{-2})] - \text{LSR}[\hat{x}_2, P_{X_2|X_1}(\cdot \mid x_1)]. \tag{4}$$

For the BTS (Mechanism 3), the information score in BTS at truth-telling strategy profile is $\text{LSR}[\hat{x}_i, Q_{-ij}^{(n)}] - \text{LSR}[\hat{x}_i, \hat{Q}_j]$ which equals to

$$\text{LSR}\left[\hat{x}_2, Q_{-ij}^{(n)}\right] - \text{LSR}\left[\hat{x}_2, P_{X_2|X_1}(\cdot \mid x_1)\right]. \tag{5}$$

The only difference between (4) and (5) is the first term: $P_{X_2|X_{-2}}(\cdot \mid x_1, x_3, \ldots, x_n)$ and $Q^{(n)}_{-ij}$. Therefore, the original BTS reduces to a special case of Mechanism 2 as $n \to \infty$, if we can show $\lim_{n \to \infty} P(X_2 \mid x_1, x_3, \ldots, x_n) = \lim_{n \to \infty} Q^{(n)}_{-ij}$. Formally,

Proposition 1. *For all $t = 1, \ldots, m$ and $w \in \Omega$,*

$$Q^{(n)}_{-ij}(w) - P_{X_2|X_{-2}}(w \mid x_1, x_3, \ldots, x_n) \xrightarrow{P_{\mathbf{X}|T}(\cdot|t)} 0 \ as \ n \to \infty.$$

That is the difference between these estimators converges to zero in probability as n goes to infinity.

5 Conclusion

We define two Differential Peer Prediction mechanisms for the single question setting which are strongly-truthful, detail-free, and only require a single item report from three agents. Moreover, the agents need not to be homogeneous and their signals may be continuous. We also show a new property of the logarithmic scoring rules, apply it to make target incentive mechanisms, and show that BTS can be seen as such a mechanism. One future direction is to use this machinery to analyse when BTS retains its strongly truthful guarantee, e.g. for what parameters of finite and/or heterogeneous agents. We define Differential Peer Prediction, a strongly-truthful, detail-free, mechanism for the single question setting that only requires a single item report from three agents. Moreover, the agents need not be homogeneous and their signals may be continuous. We provide a simple, conceptually motivated proof for the guarantees of Differential Peer Prediction, which ties together several themes in the information elicitation literature.

References

1. Cover, T.M.: Elements of Information Theory. Wiley, New York (1999)
2. Dasgupta, A., Ghosh, A.: Crowdsourced judgement elicitation with endogenous proficiency. In: Proceedings of the 22nd International Conference on World Wide Web, pp. 319–330, International World Wide Web Conferences Steering Committee (2013)
3. Gao, X.A., Mao, A., Chen, Y., Adams, R.P.: Trick or treat: putting peer prediction to the test. In: Proceedings of the Fifteenth ACM Conference on Economics and Computation, pp. 507–524. ACM (2014)
4. Kong, Y.: Dominantly truthful multi-task peer prediction with a constant number of tasks. In: Proceedings of the Fourteenth Annual ACM-SIAM Symposium on Discrete Algorithms, pp. 2398–2411. SIAM (2020)
5. Kong, Y., Ligett, K., Schoenebeck, G.: Putting peer prediction under the micro(economic)scope and making truth-telling focal. In: Cai, Y., Vetta, A. (eds.) WINE 2016. LNCS, vol. 10123, pp. 251–264. Springer, Heidelberg (2016). https://doi.org/10.1007/978-3-662-54110-4_18

132   G. Schoenebeck and F.-Y. Yu

6. Kong, Y., Schoenebeck, G.: Equilibrium selection in information elicitation without verification via information monotonicity. In: 9th Innovations in Theoretical Computer Science Conference (2018)
7. Kong, Y., Schoenebeck, G.: Water from two rocks: maximizing the mutual information. In: Proceedings of the 2018 ACM Conference on Economics and Computation, pp. 177–194. ACM (2018)
8. Kong, Y., Schoenebeck, G.: An information theoretic framework for designing information elicitation mechanisms that reward truth-telling. ACM Trans. Econ. Comput. (TEAC) **7**(1), 2 (2019)
9. Kong, Y., Schoenebeck, G., Yu, F.Y., Tao, B.: Information elicitation mechanisms for statistical estimation. In: Thirty-Fourth AAAI Conference on Arificial intelligence (AAAI 2020), February 2020
10. Miller, N., Resnick, P., Zeckhauser, R.: Eliciting informative feedback: the peer-prediction method. Manage. Sci. **51**, 1359–1373 (2005)
11. Prelec, D.: A Bayesian truth serum for subjective data. Science **306**(5695), 462–466 (2004)
12. Radanovic, G., Faltings, B.: A robust Bayesian truth serum for non-binary signals. In: Proceedings of the 27th AAAI Conference on Artificial Intelligence (AAAI 2013), pp. 833–839. EPFL-CONF-197486 (2013)
13. Radanovic, G., Faltings, B.: Incentives for truthful information elicitation of continuous signals. In: Proceedings of the 28th AAAI Conference on Artificial Intelligence (AAAI 2014), pp. 770–776. EPFL-CONF-215878 (2014)
14. Shnayder, V., Agarwal, A., Frongillo, R., Parkes, D.C.: Informed truthfulness in multi-task peer prediction. In: Proceedings of the 2016 ACM Conference on Economics and Computation, EC 2016, pp. 179–196. ACM, New York (2016). ISBN 978-1-4503-3936-0
15. Waggoner, B., Chen, Y.: Information elicitation sans verification. In: Proceedings of the 3rd Workshop on Social Computing and User Generated Content (SC13) (2013)
16. Winkler, R.L.: Scoring rules and the evaluation of probability assessors. J. Am. Stat. Assoc. **64**(327), 1073–1078 (1969)
17. Witkowski, J., Parkes, D.C.: A robust Bayesian truth serum for small populations. In: Proceedings of the 26th AAAI Conference on Artificial Intelligence (AAAI 2012) (2011)
18. Witkowski, J., Parkes, D.C.: Peer prediction without a common prior. In: Proceedings of the 13th ACM Conference on Electronic Commerce, EC 2012, pp. 964–981. Association for Computing Machinery, New York (2012). ISBN 9781450314152
19. Zhang, P., Chen, Y.: Elicitability and knowledge-free elicitation with peer prediction. In: Proceedings of the 2014 International Conference on Autonomous Agents and Multi-agent Systems, pp. 245–252. International Foundation for Autonomous Agents and Multiagent Systems (2014)

A Generic Truthful Mechanism
for Combinatorial Auctions

Hanrui Zhang[(⊠)]

Duke University, Durham, NC 27705, USA
hrzhang@cs.duke.edu

Abstract. We study combinatorial auctions with n agents and m items, where the goal is to allocate the items to the agents such that the social welfare is maximized. We present a universally truthful mechanism with polynomially many queries for combinatorial auctions. Our mechanism and analysis work adaptively for all classes of valuation functions, guaranteeing $\widetilde{O}(\min(d, \sqrt{m}))$-approximation (where $\widetilde{O}$ hides a polylogarithmic factor in m) of the optimal social welfare, where d is the degree of complementarity of the valuation functions. To our knowledge, this is the first mechanism that achieves an approximation guarantee better than $\Omega(\sqrt{m})$, when the valuations exhibit any kind of complementarity.

Keywords: Truthful combinatorial auctions · Approximate subadditivity · Pointwise approximation

1 Introduction

The field of algorithmic mechanism design studies protocols for computing an outcome to optimize a certain social objective (e.g., the social welfare), when inputs are reported by strategic agents. The main challenge in algorithmic mechanism design is twofold: algorithmically, the mechanism has to deal with the *computational hardness* of the problem; strategically, the mechanism has to take into account the *incentives* of the agents, which often do not align with the interests of the designer. One popular scheme in the field is to design *truthful* mechanisms, where the dominant strategy of all bidders are to report their true preferences. Restricted to truthful mechanisms, one no longer needs to worry about complex strategic behavior, and can therefore focus on the algorithmic properties of the mechanism.

In this paper, we consider a central problem in algorithmic mechanism design—designing truthful mechanisms for *combinatorial auctions*. In a combinatorial auction, there are n *agents* and m *items*. Each agent i has a *valuation function* v_i, that maps each subset S of the items to her value of the subset $v_i(S)$. The goal is to find an *allocation* of all items, $(A_1, \ldots, A_n)$, such that the total value (i.e., the *social welfare*) of the agents, $\sum_{i \in [n]} v_i(A_i)$, is maximized. It is standard in combinatorial auctions to assume that all valuations are *monotone*[1]

---

[1] A valuation v is monotone, if for any $S \subseteq T \subseteq [m]$, $v(S) \leq v(T)$.

© Springer Nature Switzerland AG 2020
X. Chen et al. (Eds.): WINE 2020, LNCS 12495, pp. 133–146, 2020.
https://doi.org/10.1007/978-3-030-64946-3_10

and *normalized*[2]. Previous research also studies restricted classes of valuations, e.g., *submodular*[3], *fractionally subadditive (XOS)*[4], and *subadditive*[5] valuations. It is known that all submodular valuations are fractionally subadditive, and all fractionally subadditive valuations are subadditive.

Since the size of a valuation function can be exponentially large in m, it is often impossible to use the entire functions as the input. Instead, two standard kinds of queries are allowed: (1) *value* queries, which, given an agent i and a set S, return the value of S to agent i, $v_i(S)$; (2) *demand* queries, which, given an agent i and prices $\{p_j\}_{j\in[m]}$, return a utility-maximizing set (i.e., a *demand set*) of i under the given prices. That is, the query returns a set S that maximizes $v_i(S) - \sum_{j\in S} p_j$.

Combinatorial auctions become relatively easy if we remove either one of the two aspects of the difficulty. Ignoring incentive issues, efficient approximation algorithms exist for the welfare maximization problem. Vondrak gives a $\frac{e}{e-1}$-approximation for submodular valuations, using only value queries [20], which is shown tight by Mirrokni et al. [18]. When demand queries are allowed, Feige and Vondrak give an upper bound of $\frac{e}{e-1} - 10^{-6}$ for submodular valuations [15], where a lower bound of $\frac{2e}{2e-1}$ is known [9]. Feige gives a $\frac{e}{e-1}$-approximation for XOS valuations and a 2-approximation for subadditive valuations using both queries [12]. None of these algorithms are truthful. On the other hand, the VCG mechanism is truthful and guarantees the optimal welfare. Computing the VCG outcome and payments, however, is usually algorithmically hard. In particular, approximation usually does not help in implementing the mechanism because of incentive issues.

Taking into account both computational and strategic issues, there are significant gaps between known upper and lower bounds. Under the most restrictive assumptions, for submodular valuations, Dobzinski et al. [7] give a deterministic $O(\sqrt{m})$-approximation that requires only value queries, which is tight both information theoretically [5] and complexity theoretically [9]. Allowing randomization and demand queries, a series of work improves the upper bound from $O(\log^2 m)$ for XOS valuations [8], to $O(\log m \log\log m)$ for subadditive valuations [4], to $O(\log m)$ for XOS valuations [17], to $O(\sqrt{\log m})$ for XOS valuations [6], and finally to $O((\log\log m)^3)$ for XOS valuations [1]. For general valuations, $O(\sqrt{m})$-approximation randomized mechanisms using both kinds of queries are known [4,8], accompanied by a matching $\Omega(m^{1/2-\varepsilon})$ communication complexity lower bound by Nisan [19].

All of the above mechanisms are *universally truthful*. That is, fixing the randomness of the mechanism, no agent has incentive to misreport her valuation. We focus our attention on universally truthful mechanisms, as opposed to *truthful in expectation* ones, since if the mechanism proceeds in stages, as agents observe

---

[2] A valuation v is normalized, if $v(\emptyset) = 0$.

[3] A valuation v is submodular, if for any $S, T \subseteq [m]$, $v(S) + v(T) \geq v(S\cup T) + v(S\cap T)$.

[4] A valuation v is fractionally subadditive, if for any S, $\{T_i\}$, and $\{\alpha_i\}$, $v(S) \leq \sum \alpha_i v(T_i)$, whenever the following holds: for each $j \in S$, $\sum_{i:j\in T_i} \alpha_i \geq 1$.

[5] A valuation v is subadditive, if for any $S, T \subseteq [m]$, $v(S) + v(T) \geq v(S\cup T)$.

partial realization of the randomness, truthfulness in expectation may not be able to prevent them from lying. Even if agents do not observe the realization of the randomness, their attitude toward risk may still lead them to misreport.

Despite all the upper bounds for various restricted classes of valuations, little is known for classes beyond subadditivity. Subadditive valuations are considered reasonably general, but they can only model items as *substitutes* to each other— that is, possessing some items can never make other items more desirable. While focusing on subadditive valuations usually allows better approximation ratios, real world valuations often do involve *complementarity*. For example, a TV set seems more valuable when one already has a sofa, because otherwise she might have to watch on her feet. On the other hand, the amount of complementarity is usually *limited*, in the sense that a sofa and a TV set complement each other, but neither of them would affect the value of a car, a dishwasher, or anything out of the living room. In other words, possible sets of items that complement each other are likely not too large. Such valuations with limited complementarity, while being obviously more general than the subadditive class, still seem intuitively easier to handle than arbitrary monotone valuations. So, a natural question arises:

Beyond subadditivity, can we do better than $\Omega(\sqrt{m})$, when agents have valuations exhibiting limited complementarity?

1.1 Our Results

We give a positive answer to the question above. Our main contribution is twofold:

1. Going beyond subadditive valuations, we establish welfare guarantees that degrade smoothly as the degree of complementarity of the valuations grows. We prove fine-grained upper bounds roughly proportional to the degree of complementarity, which, when the degree is small, improve substantially over the $O(\sqrt{m})$ bound for general valuations. To our knowledge, no such results were known before.
2. We provide unified design and analysis that work adaptively for all classes of valuations, guaranteeing approximation ratios that nearly match the state-of-the-art for the respective class.

In order to derive parametrized welfare guarantees for valuations beyond the complement-free class, we need to be able to measure how much complementarity the valuations exhibit (i.e., we need a *measure of complementarity*). While several measures have been proposed and referred to in various applications (e.g., the supermodular degree hierarchy [14] and the Maximum-over-Positive-Hypergraphs hierarchy [13]), it has been observed that different tasks often require different measures to capture the transition of hardness from restricted to general valuations (see, e.g., [11]). For our problem, the superadditive width hierarchy proposed by Chen et al. [2] seems the best fit. The measure builds on the concept of superadditive sets:

Definition 1 (Superadditive Sets [2]). *Let $v(S|T) = v(S \cup T) - v(T)$ be the marginal of S given T. Given a normalized monotone valuation function v over a ground set $[m]$, a set $T \subseteq [m]$ is* superadditive w.r.t. v *if*

$$\exists S \subseteq [m] \setminus T \text{ such that: } v(S|T) > \max_{T' \subsetneq T} v(S|T').$$

In words, a set T is superadditive, if it enables some set S with a larger marginal than any of its proper subsets does. Based on the concept of superadditive sets, Chen et al. define a measure of complementarity:

Definition 2 (Superadditive Widths [2]). *The* superadditive width *of a valuation function v is defined to be*

$$\text{SAW}(v) = \max\{|T| \mid T \text{ is a superadditive set w.r.t. } v\}.$$

The definition essentially says, that the degree of complementarity of a valuation is proportional to the size of the largest superadditive set with respect to the valuation.

It is known that for any monotone valuation function v over $2^{[m]}$, $0 \leq \text{SAW}(v) \leq m - 1$, and $\text{SAW}(v) = 0$ iff v is subadditive [2]. In other words, valuations can be categorized, according to their superadditive width, into m nested layers, where the lowest layer (layer 0) contains exactly the class of subadditive valuations, and the highest layer (layer $m - 1$) contains all monotone valuation functions. We denote the d-th layer, containing valuations with superadditive width at most d, by SAW-d (Table 1).

The following theorem summarizes our results:

Theorem 1 (Informal). *There is an efficient universally truthful mechanism which guarantees $\widetilde{O}(\min(d, \sqrt{m}))$-approximation[6] of the optimal welfare, where m is the number of items, and $d = \max_{i \in [n]} \text{SAW}(v_i)$ is the maximum superadditive width of agents' valuations.*

Table 1. Comparison of approximation ratios of several mechanisms.

	Submodular/XOS	Subadditive	SAW-d	General
Mechanism 1 of [4]	$O(\sqrt{m})$	$O(\sqrt{m})$	$O(\sqrt{m})$	$O(\sqrt{m})$
Mechanism 2 of [4]	$O(\log m \log \log m)$	$O(\log m \log \log m)$	?	?
[1]	$O((\log \log m)^3)$	?	?	?
This paper	$O(\log m)$	$O(\log^2 m)$	$O(d \log^2 m)$	$O(\sqrt{m \log m})$

The mechanism and analysis we present enjoy generic applicability—they require no parameters and automatically work for all kinds of valuations. Beside our result for limited-complementarity valuations, for complement-free

---

[6] $\widetilde{O}$ hides a polylog m factor.

valuations, we recover the polylog approximation ratios, and for general valuations, we match the $\Omega(\sqrt{m})$ lower bound up to a $O(\sqrt{\log m})$ factor. This adaptivity is particularly desirable when it is unrealistic to know beforehand to which class the valuations belong[7]. We also note that our mechanism is considerably simplified compared to previously proposed mechanisms—we intend to keep the mechanism as simple as possible to demonstrate the power of the underlying ideas, potentially compromising a minor factor in the approximation ratio. On the other hand, our analysis does shed light on the potential space for improvement within the framework we present, possibly by incorporating ideas from [1,4]. For further related work, see Appendix A in the full version of the paper.

1.2 Organization and Technical Overview

We present our mechanism in Sect. 2, and then proceed to establishing approximation guarantees for different classes of valuations in later sections. The overall idea is to build a framework using the strongest assumptions under which the argument remains illustrative, and then generalize gradually by adapting the framework.

We begin our investigation with *constraint homogeneous (CH)* valuations (defined in Definition 3), which is arguably the simplest class of valuations exhibiting complementarity. The class was originally introduced by Devanur et al. [3] and extended by Feldman et al. [16] to study the PoA of simple auctions. Roughly speaking, the CH class contains valuations that are additive over small disjoint bundles, where each bundle's value is proportional to its size. We show in Sect. 3 that our mechanism guarantees $\widetilde{O}(d)$-approximation for CH valuations with maximum bundle size d. More specifically, we first show that given complete information about agents' valuations, there exist prices, such that if we post these prices on the items, order agents arbitrarily, and let them purchase their demand sets, the resulting allocation is a $O(d)$-approximation of the optimal welfare. We prove this guarantee using a standard argument that decomposes the welfare into two parts: the total payment, and the total buyer surplus. The intuition is that, if we post the right prices, then when most items are sold, the payment must be high enough. Otherwise, since the unsold items are available to every agent as an option, the total buyer surplus must be high enough. The welfare bound follows since both terms are nonnegative. We then argue that without knowing agents' valuations, we can somehow guess a price, such that if we post that price on every item, the expected welfare is still reasonably high. The technique of "guessing a price" has also been shown useful in [4,8].

---

[7] One may argue that running the state-of-the-art mechanism for each class of valuations with constant probability achieves the best approximation guarantee for all classes simultaneously. The point we try to make here is, we show how one can achieve this adaptivity with coherent design and analysis, which arguably provides more insight into the problem, and is more likely to inspire future research on the topic.

We further observe that for certain truthful mechanisms, *pointwise approximation* between classes of valuations (as defined in Definition 4) in a sense preserves welfare guarantees. The notion of pointwise approximation was explicitly defined by Devanur et al. in [3], where they show such approximation approximately preserves PoA bounds. Informally, v is approximated by v' at set S, if (1) v' is always no larger than v at any subset of S, and (2) v' is not too much smaller than v at S. In Sect. 4, based on this observation, we provide a way to translate these approximation relationships into welfare guarantees, by proving the following lemma:

Lemma 1 (Informal). *There is an efficient universally truthful mechanism which guarantees $\widetilde{O}(d)$-approximation of the optimal welfare, when agents have valuations approximated by disjoint bundle (DB) valuations (as defined in Definition 5) with maximum bundle size d.*

The class of DB valuations is similar to CH, except that each bundle can have an arbitrary value. We first argue the lemma for CH valuations, and then extend to DB valuations by assigning a dummy agent to every bundle in a DB valuation. The proof of the lemma builds on the observation, that if we pretend that the agents have CH valuations that approximate the actual ones at some optimal allocation, we can borrow the argument for CH valuations with local modifications. In particular, since the welfare of the optimal allocation under the dummy valuations is not too much smaller than the actual optimal welfare, we can use the dummy welfare as the benchmark without significant loss.

The extension lemma above essentially says, in order to establish welfare guarantee for a particular class of valuations, one only needs to show approximability of the class by DB valuations. Given the extension lemma, we plug in previously known approximation results for XOS, subadditive, and SAW-d valuations by DB valuations, which immediately yields approximation guarantees for the respective classes of valuations.

Finally, in Sect. 5, we show that for general valuations, we are able to nearly recover the optimal $O(\sqrt{m})$ approximation ratio. We take a similar but slightly different approach. We argue that if the agents' shares in the optimal allocation are roughly equally distributed, then we can ignore agents who receive too many items. The intuition is, since agents receive disjoint sets of items, the number of agents who receive many items is not too large. Also, since the optimal welfare is equally distributed, a small number of agents cannot share too large a fraction of the welfare, and can therefore be removed without hurting the welfare too much. We then use the optimal allocation projected to agents who receive few items as the benchmark. We observe, that the valuation of each agent is approximated at the set she receives, by a CH valuation with reasonably small maximum bundle size. A similar argument to the one we use to prove the extension lemma gives the desired approximation guarantee.

2   A Generic Mechanism

In this section, we present our generic mechanism for truthful combinatorial auctions, and state its approximation guarantees for different classes of valuations.

Notation. Throughout the paper we use $[n]$ and $[m]$ to denote the sets of agents and items, respectively. W.l.o.g. we assume $m = 2^p$ for some integer p. In general we use i as the index of an agent, and j the index of an item.

The mechanism, as well as the frameworks presented in [4,8], uses two widely applied subroutines:

- A (grand-bundle) *second price auction*, where each agent bids on the grand bundle of all items. The agent with the highest bid wins, receives all items, and pays the second highest bid.
- A *fixed-price auction* with price p, where all agents are approached in some arbitrary order. Each agent, when being asked, can choose to purchase any subset of the items available at the time, paying p for each item she purchases. Any item purchased by some agent becomes unavailable immediately.

A generic mechanism.

1. With probability $\frac{1}{2}$, run a second price auction on the grand bundle, give all items to the winner, charge her the second highest bid, and terminate.
2. Partition all agents into two sets: STAT and FIXED. Each bidder is assigned independently, with probability $\frac{1}{2}$ to STAT, and with probability $\frac{1}{2}$ to FIXED.
3. For each agent $i \in$ STAT, query $v_i([m])$. Let $p_0 = \max_{i \in \text{STAT}} v_i([m])$.
4. Draw p uniformly at random from

$$P = \left\{ \frac{p_0}{32m^2}, \frac{p_0}{16m^2}, \ldots, \frac{p_0}{2}, p_0, 2p_0, \ldots, 8m^2 p_0, 16m^2 p_0 \right\}.$$

   Run a fixed-price auction for agents in FIXED with price p, give any purchased item to the agent who purchased it, collect the corresponding payments, and terminate.

It is easy to check that the above mechanism is universally truthful. If a grand-bundle second price auction happens, truthfulness follows from that of second price auctions. Otherwise, for an agent in STAT, since she will not receive any item anyway, there is no incentive to lie.[8] For an agent i in FIXED, when being asked, her dominant strategy is to purchase her demand set (i.e. a set S that maximizes $v_i(S) - p \cdot |S|$) according to her actual valuation. We prove in the following sections that:

---

[8] As suggested by an anonymous reviewer, a slight modification gives all agents strict incentives to report truthfully: partition agents into two sets (STAT and FIXED) uniformly at random, and run a second-price auction on the grand bundle for agents in STAT. Then with probability 1/2, allocate the grand bundle to the highest bidder in the second-price auction, and with probability 1/2, let p_0 be the highest bid, and proceed to Step 4 (the fixed-price auction) of the original mechanism.

Theorem 2 (Main Theorem). *The generic mechanism is universally truthful, makes exactly one value or demand query to each agent, and returns a $O(\min(d\log^2 m, \sqrt{m\log m}))$-approximately optimal allocation of all items in expectation, where $d = \max_{i\in[n]} \mathrm{SAW}(v_i)$. When agents have submodular or XOS valuations, the approximation ratio improves to $O(\log m)$.*

It may appear that a tighter analysis should give a bound of $\widetilde{O}(\sqrt{d})$, which becomes $\widetilde{O}(1)$ for complement-free agents (when $d = 0$) and $\widetilde{O}(\sqrt{m})$ for general monotone agents (when $d = m - 1$). However, we show that the above bound is in fact almost tight for our protocol, or any protocol within the same framework. Namely,

Proposition 1. *There exist $2m/(d+1)$ agents with SAW-d valuations such that the generic mechanism yields a $\Omega(\min\{d, m/d\})$-approximately optimal allocation.*

We postpone the proof of the above proposition to Appendix B in the full version of the paper.

3   Warmup: Constraint Homogeneous Valuations

As a warmup, we first prove an approximation guarantee of the generic framework when agents are interested in only disjoint bundles of items. The proof will also be the backbone of the limited-complementarity and general valuation cases to be discussed later. Formally, we are interested in agents with the following class of valuations:

Definition 3 (*d*-Constraint Homogeneous Valuations [16]). *A valuation v is d-constraint homogeneous (d-CH) if there exists a value p (the price-per-item), and disjoint sets $Q_1, \ldots, Q_\ell$, each of size at most d, so that $v(Q_k) = p\cdot|Q_k|$ for every Q_k, and the value of every set $S \subseteq [m]$ is the sum of values of contained Q_i's, i.e.,*

$$v(S) = \sum_{Q_k \subseteq S} v(Q_k) = p \sum_{Q_k \subseteq S} |Q_k| = p \cdot |\{j : \exists k \ s.t. \ j \in Q_k \subseteq S\}|.$$

We prove that the generic mechanism gives a $O(d\log m)$ approximation of the optimal welfare when agents have d-CH valuations. We proceed by two cases: when there is an agent whose share in the optimal allocation is large, and when there is no such agent. The former case is directly handled by the grand-bundle second price auction, while the second case requires more effort. All missing proofs in this section are postponed to Appendix C in the full version of the paper.

Notation. Let $\mathrm{OPT} = (\mathrm{OPT}_1, \ldots, \mathrm{OPT}_n)$ be an optimal allocation, where OPT_i is the set of items that agent i receives. Let $v(\mathrm{OPT}) = \sum_i v_i(\mathrm{OPT}_i)$ be the optimal welfare.

3.1   The Easy Case: When Heavy Agents Exist

First note that:

Lemma 2. *For any $t \geq 1$, if for some agent i, $v_i(\mathrm{OPT}_i) \geq \frac{v(\mathrm{OPT})}{t}$, then a grand-bundle second price auction guarantees welfare at least $\frac{v(\mathrm{OPT})}{t}$.*

Therefore, if there is an agent i whose share in the optimal allocation is at least $v_i(\mathrm{OPT}_i) \geq \frac{v(\mathrm{OPT})}{\log m}$, with probability $\frac{1}{2}$ a grand-bundle second price auctions happens, in which case the welfare is at least $\frac{v(\mathrm{OPT})}{\log m}$. The expected welfare is hence at least $\frac{v(\mathrm{OPT})}{2 \log m}$.

3.2   A Thought Experiment: Posted Prices Given Complete Information

Before proceeding to the hard case, we first consider a scenario where the valuations of all agents are known. We demonstrate that in such a case, there exist prices, using which a posted-price auction achieves a d-approximation of the optimal welfare when agents have d-CH valuations. The result does not directly imply a welfare guarantee of our mechanism. Nevertheless, the argument is instrumental for later discussion. We also note that the result in this subsection for the complete information case is not a novel contribution of this paper: for example, a similar statement appears in [10]. We present the entire argument here mainly to provide intuition about the hard case and to be self-contained.

Posted-Price Auctions. A posted price auction is similar to a fixed price auction, except that the prices for different items can be different. A price is assigned to each item before the auction begins. During the auction, agents are approached in some arbitrary order. Upon being asked, each agent can purchase any subset of the items available, and pay the total prices assigned to these items.
We claim that:

Proposition 2. *For agents with d-CH valuations, there exists prices $\{q_j\}_j$, such that a posted-price auction with prices $\{q_j\}_j$ yields an allocation with welfare at least $\frac{v(\mathrm{OPT})}{2d}$.*

3.3   The Hard Case: When No Heavy Agents Exist

Now we focus on the case where no agent has a share larger than $\frac{v(\mathrm{OPT})}{\log m}$. In such a case, we completely ignore the contribution to the welfare by the second price auction, and analyze solely the contribution of the fixed price auction.
Ideally we would like to run the posted-price auction discussed in the preceding subsection. However, there are two obstacles preventing us from implementing the auction: (1) the valuations of agents are unknown, and (2) computing an optimal allocation is computationally prohibiting. The latter issue can be solved in some sense, by running an approximation algorithm (e.g. [13]), presumably

compromising the approximation ratio. On the other hand, there seems to be no easy way around the first issue.

To overcome these difficulties, instead of posting the prices constructed in Proposition 2, our mechanism (1) estimates the interval in which the posted-prices lie, by querying agents in STAT, (2) guesses an appropriate price for agents in FIXED from the estimated interval, and (3) runs a fixed-price auction for agents in FIXED with the price guessed. We show that the expected welfare resulting from such a procedure is not too much worse than the posted-price outcome.

The first step is to show that with high probability, the optimal welfare is relatively equally distributed into STAT and FIXED, so (1) a good approximation restricted to agents in FIXED is also a good approximation with all agents, and (2) an estimation from STAT is useful for guessing the price for FIXED.

Let OPT^{STAT} and $\text{OPT}^{\text{FIXED}}$ be optimal allocations projected to agents in STAT and FIXED respectively. That is, $\text{OPT}_i^{\text{STAT}}$ (resp. $\text{OPT}_i^{\text{FIXED}}$) is OPT_i if i belongs to STAT (resp. FIXED), and $\emptyset$ otherwise.

Lemma 3. *If for some $t \geq 1$, for all $i \in [n]$, $v_i(\text{OPT}_i) \leq \frac{v(\text{OPT})}{t}$, then with probability $1 - 2e^{-t/8}$, $v(\text{OPT}^{\text{STAT}}) \geq \frac{v(\text{OPT})}{4}$ and $v(\text{OPT}^{\text{FIXED}}) \geq \frac{v(\text{OPT})}{4}$.*

Corollary 1. *If for all $i \in [n]$, $v_i(\text{OPT}_i) \leq \frac{v(\text{OPT})}{\log m}$, then with probability $1 - O(1/m)$, $v(\text{OPT}^{\text{STAT}}) \geq \frac{v(\text{OPT})}{4}$ and $v(\text{OPT}^{\text{FIXED}}) \geq \frac{v(\text{OPT})}{4}$.*

We now condition everything on the event (denoted by $\mathcal{E}$) that (1) with probability $1/2$, agents are divided into 2 groups, and (2) with probability $1 - O(1/m)$, the two groups are roughly balanced. We only need to show, that when $\mathcal{E}$ happens, the expected welfare of the mechanism is $\Omega\left(\frac{v(\text{OPT})}{d \log m}\right)$.

Let OPT' be an allocation obtained by removing from $\text{OPT}^{\text{FIXED}}$ any item allocated to an agent whose price-per-item is no larger than $\frac{v(\text{OPT}^{\text{FIXED}})}{2m}$. Observe that

Lemma 4. $v(\text{OPT}') \geq \frac{1}{2}v(\text{OPT}^{\text{FIXED}})$.

This means we can safely ignore agents with low price-per-item without losing too much.

For prices high enough, the next lemma shows that we can estimate and guess them with relatively high probability.

Lemma 5. *Conditioned on $\mathcal{E}$, for any $m \geq 512$, price $q \in \left[\frac{v(\text{OPT}^{\text{FIXED}})}{2m^2}, 4v(\text{OPT}^{\text{FIXED}})\right]$, with probability $\frac{1}{|P|} \geq \frac{1}{5\log m}$, the price p guessed in step 4 of the mechanism satisfies $\frac{1}{4}q \leq p < \frac{1}{2}q$.*

The next step is to show that the fixed-price auction approximates the sum of values of agents whose price-per-item is close to the guessed price p.

Lemma 6. *Conditioned on $\mathcal{E}$, the welfare of the allocation given by the fixed-price auction with price p is at least*

$$\frac{1}{4d} \sum_{i \in \text{FIXED}, \frac{1}{4}p_i \leq p \leq \frac{1}{2}p_i} v_i(\text{OPT}'_i).$$

We are ready to prove a lower bound on the expected welfare of the fixed-price auction.

Lemma 7. *Conditioned on $\mathcal{E}$, the expected welfare generated by the fixed-price auction is $\Omega\left(\frac{v(\text{OPT})}{d \log m}\right)$.*

Now we can put everything together and conclude:

Proposition 3. *When agents have d-CH valuations, the generic mechanism guarantees $O(d \log m)$-approximation of the optimal welfare.*

Proof. When there is a heavy agent (i.e., an agent i with $v_i(\text{OPT}_i) \geq \frac{v(\text{OPT})}{\log m}$), Lemma 2 guarantees expected welfare $\frac{v(\text{OPT})}{2 \log m}$. When there is no heavy agent, Corollary 1 and Lemma 7 guarantee expected welfare $\Omega\left(\frac{v(\text{OPT})}{d \log m}\right)$.

4   Valuations with Limited Complementarity

We show in this section, that for general valuations, the approximation guarantee of the generic mechanism degrades smoothly as the degree of complementarity grows. To establish this result, we first show that if a class of valuations $\mathcal{V}$ is approximated by disjoint bundle valuations with limited bundle size, then the mechanism gives a reasonable guarantee with valuations in $\mathcal{V}$. Then we apply various existing approximation lemmas to establish approximation guarantees of the generic mechanism for submodular, XOS, subadditive, and SAW-d valuations.

Formally, we define pointwise approximation between classes of valuations:

Definition 4 (Pointwise Approximation [3]). *A valuation class $\mathcal{V}$ is pointwise β-approximated by a valuation class $\mathcal{V}'$ if for any valuation $v \in \mathcal{V}$ and for any set $S \subseteq [m]$, there exists a valuation $v' \in \mathcal{V}'$ such that $\beta \cdot v'(S) \geq v(S)$ and for all $T \subseteq [m]$ it holds that $v'(T) \leq v(T)$. We also say such a v' β-approximates v at S.*

We first show that if d-CH β-approximates $\mathcal{V}$, then the generic mechanism guarantees $O(\beta d \log m)$-approximation of the optimal welfare, and then extend the result to d-DB valuations, a superclass of d-CH, as defined below.

Definition 5 (d-Disjoint Bundle Valuations). *A valuation v is d-disjoint bundle (d-DB) if there exists disjoints sets of size at most d and corresponding* values $(Q_1, v(Q_1)), \ldots, (Q_\ell, v(Q_\ell))$, so that the value of every set $S \subseteq [m]$ is the sum of values of contained Q_i's, i.e.,

$$v(S) = \sum_{Q_k \subseteq S} v(Q_k).$$

We first prove the d-CH version of the extension lemma, which plays a central part in our argument:

Lemma 8. When agents have valuations in class $\mathcal{V}$, for $\beta \leq m$, if $\mathcal{V}$ is pointwise β-approximated by d-CH valuations, then the generic mechanism guarantees $O(\beta d \log m)$-approximation of the optimal welfare.

We postpone the proof to Appendix D in the full version of the paper. Now observe that the above argument can be easily modified to work if we replace d-CH valuations with d-DB valuations. Formally,

Lemma 9. When agents have valuations in class $\mathcal{V}$, for $\beta \leq m$, if $\mathcal{V}$ is pointwise β-approximated by d-DB valuations, then the generic mechanism guarantees $O(\beta d \log m)$-approximation of the optimal welfare.

Again, we postpone the proof of Lemma 9 to Appendix D in the full version of the paper. Note that we do not need to know the d-CH or d-DB valuations which approximate the v_i's—the existence of the approximation suffices for our purpose.

With Lemma 9, we are now ready to translate the approximation lemmas by d-DB to welfare guarantees of the generic mechanism. Restricted to complement-free classes, it is well known that:

Lemma 10 (Folklore). Fractionally subadditive (or XOS) valuations are pointwise 1-approximated by 1-DB (i.e. additive) valuations.

Dobzinski [4] and Devanur et al. [3] independently show that:

Lemma 11 [3,4]. Subadditive valuations are pointwise $O(\log m)$-approximated by 1-CH (i.e. homogeneously additive) valuations.

And beyond complement-free classes, Chen et al. [2] show that:

Lemma 12 [2]. For any $d \geq 1$, the class SAW-d is pointwise $2H_m$-approximated by $2d$-CH, where $H_i = \sum_{k \in [i]} \frac{1}{k}$ is the i-th harmonic number.

Applying Lemma 9 to Lemmas 10, 11, and 12, we obtain:

Theorem 3. When agents have (1) submodular or XOS, (2) subadditive, or (3) SAW-d valuations for $d \geq 1$, the generic mechanism guarantees (1) $O(\log m)$-, (2) $O(\log^2 m)$-, or (3) $O(d \log^2 m)$-approximation of the optimal welfare, respectively.

Proof. The Theorem follows from Lemma 9 by setting β to (1) 1, (2) $O(\log m)$, and (3) $2H_m = O(\log m)$, and d to (1) 1, (2) 1, and (3) $2d'$ respectively.

5   General Monotone Valuations

In this section, we show that the generic mechanism guarantees $O(\sqrt{m \log m})$-approximation of the optimal welfare, thereby concluding the proof of Theorem 2. We do this, again, by modifying the outline given in Sect. 4 (proof deferred to Appendix E in the full version of the paper).

Theorem 4. *When agents have monotone valuations, the generic mechanism guarantees $O(\sqrt{m \log m})$-approximation of the optimal welfare.*

Putting Theorems 3 and 4 together, Theorem 2 follows directly.

Acknowledgements. This work is supported by NSF award IIS-1814056. The author thanks anonymous reviewers for helpful feedback.

References

1. Assadi, S., Singla, S.: Improved truthful mechanisms for combinatorial auctions with submodular bidders. In: Proceedings of the IEEE 60th Annual Symposium on Foundations of Computer Science (FOCS 2019), pp. 233–248. IEEE (2019)
2. Chen, W., Teng, S.H., Zhang, H.: Capturing complementarity in set functions by going beyond submodularity/subadditivity. In: Proceedings of the 10th Innovations in Theoretical Computer Science Conference (ITCS 2019). Schloss Dagstuhl-Leibniz-Zentrum fuer Informatik (2019)
3. Devanur, N., Morgenstern, J., Syrgkanis, V., Weinberg, S.M.: Simple auctions with simple strategies. In: Proceedings of the Sixteenth ACM Conference on Economics and Computation, pp. 305–322. ACM (2015)
4. Dobzinski, S.: Two randomized mechanisms for combinatorial auctions. In: Charikar, M., Jansen, K., Reingold, O., Rolim, J.D.P. (eds.) APPROX/RANDOM -2007. LNCS, vol. 4627, pp. 89–103. Springer, Heidelberg (2007). https://doi.org/10.1007/978-3-540-74208-1_7
5. Dobzinski, S.: An impossibility result for truthful combinatorial auctions with submodular valuations. In: Proceedings of the Forty-Third Annual ACM Symposium on Theory of Computing, pp. 139–148. ACM (2011)
6. Dobzinski, S.: Breaking the logarithmic barrier for truthful combinatorial auctions with submodular bidders. In: Proceedings of the Forty-Eighth Annual ACM Symposium on Theory of Computing, pp. 940–948. ACM (2016)
7. Dobzinski, S., Nisan, N., Schapira, M.: Approximation algorithms for combinatorial auctions with complement-free bidders. In: Proceedings of the Thirty-Seventh Annual ACM Symposium on Theory of Computing, pp. 610–618. ACM (2005)
8. Dobzinski, S., Nisan, N., Schapira, M.: Truthful randomized mechanisms for combinatorial auctions. In: Proceedings of the Thirty-Eighth Annual ACM Symposium on Theory of Computing, pp. 644–652. ACM (2006)
9. Dobzinski, S., Vondrák, J.: The computational complexity of truthfulness in combinatorial auctions. In: Proceedings of the 13th ACM Conference on Electronic Commerce, pp. 405–422. ACM (2012)
10. Düetting, P., Feldman, M., Kesselheim, T., Lucier, B.: Prophet inequalities made easy: stochastic optimization by pricing non-stochastic inputs. In: IEEE 58th Annual Symposium on Foundations of Computer Science (FOCS 2017), pp. 540–551. IEEE (2017)

11. Eden, A., Feldman, M., Friedler, O., Talgam-Cohen, I., Weinberg, S.M.: A simple and approximately optimal mechanism for a buyer with complements. In: Proceedings of the 2017 ACM Conference on Economics and Computation, p. 323 (2017)
12. Feige, U.: On maximizing welfare when utility functions are subadditive. SIAM J. Comput. **39**(1), 122–142 (2009)
13. Feige, U., Feldman, M., Immorlica, N., Izsak, R., Lucier, B., Syrgkanis, V.: A unifying hierarchy of valuations with complements and substitutes. In: Proceedings of the Twenty-Ninth AAAI Conference on Artificial Intelligence (2015)
14. Feige, U., Izsak, R.: Welfare maximization and the supermodular degree. In: Proceedings of the 4th Conference on Innovations in Theoretical Computer Science, pp. 247–256. ACM (2013)
15. Feige, U., Vondrak, J.: Approximation algorithms for allocation problems: improving the factor of 1-1/e, pp. 667–676. IEEE (2006)
16. Feldman, M., Friedler, O., Morgenstern, J., Reiner, G.: Simple mechanisms for agents with complements. In: Proceedings of the 2016 ACM Conference on Economics and Computation, pp. 251–267. ACM (2016)
17. Krysta, P., Vöcking, B.: Online mechanism design (randomized rounding on the fly). In: Czumaj, A., Mehlhorn, K., Pitts, A., Wattenhofer, R. (eds.) ICALP 2012. LNCS, vol. 7392, pp. 636–647. Springer, Heidelberg (2012). https://doi.org/10.1007/978-3-642-31585-5_56
18. Mirrokni, V., Schapira, M., Vondrák, J.: Tight information-theoretic lower bounds for welfare maximization in combinatorial auctions. In: Proceedings of the 9th ACM Conference on Electronic Commerce, pp. 70–77. ACM (2008)
19. Nisan, N.: The communication complexity of approximate set packing and covering. In: Widmayer, P., Eidenbenz, S., Triguero, F., Morales, R., Conejo, R., Hennessy, M. (eds.) ICALP 2002. LNCS, vol. 2380, pp. 868–875. Springer, Heidelberg (2002). https://doi.org/10.1007/3-540-45465-9_74
20. Vondrák, J.: Optimal approximation for the submodular welfare problem in the value oracle model. In: Proceedings of the Fortieth Annual ACM Symposium on Theory of Computing, pp. 67–74. ACM (2008)

The Price of Anarchy of Two-Buyer Sequential Multiunit Auctions

Mete Şeref Ahunbay[1(✉)] and Adrian Vetta[2]

[1] Department of Mathematics and Statistics, McGill University,
Montréal, QC, Canada
`mete.ahunbay@mail.mcgill.ca`
[2] Department of Mathematics and Statistics, School of Computer Science,
McGill University, Montréal, QC, Canada
`adrian.vetta@mcgill.ca`

Abstract. We study the efficiency of sequential multiunit auctions with two buyers and complete information. For general valuation functions, we show that the *price of anarchy* is exactly $1/T$ for auctions with T items for sale. For concave valuation functions, we show that the price of anarchy is bounded below by $1 - 1/e \simeq 0.632$. This bound is asymptotically tight as the number of items sold tends to infinity.

1 Introduction

In a *sequential multiunit auction*, T identical copies of an item are sold one at a time. We evaluate the price of anarchy in two-buyer sequential multiunit auctions with complete information, under the standard model introduced by Gale and Stegeman [6] where each item is sold via a second-price auction. Our main result is that, for concave valuation functions, the price of anarchy is at least $1 - 1/e \simeq 0.632$, and this bound is asymptotically tight as the number of items T tends to infinity. We also show that, for general valuation functions, the price of anarchy is exactly $1/T$ for sequential multiunit auctions with T items for sale. To obtain these results we show how to lower bound the price of anarchy via a linear programming formulation. Key to our analyses is a detailed examination of the properties of equilibria. These properties lead to a collection of valid constraints whose incorporation into the linear program produces the optimal lower bounds. The optimality of these bounds is certified by providing examples of two-buyer sequential auctions with matching upper bounds on the price of anarchy.

1.1 Related Work

There is an extensive literature studying the price of anarchy of sequential multiunit auctions. For the case of identical items, our price of anarchy bound of $1 - 1/e$ for two-buyer auctions with concave valuations has previously been claimed by Bae et al. [2,3]. However, those papers contain flaws and the proofs

X. Chen et al. (Eds.): WINE 2020, LNCS 12495, pp. 147–161, 2020.
https://doi.org/10.1007/978-3-030-64946-3_11

do not hold; see [1] for details. Recently, Ahunbay et al. [1] were able to prove that the price of anarchy is $1 - 1/e$ under the restriction that a buyer may not bid higher than its incremental value for winning the next item. But, even with concave valuations, equilibrium bids can be higher than incremental values – thus the results of [1] do not apply to the traditional equilibrium concept studied in this paper. The price of anarchy of sequential auctions with non-identical items has also been studied in depth; see, for example [5,8,11,12].

To evaluate the price of anarchy we apply primal-dual methods. Previously for sequential auctions, Nguyen [13] provided through a primal-dual formulation price of anarchy bounds for sequential second-price sponsored search auctions, and for sequential first-price auctions with unit-demand valuations. Primal-dual methods have also been applied to inspect the efficiency of other classes of games. For example, Nadav and Roughgarden [9] characterized the set of outcomes for which smoothness [10] arguments apply for price of anarchy bounds by a primal-dual argument, and proposed a refinement of smoothness to obtain better price of anarchy bounds for coarse correlated equilibria. Nguyen [13], in addition to the previously mentioned results on sequential auctions, also provided price of anarchy bounds for congestion games and simultaneous auctions. Bilo [4] showed that constant-ratio efficiency bounds may be obtained for weighted congestion games even with quadratic and cubic latency functions through a primal-dual formulation. Likewise, Kulkarni and Mirrokni [7] provided bounds on the robust price of anarchy for several classes of games through the use of LP and Fenchel duality.

2   The Sequential Auction Model

We study two-buyer sequential auctions under the complete information model of Gale and Stegeman [6], and our notion of efficiency is that of Bae et al. [2,3]. Here, we present the model, notation and the concept of efficiency as in Ahunbay et al. [1]. There are T identical items which are sold one by one in a sequence of second-price auctions. Buyer $i \in \{1, 2\}$ has *value* $V_i(k)$ for winning k items. Given the valuations, we will say buyer i has *incremental value* $v_i(k)$ for obtaining a kth item: formally, $v_i(k) = V_i(k) - V_i(k-1)$. We also make the standard assumption of *free disposal*. Thus, the valuation functions are non-decreasing; in particular, the incremental values are non-negative, i.e. $v_i(k) \geq 0$, for any buyer i and any $k \in [T] := \{1, 2, \ldots, T\}$. Furthermore, we say the valuation function is *concave* if the incremental values are non-increasing; that is $v_i(k) \geq v_i(k+1)$ for any $k \in [T]$.

2.1   Forward Utilities and Equilibria

To find an equilibrium in the sequential auction we make a Markov perfection assumption: in each round of the auction, buyer i makes a bid conditioned on the number of items previously won by each buyer. The set of histories is then given by $\mathbb{H} = \{\mathbf{x} \in \mathbb{Z}^2 : \mathbf{x} \geq 0, x_1 + x_2 \leq T\}$. For $\mathbf{x} \in \mathbb{H}$, if $x_1 + x_2 = T$, then $\mathbf{x}$ is called a *terminal node*; otherwise, $\mathbf{x}$ is called a *decision node*.

We can find an *equilibrium* by computing the *forward utility* $u_i(\mathbf{x})$ of each buyer i at each node $\mathbf{x} \in \mathbb{H}$. The forward utility at $\mathbf{x}$ is the profit a buyer will earn from period $x_1 + x_2$ onwards, provided that each buyer i has won x_i items. This can be calculated by backwards induction on $x_1 + x_2$. If $\mathbf{x}$ is a terminal node then the auction has ended. Hence the forward utility of each buyer is zero at such a terminal node, i.e. $u_i(\mathbf{x}) = 0$ for any $i \in \{1, 2\}$. It remains to evaluate the forward utility of each buyer at a decision node $\mathbf{x}$. Decision node $\mathbf{x}$ has two *direct successors*: the decision node $\mathbf{x} + \mathbf{e}_i$, where $\mathbf{e}_i$ is the standard basis vector with the ith coordinate equal to 1 and the other coordinate equal to 0, corresponds to buyer i winning an item at $\mathbf{x}$. Then, in a second-price auction at decision node $\mathbf{x}$, the unique bidding strategies that survive the iterative elimination of weakly dominated strategies are:

$$
\begin{aligned}
b_1(\mathbf{x}) &= v_1(x_1 + 1) + u_1(x_1 + 1, x_2) - u_1(x_1, x_2 + 1) \\
b_2(\mathbf{x}) &= v_2(x_2 + 1) + u_2(x_1, x_2 + 1) - u_2(x_1 + 1, x_2)
\end{aligned}
\tag{1}
$$

Let $p(\mathbf{x})$ denote the price paid by the winning buyer at decision node $\mathbf{x}$. As this is a second-price auction, this price is simply the minimum of the two bids:

$$
p(\mathbf{x}) = \min_{i \in \{1, 2\}} b_i(\mathbf{x})
\tag{2}
$$

Now, if $b_1(\mathbf{x}) > b_2(\mathbf{x})$ then buyer 1 wins and the utilities of the buyers are given by:

$$
\begin{aligned}
u_1(\mathbf{x}) &= v_1(x_1 + 1) - b_2(\mathbf{x}) + u_1(x_1 + 1, x_2) \\
&= v_1(x_1 + 1) + u_1(x_1 + 1, x_2) + u_2(x_1 + 1, x_2) - u_2(x_1, x_2 + 1) - v_2(x_2 + 1) \\
u_2(\mathbf{x}) &= u_2(x_1 + 1, x_2)
\end{aligned}
\tag{3}
$$

Conversely, if $b_1(\mathbf{x}) < b_2(\mathbf{x})$ then buyer 2 wins, and the utilities are defined symmetrically as:

$$
\begin{aligned}
u_1(\mathbf{x}) &= u_1(x_1, x_2 + 1) \\
u_2(\mathbf{x}) &= v_2(x_2 + 1) - b_1(\mathbf{x}) + u_2(x_1, x_2 + 1) \\
&= v_2(x_2 + 1) + u_1(x_1, x_2 + 1) + u_2(x_1, x_2 + 1) - u_1(x_1 + 1, x_2) - v_1(x_1 + 1)
\end{aligned}
\tag{4}
$$

Finally, if $b_1(\mathbf{x}) = b_2(\mathbf{x})$ then by (1), for any buyer i:

$$
u_i(\mathbf{x} + \mathbf{e}_{-i}) = v_i(x_i + 1) - b_i(\mathbf{x}) + u_i(\mathbf{x} + \mathbf{e}_i)
\tag{5}
$$

Thus in the case of a tie, the utilities are invariant to which way the tie is broken. In particular, the forward utilities and bids of the buyers at each node are uniquely determined. Observe that this means that the Markov perfection assumption does not result in any loss of generality. We remark that a two-buyer sequential multiunit auction may be represented by a labelled directed tree rooted at decision node $(0, 0)$. This notation allows for a simple description of the forward utilities at each decision node. Denote by $U(\mathbf{x}) = \sum_{i \in \{1, 2\}} u_i(\mathbf{x})$ the sum of the forward utilities of the two buyers at node $\mathbf{x} = (x_1, x_2)$.

Claim 1. *Let* $\mathbf{x}$ *be a decision node. Then* $b_i(\mathbf{x}) \geq b_{-i}(\mathbf{x})$ *if and only if:*

$$v_i(x_i + 1) + U(\mathbf{x} + \mathbf{e}_i) \geq v_{-i}(x_{-i} + 1) + U(\mathbf{x} + \mathbf{e}_{-i})$$

Proof. By (1), we have $b_i(\mathbf{x}) \geq b_{-i}(\mathbf{x})$ at decision node $\mathbf{x}$ if and only if:

$$v_i(x_i + 1) + u_i(\mathbf{x} + \mathbf{e}_i) - u_i(\mathbf{x} + \mathbf{e}_{-i}) \geq v_{-i}(x_{-i} + 1) + u_{-i}(\mathbf{x} + \mathbf{e}_{-i}) - u_{-i}(\mathbf{x} + \mathbf{e}_i)$$

Rearranging, this is equivalent to:

$$v_i(x_i + 1) + u_i(\mathbf{x} + \mathbf{e}_i) + u_{-i}(\mathbf{x} + \mathbf{e}_i) \geq v_{-i}(x_{-i} + 1) + u_i(\mathbf{x} + \mathbf{e}_{-i}) + u_{-i}(\mathbf{x} + \mathbf{e}_{-i})$$

The claim then follows by definition of $U(\mathbf{x} + \mathbf{e}_i)$ and $U(\mathbf{x} + \mathbf{e}_{-i})$. □

Together with (3) and (4), Claim 1 implies the following.

Claim 2 ([6], Eq. 7). *The forward utility of buyer* i *at decision node* $\mathbf{x}$ *is exactly:*

$$u_i(\mathbf{x}) = \max_{j \in \{1,2\}} [v_j(x_j + 1) + U(\mathbf{x} + \mathbf{e}_j)] - v_{-i}(x_{-i} + 1) - u_{-i}(\mathbf{x} + \mathbf{e}_{-i}) \quad □$$

2.2   Social Welfare and Efficiency

The purpose of this paper is to evaluate the price of anarchy in the sequential auction. This requires us to formally define the social welfare of an allocation. To wit, let $\mathbf{x}$ be a decision node and denote by $t(\mathbf{x}) = T - x_1 - x_2$ the number of items for sale starting from $\mathbf{x}$. Then the *social welfare* from decision node $\mathbf{x}$ of the allocation where buyer 1 wins exactly k more items is:

$$
\begin{aligned}
\mathrm{sw}(k|\mathbf{x}) &= V_1(x_1 + k) - V_1(x_1) + V_2(T - x_1 - k) - V_2(x_2) \\
&= \sum_{j=x_1+1}^{x_1+k} v_1(j) + \sum_{j=x_2+1}^{T-x_1-k} v_2(j)
\end{aligned}
\tag{6}
$$

The *optimal social welfare* from decision node $\mathbf{x}$ is then given by:

$$\mathrm{OPT}(\mathbf{x}) = \max_{k \in [t(\mathbf{x})] \cup \{0\}} \mathrm{sw}(k|\mathbf{x}) \tag{7}$$

Our formal treatment of *efficiency* will relate the optimal social welfare at a decision node $\mathbf{x}$ to the social welfare of some terminal node $\mathbf{x} + (k, t(\mathbf{x}) - k)$, given that there exists some equilibrium path connecting the two nodes. To do this, we first present the formal definition of an *(equilibrium) path* from [1]. A *path* from decision node $\mathbf{x}$ is a $(t(\mathbf{x}) + 1)$-tuple $P = (\mathbf{x}^{t(\mathbf{x})}, \mathbf{x}^{t(\mathbf{x})-1}, ..., \mathbf{x}^1, \mathbf{x}^0)$ such that: (i) the path starts from $\mathbf{x}$, i.e. $\mathbf{x}^{t(\mathbf{x})} = \mathbf{x}$, and (ii) each successive node follows from some buyer j acquiring an item, i.e. for each $k \in [t(\mathbf{x})]$, $\mathbf{x}^{k-1} = \mathbf{x}^k + \mathbf{e}_j$ for some $j \in \{1, 2\}$. A path P is called an *equilibrium path* if each successive node follows from some buyer j acquiring an item by outbidding the other player, i.e. for any $k \in [t(\mathbf{x})]$, if $\mathbf{x}^{k-1} = \mathbf{x}^k + \mathbf{e}_j$, then $b_j(\mathbf{x}^k) \geq b_{-j}(\mathbf{x}^k)$.

Finally, for any path $P = (\mathbf{x}^{t(\mathbf{x})}, \mathbf{x}^{t(\mathbf{x})-1}, ..., \mathbf{x}^1, \mathbf{x}^0)$ and any $s \in [t(\mathbf{x})]$, we denote by $P^s = (\mathbf{x}^s, \mathbf{x}^{s-1}, ..., \mathbf{x}^1, \mathbf{x}^0)$ the final segment of P of $s+1$ nodes.

We now present our notion of efficiency. The *efficiency along path P*, denoted $\Gamma(P)$, satisfies:

$$\Gamma(P) = \begin{cases} \frac{\text{SW}(x_1^0 - x_1^{t(\mathbf{x})} | \mathbf{x})}{\text{OPT}(\mathbf{x})} & \text{OPT}(\mathbf{x}) \neq 0 \\ 1 & \text{OPT}(\mathbf{x}) = 0 \end{cases} \tag{8}$$

The *price of anarchy* (over some class) is then the infimum of the set of possible efficiency values along equilibrium paths of auctions in class. Here, of course, the class of auctions we consider is two-buyer sequential multiunit auctions.

We remark that because the valuation functions $V_i(\cdot)$ are non-decreasing, the price of anarchy is meaningful; in particular, it always lies between 0 and 1. To see this, as the incremental valuations are non-negative, (6) and (7) imply that $\text{OPT}(\mathbf{x}) \geq \text{SW}(k|\mathbf{x}) \geq 0$ at any decision node $\mathbf{x}$, for any $0 \leq k \leq t(\mathbf{x})$. Thus $\Gamma(P) \in [0, 1]$ for any path P starting from $\mathbf{x}$.

3   A Linear Programming Formulation

In this section, we provide a linear programming approach for bounding the price of anarchy in a two-buyer sequential auction. We begin in Subsect. 3.1 by presenting a set of structural results concerning equilibria in the sequential auction. These structural properties will induce a class of linear programs that can be used to lower bound the price of anarchy. Then, in Subsect. 3.2, we motivate and generate an additional class of valid inequalities that must hold along equilibrium paths. In Sects. 4 and 5, we will prove that the incorporation of these valid inequalities into our linear programs suffices to provide tight price of anarchy bounds for concave valuation functions and general valuation functions, respectively.

3.1   Structural Results

Let us first note two results from Gale and Stegeman [6]. The first is the intuitive result that buyer i does not derive any benefit from letting buyer $-i$ win an item at no cost:

Lemma 1 ([6], Lemma 1). *Let $\mathbf{x}$ be a decision node. Then $u_i(\mathbf{x}) \geq u_i(\mathbf{x}+\mathbf{e}_{-i})$ for any buyer i. Moreover, this inequality is strict if and only if $b_i(\mathbf{x}) > b_{-i}(\mathbf{x})$, that is, buyer i wins with a strictly greater bid at decision node $\mathbf{x}$.*   □

The second result is the *declining price anomaly*: prices are non-increasing along any equilibrium path.

Lemma 2 ([6], Lemma 2). *Let $\mathbf{x}$ be a decision node such that $t(\mathbf{x}) > 1$. If buyer i wins at $\mathbf{x}$, then $p(\mathbf{x}) \geq p(\mathbf{x}+\mathbf{e}_i)$. Moreover, $p(\mathbf{x}) = p(\mathbf{x}+\mathbf{e}_i)$ if and only if buyer i also wins at decision node $\mathbf{x}+\mathbf{e}_{-i}$.*   □

Because the forward utilities are zero at each terminal node, an immediate consequence of Lemma 1 is that the forward utility of any buyer at any decision node is non-negative.

Corollary 1. *Let* $\mathbf{x} \in \mathbb{H}$ *and* $i \in \{1, 2\}$, *then* $u_i(\mathbf{x}) \geq 0$. □

Furthermore, given the assumption of non-decreasing valuation functions, Lemma 2 implies that prices are non-negative.

Lemma 3. *At any decision node* $\mathbf{x}$, $p(\mathbf{x}) \geq 0$.

We may now derive a simple upper bound on the forward utility of any buyer. Observe that, for any equilibrium path P starting at $\mathbf{x}$, the forward utility of buyer i at $\mathbf{x}$ is the value it has for the items it wins on the path P minus the total price it pays. Thus, because the prices are non-negative by Lemma 3, the total value buyer i has for the items it wins on the equilibrium path P is an upper bound on its forward utility at $\mathbf{x}$.

Lemma 4. *Let* $\mathbf{x}$ *be a decision node and* $P = (\mathbf{x}^{t(\mathbf{x})}, ..., \mathbf{x}^0)$ *an equilibrium path starting at* $\mathbf{x}$. *Then, for any* $i \in \{1, 2\}$, $u_i(\mathbf{x}) \leq \sum_{j=x_i+1}^{x_i^0} v_i(j)$. □

Claim 2 also immediately provides an explicit form for the difference of the buyers' forward utilities.

Lemma 5. *Let* $\mathbf{x}$ *be a decision node. Then:*

$$u_i(\mathbf{x}) - u_{-i}(\mathbf{x}) = v_i(x_i + 1) + u_i(\mathbf{x} + \mathbf{e}_i) - v_{-i}(x_{-i} + 1) - u_{-i}(\mathbf{x} + \mathbf{e}_{-i})$$ □

Finally, we turn our attention to the efficiency of paths. As the valuations are non-decreasing, we can show that the efficiency along a path $P = (\mathbf{x}^{t(\mathbf{x})}, \mathbf{x}^{t(\mathbf{x})-1}, ..., \mathbf{x}^1, \mathbf{x}^0)$ may be bounded below by the efficiency along a specific subpath P^s of P (which may be P itself), such that the unique optimum allocation from $\mathbf{x}^s$ has one buyer winning all the remaining items. The result generalises arguments made in the proofs of Theorem 2 in [3], and Lemma 6.2 and Lemma 6.3 in [1] to possibly non-concave valuations.

Lemma 6. *Let* $\mathbf{x}$ *be a decision node and* $P = (\mathbf{x}^{t(\mathbf{x})}, \mathbf{x}^{t(\mathbf{x})-1}, ..., \mathbf{x}^1, \mathbf{x}^0)$ *a path from* $\mathbf{x}$. *Then:*

(a) *If* $\mathbf{x}^{t(\mathbf{x})-1} = \mathbf{x} + \mathbf{e}_1$ *and* $\exists k > 0, \text{SW}(k|\mathbf{x}) = \text{OPT}(\mathbf{x})$, *then* $\Gamma(P) \geq \Gamma(P^{t(\mathbf{x})-1})$.
(b) *If* $\mathbf{x}^{t(\mathbf{x})-1} = \mathbf{x} + \mathbf{e}_2$ *and* $\exists k < t(\mathbf{x}), \text{SW}(k|\mathbf{x}) = \text{OPT}(\mathbf{x})$, *then* $\Gamma(P) \geq \Gamma(P^{t(\mathbf{x})-1})$.

Proof. It suffices to prove (a), as (b) then follows from relabelling the buyers. If $\text{OPT}(\mathbf{x}) = 0$ then, because the efficiency is between 0 and 1 along any path, we have $\Gamma(P) = 1 \geq \Gamma(P^{t(\mathbf{x})-1})$. So suppose that $\text{OPT}(x) > 0$. Note that $t(\mathbf{x}+\mathbf{e}_1) = t(\mathbf{x}) - 1$. So, by definition (6), $\text{SW}(k|\mathbf{x}+\mathbf{e}_1) = \text{SW}(k+1|\mathbf{x}) - v_1(x_1 + 1)$ for any $k \in [t(\mathbf{x} + \mathbf{e}_1)] \cup \{0\}$. By assumption, there exists $k > 0$ such that $\text{SW}(k|\mathbf{x}) = \text{OPT}(\mathbf{x})$. Thus $\text{OPT}(\mathbf{x} + \mathbf{e}_1) = \text{OPT}(\mathbf{x}) - v_1(x_1 + 1)$. Therefore:

$$\Gamma(P) = \frac{\text{SW}(x_1^0 - x_1 | \mathbf{x})}{\text{OPT}(\mathbf{x})} = \frac{\text{SW}(x^0 - x_1 - 1 | \mathbf{x} + \mathbf{e}_1) + v_1(x_1 + 1)}{\text{OPT}(\mathbf{x} + \mathbf{e}_1) + v_1(x_1 + 1)}$$

If $\text{OPT}(\mathbf{x} + \mathbf{e}_1) = 0$ then $\Gamma(P) = 1$ and so $\Gamma(P) \geq \Gamma(P^{t(\mathbf{x})-1})$, as desired. Therefore, we may assume that $\text{OPT}(\mathbf{x} + \mathbf{e}_1) > 0$. Then:

$$
\begin{aligned}
\Gamma(P) &= \frac{\text{SW}(x^0 - x_1 - 1 | \mathbf{x} + \mathbf{e}_1) + v_1(x_1 + 1)}{\text{OPT}(\mathbf{x} + \mathbf{e}_1) + v_1(x_1 + 1)} \\
&\geq \frac{\text{SW}(x^0 - (x_1 + 1) | \mathbf{x} + \mathbf{e}_1)}{\text{OPT}(\mathbf{x} + \mathbf{e}_1)} = \Gamma(P^{t(\mathbf{x})-1})
\end{aligned}
$$

Here the inequality holds because $v_1(x_1 + 1) \geq 0$.   □

Corollary 2. *Let $\mathbf{x}$ be a decision node and $P = (\mathbf{x}^{t(\mathbf{x})}, \mathbf{x}^{t(\mathbf{x})-1}, ..., \mathbf{x}^1, \mathbf{x}^0)$ a path from $\mathbf{x}$. If $\Gamma(P) < \Gamma(P^{t(\mathbf{x})-1})$ then exactly one of the following holds:*

(a) *Buyer 1 winning all the items is the unique optimal allocation but buyer 2 wins an item at $\mathbf{x}$, i.e. $\arg\max_{k \in [t(\mathbf{x})] \cup \{0\}} \text{SW}(k | \mathbf{x}) = \{t(\mathbf{x})\}$ and $\mathbf{x}^{t(\mathbf{x})-1} = \mathbf{x}^{t(\mathbf{x})} + \mathbf{e}_2$.*

(b) *Buyer 2 winning all the items is the unique optimal allocation but buyer 1 wins an item at $\mathbf{x}$, i.e. $\arg\max_{k \in [t(\mathbf{x})] \cup \{0\}} \text{SW}(k | \mathbf{x}) = \{0\}$ and $\mathbf{x}^{t(\mathbf{x})-1} = \mathbf{x}^{t(\mathbf{x})} + \mathbf{e}_1$.*   □

Corollary 2 implies that, if we are interested in obtaining a lower bound for efficiency, it is sufficient to consider auctions in which the unique optimal allocation is $(T, 0)$ but buyer 1 wins less than T items on an equilibrium path. Furthermore, any auction with efficiency less than 1 must have positive optimal welfare. Consequently, by multiplying all valuations, forward utilities and bids by a constant, we may normalize so that $\text{OPT}(\mathbf{0}) = \text{SW}(T | \mathbf{0}) = 1$.

Now, suppose further that buyer 1 wins k items on the equilibrium path. Then efficiency is equal to $\text{SW}(k | \mathbf{0})$. To obtain a lower bound on the efficiency, we may consider minimizing $\text{SW}(k | \mathbf{0})$ subject to constraints following from our assumptions. Note that the objective is linear in the incremental valuations of buyers, and so too are the constraints that imply $\text{OPT}(\mathbf{0}) = \text{SW}(T | \mathbf{0}) = 1$. We may, of course, also add in any valid inequality that holds when buyer 1 wins k items on the equilibrium path. Then the following class of linear programs provides lower bounds on the efficiency of the auction:

$$\text{minimize} \sum_{j=1}^{k} v_1(j) + \sum_{j=1}^{T-k} v_2(j) \tag{9}$$

$$\text{subject to} \qquad \sum_{j=1}^{T} v_1(j) = 1$$

$$\sum_{j=1}^{l} v_1(j) + \sum_{j=1}^{T-l} v_2(j) \le 1 \qquad \forall 0 \le l < T$$

$$v_i(j) \ge 0 \qquad \forall i \in \{1,2\}, j \in [T]$$

$$(+ \text{ valid inequalities})$$

Specifically, we obtain a lower bound for the efficiency of a T item auction by finding the minimum value of the linear program for $0 \le k < T$. Of course, the lower bound produced will depend upon the choice of additional valid inequalities. The difficulty is to select inequalities that must be satisfied at equilibrium **and** that are strong enough to provide an exact efficiency bound. Thus, our task reduces to finding such a set of inequalities.

3.2 A Set of Valid Inequalities

The following theorem will allow us to obtain a collection of valid inequalities that are strong enough to induce tight price of anarchy bounds.

Theorem 3. *Let* $\mathbf{x}$ *be a decision node and* P *an equilibrium path from* $\mathbf{x}$ *with endpoint* $(k, T - k)$. *Then:*

$$\sum_{j=0}^{t(\mathbf{x})} u_2(\mathbf{x} + j\mathbf{e}_1) \le \sum_{i=x_2+1}^{T-k} \left[(T - x_1 - i + 1) \cdot v_2(i) - \sum_{j=k+1}^{T-i+1} v_1(j) \right] \tag{10}$$

Proof. Proceed by induction on $t(\mathbf{x})$. The base case $t(\mathbf{x}) = 1$ is trivial, so consider $t(\mathbf{x}) > 1$. First suppose that, on an equilibrium path P, buyer 1 wins at decision node $\mathbf{x}$. Then:

$$\sum_{j=0}^{t(\mathbf{x})} u_2(\mathbf{x} + j\mathbf{e}_1) = u_2(\mathbf{x}) + \sum_{j=1}^{t(\mathbf{x})} u_2(\mathbf{x} + j\mathbf{e}_1) = u_2(\mathbf{x}) + \sum_{j=0}^{t(\mathbf{x}+\mathbf{e}_1)} u_2\big((\mathbf{x} + \mathbf{e}_1) + j\mathbf{e}_1\big)$$

$$\le u_2(\mathbf{x}) + \sum_{i=x_2+1}^{T-k} \left[(T - (x_1 + 1) - i + 1) \cdot v_2(i) - \sum_{j=k+1}^{T-i+1} v_1(j) \right]$$

$$\le \sum_{i=x_2+1}^{T-k} \left[(T - x_1 - i + 1) \cdot v_2(i) - \sum_{j=k+1}^{T-i+1} v_1(j) \right]$$

Here the second equality holds by the fact that $t(\mathbf{x} + \mathbf{e}_1) = t(\mathbf{x}) - 1$. The first inequality follows from the induction hypothesis, because $P^{t(\mathbf{x})-1}$ is an equilibrium path from $\mathbf{x} + \mathbf{e}_1$ to $(k, T - k)$. The second inequality arises from the upper bound on $u(\mathbf{x})$ given by Lemma 4.

Next suppose buyer 2 wins at decision node $\mathbf{x}$. Then we have:

$$\sum_{j=0}^{t(\mathbf{x})} u_2(\mathbf{x} + j\mathbf{e}_1) = v_2(x_2 + 1) + u_2(\mathbf{x} + \mathbf{e}_2) + u_1(\mathbf{x} + \mathbf{e}_2)$$

$$- v_1(x_1 + 1) - u_1(\mathbf{x} + \mathbf{e}_1) + \sum_{j=1}^{t(\mathbf{x})-1} u_2(\mathbf{x} + j\mathbf{e}_1) \qquad (11)$$

Here the equality holds by definition (4) of $u(\mathbf{x})$ and by noting that $u_2(\mathbf{x} + t(\mathbf{x})\mathbf{e}_1) = 0$ because $\mathbf{x} + t(\mathbf{x})\mathbf{e}_1$ is a terminal node.

To simplify this we make repeated applications of Lemma 5 on $-u_1(\cdot)$:

$$-u_1(\mathbf{x} + \mathbf{e}_1) = - \sum_{j=1}^{t(\mathbf{x})-1} u_2(\mathbf{x} + j\mathbf{e}_1) + (t(\mathbf{x}) - 1) \cdot v_2(x_2 + 1)$$

$$+ \sum_{j=1}^{t(\mathbf{x})-1} u_2(\mathbf{x} + \mathbf{e}_2 + j\mathbf{e}_1) - \sum_{j=x_1+2}^{T-x_2} v_1(j) \qquad (12)$$

In turn, by Lemma 4, $u_1(\mathbf{x} + \mathbf{e}_2) \leq \sum_{j=x_1+1}^{k} v_1(j)$. Plugging this and (12) into (11) and noting that $t(\mathbf{x} + \mathbf{e}_2) = t(\mathbf{x}) - 1$, we obtain:

$$\sum_{j=0}^{t(\mathbf{x})} u_2(\mathbf{x} + j\mathbf{e}_1) \leq t(\mathbf{x}) \cdot v_2(x_2 + 1) - \sum_{j=k+1}^{T-x_2} v_1(j) + \sum_{j=0}^{t(\mathbf{x}+\mathbf{e}_2)} u_2(\mathbf{x} + \mathbf{e}_2 + j\mathbf{e}_1)$$

As $P^{t(\mathbf{x})-1}$ is an equilibrium path from $\mathbf{x} + \mathbf{e}_2$ to $(k, T - k)$, by the induction hypothesis we obtain the desired inequality. □

Note that given an equilibrium path P from $\mathbf{0}$ to $(k, T - k)$, Theorem 3 and Corollary 1 imply a class of valid inequalities corresponding to each node x^t of P. However these inequalities depend on the specific form of P and we want inequalities valid for *every* equilibrium path from $\mathbf{0}$ to $(k, T - k)$. The following theorem provides such valid inequalities.

Theorem 4. *Suppose P is an equilibrium path from $\mathbf{0}$ to $(k, T - k)$. Then for any $0 \leq \ell < T - k$:*

$$\sum_{i=\ell+1}^{T-k} \left[(T - i + 1) \cdot v_2(i) - \sum_{j=k+1}^{T-i+1} v_1(j) \right] \geq 0 \qquad (13)$$

Proof. Let P be an equilibrium path from $\mathbf{0}$ to $(k, T - k)$, and $0 \leq \ell < T - k$ an integer. Observe that P must contain a decision node (x_ℓ, ℓ); otherwise, the endpoint of the path P could not have been $(k, T - k)$. Now, by Theorem 3 and Corollary 1:

$$\sum_{i=\ell+1}^{T-k} \left[(T - x_\ell - i + 1) \cdot v_2(i) - \sum_{j=k+1}^{T-i+1} v_1(j) \right] \geq 0$$

On the other hand, $\sum_{i=\ell+1}^{T-k} x_\ell \cdot v_2(i) \geq 0$ as incremental valuations are non-negative and $x_\ell \geq 0$. Summing up the two inequalities yields the desired result.

$\square$

To conclude this section, we write inequality (13) in a more amenable form. Specifically, for any given $T \in \mathbb{N}$, $0 \leq k \leq T$ and $0 \leq \ell < T - k$, an equivalent formulation is:

$$\sum_{i=\ell+1}^{T-k} (T - i + 1) \cdot v_2(i) - \sum_{i=k+1}^{T-\ell} (T - i - \ell + 1) \cdot v_1(i) \geq 0 \qquad (14)$$

In the remainder of this paper, we will show that the addition of the valid inqualities (14) will allow us to obtain sharp bounds on the efficiency of sequential auctions for both concave and general valuation functions.

4   The Price of Anarchy with Concave Valuation Functions

In this section, we prove that the price of anarchy is exactly $\left(1 - \frac{1}{e}\right)$ when both buyers have concave valuation functions. We begin by deriving a lower bound conditional on the final allocation.

Theorem 5. *Let each buyer have a non-decreasing, concave valuation function. If $(T, 0)$ is an optimal allocation and P is an equilibrium path from $\mathbf{0}$ to $(k, T - k)$ then:*

$$\Gamma(P) \geq \frac{1}{T} \left(k + \sum_{j=1}^{T-k} \frac{j}{k+j} \right)$$

Proof. Recall buyer i has a concave valuation function if and only if the incremental valuations satisfy $v_i(j) \geq v_i(j + 1)$ for all $1 \leq j \leq T - 1$. The addition of these inequalities plus the valid inequalities (14) to linear program (9) yields a linear program whose value provides a lower bound on the efficiency of the auction when $(T, 0)$ is an optimal allocation with $\text{OPT}(\mathbf{0}) = 1$ and there is an equilibrium path from $\mathbf{0}$ to $(k, T - k)$. Further, by weak duality we may lower bound this primal LP by considering its dual LP.

In the dual LP, we assign a dual variable σ_l to the welfare constraint for when buyer 1 wins l items (for $0 \leq l \leq T$). We assign a dual variable $\kappa_{i,j}$ for each concavity constraint $j \in [T-1]$ of buyer i; for convenience we also set $\kappa_{i,0} = \kappa_{i,T} = 0$. Finally, we have a dual variable μ_ℓ for the valid inequalities of type (14) for $0 \le \ell < T - k$. The dual linear program is then:

$$\text{maximize} \quad \sigma_T + \sum_{l=0}^{T-1} \sigma_l$$

$$\text{subject to} \quad \sum_{l=i}^{T} \sigma_l - \kappa_{1,i} + \kappa_{1,i-1} \le 1 \qquad \forall\, 1 \le i \le k$$

$$\sum_{l=i}^{T} \sigma_l - \kappa_{1,i} + \kappa_{1,i-1} - \sum_{\ell=0}^{T-i}(T - i - \ell + 1) \cdot \mu_\ell \le 0 \qquad \forall\, k+1 \le i \le T$$

$$\sum_{l=0}^{T-i} \sigma_l - \kappa_{2,i} + \kappa_{2,i-1} + \sum_{\ell=0}^{i-1}(T - i + 1) \cdot \mu_\ell \le 1 \qquad \forall\, 1 \le i \le T - k$$

$$\sum_{l=0}^{T-i} \sigma_l - \kappa_{2,i} + \kappa_{2,i-1} \le 0 \qquad \forall\, T - k + 1 \le i \le T$$

$$\sigma_T \in \mathbb{R}$$
$$\sigma_l \le 0 \qquad \forall\, 0 \le l < T$$
$$\kappa_{i,j} \le 0 \qquad \forall i \in \{1,2\}, j \in [T-1]$$
$$\kappa_{i,j} = 0 \qquad \forall i \in \{1,2\}, j \in \{0, T\}$$
$$\mu_\ell \ge 0 \qquad \forall\, 0 \le \ell < T - k$$

Consider the dual solution given by:

$$\sigma_T = \frac{1}{T}\left(k + \sum_{j=1}^{T-k} \frac{j}{k+j} \right) \tag{15}$$

$$\mu_0 = \frac{1}{T}$$

$$\mu_\ell = \frac{1}{T-\ell} - \frac{1}{T-\ell+1} \qquad \forall\, 0 < \ell < T - k$$

$$\kappa_{1,i} = \begin{cases} i \cdot (\sigma_T - 1) & 0 < i \le k \\ -(T - i) \cdot \sigma_T + \sum_{j=0}^{T-i-1} \frac{T-i-j}{T-j} & k \le i \le T - 1 \end{cases}$$

and all other dual variables set to 0. Through meticulous case analysis, this solution can be shown to be feasible. This dual solution has value $\sigma_T = \frac{1}{T}(k + \sum_{j=1}^{T-k} \frac{j}{k+j})$. It follows that the efficiency is at least $\frac{1}{T}(k + \sum_{j=1}^{T-k} \frac{j}{k+j})$. □

Theorem 6. *There exists a 2-buyer sequential auction with the following properties: both buyers have non-decreasing, concave valuation functions, the allocation $(T, 0)$ maximizes social welfare and there is an equilibrium path P from $\mathbf{0}$ to $(k, T - k)$ with:*

$$\Gamma(P) = \frac{1}{T}\left(k + \sum_{j=1}^{T-k} \frac{j}{k+j}\right)$$

Proof. Consider a sequential auction with the following valuation profiles:

$$v_1(j) = 1 \qquad\qquad 1 \le j \le T$$

$$v_2(j) = \begin{cases} \frac{T-k-j+1}{T-j+1} & 1 \le j \le T-k \\ 0 & \text{else} \end{cases}$$

Observe that the unique optimal allocation is $(T, 0)$ with social welfare $\text{OPT}(\mathbf{0}) = T$. Meanwhile, $\text{SW}(k|\mathbf{0}) = k + \sum_{j=1}^{T-k} \frac{j}{k+j}$. Therefore, it suffices to show that there exists an equilibrium path from $\mathbf{0}$ to $(k, T-k)$. Computation of forward utilities shows that for any $0 \le \ell < T - k$ we have $b_1(0, \ell) = b_2(0, \ell)$, and at any other decision node $\mathbf{x}$, we have $b_1(\mathbf{x}) > b_2(\mathbf{x})$. Hence by breaking all ties in favour of buyer 2, we obtain an equilibrium path P from $\mathbf{0}$ to $(k, T-k)$ on which buyer 2 wins the first $T - k$ items and buyer 1 wins the last k items. $\qquad\square$

These conditional bounds readily extend to an asymptotically tight constant lower bound for efficiency.

Theorem 7. *Given non-decreasing, concave valuation functions. For any $T \in \mathbb{N}$, any equilibrium path P from $\mathbf{0}$ has efficiency at least $1 - \frac{1}{e}$. This bound is asymptotically tight as $T \to \infty$.*

Proof. Fix T and let P be an equilibrium path from $\mathbf{0}$. By Corollary 2, we may assume that $(T, 0)$ is the unique optimal allocation. If buyer 1 wins T items then $\Gamma(P) = 1 > 1 - \frac{1}{e}$. So suppose that buyer 1 wins $k < T$ items. By Theorem 5, we have $\Gamma(P) \ge \frac{1}{T}\left(k + \sum_{j=1}^{T-k} \frac{j}{k+j}\right)$.

Next, observe that:

$$\frac{1}{T} \cdot \sum_{j=1}^{T-k} \frac{j}{k+j} = \sum_{j=0}^{T-k-1} \frac{1}{T} \cdot \frac{1 - k/T - j/T}{1 - j/T} \ge \int_0^{1-k/T} \frac{1 - k/T - x}{1 - x}\, dx$$

The inequality holds as we have an *upper Darboux sum*. Therefore:

$$\Gamma(P) \ge \min_{k \in [T] \cup \{0\}} \frac{k}{T} + \int_0^{1-k/T} \frac{1 - k/T - x}{1 - x}\, dx$$

$$\ge \inf_{\alpha \in [0,1]} \alpha + \int_0^{1-\alpha} \frac{1 - \alpha - x}{1 - x}\, dx = \inf_{\alpha \in [0,1]} 1 + \alpha \ln \alpha$$

The infimum is attained for $\alpha = \frac{1}{e}$, with value $1 - \frac{1}{e}$. Setting $k = \lfloor T/e \rfloor$ for the valuations given in Theorem 6 shows the asymptotic tightness of the bound. $\quad\square$

5   The Price of Anarchy with General Valuation Functions

In this section we consider the case of general non-decreasing valuation functions. We show that the price of anarchy is then exactly $1/T$. In particular, this bound is no longer a constant but deteriorates linearly with the number of items for sale in the auction. This value was first identified in [3] as an upper bound for the price of anarchy for general non-decreasing valuations. Again, we begin with the lower bound, and then present the matching upper bound.

Theorem 8. *Let the buyers have non-decreasing valuation functions. Then any equilibrium path has efficiency at least $1/T$, where T is the number of items.*

Proof. By induction on T. The bound holds for the base case $T = 1$ because single-item second-price auctions have full efficiency. Now consider $T > 1$ and suppose the valuations are such that there exists an equilibrium path P from $\mathbf{0}$ with $\Gamma(P) \leq 1/T$. Note it cannot be that $\Gamma(P) \geq \Gamma(P^{T-1})$; otherwise, by the induction hypothesis, $\Gamma(P) \geq 1/(T-1)$. Therefore, by Corollary 2, we may assume that the unique optimal allocation is $(T, 0)$ and that buyer 2 wins $T - k > 0$ items on the equilibrium path P.

To lower bound $\Gamma(P)$, we add the valid inequalities (14) to the linear program (9) to obtain a linear program whose value is a lower bound on the efficiency of the auction when $(T, 0)$ is an optimal allocation with $\text{OPT}(\mathbf{0}) = 1$ and there is an equilibrium path from $\mathbf{0}$ to $(k, T - k)$. Again to lower bound this primal LP we consider its dual LP. We assign a dual variable σ_l to the welfare constraint for when buyer 1 wins l items (for $0 \leq l \leq T$). We have a dual variable μ_ℓ for the valid inequalities of type (14) for $0 \leq \ell < T - k$. The dual linear program is then:

$$\text{maximize} \quad \sigma_T + \sum_{l=0}^{T-1} \sigma_l$$

$$\text{subject to} \quad \sum_{l=i}^{T} \sigma_l \leq 1 \qquad \forall\, 1 \leq i \leq k$$

$$\sum_{l=i}^{T} \sigma_l - \sum_{\ell=0}^{T-i} (T - i - \ell + 1) \cdot \mu_\ell \leq 0 \qquad \forall\, k+1 \leq i \leq T$$

$$\sum_{l=0}^{T-i} \sigma_l + \sum_{\ell=0}^{i-1} (T - i + 1) \cdot \mu_\ell \leq 1 \qquad \forall\, 1 \leq i \leq T - k$$

$$\sum_{l=0}^{T-i} \sigma_l \leq 0 \qquad \forall\, T - k + 1 \leq i \leq T$$

$$\sigma_T \in \mathbb{R}$$

$$\sigma_l \leq 0 \qquad \forall\, 0 \leq l < T$$

$$\mu_\ell \geq 0 \qquad \forall\, 0 \leq \ell < T - k$$

Now consider setting $\sigma_T = \mu_0 = 1/T$ and all other variables 0. It is easy to verify that this is dual feasible and has objective value $1/T$. This implies that $\Gamma(P) \geq 1/T$ as desired. □

Theorem 9. *There exists a 2-buyer sequential auction with the following properties: both buyers have non-decreasing valuation functions, the allocation $(T, 0)$ maximizes social welfare and there is an equilibrium path P from $\mathbf{0}$ with:*

$$\Gamma(P) = \frac{1}{T}$$

Proof. Consider a sequential auction with the following valuation profiles:

$$v_1(j) = \begin{cases} 0 & j < T \\ 1 & j = T \end{cases} \qquad v_2(j) = \begin{cases} 1/T & j = 1 \\ 0 & j > 1 \end{cases}$$

With the given valuation profile, the optimal allocation is $(T, 0)$ with a welfare of 1, while any other allocation has social welfare $1/T$. Solving for forward utilities by backwards induction yields $b_1(\mathbf{0}) = b_2(\mathbf{0}) = 1/T$, so buyer 1 and 2 tie at decision node $\mathbf{0}$. Then by breaking the tie in favour of buyer 2, there exists an equilibrium path from $\mathbf{0}$ which awards at least one item to buyer 2, attaining an efficiency of $1/T$. □

Theorem 10. *The price of anarchy for 2-buyer sequential auctions with non-decreasing valuations is exactly $1/T$.* □

References

1. Ahunbay, M., Lucier, B., Vetta, A.: Two-buyer sequential multiunit auctions with no overbidding. arXiv preprint arXiv:2006.03142 (2020)
2. Bae, J., Beigman, E., Berry, R., Honig, M.L., Vohra, R.: On the efficiency of sequential auctions for spectrum sharing. In: Proceedings of the International Conference on Game Theory for Networks, pp. 199–205 (2009)
3. Bae, J., Beigman, E., Berry, R.A., Honig, M.L., Vohra, R.: Sequential bandwidth and power auctions for distributed spectrum sharing. IEEE J. Sel. Areas Commun. **26**(7), 1193–1203 (2008)
4. Bilò, V.: A unifying tool for bounding the quality of non-cooperative solutions in weighted congestion games. In: Erlebach, T., Persiano, G. (eds.) WAOA 2012. LNCS, vol. 7846, pp. 215–228. Springer, Heidelberg (2013). https://doi.org/10.1007/978-3-642-38016-7_18
5. Feldman, M., Lucier, B., Syrgkanis, V.: Limits of efficiency in sequential auctions. In: Chen, Y., Immorlica, N. (eds.) WINE 2013. LNCS, vol. 8289, pp. 160–173. Springer, Heidelberg (2013). https://doi.org/10.1007/978-3-642-45046-4_14
6. Gale, I.L., Stegeman, M.: Sequential auctions of endogenously valued objects. Games Econ. Behav. **36**(1), 74–103 (2001). https://doi.org/10.1006/game.2000.0802
7. Kulkarni, J., Mirrokni, V.: Robust price of anarchy bounds via LP and fenchel duality. In: Proceedings of the 2015 Annual ACM-SIAM Symposium on Discrete Algorithms, pp. 1030–1049 (2015). https://doi.org/10.1137/1.9781611973730.70

8. Leme, R.P., Syrgkanis, V., Tardos, E.: Sequential auctions and externalities. In: Proceedings of the 2012 Annual ACM-SIAM Symposium on Discrete Algorithms, pp. 869–886 (2012). https://doi.org/10.1137/1.9781611973099.70

9. Nadav, U., Roughgarden, T.: The limits of smoothness: a primal-dual framework for price of anarchy bounds. In: Saberi, A. (ed.) WINE 2010. LNCS, vol. 6484, pp. 319–326. Springer, Heidelberg (2010). https://doi.org/10.1007/978-3-642-17572-5_26

10. Roughgarden, T.: Intrinsic robustness of the price of anarchy. In: Proceedings of the 41st Annual ACM Symposium on Theory of Computing, pp. 513–522. Association for Computing Machinery, New York (2009). https://doi.org/10.1145/1536414.1536485

11. Syrgkanis, V., Tardos, E.: Bayesian sequential auctions. In: Proceedings of the 13th ACM Conference on Electronic Commerce, pp. 929–944. Association for Computing Machinery, New York (2012). https://doi.org/10.1145/2229012.2229082

12. Syrgkanis, V., Tardos, E.: Composable and efficient mechanisms. In: Proceedings of 45th Annual ACM Symposium on Theory of Computing, pp. 211–220. Association for Computing Machinery, New York (2013). https://doi.org/10.1145/2488608.2488635

13. Thang, N.K.: Game efficiency through linear programming duality. arXiv Preprint arXiv:1708.06499v1 (2017)

Revenue-Optimal Deterministic Auctions for Multiple Buyers with Ordinal Preferences over Fixed-Price Items

Will Ma$^{(\boxtimes)}$ (iD)

Graduate School of Business, Columbia University, New York City, NY 10027, USA
`wm2428@gsb.columbia.edu`

Abstract. In this paper, we introduce a Bayesian revenue-maximizing mechanism design model where the items have fixed, exogenously-given prices. Buyers are unit-demand and have an ordinal ranking over purchasing either one of these items at its given price, or purchasing nothing. This model arises naturally from the assortment optimization problem, in that the single-buyer optimization problem over deterministic mechanisms reduces to deciding on an assortment of items to "show". We study its multi-buyer generalization in the simplest setting of single-winner auctions, or more broadly, any service-constrained environment. Our main result is that if the buyer rankings are drawn independently from Markov Chain ranking models, then the optimal mechanism is computationally tractable, and structurally a virtual welfare maximizer. We also show that for ranking distributions not induced by Markov Chains, the optimal mechanism may not be a virtual welfare maximizer.

Keywords: Bayesian mechanism design · Assortment optimization

1 Introduction

In this paper, we study auction design for unit-demand buyers when the prices of the products are fixed. In particular, a seller is endowed with n substitutable products with exogenously-given prices $r_1, \ldots, r_n \geq 0$. A buyer's outcome and payment from participating in the auction will always take the form "receive product j and pay price r_j", for some $j = 0, \ldots, n$, where we let $j = 0$ represent the "no-purchase" option with $r_0 = 0$.

We restrict attention to mechanisms that are *deterministic* and *dominant-strategy* (DS) truthful. Under this restriction, a buyer's preference is fully captured by a weak ordering of the options "buy product j for price r_j", for $j = 0, \ldots, n$. Our mechanisms will be DS *incentive-compatible*, where a buyer can never get a more-preferred option from lying about her ranking, and DS

The author thanks anonymous reviewers, whose detailed suggestions helped improve and polish the paper.

individually-rational, where a buyer can never get an option she ranks below the no-purchase option.

We study revenue maximization in a Bayesian setting, where the buyers' rankings are drawn from *known, independent* (non-identical) distributions. There is also a feasibility constraint on the inventory of products available to be allocated to buyers. The problem is then: maximize the expected revenue of a mechanism with respect to these random rankings, subject to it being deterministic, DS incentive-compatible and individually-rational, and satisfying the feasibility constraint in its allocations.

1.1 Motivation and Related Problems

We now explain why we believe this to be a well-motivated problem that arises naturally in relation to the streams of existing literature.

Mechanism Design Without Money. Although we use the language of "prices" and "revenue", we are technically designing mechanisms "without money", because the auctioneer cannot charge arbitrary payments. Our use of ordinal preferences with an outside option has previously appeared in the house allocation problem [17,19], and our focus on deterministic mechanisms and DS truthfulness is inherited from the more general context of allocation mechanisms under one-sided ordinal preferences [4,5,20,21]. Our paper is different from these lines of work in that we are maximizing the Bayesian expectation of a cardinal objective function, where we have been given real numbers $r_1, \ldots, r_n$ as the rewards for the successful allocations of the products. By contrast, these lines of work derive settings and conditions under which the feasible space of mechanisms can be nicely characterized, e.g. using top-trading cycles [17,19], serial dictatorships [21], or the uniform allocation rule [20].

Bayesian Mechanism Design. The difference between our mechanisms and those for Bayesian unit-demand revenue maximization [7,9,10] is that we must charge the fixed prices $r_1, \ldots, r_n$, instead of being able to tweak the payments to entice buyers into higher-valued products. Also, the distributional assumption we make on the buyers' rankings (namely, being generated by Markov chains) is combinatorial, and generally incomparable to the assumptions made in this literature (e.g. on valuations being independent across products).

Assortment Optimization and Sequential Posted Assortment. When there is a single buyer, our mechanism design problem reduces to the assortment optimization problem, where the mechanism must decide on a subset of products to show[1] the buyer. This is a standard problem in revenue management [22]

---

[1] We will formally prove this reduction using the taxation principle. Note that the optimal mechanism may not show all products, instead "hiding" some lower-priced products to prevent them from being chosen in lieu of higher-priced products.

motivated by brick-and-mortar retailers who do not control the pricing but can decide the set of products to carry. There has also been a recent line of work on the "sequential posted assortment" problem [14,15,18], motivated by online retailers who recommend personalized subsets to their heterogeneous customers.

Our problem is a generalization of the assortment optimization problem to multiple buyers. On the other hand, our mechanisms form a superclass of "sequential posted assortment" mechanisms, which is analogous to the well-known relationship between classical auctions and "sequential posted pricing" [8]. In light of these relationships, we will refer to our mechanism design problem as **assortment auction** problem.

1.2   Results for Assortment Auctions

Our results are focused on the special case of our model where the feasibility constraints are *product-independent*, only depending on the set of "winners" allocated a non-zero product but not which specific products they were allocated. It still captures the fundamental setting of a single-winner auction, as well as the single-leg revenue management problem where b identical units (e.g. flight seats, hotel rooms) could be sold using different "fare classes" with fixed prices [22]. This assumption is generally justified whenever the products correspond to different "packagings" of an underlying item, or different "services" which share the same limiting resource (e.g. different types of massages with the masseur/masseuse, different VIP packages for time backstage). These settings are also the focus in the papers by [1,2], in which they are called *service-constrained environments*. We note that our combination of fixed prices with a service-constrained environment is quite natural in the application of the airline selling b seats under different fare classes.

In the Introduction we will describe our results in the further special case of auctions with a *single winner*, and start to describe our results by relating our problem to classical single-item auctions. Suppose that the preferences are *buy-down*, where any realizable ranking prefers the non-zero products in order of low-to-high prices. Such a ranking is characterized by a *valuation*, equal to the maximum price of a product ranked higher than product 0. In this case, the well-known result of Myerson [16] says that the optimal mechanism is deterministic, dominant-strategy truthful, and can be implemented in a way where the winner always pays one of the prices in $r_1, \ldots, r_n$.[2] Hence, Myerson's mechanism is the optimal solution in our setting in the special case of buy-down preferences. Moreover, Myerson's mechanism is structurally a virtual welfare maximizer, in that each buyer, based on only her report and distribution, is assigned a univariate score called a *virtual valuation*, after which the buyer with the highest virtual valuation is declared the winner. We will call this a "Myersonian" structure.

---

[2] See [12], who derives Myerson's mechanism for discrete valuations. Although there do exist randomized, symmetric implementations of Myerson, the one which is deterministic and breaks ties in a consistent order always charges one of the prices in $r_1, \ldots, r_n$, and thus can be implemented as an assortment auction.

Our first result is a negative one, which shows that for general preference distributions, the optimal auction may not have the "Myersonian" structure described above. Namely, when non-zero products are not necessarily ranked in order of low-to-high prices, even with two IID buyers, the optimal allocation rule may want buyer 1 to win the auction when the buyers report the *same* ranking, and buyer 2 to win when they report *different* rankings. Such an allocation rule clearly cannot be defined via virtual valuations. Although it was already known that assortment optimization (the special case of our problem with a single buyer) is NP-hard for general preference distributions [3], this result shows that even structurally, one cannot hope to derive the optimal auction using only Myersonian mechanisms based on virtual valuations.

Our main positive result is that for preference distributions induced by *Markov Chain choice models*, the optimal mechanism is structurally Myersonian, and computationally tractable. This is a well-studied class of choice models where the random ranking satisfies a memorylessness property that the next product in the ranking depends probabilistically on only the current product, and not the entire history. Markov Chain choice models capture the buy-down preferences corresponding to the classical auctions setting, so our result generalizes Myerson's mechanism for discrete valuations. They also capture the commonly-used *Multi-Nomial Logit (MNL) choice model* (a.k.a. the Plackett-Luce vase model), as well as the case of single-minded buyers. Finally, we should mention that the tractability of assortment optimization for Markov Chain choice models was already known [6,11,13], so our auction extends this result to multiple buyers.

1.3 Description of Optimal Myersonian Auction

We now explain how our generalized Myersonian mechanism assigns each buyer a virtual valuation based on her reported ranking and ranking distribution. It is a generalization of how virtual valuations can be assigned in the classical auctions setting based on the "ironed revenue curve". We will consider the following example: there are four products A, B, C, D with prices $r_A = 12, r_B = 7.5, r_C = 4.5, r_D = 4$. One buyer's ranking distribution is uniform over lists $(CBA), (CB), (CD), (C)$, where e.g. list (CB) means that her first choice is to buy C at price r_C, second choice is to buy B at price r_B, and third choice is to buy nothing (we can ignore ordering after the no-purchase option).

Auction pre-processing. Fix a buyer and consider the assortment optimization problem with just that buyer. For an assortment S, let $Q(S)$ denote the probability of selling a product when S is offered, and let $R(S)$ denote the expected revenue. In the example above, if $S = \{A, B, D\}$, then $Q(S) = \frac{3}{4}$ and $R(S) = \frac{1}{2}r_B + \frac{1}{4}r_D = 4.75$.

Now, consider the two-dimensional plot consisting of points $(Q(S), R(S))$ for every assortment S. Call the upper concave envelope of these points the *revenue frontier*. The revenue frontier is formed by connecting the points for a *sequence of efficient assortments*. In the example above, this sequence is $\{A\}, \{A, D\}, \{A, B, D\}, \{A, B, C, D\}$ (see Fig. 1).

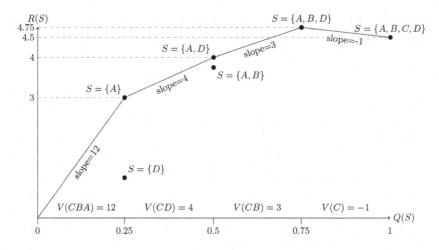

Fig. 1. The points $(Q(S), R(S))$ plotted for every S, all of which are equivalent to one of the six assortments shown. The revenue frontier is the upper concave envelope in red, formed by joining the sequence of efficient assortments. The slopes of the revenue frontier and the resulting virtual valuations V are shown in blue. (Color figure online)

Virtual Valuation Assignment. Fix a buyer and suppose that the sequence of efficient assortments for her list distribution has been identified. Now, if she reports a realized list of ℓ, then we find the first efficient assortment S which intersects ℓ, and set her virtual valuation equal to the slope of the revenue frontier on the *left* side of point $(Q(S), R(S))$.

In the example above, if $\ell = (CD)$, then $\{A, D\}$ is the first efficient assortment to intersect ℓ, since the earlier assortment in the sequence, $\{A\}$, does not. The virtual valuation is the slope of the line segment from $(Q(\{A\}), R(\{A\}))$ to $(Q(\{A, D\}), R(\{A, D\}))$, equal to 4 (see Fig. 1).

Winner and Allocation. Suppose that each buyer has been assigned a virtual valuation based on her list and distribution, as described above. The winner is then the buyer with the highest virtual valuation. She is allocated her most-preferred product from the assortment whose left-side slope represents the *minimum* virtual valuation she could have had to win the auction.

In the example above, suppose that the buyer's list realizes to (CBA) and that her virtual valuation of 12 is the highest. If the second-highest virtual valuation is 3.5, then she would get her most-preferred product from assortment $\{A, D\}$, whose left-side slope is 4 (see Fig. 1). As a result, she would end up paying 12 for product A. On the other hand, if the second-highest virtual valuation is 2.5, then she would get to choose from assortment $\{A, B, D\}$, whose left-side slope is 3. As a result, she would get her more-preferred option of B.

Like in Myerson's original mechanism, a negative virtual valuation is not allowed to win the auction, and hence even with no competition from other buyers, this buyer would still be restricted to assortment $\{A, B, D\}$ (not

$\{A, B, C, D\}$, whose left-side slope is -1). $\{A, B, D\}$ is our analogue of a *reserve price*, and is the solution to the assortment optimization problem for this single buyer.

1.4   Establishing Optimality for Markov Chain Choice Models

Nothing from the auction described in Sect. 1.2 required the list distributions to arise from Markov chains. We now explain what could go wrong without such an assumption, thereby sketching the proof of our main result.

First, we need to show that the revenue frontier and efficient assortments from Sect. 1.2 can be tractably computed. We show that for a Markov Chain choice model, the revenue frontier is always defined by a nested sequence of efficient assortments, which can be greedily constructed (Sect. 3). Our greedy procedure modifies the "externality-adjustment" technique of [11], and generates a sequence of products which yield the revenue frontier, which is different than the sequence used by [11] for their constrained assortment optimization problem.

Second, we need to show that in the allocation rule from Sect. 1.2, whenever the winner has a positive virtual valuation, the assortment she gets to "choose from" actually contains a product she wants. This is not obvious; in fact, there exist distributions (Sect. 2.3) for which the winner may choose no product. Nonetheless, we introduce a condition called *implementability*, under which the winner always chooses a product and the *virtual surplus*[3] is earned by the Myersonian mechanism (Sect. 2.2). We use the nested property of the efficient assortments of a Markov Chain choice model to establish this (Sect. 3.1).

Third, we need to show that earning the virtual surplus is optimal. This does not follow from above; in fact, in our example (Sect. 2.3) where the optimal auction is non-Myersonian, implementability is satisfied. Nonetheless, we introduce a condition called *insurmountability* which ensures that the virtual surplus cannot be exceeded by a truthful mechanism (Sect. 2.2). We show that it is satisfied under Markov Chain choice models, by proving that the cannibalization patterns from our non-Myersonian example cannot arise under the memorylessness property of Markov chains (Sect. 3.1).

We should note that our implementability and insurmountability conditions are similar to the *revenue linearity* condition from [1], who also studied the existence of Myersonian mechanisms under product-independent feasibility constraints. However, they focus on cardinal instead of ordinal preferences, and their definitions are stated with respect to Bayesian instead of dominant-strategy truthfulness, which is why we independently develop our conditions using the language of assortment optimization. Importantly, our main result for Markov Chain ordinal preferences is quite general in that it holds regardless of the prices $r_1, \ldots, r_n$ of the products, which cannot be derived from their results.

---

[3] This is the expected value of the maximum among all virtual valuations and 0.

2   Definition of Assortment Auctions

A seller has a set of products $N = \{1, \ldots, n\}$. Each product $j \in N$ has a fixed price r_j, and the products are indexed so that $0 \leq r_1 \leq \cdots \leq r_n$. We also let $j = 0$ refer to a "no-purchase" product, with $r_0 = 0$, which is always available. Throughout this paper, for an arbitrary subset of products $S \subseteq N$, we will let S_+ denote the set $S \cup \{0\}$.

There is a set of buyers $M = \{1, \ldots, m\}$. Each buyer $i \in M$ has a ranked list ℓ_i from which she is willing to purchase at most one product, at its corresponding price. For example, the ranked list $(1, 3)$ indicates that the buyer's first choice is to purchase product 1 at price r_1, second choice is to purchase product 3 at price r_3, and third choice is to make no purchase. The list omits product 0 and all the products ranked after it, which are irrelevant. We let Ω denote the universe of all possible lists, which are the ordered subsets of N.

The ranked list can be interpreted as the set of products for which the buyer's utility minus price is positive, sorted in decreasing order. We treat ℓ_i as both a set and a ranking, where $\ell_i(j)$ denotes the rank of product j in list ℓ_i, with smaller numbers meaning more preferred. We define $\ell_i(0) = |\ell_i| + 1$ and $\ell_i(j) = \infty$ for all $j \in N \setminus \ell_i$. When presented with an *assortment* of products $S \subseteq N$, a buyer i chooses her most-preferred product from S_+, i.e. $\operatorname{argmin}_{j \in S_+} \ell_i(j)$.

We let $\boldsymbol{\ell} = (\ell_1, \ldots, \ell_m)$ denote the *list profile*, which consists of all buyers' ranked lists. We often write $\boldsymbol{\ell}$ as $(\ell_i, \boldsymbol{\ell}_{-i})$, where $\boldsymbol{\ell}_{-i}$ consists of all ranked lists except that of buyer i. A *mechanism* takes in a list profile $\boldsymbol{\ell}$ and outputs an allocation vector $(j_1(\boldsymbol{\ell}), \ldots, j_m(\boldsymbol{\ell})) \in (N_+)^m$, where each buyer i receives product $j_i(\boldsymbol{\ell})$ and pays $r_{j_i(\boldsymbol{\ell})}$.

We only consider deterministic mechanisms, to avoid defining the preferences of an ordinal ranking under uncertainty. Similarly, we only consider dominant-strategy truthfulness, and say that a mechanism is *truthful* if

$$\ell_i(j_i(\ell_i, \boldsymbol{\ell}_{-i})) \leq \ell_i(j_i(\ell_i', \boldsymbol{\ell}_{-i})) \qquad \forall i \in M, \boldsymbol{\ell}_{-i} \in \Omega^{m-1}, \ell_i \in \Omega, \ell_i' \in \Omega; \qquad (1)$$

$$\ell_i(j_i(\ell_i, \boldsymbol{\ell}_{-i})) \leq \ell_i(0) \qquad \forall i \in M, \boldsymbol{\ell}_{-i} \in \Omega^{m-1}, \ell_i \in \Omega. \qquad (2)$$

(1) imposes that the mechanism is *incentive-compatible*, where a buyer i always receives a less-preferred product when she misreports her list as ℓ_i' instead of her true list ℓ_i. (2) imposes that the mechanism is *individually-rational*, where a buyer i cannot be forced into purchasing a product which is less-preferred to 0.

Hereafter, we restrict to truthful mechanisms and make no distinction between a buyer's reported list and true list. We also assume that the lists are *strictly ordered*, where we note that the truthfulness constraints (1)–(2) are only easier to satisfy if we allow for indifference in the lists. The following statement provides a useful characterization of all deterministic truthful mechanisms, and is analogous to the "taxation principle" for classical auctions.

Proposition 1 (Taxation Principle for Assortment Auctions). *Any deterministic truthful mechanism can be characterized by functions T_i for the* buyers $i \in M$, where each T_i takes in the other lists $\boldsymbol{\ell}_{-i}$ and outputs an assortment $T_i(\boldsymbol{\ell}_{-i})$, such that the allocation vector satisfies

$$j_i(\boldsymbol{\ell}) = argmin_{j \in T_i(\boldsymbol{\ell}_{-i})_+} \ell_i(j) \qquad\qquad \forall i \in M. \qquad (3)$$

Proposition 1 can be proven by for each buyer i, fixing $\boldsymbol{\ell}_{-i}$ and considering the possible products she could be allocated by the mechanism through the different lies ℓ_i' she could tell. The corresponding assortment $T_i(\boldsymbol{\ell}_{-i})$ she is allowed to choose from in Proposition 1 is then the union $\cup_{\ell_i' \in \Omega} j_i(\ell_i', \boldsymbol{\ell}_{-i})$.

2.1 Bayesian Revenue Maximization with Product-Independent Feasibility Constraints

Our paper assumes the *Bayesian* setting, where the seller has full distributional information about the buyers' private lists. We assume that the list of a buyer i is drawn *independently* from a distribution over Ω, given by its discrete probability mass function P_i, which could be different across buyers. In the Bayesian setting, we use ℓ_i to refer to the realized list of buyer i, and l to refer to an arbitrary list in Ω, with $\Pr[\ell_i = l] = P_i(l)$. We discuss how the distributions over Ω can have compact representations in the form of *choice models*, in Sect. 3.

Our paper also focuses on the case of product-independent feasibility constraint, where the auction is constrained by the set of "winners" who are allocated non-zero products, as discussed in the Introduction. Formally, such a feasibility constraint is described as

$$\{i \in M : j_i(\boldsymbol{\ell}) \neq 0\} \in \mathcal{F} \qquad\qquad \forall \boldsymbol{\ell} \in \Omega^m \qquad (4)$$

where $\mathcal{F}$ is an arbitrary downward-closed feasible family.

We are now ready to define the main problem studied in this paper.

Problem 1 (Revenue Maximization with Assortment Auctions). Find the allocation functions $j_1, \ldots, j_m : \Omega^m \to N_+$ which maximize the expected revenue $\mathbb{E}_{\boldsymbol{\ell}}[\sum_{i=1}^{m} r_{j_i(\boldsymbol{\ell})}]$, subject to truthfulness (1)–(2) and feasibility (4).

In the case of a single buyer, Problem 1 reduces (via Proposition 1) to $\max_{T_1 \subseteq N} \mathbb{E}_{\ell_1}[r_{j_1(\ell_1)}]$, where $j_1(\ell_1) = argmin_{j \in T_1 \cup \{0\}} \ell_1(j)$, which is the basic assortment optimization problem.

We will frequently reference the special case where customers "buy down", because it corresponds to known results in the classical auctions setting, which we can then build upon. In this special case, ranked lists always take the form $(1, \ldots, j)$, for some product $j \in N_+$, whose price r_j corresponds to the customer's maximum willingness-to-pay. Therefore, we can consider an instance in the classical single-item auction setting where each buyer i has an independent *valuation* v_i that equals r_j with probability $P_i((1, \ldots, j))$, for all $j \in N_+$. Myerson's optimal auction specifies an (ironed) virtual valuation function ϕ_i for each buyer i, which maps the discrete valuation set $\{r_0, \ldots, r_n\}$ to $\mathbb{R}$ [12]. This can then be translated back into an optimal assortment auction, in this special case.

Proposition 2. *Suppose that the list distribution P_i for every buyer i is supported within $\{(1,\ldots,j) : j \in N_+\}$ and that $\mathcal{F} = \{M' \subseteq M : |M'| \leq 1\}$. Then the optimal auction is: each buyer i, upon reporting list $(1,\ldots,j)$, is assigned virtual valuation $\phi_i(r_j)$; declare the winner to be the buyer i^* with the highest[4] positive[5] virtual valuation, and allocate her the lowest-priced product j whose virtual valuation $\phi_{i^*}(r_j)$ would have won the auction. Moreover, the optimal revenue equals the expected virtual surplus, defined as the expected value of the maximum virtual valuation (or zero if all virtual valuations are non-positive).*

2.2 Implementable and Insurmountable Virtual Valuations

Myerson's result for classical auctions can be interpreted as: given any valuation distributions, it is *always* possible to find functions $\phi_1,\ldots,\phi_n$ which are simultaneously "low enough", in that the virtual surplus (defined according to $\phi_1,\ldots,\phi_n$) can be earned by a mechanism which allocates to the highest virtual valuation; "high enough", in that the virtual surplus is an upper bound on the revenue of any feasible truthful mechanism. We will see in Sect. 2.3 that for general preference distributions, the two conditions above cannot always be simultaneously satisfied. Nonetheless, here we derive what it means for virtual valuations to be "low enough" and "high enough" for assortment auctions.

For assortment auctions, the natural generalization of a function ϕ which maps valuations to virtual valuations is a function V defined on lists.

Definition 1. *A virtual valuation mapping (VVM) is a function $V : \Omega \to \mathbb{R}$. Given a VVM V_i for every buyer $i \in M$ and a downward-closed feasible family $\mathcal{F}$, define the expected virtual surplus as*

$$\mathbb{E}_{\boldsymbol{\ell}} \left[\max_{M' \in \mathcal{F}} \sum_{i \in M'} V_i(\ell_i) \right]. \tag{5}$$

For convenience, a VVM V_i will often leave virtual valuations undefined for lists of measure zero. The virtual valuation of the empty list $\emptyset$ is understood to be $-\infty$, which can always be excluded since $\mathcal{F}$ is downward-closed.

We now introduce conditions on individual VVM's V, omitting the buyer subscript i. In the classical auctions setting, ϕ was a function defined based on a valuation distribution. Similarly, in our setting, a VVM V is always defined based on a specific list distribution P.

Definition 2. *Fix a list distribution P. For all assortments $S \subseteq N$, define:*

- $\mathcal{Q}^j(S) = \{l \in \Omega : j = \operatorname{argmin}_{j \in S_+} l(j)\}$, *the subset of lists l which choose product j when offered assortment S, defined for all $j \in S$;*

---

[4] With discrete valuations, we can perturb the functions $\phi_1,\ldots,\phi_m$ slightly so that different buyers cannot have the same virtual valuation. This is equivalent to using an arbitrary deterministic tie-breaking rule.

[5] Only a positive virtual valuation can win the auction; otherwise no buyer is allocated any product.

– $Q(S) = \bigcup_{j \in S} Q^j(S)$, *the subset of lists l which make a purchase under S;*
– $R(S) = \sum_{j \in S} r_j \cdot P(Q^j(S))$, *the expected revenue when offering S;*
– $Q(S) = P(Q(S))$, *the probability of getting a sale when offering S.*

We now present the first of our conditions on a VVM V for a distribution P.

Definition 3. *We say that a virtual valuation mapping V for a distribution P is implementable if for any threshold $w \in \mathbb{R}$, we can find an assortment S such that $Q(S) = \{l \in \Omega : V(l) \geq w\}$ and*

$$\sum_{l \in Q(S)} V(l)P(l) \leq R(S). \tag{6}$$

It can be checked that the virtual valuations defined for the example in Sect. 1.2 satisfy this condition. Indeed, the relevant thresholds are $w = 12, 4, 3, -1$, and for each of these thresholds we can find the respective assortments $S = \{A\}, \{A, D\}, \{A, B, D\}, \{A, B, C, D\}$ which satisfy (6) as equality. Note that in Definition 3, it is important for $V(\emptyset)$ to be understood to be $-\infty$, since the empty list $\emptyset$ cannot lie in $Q(S)$ for any assortment S.

If for every buyer, the VVM defined for her is implementable, then the virtual valuations are "low enough" in the sense described earlier.

Lemma 1. *Suppose that VVM V_i is implementable for distribution P_i for all $i \in M$. Then revenue equal to the virtual surplus (5) can be attained by a Myersonian mechanism, which on each realization of ℓ offers assortments in a way so that buyers in $\text{argmax}_{M' \in \mathcal{F}} \sum_{i \in M'} V_i(\ell_i)$ are allocated a non-zero product.*

The virtual valuations for the example from Sect. 1.2 were defined based on the efficient assortments and the revenue frontier. If these virtual valuations satisfy implementability (which is not always the case—see Sect. 2.3), then they will maximally inflate the expected virtual surplus earned by the Myersonian mechanism. One may hope that this means the Myersonian mechanism is optimal. Surprisingly though, it is not sufficient for the optimality of the Myersonian mechanism, which motivates the need for our second condition.

Definition 4. *We say that a virtual valuation mapping V for distribution P is insurmountable if for all assortments $S \subseteq N$,*

$$\sum_{l \in Q(S)} V(l)P(l) \geq R(S). \tag{7}$$

The virtual valuations defined for the example in Sect. 1.2 are also insurmountable, although this is much more difficult to check. In the special case of buy-down preferences, $Q(S)$ always corresponds to a contiguous block of lists exceeding some price threshold, and insurmountability becomes a trivial condition, which is always satisfied by Myerson's ironed virtual valuations. However, with general preference lists, there are exponentially many possibilities for $Q(S)$, and whether insurmountability holds depends on the specific substitution patterns across those preference lists. In fact, an assortment S can violate (7) even when it is "inefficient" and has a small value of $R(S)$, especially if $\mathcal{Q}(S)$ contains many lists with low virtual valuations. And when (7) is violated, a non-Myersonian mechanism can indeed surpass the expected virtual surplus.

Nonetheless, if for every buyer, the VVM defined for her is insurmountable, then the expected virtual surplus cannot be surpassed.

Lemma 2. *Suppose that VVM V_i is insurmountable for distribution P_i for all $i \in M$. Then the expected virtual surplus (5) is an upper bound on the revenue of any feasible truthful mechanism.*

Combining Lemmas 1–2, we see that if for each buyer we can find a VVM which is simultaneously implementable and insurmountable, then a Myersonian mechanism is optimal.

2.3   Examples

All examples are deferred to the full version of this paper (available online).

3   Optimal Assortment Auction for Markov Chains

In this section we derive the optimal assortment auction under Markov Chain choice models, by specifying a procedure for defining a buyer's virtual valuation based on her reported list and list distribution. Our procedure in essence efficiently constructs the revenue frontier and defines virtual valuations following the example in Sect. 1.2. We focus on a single buyer and omit the subscript i.

Definition 5 (Markov Chain Choice Model). *Under a Markov Chain choice model, the list distribution P is implicitly defined in the following way. There is a Markov Chain with node set N_+ (recall for any set S, we defined $S_+ = S \cup \{0\}$). For all nodes $j \in N$ and $j' \in N_+$, the probability of transitioning from node j to node j' is $\rho_{jj'}$. The outgoing probabilities from every node $j \in N$ satisfy $\sum_{j' \in N_+} \rho_{jj'} = 1$, and 0 is a terminal node with no outgoing transitions.*

To generate a list $\ell \in \Omega$ according to distribution P, we start at each node $j' \in N_+$ with probability $\lambda_{j'}$ (these probabilities satisfy $\sum_{j' \in N_+} \lambda_{j'} = 1$), in which case we start with the singleton list (j'). We then transition probabilistically along the Markov chain, adding every node visited to the end of the list, but only if that node doesn't already appear on the list. The list immediately ends upon terminal node 0 being reached (and 0 is never added to the list). It is assumed that 0 is the only absorbing state, so that ℓ terminates with probability 1.

Definition 6 (Notation). *In this section, we will use the following notation, which facilitates the analysis of the Markov Chain choice model.*

- *For any $j \in N_+$, we will often use j to refer to the singleton set $\{j\}$.*

- *Consider the discrete probability space defined by the Markov Chain's distribution P. For any $s \in N_+$ and $S \subseteq N_+ \setminus s$, let $s \prec S$ denote the event node s is visited before any nodes in S, and let $\mathbb{P}[s \prec S]$ denote its probability.*
- *Similarly, for any $s \in N$, $s' \in N_+ \setminus s$, and $S \subseteq N_+ \setminus \{s, s'\}$, let $\mathbb{P}[s \prec s' \prec S]$ denote the probability that s is visited before s', which in turn is visited before any of the nodes in S. Let $\mathbb{P}_s[s' \prec S]$ denote the probability that starting from node s (instead of starting according to the probabilities λ_k), s' is visited before any of the nodes in S.*
- *For $s \in N$, $s' \in N_+ \setminus s$, and $S \subseteq N_+ \setminus \{s, s'\}$, let $\mathcal{L}(s \prec s' \prec S)$ denote the subset of lists $l \in \Omega$ for which $s \prec s' \prec S$. Note that although the list l is truncated upon reaching node 0, since $s \neq 0$, whether $s \prec s' \prec S$ is fully determined by l.*

We are now ready to define our virtual valuation mapping $V : \Omega \rightarrow \mathbb{R}$. Based on the distribution P, our procedure constructs a sequence of products $s^{(1)}, \ldots, s^{(K)}$, where each product $s^{(k)}$ maximizes the *incremental efficiency* when added to assortment $S^{(k-1)} = \{s^{(1)}, \ldots, s^{(k-1)}\}$. These efficiencies are computed using *externality-adjusted prices*, which were introduced in [11]. We emphasize, however, that our procedure is different from theirs, in that our sequence of products forms the revenue frontier while theirs accomplishes a different purpose, as illustrated in Example 1 below. Having constructed the revenue frontier, we define the virtual valuation of a list l to be the incremental efficiency of the *first* product in our sequence $s^{(1)}, \ldots, s^{(K)}$ which appears in l.

Definition 7 (Procedure for Defining Virtual Valuations)

- *Initialize assortment $S^{(0)} = \emptyset$, and $r_j^{(0)} = r_j$ for all products $j \in N$.*
- *For iterations $k = 1, 2, \ldots$*
  1. *Set $s^{(k)}$ to be a product $j \in N \setminus S^{(k-1)}$ with $\mathbb{P}_j[0 \prec S^{(k-1)}] \neq 0$ which maximizes the incremental efficiency, defined as*

$$\frac{r_j^{(k-1)}}{\mathbb{P}_j[0 \prec S^{(k-1)}]}. \tag{8}$$

  If there are no such products satisfying $\mathbb{P}_j[0 \prec S^{(k-1)}] \neq 0$, then STOP.
  2. *Define the virtual valuation $V(l)$ for every list $l \in \mathcal{L}(s^{(k)} \prec 0 \prec S^{(k-1)})$ to be this maximum incremental efficiency, equal to (8) with $j = s^{(k)}$.*
  3. *Update the assortment after iteration k to be $S^{(k)} = S^{(k-1)} \cup \{s^{(k)}\}$, and update the externality-adjusted prices for all remaining products $j \in N \setminus S^{(k)}$ to be $r_j^{(k)} = r_j^{(k-1)} - r_{s^{(k)}}^{(k-1)} \mathbb{P}_j[s^{(k)} \prec S_+^{(k-1)}]$.*

After the procedure stops, define K to be last iteration on which virtual valuations were defined, i.e. $K = |S^{(k)}|$, which is at most n.

Our virtual valuation generation procedure is different from the iterative assortment optimization procedure of [11] in that at each iteration, it maximizes the incremental efficiency instead of the externality-adjusted price $r_j^{(k-1)}$. Their

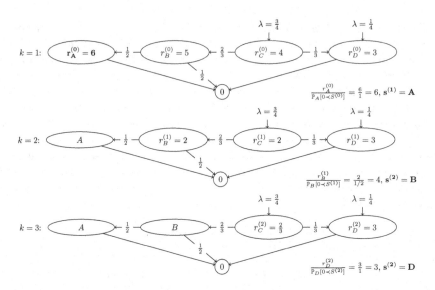

Fig. 2. The demonstration of our procedure from Definition 7 on Example 1. In the Markov chain, any arrival probabilities λ or transition probabilities ρ not depicted are 0. In each iteration k, the highest incremental efficiency (given by (8)) and the product selected $s^{(k)}$ are shown.

procedure addresses the single-buyer problem under additional capacity and knapsack constraints. By contrast, our procedure addresses the unconstrained problem for multiple buyers, where the increase in sales probability (corresponding to the term in our denominator) is highly relevant, as it prevents allocations from being made to another buyer. The following example demonstrates our procedure and the difference from their procedure.

Example 1 (Illustration of our Procedure and its difference from [11]). There are four products A, B, C, D with prices $r_A = 6, r_B = 5, r_C = 4, r_D = 3$. The ranking distribution is uniform over lists $(CBA), (CB), (CD), (D)$. It is easy to see that this distribution is generated by the Markov chain pictured in Fig. 2. Iterations $k = 1, 2, 3$ of the procedure are depicted in Fig. 2, with the externality-adjusted prices $r_j^{(k-1)}$ shown on the nodes.

In iteration $k = 1$, the highest-priced product A is selected, with a virtual valuation of $r_A = 6$.

In iteration $k = 2$, our procedure diverges from what [11] would do, in that it selects product B, instead of product D which has the highest externality-adjusted price. This is because we care about minimizing the denominator of (8), in which $\mathbb{P}_B[0 \prec S^{(1)}] = 1/2$ while $\mathbb{P}_D[0 \prec S^{(1)}] = 1$, reflecting the fact that we want to minimize the increase in sales probability. As a result, even though $r_B^{(1)} < r_D^{(1)}$ and $R(S^{(1)} \cup B) < R(S^{(1)} \cup D)$, our procedure adds product B to assortment $S^{(1)} = \{A\}$, which maximizes the gain in revenue relative to the increase in sales probability.

In iteration $k = 3$, our procedure selects product D and then stops. Even though the assortment $S^{(3)} = \{A, B, D\}$ does not contain C, the stopping criterion $\mathbb{P}_C[0 \prec S^{(3)}] = 0$ is met. It can also be checked that $r_C^{(3)} = r_C^{(2)} - r_D^{(2)}\mathbb{P}_C[D \prec S^{(2)}] = -1/3$, which is negative.

3.1 Implementability and Insurmountability of Procedure

All proofs are deferred to the full version of this paper (available online).

References

1. Alaei, S., Fu, H., Haghpanah, N., Hartline, J.: The simple economics of approximately optimal auctions. In: Proceedings of the IEEE 54th Annual Symposium on Foundations of Computer Science, pp. 628–637. IEEE (2013)
2. Alaei, S., Fu, H., Haghpanah, N., Hartline, J., Malekian, A.: Bayesian optimal auctions via multi-to single-agent reduction. In: Proceedings of the 13th ACM Conference on Electronic Commerce, p. 17 (2012)
3. Aouad, A., Farias, V., Levi, R., Segev, D.: The approximability of assortment optimization under ranking preferences. Oper. Res. **66**(6), 1661–1669 (2018)
4. Barberà, S., Jackson, M.O., Neme, A.: Strategy-proof allotment rules. Games Econ. Behav. **18**(1), 1–21 (1997)
5. Bhalgat, A., Chakrabarty, D., Khanna, S.: Social welfare in one-sided matching markets without money. In: Goldberg, L.A., Jansen, K., Ravi, R., Rolim, J.D.P. (eds.) APPROX/RANDOM -2011. LNCS, vol. 6845, pp. 87–98. Springer, Heidelberg (2011). https://doi.org/10.1007/978-3-642-22935-0_8
6. Blanchet, J., Gallego, G., Goyal, V.: A Markov chain approximation to choice modeling. Oper. Res. **64**(4), 886–905 (2016)
7. Chawla, S., Hartline, J.D., Kleinberg, R.: Algorithmic pricing via virtual valuations. In: Proceedings of the 8th ACM Conference on Electronic Commerce, pp. 243–251. ACM (2007)
8. Chawla, S., Hartline, J.D., Malec, D.L., Sivan, B.: Multi-parameter mechanism design and sequential posted pricing. In: Proceedings of the Forty-Second ACM Symposium on Theory of Computing, pp. 311–320. ACM (2010)
9. Chawla, S., Malec, D., Sivan, B.: The power of randomness in Bayesian optimal mechanism design. Games Econ. Behav. **91**, 297–317 (2015)
10. Chen, X., Diakonikolas, I., Orfanou, A., Paparas, D., Sun, X., Yannakakis, M.: On the complexity of optimal lottery pricing and randomized mechanisms. In: Proceedings of the IEEE 56th Annual Symposium on Foundations of Computer Science, pp. 1464–1479. IEEE (2015)
11. Désir, A., Goyal, V., Segev, D., Ye, C.: Capacity constrained assortment optimization under the Markov chain based choice model. Manage. Sci. (2019, Forthcoming)
12. Elkind, E.: Designing and learning optimal finite support auctions. In: Proceedings of the Eighteenth Annual ACM-SIAM symposium on Discrete Algorithms, pp. 736–745. Society for Industrial and Applied Mathematics (2007)
13. Feldman, J.B., Topaloglu, H.: Revenue management under the Markov chain choice model. Oper. Res. **65**(5), 1322–1342 (2017)
14. Golrezaei, N., Nazerzadeh, H., Rusmevichientong, P.: Real-time optimization of personalized assortments. Manage. Sci. **60**(6), 1532–1551 (2014)

15. Ma, W., Simchi-Levi, D.: Algorithms for online matching, assortment, and pricing with tight weight-dependent competitive ratios. Oper. Res. (2020)
16. Myerson, R.B.: Optimal auction design. Math. Oper. Res. **6**(1), 58–73 (1981)
17. Roth, A.E.: Incentive compatibility in a market with indivisible goods. Econ. Lett. **9**(2), 127–132 (1982)
18. Rusmevichientong, P., Sumida, M., Topaloglu, H.: Dynamic assortment optimization for reusable products with random usage durations. Manage. Sci. **66**, 2820–2844 (2020)
19. Shapley, L., Scarf, H.: On cores and indivisibility. J. Math. Econ. **1**(1), 23–37 (1974)
20. Sprumont, Y.: The division problem with single-peaked preferences: a characterization of the uniform allocation rule. Econometrica J. Econometric Soc. **59**, 509–519 (1991)
21. Svensson, L.G.: Strategy-proof allocation of indivisible goods. Soc. Choice Welfare **16**(4), 557–567 (1999)
22. Talluri, K., Van Ryzin, G.: Revenue management under a general discrete choice model of consumer behavior. Manage. Sci. **50**(1), 15–33 (2004)

Robust Revenue Maximization Under Minimal Statistical Information

Yiannis Giannakopoulos[1] (ID), Diogo Poças[2(✉)] (ID),
and Alexandros Tsigonias-Dimitriadis[1]

[1] TU Munich, Munich, Germany
{yiannis.giannakopoulos,alexandros.tsigonias}@tum.de
[2] LASIGE, Faculdade de Ciências, Universidade de Lisboa, Lisbon, Portugal
dmpocas@fc.ul.pt

Abstract. We study the problem of multi-dimensional revenue maximization when selling m items to a buyer that has additive valuations for them, drawn from a (possibly correlated) prior distribution. Unlike traditional Bayesian auction design, we assume that the seller has a very restricted knowledge of this prior: they only know the mean μ_j and an upper bound σ_j on the standard deviation of each item's marginal distribution. Our goal is to design mechanisms that achieve good revenue against an ideal optimal auction that has *full* knowledge of the distribution in advance. Informally, our main contribution is a tight quantification of the interplay between the dispersity of the priors and the aforementioned robust approximation ratio. Furthermore, this can be achieved by very simple selling mechanisms.

More precisely, we show that selling the items via separate price lotteries achieves an $O(\log r)$ approximation ratio where $r = \max_j(\sigma_j/\mu_j)$ is the maximum coefficient of variation across the items. If forced to restrict ourselves to deterministic mechanisms, this guarantee degrades to $O(r^2)$. Assuming independence of the item valuations, these ratios can be further improved by pricing the full bundle. For the case of identical means and variances, in particular, we get a guarantee of $O(\log(r/m))$ which converges to optimality as the number of items grows large. We demonstrate the optimality of the above mechanisms by providing matching lower bounds. Our tight analysis for the deterministic case resolves an open gap from the work of Azar and Micali [ITCS'13].

Keywords: Optimal auctions · Revenue maximization · Parametric auctions · Robust optimization

Supported by the Alexander von Humboldt Foundation with funds from the German Federal Ministry of Education and Research (BMBF). The last author further acknowledges the support of the German Research Foundation (DFG) within the Research Training Group AdONE (GRK 2201). A full version of this paper can be found at [27]: arxiv.org/abs/1907.04220.

1 Introduction

Optimal auction design is one of the most well-studied and fundamental problems in (algorithmic) mechanism design. In the traditional Myersonian [42] setting, an auctioneer has a single item for sale and there are n interested bidders. Each bidder has a (private) valuation for the item which, intuitively, represents the amount of money they are willing to spend to buy it. The standard Bayesian approach is to assume that the seller has only an incomplete knowledge of these valuations, in the form of a prior joint distribution F. A selling mechanism receives bids from the buyers and then decides to whom the item should be allocated (which, in general, can be a randomized rule) and for what price. The goal is to design a truthful selling mechanism that maximizes the auctioneer's revenue, in expectation over F.

Myerson [42] provided a complete and very elegant solution for this problem when bidder valuations are independent, that is, F is a product distribution. In particular, when the distributions are identical and further satisfy a regularity assumption, the optimal mechanism takes the very satisfying form of a second-price (Vickrey) auction with a reserve price. Unfortunately, in general these characterizations collapse when we move to multi-dimensional environments where there are $m > 1$ items for sale. Multi-item optimal auction design is one of the most challenging and currently active research areas of mechanism design. Given that the exact description of the revenue maximizing auctions in such settings is a notoriously hard task, there is an impressive stream of recent papers, predominantly from the algorithmic game theory community, that try to provide good approximation guarantees to the optimal revenue.

The critical common underlying assumption throughout the aforementioned optimal auction design settings is that the seller has *full knowledge* of the prior joint distribution F of the bidders' valuations. In many applications though, this might arguably be an unrealistic assumption to make: usually an auctioneer can derive some distributional properties about the bidder population, but to completely determine the actual distribution would require enormous resources. Thus, inspired by the parametric auctions of Azar and Micali [2] for the single-dimensional case, we would like to be able to design robust auctions that (1) make only use of *minimal statistical information* about the valuation distribution, namely its mean and variance; and (2) still provide good revenue guarantees even in the worst case against an adversarial selection of the actual distribution F; in particular, *no further assumptions* (e.g., independence of item valuations or regularity) should in general be made about F. This is our main goal in this paper.

1.1 Related Work

As mentioned in the introduction, there has been an impressive stream of recent work on optimal [11,22,26,29,37] and approximately-optimal [4,12,17,31,35, 44,46] multi-dimensional auction design, which tries to extend the traditional, single-dimensional auction setting studied in the seminal paper of Myerson [42].

A prominent characteristic that can often be seen in these papers is the "simplicity vs optimality" approach: knowing the computational hardness [19–21] and structural complexity [22,30] of describing exact optimality, emphasis is placed on designing both simple and practical mechanisms that can still provide good revenue guarantees. Of course, this idea can be traced back to the work of Hartline and Roughgarden [33] and Bulow and Klemperer [9] for the single-dimensional setting. For a more thorough overview we refer to the recent review article of Roughgarden and Talgam-Cohen [43] and the textbook of Hartline [32].

Related to this, and placed under the general theme of what has come to be known as "Wilson's doctrine" [45] (see also [38, Sect. 5.2]), there has also been significant effort towards the direction of *robust* revenue maximization: designing auctions that make as few assumptions as possible on the seller's prior knowledge about the bidders' valuations for the items. Examples include models where the auctioneer can perform quantile queries [18] or knows some estimate of the actual prior [7,10,36]. Another line of work studies robustness with respect to the correlation of valuations across bidders or items [6,14,28]. Other approaches regarding the parameterization of partial distributional knowledge were considered by [24] and [5]. See also the recent survey by Carroll [15].

Most relevant to our work in the present paper is the model of *parametric auctions*, introduced by Azar and Micali [2]. More specifically, they study single-dimensional (digital goods and single-item) auction settings with independent item valuations, under the assumption that the seller has only access to the mean μ_i and the variance σ_i^2 of each buyer's i prior distribution. Using Chebyshev-like tail bounds, they show that for the special single-bidder, single-item case, deterministically pricing at a multiple of the standard deviation below the mean, i.e. offering a take-it-or-leave-it price of $\mu - k \cdot \sigma$, guarantees an approximation ratio of $\tilde{\rho}(r)$, where $\tilde{\rho}$ is an increasing function taking values in $[1, \infty)$ and $r = \sigma/\mu$. Under an extra assumption of Monotone Hazard Rate (MHR), they show how the even simpler selling mechanism that just prices at μ achieves an approximation ratio of e.

It is interesting to notice here that Azar and Micali [2] provide an *exact* solution, for deterministic mechanisms, to the robust optimization problem of maximizing the expected revenue. Then, they use this maximin revenue-optimal mechanism and compare it to the optimal social welfare (which is trivially also an upper bound on the optimal revenue), to finally derive their upper bound guarantee on the approximation ratio of revenue. As such, their results are not tailored to be tight for the *ratio* benchmark. As a matter of fact, in [3] the authors also provide an explicit lower bound that can be written as $1 + r^2$. This is an important motivating factor for our work, since one of our main goals in this paper is to close these gaps and provide tight approximation ratio bounds.

Azar et al. [1] use a clever reduction (see also [16]) to show how these results can be paired with the work of Dhangwatnotai et al. [23] regarding the VCG mechanism with reserves, in order to design parametric auctions for very general single-dimensional settings. In particular, they show how in matroid-constrained environments with the extra assumption of regularity on the prior distributions (or MHR for more general downward-closed environments), using the aforementioned parametric prices as lazy reserves guarantees a $2\tilde{\rho}(r)$-approximation to the optimal (Myersonian) revenue and a $\tilde{\rho}(r)$-approximation to the optimal social welfare. Here $r = \max_i \sigma_i/\mu_i$.

Another work which is close to ours is that of Carrasco et al. [13]. The authors essentially extend the model of Azar and Micali [2] to randomized mechanisms, solving the maximin robust optimization problem with respect to revenue. Again, in principle their results cannot be immediately translated to tight bounds for the approximation ratio; however, unlike the deterministic case for which in the present paper we have to design a new mechanism in order to achieve ratio optimality, we will show that the maximin optimal lottery of Carrasco et al. [13] is actually also optimal for the ratio benchmark.

1.2   Results and Techniques

The main focus of our paper is a multi-dimensional auction setting where a single bidder has additive valuations for m items, drawn from a joint probability distribution F. We make no further assumptions on F; in particular, we do not require F to be a product distribution nor do we enforce any kind of regularity. The seller knows only the mean μ_j and (an upper bound on) the standard deviation σ_j of each item's j marginal distribution. Based on this limited statistical information, they are asked to fix a truthful (possibly randomized) mechanism to sell the items. Then, an adversary chooses the actual distribution F (respecting, of course, the statistical (μ_j, σ_j)-information) and the seller realizes the expected revenue of the auction, in the standard Bayesian way, in expectation with respect to F. The main quantity of interest, which we call the *robust approximation ratio* is the ratio of the optimal revenue (which has full knowledge of F in advance) to this revenue.

Our worst-case, min-max approach is similar in spirit to the previous work of [1,3] and [13]. However, the critical difference in the present paper is that our main goal is to optimize the *ratio* against the optimal revenue and not just the expected revenue of the selling mechanism on its own. It turns out that, similarly to the aforementioned previous work, our bounds can be stated with respect to the ratio $r_j = \sigma_j/\mu_j$ of each item's marginal distribution. This is an important statistical quantity called the *coefficient of variation (CV)*; it is essentially a "unit-independent" measure of the dispersion of the distribution (see, e.g., [40] or [34, Sect. 2.21]).

In Sect. 2 we formally introduce our model and necessary notation. In the following two sections we focus on the single-item case, since this will be the building block for all our results. In particular, in Sect. 3 we show that the robust approximation ratio of deterministic mechanisms is *exactly* $\rho_D(r) \approx 1 + 4r^2$ (see Definition 1), closing a gap open from the work of [3]. Similarly to previous work, in order to achieve this we solve exactly the corresponding min-max problem (see Lemma 2); however, the method and the solution itself have to be different, since we are dealing with the ratio, which is a more "sensitive" quantity than the revenue on its own.

Next, in Sect. 4 we deal with general randomized auctions and we show (Theorem 2) that a lottery proposed by [13], which we term *log-lottery*, although designed for a different objective, achieves an approximation ratio of $\rho(r) \approx 1 + \ln(1 + r^2)$ (see Definition 1) in our setting, which is asymptotically optimal. The construction of the lower bound instance (Theorem 3) is arguably the most technically challenging part of our paper, and is based on a novel utilization of Yao's minimax principle that might be of independent interest for deriving robust approximation lower bounds in other Bayesian mechanism design settings as well.

In Sect. 5 we demonstrate how the $O(\log r)$-approximate mechanism of the single-item case can be utilized to provide optimal approximation ratios for the multi-dimensional case of m items as well. More specifically, we show that selling each item j separately using the log-lottery guarantees an approximation ratio of $\rho(r_{\max})$ where $r_{\max} = \max_j r_j$ is the maximum CV across the items. If the seller has extra information that item valuations are independent (that is, F is a product distribution), then switching to a lottery that offers all items in a single full bundle can give an improved approximation ratio of $\rho(\bar{r})$, where $\bar{r} = \sqrt{\sum_j \sigma_j^2} / \sum_j \mu_j$ is the CV of the average valuation. We complement these upper bounds by tight lower bounds in Theorem 5; these constructions have at their core the single-item lower bound, but they take care of delicately assigning valuations to the remaining items so that they respect independence and the common prior statistical information. An interesting corollary of our upper bounds (Corollary 1) is that for the special case of independent valuations with the same mean and variance, the approximation ratio is at most $\rho\left(\frac{\sigma}{\mu\sqrt{m}}\right)$, converging to optimality as the number of items grows large.

Due to space constraints, additional material and all omitted proofs can be found at the full version of the paper [27].

2 Preliminaries

2.1 Model and Notation

A real nonnegative random variable will be called (μ, σ)-*distributed* if its expectation is μ and its standard deviation is *at most* σ. We let $\mathbb{F}_{\mu,\sigma}$ denote the class of (μ, σ) distributions.

For the most part of this paper we study auctions with m items and a single additive bidder, whose valuations $(v_1, \ldots, v_m)$ for the items are drawn from a joint distribution F over $\mathbb{R}_{\geq 0}^m$. We denote the marginal distribution of v_j by F_j, and assume that it has finite mean and variance. In general, we make no further assumptions for F; in particular, we do not assume independence of the random variables $v_1, \ldots, v_m$ nor do we enforce any regularity or continuity assumption. For vectors $\vec{\mu} = (\mu_1, \ldots, \mu_m) \in \mathbb{R}_{>0}^m$, $\vec{\sigma} = (\sigma_1, \ldots, \sigma_m) \in \mathbb{R}_{\geq 0}^m$ we denote by $\mathbb{F}_{\vec{\mu},\vec{\sigma}}$ the class of all m-dimensional distributions whose j-th marginal is (μ_j, σ_j)-distributed, for all $j = 1, \ldots, m$.

A (direct revelation, possibly randomized) selling *mechanism* for a single bidder and m items is defined by a pair (x, π) where $x : \mathbb{R}_{\geq 0}^m \to [0, 1]^m$ is the *allocation rule* and $\pi : \mathbb{R}_{\geq 0}^m \to \mathbb{R}_{\geq 0}$ is the *payment rule*. If the buyer submits as bid a valuation vector of $\vec{v}$, then they receive each item i with probability $x_i(\vec{v})$, and are charged (a total of) $\pi(\vec{v})$. We restrict our study to *truthful* mechanisms, which are characterized by the conditions $x(\vec{v}) \cdot \vec{v} - \pi(\vec{v}) \geq x(\vec{w}) \cdot \vec{v} - \pi(\vec{w})$ for all $\vec{v}, \vec{w}$ and $x(\vec{v}) \cdot \vec{v} - \pi(\vec{v}) \geq 0$ for all $\vec{v}$. Informally, the first condition states that the bidder can not be "better off" by misreporting their true valuation; the second condition, known as *individual rationality*, ensures that the bidder cannot harm themselves by truthfully participating in the mechanism.

Let $\mathbb{A}_m$ denote the space of all truthful selling mechanisms. Then, given an m-dimensional distribution F, we denote by $\mathrm{REV}(A; F) = \mathbb{E}_{\vec{v} \sim F}[\pi(\vec{v})]$ the expected *revenue* of A (the expectation is taken w.r.t. F), by $\mathrm{WEL}(A; F) = \mathbb{E}_{\vec{v} \sim F}[x(\vec{v}) \cdot \vec{v}]$ the expected *welfare* of A, by $\mathrm{OPT}(F) = \sup_{A \in \mathbb{A}_m} \mathrm{REV}(A; F)$ the optimum revenue, and by $\mathrm{VAL}(F) = \sup_{A \in \mathbb{A}_m} \mathrm{WEL}(A; F)$ the optimum welfare. By definition, this is also the welfare of a VCG auction; moreover, for a single additive bidder with a joint distribution in $\mathbb{F}_{\vec{\mu}, \vec{\sigma}}$, this is just the sum of the marginal expectations, $\mathrm{VAL}(F) = \sum_{j=1}^m \mu_j$. Note that, due to individual rationality, we immediately have the so-called *welfare bounds* for the above quantities: for any mechanism and distribution, $\mathrm{REV}(A; F) \leq \mathrm{WEL}(A; F)$ and $\mathrm{OPT}(F) \leq \mathrm{VAL}(F)$.

Our goal in this paper is to quantify the following benchmark

$$\mathrm{APX}(\vec{\mu}, \vec{\sigma}) = \inf_{A \in \mathbb{A}_m} \sup_{F \in \mathbb{F}_{\vec{\mu}, \vec{\sigma}}} \frac{\mathrm{OPT}(F)}{\mathrm{REV}(A; F)}, \tag{1}$$

which we call the *robust approximation ratio*. The semantics are the following: a seller chooses the best (revenue-maximizing) selling mechanism A, given only knowledge of the means $\vec{\mu}$ and standard deviations $\vec{\sigma}$ and then an adversary ("nature") responds by choosing a worst-case "valid" distribution that respects the statistical information $\vec{\mu}$ and $\vec{\sigma}$. At some parts of our paper, we restrict our attention to *deterministic* mechanisms A; that is, mechanisms whose allocation rule satisfies $x(\vec{v}) \in \{0, 1\}$, for all $\vec{v}$. Under this additional constraint, the quantity in (1) will be denoted by $\mathrm{DAPX}(\vec{\mu}, \vec{\sigma})$.

For the special case of a single item ($m = 1$), we know from the seminal work of [42] that an auction $A \in \mathbb{A}_1$ is truthful if and only if its allocation rule is monotone nondecreasing and the payment rule is given by $\pi(v) = v \cdot x(v) - \int_0^v x(z)\, dz$. In particular, this implies that every deterministic mechanism $A \in \mathbb{A}_1$ is completely determined by a single take-it-or-leave-it price $p \geq 0$; thus, we will feel free to sometimes abuse notation and write $\mathrm{REV}(p; F)$ instead of $\mathrm{REV}(A; F)$ if A is the deterministic auction that sells at price p.

Most importantly for our work, every randomized auction for a single item can be seen as a nonnegative random variable over prices (see [13, Footnote 10]). In particular, since the allocation rule is monotone and takes values in $[0, 1]$, it can be interpreted as the cumulative distribution of a certain randomization over prices, which assigns the item with the same probability as the original mechanism. In this way, for a randomized single-item auction we can abuse notation and write $p \sim A$ to denote that a price p is sampled according to A. In this way, $\mathrm{REV}(A; F) = \mathbb{E}_{p \sim A}[\mathrm{REV}(p; F)]$.

Finally, from [42] we also know that for single-item settings the optimum revenue can always be achieved by a deterministic mechanism, that is, $\mathrm{OPT}(F) = \sup_{p \geq 0} \mathrm{REV}(p; F) = \sup_{p \geq 0} p \cdot (1 - F(p-))$ where we use $F(\cdot)$ for the cumulative function (cdf) of distribution F and $F(p-) = \Pr[X < p] = \lim_{x \to p-} F(x)$, where $X \sim F$. We shall call $\mathrm{OPT}(\cdot)$ the *Myerson operator* and for now we simply observe that this is a functional mapping distributions to real nonnegative numbers.

2.2   Determinism vs Randomization

We would like to give some basic intuition on how randomization helps to hedge uncertainty. To this end, we present a simple example where a randomized strategy beats every price.

Example 1. Assume that we are facing a very restricted adversary who can choose between two distributions. Distribution A has just a point mass at 1. Distribution B is a two-point mass distribution, which returns either 0 or 2 with probability $1/2$ each. If the seller is restricted to deterministic pricing rules, it is not hard to see that their best strategy is to post a price equal to 1 (and for the adversary to choose distribution B), for a worst-case expected revenue of $\frac{1}{2}$. If the seller posts anything above 1, then the adversary will always respond with distribution A, resulting in zero revenue. Consider now the following randomization over prices: The seller posts a price of 1 with probability $2/3$, and a price of 2 with probability $1/3$. If the adversary chooses Distribution A, then the expected revenue will be $1 \cdot \frac{2}{3} = \frac{2}{3}$. Similarly if Distribution B is chosen, then the expected revenue becomes $1 \cdot \frac{2}{3} \cdot \frac{1}{2} + 2 \cdot \frac{1}{3} \cdot \frac{1}{2} = \frac{2}{3}$.

Regardless of the adversarial response, a randomization over two prices strictly outperforms the best deterministic pricing. In subsequent sections we formalize this intuition, by showing a significant separation between the power of deterministic and randomized mechanisms. A separation between determinism and randomization in single-dimensional settings, but under a sample access model, has been demonstrated by [25].

2.3   Auxiliary Functions and Distributions

To state our bounds, it will be convenient to define the following auxiliary functions.

Definition 1 (Functions ρ_D, ρ). *For any $r \geq 0$, let $\rho_D(r) = \rho$, resp. $\rho(r) = \rho$, be the unique positive solution of equation*

$$\frac{(\rho - 1)^3}{(2\rho - 1)^2} = r^2, \qquad resp. \qquad \frac{1}{\rho^2}\left(2e^{\rho - 1} - 1\right) = r^2 + 1.$$

Lemma 1. *For the functions ρ_D, ρ defined in Definition 1, we have the bounds and asymptotics,*

$$1 + 4r^2 \leq \rho_D(r) \leq 2 + 4r^2 \qquad \text{for all } r \geq 0; \qquad \rho(r) = 1 + (1 + o(1)) \ln(1 + r^2).$$

We now define a specific *randomized* selling mechanism, which essentially corresponds to the lottery proposed by [13, Proposition 4]:

Definition 2 (Log-Lottery). *Fix any $\mu > 0$ and $\sigma \geq 0$. A log-lottery is a randomized mechanism that sells at a price $P_{\mu,\sigma}^{\log}$, which is distributed over the nonnegative interval support $[\pi_1, \pi_2]$ according to the cdf*

$$F_{\mu,\sigma}^{\log}(x) = \frac{\pi_2 \ln \frac{x}{\pi_1} - (x - \pi_1)}{\pi_2 \ln \frac{\pi_2}{\pi_1} - (\pi_2 - \pi_1)},$$

where parameters π_1, π_2 are the (unique) solutions of the system of equations $\pi_1 \left(1 + \ln \frac{\pi_2}{\pi_1}\right) = \mu$ and $\pi_1(2\pi_2 - \pi_1) = \mu^2 + \sigma^2$.

We will sometimes slightly abuse notation and use $P_{\mu,\sigma}^{\log}$ to refer both to the log-lottery mechanism and the corresponding random variable of the prices.

3   Single Item: Deterministic Pricing

In this section we begin our study of robust revenue maximization by looking at the simplest case: one item and deterministic pricing rules. Note that [3] already established a lower bound of $1 + r^2$ for this setting, together with an upper bound which can be shown to be $1 + \left(\frac{27}{4} + o(1)\right) r^2$. Our result (Theorem 1) is a refined analysis that captures the exact robustness ratio (and in particular the "correct" constant in the quadratic term).

Our first observation (Lemma 2) will be that the worst-case adversarial response (for a specific selling price) can be characterized in terms of a two-point mass distribution, which allows the problem to be solved exactly. These types of distributions have appeared already in the results of [2] and [13], and we will start by introducing some notation to reason about them.

A two-point mass distribution F takes some value x with probability α and some value y with probability $1 - \alpha$, where without loss $x < y$. When the distribution is constrained to have mean μ and variance exactly equal to σ^2, only one free parameter remains, i.e. F can be characterized by the position x of its first point mass. The other two parameters can be obtained by solving the first and second moment conditions $\mu = \alpha x + (1 - \alpha)y$ and $\mu^2 + \sigma^2 = \alpha x^2 + (1 - \alpha)y^2$. For the remainder, we let F_x, $x \in [0, \mu)$, denote this distribution. Note that the limiting case $x \to \mu$ corresponds to $\alpha(x) \to 1$ and $y(x) \to \infty$, meaning that F_x weakly converges to μ.

By first solving the innermost optimization problem in (1), i.e. by characterizing the worst-case adversarial response against a specific *deterministic* pricing, we can derive the robustness ratio for deterministic mechanisms.

Lemma 2. *For any choice of mean μ and variance σ^2, and any deterministic pricing scheme, the worst-case robust approximation ratio is achieved over a limiting two-point mass distribution. Formally, for any μ, σ, and any price p,*

1. if $p \geq \mu$, then the worst-case response corresponds to playing F_x, with $x \to \mu^-$, and

$$\sup_{F \in \mathbb{F}_{\mu,\sigma}} \frac{\text{OPT}(F)}{\text{REV}(p; F)} = \infty;$$

2. if $0 < p < \mu$, then the worst-case response corresponds to playing F_x with $x \to p^-$, and

$$\sup_{F \in \mathbb{F}_{\mu,\sigma}} \frac{\text{OPT}(F)}{\text{REV}(p; F)} = \max \left\{ 1 + \frac{\sigma^2}{(\mu - p)^2}, \frac{\mu}{p} + \frac{\sigma^2}{p(\mu - p)} \right\}.$$

Theorem 1. *The deterministic robust approximation ratio of selling a single (μ, σ)-distributed item is exactly equal to*

$$\text{DAPX}(\mu, \sigma) = \rho_D(r) \approx 1 + 4 \cdot r^2,$$

where $r = \sigma/\mu$ and function $\rho_D(\cdot)$ is given in Definition 1. In particular, this is achieved by offering a take-it-or-leave-it price of $p = \frac{\rho_D(r)}{2\rho_D(r)-1} \cdot \mu$.

4   Single Item: Lotteries

In this section, we continue to focus on a single-item setting, but now we study the robust approximation ratio that can be achieved by a randomized mechanism, i.e. by randomizing over posted prices. Carrasco et al. [13] have given the explicit solution to the robust *absolute* revenue problem,

$$\sup_{A \in \mathbb{A}_1} \inf_{F \in \mathbb{F}_{\mu,\sigma}} \text{REV}(A; F). \tag{2}$$

We state below a proposition that can be directly derived from their work and which would be very useful for our setting.

Proposition 1. *For $\mu > 0$, $\sigma \geq 0$, the value of the maximin problem (2) is given by*

$$\sup_{A \in \mathbb{A}_1} \inf_{F \in \mathbb{F}_{\mu,\sigma}} \text{REV}(A; F) = \pi_1,$$

where π_1 is derived by the unique solution of the system in Definition 2. Moreover, this value is achieved by the log-lottery $P_{\mu,\sigma}^{\log}$ described in Definition 2.

The above characterization can be directly used to derive a logarithmic upper bound on the robust approximation ratio:

Theorem 2. *The robust approximation ratio of selling a single (μ, σ)-distributed item is at most*

$$\text{APX}(\mu, \sigma) \leq \rho(r) \approx 1 + \ln(1 + r^2),$$

where $r = \sigma/\mu$ and function ρ is given in Definition 1. In particular, this is achieved by the log-lottery described in Definition 2.

By looking at the proof of the previous theorem, it is not difficult to see that our upper bound is also an upper bound with respect to welfare (which for a single (μ, σ) distribution is simply given by μ). If we were interested in comparing the revenue of our auction to the maximum welfare, then it immediately follows from Proposition 1 that the bound is exact and tight. However, our main goal in the present paper is to provide tight bounds with respect to the optimal *revenue*, and achieving this requires some extra work.

Before we go into the actual construction of our lower bound instances, we need some technical preliminaries and to recall Yao's principle (see, e.g., [8, Sect. 8.3] or [41, Sect. 2.2.2]). As we already mentioned (see Sect. 2.1), a randomized mechanism $A \in \mathbb{A}_1$ can be interpreted as a randomization over prices $p \sim A$. From (1), we are interested in the value of a game in which the mechanism designer plays first, randomizing over posted prices, and the adversary plays second, choosing a worst-case distribution. Intuitively, Yao's principle states that this is at least the value of another game in which the adversary plays first, randomizing over their choices, and the mechanism designer plays second, choosing a deterministic response, i.e. a single posted price.

However, to define this second game formally, we would have to first explain what it means for the adversary to randomize over probability distributions, which form an infinite-dimensional space. Informally, this corresponds to a space of "distributions over distributions"; but in order to avoid technical or measure-theoretical issues, we focus on a specific model of randomization, which in the literature gives rise to the concept of *mixture* or *contagious* distribution (see, e.g., [39, Chap. III.4]).

Definition 3. *Let $\mathfrak{F}$ be a class of cumulative distribution functions over the nonnegative reals, and consider any measure space over a ground set T. By an $\mathfrak{F}$-mixture with parameter space T, we mean a pair (Θ, F), where Θ is a probability measure in T, and F is a measurable function of type $F : \mathbb{R}_{\geq 0} \times T \to \mathbb{R}$, whose sections are in $\mathfrak{F}$; i.e. for any parameter $\theta \in T$, the function $F_\theta : \mathbb{R}_{\geq 0} \to \mathbb{R}$ given by $F_\theta(x) = F(x; \theta)$ is a cumulative distribution in $\mathfrak{F}$.*

Given an $\mathfrak{F}$-mixture (Θ, F), we denote its posterior *distribution by $\mathbb{E}_{\theta \sim \Theta}[F_\theta]$; this is specified by the cdf*

$$\mathbb{E}_{\theta \sim \Theta}[F_\theta](z) = \int F(z; \theta) d\Theta(\theta) = \mathbb{E}_{\theta \sim \Theta}[F_\theta(z)].$$

When $\mathfrak{F} = \mathbb{F}_{\mu, \sigma}$ is the class of (μ, σ) distributions, we shall let $\Delta_{\mu, \sigma}$ denote the class of (μ, σ) mixtures, that is, the class of mixtures over $\mathbb{F}_{\mu, \sigma}$ (with arbitrary, unspecified parameter space). We can interpret (Θ, F) as a convex combination of distributions, so that the cdf of $\mathbb{E}_{\theta \sim \Theta}[F_\theta]$ is the convex combination of the corresponding cdfs; alternatively, $\mathbb{E}_{\theta \sim \Theta}[F]$ can be seen as the cdf of a random variable that first samples a distribution F_θ according to $\theta \sim \Theta$, and then samples a value z according to F_θ.

Now that we have carefully described the adversarial model, we are ready to state our main technical tool, whose proof makes use of a "non-standard" version of Yao's principle involving continuous spaces.

Lemma 3. *For any μ, σ, the robust approximation ratio is lower bounded by*

$$\text{APX}(\mu, \sigma) \geq \sup_{(\Theta, F) \in \Delta_{\mu,\sigma}} \frac{\mathbb{E}_{\theta \sim \Theta}[\text{OPT}(F_\theta)]}{\text{OPT}(\mathbb{E}_{\theta \sim \Theta}[F_\theta])}. \tag{3}$$

To construct an adversarial instance, we design a distribution over two-point mass distributions, finely-tuned such that the resulting mixture becomes a truncated "equal-revenue style" distribution. This gives rise to the following lower bound, which asymptotically matches that of Theorem 2.

Theorem 3. *For a single (μ, σ)-distributed item, the robust approximation ratio is at least*

$$\text{APX}(\mu, \sigma) \geq 1 + \ln(1 + r^2), \qquad \text{where } r = \sigma/\mu.$$

5 Multiple Items

In this section we finally consider the more general setting of a single additive buyer with valuations for m items. As it turns out, the main tools developed in Sect. 4 can be leveraged very naturally to produce similar upper and lower bounds. We get the following upper bounds for both correlated and independent item valuations.

Theorem 4. *The robust approximation ratio of selling m (possibly correlated) $(\vec{\mu}, \vec{\sigma})$-distributed items is at most*

$$\text{APX}(\vec{\mu}, \vec{\sigma}) \leq \rho(r_{\max}), \qquad \text{where } r_{\max} = \max_{j=1,\dots,m} r_j, \ r_j = \frac{\sigma_j}{\mu_j}$$

and function ρ is given in Definition 1. This is achieved by selling each item j separately using the log-lottery $P^{\log}_{\mu_j, \sigma_j}$ from Definition 2.

Furthermore, if the items are independently distributed, the above bound improves to

$$\text{APX}(\vec{\mu}, \vec{\sigma}) \leq \rho(\bar{r}), \qquad \text{where } \bar{r} = \frac{\bar{\sigma}}{\bar{\mu}}, \ \bar{\mu} = \sum_{j=1}^{m} \mu_j, \ \bar{\sigma} = \sqrt{\sum_{j=1}^{m} \sigma_j^2},$$

achieved by selling the items in a single full-bundle using the log-lottery $P^{\log}_{\bar{\mu}, \bar{\sigma}}$ from Definition 2.

Corollary 1. *The robust approximation ratio of selling m independently (μ, σ)-distributed items is at most*

$$\text{APX}(\vec{\mu}, \vec{\sigma}) \leq \rho\left(\frac{r}{\sqrt{m}}\right),$$

where $r = \sigma/\mu$, achieved by selling the items in a single full-bundle using the mechanism given in Theorem 2.

Although the mechanisms presented in Theorem 4 are extremely simple (lotteries over separate pricing or bundle pricing), we can actually show asymptotically matching lower bounds for *any* choice of the coefficients of variation:

Theorem 5. *Fix any positive integer m and positive real numbers $r_1, \ldots, r_m$, and let $r = \max_j r_j$. Then, for any $\varepsilon > 0$, there exist $\vec{\mu} = (\mu_1, \ldots, \mu_m) \in \mathbb{R}_{>0}^m$, $\vec{\sigma} = (\sigma_1, \ldots, \sigma_m) \in \mathbb{R}_{\geq 0}^m$ with $r_j = \sigma_j/\mu_j$, such that*

$$\mathrm{APX}(\vec{\mu}, \vec{\sigma}) \geq 1 - \varepsilon + \ln(1 + r^2).$$

Furthermore, this lower bound is achieved by independent (μ_j, σ_j)-distributions.

References

1. Azar, P., Daskalakis, C., Micali, S., Weinberg, S.M.: Optimal and efficient parametric auctions. In: Proceedings of the 24th Annual ACM-SIAM Symposium on Discrete Algorithms (SODA), pp. 596–604 (2013). https://doi.org/10.1137/1.9781611973105.43
2. Azar, P., Micali, S.: Optimal parametric auctions. Technical report, MIT-CSAIL-TR-2012-015 (2012). http://hdl.handle.net/1721.1/70556
3. Azar, P.D., Micali, S.: Parametric digital auctions. In: Proceedings of the 4th Conference on Innovations in Theoretical Computer Science (ITCS), pp. 231–232 (2013). https://doi.org/10.1145/2422436.2422464
4. Babaioff, M., Immorlica, N., Lucier, B., Weinberg, S.M.: A simple and approximately optimal mechanism for an additive buyer. In: Proceedings of the 55th Annual Symposium on Foundations of Computer Science (FOCS), pp. 21–30 (2014). https://doi.org/10.1109/FOCS.2014.11
5. Bandi, C., Bertsimas, D.: Optimal design for multi-item auctions: a robust optimization approach. Math. Oper. Res. **39**(4), 1012–1038 (2014). https://doi.org/10.1287/moor.2014.0645
6. Bei, X., Gravin, N., Lu, P., Tang, Z.G.: Correlation-robust analysis of single item auction. In: Proceedings of the 30th Annual ACM-SIAM Symposium on Discrete Algorithms (SODA), pp. 193–208 (2019). https://doi.org/10.1137/1.9781611975482.13
7. Bergemann, D., Schlag, K.: Robust monopoly pricing. J. Econ. Theory **146**(6), 2527–2543 (2011). https://doi.org/10.1016/j.jet.2011.10.018
8. Borodin, A., El-Yaniv, R.: Online Computation and Competitive Analysis. Cambridge University Press, Cambridge (1998)
9. Bulow, J., Klemperer, P.: Auctions versus negotiations. Am. Econ. Rev. **86**(1), 180–194 (1996)
10. Cai, Y., Daskalakis, C.: Learning multi-item auctions with (or without) samples. In: Proceedings of the 58th Annual Symposium on Foundations of Computer Science (FOCS), pp. 516–527 (2017). https://doi.org/10.1109/FOCS.2017.54
11. Cai, Y., Devanur, N.R., Weinberg, S.M.: A duality based unified approach to Bayesian mechanism design. In: Proceedings of the 48th Annual ACM SIGACT Symposium on Theory of Computing (STOC), pp. 926–939. ACM Press (2016). https://doi.org/10.1145/2897518.2897645
12. Cai, Y., Zhao, M.: Simple mechanisms for subadditive buyers via duality. In: Proceedings of the 49th Annual ACM SIGACT Symposium on Theory of Computing (STOC), pp. 170–183 (2017). https://doi.org/10.1145/3055399.3055465

13. Carrasco, V., Luz, V.F., Kos, N., Messner, M., Monteiro, P., Moreira, H.: Optimal selling mechanisms under moment conditions. J. Econ. Theory **177**, 245–279 (2018). https://doi.org/10.1016/j.jet.2018.05.005
14. Carroll, G.: Robustness and separation in multidimensional screening. Econometrica **85**(2), 453–488 (2017). https://doi.org/10.3982/ECTA14165
15. Carroll, G.: Robustness in mechanism design and contracting. Annu. Rev. Econ. **11**(1), 139–166 (2019). https://doi.org/10.1146/annurev-economics-080218-025616
16. Chawla, S., Fu, H., Karlin, A.R.: Approximate revenue maximization in interdependent value settings. CoRR abs/1408.4424 (2014)
17. Chawla, S., Hartline, J.D., Malec, D.L., Sivan, B.: Multi-parameter mechanism design and sequential posted pricing. In: Proceedings of the 42nd ACM Symposium on Theory of Computing (STOC), pp. 311–320 (2010). https://doi.org/10.1145/1806689.1806733
18. Chen, J., Li, B., Li, Y., Lu, P.: Bayesian auctions with efficient queries. CoRR abs/1804.07451 (2018)
19. Chen, X., Diakonikolas, I., Orfanou, A., Paparas, D., Sun, X., Yannakakis, M.: On the complexity of optimal lottery pricing and randomized mechanisms. In: Proceedings of 56th Annual Symposium on Foundations of Computer Science (FOCS), pp. 1464–1479 (2015). https://doi.org/10.1109/FOCS.2015.93
20. Chen, X., Matikas, G., Paparas, D., Yannakakis, M.: On the complexity of simple and optimal deterministic mechanisms for an additive buyer. In: Proceedings of the 29th Annual ACM-SIAM Symposium on Discrete Algorithms (SODA), pp. 2036–2049 (2018). https://doi.org/10.1137/1.9781611975031.133
21. Daskalakis, C., Deckelbaum, A., Tzamos, C.: The complexity of optimal mechanism design. In: Proceedings of the 25th Annual ACM-SIAM Symposium on Discrete Algorithms (SODA), pp. 1302–1318 (2013). https://doi.org/10.1137/1.9781611973402.96
22. Daskalakis, C., Deckelbaum, A., Tzamos, C.: Strong duality for a multiple-good monopolist. Econometrica **85**(3), 735–767 (2017). https://doi.org/10.3982/ECTA12618
23. Dhangwatnotai, P., Roughgarden, T., Yan, Q.: Revenue maximization with a single sample. Games Econ. Behav. **91**(C), 318–333 (2014)
24. Dütting, P., Roughgarden, T., Talgam-Cohen, I.: Simple versus optimal contracts. In: Proceedings of the 20th ACM Conference on Economics and Computation (EC), pp. 369–387 (2019). https://doi.org/10.1145/3328526.3329591
25. Fu, H., Immorlica, N., Lucier, B., Strack, P.: Randomization beats second price as a prior-independent auction. In: Proceedings of the 16th ACM Conference on Economics and Computation (EC), p. 323 (2015). https://doi.org/10.1145/2764468.2764489
26. Giannakopoulos, Y., Koutsoupias, E.: Duality and optimality of auctions for uniform distributions. SIAM J. Comput. **47**(1), 121–165 (2018). https://doi.org/10.1137/16M1072218
27. Giannakopoulos, Y., Poças, D., Tsigonias-Dimitriadis, A.: Robust revenue maximization under minimal statistical information. CoRR abs/1907.04220 (2019)
28. Gravin, N., Lu, P.: Separation in correlation-robust monopolist problem with budget. In: Proceedings of the 29th Annual ACM-SIAM Symposium on Discrete Algorithms (SODA), pp. 2069–2080 (2018). https://doi.org/10.1137/1.9781611975031.135

29. Haghpanah, N., Hartline, J.: Reverse mechanism design. In: Proceedings of the 16th ACM Conference on Economics and Computation (EC), pp. 757–758 (2015). https://doi.org/10.1145/2764468.2764498
30. Hart, S., Nisan, N.: The menu-size complexity of auctions. In: Proceedings of the 14th ACM Conference on Electronic Commerce (EC), pp. 565–566 (2013). https://doi.org/10.1145/2482540.2482544
31. Hart, S., Nisan, N.: Approximate revenue maximization with multiple items. J. Econ. Theory **172**, 313–347 (2017). https://doi.org/10.1016/j.jet.2017.09.001
32. Hartline, J.D.: Mechanism design and approximation (2013), manuscript. http://jasonhartline.com/MDnA/
33. Hartline, J.D., Roughgarden, T.: Simple versus optimal mechanisms. In: Proceedings of the 10th ACM Conference on Electronic Commerce (EC), pp. 225–234 (2009). https://doi.org/10.1145/1566374.1566407
34. Kendall, M.G.: The Advanced Theory of Statistics, vol. I, 4th edn. Charles Griffin, Glasgow (1948)
35. Li, X., Yao, A.C.C.: On revenue maximization for selling multiple independently distributed items. Proc. Nat. Acad. Sci. **110**(28), 11232–11237 (2013). https://doi.org/10.1073/pnas.1309533110
36. Li, Y., Lu, P., Ye, H.: Revenue maximization with imprecise distribution. In: Proceedings of the 18th International Conference on Autonomous Agents and Multi-Agent Systems (AAMAS), pp. 1582–1590 (2019). http://dl.acm.org/citation.cfm?id=3306127.3331877
37. Manelli, A.M., Vincent, D.R.: Multidimensional mechanism design: revenue maximization and the multiple-good monopoly. J. Econ. Theory **137**(1), 153–185 (2007). https://doi.org/10.1016/j.jet.2006.12.007
38. Milgrom, P.: Putting Auction Theory to Work. Cambridge University Press, Cambridge (2004). https://doi.org/10.1017/CBO9780511813825.009
39. Mood, A.M., Graybill, F.A., Boes, D.C.: Introduction to the Theory of Statistics, 3rd edn. McGraw-Hill, New York (1974)
40. Moriguti, S.: Extremal properties of extreme value distributions. Ann. Math. Stat. **22**(4), 523–536 (1951)
41. Motwani, R., Raghavan, P.: Randomized Algorithms. Cambridge University Press, Cambridge (1995)
42. Myerson, R.B.: Optimal auction design. Math. Oper. Res. **6**(1), 58–73 (1981). https://doi.org/10.1287/moor.6.1.58
43. Roughgarden, T., Talgam-Cohen, I.: Approximately optimal mechanism design. Annu. Rev. Econ. **11**(1), 355–381 (2019). https://doi.org/10.1146/annurev-economics-080218-025607
44. Rubinstein, A., Weinberg, S.M.: Simple mechanisms for a subadditive buyer and applications to revenue monotonicity. ACM Trans. Econ. Comput. **6**(3–4), 19:1–19:25 (2018). https://doi.org/10.1145/3105448
45. Wilson, R.: Game-theoretic analyses of trading processes. In: Advances in Economic Theory: Fifth World Congress, pp. 33–70. Econometric Society Monographs, Cambridge University Press (1987). https://doi.org/10.1017/CCOL0521340446.002
46. Yao, A.C.C.: An n-to-1 bidder reduction for multi-item auctions and its applications. In: Proceedings of the 26th Annual ACM-SIAM Symposium on Discrete Algorithms (SODA), pp. 92–109 (2015). https://doi.org/10.1137/1.9781611973730.8

Revenue Monotonicity Under Misspecified Bidders

Makis Arsenis[1]([✉]), Odysseas Drosis[2], and Robert Kleinberg[1]

[1] Cornell University, Ithaca, NY, USA
{marsenis,rdk}@cs.cornell.edu
[2] EPFL, Lausanne, Switzerland
odysseas.drosis@epfl.ch

Abstract. We investigate revenue guarantees for auction mechanisms in a model where a distribution is specified for each bidder, but only some of the distributions are correct. The subset of bidders whose distribution is correctly specified (henceforth, the "green bidders") is unknown to the auctioneer. The question we address is whether the auctioneer can run a mechanism that is guaranteed to obtain at least as much revenue, in expectation, as would be obtained by running an optimal mechanism on the green bidders only. For single-parameter feasibility environments, we find that the answer depends on the feasibility constraint. For matroid environments, running the optimal mechanism using all the specified distributions (including the incorrect ones) guarantees at least as much revenue in expectation as running the optimal mechanism on the green bidders. For any feasibility constraint that is not a matroid, there exists a way of setting the specified distributions and the true distributions such that the opposite conclusion holds.

1 Introduction

In a seminal paper nearly forty years ago [30], Roger Myerson derived a beautifully precise characterization of optimal (i.e., revenue maximizing) mechanisms for Bayesian single-parameter environments. One way this result has been critiqued over the years is by noting that auctioneers may have incorrect beliefs about bidders' values; if so, the mechanism recommended by the theory will actually be suboptimal.

In this paper we evaluate this critique by examining revenue guarantees for optimal mechanisms when a subset of bidders' value distributions are misspecified, but the auctioneer doesn't know which of the distributions are incorrect. Our model is inspired by the literature on *semi-random adversaries* in the theoretical computer science literature, particularly the work of Bradac et al. [8] on robust algorithms for the secretary problem. In the model we investigate here, the auctioneer is given (not necessarily identical) distributions for each of n bidders. An unknown subset of the bidders, called the *green bidders*, draw their values independently at random from these distributions. The other bidders, called the *red bidders*, draw their values from distributions other than the given ones.

O. Drosis—This work was done while the author was a student in the Masters of Engineering program at Cornell University.

© Springer Nature Switzerland AG 2020
X. Chen et al. (Eds.): WINE 2020, LNCS 12495, pp. 191–205, 2020.
https://doi.org/10.1007/978-3-030-64946-3_14

The question we ask in this paper is, "When can one guarantee that the expected revenue of the optimal mechanism for the given distributions is at least as great as the expected revenue that would be obtained by excluding the red bidders and running an optimal mechanism on the green subset of bidders?" In other words, can the presence of bidders with misspecified distributions in a market be worse (for the auctioneer's expected revenue) than if those bidders were absent? Or does the increased competition from incorporating the red bidders always offset the revenue loss due to ascribing the wrong distribution to them?

We give a precise answer to this question, for single-parameter feasibility environments. We show that the answer depends on the structure of the feasibility constraint that defines which sets of bidders may win the auction. For matroid feasibility constraints, the revenue of the optimal mechanism is always greater than or equal to the revenue obtained by running the optimal mechanism on the set of green bidders. For any feasibility constraint that is not a matroid, the opposite holds true: there is a way of setting the specified distribution and the true distributions such that the revenue of the optimal mechanism for the specified distributions, when bids are drawn from the true distributions, is *strictly less* than the revenue of the optimal mechanism on the green bidders only.

The economic intuition behind this result is fairly easy to explain. The matroid property guarantees that the winning red bidders in the auction can be put in one-to-one correspondence with losing green bidders who would have won in the absence of their red competitors, in such a way that the revenue collected from each winning red bidder offsets the lost revenue from the corresponding green bidder whom he or she displaces. When the feasibility constraint is not a matroid, this one-to-one correspondence does not always exist; a single green bidder might be displaced by two or more red bidders each of whom pays almost nothing. The optimal mechanism allows this to happen at some bid profiles, because the low revenue received on such bid profiles is compensated by the high expected revenue that would be received if the red bidders had sampled values from elsewhere in their distributions. However, since the red bidders' distributions are misspecified, the anticipated revenue from these more favorable bid profiles may never materialize.

Our result can be interpreted as a type of revenue monotonicity statement for optimal mechanisms in single-parameter matroid environments. However it does not follow from other known results on revenue monotonicity, and it is illuminating to draw some points of distinction between our result and earlier ones. Let us begin by distinguishing *pointwise* and *setwise* revenue monotonicity results: the former concern how the revenue earned on individual bid profiles varies as the bids are increased, the latter concern how (expected) revenue varies as the set of bidders is enlarged.

- VCG mechanisms are neither pointwise nor setwise revenue monotone in general, but in single-parameter matroid feasibility environments, VCG revenue satisfies both pointwise and setwise monotonicity. In fact, Dughmi et al. [19] observed that VCG revenue obeys setwise monotonicity *if and only if* the feasibility constraint is a matroid. The proof of this result in [19] rests on a slightly erroneous characterization of matroids but a part of our work (namely Lemma 4 below) can be used to correct this minor error. A complete discussion and a proposed fix is included in the full version of our paper.

- Myerson's optimal mechanism is not pointwise revenue monotone, even for single-item auctions. For example, consider using Myerson's optimal mechanism to sell a single item to Alice whose value is uniformly distributed in $[0, 4]$ and Bob whose value is uniformly distributed in $[0, 8]$. When Alice bids 0 and Bob bids 5, Bob wins and pays 4. If Alice increases her bid to 4, she wins but pays only 3.
- However, Myerson's optimal mechanism is *always* setwise revenue monotone in single-parameter environments with downward-closed feasibility constraints, regardless of whether the feasibility constraint is a matroid. This is because the mechanism's expected revenue is equal to the expectation of the maximum, over all feasible sets of winners, of the winners' combined ironed virtual value. Enlarging the set of bidders only enlarges the collection of sets over which this maximization is performed, hence it cannot decrease the expectation of the maximum.

Our main result is analogous to the setwise revenue monotonicity of Myerson revenue, except that we are considering monotonicity with respect to the operation of enlarging the set of bidders *by adding bidders whose value distributions are potentially misspecified*. We show that the behavior of Myerson revenue with respect to this stricter notion of setwise revenue monotonicity holds under matroid feasibility constraints *but not under any other feasibility constraints*, in contrast to the traditional setwise revenue monotonicity that is satisfied by Myerson mechanisms under arbitrarily downward-closed constraints.

1.1 Related Work

Semi-random models are a class of models studied in the theoretical computer science literature in which the input data is partly generated by random sampling, and partly by a worst-case adversary. Initially studied in the setting of graph coloring [7] and graph partitioning [20, 28], the study of semi-random models has since been broadened to statistical estimation [18, 26], multi-armed bandits [27], and secretary problems [8]. Our work extends semi-random models into the realm of Bayesian mechanism design. In particular, our model of green and red bidders resembles in a sense that of Bradac et al. [8] for the secretary problem which served as inspiration for this work. In both settings, green players/elements behave randomly and independently while red players/elements behave adversarially. In the secretary model of [8], red elements can choose arbitrary arrival times while green elements' arrival times are i.i.d. uniform in $[0, 1]$ and independent of the red arrival times. Similarly, in our setting red bidders can set their bids arbitrarily whereas green bidders sample their bids from known distributions, independently of the red bidders and one another.

Our work can be seen as part of a general framework of *robust mechanism design*, a research direction inspired by Wilson [34], who famously wrote,

Game theory has a great advantage in explicitly analyzing the consequences of trading rules that presumably are really common knowledge; it is deficient to the extent it assumes other features to be common knowledge, such as one agent's probability assessment about another's preferences or information. I foresee the progress of game theory as depending on successive reductions in the base of common knowledge required to conduct useful analyses of practical problems. Only by repeated weakening of common knowledge assumptions will the theory approximate reality.

This *Wilson doctrine* has been used to justify more robust solution concepts such as dominant strategy and ex post implementation. The question of when these stronger solution concepts are required in order to ensure robustness was explored in a research program initiated by Bergemann and Morris [4] and surveyed in [5]. Robustness and the Wilson doctrine have also been used to justify prior-free [21] and prior-independent [24] mechanisms as well as mechanisms that learn from samples [9–11, 15, 17, 25, 29]. A different approach to robust mechanism design assumes that, rather than being given the bid distributions, the designer is given constraints on the set of potential bid distributions and aims to optimize a minimax objective on the expected revenue. For example Azar and Micali [2] assume the seller knows only the mean and variance of each bidder's distribution, Carrasco et al. [12] generalize this to sellers that know the first N moments of each bidder's distribution, Azar et al. [1] consider sellers that know the median or other quantiles of the distributions, and Carroll [13] introduced a model in which bids are correlated but the seller only knows each bidder's marginal distribution (see [3, 22] for further work in this correlation-robust model). Bergemann and Schlag [6] develop mechanisms for the single-item/single-bidder setting with robust revenue guarantees when the seller is assumed to be given a distribution which lies in a small neighborhood of the true distribution. Brustle et al. [9] and Cai and Daskalakis [11], as part of their work, derive mechanism robustification results (where robustness is defined in a similar sense to [6]) for more general settings.

Another related subject is that of *revenue monotonicity* of mechanisms—regardless of the existence of adversarial bidders. Dughmi et al. [19] prove a result very close in spirit to ours. They consider the VCG mechanism in a single-parameter downward-closed environment and prove that it is revenue monotone if and only if the environment is a matroid akin to our Theorems 1 and 2. Devanur et al. [16] prove that optimal auction revenue is monotone under first-order stochastic dominance, a result which they apply to the study of sample complexity in auction revenue maximization. Rastegari et al. [32] study revenue monotonicity properties of mechanisms (including VCG) for Combinatorial Auctions. Under some reasonable assumptions, they prove that no mechanism can be revenue monotone when bidders have single-minded valuations. Chen et al. [14] use a type of *reverse* setwise revenue monotonicity—the revenue that optimal mechanisms extract from a fixed set of bidders is non-increasing as other bidders join the auction— to derive revenue approximation guarantees in an information elicitation setting where knowledge about the players' distributions is scattered among the players and the seller is trying to both elicit this knowledge and sell (multiple) item(s).

2 Preliminaries

2.1 Matroids

Given a finite ground set E and a collection $\mathcal{I} \subseteq 2^E$ of subsets of E such that $\emptyset \in \mathcal{I}$, we call $\mathcal{M} = (E, \mathcal{I})$ a *set system*. $\mathcal{M}$ is a *downward-closed* set system if $\mathcal{I}$ satisfies the following property: (I1) (**downward-closed axiom**) If $B \in \mathcal{I}$ and $A \subseteq B$ then $A \in \mathcal{I}$. Furthermore, $\mathcal{M}$ is called a *matroid* if it satisfies both (I1) and: (I2) (**exchange axiom**) If $A, B \in \mathcal{I}$ and $|A| > |B|$ then there exists $x \in A \backslash B$ such that $B + x \in \mathcal{I}$[1].

In the context of matroids, sets in (resp. not in) $\mathcal{I}$ are called *independent* (resp. *dependent*). An (inclusion-wise) maximal independent set is called a *basis*. A fundamental consequence of axioms (I1), (I2) is that all bases of a matroid have equal cardinality and this common quantity is called the *rank* of the matroid. A *circuit* is a minimal dependent set. The set of all circuits of a matroid will be denoted by $\mathcal{C}$. The following is a standard property of $\mathcal{C}$.

Proposition 1 ([31, **Proposition 1.4.11**]). *For any $\mathcal{C}$ which is the circuit set of a matroid $\mathcal{M}$, let $C_1, C_2 \in \mathcal{C}, e \in C_1 \cap C_2$ and $f \in C_1 \backslash C_2$. Then there exists $C_3 \in \mathcal{C}$ such that $f \in C_3 \subseteq (C_1 \cup C_2) - e$.*

For any set system $\mathcal{M} = (E, \mathcal{I})$ and any given $S \subseteq E$, define $\mathcal{I}_{|S} = \mathcal{I} \cap 2^S$ and call $\mathcal{M}_{|S} = (S, \mathcal{I}_{|S})$ the *restriction* of $\mathcal{M}$ on S. Notice that restrictions maintain properties (I1), (I2) if they were satisfied already in $\mathcal{M}$.

If $\mathcal{M} = (E, \mathcal{I})$ is equipped with a weight function $w : E \to \mathbb{R}^+$ it is called a *weighted* matroid. The problem of finding an independent set of maximum sum of weights is central to the study of matroids. A very simple greedy algorithm is guaranteed to find the optimal solution and in fact matroids are exactly the downward-closed systems for which that greedy algorithm is always guaranteed to find the optimal solution.

GREEDY. Sort the elements of E in non-increasing order of weights $w(e_1) \geq w(e_2) \geq \ldots \geq w(e_n)$. Loop through the elements in that order adding each element to the current solution as long as the current solution remains an independent set.

Lemma 1 ([31, **Lemma 1.8.3.**]). *Let $\mathcal{M} = (E, \mathcal{I})$ be a weighted downward-closed set system. Then GREEDY is guaranteed to return an independent set of maximum total weight for every weight function $w : E \to \mathbb{R}^+$ if and only $\mathcal{M}$ is a matroid.*

In what follows we're going to assume without loss of generality that the function w is one-to-one, meaning that no two element have the same weight. All proofs can be adapted to work in the general case using any deterministic tie breaking rule.

The following proposition provides a convenient way for updating the solution to an optimization problem under matroid constraints when new elements are added. The proof is standard in Matroid Theory and is omitted.

Proposition 2. *Let $\mathcal{M} = (E, \mathcal{I})$ be a weighted matroid with weight function $w : E \to \mathbb{R}^+$. Consider the max-weight independent set I of the restricted matroid $\mathcal{M}_{|E-x}$. Then*

---

[1] We use the shorthand $B + x$ (resp. $B - x$) to mean $B \cup \{x\}$ (resp. $B \backslash \{x\}$) throughout the paper.

the max-weight independent set I^* of M can be obtained from I as follows: if $(I + x) \in I$ then $I^* = I + x$, otherwise, $I^* = (I + x) - y$ where y is the minimum-weight element in the unique circuit C of $I + x$.

For a more in-depth study of matroid theory, we point the reader to the classic text of Oxley [31].

2.2   Optimal Mechanism Design

We study auctions modeled as a *Bayesian single-parameter environment*, a standard mechanism design setting in which a *seller* (or mechanism designer) holds many identical copies of an item they want to sell. A set of n bidders (or players), numbered 1 through n, participate in the auction and each bidder i has a private, non-negative value $v_i \sim F_i$, sampled (independently across bidders) from a distribution F_i known to the seller. Abusing notation, we'll use F_i to also denote the cumulative distribution function and f_i to denote the probability density function of the respective distribution. The value of each bidder expresses their valuation for receiving one item. Let V_i be the support of distribution F_i and define $V = V_1 \times \ldots \times V_n$. For a vector $\mathbf{v} \in V$, we use the standard notation $\mathbf{v}_{-i} = (v_1, \ldots, v_{i-1}, v_{i+1}, \ldots, v_n)$ to express the vector of valuations of all bidders *except* bidder i. When the index set $[n]$ is partitioned into two sets A, B and we have vectors $\mathbf{v}_A \in \mathbb{R}^A$, $\mathbf{w}_B \in \mathbb{R}^B$, we will abuse notation and let $(\mathbf{v}_A, \mathbf{w}_B)$ denote the vector obtained by interleaving $\mathbf{v}_A$ and $\mathbf{w}_B$, i.e. $(\mathbf{v}_A, \mathbf{w}_B)$ is the vector $\mathbf{u} \in \mathbb{R}^n$ such that $u_i = v_i$ for $i \in A$ and $u_i = w_i$ for $i \in B$. Similarly, when $\mathbf{v} \in V$, $i \in [n]$, and $z \in \mathbb{R}$, $(z, \mathbf{v}_{-i})$ will denote the vector obtained by replacing the ith component of $\mathbf{v}$ with z.

A *feasibility constraint* $I \subseteq 2^{[n]}$ defines all subsets of bidders that can be simultaneously declared winners of the auction. We will interchangeably denote elements of I both as subsets of $[n]$ and as vectors in $\{0, 1\}^n$. Of special interest are feasibility constraints which define the independent sets of a matroid. We will sometimes use the phrase *matroid market* to indicate this fact. Matroid markets model many real world applications. For example when selling k identical copies of an item, the market is a uniform rank k matroid. Another example is kidney exchange markets which can be modeled as transversal matroids [33].

In a *sealed-bid auction*, each bidder i submits a *bid* $b_i \in V_i$ simultaneously to the mechanism. Formally, a *mechanism* $\mathcal{A}$ is a pair (x, p) of an allocation rule $x : V \to I$ accepting the bids and choosing a feasible outcome and a *payment rule* $p : V \to \mathbb{R}^n$ assigning each bidder a monetary payment they need to make to the mechanism. We denote by $x_i(\mathbf{b})$ (or just x_i when clear from the context) the i-th component of the 0-1 vector $x(\mathbf{b})$ and similarly for p. An allocation rule is called *monotone* if the function $x_i(z, \mathbf{b}_{-i})$ is monotone non-decreasing in z for any vector $\mathbf{b}_{-i} \in V_{-i}$ and any bidder i.

We assume bidders have *quasilinear utilities* meaning that bidder's i utility for winning the auction and having to pay a price p_i is $u_i = v_i - p_i$ and 0 if they do not win and pay nothing. Bidders are selfish agents aiming to maximize their own utility.

A mechanism is called *truthful* if bidding $b_i = v_i$ is a *dominant strategy* for each bidder, i.e. no bidder can increase their utility by reporting $b_i \neq v_i$ regardless the values and bids of the other bidders. An allocation rule x is called *implementable* if there exists a payment rule p such that (x, p) is truthful. Such mechanisms are well understood and easy to reason about since we can predict how the bidders are going to behave. In what follows we focus our attention only on truthful mechanisms and thus use the terms value and bid interchangeably.

A well known result of Myerson [30] states that a given allocation rule x is implementable if and only if x is monotone. In case x is monotone, Myerson gives an explicit formula for the unique[2] payment rule such that (x, p) is truthful. In the single-parameter setting we're studying, the payment rule can be informally described as follows: p_i is equal to the minimum b_i that bidder i has to report such that they are included in the set of winners—we'll refer to such a b_i as the *critical bid* of bidder i.

The mechanism designer, who is collecting all the payments, commonly aims to maximize her *expected revenue* which for a mechanism $\mathcal{A}$ is defined as $\text{Rev}(\mathcal{A}) = \mathbb{E}_{b_i \sim F_i} \left[\sum_{i \in [n]} p_i \right]$.

Lemma 2 [30]. *For any truthful mechanism (x, p) and any bidder $i \in [n]$:*

$$\mathbb{E}[p_i] = \mathbb{E}[\phi_i(b_i) \cdot x_i(b_i, \mathbf{b}_{-i})]$$

where the expectations are taken over $b_1, \ldots, b_n \sim F_1, \ldots, F_n$, the function $\phi_i(\cdot)$ is defined as

$$\phi_i(z) = z - \frac{1 - F_i(z)}{f_i(z)}$$

and $\phi_i(b_i)$ is called the virtual value *of bidder i.*

The importance of this lemma is that it reduces the problem of revenue maximization to that of virtual welfare maximization. More specifically, consider a sequence of distributions $F_1, \ldots, F_n$ which have the property that all ϕ_i are monotone nondecreasing (such distributions are called *regular*). In this case, the allocation rule that chooses a set of bidders with the maximum total virtual value (subject to feasibility constraints) is monotone (a consequence of the regularity condition) and thus implementable. We'll frequently denote this revenue-maximizing mechanism by MyerOPT.

More precisely, the MyerOPT mechanism works as follows:

- Collect bids b_i from every bidder $i \in [n]$.
- Compute $\phi_i(b_i)$ and discard all bidders whose virtual valuation is negative.
- Solve the optimization problem $S^* = \text{argmax}_{S \in I} \sum_{i \in S} \phi_i(b_i)$.
- Allocate the items to S^* and charge each bidder $i \in S^*$ their critical bid.

Handling non-regular distributions is possible using the standard technique of *ironing*. Very briefly, it works as follows. So far, we've been expressing x, p and ϕ as a function of the random vector $\mathbf{v}$. It is convenient to switch to the quantile space and express them as a function of a vector $\mathbf{q} \in [0, 1]^n$ where for a given sample z from F_i we let $q_i = \text{Pr}_{b_i \sim F_i}[b_i \geq z]$. Another way to think of this is, instead of sampling values, we sample quantiles q_i distributed uniformly at random in the interval $[0, 1]$ which are then transformed into values $v_i(q_i) = F_i^{-1}(1 - q_i)^3$. Let $R_i(q_i) = q_i \cdot v_i(q_i)$ and notice that

---

[2] Unique up to the normalizing assumption that $p_i = 0$ whenever $b_i = 0$.

[3] In general, $v_i(q_i) = \min \{v \mid F_i(v) \geq q_i\}$.

$\phi_i(v_i(q_i)) = \left. \frac{dR_i}{dq} \right|_{q=q_i}$. Now, since $v_i(\cdot)$ is a non-increasing function we have that $\phi_i(\cdot)$ is monotone if and only if R is concave.

Now, suppose that F_i is such that R_i is not concave. One can consider the concave hull of $\overline{R_i}$ of R_i which replaces R_i with a straight line in every interval that R_i was not following that concave hull. The corresponding function $\overline{\phi}_i(\cdot) = \frac{d\overline{R_i}}{dq}$ is called *ironed virtual value function*.

Lemma 3 ([23, **Theorem 3.18**]). *For any monotone allocation rule x and any virtual value function ϕ_i of bidder i, the expected virtual welfare of i is upper bounded by their expected ironed virtual value welfare.*

$$\mathbb{E}\left[\phi_i(v_i(q_i)) \cdot x_i(v_i(q_i), \mathbf{v}_{-i}(\mathbf{q}))\right] \leq \mathbb{E}\left[\overline{\phi}_i(v_i(q_i)) \cdot x_i(v_i(q_i), \mathbf{v}_{-i}(\mathbf{q}))\right]$$

Furthermore, the inequality holds with equality if the allocation rule x is such that for all bidders i, $x_i'(q) = 0$ whenever $\overline{R}_i(q) > R_i(q)$.

As a consequence, consider the monotone allocation rule which allocates to a feasible set of maximum total ironed virtual value. On the intervals where $\overline{R}_i(q) > R_i(q)$, $\overline{R}_i$ is linear as part of the concave hull so the ironed virtual value function, being a derivative of a linear function, is a constant. Therefore, the allocation rule is not affected when q ranges in such an interval.

A crucial property of any (ironed) virtual value function ϕ corresponding to a distribution F is that $z \geq \phi(z)$ for all z in the support of F. This is obvious for ϕ as defined in Lemma 2. We claim it also holds for ironed virtual value functions: if z lies in an interval where $\overline{\phi} = \phi$ it holds trivially. Otherwise, if $z \in [a, b]$ for some interval where ϕ needed ironing (i.e. $\overline{R}(q) > R(q)$ in the quantile space), we have: $z \geq a \geq \phi(a) = \overline{\phi}(a) = \overline{\phi}(z)$. We've thus proven:

Proposition 3. *Any (possibly non-regular) distribution F having an ironed virtual value function $\overline{\phi}$ satisfies $z \geq \overline{\phi}(z)$ for any z in the support of F.*

Remark 1. For simplicity, in the remainder of the paper we'll use ϕ and $\overline{\phi}$ interchangeably and we will refer to ϕ as virtual value function. The reader should keep in mind that if the associated distribution is non-regular, then *ironed* virtual value functions should be used instead.

3   Revenue Monotonicity on Matroid Markets

We extend the standard single-parameter environment to allow for bidders with misspecified distributions. Formally, the n bidders are partitioned into sets G and R; the former are called *green* and the latter *red*. The color of each bidder (green or red) is not revealed to the mechanism designer at any point. Green bidders sample their values from their respective distribution F_i but red bidders are sampling $v_i \sim F_i'$ for some $\{F_i'\}_{i \in R}$ which are completely unknown to the mechanism designer and can be adversarially chosen.

In this section we are interested in studying the behavior of Myerson's optimal mechanism when designed under the (wrong) assumption that $v_i \sim F_i$ for all $i \in [n]$.

Specifically, we ask the question of whether the existence of the red bidders could harm the expected revenue of the seller compared to the case where the seller was able to identify and exclude the red bidders, thus designing the optimal mechanism for the green bidders alone. The following definition makes this notion of revenue monotonicity more precise.

Definition 1 (RMMB). *Consider a single-parameter, downward-closed market* $M = (E, I)$ *of* $|E| = n$ *bidders. A mechanism* $\mathcal{A}$ *is* Revenue Monotone under Misspecified Bidders (RMMB) *if for any distributions* $F_1, \ldots, F_n$, *any number* $1 \leq k \leq n$ *of green bidders and any fixed misspecified bids* $\mathbf{b}_R \in \mathbb{R}^R$ *of the red bidders:*

$$\mathbb{E}\left[Rev(\mathcal{A}(\mathbf{b}_G, \mathbf{b}_R))\right] \geq \mathbb{E}\left[Rev(\mathcal{A}(\mathbf{b}_G))\right] \tag{1}$$

where both expectation are taken over $\mathbf{b}_G \sim \prod_{i \in G} F_i$.

An alternative definition of the revenue monotonicity property allows red bidders to have stochastic valuations drawn from distributions $F'_i \neq F_i$ instead of fixed bids. We note that the two definitions are equivalent: if $\mathcal{A}$ is RMMB according to Definition 1 then inequality (1) holds pointwise for any fixed misspecified bids and thus would also hold in expectation. For the other direction, if inequality (1) holds in expectation over the red bids, regardless of the choice of distributions $\{F'_i \mid i \in R\}$ then we may specialize to the case when each F'_i is a point-mass distribution with a single support point b_i for each $i \in R$, and then Definition 1 follows.

In what follows we assume bidders always submit bids that fall within the support of their respective distribution. Green bidders obviously follow that rule and red bidders should do as well, otherwise the mechanism could recognize they are red and just ignore them.

Consider first the simpler case of selling a single item. This corresponds to a uniform rank 1 matroid market. Intuitively when the item is allocated to a green bidder, the existence of the red bidders is not problematic and in fact could help increase the critical bid and thus the payment of the winner. On the other hand, when a red bidder wins one has to prove that they are not charged too little and thus risk bringing the expected revenue down.

Let $m = \max(\max_{i \in G} \phi_i(b_i), 0)$ be the random variable denoting the highest non-negative virtual value in the set of green bidders. Let also X be an indicator a random variable which is 1 if the winner belongs to G and Y denote an indicator random variable which is 1 if the winner belongs to R. For the mechanism MyerOPT have:

$$\mathbb{E}\left[\text{revenue from green bidders}\right] = \mathbb{E}\left[m \cdot X\right] \tag{2}$$

$$\mathbb{E}\left[\text{revenue from red bidders}\right] \geq \mathbb{E}\left[m \cdot Y\right] \tag{3}$$

where (2) follows from Myerson's lemma and (3) follows from the observation that the winner of the optimal auction never pays less than the second-highest virtual value. To see why the latter holds, let ϕ_s be the second highest virtual value, r be the red winner and g is the green player with the highest virtual value. The critical bid of the red winner is at least $\phi_r^{-1}(\phi_s) \geq \phi_r^{-1}(\phi_g(b_g)) \geq \phi_g(b_g)$ where we applied the fact that $x \geq \phi(x)$ to the virtual value function $\phi = \phi_r$ and the value $x = \phi_r^{-1}(\phi_g(b_g))$.

Summing (2) and (3) and using the fact that $X + Y = 1$ whenever $m > 0$, we find:

$$\mathbb{E}[\text{Revenue from all bidders } 1, \ldots, n] \geq \mathbb{E}[m \cdot X] + \mathbb{E}[m \cdot Y]$$
$$= \mathbb{E}[m]$$
$$= \mathbb{E}[\text{revenue of MyerOPT on } G]$$

We therefore concluded that Myerson's optimal mechanism is RMMB in the single-item case. We are now ready to generalize the above idea to any matroid market.

Theorem 1. *Let $\mathcal{M} = (E, \mathcal{I})$ be any matroid market. Then MyerOPT in $\mathcal{M}$ is RMMB.*

Proof. Call G the set of green bidders and R the set of red bidders. Let (x, p) denote the allocation and payment rules for the mechanism MyerOPT that runs Myerson's optimal mechanism on all n bidders, using the given distribution of each. Let (x', p') denote the allocation and payment rules for the mechanism MyerOPT$_G$ that runs Myerson's optimal mechanism in the bidder set G only. For a set $S \subseteq [n]$, let T_S be the random variable denoting the independent subset of S that maximizes the sum of ironed virtual values. In other words, T_S is the set of winners chosen by Myerson's optimal mechanism on bidder set S.

By Myerson's Lemma, the revenue of MyerOPT$_G$ satisfies:

$$\mathbb{E}\left[\sum_{i \in G} p'_i(\mathbf{b})\right] = \mathbb{E}\left[\sum_{i \in G} x'_i(\mathbf{b}) \cdot \phi_i(b_i)\right] \tag{4}$$

By linearity of expectation, we can break up the expected revenue of MyerOPT into two terms as follows:

$$\mathbb{E}\left[\sum_{i \in [n]} p_i(\mathbf{b})\right] = \mathbb{E}\left[\sum_{i \in G} p_i(\mathbf{b})\right] + \mathbb{E}\left[\sum_{i \in R} p_i(\mathbf{b})\right] \tag{5}$$

The first term on the right side of (5) expresses the revenue original from the green bidders. Using Myerson's Lemma, we can equate this revenue with the expectation of the green winners' combined virtual value:

$$\mathbb{E}\left[\sum_{i \in G} p_i(\mathbf{b})\right] = \mathbb{E}\left[\sum_{i \in G} x_i(\mathbf{b}) \cdot \phi_i(b_i)\right]. \tag{6}$$

To express the revenue coming from the red bidders in terms of virtual valuations, we provide the argument that follows. One way to derive T_{G+R} from T_G is to start with T_G and sequentially add elements of $T_{G+R} \cap R$ in arbitrary order while removing at each step the least weight element in the circuit that potentially forms (repeated application of Proposition 2). Let e be the i-th red element we're adding. If no circuit forms after the addition, then e pays the smallest value in its support which is a non-negative quantity. Otherwise, let C be the unique circuit that forms after that addition. Let f be the minimum weight element in C and let b_f be the associated bid made by player f. Notice that f must be green; by assumption, every red element we're adding is part of the eventual optimal solution so it cannot be removed at any stage of this process. The price charged to e is their critical bid which we claim is at least $\phi_e^{-1}(\phi_f(b_f))$. The reason is that e is part of circuit C and f is the min-weight element of that circuit. The min-weight element of a circuit is never in the max-weight independent set[4] so if bidder e bids any value v such that $\phi_e(v) < \phi_f(b_f)$ they will certainly *not* be included in the set of winners, T_{G+R}. By Proposition 3 it follows that $\phi_e^{-1}(\phi_f(b_f)) \geq \phi_f(b_f)$ thus $p_e(\mathbf{b}) \geq \phi_f(b_f)$.

The above reasoning allows us "charge" each red bidder's payment to a green player's virtual value in $T_G \setminus T_{G+R}$:

$$\mathbb{E}\left[\sum_{i\in R} p_i(\mathbf{b})\right] \geq \mathbb{E}\left[\sum_{i\in T_G\setminus T_{G+R}} \phi_i(b_i)\right] = \mathbb{E}\left[\sum_{i\in G}(x_i'(\mathbf{b}) - x_i(\mathbf{b})) \cdot \phi_i(b_i)\right] \tag{7}$$

The second line is justified by observing that for $i \in G$, $x_i'(\mathbf{b}) = x_i(\mathbf{b})$ unless $i \in T_G \setminus T_{G+R}$, in which case $x_i'(\mathbf{b}) - x_i(\mathbf{b}) = 1$.

Combining Inequalities/Equations (4)–(7) we get:

$$\mathbb{E}\left[\sum_{i\in[n]} p_i(\mathbf{b})\right] \geq \mathbb{E}\left[\sum_{i\in G} x_i(\mathbf{b}) \cdot \phi_i(b_i)\right] + \mathbb{E}\left[\sum_{i\in G}(x_i'(\mathbf{b}) - x_i(\mathbf{b})) \cdot \phi_i(b_i)\right]$$

$$= \mathbb{E}\left[\sum_{i\in G} x_i'(\mathbf{b}) \cdot \phi_i(b_i)\right] = \mathbb{E}\left[\sum_{i\in G} p_i'(\mathbf{b})\right]$$

In other words, the expected revenue of MyerOPT is greater than or equal to that of MyerOPT$_G$.

4 General Downward-Closed Markets

When the market is not a matroid, the existence of red bidders can do a lot of damage to the revenue of the mechanism as shown in the following simple example.

Example 1. Consider a 3-element downward-closed set system on $E = \{a, b, c\}$ with maximal feasible sets: $\{a, b\}$ and $\{c\}$. Let c be a green bidder with a deterministic value of 1 and a, b be red bidders each with a specified value distribution given by the following cumulative distribution function $F(x) = 1 - (1 + x)^{1-N}$ for some parameter N. Note that the associated virtual value function is $\phi(x) = \left(1 - \frac{1}{N-1}\right)x - \frac{1}{N-1}$. For this virtual value function we have $\phi^{-1}(0) = \frac{1}{N-2}$, $\phi^{-1}(1) = \frac{N}{N-2}$.

Consider the revenue of Myerson's mechanism when the red bidders, instead of following their specified distribution, they each bid $\phi^{-1}(1)$—and the green bidder bids 1, the only support point of their distribution. The set $\{a, b\}$ wins over $\{c\}$ since the former sums to a total virtual value of 2 over the latter's virtual value 1 so bidders a, b pay their critical bid.

---

[4] This is a consequence of the optimality of the GREEDY algorithm since the min-weight element of a circuit is the last to be considered among the elements of the circuit and its inclusion will violate independence.

To compute that, notice that each of the bidders a, b could unilaterally decrease their bid to any $\varepsilon > \frac{1}{N-2}$ and they would still win the auction since the set $\{a, b\}$ would still have a total virtual value greater than 1. Therefore, each of a, b pays $\frac{1}{N-2}$ for a total revenue of $\frac{2}{N-2}$.

On the other hand, the same mechanism when run on the set $\{c\}$ of only the green bidder, always allocates an item to c and collects a total revenue of 1.

Letting $N \to \infty$ we see that the former revenue tends to zero while the latter remains 1, violating the revenue monotonicity property of Definition 1 by an unbounded multiplicative factor.

To generalize the above idea to any non-matroid set system we need the following lemma.

Lemma 4. *A downward-closed set system $S = (E, \mathcal{I})$ is* not *a matroid if and only if there exist $I, J \in \mathcal{I}$ with the following properties:*

1. *For every $K \in \mathcal{I}|_{I \cup J}$, if $|K| \geq |I|$ then $K \supseteq I \backslash J$.*
2. *$|J \backslash I| \geq 1$.*
3. *I is a maximum cardinality element of $\mathcal{I}|_{I \cup J}$.*

Proof. For the forward direction, suppose S is *not* a matroid and let V be a minimum-cardinality subset of E that is not a matroid. Since $\mathcal{I}|_V$ is downward-closed and non-empty, it must violate the exchange axiom. Hence, there exist sets $I, J \in \mathcal{I}|_V$ such that $|I| > |J|$ but $J + x \notin \mathcal{I}$ for all $x \in I \backslash J$. Note that $V = I \cup J$, since otherwise $I \cup J$ is a strictly smaller subset of E satisfying the property that $(I \cup J, \mathcal{I}|_{I \cup J})$ is not a matroid.

Observe that J is a maximal element of $\mathcal{I}_V$. The reason is that $V = I \cup J$, so every element of $V \backslash J$ belongs to I. By our assumption on the pair I, J, there is no element $y \in I$ such that $J + y \in \mathcal{I}|_V$. Since $\mathcal{I}|_V$ is downward-closed, it follows that no strict superset of J belongs to $\mathcal{I}|_V$.

We now proceed to prove that I, J satisfy the required properties of the lemma:

(1) Let $K \in \mathcal{I}_V$ with $|K| \geq |I|$. It follows that $|K| > |J|$, but J is maximal in $\mathcal{I}|_V$, so K and J must violate the exchange axiom. Thus, $\mathcal{I}|_{K \cup J}$ is not a matroid. By the minimality of V, this implies $K \cup J = V$ hence $K \supseteq I \backslash J$.

(2) If $J \backslash I = \emptyset$ then $J \subseteq I$ which contradicts the fact that I, J violate the exchange axiom.

(3) Suppose there exists $I' \in \mathcal{I}|_V$ with $|I'| > |I|$, then by property (1) we have $I' \supseteq I \backslash J$. Remove elements of $I \backslash J$ from I' one by one, in arbitrary order, until we reach a set $K \in \mathcal{I}_V$ such that $|K| = |I|$. This is possible because after the entire set $I \backslash J$ is removed from I', what remains is a subset of J, hence has strictly fewer elements than I. The set K thus constructed has $|K| = |I|$ but $K \not\supseteq I \backslash J$, violating property (1).

For the "only if" direction, supposing that S is a matroid, we must show that no $I, J \in \mathcal{I}$ satisfy all three properties. To this end, suppose I and J satisfy (2) and (3). Since $S|_{I \cup J}$ is a matroid, there exists $K \supseteq J$ such that $K \in \mathcal{I}|_{I \cup J}$ and $|K| = |I|$. By property (2), we know that no $|I|$-element superset of J contains $I - J$ as a subset. Therefore, the set K violates property (1). $\square$

We are now ready to generalize Example 1 to every non-matroid set system.

Theorem 2. *For any* $M = (E, \mathcal{I})$ *which is* not *a matroid, MyerOPT is* not *RMMB.*

Proof. Consider a downward-closed $M = (E, \mathcal{I})$ which is *not* a matroid. We are going to show there exists a partition of players into green and red sets and a choice of valuation distributions and misspecified red bids such that the RMMB property is violated.

Let $I, J \subseteq E$ be the subsets whose existence is guaranteed by Lemma 4. Define $G = J$ to be the set of green bidders, $R = I \backslash J$ to be the set of red bidders. All other bidders are irrelevant and can be assumed to be bidding zero. Set the value of each green bidder to be deterministically equal to 1. For each red bidder r, the specified value distribution has the same cumulative distribution function $F(x) = 1 - (1 + x)^{1-N}$ defined in Example 1.

Now let's consider the expected revenue of Myerson's mechanism when every bidder in R bids $\phi^{-1}(1)$.[5] Every bidder's virtual value is 1, so the mechanism will choose any set of winners with maximum cardinality which, according to Lemma 4, property (3), is $|I|$. For example, the set of winners could be I.

A consequence of Lemma 4, property (1) is that for every red bidder r there is no set of bidders disjoint from $\{r\}$ with combined virtual value greater than $|I| - 1$. Thus each red bidder pays $\phi^{-1}(0)$. Elements of $I \cap J$ correspond to green bidders who win the auction and pay 1, because a green bidder pays 1 whenever they win. There are $|I \cap J|$ such bidders. Thus, the Myerson revenue is $|I \cap J| + \frac{1}{N-2}|I \backslash J|$. The optimal auction on the green bidders alone charges each of these bidders a price of 1, receiving revenue $|J| = |I \cap J| + |J \backslash I|$. This exceeds $|I \cap J| + \frac{1}{N-2}|I \backslash J|$ as long as $(N - 2) \cdot |J \backslash I| > |I \backslash J|$. This inequality is satisfied, for example, when $N = |I \backslash J| + 3$, because $J \backslash I$ has at least one element (Lemma 4, property (2)).

Acknowledgements. The authors thank Jason Hartline for a helpful discussion about this work. Makis Arsenis and Robert Kleinberg gratefully acknowledge the support of NSF Grant CCF-1512964.

References

1. Azar, P., Micali, S., Daskalakis, C., Weinberg, S.M.: Optimal and efficient parametric auctions. In: SODA, pp. 596–604 (2013)
2. Azar, P.D., Micali, S.: Parametric digital auctions. In: ITCS 2013, pp. 231–232. ACM, New York (2013)
3. Bei, X., Gravin, N., Lu, P., Tang, Z.G.: Correlation-robust analysis of single item auction. In: SODA, pp. 193–208. SIAM (2019)
4. Bergemann, D., Morris, S.: Robust mechanism design. Econometrica **73**(6), 1771–1813 (2005)
5. Bergemann, D., Morris, S.: An introduction to robust mechanism design. Found. Trends® Microecon. **8**(3), 169–230 (2013)
6. Bergemann, D., Schlag, K.: Robust monopoly pricing. J. Econ. Theory **146**(6), 2527–2543 (2011)

---

[5] Members of G bid as well, but it hardly matters, because their bid is always 1—the only support point of their value distribution—so the auctioneer knows their value without their having to submit a bid.

7. Blum, A., Spencer, J.H.: Coloring random and semi-random k-colorable graphs. J. Algorithms **19**, 204–234 (1995)
8. Bradac, D., Gupta, A., Singla, S., Zuzic, G.: Robust algorithms for the secretary problem. In: ITCS (2019)
9. Brustle, J., Cai, Y., Daskalakis, C.: Multi-item mechanisms without item-independence: learnability via robustness. In: EC 2020, pp. 715–761. ACM, New York (2020)
10. Bubeck, S., Devanur, N., Huang, Z., Niazadeh, R.: Multi-scale online learning: theory and applications to online auctions and pricing. J. Mach. Learn. Res. **20**, 1–37 (2019). https://www.jmlr.org/papers/v20/17-498.bib
11. Cai, Y., Daskalakis, C.: Learning multi-item auctions with (or without) samples. In: FOCS, pp. 516–527. IEEE (2017)
12. Carrasco, V., Farinha Luz, V., Kos, N., Messner, M., Monteiro, P., Moreira, H.: Optimal selling mechanisms under moment conditions. J. Econ. Theory **177**, 245–279 (2018)
13. Carroll, G.: Robustness and separation in multidimensional screening. Econometrica **85**(2), 453–488 (2017)
14. Chen, J., Li, B., Li, Y.: Information elicitation for Bayesian auctions. In: Deng, X. (ed.) SAGT 2018. LNCS, vol. 11059, pp. 43–55. Springer, Cham (2018). https://doi.org/10.1007/978-3-319-99660-8_5
15. Cole, R., Roughgarden, T.: The sample complexity of revenue maximization. In: Proceedings of the Forty-Sixth Annual ACM Symposium on Theory of Computing, pp. 243–252 (2014)
16. Devanur, N., Huang, Z., Psomas, C.A.: The sample complexity of auctions with side information. In: STOC, pp. 426–439 (2016)
17. Dhangwatnotai, P., Roughgarden, T., Yan, Q.: Revenue maximization with a single sample. Games Econ. Behav. **91**, 318–333 (2015)
18. Diakonikolas, I., Kamath, G., Kane, D., Li, J., Moitra, A., Stewart, A.: Robust estimators in high-dimensions without the computational intractability. SIAM J. Comput. **48**(2), 742–864 (2019)
19. Dughmi, S., Roughgarden, T., Sundararajan, M.: Revenue submodularity. In: EC 2009, pp. 243–252. Association for Computing Machinery, New York (2009)
20. Feige, U., Kilian, J.: Heuristics for semirandom graph problems. J. Comput. Syst. Sci. **63**(4), 639–671 (2001)
21. Goldberg, A.V., Hartline, J.D., Karlin, A.R., Saks, M., Wright, A.: Competitive auctions. Games Econ. Behav. **55**(2), 242–269 (2006). Mini Special Issue: Electronic Market Design
22. Gravin, N., Lu, P.: Separation in correlation-robust monopolist problem with budget. In: SODA, pp. 2069–2080. SIAM (2018)
23. Hartline, J.D.: Mechanism design and approximation. http://jasonhartline.com/MDnA/MDnA-ch3.pdf. Accessed 13 July 2020
24. Hartline, J.D., Roughgarden, T.: Simple versus optimal mechanisms. In: EC (2009)
25. Huang, Z., Mansour, Y., Roughgarden, T.: Making the most of your samples. SIAM J. Comput. **47**(3), 651–674 (2018)
26. Lai, K.A., Rao, A.B., Vempala, S.: Agnostic estimation of mean and covariance. In: FOCS, pp. 665–674. IEEE (2016)
27. Lykouris, T., Mirrokni, V., Paes Leme, R.: Stochastic bandits robust to adversarial corruptions. In: STOC, pp. 114–122 (2018)
28. Makarychev, K., Makarychev, Y., Vijayaraghavan, A.: Approximation algorithms for semirandom partitioning problems. In: STOC, pp. 367–384 (2012)
29. Morgenstern, J., Roughgarden, T.: Learning simple auctions. In: CoLT (2016)
30. Myerson, R.B.: Optimal auction design. Math. Oper. Res. **6**(1), 58–73 (1981)
31. Oxley, J.G.: Matroid Theory (Oxford Graduate Texts in Mathematics). Oxford University Press Inc., Oxford (2006)

32. Rastegari, B., Condon, A., Leyton-Brown, K.: Revenue monotonicity in combinatorial auctions. SIGecom Exch. **7**(1), 45–47 (2007)
33. Roth, A., Sönmez, T., Unver, U.: Pairwise kidney exchange. In: Game Theory and Information. University Library of Munich, Germany (2005)
34. Wilson, R.: Game-theoretic analyses of trading processes. In: Econometric Society Monographs, pp. 33–70. Cambridge University Press (1987)

On the Power and Limits of Dynamic Pricing in Combinatorial Markets

Ben Berger[1], Alon Eden[2(✉)], and Michal Feldman[1]

[1] Tel-Aviv University, Tel Aviv, Israel
benberger1@tauex.tau.ac.il, michal.feldman@cs.tau.ac.il
[2] Harvard University, Cambridge, USA
aloneden@seas.harvard.edu

Abstract. We study the power and limits of *optimal dynamic pricing* in combinatorial markets; i.e., dynamic pricing that leads to optimal social welfare. Previous work by Cohen-Addad *et al.* [EC'16] demonstrated the existence of optimal dynamic prices for unit-demand buyers, and showed a market with coverage valuations that admits no such prices. However, finding the most general class of markets (i.e., valuation functions) that admit optimal dynamic prices remains an open problem. In this work we establish positive and negative results that narrow the existing gap.

On the positive side, we provide tools for handling markets beyond unit-demand valuations. In particular, we characterize all optimal allocations in multi-demand markets. This characterization allows us to partition the items into equivalence classes according to the role they play in achieving optimality. Using these tools, we provide a poly-time optimal dynamic pricing algorithm for up to 3 multi-demand buyers.

On the negative side, we establish a maximal domain theorem, showing that for every non-gross substitutes valuation, there exist unit-demand valuations such that adding them yields a market that does not admit an optimal dynamic pricing. This result is the dynamic pricing equivalent of the seminal maximal domain theorem by Gul and Stacchetti [JET'99] for Walrasian equilibrium. Yang [JET'17] discovered an error in their original proof, and established a different, incomparable version of their maximal domain theorem. En route to our maximal domain theorem for optimal dynamic pricing, we provide the first complete proof of the original theorem by Gul and Stacchetti.

1 Introduction

We study the power and limitations of pricing schemes for social welfare optimization in combinatorial markets. We consider combinatorial markets with m

This project has received funding from the European Research Council (ERC) under the European Union's Horizon 2020 research and innovation program (grant agreement No. 866132), and by the Israel Science Foundation (grant number 317/17). The work of A. Eden was supported by the National Science Foundation under Grant No. CCF-1718549.

© Springer Nature Switzerland AG 2020
X. Chen et al. (Eds.): WINE 2020, LNCS 12495, pp. 206–219, 2020.
https://doi.org/10.1007/978-3-030-64946-3_15

heterogeneous, indivisible goods, and n buyers with publicly known valuation function $v_i : 2^{[m]} \to \mathbb{R}_{\geq 0}$ over bundles of items. The goal is to allocate items to buyers in a way that maximizes the social welfare.

Apart from being simple, pricing schemes are attractive since they do not require an all powerful central authority. Once the prices are set, the buyers arrive and simply choose a desired set of items from the available inventory. This is the mechanism we see everywhere, from supermarkets to online stores. Formally, the seller sets items prices $\mathbf{p} = (p_1, \ldots, p_m) \in \mathbb{R}_{\geq 0}^m$, buyers arrive sequentially in an arbitrary order, and every buyer chooses a bundle T from the remaining items that maximizes the utility: $u_i(T, \mathbf{p}) = v_i(T) - \sum_{j \in T} p_j$, breaking ties arbitrarily.

A reader familiar with the fundamental notion of Walrasian equilibrium, may conclude that the problem is solved for any market that admits a Walrasian equilibrium. A Walrasian equilibrium is a pair of an allocation $\mathbf{S} = (S_1, \ldots, S_n)$ and prices $\mathbf{p}$, such that for every buyer i, S_i maximizes i's utility given $\mathbf{p}$. By the first welfare theorem, every Walrasian equilibrium maximizes social welfare.

Are Walrasian prices a solution to our problem? The answer is no [1,3]. Walrasian prices cannot resolve a market without coordinating the tie breaking. If a buyer is faced with multiple utility-maximizing bundles, it is crucial that a central authority coordinates the tie breaking in accordance with the corresponding optimal allocation. In real-world markets, however, buyers are only faced with prices and choose a desired bundle by themselves without caring about global efficiency. [1] demonstrated that lacking a tie-breaking coordinator, Walrasian pricing can lead to arbitrarily bad welfare. Moreover, they showed that no fixed prices whatsoever can guarantee more than $2/3$ of the optimal social welfare, even when restricted to unit-demand buyers.[1]

In order to circumvent this state of affairs, [1] proposed a more powerful pricing scheme, *dynamic pricing*, in which the seller updates prices in between buyer arrivals. The updated prices are set based on the remaining buyers and the current inventory. The main result of [1] is that every unit-demand market admits an optimal dynamic pricing. They also showed an example of a market with coverage valuations (a strict sub-class of submodular valuations) in which dynamic prices cannot guarantee optimal welfare. A natural question arises:

What markets (i.e., what valuation classes) can be resolved optimally using dynamic pricing?

A similar question was considered for Walrasian equilibrium, where it was shown that every market with gross-substitutes buyers admits a Walrasian equilibrium [4]. Moreover, [2] show that gross-substitutes valuations are also maximal with respect to guaranteed existence of a Walrasian equilibrium:

Theorem 1 (Maximal Domain Theorem for Walrasian Equilibrium [2]). *Let v_1 be a non gross-substitutes valuation. Then, there exist unit-demand*

---

[1] A unit demand buyer has a value for every item, and the value for a set is the maximum value of any item in the set.

valuations $v_2, \ldots, v_\ell$ *for some* ℓ *such that the valuation profile* $(v_1, v_2, \ldots, v_\ell)$ *does not admit a Walrasian equilibrium.*

Although the notions of dynamic pricing and Walrasian are incomparable, Cohen-Addad *et al.* [1] conjectured that GS valuations are also maximal and sufficient with respect to the existence of dynamic prices. For the special case of markets with a unique optimal allocation, they showed that every GS market admits static prices guaranteeing optimal welfare, and there exists a market with non-GS (though submodular) valuations such that no pricing, even dynamic, guarantee optimal welfare.

1.1   Our Results and Techniques

In this work we shrink the known gap between markets that can and cannot be resolved optimally via dynamic pricing, from both ends.

A natural extension of unit-demand valuations is *multi-demand* valuations, where every buyer i has a public *cap* $k_i \in \mathbb{N}$ on the number of desired items, and the value for a set is the sum of the values for the k_i most valued items in the set. The case of $k_i = 1$ is simply unit-demand. Every multi-demand valuation is gross-substitutes. Our main positive result is the following:

Theorem 2. *Every market with up to 3 buyers, each with a multi-demand valuation function, admits an optimal dynamic pricing. Moreover, the prices can be computed in polynomial (in the number of items m) time, using value queries*[2].

On the negative side, we show the first general negative result for dynamic prices, which takes the form of a maximal domain result in the spirit of [2]:

Theorem 3. *Let* v_1 *be a non gross-substitutes valuation. Then, there are unit-demand valuations* $v_2, \ldots, v_\ell$ *such that the valuation profile* $(v_1, v_2, \ldots, v_\ell)$ *does not admit an optimal dynamic pricing.*

En route, we provide *the first complete proof of the maximal domain theorem by Gul-Stacchetti* (Theorem 1 above), whose original proof was imprecise.

Techniques: Positive Results. We first review the solution of Cohen-Addad *et al.* [1] for unit-demand valuations, and show why we need a more fundamental technique in order to get past unit-demand bidders. Their scheme computes an optimal allocation $\mathbf{X} = (x_1, \ldots, x_n)$, where item x_i is allocated to buyer i, and then constructs a *complete*, weighted directed graph in which the vertices are the items. An edge $x_i \rightarrow x_j$ in this graph represents a *preference constraint*, requiring that buyer i *strongly* prefers item x_i over x_j, relative to the output prices. Hereafter, we term this graph the *preference graph*.

If there exist prices $\mathbf{p}$ that satisfy all edge constraints, then all buyers strongly prefer their items over the rest, and the allocation obtained after the last buyer

---

[2] A value query for a valuation v receives a set S as input, and returns $v(S)$.

leaves the market is precisely $\mathbf{X}$, which is optimal. Unfortunately, in some cases such prices do not exist. In order to circumvent this problem, [1] proves the following two claims:

- An edge $x_i \to x_j$ participates in a 0-weight cycle iff there is an alternative optimal allocation in which x_j is allocated to buyer i.
- If 0-weight cycles are removed from the graph, then one can compute prices that satisfy the remaining edge constraints.

Their pricing scheme removes every edge that participates in a 0-weight cycle, and then computes the prices as per the second bullet above. Relative to these prices, every buyer strongly prefers her allocated item to every other item, except perhaps for the set of items that are allocated to her in some alternative optimal allocation. Since every buyer takes at most one favorite item, as the buyers are unit-demand, this property guarantees that allocating this item to the buyer is consistent with an optimal allocation (not necessarily $\mathbf{X}$), as desired. When agents are multi-demand, they might take multiple items, and this breaks the solution by [1].

To illustrate this, consider the example given in Fig. 1, which serves as a running example throughout the paper. Removing the given 0-weight cycles could result in buyer 1 taking c and d instead of a and b, and the only remaining item that gives buyer 2 any positive value is e. This decreases the maximum attainable welfare from 5 to 4. The reason for this is that the two cycles intersect, and item e acts as a bottleneck for the two cycles. The machinery developed in [1] can-

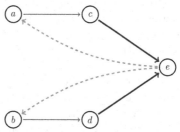

Fig. 1. Consider a market with 5 items a, b, c, d, e and 3 buyers, 1, 2, 3. Buyers 1 and 2 are both 2-demand, and buyer 3 is unit-demand. Buyer 1 values a, b, c, d at 1 and e at 0, Buyer 2 values c, d, e at 1 and a, b at 0, and buyer 3 values a, b, e at 1 and c, d at 0. One can verify that allocating a, b to 1, c, d to 2 and e to 3 maximizes social welfare. The figure depicts two 0-weight cycles in the preference graph constructed in the running example (edge weights are omitted). The thin red, thick blue and dashed green arrows correspond to the constraints of buyers 1, 2, 3 respectively.

not identify the special role of item e, which is crucial for resolving this instance.

Our first step is to gain a better structural understanding of optimal allocations in multi-demand markets. This is cast in the following theorem that characterizes the set of optimal allocations in multi-demand markets with any number of buyers. For the sake of simplicity, we present the theorem for markets in which all m items are allocated in every optimal allocation, and in which the total demand of the players equals supply, i.e. $m = \sum_{i=1}^{n} k_i$, where k_i is the cap of buyer i. In the full version, we show that an analogous result holds in the general case.

Theorem *(Informal. See Theorem* 4). *In a market with multi-demand buyers, an allocation is optimal if and only if the following hold:*

- *Every buyer i receives k_i items.*
- *If item x is allocated to buyer i, then there exists an optimal allocation where x is allocated to i.*

Put informally, the above states that one can mix-and-match items given to a buyer in *different* optimal allocations, and as long as each buyer i receives *exactly* k_i items, the resulting allocation is also optimal. While the only if direction is straightforward, it is not a-priori clear that the other direction holds as well. We prove this direction by reducing the problem to unit-demand valuations and proving for this case.

This characterization significantly simplifies the problem. It allows us to ignore the concrete values, and consider for each item only the set of buyers that receives it in some optimal allocation. Two items are essentially equivalent if their corresponding sets of buyers coincide. Thus, we group items into *equivalence classes*, providing a compact view of the market. For example, in markets with up to 3 multi-demand buyers, there are at most 8 (non-empty) equivalence classes corresponding to the possible subsets of players, while the total number of items can be arbitrarily large. We construct a new directed graph, termed the *item-equivalence graph*, where the vertices are these equivalence classes (refined after intersecting them with the bundles from the initial optimal allocation $\mathbf{X}$), and there is an edge $C \rightarrow D$ whenever the buyer that receives the items in C in the allocation $\mathbf{X}$ also receives every item in D in some optimal allocation. Figure 2 depicts the item-equivalence graph for the running example.

We show that there is a correspondence between cycles in the item-equivalence graph and 0-weight cycles in the preference graph. Thus our challenge is reduced to removing enough edges from the first (and translating these removals back to the second), in a way that eliminates all cycles, but also guarantees the following: every deviation by any buyer from her pre-

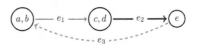

Fig. 2. The item-equivalence graph for the running example. E.g., the items a, b are equivalent since the set of buyers that receive any of them in some optimal allocation is the same ($\{1, 3\}$).

scribed bundle, implied by the edge removals, allows the other buyers to simultaneously compensate for their "stolen" items by replacing them with items from other relevant equivalence classes. The optimal allocation characterization theorem then guarantees that the obtained allocation is indeed optimal. We devise an edge-removal method satisfying these requirements whenever the number of buyers is at most 3.

We believe this characterization theorem and the item equivalence graph may prove useful in other problems related to multi-demand markets.

Techniques: Negative Results. The original proof of Theorem 1 by Gul and Stacchetti considers two cases, and for each case, they construct a different market that does not admit a Walrasian equilibrium. Yang [7] showed one of the constructions does not work by finding an instance such that the constructed market does admit a Walrasian equilibrium. The error could not be easily fixed, and Yang proceeded by establishing an alternative, incomparable theorem; namely, that for every non gross-substitutes valuation there is a (single) gross-substitutes valuation for which the obtained market has no Walrasian equilibrium. While Yang's version of the assertion requires only a single valuation, this valuation has a complex structure compared with the simple unit-demand valuations in the original version. In the full version, we prove the maximal domain theorem *as originally stated*. The proof relies on a theorem which allows us to consider only the case with the correct construction in the original proof.

Our proof of Theorem 3, which is deferred to the full version, is driven by the following lemma from Cohen-Addad *et al.* [1]—in the case of a unique optimal allocation, the existence of optimal dynamic prices implies the existence of Walrasian prices. We modify the construction of Gul and Stacchetti to a market with an optimal allocation that is "almost" unique. This market still does not admit a Walrasian equilbrium. We then adapt the lemma in [1] to show that the existence of optimal dynamic prices in this market also implies the existence of Walrasian prices. The non-existence of Walrasian prices now implies non-existence of dynamic prices.

2   Preliminaries

We consider a setting with a finite set of indivisible items M (with $m := |M|$) and a set of n buyers (or players). Every buyer has a valuation function $v : 2^M \to \mathbb{R}_{\geq 0}$. As standard, we assume monotonicity and normalization of all valuations, i.e. $v(S) \leq v(T)$ whenever $S \subseteq T$, and $v(\emptyset) = 0$. A valuation profile of n buyers is denoted $\mathbf{v} = (v_1, \ldots, v_n)$ and we assume that it is known by all. An *allocation* is a vector $\mathbf{A} = (A_1, \ldots, A_n)$ of disjoint subsets of M, indicating the bundles of items given to each player (not all items have to be allocated). The *social welfare* of an allocation $\mathbf{A}$ is given by $\mathsf{SW}(\mathbf{A}) = \sum_{i=1}^{n} v_i(A_i)$. An *optimal allocation* is an allocation that achieves the maximum social welfare among all allocations.

A *pricing* or a *price vector* is a vector $\mathbf{p} \in \mathbb{R}_{\geq 0}^n$ indicating the price of each item. We assume a quasi-linear utility, i.e. the *utility* of a buyer i from a bundle $S \subseteq M$ given prices $\mathbf{p}$ is $u_i(S, \mathbf{p}) = v_i(S) - \sum_{x \in S} p_x$. The *demand correspondence* of buyer i given $\mathbf{p}$ is the collection of utility maximizing bundles $D_{\mathbf{p}}(v) := \arg\max_{S \subseteq M} \{u(S, \mathbf{p})\}$.

Dynamic Pricing. In the dynamic pricing problem buyers arrive to the market in an arbitrary and unknown order. Before every buyer arrival new prices are set to the items that are still available, and these prices are based only on the set of buyers that have not yet arrived (their arrival order remains unknown). The arriving buyer then chooses an arbitrary utility-maximizing bundle based on the current prices and available items. The goal is to set the prices so that for any arrival order and any tie breaking choices by the buyers, the obtained social welfare is optimal.

We are interested in proving the guaranteed existence of an optimal dynamic pricing for any market composed entirely of buyers from a given valuation class C. It can be easily shown by induction that the problem is reduced to proving the guaranteed existence of item prices $\mathbf{p}$ such that any utility-maximizing bundle of any buyer can be completed to an optimal allocation. In other words, we can rephrase dynamic pricing as follows:

Definition 1. *An optimal dynamic pricing (hereafter, dynamic pricing) for the buyer profile* $\mathbf{v} = (v_1, \ldots, v_n)$ *is a price vector* $\mathbf{p} \in \mathbb{R}^m_{\geq 0}$ *such that for any buyer i and any $S \in D_{\mathbf{p}}(v_i)$ there is an optimal allocation in which player i receives S.*

3   Dynamic Pricing for Multi-demand Buyers

In this section we prove Theorem 2, namely we establish a dynamic pricing scheme for up to $n = 3$ multi-demand buyers that runs in $poly(m)$ time. As we shall see most of the tools we use hold for any number of buyers n. We fix a multi-demand buyer profile $\mathbf{v} = (v_1, \ldots, v_n)$ over the item set M, where each v_i is k_i-demand. We assume w.l.o.g. that all items are essential for optimality (i.e. all items are allocated in every optimal allocation) since otherwise we can price all unnecessary items at ∞ in every round to ensure that no player takes any of them (and price the rest of the items as if the unnecessary items do not exist). Note that under this assumption, each optimal allocation gives buyer i at most k_i items, for every i. In particular we have $m \leq \sum_{i=1}^{n} k_i$. For the sake of simplicity we further assume for the rest of this section that every optimal allocation gives each buyer i exactly k_i items, and thus $m = \sum_{i=1}^{n} k_i$. The case $m < \sum k_i$ introduces substantial technical difficulty. We show the solution for the general case in the full version. We first go over the tools used in our dynamic pricing scheme. We then present the dynamic pricing scheme for $n = 3$ buyers.

3.1   Tools and Previous Solutions

We start by presenting the main combinatorial construct of our solution, namely the preference-graph, which generalizes the construct given by [1] in their solution for unit-demand buyers. Then we explain the obstacles for generalizing the approach of [1] to the multi-demand setting. Finally, we develop the necessary machinery needed to overcome these obstacles. All the tools we develop and their properties hold for any number of buyers n.

The Preference Graph and an Initial Pricing Attempt. Let $\mathbf{O}$ be an arbitrary optimal allocation. The preference graph based on $\mathbf{O}$ is the directed graph H whose vertices are the items in M. Furthermore there is a special 'source' vertex denoted s. For any two different players i, j and items $x \in O_i, y \in O_j$ we have a directed edge $e = x \to y$ with weight $w(e) = v_i(x) - v_i(y)$. We also have a 0-weight edge $s \to x$ for every item $x \in M$. Since an optimal allocation can be computed in $poly(n, m)$ time with value queries (since the valuations are gross substitutes, see [5]), it follows that the preference graph can also be computed in $poly(n, m)$ time with value queries. When $|O_i| = 1$ for every i, the graph is exactly the one introduced by [1] in their unit-demand solution[3]. The proofs of the following two lemmas and corollary are deferred to the full version.

Lemma 1. *Let $C := x_1 \to x_2 \to \cdots x_k \to x_1$ be a cycle in H, where x_i is allocated to player i in $\mathbf{O}$ and $x_i \neq x_j$ for every $i \neq j$. Then the weight of the cycle is $w(C) = \mathsf{SW}(\mathbf{O}) - \mathsf{SW}(\mathbf{A})$ where $\mathbf{A}$ is the allocation obtained from $\mathbf{O}$ by transferring x_{i+1} to player i for every i (we identify player $k+1$ with player 1).*

Corollary 1. *Every cycle in H has non-negative weight.*

Corollary 1 implies that the weight of the min-weight path from s to x, denoted $\delta(s, x)$, is well-defined for any item x.

Lemma 2. *Let $p_x := -\delta(s, x)$ for every item x. Let i be some player, and let x, y be items such that $x \in O_i, y \notin O_i$. Then: (1) $p_x \geq 0$. (2) $v_i(x) - p_x \geq v_i(y) - p_y$ (3) $v_i(x) - p_x \geq 0$.*

Note that the utility player i obtains from any bundle of size at most k_i is the sum of the individual utilities obtained by the individual items. Thus, Lemma 2 shows that setting the prices $p_x = -\delta(s, x)$ almost achieves the requirements of dynamic pricing. However, since the inequalities in Lemma 2 are not strict, the incoming player might deviate from the designated bundle.

Solution for Unit-Demand Valuations and its Failure to Generalize. The inequalities of Lemmas 2 can be made strict by decreasing the weight of all edges by an appropriately selected $\varepsilon > 0$, but in the case H has zero-weight cycles, this can introduce negative cycles to H, in which case $\delta(s, x)$ is not defined for any x in such cycle. To circumvent this issue, [1] remove every edge that participates in a 0-weight cycle in H. Therefore, by choosing a small enough ϵ to decrease from the remaining edges, the remaining cycles are guaranteed to be strictly positive. Removing an edge $x \to y$ for $x \in O_i, y \notin O_i$ cancels the preference guarantee of Lemma 2 (part 2), leading to a possible deviation by buyer i from taking x to taking y. However, since 0-weight cycles correspond to alternative optimal allocations (see Lemma 1 with $w(C) = 0$), then this is not a problem: if the edge $x \to y$ was removed, then there is an optimal allocation in which player i receives y instead of x. As for the edges $x \to y$ that were not removed, the ϵ decrement causes i to strongly prefer x over y. The other inequalities of Lemma 2 would also be strict, and we are thus guaranteed that the incoming player indeed takes a one-item bundle that is part of some optimal allocation, as desired.

This approach works in the unit-demand setting, but poses problems in the multi-demand setting, as illustrated in the running example (presented in the

---

[3] A similar graph structure has been used by Murota in order to compute Walrasian equilibria in gross-substitutes markets [6].

introduction, see Fig. 1). Therefore, a more sophisticated method of eliminating 0-weight cycles must be employed instead of simply removing all edges that participate in some 0-weight cycle. Our informal goal is:

> Remove a set of edges from the preference graph so that no 0-weight cycles are left, and every possible deviation implied by the removed edges is consistent with some optimal allocation.

Legal Allocations.

Definition 2

- An item $x \in M$ is legal for player i if there is some optimal allocation $\mathbf{X} = (X_1, \ldots, X_n)$ such that $x \in X_i$.
- A bundle $S \subseteq M$ is legal for player i if $|S| = k_i$ and every $x \in S$ is legal for player i.
- A legal allocation $\mathbf{A} = (A_1, \ldots, A_n)$ is an allocation in which A_i is legal for player i, for every i.

In a legal allocation every player i receives exactly k_i items, each of which is allocated to her in some optimal allocation. Note that a legal bundle for buyer i might not form a part of any optimal allocation (e.g., the bundle $\{c, d\}$ for buyer 1 in the running example). The following theorem provides a characterization of the collection of optimal allocations in the given market $\mathbf{v}$. The subsequent Corollary follows directly from the theorem and Definition 1. We next provide a proof sketch, for the full proof, we refer the reader to the full version.

Theorem 4. *An allocation is legal if and only if it is optimal.*

Proof (sketch). We first show that the theorem holds for unit-demand valuations, and then reduce the case of multi-demand valuations to unit-demand valuations. The *if* direction is trivial; we show the *only if* direction in this sketch. Let OPT denote the optimal welfare, and let $M_L = \{(i, \ell_i)\}_{i \in [n]}$ be a legal allocation (which is also a perfect matching since $m = \sum_i k_i = n$). For each edge (i, ℓ_i) in M_L, let M^i represent an optimal allocation, which is also a max-weight matching, in which (i, ℓ_i) participates (there must exist such a matching by the definition of legal allocations). Let $G = \bigcup_i M^i$ be the bipartite multigraph that is the union of all the perfect matchings. This is an n-regular bipartite graph which has M_L as a subgraph. We decompose G as follows—we first remove the matching M_L from G, resulting in an $n - 1$ regular graph. We then decompose this graph into $n - 1$ perfect matchings $M'_1, \ldots, M'_{n-1}$ (which is possible due to the regularity of the graph). For a matching M, we use $w(M)$ to denote its weight. We notice that $w(M_L) + \sum_{i=1}^{n-1} w(M'_i) = \sum_{i=1}^{n} w(M^i) = n \cdot \text{OPT}$. Since $w(M'_i) \leq \text{OPT}$ for every i, it follows that $w(M_L) \geq \text{OPT}$. Therefore, M_L is optimal.

We now describe the reduction: each k_i-demand buyer is decomposed into k_i identical unit-demand buyers, each of whom has the same value as the original buyer for every item j. The corresponding allocations are naturally defined: A single multi-demand buyer receiving $k \leq k_i$ items in the original market corresponds to allocating these k items to k copies of this agent in the unit-demand market (one item to each copy). In the other direction, all the items allocated to copies of a particular multi-demand buyer are allocated to that buyer in the original market. It is not hard to see that an allocation is legal (resp. optimal) in the original market if and only if the corresponding allocation is legal (resp. optimal) in the corresponding unit-demand market.   □

Corollary 2. *A price vector* **p** *is a dynamic pricing if for every player i and $S \in D_{\mathbf{p}}(i)$, S is legal for player i and there exists an allocation of the items $M \setminus S$ to the other players in which every player receives a legal bundle.*

Going back to our informal goal, Theorem 4 determines the deviations from the bundles O_i which are tolerable. A buyer can only deviate to a bundle which is legal for her, in a way that the leftover items can be partitioned "legally" among the rest of the buyers. The proof of Theorem 4 is deferred to the full version.

The Item-Equivalence Graph. Let **O** be some optimal allocation and H the corresponding preference graph. For every player i and set of players $C \subseteq [n]\setminus\{i\}$, we denote by $B_{i,C}$ the set of items allocated to buyer i in **O**, and whose set of players to which they are legal is exactly $\{i\} \cup C$. For example, $B_{1,\{2,3\}}$ is the set of items $x \in O_1$ such that there are optimal allocations $\mathbf{O'}, \tilde{\mathbf{O}}$ in which x is allocated to players 2, 3 (respectively), and for any other player $j \notin \{1,2,3\}$, there is no optimal allocation in which x is allocated to j. Formally,

$$B_{i,C} := \left\{ x \in O_i \;\middle|\; \begin{array}{l} \forall j \in \{i\} \cup C \; x \text{ is legal for } j \\ \forall j \notin \{i\} \cup C \; x \text{ is not legal for } j \end{array} \right\}$$

We make a few observations:

- The sets $B_{i,C}$ form a partition of M (some of these sets might be empty sets).
- Let $x \in O_i$ and $y \in O_j$ for $i \neq j$. If $x \to y$ participates in a 0-weight cycle in H and $y \in B_{j,C}$, then $i \in C$.

The second observation holds since if $x \to y$ participates in a 0-weight cycle, then there is an alternative optimal allocation in which y is allocated to player i (see Lemma 1 with $w(C) = 0$).

Definition 3 (Item-Equivalence Graph). *Given an optimal allocation* **O**, *its associated item-equivalence graph is the directed graph $B = (T, D)$ with vertices $T = \{B_{i,C} \neq \emptyset \mid i \in [n], C \subseteq [n] \setminus \{i\}\}$ and directed edges $D = \{B_{i,C_1} \to B_{j,C_2} \mid i \in C_2\}$.*

For example, $(B_{1,\emptyset} \to B_{2,\{1,4\}})$ and $(B_{2,\{1,5\}} \to B_{6,\{2\}})$ are edges in the item-equivalence graph (assuming that the participating sets are non-empty), whereas, for example, $(B_{1,\emptyset} \to B_{1,\{2\}})$ and $(B_{2,\{1\}} \to B_{3,\{1,4\}})$ are not. Note also that the number of vertices is at most m.

The next Lemma shows that the item-equivalence graph can be computed efficiently. The proof is deferred to the full version.

Lemma 3. *Given an optimal allocation* **O**, *its associated item-equivalence graph can be computed in poly(m, n) time and value queries.*

The following lemma uses Theorem 4 to establish a correspondence between 0-weight cycles in H and cycles in B. Its proof is deferred to the full version.

Lemma 4. *Let* **O** *be an optimal allocation and let H and B be the corresponding preference graph and item-equivalence graph, respectively. Then:*

1. *If $B_{i_1,C_1} \to \cdots \to B_{i_k,C_k} \to B_{i_1,C_1}$ is a cycle in B then for any items $x_1 \in B_{i_1,C_1}, \ldots, x_k \in B_{i_k,C_k}$, the cycle $C = x_1 \to x_2 \to \cdots \to x_k \to x_1$ is a 0-weight cycle in H.*
2. *If $C = x_1 \to x_2 \to \cdots \to x_k \to x_1$ is a 0-weight cycle in H, and $x_\ell \in B_{i_\ell,C_\ell}$ for every $1 \leq \ell \leq k$ then $C' := B_{i_1,C_1} \to \cdots \to B_{i_k,C_k} \to B_{i_1,C_1}$ is a cycle in B.*

As explained before, our main challenge in the dynamic pricing problem is to come up with a method to remove all 0-weight cycles from H in a way that each potential deviation of any player i from the designated bundle O_i, that emanates from the edge removals, is consistent with some optimal allocation. In particular the method must overcome the "bottleneck problem" (as illustrated in Fig. 1). Lemma 4 allows us to shift the focus from removing 0-weight cycles in H to removing cycles in B and translate these removals back to H.

[**Running Example**]. Figure 2 shows the item-equivalence graph obtained from the initial optimal allocation. Each of the items a, b is allocated to buyer 3 in some other optimal allocation, and is never allocated to buyer 2. Thus $a, b \in B_{1,\{3\}}$. Similarly we have $c, d \in B_{2,\{1\}}$ and $e \in B_{3,\{2\}}$. Removing any edge of the item-equivalence graph makes it cycle-free. Thus, by Lemma 4, if we choose one of the edges e_1, e_2, e_3 and remove all edges in the preference graph corresponding to the chosen edge, then the preference graph will remain cycle-free. Removing the edges corresponding to e_1 could cause player 1 to take the bundle $\{c, d\}$ instead of the designated bundle $\{a, b\}$, which cannot be completed to an optimal allocation. On the other hand, removing the preference graph edges that correspond to the edges e_2, e_3 is fine. If player 2 arrives first to the market, then the removal of edge e_2 might cause her to take the item e instead of c or d, and both options are consistent with some optimal allocation. Likewise if player 3 arrives first and takes a or b instead of e then this too can be completed to an optimal allocation. The important property here is that $B_{3,\{2\}}$ has minimal size in the cycle, and thus removing its incoming and outgoing edges introduces tolerable potential deviations.

3.2   Solution for Up to 3 Multi-demand Buyers

We are now ready to present the dynamic pricing scheme for up to $n = 3$ multi-demand buyers. The algorithm makes use of the item-equivalence graph. We abuse notation and instead of writing $B_{i,\{j\}}$ ($B_{i,\{j,k\}}$) we write B_{ij} (B_{ijk}). Thus the vertices of the item-equivalence graph for 3 buyers are $B_{1,\emptyset}, B_{2,\emptyset}, B_{3,\emptyset}$, $B_{12}, B_{21}, B_{31}, B_{123}, B_{213}, B_{312}, B_{13}, B_{23}, B_{32}$ (only the non-empty sets out of these appear in the graph). For 2 buyers there are at most 4 vertices in the graph: $B_{1,\emptyset}$, $B_{2,\emptyset}$, B_{12}, B_{21}. Step 4 is only relevant for the case of 3 buyers.

ALGORITHM 1: Dynamic Pricing Scheme for up to 3 Multi-Demand Buyers.

Input: Multi-demand valuations v_1, v_2, and also v_3 when $n = 3$.

Output: prices $\mathbf{p} = (p_x)_{x \in M}$.

1 Compute some optimal allocation **O**.

2 Compute the preference graph H and the item-equivalence graph B based on **O**.

3 Mark all edges that participate in a cycle of size 2 in B.

4 In each of the cycles $B_{13} \to B_{21} \to B_{32} \to B_{13}$ and $B_{12} \to B_{31} \to B_{23} \to B_{12}$ (if these exist) choose a set of minimal size and mark its incoming edge and outgoing edge in the cycle.

5 For every edge $B_{i_1,C_1} \to B_{i_2,C_2}$ in B that was marked, and for every $x \in B_{i_1,C_1}, y \in B_{i_2,C_2}$, remove the edge $x \to y$ from H. Denote the obtained graph by H'.

6 Let $\Delta > 0$ be the difference in social welfare between the optimal and 2nd optimal allocation. Denote $\epsilon := \frac{\Delta}{m+1}$ and for every edge e that was not removed (except for edges starting at the source vertex s) update its weight to $w'(e) = w(e) - \epsilon$.

7 Compute the min-weight paths from s to every x in H', and let $\delta(s,x)$ be its weight. For every item x set the price $p_x = -\delta(s,x) + \epsilon$.

8 **return** $(p_x)_{x \in M}$

When $n = 2$, the only cycle in the item-equivalence graph is $B_{12} \to B_{21} \to B_{12}$ (assuming both of these are non-empty sets), and both of its edges were marked in step 3. Thus, by Lemma 4, all edges that participate in a 0-weight cycle in the preference graph were removed in step 5. Thus for $n = 2$ Algorithm 1 is, effectively, the straightforward generalization of the Cohen-Addad et al. [1] unit-demand solution to multi-demand buyers.

As stated before, computing **O**, H and B can be done in polynomial time. Finding the cycles in B can also be done efficiently (B has a constant number of vertices) as well as computing min-weight paths. Thus the algorithm indeed runs in $poly(m)$ time as desired. The proofs of the following 4 lemmas are deferred to the full version.

Lemma 5. *After step 5 every cycle in H' has strictly positive weight.*

Lemma 6. *For any item x, $p_x > 0$.*

Lemma 7. *For any player i, $x \in O_i$ and $y \notin O_i$, if $e = x \to y \in H'$ then $u_i(x, \mathbf{p}) > u_i(y, \mathbf{p})$.*

Lemma 8. *For any player i and item $x \in O_i$ we have $v_i(x) - p_x > 0$.*

We are now ready to prove that the output of our dynamic pricing scheme meets the requirements of Corollary 2. This is cast in the following lemma:

Lemma 9. *Let $\mathbf{p}$ be the price vector output by Algorithm 1. Then, for every player i and $S \in D_{\mathbf{p}}(i)$, (a) S is legal for player i; and (b) S can be completed to a legal allocation, i.e. there exists an allocation of the items $M \setminus S$ to the other players in which every player receives a bundle that is legal for her.*

Proof. We prove for $i = 1$ (the same proof applies also for $i = 2, 3$). We first prove part (a). We start by showing that every $S \in D_{\mathbf{p}}(1)$ is of size k_1. Since all item prices are positive (Lemma 6) and player 1 is k_1-demand, it cannot be the case that player 1 maximizes utility with a bundle consisting of more than k_1 items. Furthermore, by Lemma 8 there are at least k_1 legal items from which she derives positive utility. Combining, every demanded bundle has exactly k_1 items. Now, for any two items x, y where $x \in O_1$ and y is not legal for player 1, the edge $x \to y$ was not removed in the transition from H to H' (since there is no corresponding edge in the item-equivalence graph that could have been marked). Thus, player 1 strongly prefers x over y (by Lemma 7) and we conclude that every demanded bundle contains only legal items, as desired.

We proceed to prove part (b). Let $S \in D_{\mathbf{p}}(1)$. We refer to the items in $S \setminus O_1$ as the items that player 1 'stole' from players 2 (and 3 if $n = 3$), and to the items in $O_1 \setminus S$ as those player 1 'left behind'. We need to show that players 2 and 3 can compensate for their stolen items in a 'legal manner', that is, by completing their leftover bundles $O_2 \setminus S$ and $O_3 \setminus S$ to k_2 and k_3 legal items, respectively. The first step is to determine where the stolen and left behind items are taken from. Since $B_{1,\emptyset}$ does not participate in any cycle in the item-equivalence graph (as it has no incoming edge), then none of its outgoing edges were marked, implying (by Lemma 7) that player 1 strongly prefers every item of $B_{1,\emptyset}$ over every item $y \notin O_1$. Since buyer 1 derives positive utility from these items (Lemma 8), we conclude that $B_{1,\emptyset}$ is contained in every demanded bundle and in particular in S. In other words, all the items player 1 left-behind are in B_{12} if $n = 2$, or in $B_{12} \cup B_{13} \cup B_{123}$ if $n = 3$. Thus, if $n = 2$ we are done: buyer 2 can compensate for her stolen items by taking the leftover items in B_{12} which are legal for her (the amount of stolen items equals the amount of leftover items since $|O_1| = |S| = k_1$). We assume for the rest of the proof that $n = 3$. Since S is legal for buyer 1, the stolen items $S \setminus O_1$ are contained in $B_{21} \cup B_{213} \cup B_{31} \cup B_{312}$.

Denote $a_2 := |(O_1 \setminus S) \cap B_{12}|, a_3 := |(O_1 \setminus S) \cap B_{13}|, a_{23} := |(O_1 \setminus S) \cap B_{123}|, b_2 := |(S \setminus O_1) \cap B_{21}|, b_{23} := |(S \setminus O_1) \cap B_{213}|, b_3 := |(S \setminus O_1) \cap B_{31}|, b_{32} := |(S \setminus O_1) \cap B_{312}|$.

In words, a_2 is the number of items player 1 left behind in B_{12}, b_2 is the number of items she 'stole' from player 2 out of the items in B_{21}, b_{32} is the amount she 'stole' from player 3 out of the items in B_{312}, etc. By the discussion in the previous paragraph, these account for all stolen and leftover items, and we get

$$b_2 + b_{23} + b_3 + b_{32} = |S \setminus O_1| = |O_1 \setminus S| = a_2 + a_{23} + a_3. \tag{1}$$

Consider the bipartite graph G whose left side consists of the items in $S \setminus O_1$ and whose right side consists of the items in $O_1 \setminus S$, with edges (x, y) whenever the stolen item x can be replaced by the leftover item y legally (e.g., if $x \in O_2$, then $y \in B_{12} \cup B_{123}$). Specifically, G is composed of a bi-clique between the stolen items from $B_{21} \cup B_{213}$ (the stolen items of player 2) and the leftover items from $B_{12} \cup B_{123}$ (these are the leftover items that are legal for player 2), and of another bi-clique between the stolen items of $B_{31} \cup B_{312}$ (the stolen items of player 3) and the leftover items of $B_{13} \cup B_{123}$ (the leftover items that are legal for player

3). If there is a perfect matching in G, then every stolen item can be replaced with the item it was matched to in the perfect matching, resulting in a legal allocation, and we are done. Thus we assume that there is no perfect matching in G. Since Hall's condition does not hold, we have that either $b_2 + b_{23} > a_2 + a_{23}$, or $b_3 + b_{32} > a_3 + a_{23}$. Assume w.l.o.g. that $b_2 + b_{23} > a_2 + a_{23}$. Then, by Eq. (1), we have $a_3 > b_3 + b_{32} \geq 0$. We claim that this implies $b_{23} = 0$. The reason is that otherwise, player 1 stole some item, denoted y, from B_{213} and left behind some item, denoted x, in B_{13}. But this cannot be the case since this would imply (by Lemma 7) that the edge $x \to y$ was removed in the transition from H to H', but the edge $B_{13} \to B_{213}$ was never marked in the pricing scheme. Therefore $b_{23} = 0$ and $b_2 > a_2 + a_{23} \geq 0$. The combination of $b_2 > 0$ and $a_3 > 0$ implies that the edge $B_{13} \to B_{21}$ was marked in step 4, and so one of B_{13}, B_{21} is of minimal size in the cycle $B_{13} \to B_{21} \to B_{32} \to B_{13}$. In particular,

$$|B_{32}| \geq \min\{|B_{13}|, |B_{21}|\} \geq \min\{a_3, b_2\}$$
$$\geq \min\{a_3 - (b_3 + b_{32}), b_2 - (a_2 + a_{23})\} = b_2 - (a_2 + a_{23}),$$

where the equality holds by Eq. (1). In order to complete S to a legal allocation, player 2 compensates for his stolen b_2 items by taking the $a_2 + a_{23}$ items player 1 left behind in $B_{12} \cup B_{123}$ and by "stealing" $b_2 - (a_2 + a_{23})$ items from B_{32} (indeed there are enough items there for player 2 to steal). Player 3 now has to compensate for the items stolen from her by both players, a total of $(b_{32} + b_3) + (b_2 - (a_2 + a_{23})) = a_3$ items. Since player 1 left precisely this number of items in B_{13}, player 3 can take them. Note that the resulting allocation is indeed legal and thus optimal. □

Acknowledgments. We deeply thank Amos Fiat and Renato Paes-Leme for helpful discussions.

References

1. Cohen-Addad, V., Eden, A., Feldman, M., Fiat, A.: The invisible hand of dynamic market pricing. In: Proceedings of the 2016 ACM Conference on Economics and Computation, EC 2016, Maastricht, NL, 24–28 July 2016, pp. 383–400 (2016)
2. Gul, F., Stacchetti, E.: Walrasian equilibrium with gross substitutes. J. Econ. Theory **87**(1), 95–124 (1999)
3. Hsu, J., Morgenstern, J., Rogers, R.M., Roth, A., Vohra, R.: Do prices coordinate markets? In: Proceedings of the 48th Annual ACM SIGACT Symposium on Theory of Computing, STOC 2016, Cambridge, MA, USA, 18–21 June 2016, pp. 440–453 (2016)
4. Kelso Jr., A.S., Crawford, V.P.: Job matching, coalition formation, and gross substitutes. Econ. J. Econ. Soc., 1483–1504 (1982)
5. Leme, R.P.: Gross substitutability: an algorithmic survey. Games Econ. Behav. **106**, 294–316 (2017)
6. Murota, K.: Valuated matroid intersection I: optimality criteria. SIAM J. Discrete Math. **9**(4), 545–561 (1996)
7. Yang, Y.: On the maximal domain theorem: a corrigendum to "Walrasian equilibrium with gross substitutes". J. Econ. Theory **172**, 505–511 (2017)

Competitively Pricing Parking in a Tree

Max Bender[1]([⊠]), Jacob Gilbert[1], Aditya Krishnan[2], and Kirk Pruhs[1]

[1] University of Pittsburgh, Pittsburgh, PA 15260, USA
{mcb121,jmg264}@pitt.edu, kirk@cs.pitt.edu
[2] Johns Hopkins University, Baltimore, MD 21218, USA
aditya.krishnan94@gmail.com

Abstract. Motivated by demand-responsive parking pricing systems we consider posted-price algorithms for the online metrical matching problem and the online metrical searching problem in a tree metric. Our main result is a poly-log competitive posted-price algorithm for online metrical searching.

1 Introduction

Since 2011 SFpark has been San Francisco's system for managing the availability of on-street parking [2,3,28]. The goal of the system is to reduce the time and fuel wasted by drivers searching for an open space. The system monitors parking usages via sensors embedded in the pavement and distributes this information in real-time to drivers via SFpark.org and phone apps. SFpark periodically adjusts parking meter pricing to manage demand, to lower prices in underutilized areas, and to raise prices in overutilized areas. Prices can range from a minimum of 25 cents to a maximum of 7 dollar per hour during normal hours with a 18 dollars per hour cap for special events such as baseball games or street fairs. Several other cities in the world have similar demand-responsive parking pricing systems, for example Calgary has had the ParkPlus system since 2008 [1].

The problem of centrally assigning drivers to parking spots to minimize time and fuel usage is naturally modeled by the online metrical matching problem. The setting for online metrical matching consists of a collection of k servers (the parking spots) located at various locations within a metric space. The algorithm then sees an online sequence of requests over time that arrive at various locations in the metric space (the drivers arriving to look for a parking spot). In response to a request, the online algorithm must match the request (car) to some server (parking spot) that has not been previously matched; Conceptually we interpret this matching as the request (car) moving to the location of the matched server (parking spot). The objective goal is to minimize the aggregate distance traveled by the requests (cars).

A. Krishnan—This work was done in part while this author was a student at Carnegie Mellon University advised by Anupam Gupta.

K. Pruhs—Supported in part by NSF grants CCF-1421508, CCF-1535755, CCF-1907673, CCF-2036077 and an IBM Faculty Award.

X. Chen et al. (Eds.): WINE 2020, LNCS 12495, pp. 220–233, 2020.
https://doi.org/10.1007/978-3-030-64946-3_16

We also consider what we call the online metrical search problem, which is an important special case of the online metrical matching problem. This is a promise problem in that the adversary is constrained to guarantee that there is an optimal matching for which only one edge has positive cost. It is useful to conceptually think of online metrical search as the following parking problem: the setting consists of many parking spots at various locations in a metric space and a single car that is initially parked at some location in the metric space. Over time the parking spots are decommissioned one by one until only one parking spot is left in commission. If at any time the car is not parked at an in-commission parking spot, then the car must move to a parking spot that is still in commission. The objective is to minimize the aggregate distance traveled by the car. The optimal solution is to move the car directly to the last remaining parking spot.

The online metrical search problem is a special case of the online metrical matching problem because the parking spots can be viewed as servers and the decommissioning of a parking spot can be simulated by the arrival of a request at the location of that parking spot. So a lower bound on the competitive ratio for the online metrical search problem for a particular metric space also gives a lower bound for the online metrical matching problem on the metric space. Conversely it seems that in terms of the optimal competitive ratio, online metric search is no easier than metric matching. In particular, there is no known example of a metric space where the optimal competitive ratio for online metrical matching is known to be significantly greater than the optimal competitive ratio for online metrical search on that metric space. For example on a line metric, the online metrical search problem is better known as the "cow path problem", and the optimal deterministic competitive ratio is known to be 9 [13], while the best known lower bound on the deterministic competitive ratio for online metrical matching on a line metric is 9.001 [18], worse only by a minuscule factor.

In order to be implementable within the context of SFpark, online algorithms must be posted-price algorithms. In this setting, posted-price means that before each request arrives, the online algorithm sets a price on each unused server (parking spot) without knowing the location where the next request will arrive. Furthermore, each request is assumed to be a selfish agent who moves to the available server (parking spot) that minimizes the sum of the price of and distance to that server. The objective remains to minimize the aggregate distance traveled by the requests. So conceptually the objective of the parking pricing agency is minimizing social cost, not maximizing revenue.

Research into posted-price algorithms for online metrical matching was initiated in [14] as part of a line of research to study the use of posted-price algorithms to minimize social cost in online optimization problems. As a posted-price algorithm is a valid online algorithm, one can not expect to obtain a better competitive ratio for posted-price algorithms than what is achievable by online algorithms. So this research line has primarily focused on problems where the optimal competitive ratio achievable by an online algorithm is (perhaps approximately) known and seeks to determine whether a similar competitive ratio can be (again perhaps approximately) achieved by a posted-price algorithm. The higher level goal is to determine the increase in social cost that is necessitated by the restriction that an algorithm has to use posted prices to incentivize selfish agents, instead of being able to mandate agent behavior.

An $O(\log \Delta)$-competitive randomized posted-price algorithm for metric matching on a line metric is given in [14] where Δ is the ratio of the distance between the furthest two servers and the distance between the closest two servers. No $o(\log k)$-competitive (not necessarily posted-price) algorithm is known for online metric matching on a line metric. So arguably, on a line metric there is a posted-price algorithm that is nearly as competitive as the best known centralized online algorithm.

Our original research goal was to determine whether posted-price algorithms can be similarly competitive with a centralized online algorithm for tree metrics for online metrical matching. In order to be more specific about our goal, we need to review a bit. A tree metric is represented by a tree $T = (V, E)$ with positive real edge weights where the distance $d_T(u, v)$ between vertices $u, v \in V$ is the shortest path between vertices u and v in T. There is a deterministic online algorithm that is $(2k - 1)$-competitive for online metric matching in any metric space, and no deterministic online algorithm can achieve a better competitive ratio for online metric searching in a tree metric [21, 22]. An $O(\log k)$-competitive randomized algorithm for online metric matching in $O(\log k)$-HST's (Hierarchically Separated Trees) is given in [25]. By combining this result with results about randomly embedding metric spaces into HST's [10, 11, 16, 25] obtained an $O(\log^3 k)$-competitive randomized algorithm for online metric matching in a general metric space. Following this general approach, [9] later obtained an $O(\log^2 k)$-competitive randomized algorithm for online metrical search in an arbitrary metric by giving an $O(\log k)$-competitive randomized algorithm for 2-HST's. No better results are known for tree metrics, so all evidence points to tree metrics as being as hard as general metrics for online metrical matching. Thus, more specifically our original research goal was to determine whether there is poly-log competitive randomized posted-price algorithm for the online metrical matching problem on a tree metric. Before stating our progress toward this goal, it will be useful to review the literature a bit more.

1.1   Prior Related Work

The most obvious algorithmic design approach for posted-price problems is to directly design a pricing algorithm from scratch, as is done for metrical task systems in [14], but this is not the most common approach in the literature. Two less direct algorithmic design paradigms have emerged in the literature. The first algorithmic design paradigm is what we will call *mimicry*. A posted-price algorithm A *mimics* an online algorithm B if the probability that B will take a particular action is equal the probability that a self-interested agent will choose this same action when the prices of actions are set using A. For example, [14] shows how to set prices to mimic the $O(\log \Delta)$-competitive Harmonic algorithm for online metric matching on a line metric from [19]. As another example, [17] shows how to set prices to mimic the $O(1)$-competitive algorithm Slow-Fit from [7,8] for the problem of minimizing makespan on related machines. However, for some problems it is not possible to mimic known competitive algorithms using posted prices. For such problems, another algorithmic design paradigm is what we will call *monotonization*. In the monotonization algorithm design approach, one first seeks to characterize the online algorithms that can be mimicked, and then designs such an online algorithm. In the examples in the literature, this characterization involves some sort of monotonicity property. For example, monotonization is used in [14] to obtain an $O(k)$-competitive posted-price algorithm for the k-server problem on a line metric, and in [15] to obtain an $O(k)$-competitive posted-price algorithm for the k-server problem on a tree metric. Since no deterministic algorithm can be better than k-competitive for the k-server problem in any metric [24], this shows that in these settings, there is minimal increase in social cost necessitated by the use of posted-prices. As another example, monotonization is used in [20] to obtain an $O(1)$-competitive posted-price algorithm for minimizing maximum flow time on related machines.

For online metric matching on a line metric, better competitive ratios are achievable. An $O(k^{.59})$-competitive deterministic online algorithm was given in [4]. Subsequently several different $O(\log n)$-competitive randomized online algorithms for a line are given in [19]; these algorithms leverage special properties of HST's constructed from a line metric. As already mentioned, [19] also showed that the natural Harmonic algorithm is $O(\log \Delta)$-competitive. An $O(\log^2 k)$-competitive deterministic online algorithm was given in [26], and this was later improved to $O(\log k)$ in [27]. Super-constant lower bounds for various types of algorithms are given in [5,23]. More generally, the algorithm for online metric matching given in [26] has the property that for every metric space, its competitive ratio is at most $O(\log^2 k)$ times the optimal competitive ratio achievable by any deterministic algorithm on that metric space.

1.2   Our Contribution

There is no hope to mimic any of the online algorithms for online metrical matching that are based on HST's as HST's by their very nature lose too much information about the structure of a tree metric. Therefore we adopt the monotonization approach. In Sect. 2 we identify a monotonicity property that characterizes mimicable algorithms for online metrical matching in tree metrics. Roughly speaking this property says that if a request were to have arrived on the route to its desired server, then the probability that the request would still have been matched to this server can not decrease. Thus we reduce finding a post-priced algorithm to finding a monotone algorithm.

In Sect. 3 we give an algorithm TreeSearch for the online metrical search problem on a tree metric. The algorithm is based on the classic multiplicative weights algorithm for online learning from experts [6]. Conceptually there is one expert E^ℓ for each leaf ℓ of the tree T. Expert E^ℓ always recommends that the car/request travels toward the leaf ℓ. Thus expert E^ℓ pays a cost of one whenever a parking spot on the path from the root to ℓ is decommissioned, a cost of zero when other parking spots are decommissioned, and an infinite cost if there are no remaining parking spots on the path from the root to ℓ. Let π_t^ℓ be the probability that the multiplicative weights algorithm has associated with expert E^ℓ right before request r_t arrives. Let v_t^ℓ be the location of the car just before request r_t arrives if the advice of expert E^ℓ had always been followed. The algorithm TreeSearch maintains the invariant that right before request r_t arrives, the probability that the car is at a vertex v is $\sum_{\ell:v_t^\ell=v} \pi_t^\ell$, the sum of the probabilities of the experts that recommend that the car should be parked at v. The most technically difficult part of the algorithm design process was maintaining this invariant. We then upper bound the expected number of jumps made by the TreeSearch algorithm, where a jump is a movement of the car by a positive amount. Finally, we show how to extend TreeSearch to be a monotone algorithm TreeMatch for online metrical matching on a tree metric.

In Section algorithm for online metric searching on a tree metric. Before any requests arrive, an algorithm GroveBuild embeds the tree metric into what we will call a grove, which is a refinement of an HST that retains more information about the topology of the original metric space. It is probably easiest to explain what a grove is by explaining the difference in how one is constructed in comparison to how an HST is constructed. The construction of each starts with a Low Diameter Decomposition (LDD) of the metric space. A LDD is a partition $\mathcal{P} = \{P_1, \ldots, P_n\}$ of the vertices of the metric space where each part is connected and the diameter of each part is an α factor smaller than the diameter of the whole metric space. The top of the HST consists of a star where the center of the star is the root of the HST, and there is one child of the root for each part P_i. In contrast, the top of a grove consists of the tree that remains after collapsing each part to a single vertex. For both an HST and a grove, the construction then proceeds recursively on each part. So intuitively the key difference is that groves retain information about the distances between parts in the LDD that the HST instead discards. See Fig. 1 for a comparison of an HST and a grove constructed from the same LDD.

We then give a monotone algorithm GroveMatch for online metrical matching on a tree metric that utilizes the algorithm TreeMatch on each tree in the grove constructed from the tree metric. We show that GroveMatch is poly-log competitive (more precisely $O(\log^6 \Delta \log^2 n)$-competitive) on metric search instances by induction on the levels of the grove. This is an extension of a similar induction argument in [25] that shows that a $O(\log n)$-competitive algorithm for a star (or a complete unit metric) can be extended to an algorithm for a $O(\log n)$-HST with the loss of a poly-log factor in the competitiveness. However, our situation is complicated by the fact the possible ways that a request can potentially move within a grove is more complicated than the possible ways a request can move within an HST, and thus the induction is more complicated as the induction depends on when the request is moving "up" and when the request is moving "down" in trees within the grove. The bound on the number of jumps made by TreeSearch translates to a bound on the number of recursive calls made by GroveMatch. There is not a lot of wiggle room in our analysis, and thus both the algorithm design and algorithm analysis process are necessarily quite delicate. For example, if `TreeSearch` made just 1% more jumps than the bound that we can show, then the resulting competitiveness of `GroveMatch` would not be poly-logarithmic. One consequence of this delicateness is that we can not use a black box LDD construction to build our grove, we need to construct our LDD in a way that tightly controls the variance of random properties of our grove.

Due to space requirements, proofs have mostly been removed. See [12] for the full paper with complete proofs.

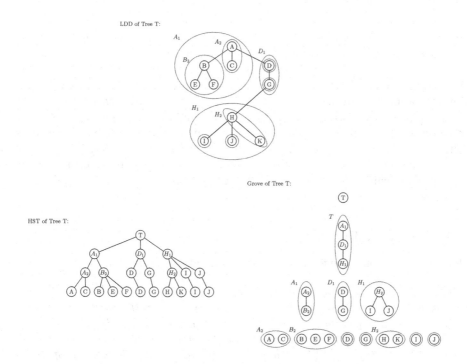

Fig. 1. An example of a LDD, the corresponding HST, and the corresponding grove.

2 Pricing Monotone Algorithms

In this section, we show that an algorithm for the online metrical matching can be implemented as a posted-price algorithm if and only if the algorithm satisfies the following monotonicity property. We note that monotonicity does not have a natural interpretation within the context of online metrical searching, which explains why we give a monotone algorithm for online metrical matching, even though we only analyze its competitiveness for online metrical search.

Definition 1. *An algorithm A for online metric matching is monotone if for every instance, every request r_t in that instance, every possible sequence R of* *random events internal to A prior to r_t's arrival, and all vertices u, v, s where v is on the path from u to s it is the case that:* $\boldsymbol{Pr}[A_R(r_t) = s \mid E_R$ *and* $r_t = u] \leq$ $\boldsymbol{Pr}[A_R(r_t) = s \mid E_R$ *and* $r_t = v]$ *where* $A_R(r_t)$ *is the event that A matches* r_t *to s, and* E_R *is the event that the past random events internal to A are equal to R.*

Theorem* 1. *Any algorithm A for the online metrical matching problem can be implemented as a posted-price algorithm if and only if A is monotone.*

3 The Algorithm `TreeMatch`

In Subsect. 3.1 we define algorithm `TreeSearch` for the metric search problem on a tree $T = (V, E)$ rooted at vertex a ρ. The distance metric on T will not be of interest to us in this section. We will use the interpretation of a car moving when its parking spot is decommissioned, as introduced earlier, as we think that this interpretation is more intuitive. The description of `TreeSearch` in Subsect. 3.1 uses a probability distribution $q_t^\sigma(\tau)$ that is complicated to define, so its exact definition is postponed until Subsect. 3.2, in which we also show that it achieves our goal of matching the experts distribution. Finally in Subsect. 3.3, we show how to convert `TreeSearch` into a monotone algorithm `TreeMatch` for online metrical matching that is identical to `TreeSearch` on online metrical search instances.

3.1 Algorithm Description

We start with some needed definitions and notation.

Definition 2. *A parking spot s_i in the collection S of parking spots is a leaf-spot if there are no other parking spots in the subtree rooted at s_i. Let $L(T) = \{\ell_1, ..., \ell_d\}$ denote the collection of leaf-spots. Let H be the maximum initial number of parking spots in T on the path from the root ρ to a leaf-spot in $L(T)$. For $\sigma \in [d]$, define $T_\sigma \subseteq V$ as the set of parking spots on the path from the root ρ to ℓ_σ, inclusive. We define T_σ to be alive if there is still an in-commission parking spot in T_σ, and dead otherwise. A T_σ is killed by r_t if r_t is the last parking spot to be decommissioned in T_σ. Let $\mathcal{A}_t = \{\sigma \in [d] \mid T_\sigma$ is alive just before the arrival of $r_t\}$. For a vertex $v \in V$, let $L(v)$ denote the collection of leaf-spots that are descendants of v in T. Let c_t be the location of the car just before the arrival of request r_t.*

Algorithm `TreeSearch`: The algorithm has two phases: the prologue phase and the core phase. The algorithm starts in the prologue phase and transitions to the core phase after the first time m when there is no available parking space on the path from the new parking spot c_{m+1} to the root ρ, inclusive. The algorithm then remains in the core phase until the end. In the prologue phase, whenever the car is not parked at a vertex with an in-commission parking spot, the following actions are taken:

1. If there is an in-commission parking spot at c_t then no action is taken.
2. Else if there is an in-commission parking spot on the path between c_t and the root ρ, inclusive, then the car moves to the first in-commission parking spot on this path nearest to c_t.
3. Else the car moves to the root ρ and enters the core phase to determine where to go from there. So for analysis purposes, the movement to ρ counts as being part of the prologue phase, and the rest of the movement counts as being in the core phase.

If the car is at the root ρ and the algorithm is just transitioning into the core phase, then a live T_τ is picked uniformly at random from $\mathcal{A}_{t+1}$, an internal variable γ is set to be τ, and the car moves to the first in-commission parking spot on the path from ρ to ℓ_τ. Subsequently in the core phase, when a parking spot r_t is decommissioned then:

1. If the car is not parked at r_t, that is if $c_t \neq r_t$, then no action is taken.
2. Else the car moves to the first in-commission parking spot in T_τ with probability $q_t^\gamma(\tau)$ and sets γ to be τ. ($q_t^\gamma(\tau)$ is defined in the next subsection.)

Intuitively γ stores the last random choice of the algorithm.

3.2   The Definition of $q_t^\sigma(\tau)$

In this section we only consider times in the core phase. We conceptually divide up the tree T into three regions. Given vertex v and time t, we let z_t^v be the number of in-commission parking spots on the path from v to ρ, inclusive, just before decommission r_t. We then define the regions as follows:

1. The *root region* is the set of all vertices v such that $z_t^v = 0$. Note that this region is connected, and no decommissioning can occur in this region since there are no parking spots left.
2. The *frontier region* is the set of all vertices v such that $z_t^v = 1$. A decommissioning r_t is called a frontier decommissioning if r_t is in the frontier region.
3. The *outer region* is the set of all vertices v such that $z_t^v > 1$. A decommissioning r_t is called a outer decommissioning if r_t is in the outer region.

Observe that these regions have no dependence on random events internal to the algorithm. Further observe that step 2 of the core phase in algorithm TreeSearch maintains the invariant that the car is always parked at a spot in the frontier region. This means that any outer decommissionings will not move the car from its current parking spot.

Definition 3. *Let r_m be the last decommissioning handled in the prologue phase of TreeSearch. Define $\mathcal{X}_t = \mathcal{A}_t \cap L(r_t)$ to be the collection of σ's such that T_σ is alive and contains r_t and define $\mathcal{Y}_t = \mathcal{A}_t \setminus \mathcal{X}_t = \mathcal{A}_t \cap \overline{L(r_t)}$ to be the collection of σ's such that T_σ is alive and doesn't contain r_t. Define $\mathcal{F}_t = \mathcal{X}_t \cap \overline{\mathcal{A}_{t+1}}$ to be the collection of σ's such that T_σ is killed by r_t. Let n_t^σ denote the number of frontier decommissionings strictly before time t from T_σ. Define $w_t^\sigma = (1-\epsilon)^{n_t^\sigma}$ for each*

$\sigma \in [d]$. Define $W_t(\mathcal{J}) = \sum_{\sigma \in \mathcal{J}} w_t^\sigma$ for any $\mathcal{J} \subseteq \{1, ..., d\}$. Define π_t^σ as the probability the experts algorithm would give to expert σ, that is $\pi_t^\sigma = \frac{w_t^\sigma}{\sum_{\tau \in [d]} w_t^\tau}$. Define $\tilde{\pi}_t^\sigma$ as π_t normalized amongst all experts in $\mathcal{A}_t$, that is $\tilde{\pi}_t^\sigma = \frac{w_t^\sigma}{\sum_{\tau \in \mathcal{A}_t} w_t^\tau}$ if $\sigma \in \mathcal{A}_t$, and 0 otherwise. Define p_t^σ as the probability that $\gamma = \sigma$ right before time t.

We are now ready to define $q_t^\sigma(\tau)$. Note that by the definition of TreeSearch, $q_t^\sigma(\tau)$ is only used for $\sigma \in \mathcal{X}_t$ since the algorithm only reaches step 2 of the core phase when $r_t \in T_\gamma$. We show in Lemma 1 that this definition of $q_t^\sigma(\tau)$ indeed defines a probability distribution over $\tau \in [d]$. We then show in Lemma 2 that the definition of $q_t^\sigma(\tau)$ guarantees that our desired invariant $p_t^\sigma = \tilde{\pi}_t^\sigma$ holds.

Definition 4

$$
q_t^\sigma(\tau) = \begin{cases} \frac{\epsilon w_t^\tau}{(1-\epsilon)W_t(\mathcal{X}_t \setminus \mathcal{F}_t) + W_t(\mathcal{Y}_t)} & \text{if } \tau \in \mathcal{Y}_t \text{ and } \sigma \in \mathcal{X}_t \setminus \mathcal{F}_t \\[2mm] \frac{w_t^\tau}{(1-\epsilon)W_t(\mathcal{X}_t \setminus \mathcal{F}_t) + W_t(\mathcal{Y}_t)} & \text{if } \tau \in \mathcal{Y}_t \text{ and } \sigma \in \mathcal{F}_t \\[2mm] \frac{1 - \sum_{\varsigma \in \mathcal{Y}_t} q_t^\sigma(\varsigma)}{|\mathcal{X}_t \setminus \mathcal{F}_t|} & \text{if } \tau \in \mathcal{X}_t \setminus \mathcal{F}_t \\[2mm] 0 & \text{if } \tau \in \mathcal{F}_t \text{ or } \tau \in \overline{\mathcal{A}_t} \end{cases}
$$

Lemma* 1. *For all times t in the core phase and for all $\sigma \in \mathcal{X}_t$, $q_t^\sigma(\tau)$ forms a distribution over $\tau \in [d]$.*

Lemma* 2. *For all times t during the core phase and for all $\sigma \in [d]$, $p_t^\sigma = \tilde{\pi}_t^\sigma$.*

Definition 4 and Lemmas 1 and 2 give us the following bound on the cost:

Theorem* 2. *During the prologue phase, $\sum_{t=1}^m \mathbf{1}^{\text{TM}}(t) \leq H$ and during the core phase, $\mathbf{E}\left[\sum_{t=m+1}^{k-1} \mathbf{1}^{\text{TM}}(t)\right] \leq (1+\epsilon)H + \frac{\ln d}{\epsilon}$ where $\mathbf{1}^{\text{TM}}(t)$ is an indicator random variable that is 1 if TreeSearch moves the car to a new parking spot on the decommissioning r_t and 0 otherwise.*

3.3 Monotonicity

We show that any neighbor algorithm for online metrical search can be extended to a monotone algorithm for online metrical matching, where a neighbor algorithm has the property that if it moves the car to a parking spot s_i with positive probability then it must be the case that there is no in-commission parking spot on the route to s_i. As TreeSearch is obviously a neighbor algorithm, it then follows that it can be extended to a monotone algorithm for online metrical matching, which we will call TreeMatch.

Lemma* 3. *Let A be a neighbor algorithm for online metrical search. Then there exists a monotone algorithm B for online metrical matching on a tree metric that is identical to A for online metrical search instances.*

4   The GroveMatch Algorithm

In Subsect. 4.1 we describe an algorithm GroveBuild that builds a grove G from a tree metric T with distance metric d_T before any request arrives. We assume without loss of generality that the minimum distance in T is 1. In Subsect. 4.2 we then give an algorithm GroveMatch for online metrical matching on a tree metric that utilizes the algorithm TreeMatch on each tree in the grove constructed by GroveBuild, and we prove some basic properties of the grove G. In Subsect. 4.3 we show that GroveMatch is a monotone online metrical matching algorithm on a tree metric, and is $O(\log^6 \Delta \log^2 n)$-competitive for online metrical search instances.

4.1   The GroveBuild Algorithm

Definition 5. *A grove G is either: a rooted tree X consisting of a single vertex, or an unweighted rooted tree X with a grove $X(v)$ associated with each vertex $v \in X$. The tree X is the canopy of the grove G. Each $X(v)$ is a subgrove of X. The canopy of a subtree $X(v)$ is a child of X. Trees in G are descendants of X.*

GroveBuild **Description:** GroveBuild is a recursive algorithm that takes as input a tree metric T, a designated root ρ of T, positive real R, a positive real α and a positive integer d. In the initial call to GroveBuild, T is the original tree metric, ρ is an arbitrary vertex in T, R is the maximum distance Δ between ρ and any other vertex in T, d is 1, and α is a parameter to be determined later in the analysis.

If T consists of a single vertex v, then the recursion ends and the algorithm outputs a rooted tree consisting of only the vertex v. We call this tree a leaf of the grove. Otherwise the algorithm's first goal is to partition the vertices of T into parts $P_1, \ldots, P_k$, and designate one vertex ℓ_i of each partition P_i as being the leader of P_i. To accomplish this, the algorithm sets partition P_1 to consist of the vertices in T that are within a distance z of ρ, where z is selected uniformly at random from the range $[0, \frac{R}{\alpha}]$. The leader ℓ_1 is set to be ρ. To compute P_i and ℓ_i after the first $i - 1$ parts and leaders are computed the algorithm takes the following steps. Let ℓ_i be a vertex such that $\ell_i \notin \cup_{j=1}^{i-1} P_j$ and for each vertex v on the path (ℓ_i, ρ) it is the case that $v \in \cup_{j=1}^{i-1} P_j$. So ℓ_i is not in but adjacent to the previous partitions. Then P_i consists of all vertices $v \in T - \cup_{j=1}^{i-1} P_j$ that are within distance $\frac{R}{\alpha}$ from ℓ_i in T. So P_i intuitively is composed of vertices that are not in previous partitions and that are close to ℓ_i.

The tree X at this point in the recursion has a vertex for each part in the partition of T. There is an edge between vertices/parts P_i and P_j in X if and only if there is an edge (v, w) in T such that $v \in P_i$ and $w \in P_j$. We identify this edge in X with the edge $(v, w) \in T$. The root of X is the vertex/part P_1. The tree X is at depth d in the grove. The grove $X(P_i)$ associated with vertex P_i in X is the result of calling GroveBuild on the subtree of T induced by the vertices in P_i, with ℓ_i designated as the root, parameter R decreased by an α factor, parameter α unchanged, and parameter d incremented by 1.

So from here on, let G denote the grove built by GroveBuild on the original tree metric T.

Definition 6

- *For an edge $(u, v) \in T$, let $\delta(u, v)$ be the depth in the grove G of the tree X that contains (u, v). Note that each edge in T occurs in exactly one tree in G.*
- *For an edge $(u, v) \in T$, define $d_G(u, v)$ to be $\frac{\Delta}{\alpha^{\delta(u,v)-1}}$.*
- *For vertices $u_0, u_h \in T$, connected by the simple path $(u_0, u_1, \ldots, u_h)$ in T, define $d_G(u_0, u_h)$ to be $\sum_{i=0}^{h-1} d_G(u_i, u_{i+1})$. Obviously d_G forms a metric on the vertices of T.*

Lemma* 4. *Recall that $d_T(u, v)$ is the shortest path distance between two vertices u, v of tree T. For all vertices $u, v \in T$, we have that $d_G(u, v) \geq d_T(u, v)$ and $\boldsymbol{E}\left[d_G(u, v)\right] \leq \alpha(1 + \log \Delta) \cdot d_T(u, v)$.*

Corollary* 1. *An algorithm $\boldsymbol{B}$ that is c-competitive for online metric matching on T with distance metric d_G is $O(c \cdot \alpha \log \Delta)$-competitive for online metric matching on T with distance metric d_T.*

4.2 GroveMatch **Description**

We now describe an algorithm GroveMatch for online metrical matching for tree metrics.

GroveMatch **Description:** Conceptually within GroveMatch, a separate copy TreeMatch(X) of the online metric matching algorithm TreeMatch will be run on each tree X in the grove G constructed by the algorithm GroveBuild. In order to accomplish this, we need to initially place servers at the vertices in X. We set the number of servers initially located at each vertex $x \in X$ to the number of servers in T that are located at vertices $v \in T$ such that $v \in x$ (recall that each vertex in a tree in the grove G corresponds to a collection of vertices in T).

When a request r_t arrives at a vertex v in T, the algorithm GroveMatch calls the algorithm TreeMatch on a sequence $(X_1, x_1), (X_2, x_2), \ldots$ where each X_i is a tree of depth i in G and x_i is a vertex in X_i. Initially X_1 is the depth 1 tree in G, and x_1 is the vertex in X_1 that contains v. Assume that TreeMatch has already been called on $(X_1, x_1), (X_2, x_2), \ldots (X_{i-1}, x_{i-1})$, then the algorithm GroveMatch processes (X_i, x_i) in the following manner. First, TreeMatch(X_i) is called to respond to a request at x_i. Let y_i be the vertex in X_i that TreeMatch(X_i) moved this request to. If X_i is a leaf in G, then TreeMatch(X_i) sets $y_i = x_i$, and GroveMatch moves request r_t to the unique vertex in T corresponding to x_i. If X_i is not a leaf in G, then X_{i+1} is set to be the canopy of the grove $X_i(y_i)$, and $x_{i+1} = \arg\min_{w \in T : w \in X_{i+1}} d_T(v, w)$ or equivalently x_{i+1} is the first vertex in X_{i+1} that one encounters if one walks in T from v to the vertices of X_{i+1}.

Lemma* 5. *Consider a tree X at depth δ with root ρ in grove G. For any vertex v in X, the number of hops in X between ρ and v is at most $\alpha+1$. Furthermore, by the time that $\mathtt{TreeMatch}(X)$ enters its core phase, it must be the case that for every descendent tree Y of X in G there will be no future movement of the car on edges in Y while $\mathtt{TreeMatch}(Y)$ is in its prologue phase.*

4.3 GroveMatch Analysis

We now analyze $\mathtt{GroveBuild}$ and $\mathtt{GroveMatch}$ under the assumption that $\alpha = (\ln n)(\log_\alpha^2 \Delta)$ and $\epsilon = \frac{1}{\log_\alpha \Delta}$.

Lemma 6. *The algorithm $\mathtt{GroveMatch}$ is $O(\log n \log^3 \Delta)$-competitive for online metrical search instances with the metric d_G.*

Proof. If $\mathtt{GroveMatch}$ directs a request to traverse an edge $(u,v) \in T$, we will say that the cost of this traversal is charged to the unique tree in G that contains (u,v). Define $P(\delta)$ to be the charge incurred by a tree X of depth δ in G and all subgroves $X(v)$ of X during the prologue phase of $\mathtt{TreeMatch}(X)$. Define $C(\delta)$ to be the charge incurred by a tree X of depth δ in G and all subgroves $X(v)$ of X during the core phase of $\mathtt{TreeMatch}(X)$.

Recall that the distance under the d_G metric of ever edge in X is $\frac{\Delta}{\alpha^{\delta-1}}$ and by Lemma 5 there are at most $\alpha+1$ vertices on the path from any leaf to the root of X. This gives us that the distance in X under d_G from the root to any leaf is at most $\alpha \frac{\Delta}{\alpha^{\delta-1}} = \frac{\Delta}{\alpha^{\delta-2}}$ and that the diameter of X is at most $2\frac{\Delta}{\alpha^{\delta-2}}$. The only subgroves $X(v)$ of X that incur costs during the prologue phase of $\mathtt{TreeMatch}(X)$ are those subgroves for which v is traversed by the car on its path to the root of X. Thus we obtain the following recurrence:

$$P(\delta) \le (\alpha+1)\left(P(\delta+1) + C(\delta+1)\right) + \frac{\Delta}{\alpha^{\delta-2}}. \tag{1}$$

Note that once the core phase begins in $\mathtt{TreeMatch}(X)$, by Lemma 5 all instances of $\mathtt{TreeMatch}(Y)$ on any tree Y that is a descendent of X in G can incur no most costs in their prologue phase. By Theorem 2 the core phase cost on X is at most $(1+\epsilon)(\alpha+1) + \frac{\ln n}{\epsilon}$ times the diameter of X, which is at most $2\frac{\Delta}{\alpha^{\delta-2}}$. Thus we obtain the following recurrence:

$$C(\delta) \le \left(C(\delta+1) + 2\frac{\Delta}{\alpha^{\delta-2}}\right)\left((1+\epsilon)(\alpha+1) + \frac{\ln n}{\epsilon}\right) \tag{2}$$

We expand the recurrence relation for $C(\delta)$ first. Treating $((1+\epsilon)(\alpha+1) + \frac{\ln(n)}{\epsilon})$ as a constant Z, and expanding $C(\delta)$ we obtain:

$$C(\delta) \le \left(C(\delta+1) + 2\frac{\Delta}{\alpha^{\delta-2}}\right) Z \le \frac{2\Delta \log_\alpha \Delta}{\alpha^{\delta-1}}\left(\frac{Z}{\alpha}\right)^{\log_\alpha(\Delta)} \le \frac{2e^4 \Delta \log_\alpha \Delta}{\alpha^{\delta-1}}$$

Now expanding the recurrence relation for $P(\delta)$ we obtain:

$$P(\delta) \le (\alpha + 1)\left(P(\delta + 1) + C(\delta + 1)\right) + \frac{\Delta}{\alpha^{\delta - 2}} \le \frac{3e^5 \Delta \log_\alpha^2 \Delta}{\alpha^{\delta - 2}}$$

Hence the cost of the algorithm `GroveMatch` is $O\left(\frac{\Delta}{\alpha^{\delta - 2}} \log^2 \Delta\right)$. However, note that `TreeMatch` only pays positive cost on X if for any optimal solution there is at least one request that such a solution must pay positive cost for in X. The reason for this is that if `TreeMatch`(X) moves the car out of a vertex v in X, then there are no in-commission parking spots left in v, and therefore every algorithm would have to move the car out of v. Since every edge in X has distance $\frac{\Delta}{\alpha^{\delta - 1}}$, this gives us that `GroveMatch` must be $O(\alpha \log^2 \Delta) = O(\log n \log^3 \Delta)$ competitive on the metric d_G.

Together with Corollary 1, Lemma 6 gives us the following theorem:

Theorem 3. *`GroveMatch` is $O(\log^6 \Delta \log^2 n)$-competitive for online metrical search instances.*

Lemma* 7. *`GroveMatch` is a monotone algorithm for online metrical matching.*

Acknowledgements. We thank Anupam Gupta for his guidance, throughout the research process, that was absolutely critical to obtaining these results. We thank Amos Fiat for introducing us to this posted-price research area, and for several helpful discussions.

References

1. Calgar ParkPlus Homepage. https://www.calgaryparking.com/parkplus
2. SFpark Homepage. http://sfpark.org/
3. SFpark Wikipedia page. https://en.wikipedia.org/wiki/SFpark
4. Antoniadis, A., Barcelo, N., Nugent, M., Pruhs, K., Scquizzato, M.: A $o(n)$-competitive deterministic algorithm for online matching on a line. In: Workshop on Approximation and Online Algorithms, pp. 11–22 (2014)
5. Antoniadis, A., Fischer, C., Tönnis, A.: A collection of lower bounds for online matching on the line. In: Bender, M.A., Farach-Colton, M., Mosteiro, M.A. (eds.) LATIN 2018. LNCS, vol. 10807, pp. 52–65. Springer, Cham (2018). https://doi.org/10.1007/978-3-319-77404-6_5
6. Arora, S., Hazan, E., Kale, S.: The multiplicative weights update method: a meta-algorithm and applications. Theory Comput. **8**, 121–164 (2012)
7. Aspnes, J., Azar, Y., Fiat, A., Plotkin, S., Waarts, O.: On-line routing of virtual circuits with applications to load balancing and machine scheduling. J. ACM **44**(3), 486–504 (1997)
8. Azar, Y., Kalyanasundaram, B., Plotkin, S.A., Pruhs, K., Waarts, O.: On-line load balancing of temporary tasks. J. Algorithms **22**(1), 93–110 (1997)
9. Bansal, N., Buchbinder, N., Gupta, A., Naor, J.: A randomized $O(\log^2 k)$-competitive algorithm for metric bipartite matching. Algorithmica **68**(2), 390–403 (2014)

10. Bartal, Y.: Probabilistic approximation of metric spaces and its algorithmic applications. In: Symposium on Foundations of Computer Science, pp. 184–193 (1996)
11. Bartal, Y.: On approximating arbitrary metrics by tree metrics. In: ACM Symposium on Theory of Computing, pp. 161–168 (1998)
12. Bender, M.E., Gilbert, J., Krishnan, A., Pruhs, K.: Competitively pricing parking in a tree. arXiv, abs/2007.07294 (2020)
13. Borodin, A., El-Yaniv, R.: Online Computation and Competitive Analysis. Cambridge University Press, Cambridge (1998)
14. Cohen, I.R., Eden, A., Fiat, A., Jez, L.: Pricing online decisions: beyond auctions. In: ACM-SIAM Symposium on Discrete Algorithms, pp. 73–91 (2015)
15. Cohen, I.R., Eden, A., Fiat, A., Jez, L.: Dynamic pricing of servers on trees. In: Approximation, Randomization, and Combinatorial Optimization. Algorithms and Techniques. LIPIcs, vol. 145, pp. 10:1–10:22 (2019)
16. Fakcharoenphol, J., Rao, S., Talwar, K.: A tight bound on approximating arbitrary metrics by tree metrics. J. Comput. Syst. Sci. **69**(3), 485–497 (2004)
17. Feldman, M., Fiat, A., Roytman, A.: Makespan minimization via posted prices. In: ACM Conference on Economics and Computation, pp. 405–422 (2017)
18. Fuchs, B., Hochstättler, W., Kern, W.: Online matching on a line. Theor. Comput. Sci. **332**(1–3), 251–264 (2005)
19. Gupta, A., Lewi, K.: The online metric matching problem for doubling metrics. In: Czumaj, A., Mehlhorn, K., Pitts, A., Wattenhofer, R. (eds.) ICALP 2012. LNCS, vol. 7391, pp. 424–435. Springer, Heidelberg (2012). https://doi.org/10.1007/978-3-642-31594-7_36
20. Im, S., Moseley, B., Pruhs, K., Stein, C.: Minimizing maximum flow time on related machines via dynamic posted pricing. In: European Symposium on Algorithms, pp. 51:1–51:10 (2017)
21. Kalyanasundaram, B., Pruhs, K.: Online weighted matching. J. Algorithms **14**(3), 478–488 (1993)
22. Khuller, S., Mitchell, S.G., Vazirani, V.V.: On-line algorithms for weighted bipartite matching and stable marriages. Theor. Comput. Sci. **127**(2), 255–267 (1994)
23. Koutsoupias, E., Nanavati, A.: The online matching problem on a line. In: Solis-Oba, R., Jansen, K. (eds.) WAOA 2003. LNCS, vol. 2909, pp. 179–191. Springer, Heidelberg (2004). https://doi.org/10.1007/978-3-540-24592-6_14
24. Manasse, M., McGeoch, L., Sleator, D.: Competitive algorithms for on-line problems. In: ACM Symposium on Theory of Computing, pp. 322–333 (1988)
25. Meyerson, A., Nanavati, A., Poplawski, L.J.: Randomized online algorithms for minimum metric bipartite matching. In: ACM-SIAM Symposium on Discrete Algorithms, pp. 954–959 (2006)
26. Nayyar, K., Raghvendra, S.: An input sensitive online algorithm for the metric bipartite matching problem. In: Symposium on Foundations of Computer Science, pp. 505–515 (2017)
27. Raghvendra, S.: Optimal analysis of an online algorithm for the bipartite matching problem on a line. In: Symposium on Computational Geometry. LIPIcs, vol. 99, pp. 67:1–67:14 (2018)
28. Shoup, D., Pierce, G.: SFpark: Pricing Parking by Demand (2013). https://www.accessmagazine.org/fall-2013/sfpark-pricing-parking-demand/

Routing, Scheduling, Load Balancing

The Price of Anarchy for Instantaneous Dynamic Equilibria

Lukas Graf$^{(\boxtimes)}$ [iD] and Tobias Harks

Institute of Mathematics, Augsburg University, 86135 Augsburg, Germany
{lukas.graf,tobias.harks}@math.uni-augsburg.de

Abstract. We consider flows over time within the deterministic queue-ing model and study the solution concept of instantaneous dynamic equi-librium (IDE) in which flow particles select at every decision point a currently shortest path. The length of such a path is measured by the physical travel time plus the time spent in queues. Although IDE have been studied since the eighties, the efficiency of the solution concept is not well understood. We study the price of anarchy for this model and show an upper bound of order $\mathcal{O}(U \cdot \tau)$ for single-sink instances, where U denotes the total inflow volume and τ the sum of edge travel times. We complement this upper bound with a family of quite complex instances proving a lower bound of order $\Omega(U \cdot \log \tau)$.

Keywords: Dynamic flows · Flows over time · Price of anarchy

1 Introduction

Dynamic flows have gained substantial interest over the last decades in modeling dynamic network systems such as urban traffic or the Internet. A widely used model for describing dynamic flows is based on the fluid queueing model due to Vickrey [23]. There is a directed graph $G = (V, E)$, where edges $e \in E$ are associated with a queue with positive rate capacity $\nu_e \in \mathbb{R}_+$ and a physical transit time $\tau_e \in \mathbb{R}_+$. If the total inflow into an edge $e = vw \in E$ exceeds the rate capacity ν_e, a queue builds up and arriving flow particles need to wait in the queue before they are forwarded along the edge. The total travel time along e is thus composed of the waiting time spent in the queue plus the physical transit time τ_e.

Due to the decentralized nature of the above mentioned applications, the physical flow model needs to be complemented by a *behavioral model* prescrib-ing the actions of flow particles. Most works in the transportation science litera-ture as well as recent works in the mathematics and computer science literature adopt the *full information model*, i.e., all flow particles have complete infor-mation on the state of the network for all points in time (including the future evolution of all flow particles) and based on this information travel along a short-est path. This leads to the concept of *dynamic equilibrium* (Nash equilibrium) and has been analyzed in the transportation science literature for decades, see

© Springer Nature Switzerland AG 2020
X. Chen et al. (Eds.): WINE 2020, LNCS 12495, pp. 237–251, 2020.
https://doi.org/10.1007/978-3-030-64946-3_17

Friesz et al. [7], Meunier and Wagner [18], Zhu and Marcotte [24] and the more recent works by Koch and Skutella [16] and Cominetti, Correa and Larré [3]. The full information assumption has been justified by assuming that the game is played repeatedly and a dynamic equilibrium is then an attractor of a learning process. In light of the wide-spread use of navigation devices, this concept may not be completely realistic anymore, because drivers are informed in real-time about the current traffic situation and, if beneficial, reroute instantaneously no matter how good or bad that route was in hindsight. This aspect is also discussed in Marcotte et al. [17], Hamdouch et al. [12] and Unnikrishnan and Waller [22].

Instead of the (classical) dynamic equilibrium, we consider in this paper *instantaneous dynamic equilibria (IDE)*, where for every point in time and at every decision node, flow only enters those edges that lie on a currently shortest path towards the respective sink. This concept assumes far less information (only the network-wide queue length which are continuously measured) and leads to a distributed dynamic using only present information that is readily available via real-time information. IDE have been proposed already in the late 80's (cf. Ran and Boyce [19, § VII-IX], Boyce, Ran and LeBlanc [2,20], Friesz et al. [8]) and it is known that IDE do exist under quite general conditions, see Graf, Harks and Sering [11].

Price of Anarchy. In comparison to dynamic equilibrium, an IDE flow behaves quite differently and several fundamental aspects of IDE are not well understood. There are, for instance, simple single-source single-sink instances in which the unique IDE flow exhibits cycling behavior, that is, some flow particles travel along cycles before they reach the sink. This behavior is impossible for dynamic equilibria as every particle chooses a path once and never gets into a cycle. This raises the question of the (time) price of anarchy of IDE flows.

Question (PoA): Assuming single-sink instances with constant inflow rates for a finite time interval, what is the maximum time needed so that every flow particle reaches the sink?[1]

1.1   Our Results and Proof Techniques

We study the termination time of IDE flows for single-sink instances and derive the first quantitative upper bound on the termination of IDE flows. Our bound is parameterized in the numbers U and τ denoting the total flow volume injected into the sources and the sum of physical travel times, respectively. We denote by $\text{PoA}(U, \tau)$ the price of anarchy over the family of instances parameterized by U and τ.

Theorem 1: For multi-source single-sink networks, any IDE flow over time terminates after at most $\mathcal{O}(U\tau)$ time. Moreover, $\text{PoA}(U, \tau) \in \mathcal{O}(U\tau)$.

---

[1] For multi-sink instances, it is known that IDE flows may cycle forever, thus, the termination time and the PoA is infinity in this case.

We prove this bound by first deriving a general termination bound for acyclic graphs. Using this bound, we then show that there exist so-called sink-like subgraphs that can effectively be treated as acyclic graphs. This way, we can argue that at all times a sufficiently large flow volume enters the current sink-like subgraph and, by the bound for acyclic graphs, reaches the sink within the claimed time. The proof technique and the bound itself are completely different to those for dynamic equilibria in [4].

We then turn to lower bounds on the termination time (PoA) of IDE flows.

Theorem 4: For $(U, \tau) \in \mathbb{N}^* \times \mathbb{N}^*$ with $U \geq 2\tau$, we have $\text{PoA}(U, \tau) \in \Omega(U \log \tau)$.

The lower bound is based on a quite complex instance (see Fig. 2) that works roughly as follows. We combine two gadgets: A "cycling gadget" consisting of a large cycle made of edges with capacity $\approx U$ and a "blocking gadget" consisting of paths with low capacity and length of about τ connecting the nodes on the cycle to the sink node. An IDE flow within this graph can then alternate between two different phases: A "charging phase", wherein the main amount of flow travels once around the big cycle, loosing a small amount of flow to each of the paths leading towards the sink, and a "blocking phase", in which the particles traveling along the paths form queues again and again in just the right way as to keep the main amount of flow traveling around on the large cycle without loosing any more flow. In order to derive a lower bound on the price of anarchy we then augment this instance in such a way that the optimal flow can just bypass the two gadgets and reach the sink in constant time while any IDE flow gets diverted into the cycling gadget.

1.2   Further Related Work

The concept of flows over time was studied by Ford and Fulkerson [5]. Shortly after, Vickrey [23] introduced a game-theoretic variant using a deterministic queueing model. Since then, dynamic equilibria have been studied extensively in the transportation science literature, see Friesz et al. [8]. New interest in this model was raised after Koch and Skutella [16] gave a novel characterization of dynamic equilibria in terms of a family of static flows (thin flows). Cominetti, Correa and Omar [3] refined this characterization and Koch and Sering [21] incorporated spillbacks in the fluid queueing model.

Regarding the price of anarchy of dynamic equilibria, Koch and Skutella [16] derived the first results on the price of anarchy for dynamic equilibria, which were recently improved by Correa, Cristi and Oosterwijk [4] devising a tight bound of $\frac{e}{e-1}$, provided that a certain monotonicity conjecture holds. Israel and Sering [14] investigated the price of anarchy for the model with spillbacks. Bhaskar, Fleischer and Anshelevich [1] devised Stackelberg strategies in order to improve the efficiency of dynamic equilibria. Recently, Frascaria and Olver [6] considered a flexible departure choice model from an optimization point of view and derived insights into devising tolls for improving the performance of dynamic equilibria.

Ismaili [13] considered a discrete version of IDEs and investigated the price of anarchy. He used the utilitarian social cost (not the makespan as we do) and derived lower bounds of order $\Omega(|V| + n)$ for the setting that only simple paths are allowed. Here n denotes the number of discrete players in the game. For general multi-commodity instances allowing also cycles, he proves that the price of anarchy is unbounded. Similarly, Graf, Harks and Sering [11] showed that for the continuous version multi-commodity IDE flows may cycle forever and, thus, the price of anarchy is infinity. For IDE flows in single-sink networks, on the other hand, they showed that termination is always guaranteed. However, due to the non-constructive nature of their proof they could not derive any explicit bound on the termination time or the price of anarchy for those instances.

2   Model

Let $\mathcal{N} = (G, (\nu_e)_{e \in E}, (\tau_e)_{e \in E}, (u_v)_{v \in V \setminus \{t\}}, t)$ be a network consisting of a directed graph $G = (V, E)$, edge capacities $\nu_e \in \mathbb{N}^*$, edge travel times $\tau_e \in \mathbb{N}^*$,[2] a single sink node $t \in V$ reachable from every other node and for every node $v \in V \setminus \{t\}$ a corresponding integrable (network) inflow rate $u_v : \mathbb{R}_{\geq 0} \to \mathbb{R}_{\geq 0}$. The idea then is that, at all times $\theta \in \mathbb{R}_{\geq 0}$ infinitesimal small agents enter the network at node v at a rate according to $u_v(\theta)$ and start traveling through the graph towards the common sink t. Such a dynamic can be described by a *flow over time*, a tuple $f = (f^+, f^-)$ where $f^+, f^- : E \times \mathbb{R}_{\geq 0} \to \mathbb{R}_{\geq 0}$ are integrable functions. For any edge $e \in E$ and time $\theta \in \mathbb{R}_{\geq 0}$ the value $f_e^+(\theta)$ describes the *(edge) inflow rate* into e at time θ and $f_e^-(\theta)$ is the *(edge) outflow rate* from e at time θ.

For any such flow over time f we define the *cumulative (edge) in- and outflow rates* F^+ and F^- as

$$F_e^+(\theta) := \int_0^\theta f_e^+(\zeta)d\zeta \quad \text{and} \quad F_e^-(\theta) := \int_0^\theta f_e^-(\zeta)d\zeta,$$

respectively. The queue length of edge e at time θ is then defined as

$$q_e(\theta) := F_e^+(\theta) - F_e^-(\theta + \tau_e). \tag{1}$$

We call such a flow f a *feasible flow* for a given set of network inflow rates $u_v : \mathbb{R}_{\geq 0} \to \mathbb{R}_{\geq 0}$ for each node $v \in V \setminus \{t\}$, if it satisfies the following constraints (2) to (5). The *flow conservation constraints* are modeled for all nodes $v \neq t$ as

$$\sum_{e \in \delta_v^+} f_e^+(\theta) - \sum_{e \in \delta_v^-} f_e^-(\theta) = u_v(\theta) \quad \text{for all } \theta \in \mathbb{R}_{\geq 0}, \tag{2}$$

---

[2] Throughout this paper we will restrict ourselves to integer travel times and edge capacities to make the statements and proofs cleaner. However, all results can be easily applied to instances with rational travel times and capacities by simply rescaling the instance appropriately. Note, however, that all bounds will then scale accordingly.

where $\delta_v^+ := \{\, vu \in E \,\}$ and $\delta_v^- := \{\, uv \in E \,\}$ are the sets of outgoing edges from v and incoming edges into v, respectively. For the sink node t we require

$$\sum_{e \in \delta_t^+} f_e^+(\theta) - \sum_{e \in \delta_t^-} f_e^-(\theta) \leq 0 \tag{3}$$

and for all edges $e \in E$ we always assume

$$f_e^-(\theta) = 0 \text{ f.a. } \theta < \tau_e. \tag{4}$$

Finally we assume that the queues operate at capacity which can be modeled by

$$f_e^-(\theta + \tau_e) = \begin{cases} \nu_e, & \text{if } q_e(\theta) > 0 \\ \min\{\, f_e^+(\theta), \nu_e \,\}, & \text{if } q_e(\theta) \leq 0 \end{cases} \quad \text{for all } e \in E, \theta \in \mathbb{R}_{\geq 0}. \tag{5}$$

Termination Time for Flows over Time. We will now introduce some additional notation in order to formally define the termination time of a feasible flow. Since termination is only relevant for flows with finitely lasting inflow rates, from here on we will always assume that there exists some time θ_0, such that the supports of all network inflow rates u_v are contained in $[0, \theta_0]$.

Following [21], for any feasible flow f and every edge $e \in E$ we define the *edge load* function F_e^Δ that gives us for any time θ the total amount of flow currently on edge e (either waiting in its queue or traveling along the edge):

$$F_e^\Delta : \mathbb{R}_{\geq 0} \to \mathbb{R}_{\geq 0}, \theta \mapsto F_e^+(\theta) - F_e^-(\theta).$$

The function $F^\Delta(\theta) := \sum_{e \in E} F_e^\Delta(\theta)$ then gives the *total amount of flow in the network at time* θ. It is a straightforward calculation to show that after θ_0 the function F^Δ is monotonically decreasing.

Lemma 1. *Let f be a feasible flow. Then for all $\theta_2 \geq \theta_1 \geq \theta_0$, we have $F^\Delta(\theta_2) \leq F^\Delta(\theta_1)$. In particular, for $\hat{\theta} \geq \theta_0$ with $F^\Delta(\hat{\theta}) = 0$, we have $F^\Delta(\hat{\theta}) = 0$ for all $\theta \geq \hat{\theta}$.*

This motivates the following definition of termination time.

Definition 1. A feasible flow over time f *terminates* if it satisfies

$$\inf\{\, \theta \geq \theta_0 \mid F^\Delta(\theta) = 0 \,\} < \infty.$$

We then say that $\Theta := \inf\{\, \theta \geq \theta_0 \mid F^\Delta(\theta) = 0 \,\}$ is the *termination time* of f or f *terminates by time* Θ. Lemma 1 then implies $F^\Delta(\theta) = 0$ for all $\theta > \Theta$.

IDE Flows and their PoA. Following [11] we define an IDE flow as a feasible flow with the property that whenever a particle arrives at a node $v \neq t$, it can only enter an edge that is the first edge on a currently shortest v-t path. Here, the *current* or *instantaneous travel time* is defined for any edge e and time θ as

$$c_e(\theta) := \tau_e + \frac{q_e(\theta)}{\nu_e}. \tag{6}$$

We then define time dependent node labels $\ell_v(\theta)$ corresponding to current shortest path distances from v to the sink t. For the sink t we set $\ell_t(\theta) = 0$ for all times $\theta \in \mathbb{R}_{\geq 0}$, while for all other nodes $v \in V \setminus \{t\}$ and $\theta \in \mathbb{R}_{\geq 0}$ we recursively define $\ell_v(\theta) = \min\limits_{e=vw \in E} \{\ell_w(\theta) + c_e(\theta)\}$. We say that an edge $e = vw$ is *active* at time θ, if $\ell_v(\theta) = \ell_w(\theta) + c_e(\theta)$ and we denote the set of active edges by $E_\theta \subseteq E$. We call a v-t path P an *active v-t path at time* θ, if all edges of P are active for i at θ or, equivalently, $\sum_{e \in P} c_e(\theta) = \ell_v(\theta)$. For differentiation we call paths that are minimal with respect to the transit times τ *physical shortest paths*.

Definition 2. A feasible flow over time f is an *instantaneous dynamic equilibrium (IDE)*, if for all $\theta \in \mathbb{R}_{\geq 0}$ and $e \in E$ it satisfies

$$f_e^+(\theta) > 0 \Rightarrow e \in E_\theta. \tag{7}$$

Since in an IDE flow particles act selfishly and without cooperation we should expect that the termination time of an IDE flow is not optimal. To quantify this difference between termination times of IDE flows and optimal flows we will use the price of anarchy, which we define as follows: For any instance $\mathcal{N} = (G, (\nu_e)_{e \in E}, (\tau_e)_{e \in E}, (u_v)_{v \in V \setminus \{t\}}, t)$ we define the worst case termination time of an IDE flow in $\mathcal{N}$ as

$$\Theta_{\mathrm{IDE}}(\mathcal{N}) := \sup \{\Theta \text{ termination time of } f \mid f \text{ an IDE flow in } \mathcal{N}\}$$

and the optimal termination time in $\mathcal{N}$ as

$$\Theta_{\mathrm{OPT}}(\mathcal{N}) := \inf \{\Theta \text{ termination time of } f \mid f \text{ a feasible flow in } \mathcal{N}\}.$$

Definition 3. For any pair of whole numbers (U, τ) we define the *Price of Anarchy (PoA)* for instances with total flow volume U and total edge length τ as

$$\mathrm{PoA}(U, \tau) := \sup \left\{ \frac{\Theta_{\mathrm{IDE}}(\mathcal{N})}{\Theta_{\mathrm{OPT}}(\mathcal{N})} \;\middle|\; \mathcal{N} \text{ s.th. } \sum_{v \in V \setminus \{t\}} \int_0^{\theta_0} u_v(\theta) d\theta = U, \sum_{e \in E} \tau_e = \tau \right\}.$$

Remark 1. At first it might seem strange that the PoA depends only on U and τ while being independent of the capacities ν_e. However, this is only the case here because we always assume that all capacities are at least 1 throughout this paper. In order to transfer our results to networks with arbitrary capacities one has to rescale the network and, in particular, replace U by $\frac{1}{\nu_{\min}} U$, where $\nu_{\min} := \min \{\nu_e \mid e \in E\}$.

3   Upper Bounds

In this section we will show an upper bound for the termination time of IDE flows in terms of $\tau(G) := \sum_{e \in E} \tau_e$ and $U := \sum_{v \in V \setminus \{t\}} \int_0^{\theta_0} u_v(\theta) d\theta$. From this we can then derive an upper bound for the PoA. However, before we can turn to these general termination results we first have to look at acyclic graphs and give a termination bound for *all* feasible flows in such networks in terms of U and $\tau(P_{\max})$, where the latter denotes the physical length of a longest v-t path. Even though the bound may seem obvious its proof requires a quite lengthy and careful analysis which can be found in the full version of this paper [10].

Lemma 2. *In an acyclic network, every feasible flow over time terminates before $\theta_0 + \tau(P_{\max}) + U$.*

Similarly to the proof of termination in [11, Theorem 4.6] we will apply our result for feasible flows in acyclic graphs to IDE flows in general graphs by using the fact ([11, Lemma 4.4]) that, whenever the total flow volume in a subgraph is small enough, only the physically shortest paths in this subgraph can be active. Since these edges form an acyclic subgraph, for an IDE flow we can then apply Lemma 2. For the following proof we will look at a particular type of subgraph, which we will call a sink-like subgraph: a subgraph containing all physically shortest paths from its nodes towards the sink, with a sufficiently low flow volume at the beginning of some interval as well as a low inflow into this subgraph over the course of said interval.

Definition 4. *An induced subgraph $T \subseteq G$ is a* sink-like subgraph *on an interval $[\theta_1, \theta_2]$ with $\theta_1 \geq \theta_0$ if the following two properties hold:*

- *For each node $v \in V(T)$ all physically shortest v-t paths are contained in T.*
- *T satisfies* $\mathrm{vol}_T(\theta_1, \theta_2) := \sum_{e \in E(T)} F_e^\Delta(\theta_1) + \sum_{e \in \delta_T^-} \int_{\theta_1}^{\theta_2} f_e^-(\theta) d\theta < \frac{1}{2}$.

Here $\delta_T^- := \{\, vw \in E \mid v \notin V(T), w \in V(T) \,\}$ denotes the set of edges entering the subgraph T. Using [11, Lemma 4.4] we can show that inside a sink-like subgraph only physically shortest paths towards the sink can be active (see [10] for the full proof).

Lemma 3. *Let T be a sink-like subgraph on an interval $[\theta_1, \theta_2]$. Then during this interval only physically shortest paths towards t can be active.*

Together with Lemmas 1 and 2 this implies that any IDE flow will terminate once the whole graph is sink-like.

Corollary 1. *Let f be an IDE flow and $\tilde{\theta} \geq \theta_0$ such that the whole graph G is sink-like at time $\tilde{\theta}$. Then, the flow terminates before $\tilde{\theta} + \tau(P_{\max}) + \frac{1}{2}$.*

To get an upper bound on the termination time of an IDE flow it now suffices to find a large enough time horizon such that it contains at least one point in time where the whole graph is sink-like. To determine such a time, we first show that if we have a sink-like subgraph over a sufficiently long period of time, we can extend this subgraph to a larger sink-like subgraph over a slightly smaller subinterval. Note, that the proof of [11, Theorem 4.6] uses a similar strategy, but is non-constructive and, therefore, only establishes the existence of a termination time without revealing anything about the length of this time. Thus, a more thorough analysis is needed here.

Lemma 4. *Let $T \subsetneq G$ be an induced subgraph, v the closest node to t not in T and T' the subgraph of G induced by $V(T) \cup \{v\}$. Let θ_1 be some time after θ_0, $\theta_2 := \theta_1 + \sum_{e \in E \backslash E(T)} (\tau_e + \frac{1}{2\nu_e})$ and $\theta'_2 := \theta_1 + \sum_{e \in E \backslash E(T')} (\tau_e + \frac{1}{2\nu_e})$.*
  If T is sink-like on $[\theta_1, \theta_2]$, then T' is a sink-like subgraph on $[\theta_1, \theta'_2]$.

Proof. Since it is clear that T' fulfills the first property of being sink-like (by the choice of v), we only need to show that $\mathrm{vol}_{T'}(\theta_1, \theta'_2) \leq \mathrm{vol}_T(\theta_1, \theta_2)$, from which the lemma follows immediately (as T is sink-like on $[\theta_1, \theta_2]$). More precisely we will show that the flow volume on edges between v and T (i.e. edges in $E(T') \backslash E(T) = (\delta_v^+ \cap \delta_T^-) \cup (\delta_v^- \cap \delta_T^+))$ at time θ_1 as well as the inflow into v over the interval $[\theta_1, \theta'_2]$ is already accounted for by the inflow into T on the interval $[\theta_1, \theta_2]$ via edges from v to T. This is formalized in the following three claims:

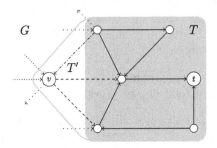

Fig. 1. A sink-like subgraph T and a closest node $v \in V \setminus V(T)$ as in the statement of Lemma 4. By Claim 1 all flow on the dash-dotted edge from T to v will reach v before time θ_v. By Claim 2 between θ_1 and θ_v all flow reaching v (either via the dotted or via the dash-dotted edges) will travel towards T from there (i.e. enter one of the dashed edges). By Claim 3 the dashed edges will never carry a larger flow volume than $\frac{1}{2}$ between θ_1 and θ_v and all flow particles using these edges within this time interval will reach T before θ_2.

Claim 1. *All flow on edges from T to v (dash-dotted edges in Fig. 1) at time θ_1 reaches v before $\theta_v := \theta_1 + \sum_{e \in E \backslash E(T')} (\tau_e + \frac{1}{2\nu_e}) + \sum_{e \in \delta_T^- \cap \delta_T^+} (\tau_e + \frac{1}{2\nu_e})$, i.e.*

$$F_e^\Delta(\theta_1) \leq \int_{\theta_1}^{\theta_v} f_e^-(\theta) d\theta \text{ for all } e \in \delta_T^+ \cap \delta_v^-.$$

Claim 2. *All flow reaching v (from T or $G \setminus T'$, i.e. via the dash-dotted or via the dotted edges in Fig. 1) between θ_1 and θ_v will enter an edge towards T (dashed edges in Fig. 1), i.e.*

$$\sum_{e \in \delta_v^-} \int_{\theta_1}^{\theta_v} f_e^-(\theta) d\theta = \sum_{e \in \delta_v^+ \cap \delta_T^-} \int_{\theta_1}^{\theta_v} f_e^+(\theta) d\theta.$$

Claim 3. *For any edge from v to T (dashed edges in Fig. 1) the total amount of flow currently traveling on this edge at any time $\theta \in [\theta_1, \theta_v]$ is less than $\frac{1}{2}$, i.e.*

$$F_e^{\Delta}(\theta) < \frac{1}{2} \text{ for all } e \in \delta_v^+ \cap \delta_T^- \text{ and } \theta \in [\theta_1, \theta_v].$$

Additionally all this flow will reach T before θ_2, i.e.

$$F_e^{\Delta}(\theta_1) + \int_{\theta_1}^{\theta_v} f_e^+(\theta)d\theta \leq \int_{\theta_1}^{\theta_2} f_e^-(\theta)d\theta \text{ for all } e \in \delta_v^+ \cap \delta_T^-.$$

From Claims 1 to 3 we then directly get

$$\sum_{e \in E(T') \setminus E(T)} F_e^{\Delta}(\theta_1) + \sum_{e \in \delta_{T'}^-} \int_{\theta_1}^{\theta_v} f_e^-(\theta)d\theta$$

$$= \sum_{e \in \delta_v^+ \cap \delta_v^-} F_e^{\Delta}(\theta_1) + \sum_{e \in \delta_v^+ \cap \delta_T^-} F_e^{\Delta}(\theta_1) + \sum_{e \in \delta_T^- \setminus \delta_v^+} \int_{\theta_1}^{\theta_v} f_e^-(\theta)d\theta + \sum_{e \in \delta_v^- \setminus \delta_T^+} \int_{\theta_1}^{\theta_v} f_e^-(\theta)d\theta$$

$$\overset{\text{Cl. 1}}{\leq} \sum_{e \in \delta_T^+ \cap \delta_v^-} \int_{\theta_1}^{\theta_v} f_e^-(\theta)d\theta + \sum_{e \in \delta_v^+ \cap \delta_T^-} F_e^{\Delta}(\theta_1) + \sum_{e \in \delta_T^- \setminus \delta_v^+} \int_{\theta_1}^{\theta_v} f_e^-(\theta)d\theta + \sum_{e \in \delta_v^- \setminus \delta_T^+} \int_{\theta_1}^{\theta_v} f_e^-(\theta)d\theta$$

$$\overset{\text{Cl. 2}}{=} \sum_{e \in \delta_v^+ \cap \delta_T^-} F_e^{\Delta}(\theta_1) + \sum_{e \in \delta_T^- \setminus \delta_v^+} \int_{\theta_1}^{\theta_v} f_e^-(\theta)d\theta + \sum_{e \in \delta_v^+ \cap \delta_T^-} \int_{\theta_1}^{\theta_v} f_e^+(\theta)d\theta$$

$$\overset{\text{Cl. 3}}{\leq} \sum_{e \in \delta_T^- \setminus \delta_v^+} \int_{\theta_1}^{\theta_v} f_e^-(\theta)d\theta + \sum_{e \in \delta_v^+ \cap \delta_T^-} \int_{\theta_1}^{\theta_2} f_e^-(\theta)d\theta,$$

implying $\text{vol}_{T'}(\theta_1, \theta_2') \leq \text{vol}_{T'}(\theta_1, \theta_v) = \sum_{e \in E(T')} F_e^{\Delta}(\theta_1) + \sum_{e \in \delta_{T'}^-} \int_{\theta_1}^{\theta_v} f_e^-(\theta)d\theta$ $\leq \sum_{e \in E(T)} F_e^{\Delta}(\theta_1) + \sum_{e \in \delta_T^-} \int_{\theta_1}^{\theta_2} f_e^-(\theta)d\theta = \text{vol}_T(\theta_1, \theta_2) < \frac{1}{2}$. This shows that T' is indeed sink-like on $[\theta_1, \theta_2']$. The proofs of the claims are relatively straightforward calculations (see [10]) using [11, Lemma 4.4] and a strengthened version of [11, Lemma 4.2]. Note, that the proofs have to be done in reverse order, as the proof of Claim 2 uses Claim 3 and the proof of Claim 1 uses both Claims 2 and 3. $\qquad\square$

Theorem 1. *For multi-source single-sink networks, any IDE flow over time terminates before $\hat{\theta} := \theta_0 + 2U \sum_{e \in E}(\tau_e + \frac{1}{2\nu_e}) + \tau(P_{\max}) + \frac{1}{2}$.*

Proof. Starting with the subgraph consisting only of the sink node t (which trivially contains all shortest paths towards t) and iteratively applying Lemma 4 we immediately get

Claim 4. *If, after time θ_0, the sink node t has a total cumulative inflow of less than $\frac{1}{2}$ for some interval of length $\sum_{e \in E}(\tau_e + \frac{1}{2\nu_e})$, then the whole graph is sink-like at the beginning of this interval.* $\qquad\blacksquare$

Since all flow reaching t vanishes from the network there can be at most $2U$ (pairwise disjoint) intervals of length $\sum_{e \in E}(\tau_e + \frac{1}{2\nu_e})$ with inflow of at least $\frac{1}{2}$ into t. Thus, there must be some time $\tilde{\theta} \leq 2U \sum_{e \in E}(\tau_e + \frac{1}{2\nu_e})$ which is the beginning of an interval of length $\sum_{e \in E}(\tau_e + \frac{1}{2\nu_e})$ with total inflow of less than $\frac{1}{2}$ into t. So, by Claim 4, the whole graph is sink-like at $\tilde{\theta}$, which, by Claim 1, implies that the flow terminates before $\tilde{\theta} + \tau(P_{\max}) + \frac{1}{2} \leq \hat{\theta}$.   □

Remark 2. This means that for any single-sink network any IDE flow terminates within $\mathcal{O}(U\tau(G))$.

Since Θ_{OPT} is trivially bounded below by $\theta_0 + 1$ this immediately leads to the following upper bound on the PoA for IDE flows:

Theorem 2. *For any pair of integers (U, τ) we have* $\text{PoA}(U, \tau) \in \mathcal{O}(U\tau)$.   □

4   Lower Bounds on the Termination Time of IDE Flows

It is easy to see that a general bound for the termination time cannot be better than $\mathcal{O}(U + \tau(G))$, since any feasible flow in the network consisting of one source node with an inflow rate of U over the interval $[0, 1]$, one sink node and a single edge between the two nodes with capacity 1 and some travel time τ terminates by $U + \tau(G)$. In the following, we will construct a family of instances, parameterized by $K, L \in \mathbb{N}^*$, that provide a lower bound on the termination time in single-sink networks of order $\Omega(U \cdot \log(\tau(G)))$ – which is strictly larger than $\mathcal{O}(U + \tau(G))$.

For any given pair of positive integers $K, L \in \mathbb{N}^*$ the instance is of the form sketched in Fig. 2, with u_{3^K+1} as source node and t as its sink. The graph has a "width" (i.e. length of the horizontal paths from u_1 to u_{3^K+1}) of $\approx 3^{K+1}$ and a "height" (length of the vertical paths from nodes u_i, v_i and w_i to t) of $\approx K3^{K+1}$. All edges on the horizontal path (including the one edge back to u_1) have a capacity of $2U$ with $U \approx L3^{K+1}$, while all the edges on the vertical paths have capacities of either 1 or 3.

If we let flow enter at node u_{3^K+1} at a rate of $2U$ over the interval $[-0.5, 0]$, we will observe the following behavior: At first, all flow enters the direct downwards path towards the sink t until a queue of length 1 has built up on the first edge of this path. After that almost all flow will enter the edge towards u_1 and some flow will go downwards to keep the queue length constant. Assuming $U \gg 1$, most of the flow will travel towards u_1 and arrive there one time step later with a slightly lower inflow rate and over a slightly shorter interval as at u_{3^K+1}. At u_1 the same flow split happens again: First all flow enters the edge to u_1' until a queue of sufficient length to induce a waiting time of 1 has formed, then most of flow travels towards the next node v_1. Similarly, at all the following nodes on the horizontal path, this pattern repeats, i.e., a small amount of flow (of volume ≈ 3) starts traveling downwards while most of the flow is diverted further to the right. Finally the main block of flow arrives at u_{3^K+1} and is diverted back to u_1 (having lost a total volume of $\approx 3^{K+1}$ to the downwards paths). By the time this

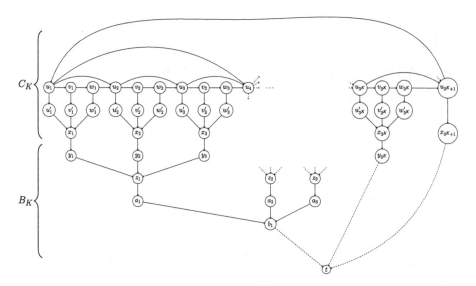

Fig. 2. A network with a total edge travel time of $\approx 3^{2K}$ that, given an inflow volume of $\approx L3^{K+1}$, has a termination time of more than $KL3^{K+1}$.

flow arrives at u_1 again, the flow particles that traveled along the edges u_1u_1', v_1v_1' and w_1w_1' join up again at node x_1 in such a way that they form a queue of length ≈ 3 on the edge y_1z_1. This queue is long enough to divert the main block of flow away towards u_2 (over the direct edge u_1u_2 of length 3). This pattern, again, repeats at all subsequent nodes u_i until the main flow finally arrives at node u_{3^K+1} (having lost no additional flow volume) and is again diverted back to u_1. This time, the flow particles from the queues on the edges y_1z_1, y_2z_1 and y_3z_1 met at node z_1 and now form a queue of length ≈ 9 on edge a_1b_1. Thus, our main flow can now be diverted away directly to node u_4 and so on. This way, the main amount of flow can travel along the horizontal path for $\approx K$ times without losing a significant amount of flow until all the flow on the vertical paths finally reaches the sink t. After that the pattern described until now repeats. Thus, flow remains in the network until at least time $\approx 3^{K+1}K\frac{U}{3^{K+1}} = 3^{K+1}KL$.

Theorem 3. *Given any pair $K, L \in \mathbb{N}^*$, there exists an instance $G_{K,L}$ with $\tau(G_{K,L}) \in \mathcal{O}(3^{2K})$ and $U_{K,L} \in \mathcal{O}(L3^K)$ such that there exists an IDE flow that does not terminate before $LK(3^{K+1} + 1)$.*

Proof. The detailed construction as well as the formal proof of its correctness can be found in [10]. □

In order to derive a lower bound on the price of anarchy from Theorem 3, we will slightly modify the instance used there in such a way that the termination time of the worst case IDE flow remains approximately the same, while there exists an optimal termination time in $\mathcal{O}(1)$.

Theorem 4. *For any pair of positive integers (U, τ) satisfying $U \geq 2\tau$, we have* $\mathrm{PoA}(U, \tau) \in \Omega(U \log \tau)$.

Proof. Wlog assume that there exist positive integers $L \geq 3^K$ such that $U = (L + 3^K)3^K$ and $\tau = 3^{2K}$. Then we take the graph $G_{K,L}$ constructed in the proof of Theorem 3 and modify it by adding two new vertices s and v and four new edges as indicating in Fig. 3.

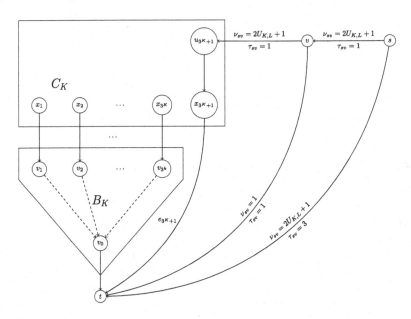

Fig. 3. The instance from the proof of Theorem 3 (on the left), two additional nodes s and v as well as four new edges.

We now use s as our new source node and a constant inflow rate of $2U_{K,L} + 1$ over the interval $[-0.5 - \varepsilon, 0]$, where $\varepsilon := \frac{4 + \tau_{e_{3K+1}}}{2U_{K,L}} \leq \frac{1}{2}$. The optimal termination time of the resulting network $\mathcal{N}$ is then at most 3, since we can just send all flow on the direct edge from s to t, where the last particle arrives 3 time steps later.

In an IDE flow, however, all flow particles travel first to v (as the path s-v-t is shorter than the path s-t), where they enter the edge towards t. This continues until a queue of length $\tau_{e_{3K+1}} + 3$ has built up at edge vt and the edge towards u_{3^K+1} becomes active, which happens at time $\theta = 0.5$. From there on, flow splits between the two edges, entering edge vt at a rate of 1 and edge vu_{3^K+1} at a rate of $2U_{K,L}$ throughout the interval $[0.5, 1]$. Thus, over the interval $[1.5, 2]$ flow arrives at node u_{3^K+1} at a rate of $2U_{K,L}$. Continuing with the flow described before the statement of Theorem 3 is then again an IDE flow. This shows that $\Theta_{\mathrm{IDE}}(\mathcal{N}) \geq LK(3^{K+1} + 1)$.

From $\tau(\mathcal{N}) = \tau(G_{K,L}) + 4 \in \mathcal{O}(3^{2K})$ and $U_{\mathcal{N}} = \left(\frac{1}{2} + \varepsilon\right)(2U_{K,L} + 1) \in \mathcal{O}(L3^K + 3^{2K}) = \mathcal{O}(L3^K)$ we get $3^{2K} \in \Omega(\tau(\mathcal{N}))$ and $L3^K \in \Omega(U_{\mathcal{N}})$, which implies $\Theta_{\text{IDE}}(\mathcal{N}) \geq LK(3^K + 1) \in \Omega(U_{\mathcal{N}} \log \tau(\mathcal{N}))$. Thus, in particular, $\text{PoA}(U, \tau) \geq \frac{\Theta_{\text{IDE}}(\mathcal{N})}{\Theta_{\text{OPT}}(\mathcal{N})} \in \Omega(U \log \tau)$.   □

Remark 3. Expanding the network constructed in the proof of Theorem 4 into an acyclic network results in an instance with constant optimal termination time, but IDE termination time of $\tau(P_{\max}) \gg \tau(P_{\min})$, where $\tau(P_{\min})$ is the physical length of a shortest path from the source to the sink node.

Together with the upper bound from Lemma 2 this implies the following bounds for the IDE price of anarchy for acyclic networks:

$$\text{PoA}\big|_{\text{acyclic}} \in \Omega(\tau(P_{\max})) \cap \mathcal{O}(U + \tau(P_{\max})).$$

5 Conclusions and Open Questions

We studied the efficiency of IDE flows and derived the first upper and lower bounds on the time price of anarchy of IDE flows. These bounds are of order $\mathcal{O}(U\tau)$ and $\Omega(U \log \tau)$, respectively. Comparing these bounds to the constant bound of $\frac{e}{e-1}$ for dynamic equilibria (cf. Correa, Cristi and Oosterwijk [4]) shows in some sense a "price of shortsightedness". While instantaneous dynamic equilibria may be significantly less efficient than dynamic equilibria, in many situations this might be a price one has to pay as the full information needed for dynamic equilibria might just not be available.

Generally, it would be interesting to test the different equilibria on real instances and see how their efficiency compares there. A large-scale computational study seems more feasible for IDEs compared to dynamic equilibria, as already calculating a single α-extension is much more difficult for the full information model, while it is easy for IDE flows using a simple water-filling procedure. Indeed, for calculating a single extension phase the only positive result for dynamic equilibria is based on a recent work of Kaiser [15] showing that for series-parallel graphs a single phase can be computed in polynomial time. The question of whether a finite number of such extensions is enough to compute a complete equilibrium flow is still open for dynamic equilibria, while we were able to answer this question positively for IDE flows in an upcoming paper [9].

Acknowledgments. We thank Kathrin Gimmi for sparking the initial idea that allowed us to prove the explicit upper bound on the termination time of IDE flows. We are also grateful to the anonymous reviewers for their valuable feedback. Finally, we thank the Deutsche Forschungsgemeinschaft (DFG) for their financial support.

References

1. Bhaskar, U., Fleischer, L., Anshelevich, E.: A Stackelberg strategy for routing flow over time. Games Econom. Behav. **92**, 232–247 (2015)

2. Boyce, D.E., Ran, B., LeBlanc, L.J.: Solving an instantaneous dynamic user-optimal route choice model. Transp. Sci. **29**(2), 128–142 (1995)
3. Cominetti, R., Correa, J.R., Larré, O.: Dynamic equilibria in fluid queueing networks. Oper. Res. **63**(1), 21–34 (2015)
4. Correa, J., Cristi, A., Oosterwijk, T.: On the price of anarchy for flows over time. In: Proceedings of the 2019 ACM Conference on Economics and Computation, EC 2019, New York, NY, USA, pp. 559–577 (2019). Association for Computing Machinery
5. Ford, L.R., Fulkerson, D.R.: Flows in Networks. Princeton University Press, Princeton (1962)
6. Frascaria, D., Olver, N.: Algorithms for flows over time with scheduling costs. arXiv (2019). https://arxiv.org/abs/1912.00082, to appear in IPCO 2020
7. Friesz, T.L., Bernstein, D., Smith, T.E., Tobin, R.L., Wie, B.-W.: A variational inequality formulation of the dynamic network user equilibrium problem. Oper. Res. **41**(1), 179–191 (1993)
8. Friesz, T.L., Luque, J., Tobin, R.L., Wie, B.-W.: Dynamic network traffic assignment considered as a continuous time optimal control problem. Oper. Res. **37**(6), 893–901 (1989)
9. Graf, L., Harks, T.: A finite time combinatorial algorithm for instantaneous dynamic equilibrium flows (2020). https://arxiv.org/abs/2007.07808. (working paper)
10. Graf, L., Harks, T.: The price of anarchy for instantaneous dynamic equilibrium flows. https://arxiv.org/abs/2007.07794 (2020)
11. Graf, L., Harks, T., Sering, L.: Dynamic flows with adaptive route choice. Math. Program., 309–335 (2020). https://doi.org/10.1007/s10107-020-01504-2
12. Hamdouch, Y., Marcotte, P., Nguyen, S.: A strategic model for dynamic traffic assignment. Netw. Spat. Econ. **4**(3), 291–315 (2004)
13. Ismaili, A.: Routing games over time with FIFO policy. In: Devanur, N.R., Lu, P. (eds.) WINE 2017. LNCS, vol. 10660, pp. 266–280. Springer, Cham (2017). https://doi.org/10.1007/978-3-319-71924-5_19. There is also a version available on arXiv: http://arxiv.org/abs/1709.09484
14. Israel, J., Sering, L.: The impact of spillback on the price of anarchy for flows over time. In: Harks, T., Klimm, M. (eds.) SAGT 2020. LNCS, vol. 12283, pp. 114–129. Springer, Cham (2020). https://doi.org/10.1007/978-3-030-57980-7_8
15. Kaiser, M.: Computation of dynamic equilibria in series-parallel networks. Math. Oper. Res. (2020, forthcoming)
16. Koch, R., Skutella, M.: Nash equilibria and the price of anarchy for flows over time. Theory Comput. Syst. **49**(1), 71–97 (2011)
17. Marcotte, P., Nguyen, S., Schoeb, A.: A strategic flow model of traffic assignment in static capacitated networks. Oper. Res. **52**(2), 191–212 (2004)
18. Meunier, F., Wagner, N.: Equilibrium results for dynamic congestion games. Transp. Sci. **44**(4), 524–536 (2010)
19. Ran, B., Boyce, D.E.: Dynamic Urban Transportation Network Models: Theory and Implications for Intelligent Vehicle-highway Systems. LNE. Springer, Berlin (1996)
20. Ran, B., Boyce, D.E., LeBlanc, L.J.: A new class of instantaneous dynamic user-optimal traffic assignment models. Oper. Res. **41**(1), 192–202 (1993)
21. Sering, L., Vargas-Koch, L.: Nash flows over time with spillback. In: Proceedings of the 30th Annual ACM-SIAM Symposium on Discrete Algorithms. ACM (2019)
22. Unnikrishnan, A., Waller, S.: User equilibrium with recourse. Netw. Spat. Econ. **9**(4), 575–593 (2009)

23. Vickrey, W.S.: Congestion theory and transport investment. Am. Econ. Rev. **59**(2), 251–60 (1969)
24. Zhu, D., Marcotte, P.: On the existence of solutions to the dynamic user equilibrium problem. Transp. Sci. **34**(4), 402–414 (2000)

Data-Driven Models of Selfish Routing: Why Price of Anarchy Does Depend on Network Topology

Francisco Benita[1] , Vittorio Bilò[2] , Barnabé Monnot[3] ,
Georgios Piliouras[1] , and Cosimo Vinci[4(✉)]

[1] Singapore University of Technology and Design, Singapore, Singapore
{francisco_benita,georgios}@sutd.edu.sg
[2] University of Salento, Lecce, Italy
vittorio.bilo@unisalento.it
[3] Ethereum Foundation, Zug, Switzerland
barnabemonnot@gmail.com
[4] Gran Sasso Science Institute, L'Aquila, Italy
cosimo.vinci@gssi.it

Abstract. We investigate traffic routing both from the perspective of real world data as well as theory. First, we reveal through data analytics a natural but previously uncaptured regularity of real world routing behavior. Agents only consider, in their strategy sets, paths whose free-flow costs (informally their lengths) are within a small multiplicative $(1 + \theta)$ constant of the optimal free-flow cost path connecting their source and destination where $\theta \geq 0$. In the case of Singapore, $\theta = 1$ is a good estimate of agents' route (pre)selection mechanism. In contrast, in Pigou networks the ratio of the free-flow costs of the routes and thus θ is *infinite*, so although such worst case networks are mathematically simple they correspond to artificial routing scenarios with little resemblance to real world conditions, opening the possibility of proving much stronger Price of Anarchy guarantees by explicitly studying their dependency on θ. We provide an exhaustive analysis of this question by providing provably tight bounds on PoA(θ) for arbitrary classes of cost functions both in the case of general congestion/routing games as well as in the special case of path-disjoint networks. For example, in the case of the standard Bureau of Public Roads (BPR) cost model, $c_e(x) = a_e x^4 + b_e$ and more generally quartic cost functions, the standard PoA bound for $\theta = \infty$ is 2.1505 [21] and it is tight both for general networks as well as path-disjoint and even parallel-edge networks. In comparison, in the case of $\theta = 1$, the PoA in the case of general networks is only 1.6994, whereas

Full paper can be found at https://arxiv.org/abs/2009.12871. F. Benita would like to acknowledge Ministry of Education, Singapore Grant SGPCTRS1804. B. Monnot acknowledges the SUTD Presidential Graduate Fellowship. G. Piliouras gratefully acknowledges AcRF Tier 2 grant 2016-T2-1-170, grant PIE-SGP-AI-2020-01, NRF2019-NRF-ANR095 ALIAS grant and NRF 2018 Fellowship NRF-NRFF2018-07. C. Vinci would like to acknowledge the Italian MIUR PRIN 2017 Project ALGADIMAR "Algorithms, Games, and Digital Markets".

X. Chen et al. (Eds.): WINE 2020, LNCS 12495, pp. 252–265, 2020.
https://doi.org/10.1007/978-3-030-64946-3_18

for path-disjoint/parallel-edge networks is even smaller (1.3652), showing that both the route geometries as captured by the parameter θ as well as the network topology have significant effects on PoA (Fig. 1).

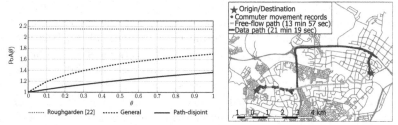

(a) Comparison between PoA(θ) in the case of quartic costs for general/path-disjoint networks resp. and the bound PoA(∞)=2.1505 from [21]. More results can be found in Table 1.

(b) Shortest free-flow path versus chosen path. Discussion on the standard data analytics can be found in Section 2.

Fig. 1. Improved Price of Anarchy bounds in data-driven routing models

1   Introduction

Modern cities are wonders of emergent, largely self-organizing, behavior. Major capitals buzz with the collective hum of millions of people whose lives are intertwined and coupled in myriad and diverse ways. One of the most palpable such phenomena of collective behavior is the emergence and diffusion of traffic throughout the city. A bird's eye view of any major city would reveal a complex and heterogeneous landscape of thousands upon thousands of cars, buses, trucks, motorcycles, running though the veins of a maze of remarkable complexity and scale consisting of a vast number of streets and highways. As Fig. 2 suggests, the full magnitude of the multi-scale complexity of these real-life networks lies outside the perceptive capabilities of any single individual. Nevertheless, as a phenomenon that we get to experience daily, such as the weather, we would like to understand at least some macroscopic, high level characteristics of traffic routing. Quite possibly, one of the most interesting such questions is how efficient is a traffic network?

This question has received a lot of attention within algorithmic game theory. Using the model of congestion games, seminal papers in the area established tight bounds on their Price of Anarchy (PoA), i.e., the worst case inefficiency of traffic routing [13,23]. For example, the Price of Anarchy of linear non-atomic congestion games is 4/3, whereas if we apply the standard Bureau of Public Roads (BPR) cost functions that are polynomials of degree four, then the Price of Anarchy is roughly 2.151. On the positive side, these bounds apply to all networks (within the prescribed class of delay/cost functions) regardless of their size or their total demand, or number of agents and are tight even for the simplest possible network instances, i.e., Pigou networks with just two parallel links.

The common interpretation of these bounds is that they are strong and a PoA anywhere in that range (e.g. PoA = 2) immediately translates to practical guarantees about real traffic. Some recent purely experimental work, however, has produced new insights that allow us to reexamine these results from a different perspective. For example, [16] showed that the efficiency of real-life traffic networks, as estimated from traffic measurements alone, is really close to optimal even when compared to very optimistic estimates of optimal performance. A Price of Anarchy of 2 implies that the average commuter can increase their mean speed by 100%. Measurements suggest that this level of inefficiencies/improvements is rather unlikely. Since Price of Anarchy is a macroscopic characteristic of a system with countless moving parts, a more useful analogy is that of weather or climate (e.g., average temperature). The differences between 10% and 20% increase to system inefficiency are significant and a 100% increase, i.e., PoA of 2 would have catastrophic consequences.

A Natural Question Emerges: Can we create classes of models, i.e., congestion games, which come closer to representing real world traffic? In this paper we do, by leveraging an intuitive but largely unexplored characteristic of real world traffic routing. Commuters only consider in their strategy sets paths/routes whose free-flow costs (informally their lengths) are approximately equal to each other (within a multiplicative factor of $1 + \theta$). We call such games θ-free flow games. We generalize the special case of linear congestion θ-free flow games [4] to the case of arbitrary classes of cost functions as well as simultaneously studying both general networks as well as path-disjoint networks. $\theta = 0$ means that all paths considered by each user have exactly equal free-flow cost/length, whereas $\theta = 1$ allows for paths whose lengths are within a factor of 2. Pigou networks may feel intuitively very simple and thus natural due to their small size, but they fail to satisfy this property in the most extreme sense. The ratio of the free-flow costs of the two edges is infinite ($\theta = \infty$). It is like considering two possible paths from home to work, one which is the shortest distance route and one that circumnavigates the globe along the way. Such unnatural paths may indeed be available to us, but we unconsciously and automatically prune them out from the set of alternatives that we consider. Amazingly, enforcing such a natural property on the set of models (routing games) we consider immediately removes from consideration Pigou networks, the worst case examples from a PoA perspective, and thus opens up the possibility of proving stronger Price of Anarchy guarantees. What are the implications of such characteristics to PoA? What other type of attributes can we take advantage of when creating new models? Finally, how well do they match real traffic conditions?

We hope that this paper opens up a new direction for tighter coupling between data analytics, modelling and theory in congestion games and beyond. Analyzing different cities as well as introducing models that take into account the difference between public and private transport seem like an exciting direction for future work.

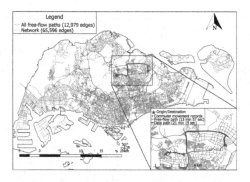

Fig. 2. For each trip segment, we find the best free-flow time and the data free-flow time. The reconstruction of the selected route uses datapoints logged along the trip. In yellow, the fastest route in free-flow condition is highlighted. The reconstructed route is in green, along which we find the data free-flow time.

1.1 Our Contribution

In Sect. 2, we start off by experimentally computing estimates of θ from real world traffic data. We employ an experimental dataset that contains detailed information (sampled every 13 s) on the routing behavior of tens of thousands of commuters in Singapore. Based on this fine-grained information and in combination with a graph representation of the road network of Singapore that we have created we can estimate numerous characteristics of the actual routing behavior at an unprecedented level of accuracy. Using these tools that we believe are of independent interest as well, we find that the θ values for the vast majority of commuters (close to 80%) are below 1.

Inspired by the above evidence, we introduce a new class of congestion games, that we call free-flow games, parametrized by θ (Sect. 3). We provide two parametric *tight bounds* on the Price of Anarchy of free-flow games under general latency functions satisfying mild assumptions, thus largely extending the results given in [4] which are restricted to affine latencies only. The first of these bounds applies to the general case of unrestricted network topologies (indeed, it applies even to congestion games) (Theorem 1), while the second one holds for path-disjoint networks (Theorem 2) which includes the fundamental parallel-links topology. These bounds are never equal as long as $\theta \notin \{0, \infty\}$. In fact, differently from what happens in the classical setting without the free-flow assumption, where the worst-case situation already arises in a two parallel-links network (the Pigou network), for free-flow games the absence of intersections among paths allows for more efficient equilibria. More precisely, as θ goes to infinity, both bounds converge to the same limit, but the convergence of the one for parallel-link networks can be significantly slower (see, for instance, Fig. 1(a)). We also stress that, with respect to the case of affine latency functions, our findings improve on the results given in [4], as we close the gap between upper and lower bound on the Price of Anarchy for parallel-link networks that was left as an open problem.

One of the most important messages coming from our investigation is that the separation outlined by Theorems 1 and 2 sheds new light on the question of whether the Price of Anarchy is affected by the network topology. In fact, a famous, and perhaps counter-intuitive, result by Roughgarden [21] states that the PoA is independent of the network topology as, in almost all notable cases, worst-case instances are already attained by simple networks, such as parallel-link graphs. Under the free-flow assumption, however, this situation ceases to hold, and the network topology begins to play a critical, if not dominant, role in the efficiency of equilibria. This evidence has major practical implications, as it signifies the fundamental importance of careful road network design and planning for selfish routing. As shown in Fig. 1 and in more details in Table 1, in the case of the standard Bureau of Public Roads (BPR) cost model, $c_e(x) = a_e x^4 + b_e$ and more generally quartic cost functions, applying the constraint $\theta = 1$ nearly *halves the percentage of inefficiency*, and applying the additional constraint of a path-disjoint network *halves it once again*.

At the technical level, our general formulas depend on whether the free-flow traversing time of some edges is larger than zero, i.e., whether the limit of the edge cost/latency as its load goes to zero is strictly positive. Latency functions for which this does not hold have been termed *homogeneous* by Roughgarden [21] and they represent one of the few exceptions for which he could not prove that the PoA is independent of the network topology. Since under homogeneous latency functions any congestion game is a 0-free flow game, as a by-product of our results, we also obtain that, for (free-flow) games with homogeneous latency functions, the Price of Anarchy is lower than the one attained by non-homogeneous latencies, and it is tight even for parallel-links topologies (Theorem 2), thus answering the open question posed by Roughgarden in [21].

To summarize, we obtain that the Price of Anarchy is independent of the network topology (i.e., the worst-case PoA is attained by parallel-link games) if and only if one of the following cases occurs: (i) $\theta = 0$ (which include the case of homogeneous latency functions as a special case) and (ii) $\theta = \infty$.

For the sake of a more concrete exposition of our results and for empirical purposes, we provide explicitly an instantiation of the PoA bounds in the case of polynomial latency functions. The resulting bounds depend on both the maximum and minimum degree of the polynomials and, in the case of non-homogeneous polynomials only, they also depend on θ. A quantitative representation of our results is partially summarized in Table 1.

Due to the lack of space, a detailed discussion of the results and some missing proofs are deferred to the full version of this paper [1].

Table 1. The Price of Anarchy of free-flow games with non-homogeneous (i.e., with constant terms allowed) polynomial latency functions of maximum degree $p \leq 4$ and minimum degree q. Unlabelled bounds are proven in this paper. Bounds for homogeneous (i.e., without constant terms) polynomials can be obtained from the case $\theta = 0$ (the same upper bounds have been given in [9], but tight lower bounds were only conjectured to exist). As it can be appreciated, the PoA depends on the network topology whenever $0 < \theta < \infty$.

(p, q)	$\theta = 0$		$\theta = 1/2$		$\theta = 1$		$\theta = \infty$	
	General	Path-disjoint	General	Path-disjoint	General	Path-disjoint	General	Path-disjoint
$(1, 1)$	1 [4]	1	1.1547 [4]	1.0909	1.2071 [4]	1.1429	1.3333 [23]	1.3333 [23]
$(2, 1)$	1.0355	1.0355	1.2873	1.1472	1.3852	1.2383	1.6258 [21]	1.6258 [21]
$(2, 2)$	1	1	1.2873	1.1472	1.3852	1.2383	1.6258 [21]	1.6258 [21]
$(3, 1)$	1.0982	1.0982	1.4078	1.1869	1.5475	1.3093	1.8956 [21]	1.8956 [21]
$(3, 2)$	1.0147	1.0147	1.4078	1.1869	1.5475	1.3093	1.8956 [21]	1.8956 [21]
$(3, 3)$	1	1	1.4078	1.1869	1.5475	1.3093	1.8956 [21]	1.8956 [21]
$(4, 1)$	1.1676	1.1676	1.5202	1.2170	1.6994	1.3652	2.1505 [21]	2.1505 [21]
$(4, 2)$	1.0450	1.0450	1.5202	1.2170	1.6994	1.3652	2.1505 [21]	2.1505 [21]
$(4, 3)$	1.0080	1.0080	1.5202	1.2170	1.6994	1.3652	2.1505 [21]	2.1505 [21]
$(4, 4)$	1	1	1.5202	1.2170	1.6994	1.3652	2.1505 [21]	2.1505 [21]

1.2   Related Work

Price of Anarchy in Routing Games: Introduced by Koutsoupias and Papadimitriou [13], the ratio between the social cost of the worst equilibrium of a game and its optimum was given the name Price of Anarchy (PoA) in [20]. For networks of linear latency and general topology, PoA was bounded tightly by 4/3 [23] and 5/2 in the atomic case [6]. Following results by Roughgarden [22] studied more general latency functions and atomic routing games and again gave tight bounds on PoA. However, for a large class of natural latency functions, PoA tends to 1 as the demand on the network approaches infinitesimally small or infinitely high levels [7,8]. This casts doubts on the predictive power of PoA on the state of a real system, as noted in Monnot et al. [16].

Strategy sets of routing games are typically exponential in the number of vertices, hence restricting them is a common assumption. The unnatural character of Pigou in real systems was noted by Lu and Yu [15], who assume players have at least one strategy that is not more than λ away from the fastest strategy in congestion games. Restricting the strategy sets to obtain tighter bounds for PoA is also employed in [3], [?] for load balancing games (i.e., congestion games where the strategies of players are singleton sets). Fotakis [10] proved a pure PoA bound for symmetric atomic congestion games on extension-parallel networks, an interesting class of networks with linearly independent paths, that is equal to that of non-atomic congestion games.

Primal-dual techniques for bounding the Price of Anarchy in non-cooperative games have been proposed by Bilò [2], Kulkarni and Mirrokni [14], Nadav and Roughgarden [18] and Thang [24]. The methods proposed in [2] and [18] operate by explicitly formulating the problem of maximizing the Price of Anarchy of a class of games. Despite using the same formulation, they differ in the choice of the variables. While [18] uses the probability distributions defining the outcomes occurring in the formulation, [2] adopts suitable multipliers for the resource cost functions. The methods in [14] and [24], instead, build on a formulation for the problem of optimizing the social function, and then implement the equilibria conditions within the choice of the dual variables. We adopt the method proposed in [2] as it appears to be more flexible and powerful in our realm of application. The first advantage is that it generalizes to any type of cost functions, while all the others require some restrictions: the method in [18] can only be applied to affine functions, the one in [14] requires convex functions, while that of [24] needs non-decreasing ones. Secondly, the method (if properly used) always yields tight bounds on the Price of Anarchy, while those in [14] and [24] are limited by the integrality gap of the formulation. Last but not least, it models in a simple, direct and intuitive way any new twist, as the free-flow property considered in this work, one may want to add to the scenario of application.

Transportation Research: The seminal work of Wardrop [26] introduces and formalizes one of the first notions of equilibrium in transportation networks. A proof of the equal social costs for equilibria and optimum (i.e., PoA = 1) in parallel links routing games appears in Nagurney and Qiang [19]. Related ideas from sensitivity analysis for edge cost functions are treated in Tobin and Friesz [25]. The Price of Anarchy was estimated for the city of Boston with different means from our study by Zhang et al. [27], where the sensitivity of the social cost at equilibrium with respect to edge parameters is also discussed. The previously cited works rely on the BPR estimation of cost functions [5], which are included in the family of weakly monomial latency functions we define in Sect. 3. The free-flow property in transportation networks has been first proposed by Jahn et al. [12] with respect to the problem of optimizing a centralized traffic flow without imposing too longer detours to some users.

2   Experimental Evidence for θ-Free-Flow Time in Singapore

We look for experimental evidence that commuters use the heuristic presented in the introduction to guide their routing decisions. Namely, we make the conjecture that commuters consider only paths with "length" at most a mutliplicative factor $1 + \theta$ away from the shortest path taking them to their destination (where "length" is measured as a latency, or travel time). Does this conjecture hold in practice? To answer, we obtain data on the routing behavior of a sampled population. Modelling assumptions and a formal definition of θ are presented in the next Sect. 3.

2.1   The National Science Experiment

The NSE is a nationwide project in Singapore in which over 90,000 students from primary, secondary and junior college wore a sensor, called SENSg, for up to one week per student in 2015 and 2016. The SENSg sensors collect various environmental data, and 9-degree of freedom motion data sampled every 13 s using the Wi-Fi based localization system. The semantic data covers the identification of individual trips within the discrete stream of locations [11], inference of the activity performed at each endpoint and transportation mode classification [16,17].

We use the NSE 2016 dataset which contains data from 49,526 students, and we implement the mode identification algorithm developed in [28] where five different modes can be identified, namely: (a) stationary; (b) walking; (c) riding a train; (d) riding a bus; and (e) riding a car. To ensure the quality of our empirical results, we perform a strict data cleaning process over the complete dataset. A total of 34,121 clean trips are considered, with 16,563 unique students and 89 different schools. This work focuses on morning travels of students who get to their schools from their homes.

Our dataset contains highly granular information concerning the routing decisions of the subjects. With the help of the onboard sensors in the device and the mode identification algorithm, we are able to obtain for each trip an accurate representation of its segments and their endpoints. For instance, typical segments making up a trip may be "Walk - Car - Walk", or "Walk - Bus - Train - Bus - Walk". The following study focuses on car trip segments. In this dataset [16], looking at the population of public transport users only, Price of Anarchy was upper bounded by 1.18. Converserly, Price of Anarchy for car users only was bounded by 1.86. Putting both populations together, Price of Anarchy was bounded by 1.34.

2.2   Estimation of Free-Flow Time for Selected Route

We compute a graph representation from a road map of Singapore, where each vertex is located at an intersection or a bend in the road. Every edge is assigned with a cost representing how much time is needed to traverse it. This latency is obtained from edge features such as the road type and the posted speed limit on the road. For each private transportation trip segment in the dataset, we associate its origin and destination with the closest vertex in the graph. We run a shortest path algorithm to estimate the free-flow travel time of the trip segment, referred to in the following as the *best free-flow time*. This best free-flow time is compared with the *data free-flow time*, or the time it would take the subject to travel its selected route if no one was on the road. We describe how the data free-flow time is estimated in the following paragraph.

A segment measured by the sensor consists of a stream of geographical locations. For each datapoint, we associate the closest edge in the graph. The size of the graph (61,151 vertices and 65,596 edges) implies a lengthy lookup phase to associate the point to its closest edge. For this reason, we consider a smaller dataset of 449 car segments out of the 17,897 segments in the larger dataset. These selected segments are well distributed across Singapore as depicted by Fig. 2. By adding the free-flow time of traversing each edge associated to the data points, connected via heuristics detailed in our online version [1], we obtain the *data free-flow time*.

2.3 Estimate of θ

We compare the best free-flow time to the data free-flow time for each sample in our dataset, and denote by θ the percent increase between the two. A small value of θ yields support to the hypothesis that agents only consider routes which connect origin and destination in a straightforward manner (under no congestion) as part of their strategy set, see Fig. 3.

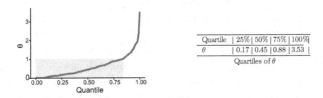

Quartile	25%	50%	75%	100%
θ	0.17	0.45	0.88	3.53

Quartiles of θ

Fig. 3. The deviation is measured by the ratio of the selected route free-flow time to the minimum free-flow time among all routes between the origin and the destination. Close to 80% of the θ values are below 1, implying that the free-flow time of the selected route is rarely twice as long as the best free-flow time.

This experimental result provides justification for the upper bound of PoA estimated from the same dataset in previous work [16]. This benchmark is meaningful for real road networks, as latency functions are typically estimated using affine quartic monomials [5]. As noted in our introduction as well as in more details in the next section, our model is based on the assumption of a uniform θ bound over the whole population. We should note that this assumption is consistent with our experimental measurements, since these measurements provide us with estimates on the lower bounds of the agents' θ's. More detailed models with a heterogeneous population/distribution of θ's is an interesting direction for future work.

3   Model and Definitions

For a positive integer i, let $[i] := \{1, 2, \ldots, i\}$. Given a set A and a set $B \supseteq A$, let $\chi_A : B \to \{0, 1\}$ denote the indicator function, i.e., $\chi_A(x) = 1$ if $x \in A$ and $\chi_A(x) = 0$ if $x \notin A$. Given a tuple of numbers $(\alpha_1, \alpha_2, \ldots, \alpha_k)$, we write $(\alpha_1, \alpha_2, \ldots, \alpha_k) > 0$ if $\alpha_i \geq 0$ for any $i \in [k]$ and $\alpha_i > 0$ for some $i \in [k]$.

Non-atomic Congestion Games. A *non-atomic congestion game* (from now on, simply a *congestion game*) is a tuple $\mathsf{CG} = ([n], (r_i)_{i \in [n]}, E, (\ell_e)_{e \in E}, (\Sigma_i)_{i \in [n]})$, where $[n]$ is a set of types, E is a set of resources, $\ell_e : \mathbb{R}_{>0} \to \mathbb{R}_{>0}$ is the *latency function* of resource $e \in E$, and, for each $i \in [n]$, $r_i \in \mathbb{R}_{\geq 0}$ is the *amount of players* of type i and $\Sigma_i \subseteq 2^E \setminus \emptyset$ is the *set of strategies* for players of type i (i.e. a strategy is a non-empty subset of resources). We assume that latency functions are non-decreasing, positive, and continuous.

Classes of Congestion Games. A *network congestion game* is a congestion game based on a graph $G = (V, E)$, where the set of resources coincides with E, each type i is associated with a pair of nodes $(u_i, v_i) \in V \times V$, so that the set of strategies of players of type i is the set of paths from u_i to v_i in graph G. If there exists $u^* \in V$ such that $u^* = u_i$ for any $i \in [n]$, the game is called *single-source network congestion game*. Let $\mathcal{P}$ be the set of all the paths P connecting source u_i with destination v_i, for any pair source-destination (u_i, v_i). The game is called *path-disjoint network congestion game* if all the paths in $\mathcal{P}$ are pair-wise node-disjoint.

A *load balancing game* is a congestion game in which each strategy is a singleton, i.e., $S = \{e\}$ for some $e \in E$, for any strategy $S \in \Sigma_i$ and type $i \in [n]$. A *parallel-link game* (or *symmetric load balancing game*) is a load balancing game in which all players have the same set of strategies. It is well-known that each load balancing game (resp. parallel-link game) can be modelled as a single-source congestion game (resp. path-disjoint network congestion game).

Latency Functions. For the sake of simplicity, we extend the domain of each latency function $\ell(x)$ to $x = 0$ in such a way that $\ell(0) = \lim_{x \to 0^+} \ell(x)$. Given a class of latency functions $\mathcal{F}$, let $[\mathcal{F}]_H := \{f : f(x) = g(x) - g(0), \ g \in \mathcal{F}\}$. Observe that $f(0) = 0$ for any $f \in [\mathcal{F}]_H$ by definition. In the following, we use similar definitions as in [21]. $\mathcal{F}$ is *homogeneous* if $\mathcal{F} = [\mathcal{F}]_H$. $\mathcal{F}$ is *weakly diverse* if $[\mathcal{F}]_H \subseteq \mathcal{F}$ and it contains at least one constant function (i.e., a function f such that $f(x) = \beta$ for any $x > 0$, for some $\beta > 0$). $\mathcal{F}$ is *scale-closed* if it contains all the functions f such that $f(x) = \alpha g(x)$, for any $g \in \mathcal{F}$ and $\alpha > 0$. $\mathcal{F}$ is *strongly diverse* if contains all the functions f such that $f(x) = \alpha g(x) + \beta$, for any $g \in [\mathcal{F}]_H$ and $(\alpha, \beta) > 0$. A *polynomial latency function* of maximum degree p and minimum degree q (with $p \geq q \geq 1$) is defined as $\ell_e(x) := \sum_{d=q}^{p} \alpha_{e,d} x^d + \beta_e$, where $\alpha_{e,q}, \alpha_{e,q+1}, \ldots, \alpha_{e,p}, \beta_e > 0$. Let $\mathcal{P}_{p,q}$ denote the class of polynomial latency functions of maximum degree p and minimum (non-zero) degree q. A latency function ℓ_e is *affine* if $\ell_e \in \mathcal{PP}_1$.

Strategy Profiles and Pure Nash Equilibria. A *strategy profile* is a tuple $\boldsymbol{\sigma} := (\sigma_{i,S})_{i \in [n], S \in \Sigma_i}$ with $\sum_{S \in \Sigma_i} \sigma_{i,S} = r_i$ for any $i \in [n]$, that is a state of the game where $\sigma_{i,S} \geq 0$ is the total amount of players of type i selecting strategy S for any $i \in [n]$ and $S \in \Sigma_i$. Given a strategy profile $\boldsymbol{\sigma}$, $k_e(\boldsymbol{\sigma}) := \sum_{i \in [n], S \in \Sigma_i : e \in S} \sigma_{i,S}$ is the *congestion* of e in $\boldsymbol{\sigma}$, i.e., the total amount of players selecting e in $\boldsymbol{\sigma}$, and given a strategy S, $c_S(\boldsymbol{\sigma}) := \sum_{e \in S} \ell_e(k_e(\boldsymbol{\sigma}))$ is the *cost* of players selecting S in $\boldsymbol{\sigma}$. A strategy profile $\boldsymbol{\sigma}$ is a *pure Nash equilibrium* (or *Wardrop equilibrium*, or *equilibrium flow*) if and only if, for each $i \in [n]$, $S \in \Sigma_i : \sigma_{i,S} > 0$ and $S' \in \Sigma_i$, it holds that $c_S(\boldsymbol{\sigma}) \leq c_{S'}(\boldsymbol{\sigma})$.

Quality of Equilibria. A *social function* that is usually used as a measure of the quality of a strategy profile in congestion games is the *total latency*, defined as $\mathsf{SUM}(\boldsymbol{\sigma}) := \sum_{e \in E} k_e(\boldsymbol{\sigma}) \ell_e(k_e(\boldsymbol{\sigma})) = \sum_{i \in [n]} r_i c_i(\boldsymbol{\sigma})$ at equilibrium $\boldsymbol{\sigma}$. A *social optimum* is a strategy profile $\boldsymbol{\sigma}^*$ minimizing SUM.

The *Price of Anarchy* of a congestion game CG (with respect to the social function SUM), denoted as $\mathsf{PoA}(\mathsf{CG})$, is the supremum of the ratio $\mathsf{SUM}(\boldsymbol{\sigma})/\mathsf{SUM}(\boldsymbol{\sigma}^*)$, where $\boldsymbol{\sigma}$ is a pure Nash equilibrium for CG and $\boldsymbol{\sigma}^*$ is a social optimum for CG. As shown in [23], all pure Nash equilibria of any congestion game have the same total latency. Thus, the Price of Anarchy can be redefined as the ratio $\mathsf{SUM}(\boldsymbol{\sigma})/\mathsf{SUM}(\boldsymbol{\sigma}^*)$, where $\boldsymbol{\sigma}$ is an arbitrary pure Nash equilibrium for CG and $\boldsymbol{\sigma}^*$ is a social optimum for CG.

Free-Flow Congestion Games. Given $\theta \in [0, \infty]$, a θ-free-flow congestion game CG_θ is a congestion game in which, for each $i \in [n]$ and $S, S' \in \Sigma_i$, it holds that $\sum_{e \in S} \ell_e(0) \leq (1 + \theta) \sum_{e \in S'} \ell_e(0)$, i.e., all the strategies available to players of type i, when evaluated in absence of congestion, are within a factor $1 + \theta$ one from the other. Observe that free-flow congestion games are congestion games obeying some special properties. Thus, all positive results holding for congestion games carries over to θ-free-flow congestion games for any value of θ. Moreover, for $\theta = \infty$, any congestion game is a θ-free-flow congestion game.

4   Price of Anarchy of Free-Flow Congestion Games

In this section, we give tight bounds on the Price of Anarchy of free-flow congestion games. A detailed discussion of the implications of our theoretical results on the Price of Anarchy and how they relate to previous work, is given in the full version of this paper. Before going into details, we sketch the high level building blocks of the proofs of the upper bounds. For the general case, by adapting [2], we formulate the problem of bounding the Price of Anarchy of θ-free-flow congestion games by means of a factor-revealing pair of primal-dual linear programs. The techniques work as follows.

Given a θ-free-flow congestion game CG_θ and a family of latency functions $\mathcal{F}$, we know that we can model the latency of every resource $e \in E$ as $\ell_e(x) = \alpha_e f_e(x) + \beta_e$, with $f_e \in [\mathcal{F}]_H$, $\alpha_e \in \{0, 1\}$ and $\beta_e \geq 0$. We fix a Nash equilibrium $\boldsymbol{\sigma}$ and a social optimum $\boldsymbol{\sigma}^*$ for CG_θ. Hence, for every $e \in E$, the congestions $k_e(\boldsymbol{\sigma})$ and $k_e(\boldsymbol{\sigma}^*)$ of e in $\boldsymbol{\sigma}$ and $\boldsymbol{\sigma}^*$, respectively, become fixed constants. As the Price of Anarchy measures the worst-case ratio of $\mathsf{SUM}(\boldsymbol{\sigma})$ over $\mathsf{SUM}(\boldsymbol{\sigma}^*)$, our goal becomes that of choosing suitable values for α_e and β_e, for every $e \in E$, so as to maximize $\mathsf{SUM}(\boldsymbol{\sigma})$ under the assumption that $\mathsf{SUM}(\boldsymbol{\sigma}^*) = 1$, $\boldsymbol{\sigma}$ is a Nash equilibrium and CG_θ is a θ-free-flow game. In particular, constraint $\mathsf{SUM}(\boldsymbol{\sigma}^*) = 1$ can be assumed without loss of generality by a simple scaling argument, provided we relax the condition $\alpha_e \in \{0, 1\}$ with $\alpha_e \geq 0$. Thus, an optimal solution to the resulting linear program, call it LP, provides an upper bound to the Price of Anarchy of CG_θ. Next step is to compute and analyze the dual of LP, that we call DLP. DLP has three variables, namely x, y and γ, with $x \geq 0$, $y \geq 0$ and γ defining its objective value. Thus, by the Weak Duality Theorem, any feasible solution (x^*, y^*, γ^*) for DLP yields an upper bound of γ^* to the optimal solution of LP and so an upper bound to the Price of Anarchy of CG_θ. For each function $f_e \in \mathcal{F}_H$, DLP has two constraints, namely $c_1(f_e, k_e(\boldsymbol{\sigma}), k_e(\boldsymbol{\sigma}^*), x, \gamma)$ and $c_2(f_e, k_e(\boldsymbol{\sigma}), k_e(\boldsymbol{\sigma}^*), y, \gamma)$, providing two lower bounds on γ, denoted as $\gamma(\mathcal{G}) := \inf_{x \geq 1} \sup_{l > 0, f \in \mathcal{G}} \left(\frac{k + x(-k+l)}{l} \right) \frac{f(k)}{f(l)}$ and $\gamma_\theta(\mathcal{G}) :=$ $\sup_{k > l > 0, f \in \mathcal{G}} \frac{f(k)(k(1+\theta)-l)}{f(k)(k-l)(1+\theta)+lf(l)\theta}$.

An important advantage of the primal-dual method is that, whenever LP provides a tight characterization of the properties possessed by the games and the equilibria under analysis, an optimal solution to DLP can be fruitfully exploited to construct, quite systematically, but not without effort, matching lower bounding instances. We manage to achieve this result also in this case, but, given the very technical nature of the constructions, we refer the interested reader to the full version of this paper.[1]

For the case of parallel-links and path-disjoint games, we apply a similar, although more direct approach. We fix once again CG_θ, the family of latency functions $\mathcal{F}$, the latency of every resource $e \in E$, a Nash equilibrium $\boldsymbol{\sigma}$ and a social optimum $\boldsymbol{\sigma}^*$ for CG_θ, so as to obtain constant values for both $k_e(\boldsymbol{\sigma})$ and $k_e(\boldsymbol{\sigma}^*)$. This time, instead of resorting to linear programming, we write down the parametric expression of the Price of Anarchy as a function of $k_e(\boldsymbol{\sigma})$, $k_e(\boldsymbol{\sigma}^*)$ and the latency functions of the resources in the game. A key feature of this case, that makes it different from the general setting analyzed before, is that, here, we need have $\sum_{e \in E} k_e(\boldsymbol{\sigma}) = \sum_{e \in E} k_e(\boldsymbol{\sigma}^*)$. By exploiting this equality, together with the equilibrium conditions and the θ-free-flow property of CG_θ, we create a sequence of more and more relaxed upper bounds for the Price of Anarchy, until we end up to a sufficiently simple formula. Also in this case, we can show that the performed analysis is tight by providing matching lower bounding instances whose description is again deferred to the full version of this paper.

4.1 The Main Theorems

Theorem 1. *Let* CG_θ *be a* θ-*free-flow congestion game with latency functions in* $\mathcal{F}$ *and* $\theta \in [0, \infty]$. *We have* $\mathsf{PoA}(\mathsf{CG}_\theta) \leq \gamma([\mathcal{F}]_H)$ *if* $\theta = 0$, $\mathsf{PoA}(\mathsf{CG}_\theta) \leq \gamma(\mathcal{F})$ *if* $\theta = \infty$, *and* $\mathsf{PoA}(\mathsf{CG}_\theta) \leq \max\{\gamma([\mathcal{F}]_H), \gamma_\theta([\mathcal{F}]_H)\}$ *if* $\theta \in (0, \infty)$. *These bounds are tight for single-source network games if* $\mathcal{F}$ *is weakly diverse and even for load balancing games if* $\mathcal{F}$ *is strongly diverse.*

We now show that, when considering either parallel-links games or path-disjoint network congestion games, a better bound on the Price of Anarchy can be achieved. To this aim, given a class of latency functions $\mathcal{G}$, let us define $\eta_\theta(\mathcal{G}) := \sup_{k > l > 0, f \in \mathcal{G}} \frac{kf(k)(1+\theta)}{kf(k)(1+\theta)+(lf(l)-lf(k))\theta}$.

Theorem 2. *Fix a value* $\theta \in [0, \infty)$ *and a class of latency functions* $\mathcal{F}$. *Let* PLG_θ *be a* θ-*free-flow path-disjoint network congestion game with latency functions in*

---

[1] In the related literature, bounds on the Price of Anarchy are often obtained by exploiting Roughgarden's smoothness framework [22]. Similarities and differences between such framework and the primal-dual method are given in the full version of this paper [1].

$\mathcal{F}$. Then, $\mathsf{PoA}(\mathsf{PLG}_\theta) \leq \max\{\gamma([\mathcal{F}]_H), \eta_\theta([\mathcal{F}]_H)\}$. The bound is tight in general and even for parallel-links networks if $\mathcal{F}$ is scale-closed.

By using Theorems 1 and 2, we can determine the exact Price of Anarchy of free-flow congestion games with polynomial latency functions in $\mathcal{P}_{p,q}$. In particular, we show that $\gamma_\theta([\mathcal{P}_{p,q}]_H) = \sup_{t>1} \frac{t^p(t(1+\theta)-1)}{t^p(t-1)(1+\theta)+\theta}$, $\gamma([\mathcal{P}_{p,q}]_H) =$

$$\frac{p^p}{(p+1)^{p+1}} \left(\sqrt[p-q]{\left(\frac{(p+1)^{p+1}q^q}{(q+1)^{q+1}p^p}\right)^{p+1}} \right) \left(\sqrt[p-q]{\frac{(p+1)^{p+1}q^q}{(q+1)^{q+1}p^p}} - 1 \right)^{-1} \chi_{[p-1]}(q) + \chi_{\{p\}}(q),$$

$\eta_\theta([\mathcal{P}_{p,q}]_H) = \sup_{t>1} \frac{t^{p+1}(1+\theta)}{t^{p+1}(1+\theta)+(1-t^p)\theta}$, and by using such values in Theorems 1 and 2 we are able to derive tight bounds on the Price of Anarchy.

References

1. Benita, F., Bilò, V., Monnot, B., Piliouras, G., Vinci, C.: Data-driven models of selfish routing: why price of anarchy does depend on network topology. arXiv preprint arXiv:2009.12871 (2020)
2. Bilò, V.: A unifying tool for bounding the quality of non-cooperative solutions in weighted congestion games. Theory Comput. Syst. **62**(5), 1288–1317 (2018)
3. Bilò, V., Vinci, C.: On the impact of singleton strategies in congestion games. In: 25th Annual European Symposium on Algorithms (ESA 2017). Schloss Dagstuhl-Leibniz-Zentrum fuer Informatik (2017)
4. Bilò, V., Vinci, C.: The price of anarchy of affine congestion games with similar strategies. Theor. Comput. Sci. **806**, 641–654 (2020)
5. Bureau of Public Roads: Traffic assignment manual. US Department of Commerce (1964)
6. Christodoulou, G., Koutsoupias, E.: The price of anarchy of finite congestion games. In: Proceedings of the Thirty-seventh Annual ACM Symposium on Theory of Computing, pp. 67–73. ACM (2005)
7. Colini-Baldeschi, R., Cominetti, R., Mertikopoulos, P., Scarsini, M.: The asymptotic behavior of the price of anarchy. In: Devanur, N.R., Lu, P. (eds.) WINE 2017. LNCS, vol. 10660, pp. 133–145. Springer, Cham (2017). https://doi.org/10.1007/978-3-319-71924-5_10
8. Colini-Baldeschi, R., Cominetti, R., Scarsini, M.: On the price of anarchy of highly congested nonatomic network games. In: Gairing, M., Savani, R. (eds.) SAGT 2016. LNCS, vol. 9928, pp. 117–128. Springer, Heidelberg (2016). https://doi.org/10.1007/978-3-662-53354-3_10
9. Dumrauf, D., Gairing, M.: Price of anarchy for polynomial wardrop games. In: Spirakis, P., Mavronicolas, M., Kontogiannis, S. (eds.) WINE 2006. LNCS, vol. 4286, pp. 319–330. Springer, Heidelberg (2006). https://doi.org/10.1007/11944874_29
10. Fotakis, D.: Congestion games with linearly independent paths: convergence time and price of anarchy. Theory Comput. Syst. **47**(1), 113–136 (2010)
11. Gemici, K., Koutsoupias, E., Monnot, B., Papadimitriou, C.H., Piliouras, G.: Wealth inequality and the price of anarchy. In: 36th International Symposium on Theoretical Aspects of Computer Science (STACS 2019). Schloss Dagstuhl-Leibniz-Zentrum fuer Informatik (2019)
12. Jahn, O., Möhring, R.H., Schulz, A.S., Moses, N.E.S.: System-optimal routing of traffic flows with user constraints in networks with congestion. Oper. Res. **53**(4), 600–616 (2005)

13. Koutsoupias, E., Papadimitriou, C.: Worst-case equilibria. In: Meinel, C., Tison, S. (eds.) STACS 1999. LNCS, vol. 1563, pp. 404–413. Springer, Heidelberg (1999). https://doi.org/10.1007/3-540-49116-3_38

14. Kulkarni, J., Mirrokni, V.S.: Robust price of anarchy bounds via LP and fenchel duality. In: Proceedings of the 26th Annual ACM-SIAM Symposium on Discrete Algorithms (SODA 2015), pp. 1030–1049. SIAM (2015)

15. Lu, P.Y., Yu, C.Y.: Worst-case Nash equilibria in restricted routing. J. Comput. Sci. Technol. **27**(4), 710–717 (2012)

16. Monnot, B., Benita, F., Piliouras, G.: Routing games in the wild: efficiency, equilibration and regret. In: Devanur, N.R., Lu, P. (eds.) WINE 2017. LNCS, vol. 10660, pp. 340–353. Springer, Cham (2017). https://doi.org/10.1007/978-3-319-71924-5_24

17. Monnot, B., et al.: Inferring activities and optimal trips: lessons from Singapore's national science experiment. In: Cardin, M.-A., Fong, S.H., Krob, D., Lui, P.C., Tan, Y.H. (eds.) Complex Systems Design & Management Asia. AISC, vol. 426, pp. 247–264. Springer, Cham (2016). https://doi.org/10.1007/978-3-319-29643-2_19

18. Nadav, U., Roughgarden, T.: The limits of smoothness: a primal-dual framework for price of anarchy bounds. In: Saberi, A. (ed.) WINE 2010. LNCS, vol. 6484, pp. 319–326. Springer, Heidelberg (2010). https://doi.org/10.1007/978-3-642-17572-5_26

19. Nagurney, A., Qiang, Q.: A relative total cost index for the evaluation of transportation network robustness in the presence of degradable links and alternative travel behavior. Int. Trans. Oper. Res. **16**(1), 49–67 (2009)

20. Papadimitriou, C.: Algorithms, games, and the internet. In: Proceedings of the Thirty-third Annual ACM Symposium on Theory of Computing, pp. 749–753. ACM (2001)

21. Roughgarden, T.: The price of anarchy is independent of the network topology. J. Comput. Syst. Sci. **67**(2), 341–364 (2003)

22. Roughgarden, T.: Intrinsic robustness of the price of anarchy. J. ACM (JACM) **62**(5), 32 (2015)

23. Roughgarden, T., Tardos, É.: How bad is selfish routing? J. ACM (JACM) **49**(2), 236–259 (2002)

24. Thang, N.K.: Game efficiency through linear programming duality. In: Proceedings of the 10th Innovations in Theoretical Computer Science Conference (ITCS 2019), vol. LIPIcs 124, pp. 66:1–66:20. Schloss Dagstuhl - Leibniz-Zentrum für Informatik (2019)

25. Tobin, R.L., Friesz, T.L.: Sensitivity analysis for equilibrium network flow. Transp. Sci. **22**(4), 242–250 (1988)

26. Wardrop, J.: Some Theoretical Aspects of Road Traffic Research. Road paper, Institution of Civil Engineers (1952). https://books.google.it/books?id=9zEpAQAAMAAJ

27. Zhang, J., Pourazarm, S., Cassandras, C.G., Paschalidis, I.C.: The price of anarchy in transportation networks: data-driven evaluation and reduction strategies. Proc. IEEE **106**(4), 538–553 (2018)

28. Zhou, Y., Wang, J., Shi, P., Dahlmeier, D., Tippenhauer, N., Wilhelm, E.: Power-saving transportation mode identification for large-scale applications. arXiv preprint arXiv:1701.05768 (2017)

Competition Alleviates Present Bias
in Task Completion

Aditya Saraf[(✉)], Anna R. Karlin, and Jamie Morgenstern

University of Washington, Seattle, WA, USA
{sarafa,karlin,jamiemmt}@cs.washington.edu

Abstract. We build upon recent work by Kleinberg, Oren, and Ragha-van [10–12] that considers *present biased* agents, who place more weight on costs they must incur now than costs they will incur in the future. They consider a graph theoretic model where agents must complete a task and show that present biased agents can take exponentially more expensive paths than optimal. We propose a theoretical model that adds *competition* into the mix – two agents compete to finish a task first. We show that, in a wide range of settings, a small amount of competition can alleviate the harms of present bias. This can help explain why biased agents may not perform so poorly in naturally competitive settings, and can guide task designers on how to protect present biased agents from harm. Our work thus paints a more positive picture than much of the existing literature on present bias.

Keywords: Present bias · Behavioral economics · Incentive design

1 Introduction

One of the most influential lines of recent economic research has been *behavioral* game theory [3,9]. The majority of economics research makes several idealized assumptions about the behavior of rational agents to prove mathematical results. Behavioral game theory questions these assumptions and proposes models of agent behavior that more closely align with human behavior. Through experimental research [5,6], behavioral economists have observed and codified several common types of cognitive biases, from loss aversion [9] (the tendency to prefer avoiding loss to acquiring equivalent gains) to the sunk cost fallacy [4] (the tendency to factor in previous costs when determining the best future course of action) to present bias [7] (the current topic). One primary goal of theorems in game theory is to offer predictive power. This perspective is especially important in the many computer science applications of these results, from modern ad auctions to cryptocurrency protocols. If these theorems are to predict human behavior, the mathematical models ought to include observed human biases. Thus, rather than viewing behavioral game theory as conflicting with the

---

A full version is available from https://arxiv.org/abs/2009.13741.

© Springer Nature Switzerland AG 2020
X. Chen et al. (Eds.): WINE 2020, LNCS 12495, pp. 266–279, 2020.
https://doi.org/10.1007/978-3-030-64946-3_19

standard mathematical approach, the experimental results of behavioral game theory can inform more sophisticated mathematical models. This paper takes a step towards this goal, building on seminal work of Kleinberg, Oren, and Raghavan [10–12] who formulated a mathematical model for planning problems where agents are present biased.

Present bias refers to overweighting immediate costs relative to future costs. This is a ubiquitous bias in human behavior that explains diverse phenomena. The most natural example is procrastination, the familiar desire to delay difficult work, even when this predictably leads to negative consequences later. Present bias can also model the tendency of firms to prefer immediate gains to long-term gains and the tendency of politicians to prefer immediate results to long-term plans. One simple model of present bias [10–12] is to multiply costs in the current time period by present bias parameter b when making plans. This model is a special case of hyperbolic discounting, where costs are discounted in proportion to how much later one would experience them. But even this special case suffices to induces *time-inconsistency*, resulting in a rich set of strategies consistent with human behavior.

Examples of time inconsistent behavior extend beyond procrastination. For example, one might undertake a project, and abandon it partway through, despite the underlying cost structure remaining unchanged. One might fail to complete a course with no deadlines, but pass the same course with weekly deadlines. Many people pay for a gym membership but never use it. Kleinberg and Oren [10] presented the key insight that this diverse range of phenomena can all be expressed in a single graph-theoretic framework, which we describe below.

Fix a directed, acyclic graph G, with designated source s and sink t. Refer to G as a task graph, where s is the start of the task and t the end. A path through this graph corresponds to a plan to complete the task; each edge represents one step of the plan. Each edge has a weight corresponding to the cost of that step.

The goal of an agent is to complete the task while incurring the least cost (i.e., to take the cheapest path from s to t). An optimal agent will simply follow such a cheapest path. A *naive* present biased agent with bias parameter b behaves as follows. At s, they compute their perceived cost for taking each path to t by summing the weights along this path with the first edge scaled up by $b > 1$. They choose the path with the lowest perceived cost and take *one* step along this path, say to v, and recompute their perceived cost along each the path from v to t. Notice that such an agent may choose a path at s, take one edge along that path, and then deviate away from it. This occurs because the agent believes that, after the current choice of edge, they will pick the path from v to t with lowest true cost. But once they arrive at v, their perceived cost of a path differs from the true cost, and they pick a path with lowest perceived cost. This is why the agents are considered naive: they incorrectly assume their future self will behave optimally, and thus exhibit time-inconsistent behavior. See Fig. 1 for an example.   The power of this graph theoretic model is that it allows us to answer questions over a range of planning problems, and to formally investigate which tasks represent the "worst-case" cost of procrastination. This is useful

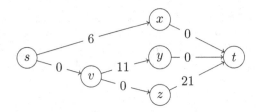

Fig. 1. The optimal path is (s, x, t) with total cost 6. However, an agent with bias $b = 2$ will take path (s, v, z, t), with cost 21. Importantly, when the agent is deciding which vertex to move to from s, they evaluate x as having total cost 12, while v has total cost 11. This is because they assume they will behave optimally at v by taking path (v, y, t). However, they apply the same bias at v and deviate to the worst possible path.

both to understand how present-biased behavior differs from optimal behavior and to design tasks to accommodate present bias. We now briefly summarize the existing literature, to motivate our introduction of competition to the model.

1.1 Prior Work

The most striking result is that there are graphs where the *cost ratio* (the ratio of the optimal agent's cost to the biased agent's cost) is exponential in the size of the graph. In addition, all graphs with exponential cost ratio have a shared structure – they all have a large n-fan as a graph minor (and graphs without exponential cost ratio do not) [10,15]. So this structure encodes the worst-case behavior for present bias in the standard model (and we later show how competition is especially effective in this graph). An n-fan is pictured in Fig. 2.

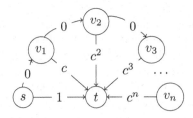

Fig. 2. A naive agent with bias $b > c > 1$ will continually choose to delay finishing the task.

The exponential cost ratio demonstrates the severe harm caused by present bias. How, then, can designers of a task limit the negative effects of present bias? Kleinberg and Oren [10] propose a model where a reward is given after finishing the task, and where the agent will abandon the task if at any point, they perceive the remaining cost to be higher than the reward. Unlike an optimal agent, a biased agent may abandon a task partway through. As a result, they give the task designer the power to arbitrarily delete vertices and edges, which can model deadlines. They then investigate the structure of *minimally motivating subgraphs* – the smallest subgraph where the agent completes the task, for some fixed reward. Follow-up work of Tang et al. [15] shows that finding *any* motivating subgraph is NP-hard. Instead of deleting edges, Albers and Kraft [2] consider the problem of spreading a fixed reward onto arbitrary vertices to motivate an agent, and find that this too is NP-hard (with a constrained budget). For other recent work involving present bias, see [1,8,13,14,16].

The above results all focus on *accommodating* present bias rather than *alleviating* it. By that, we mean that the approaches all focus on whether the agent can be convinced to complete the task – via edge deletion or reward dispersal – but not on guarding the agent from suboptimal behavior induced by their bias. [11] partially investigates the latter question in a model involving *sophisticated* agents, who plan around their present bias. They consider several types of *commitment devices* – tools by which sophisticated agents can constrain their future selves. However, these tools may require more powerful agents or designers and don't necessarily make sense for naive agents. We take a different approach – we show that adding competition can simultaneously explain why present-biased agents may not perform exponentially poorly in "natural" games and guide task designers in encouraging biased agents towards optimal behavior.

1.2 Our Model

In our model, a task is still represented by a directed, acyclic graph G, with a designated source s and sink t. There are two naive present-biased agents, A_1 and A_2, both with bias b, who compete to get to t first. The cost of a path is the sum of the weights along the path, and time is represented by the number of edges in the path, which we call the *length* of the path. In other words, each edge represents one unit of time. The first agent to get to t gets a reward of r; ties are resolved by evenly splitting the reward. Recall that naive agents believe that they will behave optimally in the future. Thus, an agent currently at u considers the cost to reach the target t to be $bc(u,v)$ plus the cost of the optimal path from v to t minus the reward of that path. More formally, let $\mathcal{P}(v \to t)$ denote the set of paths from $v \to t$ and let $P(s \to u)$ denote the path the agent has taken to u. Let $C_n(u,v)$ denote the remaining cost that the naive agent believes they will incur while at u and planning to go to v. The subscript n stands for "naive" (to help distinguish from $c(u,v)$, the cost of the edge (u,v)). Then:

$$C_n(u,v) = b \cdot c(u,v) + \min_{P(v \to t) \in \mathcal{P}(v \to t)} c(P(v \to t)) - R_{A_2}(P(s \to u) \cup (u,v) \cup P(v \to t)), \quad (1)$$

where $c(P) = \sum_{e \in P} c(e)$ denotes the cost of path P and $R_{A_2}(P)$ denotes the reward of taking path P from s to t. This reward depends on the path the other agent A_2 takes. Specifically, if A_2 takes a path of length k, and $Q := P(s \to u) \cup (u,v) \cup P(v \to t)$ is a path of length ℓ, then $R(Q)$ is r if $\ell < k$, $r/2$ if $\ell = k$ and 0 if $\ell > k$. We will often rewrite the second term in (1), for ease of notation, as $\min_{P_v} c(P_v) - R_{A_2}(P_{s \to u, v \to t})$. We sometimes refer instead to the naive agent's *utility*, which is the negation of this cost. Given this cost function, the naive agent chooses the successor of node u via $S(u) = \operatorname{argmin}_{v:(u,v) \in E} C_n(u,v)$. See Fig. 3 for an example.

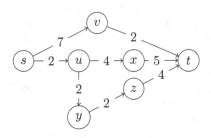

Fig. 3. Suppose $r = 5$, the bias $b = 2$, and assume A_2 takes path (s, u, x, t). Then at s, A_1 prefers to take u for perceived cost $4 + 4 + 5 - 2.5 = 10.5$. Notice that, due to the reward, the path A_1 believes he will take from u is (u, x, t), despite (u, y, z, t) having lower cost. However, at u, A_1 evaluates the lower path to be cheaper, despite losing the race. This shows that a reward of 5 does not ensure a Nash equilibrium on (s, u, x, t) when $b = 2$.

We now consider how this model of competition might both explain the outcomes of natural games and inform task designers on how to elicit better behavior from biased agents. For a natural game, consider the classic example of two companies competing to expand into a new market. Both companies want to launch a similar product, and are thus considering the same task graph G. The companies are also present biased, since shareholders often prefer immediate profit maximization/loss minimization over long term optimal behavior. The first company to enter the market gains an insurmountable advantage, represented by reward r. If the companies both enter the market at the same time, they split the market share, each getting reward $r/2$. This arrangement can be modeled within our framework, and the competition between the companies should lead them to play a set of equilibrium strategies.

For a designed game, consider the problem of encouraging students to submit final projects before they are due. The instructor sets a deadline near the end of finals week to give students flexibility to complete the project when it best fits their schedule. The instructor also knows that (1) students tend to procrastinate and (2) trying to complete the final project in a few days is much more challenging than spreading it out. They would like to convince students to work on and possibly submit their assignments early, *without* changing the deadline (to allow flexibility for the students whom it suits best). One possible solution would be to give a small amount of extra credit to the first submission. How might they set this reward to encourage early submissions?

In both these examples, the intuition is that competition will alleviate the harms of present bias by driving agents towards optimal behavior.

1.3   Summary of Results

We have introduced a model of competition for completing tasks along some graph. We warm up by analyzing these games absent present bias. Namely, we classify all Nash equilibria for an arbitrary task graph with unbiased agents, by first defining and eliminating all dominated paths.

We then analyze the model where agents have equal present bias. We show that a very small reward induces a Nash equilibrium on the optimal path, for any graph with a *dominant* path. This is a substantial improvement over the exponential worst case cost ratio experienced without competition. We then discuss how time-inconsistency defeats the intuition that higher rewards cause agents to prefer quicker paths. Despite this complication, we describe an algorithm that, given arbitrary graph G and path Q, determines the minimum reward needed to get a Nash equilibrium on Q, if possible.

Finally, we add an element of *bias uncertainty* to the model, by drawing agents' biases iid from distribution F and, for the n-fan, describe the relationship between F and the reward required for a Bayes-Nash equilibrium on the optimal path. For a wide range of distributions, we find small rewards suffice to ensure that agents behave optimally (with high probability) in equilibrium. For the stronger goal of ensuring a constant expected cost ratio, it suffices to offer reward linear in n when F is not heavy-tailed; competition thus helps here as well.

2   Nash Equilibria with Unbiased Competitors

To build intuition, we first describe the Nash equilibria of these games when agents have no present bias. We also pinpoint where the analysis will change with the introduction of bias. Notice that each path P in the graph is a strategy, with payoffs either $u_w = r - c(P)$, $u_t = r/2 - c(P)$ or $u_l = -c(P)$, depending on whether the agent wins, ties or loses, respectively. (These in turn depend on the path taken by the opponent.) We first rule out dominated paths. Notice that if $u_l(P) \geq u_w(P')$, path P' is dominated by path P, regardless of the path taken by the opponent. Also, if $u_w(P) \geq u_w(P')$ and $|P| \leq |P'|$ (where $|P|$ is the number of edges in P), then P' is dominated. Therefore, for any length k, a single cheapest path of length k will (weakly) dominate all other paths of length k.

For a given graph G, let $P_1, \ldots, P_n$ be a minimal set of non-dominated paths, where $|P_i| < |P_{i+1}|$ for each $1 \leq i < n$. Thus, P_1 is the *quickest* path, the remaining path of minimum length. Summarizing what we know about these paths:

1. *Winning is better than losing*: for any pair of paths (P_i, P_j), we know that $u_w(P_i) > u_l(P_j)$. Thus, in particular, $c(P_1) - c(P_n) \leq r$.
2. *Longer paths are more rewarding*: That is, $c(P_i) > c(P_{i+1})$ for each i. Otherwise, P_{i+1} would be dominated since its length is greater. Therefore, in particular, P_n is the *cheapest* path, i.e., the lowest cost/weight path from s to t.

We're interested in characterizing, across all possible task graphs, the pure Nash equilibria, restricting attention to paths in $P_1, \ldots, P_n$.

Proposition 1. *Let G be an arbitrary task graph. As above, let $P_1, \ldots, P_n$ be a minimal set of (non-dominated) paths ordered so P_1 is the quickest and P_n the cheapest. Suppose $n \geq 3$. Then, path P_i, where $i > 1$, is a symmetric Nash equilibrium if and only if $c(P_{i-1}) - c(P_i) \geq r/2$. P_1 is a symmetric Nash if and only if $c(P_1) - c(P_n) \leq r/2$. There are no other pure Nash equilibria. Therefore, there can be either 0, 1 or 2 pure Nash equilibria.*

If $n = 2$, there is an additional asymmetric pure Nash equilibrium where one player plays the quickest path P_1 and the other plays the cheapest path P_2 if $c(P_1) - c(P_2) = r/2$.

The proof can be found in the full version. We next turn our attention to the biased version of this problem. In the unbiased case, we could take a "global" view of the graph, and think about paths purely in terms of their overall length and cost. But when agents are biased, the actual structure of the path is very important; time-inconsistency means that agents look at paths *locally*, not globally. It is thus very difficult to cleanly rule out dominated paths – even paths with exponentially high cost may be taken, as we see next.

3 Nash Equilibria to Elicit Optimal Behavior from Biased Agents

We assume that the agents are both naive, present biased agents, with shared bias parameter b.[1] Our high-level goal is to show that competition convinces biased agents to take cheap paths, as unbiased agents do without competition. To this end, we show that a small amount of reward creates a Nash equilibrium on the cheapest path, for all graphs which have a *dominant* path – a cheapest path that is also the *uniquely* quickest path.

3.1   Graphs with an Unbiased Dominant Strategy

To focus exclusively on the irrationality of present bias rather than the optimization problem of choosing between cheap, long paths and short, expensive paths, we focus on graphs with a *dominant path* – a cheapest path[2] that is also the *uniquely* quickest path. An example of such a graph is the n-fan. In this setting, the problem is trivial for unbiased agents; simply take this dominant path. But for biased agents, the problem is still interesting; as the n-fan shows, they may take paths that are exponentially more costly than the dominant path. However, we prove that a small amount of competition and reward suffices to ensure the existence of a Nash equilibrium where both agents take the dominant path.

---

[1] The homogeneity of the agents is not particularly important to our results in this section. If the agents have different bias parameters, our results go through by setting b equal to the larger of the two biases.

[2] There may be other cheapest paths which are longer.

Theorem 1. *Suppose G is a task graph that has a dominant path, O. Then, a reward of $r \geq 2b \cdot \max_{e \in O} c(e)$ guarantees a Nash equilibrium on O, for two agents with bias b.*

Proof. Assume that A_2 takes O. Recall that a biased agent perceives the remaining traversal cost of going to v from t as $C_n(u,v) = b \cdot c(u,v) + \min_{P_v} c(P_v) - R_{A_2}(P_{s \to u, v \to t})$. We know that for any vertex v^* on the dominant path, the path that minimizes the second term is just the fragment of the dominant path from $v^* \to t$ (it is both the quickest and cheapest way to get from v^* to t). Further, any deviation from the dominant path results in no reward. So, for any v not on the dominant path, the path that minimizes the second term is again the cheapest path from $v \to t$. Thus, the cost equation simplifies to $C_n(u,v) = b \cdot c(u,v) + d(v) - r/2 \cdot 1\{D\}$, where $d(v)$, the *distance* from $v \to t$, denotes the cost of the cheapest path from v to t (ignoring rewards) and $1\{D\}$ is simply an indicator variable that's 1 if the agent has not deviated from the dominant path.

Now, let $O = (s = v_0^*, v_1^*, v_2^*, \ldots, t = v_l^*)$ be the dominant path and suppose A_2 takes this path. In order for A_1 to choose O, we require, for all i:

$$S(v_i^*) = v_{i+1}^*$$
$$\iff v_{i+1}^* = \underset{v:(v_i^*,v) \in E}{\operatorname{argmin}} \; b \cdot c(v_i^*, v) + d(v) - r/2 \cdot 1\{D\}$$
$$\iff \forall v : (v_i^*, v) \in E, bc(v_i^*, v) + d(v) \geq bc(v_i^*, v_{i+1}^*) + d(v_{i+1}^*) - r/2$$

Now, let i be arbitrary, let $v \neq v_i^*$ be an arbitrary neighbor of v_i^*, and for ease of notation, let $c = c(v_i^*, v), c^* = c(v_i^*, v_{i+1}^*), d = d(v)$, and $d^* = d(v_{i+1}^*)$. Then, we get the following bound on the reward: $r/2 \geq b(c^* - c) + d^* - d$. To get a rough sufficient bound, notice that $c + d \geq c^* + d^*$, since O is the cheapest path. This implies that $bc^* > b(c^* - c) + d^* - d$. Thus, it suffices to set $r \geq 2bc^*$ in order to ensure $S(v_i^*) = v_{i+1}^*$. Repeating this argument for all i, we see that a sufficient reward is $r = 2b \cdot \max_{e \in O} c(e)$. $\qquad\square$

One might object to our claim that $r = 2b \max_{e \in O} c(e)$ is "small". To calibrate our expectations, notice that we can view this problem as an agent trying to pick between several options (i.e. paths), each with their own reward and cost structure. We want to convince the agent to pick one particular option – namely, the cheapest path. But it would be unreasonable to expect that a reward significantly smaller than the cost of *any* option would sway the agent's decision. Our theorem above shows that a reward that is at most proportional to the *cheapest* option suffices; and in many cases the reward is only a fraction of the cost of the optimal path (e.g. when the optimal path has balanced cost among many edges).

For a point of comparison, even internal edge rewards (which required the same reward budget as competitive rewards for the n-fan) can require $O(n)$ times as much reward in some instances. To see the intuition, notice that internal edge rewards must be applied at every step where the agent might want to deviate. The agent also immediately "consumes" this reward; it doesn't impact his future

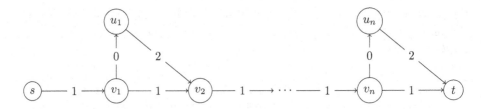

Fig. 4. A graph with many suboptimal deviations. For an agent with bias $b > 2$, a designer with access to only edge rewards must spend $O(n)$ total reward for optimal behavior ($b - 2$ on each (v_i, v_{i+1}) edge). In our competitive setting, only $2(b - 2)$ total reward is required.

decision making. However, the competitive reward is "at stake" whenever the agent considers deviating; this reward can sway the agent's behavior without being immediately consumed. For a concrete example, see Fig. 4.

3.2   Increasing the Number of Competitors

A very natural extension to this model would involve more than 2 agents competing. The winner takes all, and ties are split evenly among those who tied. However, this modification doesn't change much *when trying to get a Nash equilibrium on the dominant path*. The only change is that if m agents are competing, the reward needed is $O(m)$, as a single agent will get a $1/m$ fraction of the reward in a symmetric equilibrium. This is true because there is no way for any agent to beat the dominant path, and claim the entire $O(m)$ reward for themselves. So if the reward is scaled appropriately (i.e. in Theorem 1 set $r \geq mb \cdot \max_{e \in O} c(e)$), we will still guarantee a Nash equilibrium. Put another way, the *per-agent* reward needed for a Nash equilibrium on the dominant path does not change as the number of competitors varies.

4   General Nash Equilibria

In this section, we describe a polynomial time algorithm that, given an arbitrary graph G, path Q and bias b, determines if Q can be made a Nash equilibrium, and if so, the minimum required reward to do so. Finding and using this minimum required reward will generally cost much less than the bound given by Theorem 1. Moreover, this algorithm does not assume the existence of a dominant path. We start by describing how time-inconsistency defeats the intuition that higher rewards cause agents to prefer quicker paths. We then present a very high level overview of how to compute the minimum reward that results in Q being a symmetric Nash equilibrium.

4.1   Higher Rewards Need Not Encourage Quicker Paths

The proof of Theorem 1 suggests the following algorithm for this problem. Start with a reward of 0, and step along each vertex $u \in Q$, increasing the reward by just enough to ensure A_1 stays on Q for one more step (assuming A_2 is taking Q). However, if A_1 wants to deviate onto a quicker/tied path at any point, return $\perp$; decreasing the reward would cause them to deviate earlier, and, intuitively, it seems that increasing the reward could not cause them to switch back to Q from the quicker/tied path. After one pass, simply pass through again to ensure that the final reward doesn't cause A_1 to deviate early on. The following lemma, which we prove in the full version, shows that this algorithm is tractable, by showing that we can compute the minimum reward required for A_1 to stay on Q at any step (and determine whether A_1 wants to deviate onto a quicker path).

Lemma 1. *Assuming that A_2 takes path Q, A_1 can efficiently compute $\min_{P_v} c(P_v) - R_{A_2}(P_{s \to u, v \to t})$ by considering the cheapest path (from $v \to t$), the cheapest path where A_1 ties A_2, and the cheapest path where A_1 beats A_2. (Some of these paths may coincide, and at least one must exist).*

Unfortunately, while tractable, the approach described above does not yield a correct algorithm. This is because it relies implicitly on the following two properties, which formalize the intuition that increasing the reward causes agents to favor quicker paths.

Property 1. If a reward r guarantees a Nash equilibrium on some path Q, any reward $r' > r$ will either (a), still result in a Nash equilibrium on Q, or (b), cause an agent to deviate to a *quicker* path Q'.

Property 2. If A_1 deviates from Q onto a quicker/tied path for some reward r, increasing the reward will not cause them to follow Q

Both properties are intuitive – if we increase the reward, that should motivate the agent to take a path that beats their opponent. And vice versa – increasing the reward shouldn't cause them to shift onto a slower path or shift between equal length paths. But surprisingly, both properties are false, as Fig. 5 demonstrates.

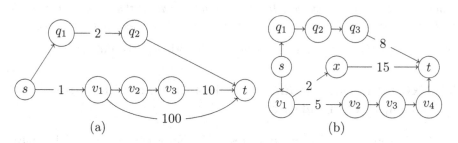

Fig. 5. Graphs which do not exhibit the two expected properties. Unlabeled edges have cost 0.

For Property 1, consider the graph in Fig. 5(a) and define paths $Q = (s, q_1, q_2, t)$, $V = (s, v_1, v_2, v_3, t)$, and $X = (s, v_1, t)$. Suppose both agents have bias 10 and that A_2 takes Q. Then a reward of 1 guarantees that A_1 takes Q, as the optimal path from $v_1 \to t$ would follow V. However, if $r = 300$, the optimal path from $v_1 \to t$ follows X. So, A_1 goes to v_1, intending to beat A_2. But at v_1, the perceived cost of (v_1, t) is actually 1000, and so the agent prefers to take path V. Thus, increasing the reward from 1 to 300 causes the agent to deviate from Q onto a slower path!

For Property 2, consider the graph in Fig. 5(b) and define paths Q, V, and X in the obvious manner. Again, suppose both agents have bias 10 and that A_2 takes Q. Then, with a reward of 10, A_1 to stick to Q as well. But if $r = 2$, the optimal path from $v_1 \to t$ follows V and thus loses, which is not as meaningful. So A_1 goes to v_1, intending to follow V. But there, with $b = 10$, deviating to X is more attractive than remaining on V, and thus the agent takes X. So, although A_1 deviates from Q to a quicker path for reward 2, they remain on Q with reward 10.

To summarize, Property 1 fails because present biased agents can take slower paths than they planned and Property 2 fails because present biased agents can take quicker paths than they planned. In other words, while higher rewards do *tempt* agents to take quicker paths, and lower rewards tempt agents towards cheaper paths, their time inconsistency may make them do the opposite.

4.2 A Description of the Algorithm

We now describe, at a very high level, how to efficiently find the set of rewards which induce a symmetric Nash equilibrium on a path Q. The algorithm narrows down the set of *feasible* rewards (rewards that ensure that Q is a Nash equilibria) by computing the set of rewards that ensure that A_1 takes (u, v) for every $(u, v) \in Q$. The key idea is that we can efficiently compute all r that ensures that A_1 prefers (u, v) over (u, v') by splitting into cases based on whether the optimal paths from $v \to t$ and $v' \to t$ involve winning, tying, or losing. From this algorithm, we get the following theorem:

Theorem 2. *There exists a polynomial time algorithm that returns the minimum r that ensures that Q is a Nash equilibrium, or $\perp$ if no such r exists.*

We prove this theorem and fully define the algorithm in the full version.

5 Extending the Model with Bias Uncertainty and Multiple Competitors

One of the shortcomings of the prior results is that agents are assumed to have publicly known, identical biases, which seems unrealistic. We therefore add the agents' uncertainty about their competitors bias to the model. The agents' biases are now represented by random variables B_1 and B_2 drawn iid from distribution F, which is publicly known to both the agents and the designer. b_1 and b_2 correspond to the realizations of these random variables. Our goal is now to construct, as cheaply as possible, Bayes-Nash equilibria (BNE) where agents behave optimally with high probability. In this setting, the cost equation becomes $C_n(u,v) = b \cdot c(u,v) + \min_{P_v} c(P_v) - \mathbb{E}_{A_2}[R_{A_2}(P_{s \to u, v \to t})]$, where the expectation is over A_2's choice of paths.

In this section, we provide a closed form BNE for the n-fan. We start with the case of two agents and then briefly consider m competing agents. Since we are searching for BNE, we assume that the agents know their competitor's strategy.

5.1 Bayes-Nash Equilibria on the n-fan

As before, let P_i represent the path that includes edge (v_i, t), and let P_0 represent the optimal path. Then, the following strategy is a Bayes-Nash equilibrium.

Theorem 3. *Let G be an n-fan with reward r and suppose B_1, B_2 are drawn from distribution B with CDF F. Let p be the solution to $F(\frac{rp}{2} + c) = p$. If $p > \frac{1}{c^{n-1}+1}$, then the following strategy is a Bayes-Nash equilibrium:*

$$P(b) = \begin{cases} take\ P_0, & b \le \frac{rp}{2} + c \\ take\ P_n, & otherwise \end{cases}$$

In this equilibrium, for either agent, the probability that they take P_0 is p. So the expected cost ratio will be $p + (1-p)c^n$.

We prove this in the full version. Notice that while the trivial solution $p = 0$ satisfies $F(\frac{rp}{2} + c) = p$, this is not above $\frac{1}{c^{n-1}+1}$, so the trivial solution is not relevant for finding Bayes-Nash equilibria. One might wonder if there's a straightforward generalization of this BNE to other graphs with a dominant path, as in the case without bias uncertainty. In the full version, we discuss challenges that we encountered trying to do this.

We now use the theorem to understand how much reward is required for optimal behavior with high probability, or a low expected cost ratio (which is a much stronger requirement). Since the expected cost is $p + c^n(1-p)$, in order for this to be low, $1 - p$ has to be close to $1/c^n$. Plugging this in to the CDF, we see that for this to happen, we must have

$$F\left(\frac{r}{2}\left(1 - \frac{1}{c^n}\right) + c\right) = 1 - \frac{1}{c^n}$$

which essentially requires that exponentially little probability mass (in n) remains after $r/2$ distance from c. For an exponential distribution, this requires r to be linear in n, and with a heavier tailed distribution like the Equal Revenue distribution, this requires r to be exponential in n. But we may be content with simply guaranteeing optimal behavior with high probability. In that case, so long as r is increasing in n, the agents will take the optimal path with high probability for at least the equal revenue, exponential, and uniform distributions. We more precisely explore the probability of optimal behavior and the cost ratios for these distributions in the full version.

5.2   Increasing Number of Competitors

We saw earlier that increasing the number of competitors doesn't change the *per-agent* reward needed for optimal behavior. But one might hope that in Bayesian settings such as bias uncertainty, increasing the number of agents significantly decreases the per-agent reward needed to encourage optimal behavior – in particular, as the number of agents increases, the probability of *some* agent having a very low bias increases. In the full version, we provide evidence against this belief. We first show that the BNE in Theorem 3 can be tweaked slightly to remain a BNE with a variable number of agents. We then consider the equal revenue distribution, which required an exponentially high reward to get a low expected cost ratio with just two competitors. But we show that even as number of competing agents goes to ∞, this relationship between the reward and the probability of optimal behavior doesn't significantly change. We conjecture that, in general, increasing the number of agents does not significantly decrease the per-agent reward required for optimal behavior.

6   Conclusion

We studied the impact of competition on present bias, showing that in many settings where naive agents can experience exponentially high cost ratio, a small amount of competition drives agents to optimal behavior. This paper is a first step towards painting a more optimistic picture than much of the work surrounding present bias. Our results highlight why, in naturally competitive settings, otherwise biased agents might behave optimally. Further, task/mechanism designers can use our results to directly alleviate the harms of present bias. This competitive model might be a more natural model than other motivation schemes, such as internal edge rewards, and is able to more cheaply ensure optimal behavior. Our work also leaves open many exciting questions.

First, with bias uncertainty, we only obtain concrete results on the n-fan. So one obvious direction is to determine which graphs have Bayes-Nash equilibria on the optimal path, and what these equilibria look like. Second, we explore two "dimensions" of competition – the amount of reward and the number of competitors, finding that the latter is unlikely to be significant. Another interesting goal is thus to explore new dimensions of competition.

Lastly, we could extend our work beyond cost ratios, moving to the model where agents can abandon their path at any point. For one, this move would allow us to integrate results on *sunk-cost* bias, represented as an intrinsic cost for abandoning a task that's proportional to the amount of effort expended. Previous work [12] has shown that agents who are sophisticated with regard to their present-bias, but naive with respect to their sunk cost bias can experience exponentially high cost before abandoning their traversal (this is especially interesting because sophisticated agents without sunk cost bias behave nearly optimally). Can competition alleviate this exponential worst case? There are also interesting computational questions in this model. For instance, given a fixed reward budget r, is it possible to determine in polynomial time if one can induce an equilibrium where both agents traverse the graph? Such problems are NP-hard for other reward models, but may be tractable with competition. Overall, the abandonment setting has several interesting interactions with competition that we have not explored.

References

1. Albers, S., Kraft, D.: On the value of penalties in time-inconsistent planning. arXiv preprint arXiv:1702.01677 (2017)
2. Albers, S., Kraft, D.: Motivating time-inconsistent agents: a computational approach. Theory Comput. Syst. **63**(3), 466–487 (2019). https://doi.org/10.1007/s00224-018-9883-0
3. Ariely, D., Jones, S.: Predictably Irrational. Harper Audio, New York (2008)
4. Arkes, H.R., Blumer, C.: The psychology of sunk cost. Organ. Behav. Hum. Decis. Processes **35**(1), 124–140 (1985)
5. DellaVigna, S.: Psychology and economics: evidence from the field. J. Econ. Lit. **47**(2), 315–72 (2009)
6. DellaVigna, S., Malmendier, U.: Paying not to go to the gym. Am. Econ. Rev. **96**(3), 694–719 (2006)
7. Frederick, S., Loewenstein, G., O'donoghue, T.: Time discounting and time preference: a critical review. J. Econ. Lit. **40**(2), 351–401 (2002)
8. Gravin, N., Immorlica, N., Lucier, B., Pountourakis, E.: Procrastination with variable present bias. arXiv preprint arXiv:1606.03062 (2016)
9. Kahneman, D., Tversky, A.: Prospect theory: an analysis of decision under risk. Econometrica **47**(2), 263–292 (1979)
10. Kleinberg, J., Oren, S.: Time-inconsistent planning: a computational problem in behavioral economics. In: Proceedings of the Fifteenth ACM Conference on Economics and Computation, pp. 547–564 (2014)
11. Kleinberg, J., Oren, S., Raghavan, M.: Planning problems for sophisticated agents with present bias. In: Proceedings of the 2016 ACM Conference on Economics and Computation, pp. 343–360 (2016)
12. Kleinberg, J., Oren, S., Raghavan, M.: Planning with multiple biases. In: Proceedings of the 2017 ACM Conference on Economics and Computation, pp. 567–584 (2017)
13. Ma, H., Meir, R., Parkes, D.C., Wu-Yan, E.: Penalty bidding mechanisms for allocating resources and overcoming present bias. arXiv preprint arXiv:1906.09713 (2019)
14. Oren, S., Soker, D.: Principal-agent problems with present-biased agents. In: Fotakis, D., Markakis, E. (eds.) SAGT 2019. LNCS, vol. 11801, pp. 237–251. Springer, Cham (2019). https://doi.org/10.1007/978-3-030-30473-7_16
15. Tang, P., Teng, Y., Wang, Z., Xiao, S., Xu, Y.: Computational issues in time-inconsistent planning. In: Thirty-First AAAI Conference on Artificial Intelligence (2017)
16. Yan, W., Yong, J.: Time-inconsistent optimal control problems and related issues. Modeling, Stochastic Control, Optimization, and Applications. TIVMA, vol. 164, pp. 533–569. Springer, Cham (2019). https://doi.org/10.1007/978-3-030-25498-8_22

Improving Approximate Pure Nash Equilibria in Congestion Games

Vipin Ravindran Vijayalakshmi[1(✉)] and Alexander Skopalik[2]

[1] Chair of Management Science, RWTH Aachen, Aachen, Germany
vipin.rv@oms.rwth-aachen.de
[2] Mathematics of Operations Research, University of Twente, Enschede, Netherlands
a.skopalik@utwente.nl

Abstract. Congestion games constitute an important class of games to model resource allocation by different users. As computing an exact [18] or even an approximate [34] pure Nash equilibrium is in general PLS-complete, Caragiannis et al. [9] present a polynomial-time algorithm that computes a $(2 + \epsilon)$-approximate pure Nash equilibria for games with linear cost functions and further results for polynomial cost functions. We show that this factor can be improved to $(1.61 + \epsilon)$ and further improved results for polynomial cost functions, by a seemingly simple modification to their algorithm by allowing for the cost functions used during the best response dynamics be different from the overall objective function. Interestingly, our modification to the algorithm also extends to efficiently computing improved approximate pure Nash equilibria in games with arbitrary non-decreasing resource cost functions. Additionally, our analysis exhibits an interesting method to optimally compute universal load dependent taxes and using linear programming duality prove tight bounds on the PoA under universal taxation, e.g., 2.012 for linear congestion games and further results for polynomial cost functions. Although our approach yield weaker results than that in Bilò and Vinci [6], we remark that our cost functions are locally computable and in contrast to [6] are independent of the actual instance of the game.

Keywords: Congestion games · Approximate pure Nash equilibria · Price of anarchy · Universal taxes

1 Introduction

Congestion games constitute an important class of games that succinctly represents a game theoretic model for resource allocation among non-cooperative users. A canonical example for this is the road transportation network, where the time needed to commute is a function on the total amount of traffic in the network. A congestion game is a cost minimization game defined by a set of

V. R. Vijayalakshmi—This work is supported by the German research council (DFG) Research Training Group 2236 UnRAVeL

resources E, a set of N players with strategies $S_1, \ldots, S_N \subseteq 2^E$, and for each resource $e \in E$, a cost function $f_e : \mathbb{N} \mapsto \mathbb{R}_+$. Congestion games were first introduced by Rosenthal [28], and using a potential function argument proved that it belongs to a class of games in which a pure Nash equilibrium always exists, i.e., the game always consists of a self-emerging solution in which no user is able to improve by unilaterally deviating.

Convergence to Pure Nash Equilibria. Fabrikant et al. [18] show that computing a pure Nash equilibrium is PLS-complete. They show that regardless of the order in which local search is performed, there are initial states from where it could take exponential number of steps before the game converges to a pure Nash equilibrium. Also, they show PLS-completeness for network congestion games with asymmetric strategy spaces. As a positive result, Fabrikant et al. [18] present a polynomial time algorithm to compute a pure Nash equilibrium in certain restricted strategy spaces e.g., symmetric network congestion games. Ackermann et al. [1] show that network congestion games with linear cost functions are PLS-complete. However, if the set of strategies of each player consists of the bases of a matroid over the set of resources, then they show that the lengths of all best response sequences are polynomially bounded in the number of players and resources. This alludes to studying *approximate* pure Nash equilibria in congestion games.

To our knowledge, the concept of α-approximate equilibria[1] was introduced by Roughgarden and Tardos [29] in the context of non-atomic selfish routing games. An α-approximate pure Nash equilibrium is a state in which none of the users can unilaterally deviate to improve by a factor of at least α. Orlin et al. [25] show that every local search problem in PLS admits a fully polynomial time ϵ-approximation scheme. Although their approach can be applied to congestion games, this does not yield an approximate pure Nash equilibrium, but rather only an approximate local optimum of the potential function. In case of congestion games, Skopalik and Vöcking [34] show that in general for arbitrary cost functions, finding a α-approximate pure Nash equilibrium is PLS-complete, for any $\alpha > 1$. However, for polynomial cost function (with non-negative coefficients) of maximum degree d, Caragiannis et al. [9] present an approximation algorithm. They present a polynomial-time algorithm that computes $(2 + \epsilon)$-approximate pure Nash equilibria for games with linear cost functions and an approximation guarantee of $d^{O(d)}$ for polynomial cost functions of maximum degree d. Interestingly, they use the convergence of subsets of players to a $(1 + \epsilon)$-approximate Nash equilibrium (of that subset) as a subroutine to generate a state which is an approximation of the minimal potential function value (of that subset), e.g. $2 \cdot$ OPT for linear congestion games. This approximation factor of the minimal potential then essentially turns into the approximation factor of the approximate equilibrium. Feldotto et al. [19] using a *path-cycle decomposition* technique bound this approximation factor of the potential for arbitrary cost functions.

---

[1] Here we refer to the multiplicative notion of approximation. There is also a additive variant which is often denoted by ϵ-Nash.

Our Contribution. In this paper we improve the approximation guarantee achieved in the computation of approximate pure Nash equilibrium with the algorithm in Caragiannis et al. [9], using a linear programming approach which generalizes the smoothness condition in Roughgarden [30], to modify the cost functions that users experience in the algorithm. Although we only make a seemingly simple modification to their algorithm in [9], we would like to remark that the analysis is significantly involved, and does not immediately follow from [9], since the sub-game induced by the algorithm with the modified costs is not a potential game anymore. Table 1 lists the results for resource cost functions that are bounded degree polynomials of maximum degree d. Our main contribution in this paper is presented as Theorem 1.

Table 1. Approximate pure Nash equilibria of congestion games with polynomial cost functions of degree at most d.

d	Previous Approx. [9,19]	Our Approx. $\rho_d + \epsilon$
1	$2 + \epsilon$	$1.61 + \epsilon$
2	$6 + \epsilon$	$3.35 + \epsilon$
3	$20 + \epsilon$	$8.60 + \epsilon$
4	$111 + \epsilon$	$27.46 + \epsilon$
5	$571 + \epsilon$	$98.14 + \epsilon$

Theorem 1. *For every $\epsilon > 0$, the algorithm computes a $(\rho_d + \epsilon)$-approximate equilibrium for every congestion game with non-decreasing cost functions that are polynomials of maximum degree d in a number of steps which is polynomial in the number of players and $1/\epsilon$.*

Our approach also yields a simple and distributed method to compute load dependent universal taxes that improves the inefficiency of equilibria in congestion games. Table 2 lists our results for the price of anarchy (PoA) under refundable taxation for resource cost functions that are bounded degree polynomials. Bilò and Vinci [6] present an algorithm to compute load dependent taxes that improve the price of anarchy e.g., for linear congestion games from 2.5 to 2. Although our methods yield slightly weaker results, our cost functions are locally computable and in contrast to [6] are independent of the actual instance of the game. Furthermore, using linear programming duality we derive a reduction to a selfish scheduling game on identical machines, which implies a matching lower bound on the approximation factor. We would like to remark that our results for PoA were achieved independently of that in Paccagnan et al. [26] by a very similar technique.

2   Preliminaries

A strategic game denoted by the tuple $\left(\mathcal{N}, (S_u)_{u \in \mathcal{N}}, (c_u)_{u \in \mathcal{N}}\right)$ consists of a finite set of players $\mathcal{N}$, and for each player $u \in \mathcal{N}$, a finite set of strategies S_u and

Table 2. PoA under taxation in congestion games with polynomial cost functions of degree at most d.

d	PoA without taxes Aland et al. [2]	Optimal taxes Bilò and Vinci [6]	Universal taxes Ψ_d Local search w.r.t ζ_{sc}
1	2.5	2	2.012
2	9.583	5	5.10
3	41.54	15	15.56
4	267.6	52	55.46
5	1514	203	220.41

a cost function $c_u : S \to \mathbb{R}_+$ mapping a state $s \in S := S_1 \times S_2 \times \cdots \times S_N$ to the cost of player $u \in \mathcal{N}$. A congestion game is a strategic game that succinctly represents a decentralized resource allocation problem involving selfish users.

A congestion game denoted by $G = \left(\mathcal{N}, E, (S_u)_{u \in N}, (f_e)_{e \in E}\right)$ consists of a set of N players, $\mathcal{N} = \{1, 2, \ldots, N\}$, who compete over a set of resources E. Each player $u \in \mathcal{N}$ has a set of strategies denoted by $S_u \subseteq 2^E$. Each resource $e \in E$ has a non-negative and non-decreasing cost function $f_e : \mathbb{N} \mapsto \mathbb{R}_+$ associated with it. Let $n_e(s)$ denote the number of players on a resource $e \in E$ in the state s, then the cost contributed by a resource $e \in E$ to each player using it is denoted by $f_e(n_e(s))$. Therefore, the cost of a player $u \in \mathcal{N}$ in a state $s = (s_1, \ldots, s_N)$ of the game is given by $c_u(s) = \sum_{e \in E : e \in s_u} f_e(n_e(s))$. For a state s, $c_u(s'_u, s_{-u})$ denotes the cost of player u, when only u deviates. A best-response move denoted by $\mathcal{BR}_u(s)$ is a move that minimizes a player's cost while all the other players are fixed to their strategy in s. With some abuse of notation, $\mathcal{BR}_u(0)$ denotes the best response of a player u assuming that no other player participates in the game.

A state $s \in S$ is a pure Nash equilibrium (PNE), if there exists no player who could deviate to another strategy and decrease their cost, i.e., $\forall u \in \mathcal{N}$, and $\forall s'_u \in S_u, c_u(s) \leq c_u(s'_u, s_{-u})$. A weaker notion of PNE is the α-approximate pure Nash equilibrium for $\alpha \geq 1$, which is a state s in which no player has an improvement that decreases their cost by a factor of at least α, i.e, $\forall u \in \mathcal{N}$, and $\forall s'_u \in S_u \ \alpha \cdot c_u(s'_u, s_{-u}) \geq c_u(s)$. For congestion games the exact potential function $\phi(s) = \sum_{e \in E} \sum_{i=1}^{n_e(s)} f_e(i)$, guarantees the existence of a PNE by proving that every sequence of unilateral improving strategies converges to a PNE. We denote social or global cost of a state s as $c(s) = \sum_{u \in \mathcal{N}} c_u(s)$ and the state that minimizes social cost is called the optimal, i.e., $s^* = \arg\min_{s \in S} c(s)$. The inefficiency of equilibria is measured using the price of anarchy (PoA) [22], which is the worst case ratio between the social cost of an equilibrium and the social optimum.

A local optimum is a state s in which there is no player $u \in \mathcal{N}$ with an alternative strategy s'_u such that $c(s'_u, s_{-u}) < c(s)$, and an α-approximate local optimum is a state s in which there is no player u who has an α-move with a strategy s'_u such that $\alpha \cdot c(s'_u, s_{-u}) < c(s)$. Let us remark that there is an interesting connection between a local optimum and a PNE. A PNE is a local optimum of the potential function ϕ, and similarly, a local optimum is a Nash equilibrium of a game in which we change the resource cost functions from $f(x)$ to the marginal contribution to social cost, e.g., to $f'(x) = xf(x) - (x-1)f(x-1)$. Analogous to the PoA, the *stretch* of a congestion game is the worst case ratio between the value of the potential function at an equilibrium and the potential minimizer.

3   Approximate Equilibria in Congestion Games

In this section we aim at improving the approximation factor of an approximate pure Nash equilibria in congestion games with arbitrary non-decreasing resource cost functions. We extend an algorithm based on Caragiannis et al. [9] to compute an approximate pure Nash equilibrium in congestion games with polynomial cost functions with non-negative coefficients. A key element of this algorithm is the so called stretch of a (sub-) game. This is the worst case ratio of the potential function at an equilibrium and the global minimum of the potential.

This algorithm generates a sequence of improving moves that converges to an approximate PNE in polynomial number of best-response moves. The idea is to divide the players into blocks based on their costs and hence their prospective ability to drop the potential of the game. In each phase of the algorithm, players of two consecutive blocks are scheduled to make improving moves starting with the blocks of players with high costs. One block only makes q-moves, which are improvements by a factor of at least q which is close to 1. The other block does p-moves, where p is slightly larger than the stretch of a q-approximate equilibrium, and slightly smaller than the final approximation factor.

The key idea here is that blocks first converge to a q-approximate equilibrium, and thereby generate a state with a stretch of approximately p. Later, when players of a block are allowed to do p-moves, there is not much potential left to move. In particular, there is no significant influence on players of blocks that moved earlier possible. This finally results in the approximation factor of roughly p. We modify the algorithm in [9] by changing the cost seen by the players during their q-moves to be the modified cost generated using a linear programming approach, to achieve a significantly smaller stretch, and this results in an improved approximation factor. For the sake of completeness we present the algorithm as Algorithm 1, but note that only the definition of $\theta(q)$ using $\lambda := \max_{e \in E} \lambda_e$, the definition of p in Line 1, and the use of the modified cost functions in Line 11 has been changed. Before we analyze the correctness of the algorithm, we describe how the modified cost functions can be computed.

Modified Cost Functions

After a long series of papers in which various authors (e.g. [2,3,14]) show upper bounds on the price of anarchy, Roughgarden exhibited that most of them essentially used the same technique, which is formalized as (λ, μ)-smoothness [30]. A game is called (λ, μ)-smooth, if for every pair of outcomes s, s^*, it holds that,

---

Algorithm 1. Computing a $\lambda(1 + \epsilon)$-approximate pure Nash equilibria in congestion games.

Input: Congestion game $G = \left(\mathcal{N}, E, (S_u)_{u \in \mathcal{N}}, (f_e)_{e \in E}\right)$ and $\epsilon > 0$.
Output: A state of G in $\lambda(1 + \epsilon)$-approximate pure Nash equilibrium.

1: Set $q = \left(1 + \frac{1}{N^c}\right)$, $p = \left(\frac{1}{\theta(q)} - \frac{1 + q + 2\lambda}{N^c}\right)^{-1}$, $c = 10 \log\left(\frac{\lambda}{\epsilon}\right)$, $\Delta = \max_{e \in E} \frac{f_e(N)}{f_e(1)}$ and
   $\theta(q) = \frac{\lambda}{1 + \frac{1-q}{q} N \lambda}$, where $\lambda := \max_{e \in E} \lambda_e$
2: **foreach** $u \in \mathcal{N}$ **do**
3:    set $\ell_u = c_u\left(\mathcal{BR}_u(0)\right)$;
4: **end for**
5: Set $\ell_{min} = \min_{u \in \mathcal{N}} \ell_u$, $\ell_{max} = \max_{u \in \mathcal{N}} \ell_u$ and $\hat{z} = 1 + \lceil \log_{2\Delta N^{2c+2}}(\ell_{max}/\ell_{min}) \rceil$;
6: Assign players to blocks $B_1, B_2, \cdots, B_{\hat{z}}$ such that
   $$u \in B_i \Leftrightarrow \ell_u \in \left(\ell_{max}\left(2\Delta N^{2c+2}\right)^{-i}, \ell_{max}\left(2\Delta N^{2c+2}\right)^{-i+1}\right];$$
7: **foreach** $u \in N$ **do**
8:    set the player u to play the strategy $s_u \leftarrow \mathcal{BR}_u(0)$;
9: **end for**
10: **for** phase $i \leftarrow 1$ to $\hat{z} - 1$ such that $B_i \neq \emptyset$ **do**
11:    **while** $\exists u \in B_i$ with a p-move w.r.t the original cost f or $\exists u \in B_{i+1}$ with a q-move w.r.t to modified cost f' **do**
12:       u deviates to that best-response strategy $s_u \leftarrow \mathcal{BR}(s_1, \cdots, s_n)$.
13:    **end while**
14: **end for**

$\sum_{u \in \mathcal{N}} c_u(s_u^*, s_{-u}) \leq \lambda \cdot c(s^*) + \mu \cdot c(s)$. The price of anarchy of a (λ, μ)-smooth game with $\lambda > 0$ and $\mu < 1$ is then at most $\frac{\lambda}{1-\mu}$. Observe that the original smoothness definition can be extended to allow for an arbitrary objective function $h(s)$ instead of the social cost function $c(s) = \sum_{u \in \mathcal{N}} c_u(s)$.

Definition 1. *A game is* (λ, μ)-*smooth with respect to an objective function* h, *if for every pair of outcome* s, s^*, $\lambda \cdot h(s^*) \geq \sum_{u \in \mathcal{N}} c_u(s_u^*, s_{-u}) - \sum_{u \in \mathcal{N}} c_u(s) + (1 - \mu)h(s)$.

From the definition above, we restate the central smoothness theorem [30].

Theorem 2. *Given a* (λ, μ)-*smooth game* G *with* $\lambda > 0$, $\mu < 1$, *and an objective function* h, *then for every equilibrium* s *and the global optimum* s^*, $h(s) \leq \frac{\lambda}{1-\mu} h(s^*)$.

The proof is analogous to Roughgarden's proof [30]. We remark that a variant to our extension of Roughgarden's smoothness framework is independently introduced as *generalized smoothness* in [11–13].

In the following we study games in which we change the cost functions c_u experienced by the players. By scaling the cost functions appropriately, we always ensure that we can satisfy the above inequality with $\mu = 0$. Observe that, given a game $G = \left(\mathcal{N}, (S_u)_{u \in \mathcal{N}}, (c_u)_{u \in \mathcal{N}}\right)$, we can determine new cost functions c_u' for which the value of λ is minimized, for all pairs of solutions s, s^*. However, observe that since the state space S grows exponentially in the number of players, this would be computationally inefficient. Therefore, we typically have to work with games in which the players' costs and the objective function h can be represented in a succinct way. In congestion games, the players cost and the global objective function are implicitly defined by the resource cost function. In the following, we allow for an arbitrary, additive objective function $h(s)$, i.e., of the form $h(s) = \sum_{e \in E} h_e(n_e(s))$, and we can conveniently restate the smoothness condition as follows.

Lemma 1. *A congestion game is* $(\lambda, 0)$-*smooth with respect to an objective function* $h(s) = \sum_{e \in E} h_e(n_e(s))$, *if for every non-decreasing cost function* $f'_e : \mathbb{N} \mapsto \mathbb{R}_+$ *and for every* $0 \leq n, m \leq N$, $\lambda \cdot h_e(m) \geq m f'_e(n+1) - n f'_e(n) + h_e(n)$.

Lemma 1 immediately gives rise to the following optimization problem: Given an objective function $h(s) = \sum_{e \in E} h_e(n_e(s))$, find functions f'_e that minimize λ. For a resource objective function h_e and a bound on the number of players N this can be easily solved by the following linear program LP_h with the variables $f'_e(0), \dots, f'_e(N+1)$ and λ_e.

$$\min \lambda_e$$

$$\lambda_e \cdot h_e(m) - m f'_e(n+1) + n f'_e(n) \geq h_e(n) \quad \text{for all } n \in [0, N], m \in [0, N]$$
$$f'_e(n+1) \geq f'_e(n) \quad \text{for all } n \in [0, N]$$
$$f'_e(n) \geq 0 \quad \text{for all } n \in [0, N+1]$$

Henceforth, we use $f' = (f'_e)_{e \in E}$ whenever we refer to cost functions that are the solution to an optimization problem and denote the players cost by $c'_u(s) = \sum_{e \in s_u} f'_e(n_e(s))$. Observe that LP_h is compact, i.e, the number of constraints and variables are polynomially bounded in the number of players. Hence, we state the following theorem.

Theorem 3. *Optimal resource cost functions* f'_e *for objective functions* h_e *can be computed in polynomial time.*

Improving the Approximation Factor
In order to achieve a better approximation factor than that in Caragiannis et al. [9] we modify the algorithm in [9] by changing the cost functions seen by the players during their q-moves to be the modified cost generated by the linear program LP_ϕ arising from Lemma 1 with the potential as its objective function. This results in an improved approximation factor $\lambda(1 + \epsilon)$ for $\epsilon > 0$, where $\lambda := \max_{e \in E} \lambda_e$ is the optimal solution value of LP_ϕ that we state below. Unfortunately, it is not possible to simply use the LP above with the potential function as its objective function, since Algorithm 1 uses the potential function argument for a subset of players $F \subseteq \mathcal{N}$. More precisely, it needs that the approximation factor also holds for an arbitrary subset of players and its induced subgame. Let us denote by $n_e^F(s)$ the number of players in F that use the resource e in the state s. Define the potential of this subset as the potential in the subgame induced by these players in s, i.e, $\phi^F(s) := \sum_{i=1}^{n_e^F(s)} f_e(i + n_e^{\mathcal{N} \setminus F}(s))$. With slight abuse of notation, we remark that $\phi^F(s)$ and $\phi_F(s)$ are equivalent. Now consider an arbitrary subset of players $F \subseteq \mathcal{N}$ and a state s.

Then, $G_s^F := (F, E, (S_u)_{u \in F}, (f_e^F)_{e \in E})$ is the subgame induced by freezing the remaining players from $\mathcal{N} \setminus F$, with $f_e^F(x) := f_e(x + n_e^{\mathcal{N} \setminus F}(s))$, where $n_e^{\mathcal{N} \setminus F}(s)$ is the number of players outside of F on resource e in the state s. Henceforth, for our purposes, the following definition is a stronger notion of the $(\lambda, 0)$-smoothness.

Definition 2. *A strategic game is strongly $(\lambda, 0)$-smooth with respect to an objective function h, and for some $\lambda > 0$, if for every subset $F \subseteq \mathcal{N}$ and for every $s, s^* \in S$, $\lambda \cdot h^F(s^*) \geq \sum_{u \in F} c_u'(s_u^*, s_{-u}) - \sum_{u \in F} c_u'(s) + h^F(s)$, where $h^F(s) := \sum_{e \in E} h_e(n_e(s)) - h_e(n_e^{\mathcal{N} \setminus F}(s))$.*

We would like to remark that all future references to $(\lambda, 0)$-smoothness in Sect. 3 imply strong $(\lambda, 0)$-smoothness. As a consequence of Definition 2, we state the following lemma.

Lemma 2. *For every congestion game G with non-decreasing cost functions $f_e' : \mathbb{N} \mapsto \mathbb{R}_+$, which is $(\lambda, 0)$-smooth with respect to the potential function ϕ_e for every subgame G_s^F induced by an arbitrary subset $F \subseteq \mathcal{N}$, and arbitrary states $s, s^* \in S$, i.e., $\lambda \cdot \phi_e^F(s^*) - n_e^F(s^*) \cdot f_e'(n_e(s) + 1) + n_e^F(s) \cdot f_e'(n_e(s)) \geq \phi_e^F(s)$, with $\lambda > 0$, is also strongly $(\lambda, 0)$-smooth.*

This subset property is of particular importance for the algorithm to compute an approximate equilibrium, but may be of independent interest as well. We are not aware of other approximation algorithms that can guarantee this property as well. From Lemma 2, for any resource $e \in E$, the modified cost functions f_e' are computed by the following linear program LP_ϕ.

$$\min \lambda_e$$

$$\lambda_e \sum_{i=z+1}^{m+z} f_e(i) - m f_e'(n + z + 1) + n f_e'(n + z) \geq \sum_{i=z+1}^{n+z} f_e(i) \quad \forall (n + z), m \in [0, N]$$

$$f_e'(n + 1) \geq f_e'(n) \qquad \forall n \in [0, N]$$

$$f_e'(n) \geq 0 \qquad \forall n \in [0, N + 1]$$

We are now ready to prove Theorem 1, by restating it as follows.

Theorem 4. *For every constant $\epsilon > 0$, Algorithm 1 computes a $\lambda(1 + \epsilon)$-approximate equilibrium for every congestion game with non-decreasing cost functions, and $\lambda = \max_{e \in E} \lambda_e$, in number of steps which is polynomial in the number of players, $\Delta := \frac{f(N)}{f(1)}$ and $1/\epsilon$.*

The proof of the theorem follows the proof scheme of Caragiannis et al. [9], which we have to rework to accommodate for our modification. The complete proof of the theorem is omitted due to space constraints (see full version [33]). Note that for cost functions which are polynomials of maximum degree d with non negative coefficients, Δ is polynomial in the number of players. In the following, we sketch the main proof idea. Here, we have to take into account that the game played by the players from $B_i \cup B_{i+1}$ in phase i is no longer a potential game as the players use different cost functions. However, we can show that the strong smoothness constraints of the LP guarantees that the values of the new cost functions can be conveniently bounded.

Lemma 3. *Let f' to be the modified cost functions generated by the LP_ϕ and f to be the original cost functions. Then for all $i \geq 1$, $f_e(i) \leq f'_e(i) \leq \lambda f_e(i)$.*

To bound the stretch of any (sub-)game in a q-approximate equilibrium the following lemma is useful. We remark that for this lemma, the property that the induced subgames are also smooth (Lemma 2) is crucial.

Lemma 4. *Let s be any q-approximate equilibrium with respect to the modified cost function, and s^* be a strategy profile with minimal potential. Then for every $F \subseteq \mathcal{N}$, $\phi_F(s) \leq \theta(q) \cdot \phi_F(s^*)$.*

We now bound the potential of the set of players $R_i \subseteq B_i \cup B_{i+1}$ that move in phase i. Most importantly, the players of B_i, were in an q-approximate equilibrium with respect to c'_u at the end of the previous round. Hence, for every subset of B_i, we can exploit Lemma 4 to obtain a small upper bound on the potential amongst players R_i participating in a phase i at the beginning of the phase. For a phase i, let $b_i := \ell_{max} \left(2\Delta N^{2c+2}\right)^{-i+1}$ and s^i denote the state of the game after the execution of phase i.

Lemma 5. *For every phase $i \geq 2$, it holds that $\phi_{R_i}(s^{i-1}) \leq \frac{b_i}{N^c}$.*

To analyze convergence, we have to take into account the fact that players use different latency functions. However, it turns out that the Rosenthal potential with respect to the modified cost functions can serve as an approximate potential function, i.e., it also decreases for the p-moves of players using the original cost functions.

Lemma 6. *Let $u \in \mathcal{N}$ be a player that makes a p-move with respect to the original cost function f. Then, $p \cdot c_u(s'_u, s_{-u}) - c_u(s) \geq q \cdot c'_u(s'_u, s_{-u}) - c'_u(s)$, where c_u and c'_u are the cost of the player u with respect to f and f', respectively.*

Using Lemma 5 and Lemma 6, we can bound the runtime which has to be slightly larger and has to depend on Δ to allow for arbitrary non-decreasing functions.

Lemma 7. *The algorithm terminates after at most $\mathcal{O}(\lambda \Delta^3 N^{5c+5})$ best-response moves.*

The next lemma shows that when players involved in phases $i \geq 2$ make their moves, they do not increase the cost of players in the blocks $B_1, B_2, \cdots, B_{i-1}$ significantly.

Lemma 8. *Let u be a player in the block B_t, where $t \leq \hat{z} - 2$. Let s'_u be a strategy different from the one assigned to u by the algorithm at the end of the phase t. Then, for each phase $i \geq t$, it holds that, $c_u(s^i) \leq p \cdot c_u(s'_u, s^i_{-u}) + \frac{2p+1}{N^c} \sum_{k=t+1}^{i} b_k$.*

As no players' costs and alternatives is significantly influenced by moves in later blocks, they remain in an approximate equilibrium which can be used to finally prove the correctness of the algorithm.

Lemma 9. *The state computed by the algorithm is a $p\left(1 + \frac{5}{N^c}\right)$-approximate equilibrium.*

Linear and Polynomial Cost Functions. We now turn to the important class of polynomial cost functions with non-negative coefficients. We can show that for polynomials of small degree, it is sufficient to restrict the attention to the first $K = 150$ values of the cost functions. Hence, we only need to solve a linear program of constant size. The following lemma states that for the larger values of n and appropriate values of λ_d and ν, we can easily obtain $(\lambda_d, 0)$-smoothness by choosing $f'(n) = \nu n^d$. We further note, that for a given $\lambda_d > 0$, and for each n and z we only need to consider a limited range for m.

Lemma 10. *For $d \leq 5$ and $n \geq 150$, the function $f'(n) = \nu n^d$ with $\nu = \sqrt[d+1]{\lambda_d}$ is $(\lambda_d, 0)$-smooth with respect to the potential function ϕ for an appropriate λ_d.*

Lemma 11. *For fixed n, z, if $\lambda_d \cdot \sum_{i=z+1}^{m+z} i^d - mf'(n+z+1) + nf'(n+z) \geq \sum_{i=z+1}^{n+z} i^d$ is true $\forall m \leq (n+z+1)^2(d+1)$, it also holds $\forall m > (n+z+1)^2(d+1)$.*

By Lemma 10 and 11 it remains to solve a linear program of constant size to obtain our results ρ_d as listed in Table 1 for $d \leq 5$.

Corollary 1. *For every congestion game with polynomial cost functions of degree $d \leq 5$, and for every constant $\epsilon > 0$, the algorithm computes a $(\rho_d + \epsilon)$-approximate pure Nash equilibrium in polynomial time.*

Lower Bound. Any feasible solution to the linear program LP_h emerging from Lemma 1 are cost functions $f'_e : \mathbb{N} \mapsto R_+$ that guarantees that the objective value associated with the function h is at most λ. We can show that this is in fact optimal. That is, LP_h is not only optimizing the smoothness inequality, but also that there exists no other resource cost function that can guarantee a smaller objective value than λ. To that end, we consider the dual of LP_h (LPD_h) and show that for every feasible solution of the dual, we can construct an instance of a selfish scheduling game on identical machines with an objective value that is equal to the value of the dual LP solution, regardless of the actual cost function of the game.

Lemma 12. *Every optimal solution of LPD_h with objective value λ can be turned into an instance of selfish scheduling on identical machines with an objective value of $\lambda - \epsilon$ for an arbitrary $\epsilon > 0$.*

4   Extensions

The smoothness framework introduced by Roughgarden [30] also extends to equilibrium concepts such as mixed Nash and (coarse) correlated equilibria. The same is true for our variant with respect to an arbitrary objective function h. We now look at an extension of Lemma 1 for computing load dependent universal taxes in congestion games.

Load Dependent Universal Taxes. One of the many approaches used to improve the PoA is the introduction of taxes. For a set of resources E, the load dependent tax function t, is the excess cost incurred by the user on a resource $e \in E$ with cost $f(x)$, e.g., $f'(x) = f(x) + t(x)$. We remark that the taxes we consider in this work are refundable, and do not contribute to the overall cost of the game.

Meyers and Schulz [24] studied the complexity of computing an optimal solution in a congestion game and prove NP-hardness. Makarychev and Sviridenko [23] give the best known approximation algorithm using randomized rounding on a natural feasibility LP with approximation factor $\mathcal{B}_{d+1}$ which is the $d+1^{\text{th}}$ Bell number, where d is the maximum degree of the polynomial cost function. Interestingly, the same was later achieved using load dependent taxes by Bilò and Vinci [6], where they apply the *primal-dual* method [4] to upper bound the PoA under refundable taxation in congestion games. They determine a load specific taxation to show that the PoA is at most $[O(d/\log d)]^{d+1}$ under refundable taxation. However, we remark that the load dependent taxes computed in [6] aren't universal, i.e, they are sensitive to the instance of the game.

We give a rather simple approach to locally (on resource) compute load dependent *universal* taxes. Table 2 lists the improved PoA bounds under refundable taxation using our technique for congestion games with resource cost functions that are bounded degree polynomials of maximum degree d. By the smoothness argument [30] the new bounds immediately extends to mixed, (coarse) correlated equilibria and outcomes generated by no-regret sequences. Moreover, since the linear program that computes the cost or tax function does only depend on the original cost function of that resource, the computed taxes are robust against perturbations of the instance such as adding or removing of resources or players.

Optimal Universal Taxes. We seek to compute universal load dependent taxes that minimize the PoA under refundable taxation. We consider the following optimization problem. For an objective function $h(s) = \sum_{e \in E} n_e(s) \cdot f_e(n_e(s))$, find functions f'_e that satisfies Lemma 1 minimizing λ. For a resource objective function $h_e(n_e(s)) = n_e(s) \cdot f_e(n_e(s))$ and a bound on the number of players N, this can be easily solved by the following linear program LP_{SC} with the variables $f'_e(0), \ldots, f'_e(N+1)$ and λ_e.

$$\min \lambda_e$$
$$\lambda_e \cdot h_e(m) - mf'_e(n+1) + nf'_e(n) \geq h_e(n) \quad \text{for all } n \in [0, N], m \in [0, N]$$

$$f'_e(n+1) \geq f'_e(n) \qquad\qquad \forall n \in [0, N]$$
$$f'_e(n) \geq 0 \qquad\qquad \text{for all } n \in [0, N+1]$$

Observe that we can solve LP_{SC} locally for each resource with cost function f_e. For the LP solution λ_e and $f'_e(n)$, define the tax function as $t_e(n) := f'_e(n) - f_e(n)$. The resulting price of anarchy under taxation is then $\lambda := \max_{e \in E} \lambda_e$. From Lemma 12 we remark that the taxes computed by LP_{SC} are optimal. Evidently our lower bound of 2.012 for congestion games with linear cost functions matches the price of anarchy bound for selfish scheduling games on identical machines [10]. For any (distributed) local search algorithm (such as Bjelde et al. [8]) that seeks to minimizes the social cost $c(s) = \sum_{e \in E} n_e(s) f_e(n_e(s))$, we define $\zeta_{\text{SC}}(s) := \sum_{e \in E} \sum_{i=1}^{n_e(s)} f'_e(i)$ as a pseudo-potential function. Then, from Lemma 1 it is guaranteed that every local optimum with respect to $\zeta_{\text{SC}}(s)$ has an approximation factor of at most $\lambda := \max_{e \in E} \lambda_e$ with respect to the social cost $c(s)$. Using approximate local search by Orlin et al. [25], we can compute a solution close to that in polynomial time, and more so to state the following.

Corollary 2. *For every congestion game the ϵ-local search algorithm using $\zeta_{\text{SC}}(s)$, produces a $\lambda(1 + \epsilon)$ local optimum in running time polynomial in the input length and $1/\epsilon$.*

Linear and Polynomial Cost Functions. For the interesting case of polynomial resource cost functions of maximum degree d, similar to Sect. 3, we show that for polynomials of small degree, it is sufficient to restrict the attention to the first 1154 values of the cost functions. Hence, we only need solve a linear program of constant size. We further note, that for a fixed $\lambda_d > 0$, and for each n we only need to consider a limited range for m in the LP_{SC}.

Lemma 13. *For $d \leq 5$ and $n \geq 1154$, the function $f'(n) = \nu n^d$ with $\nu = \sqrt[d+1]{(d+1)\lambda_d}$ is $(\lambda_d, 0)$-smooth with respect to $h(n) = n^{d+1}$ and an appropriate λ_d.*

Lemma 14. *For a fixed n, if $\lambda_d \cdot m^{d+1} - mf(n+1) + nf(n) \geq n^{d+1}$ is true for all $m \leq (n+1)^2$, it also holds for all $m > (n+1)^2$.*

As a consequence of Lemma 13 and 14 it only remains to solve a linear program of constant size for each $d \leq 5$ to obtain our results Ψ_d (listed in Table 2). Our results match the recent results that were obtained independently by Paccagnan et al. [26].

Corollary 3. *For every congestion game with polynomial cost functions of degree $d \leq 5$, each cost function f'_e can be computed in constant time and the resulting game is $(\Psi_d, 0)$-smooth with respect to social cost.*

5   Conclusion and Open Problems

The most interesting question which was the initial motivation for this work is the complexity of approximate equilibria. We find it very surprising that the technique yields such a significant improvement, e.g., for linear congestion games from 2 to 1.61, by using essentially the same algorithm of Caragiannis et al. [9]. However, the algorithmic technique is limited only by the lower bound for approximation factor of the stretch implied in Roughgarden [31]. Hence, further significant improvements may need new algorithmic ideas. On the lower bound side, not much is known for linear or polynomial congestion games. The only computational lower bound for approximate equilibria is from Skopalik and Vöcking [34] using unnatural, and very steep cost functions.

We believe that the technique of perturbing the instance of an (optimization) problem such that a simple local search heuristic (or an equilibrium) guarantees an improved approximation ratio can be applied in other settings as well. It would be interesting to see, whether one can achieve similar results for variants and generalizations of congestion games such as weighted [3], atomic- or integer-splittable [27,32] congestion games, scheduling games [16,17,20], etc. Considering other heuristics such as greedy or one-round walks [5,7,15,21] would be another natural direction.

References

1. Ackermann, H., Röglin, H., Vöcking, B.: On the impact of combinatorial structure on congestion games. J. ACM **55**(6), 25:1–25:22 (2008)
2. Aland, S., Dumrauf, D., Gairing, M., Monien, B., Schoppmann, F.: Exact price of anarchy for polynomial congestion games. SIAM J. Comput. **40**(5) (2011)
3. Awerbuch, B., Azar, Y., Epstein, A.: The price of routing unsplittable flow. In: Proceedings of the Thirty-Seventh Annual ACM Symposium on Theory of Computing. STOC (2005)
4. Bilò, V.: A unifying tool for bounding the quality of non-cooperative solutions in weighted congestion games. Theor. Comp. Syst. **62**(5), 1288–1317 (2018). https://doi.org/10.1007/978-3-642-38016-7_18
5. Bilò, V., Fanelli, A., Flammini, M., Moscardelli, L.: Performance of one-round walks in linear congestion games. Theory Comput. Syst. **49**(1), 24–45 (2011). https://doi.org/10.1007/s00224-010-9309-0
6. Bilò, V., Vinci, C.: Dynamic taxes for polynomial congestion games. In: Proceedings of the 2016 ACM Conference on Economics and Computation. EC (2016)
7. Bilò, V., Vinci, C.: On the impact of singleton strategies in congestion games. In: 25th Annual European Symposium on Algorithms (ESA) (2017)
8. Bjelde, A., Klimm, M., Schmand, D.: Brief announcement: approximation algorithms for unsplittable resource allocation problems with diseconomies of scale. In: Proceedings of the 29th ACM Symposium on Parallelism in Algorithms and Architectures. SPAA 2017, ACM, New York, NY, USA (2017)
9. Caragiannis, I., Fanelli, A., Gravin, N., Skopalik, A.: Efficient computation of approximate pure Nash equilibria in congestion games. In: Proceedings of the 2011 IEEE 52nd Annual Symposium on Foundations of Computer Science. FOCS (2011)
10. Caragiannis, I., Flammini, M., Kaklamanis, C., Kanellopoulos, P., Moscardelli, L.: Tight bounds for selfish and greedy load balancing. In: Bugliesi, M., Preneel, B., Sassone, V., Wegener, I. (eds.) ICALP 2006. LNCS, vol. 4051, pp. 311–322. Springer, Heidelberg (2006). https://doi.org/10.1007/11786986_28

11. Chandan, R., Paccagnan, D., Marden, J.R.: When smoothness is not enough: toward exact quantification and optimization of the price-of-anarchy. In: 2019 IEEE 58th Conference on Decision and Control (CDC) (2019)
12. Chandan, R., Paccagnan, D., Ferguson, B.L., Marden, J.R.: Computing optimal taxes in atomic congestion games. In: Proceedings of the 14th Workshop on the Economics of Networks, Systems and Computation. NetEcon (2019)
13. Chandan, R., Paccagnan, D., Marden, J.R.: Optimal mechanisms for distributed resource-allocation. Preprint (2019). http://arxiv.org/abs/1911.07823
14. Christodoulou, G., Koutsoupias, E.: The price of anarchy of finite congestion games. In: Proceedings of the Thirty-seventh Annual ACM Symposium on Theory of Computing. STOC 2005, ACM, New York, NY, USA (2005)
15. Christodoulou, G., Mirrokni, V.S., Sidiropoulos, A.: Convergence and approximation in potential games. Theoret. Comput. Sci. **438** (2012)
16. Cole, R., Correa, J., Gkatzelis, V., Mirrokni, V., Olver, N.: Decentralized utilitarian mechanisms for scheduling games. Games Econ. Behav. **92**, 306–326 (2015)
17. Correa, J., Queyranne, M.: Efficiency of equilibria in restricted uniform machine scheduling with total weighted completion time as social cost. Naval Res. Logistics **59**(5), 384–395 (2012)
18. Fabrikant, A., Papadimitriou, C., Talwar, K.: The complexity of pure Nash equilibria. In: Proceedings of the Thirty-Sixth Annual ACM Symposium on Theory of Computing. STOC 2004, ACM, New York, NY, USA (2004)
19. Feldotto, M., Gairing, M., Skopalik, A.: Bounding the potential function in congestion games and approximate pure Nash equilibria. In: Liu, T.-Y., Qi, Q., Ye, Y. (eds.) WINE 2014. LNCS, vol. 8877, pp. 30–43. Springer, Cham (2014). https://doi.org/10.1007/978-3-319-13129-0_3
20. Gairing, M., Lücking, T., Mavronicolas, M., Monien, B.: Computing Nash equilibria for scheduling on restricted parallel links. Theory of Computing Systems **47**(2), 405–435 (2010). https://doi.org/10.1007/s00224-009-9191-9
21. Klimm, M., Schmand, D., Tönnis, A.: The online best reply algorithm for resource allocation problems. In: Fotakis, D., Markakis, E. (eds.) SAGT 2019. LNCS, vol. 11801, pp. 200–215. Springer, Cham (2019). https://doi.org/10.1007/978-3-030-30473-7_14
22. Koutsoupias, E., Papadimitriou, C.: Worst-case equilibria. In: Proceedings of the 16th Annual Conference on Theoretical Aspects of Computer Science. STACS (1999)
23. Makarychev, K., Sviridenko, M.: Solving optimization problems with diseconomies of scale via decoupling. In: Proceedings of the 2014 IEEE 55th Annual Symposium on Foundations of Computer Science. FOCS (2014)
24. Meyers, C.A., Schulz, A.S.: The complexity of welfare maximization in congestion games. Networks **59**(2), 252–260 (2012)
25. Orlin, J.B., Punnen, A.P., Schulz, A.S.: Approximate local search in combinatorial optimization. In: Proceedings of the Fifteenth Annual ACM-SIAM Symposium on Discrete Algorithms. SODA (2004)
26. Paccagnan, D., Chandan, R., Ferguson, B.L., Marden, J.R.: Incentivizing efficient use of shared infrastructure: optimal tolls in congestion games. Preprint (2020). http://arxiv.org/abs/1911.09806
27. Rosenthal, R.W.: The network equilibrium problem in integers. Networks **3**(1), 53–59 (1973)
28. Rosenthal, R.W.: A class of games possessing pure-strategy Nash equilibria. Int. J. Game Theory **2**(1), 65–67 (1973). https://doi.org/10.1007/BF01737559

29. Roughgarden, T., Tardos, E.: How bad is selfish routing? In: Proceedings 41st Annual Symposium on Foundations of Computer Science, pp. 93–102, November 2000
30. Roughgarden, T.: Intrinsic robustness of the price of anarchy. In: Proceedings of the Forty-First Annual ACM Symposium on Theory of Computing. STOC (2009)
31. Roughgarden, T.: Barriers to near-optimal equilibria. In: Proceedings of the 2014 IEEE 55th Annual Symposium on Foundations of Computer Science. FOCS (2014)
32. Roughgarden, T., Schoppmann, F.: Local smoothness and the price of anarchy in atomic splittable congestion games. In: Proceedings of the Twenty-second Annual ACM-SIAM Symposium on Discrete Algorithms. SODA (2011)
33. Skopalik, A., Vijayalakshmi, V.R.: Improving approximate pure Nash equilibria in congestion games. Preprint (2020). https://arxiv.org/abs/2007.15520
34. Skopalik, A., Vöcking, B.: Inapproximability of pure Nash equilibria. In: Proceedings of the 40th Annual ACM Symposium on Theory of Computing. STOC (2008)

The Curse of Rationality in Sequential Scheduling Games

Cong Chen[1]([⊠])[iD] and Yinfeng Xu[2]

[1] School of Business Administration, South China University of Technology,
Guangzhou, China
chencong@scut.edu.cn
[2] School of Management, Xi'an Jiaotong University, Xi'an, China

Abstract. Despite the emphases on computability issues in research of
algorithmic game theory, the limited computational capacity of players
have received far less attention. This work examines how different levels
of players' computational ability (or "rationality") impact the outcomes
of *sequential scheduling games*. Surprisingly, our results show that a lower
level of rationality of players may lead to better equilibria.

More specifically, we characterize the sequential price of anarchy
(SPoA) under two different models of bounded rationality, namely, *players with k-lookahead* and *simple-minded players*. The model in which
players have k-lookahead interpolates between the "perfect rationality"
($k = n - 1$) and "online greedy" ($k = 0$). Our results show that the
inefficiency of equilibria (SPoA) increases in k the degree of lookahead:
SPoA $= O(k^2)$ for two machines and SPoA $= O\left(2^k \min\{mk, n\}\right)$ for
m machines, where n is the number of players. Moreover, when players are simple-minded, the SPoA is exactly m, which coincides with the
performance of "online greedy".

Keywords: Scheduling game · Subgame-perfect equilibrium ·
Bounded rationality · Sequential price of anarchy

1 Introduction

Research on algorithmic game theory – a fascinating fusion of both game theory
and algorithms – has attracted a lot of computer scientists and economists. The
core of this research field is to take the computability (computational complexity)
into consideration while studying game theory problems, such as the complexity
of finding Nash equilibria and the computational issues in mechanism design.
However, the computational ability of players has received little attention from
the community, despite its strong ties to computational complexity and the

Cong Chen gratefully acknowledges support from the China Postdoctoral Science Foundation (No. 2020M672646), the National Natural Science Foundation of China (No.
71720107002) and the National Natural Science Foundation of China-Guangdong Joint
Fund (No. U1901223).

X. Chen et al. (Eds.): WINE 2020, LNCS 12495, pp. 295–308, 2020.
https://doi.org/10.1007/978-3-030-64946-3_21

Table 1. An example from [4] with 5 jobs and 2 machines, where the SPE is shown as gray boxes.

	Job 1	Job 2	Job 3	Job 4	Job 5
Machine 1	$3 - 11\epsilon$	ϵ	ϵ	$1 - 2\epsilon$	$2 - 8\epsilon$
Machine 2	ϵ	$2 - 9\epsilon$	$2 - 8\epsilon$	$1 - 2\epsilon$	$1 - 2\epsilon$

actual behavior of players playing a game. Most research assumes the players always have the ability to compute an optimal decision, even though sometimes finding an optimal decision is a very difficult problem (e.g. NPC problem). Our work examines the impact of different levels of computational ability (also termed as "rationality" in this paper) of players on the outcomes of *sequential scheduling games*. Surprisingly, the results show that a lower level of rationality may produce better equilibrium outcomes.

Sequential Scheduling Game (On Unrelated Machines). There are n jobs $N = \{1, 2, \ldots, n\}$ as players and m machines $M = \{1, 2, \ldots, m\}$ as strategies. Each job j will take $p_{i,j}$ units of time if processed by machine i. The jobs sequentially choose one of the machines for processing, starting with job 1 and ending with job n. The load of a machine is the total processing times of the jobs processed on it. The goal of each job is to choose a machine with a smallest possible load.

When a job makes decision, he knows the choices made by his predecessors as well as the processing times of his successors. However, it is very hard for the job to compute an optimal decision. Indeed, [11] showed that for the unrelated machine scheduling computing a *subgame-perfect equilibrium* (SPE) is PSPACE-complete. One can glance at the example shown in Table 1 to see how hard to find the optimal decision (in gray box) for job 1, and how easily the job may deviate from his optimal choice (to choose machine 2 with a very small processing time ϵ) without enough computational ability.

Price of Anarchy and the Curse of Rationality. The concept of the price of anarchy (PoA), proposed by [8] to assess the inefficiency of equilibria outcomes, has attracted many research over the past two decades. To further understand the quality of SPEs outcomes of a game, [11] introduced the *sequential price of anarchy* (SPoA). While the PoA compares the cost of a worst case Nash equilibrium to the optimal social cost, the SPoA considers the outcomes of a sequential game where players, instead of choosing their strategies simultaneously, choose their strategies sequentially in some arbitrary order.

It turns out the PoA is very bad (unbounded) for even two unrelated machines, and introducing sequentiality only slightly improves the outcomes – the SPoA grows linearly with the number n of players [4]. However, when we look carefully at the worst case scenario, which gives the lower bound of SPoA for two unrelated machines in [4], we find that the equilibrium is very unnatural and can hardly be achieved in reality, unless each player can solve a PSPACE-complete problem while making decision. The example in Table 1 already reveals the phenomenon that the first two players have to make a very complex computation to counter-intuitively choose a machine with a very high processing time rather than the one with almost 0 processing time.

Perhaps surprisingly, instead of assuming all the players have such strong rationality, if players are myopic (i.e., decisions are made only based on the predecessors' decision), the SPoA will be significantly improved to 2 for two unrelated machines, where the result can be deduced from the online greedy scheduling problem [1]. This result illustrates that full rationality may have a negative effect on the quality of outcomes. Our work mainly investigates the impact of different levels of rationality on the SPoA for the unrelated machines scheduling game.

Modeling the Bounded Rationality. The notion of *bounded rationality* can be traced back to the pioneering work of [14]. Herbert Simon defines bounded rationality as "rational choice that takes account the cognitive limitations of the decision-maker – limitations of both knowledge and computational capacity". Frank Hahn remarks that "there is only one way to be perfectly rational, while there are an infinity of ways to be partially rational..." [10]. Indeed, there are tons of literature tried to model the bounded rationality. We refer the readers to some surveys (see, e.g., [6,10,15]) for details.

This paper propose two ways to model the bounded rationality of players:

1. *Players with k-lookahead.* We suppose each player only considers the next few successors' information for computing his decision, in addition to the known predecessors' decisions. We say a player has a *k-lookahead* ability if he can compute the optimal decision depending on his next k successors' information and the predecessors' decisions. Specifically, when a player makes decision, he will draw a $(k+1)$-level game tree (including the node of himself), assign the corresponding costs to the leaves, and then perform backward induction to decide which move to make. Similar setting can also be found in [2,7,9,12].

2. *Simple-minded players.* As an extension, we also examine a situation where players make decisions only via simple calculations. When a so-called simple-minded player makes decision, he simply assumes the successors will choose machines with minimum processing times, so he can easily find a best choice depending on the assumption. The setting is also very natural in the unrelated machine scheduling, since choosing a machine with minimum processing time is mostly not a bad idea, and assuming other players doing so makes the prediction of other players' behaviors much simpler.

Our Contributions. This paper mainly investigates how the degree of rationality impacts the efficiency of SPEs. We characterize the SPoA under two different models of bounded rationality, namely, *players with k-lookahead* and *simple-minded players*. In general, quantifying the SPoA is a challenging task, and no general techniques are known in the literature. In this paper, the key idea of most of our proofs is to characterize the amount of increase of the makespan or load of machine due to an additional job or set of jobs. Out main results are as follows (see also Table 2):

Table 2. A summary of results, some of which achieved in this paper are marked with "$*$"

	2 machines	m machines
Online greedy (0-lookahead)	2	m
1-lookahead	2 $*$	$O(m)$ $*$
k-lookahead	$O(k^2)$ $*$	$O\left(2^k \min\{mk, n\}\right)$ $*$
Perfect rationality (n-lookahead)	$\Theta(n)$	$O(2^n)$
Simple-minded	2 $*$	m $*$

1. In Sect. 3, we first show that for sequential scheduling game on 2 unrelated machines the SPoA is 2 for players with 1-lookahead, which coincides with the case of 0-lookahead – i.e., online greedy. This result perhaps suggests that the strategic behavior of only one player foreseen does not bring any negative influence on the current decision-maker. However, we will show in the following that the interaction of more than 2 players (i.e., 2-lookahead) may have a negative effect on the decision being made.

2. For the players with k-lookahead, we obtain that SPoA $= O(k^2)$ for 2 unrelated machines. This shows that the more lookahead the players have the worst the SPoA will be. But if we compare this result to the "perfect rationality" case where the SPoA is $\Theta(n)$ [4], which grows linearly with the number of players n, bounded rationality significantly improves the quality of SPEs. (These results are presented in Sect. 4.)

3. We also characterize the SPoA for general m unrelated machines case. We prove that SPoA $= O\left(2^k \min\{mk, n\}\right)$ for players with k-lookahead, which also improves the $O(2^n)$ upper bound for the perfect rationality case. (See Sect. 4.)

4. At last, another bounded rationality model where the players are *simple-minded* is discussed. It turns out that if assuming all the predecessors follow a simple rule – choosing the machine with minimum processing time – the player will make a decision as good as the online greedy, that is, SPoA $= m$. (The results can be found in Sect. 5.)

Further Related Work. The idea of *limited lookahead* first appeared in the 1950s [13]. Recently, the idea has been investigated in some game-theoretic setting by several research [2,7,9,12]. In particular, [2] and [7] have very similar setting to our *k-lookahead* model. However, they both focused on the congestion games. [2] studied the existence of k-lookahead equilibria and the PoA for 2-lookahead (corresponding to 1-lookahead in our setting) equilibria in congestion games with linear latencies. [7] focused on the equilibria which are not only SPEs but also Nash equilibria. They show that for generic simple congestion games the SPoA coincides with the PoA (independently of k). In fact, both of the above work failed to reveal what the role of k plays in the game, which is distinguished in the unrelated machines scheduling game by our work.

The SPoA for unrelated machines was first analyzed by [11], showing that $n \leq \text{SPoA} \leq m \cdot 2^n$. The bounds are improved to $2^{\Omega(\sqrt{n})} \leq \text{SPoA} \leq 2^n$ by [3]. However, the above lower bounds use a non-constant number of machines, which means it is still unclear whether the lower bound is constant for constant number of machines. [4] answered the question, showing that the SPoA is not constant for even two machines, that is, $\text{SPoA} = \Omega(n)$. They also provided a matching upper bound, concluding that $\text{SPoA} = \Theta(n)$ for two unrelated machines.

2 Preliminaries

We formally define the *sequential scheduling game on unrelated machines* and our two models of bounded rationality – *players with k-lookahead* and *simpleminded players*.

Sequential Scheduling Game on Unrelated Machines. Let $[a : b] = \{a, a+1, \ldots, b\}$ and $[b] = [1 : b]$ where $a, b \in \mathbb{N}$. Unrelated machine scheduling can be defined as a tuple $(N, M, (p_{i,j})_{i \in N, j \in M})$, where $N = [n]$ is the a set of jobs/players, $M = [m]$ is the set of machines/strategies, and $p_{i,j}$ is the processing time of job j on machine i. In sequential scheduling game, the jobs sequentially choose one of the machines for processing, starting with job 1 and ending with job n. A schedule $\sigma = (\sigma_1, \sigma_2, \ldots, \sigma_n)$ represents the decisions of the jobs, where σ_j is the machine which job j chooses. The *load* $L_i(N)$ of a machine i in schedule σ of jobs N is the sum of the processing times of all jobs who choose machine i, that is, $L_i(N) = \sum_{j : \sigma_j = i} p_{i,j}$. When job j makes decision, he will try to minimize his own cost $L_{\sigma_j}(N)$ – the load of machine he chooses – taking into account all his predecessors and successors. The schedule σ is thus decided. This is an *extensive form game*, and so it always possesses *subgame-perfect equilibria*, which can be calculated by backward induction.

Figure 1 gives an example of 3 jobs, in which the "perfect rationality" part depicts the game tree for this example. In this game, job 1 has to draw the whole tree, calculate the costs at each of the $2^3 = 8$ leaves, and find the best choice by backward induction. The following jobs will also go through an associated subtree in a similarly fashion. The bold lines show the subgame-perfect strategies, and the (unique) path from the root to the leaf corresponding to the black circle is the equilibrium solution (i.e., the schedule is $(2, 1, 1)$).

Players with k-Lookahead. In this model, we suppose each player can only foresee the next k players. Let $K_j = [j + 1 : j + k]$ be the lookahead set for job j, where $|K_j| = k$. When a player makes decision, he needs to draw a $(k + 1)$-level game tree (consists of himself and the successors K_j), calculate the costs for this tree (with only 2^k leaves), and find the best choose by backward induction.

The "1-lookahead" part in Fig. 1 gives an example of 3 jobs when players have 1-lookahead. In this game, job 1 only knows the information of the next job (i.e., job 2), and considers the job as the last job. After job 1 makes decision by backward induction, job 2 will compute a best choose according to job 1's

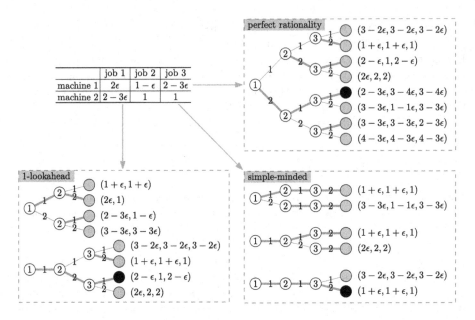

Fig. 1. An example of 3 jobs and 2 machines.

decision and the next job's information. As shown in the figure, the SPE for this example is $(1, 2, 1)$.

Simple-Minded Players. Simple-minded players ignore the strategical behaviors of their successors, and simply assume the successors will choose machines with minimum processing times. According to this, the players can directly calculate the load of each machine and find a best one.

In Fig. 1, the "simple-minded" part illustrates the decision process for each player. It shows that each player just needs to calculate the costs for only 2 leaves, and selects one machine with a lower cost. The resulting SPE for this example is $(1, 1, 2)$.

Inefficiency of Equilibria. The (social) cost of a schedule/equilibrium is often defined as the *makespan*, the maximum load over all machines. To quantify the inefficiency of SPEs, [11] introduced the sequential price of anarchy (SPoA) which compares the worst SPE with the optimal social cost:

$$\text{SPoA} = \sup_J \frac{L_{\max}(J)}{OPT(J)},$$

where J takes over all possible job sets, and $OPT(J)$ is the makespan of the optimal schedule (a schedule generated by a central authority to minimize the social cost, and is not necessary an equilibrium) for jobs J.

For example, see the instance in Fig. 1. The optimal schedule is $(1, 1, 2)$ with a makespan of $1 + \epsilon$. Since the SPE under perfect rationality is $(2, 1, 1)$ with a makespan of $3 - 4\epsilon$, the SPoA for this example is 3 (taking $\epsilon \to 0$). However, when players have only 1-lookahead, the SPoA is 2 (taking $\epsilon \to 0$). Surprisingly, the SPE generated by simple-minded players is exactly the optimal schedule, that is, SPoA = 1.

Additional Notation. We introduce a notation of initial load $\mathbf{D} = (D_1, D_2, \ldots, D_m)$ on the machines, meaning the machines already have some initial load before the jobs playing a game. Thus, $L_i(\mathbf{D}, J)$ is the load of machine i after the set J of jobs play sequentially on the machines with a initial load $\mathbf{D}$, and $L_{\max}(\mathbf{D}, J) = \max_{i \in M} L_i(\mathbf{D}, J)$ is the corresponding makespan. Notice that when $J = \emptyset$, $L_{\max}(\mathbf{D}, \emptyset) = \|\mathbf{D}\|_\infty$. Sometimes we use $\mathbf{D}(\ell) = (D_1(\ell), D_2(\ell), \ldots, D_m(\ell))$ to represent the load of each machine due to the first $\ell \in N$ jobs, where $D_i(\ell) = \sum_{j \in \{j | \sigma_j = i, 1 \le j \le \ell\}} p_{i,j}$ for $i = 1, \ldots, m$.

To denote the maximum possible increase of the makespan due to the set J of jobs for any initial load $\mathbf{D} \in \mathbb{R}_+^M$, we define:

$$\Delta L(J) = \sup_{\mathbf{D} \in \mathbb{R}_+^M} \{L_{\max}(\mathbf{D}, J) - \|\mathbf{D}\|_\infty\}.$$

For each specific machine, we also define:

$$\Delta L_i(\mathbf{D}, J) = L_i(\mathbf{D}, J) - \|\mathbf{D}\|_\infty.$$

For simplicity, we let $p_j = \min_{i \in M} p_{i,j}$ be the minimum processing time of job j, and $x_{i,j}$ represent whether job j chooses machine i in the sequential game, i.e.,

$$x_{i,j} = \begin{cases} 1, & \text{if job } j \text{ chooses machine } i, \text{ that is, } \sigma_j = i; \\ 0, & \text{otherwise.} \end{cases}$$

3   Players with 1-Lookahead on Two Unrelated Machines

In this section, we analyze the SPoA for two unrelated machine when players has 1-lookahead. We first prove a main lemma showing that the makespan is bounded by the total minimum processing time:

Lemma 1. $L_{\max}(\mathbf{0}, N) \le \sum_{j \in N} p_j$.

Proof. Since $L_{\max}(\mathbf{0}, N) = \|\mathbf{D}(n)\|_\infty$ by definition, we just prove that $\|\mathbf{D}(n)\|_\infty \le \sum_{j \in N} p_j$. First, we will define a set of $\{n_0, n_1, \ldots, n_u\}$ where $n_\ell \in \{0, 1, \ldots, n\}$ for $\ell = 0, 1, \ldots, u$ and $n_u = n$. Then we prove a claim that $\|\mathbf{D}(n_\ell)\|_\infty \le \sum_{j=1}^{n_\ell} p_j$ for $\ell = 0, 1, \ldots, u$, which indicates $\|\mathbf{D}(n)\|_\infty \le \sum_{j \in N} p_j$ and proves this lemma.

For a given set N of jobs, their processing times $p_{i,j}$ and decisions $x_{i,j}$ in the sequential game, we define a set of $\{n_0, n_1, \ldots, n_u\}$ by Algorithm 1.

We next show that the two "while loops" in Algorithm 1 (Line 5 and 8) will end at some $v \le n$. In other words, for example, if $D_1(v-1) + p_{1,v} \le D_2(v-1) + p_{2,v}$ (the first "while loop"), there must be some v' ($v \le v' \le n$) that $x_{1,v'} = 1$.

Algorithm 1: Definition of $\{n_0, n_1, \ldots, n_u\}$

Input: $p_{i,j}$ and $x_{i,j}$ for $i = 1, 2$ and $j = 1, \ldots, n$.
Output: $\{n_0, n_1, \ldots, n_u\}$.

1 $u = 0$; $v = 1$; $D_1(0) = 0$; $D_2(0) = 0$; $n_0 = 0$;
2 $D_i(\ell) = \sum_{1 \le j \le \ell} p_{i,j} \cdot x_{i,j}$ for $\ell = 1, \ldots, n$ and $i = 1, 2$;
3 **while** $v \le n$ **do**
4   **if** $D_1(v-1) + p_{1,v} \le D_2(v-1) + p_{2,v}$ **then** (n_u is the next v that $x_{1,v} == 1$)
5   **while** $x_{1,v} == 0$ **do** $v{+}{+}$;
6        $u{+}{+}$; $n_u = v$; $v{+}{+}$;
7   **else** (n_u is the next v that $x_{2,v} == 1$)
8   **while** $x_{2,v} == 0$ **do** $v{+}{+}$;
9        $u{+}{+}$; $n_u = v$; $v{+}{+}$;

We take the first "while loop" as an example and the analysis for the second one is similar. When $D_1(v-1) + p_{1,v} \le D_2(v-1) + p_{2,v}$, machine 1 is a better choice for player v regardless the decision of next player $v + 1$. If player v chooses machine 1 (i.e., $x_{1,v} = 1$), the loop ends. However, if player v chooses machine 2 (i.e., $x_{1,v} = 0$), the only reason is that player v knows player $v+1$ will choose machine 1 and $D_1(v-1) + p_{1,v} + p_{1,v+1} \ge D_2(v-1) + p_{2,v}$. What makes layer v believe player $v+1$ will choose machine 1 is that $D_1(v-1) + p_{1,v} + p_{1,v+1} \le D_2(v-1) + p_{2,v+1}$. Therefore, for player $v+1$ (after player v has made his/her decision), machine 1 is a better choice regardless the decision of next player $v+2$. Similarly, if player $v+1$ chooses machine 2 (i.e., $x_{1,v+1} = 0$), it holds that player $v+1$ believes the next player $v+2$ will also choose machine 1. In a similar fashion, we know that if player v'' chooses machine 2 (i.e., $x_{1,v''} = 0$), player $v''+1$ will choose machine 1 regardless the decision of next player $v''+2$. Therefore, when player $v''+1$ is the last player (i.e. $v''+1 = n$), player $v''+1$ will surely choose machine 1 (i.e., $x_{1,v''+1} = 1$) and the loop ends.

Given the set $\{n_0, n_1, \ldots, n_u\}$ where $n_0 = 0$ and $n_u = n$, we claim that:

Claim 1. $\|\mathbf{D}(n_\ell)\|_\infty \le \sum_{j=1}^{n_\ell} p_j$ for $\ell = 0, 1, \ldots, u$.

We prove the claim by induction on $\ell = 0, 1, \ldots, u$. The base case ($\ell = 0$) is trivial, since $\|\mathbf{D}(0)\|_\infty = 0$ and $\sum_{j=1}^{0} p_j = 0$. Assume $\|\mathbf{D}(n_\ell)\|_\infty \le \sum_{j=1}^{n_\ell} p_j$ holds for $\ell = v$. We then prove that

$$\|\mathbf{D}(n_{v'})\|_\infty \le \sum_{j=1}^{n_{v'}} p_j \,, \tag{1}$$

where $v' = v+1$. Since the first n_v jobs create load $\mathbf{D}(n_v)$ on the machines (with a makespan $\|\mathbf{D}(n_v)\|_\infty$), we only need to show that the increment of makespan after the allocation of job $\{n_v + 1, n_v + 2, \ldots, n_{v'}\}$ is no greater than the total minimum processing times of jobs $\{n_v + 1, n_v + 2, \ldots, n_{v'}\}$, namely,

$$\|\mathbf{D}(n_{v'})\|_\infty - \|\mathbf{D}(n_v)\|_\infty \le \sum_{j=n_v+1}^{n_{v'}} p_j.$$

Therefore, we focus on the subgame played by players $\{n_v + 1, n_v + 2, \ldots, n_{v'}\}$. Without loss of generality, we consider the case $D_1(n_v) + p_{1,n_v+1} \le D_2(n_v) + p_{2,n_v+1}$ (the proof for the other case $D_1(n_v) + p_{1,n_v+1} > D_2(n_v) + p_{2,n_v+1}$ is similar). According to Algorithm 1, jobs $\{n_v + 1, n_v + 2, \ldots, n_{v'} - 1\}$ choose machine 2 and job $n_{v'}$ chooses machine 1 (as shown in the following Table 3 where gray boxes represent the choices). We know that

$$\|\mathbf{D}(n_{v'})\|_\infty = \max\left\{ D_1(n_v) + p_{1,n_{v'}}\, , \ D_2(n_v) + \sum_{j=n_v+1}^{n_{v'}-1} p_{2,j} \right\}. \tag{2}$$

Table 3. Decisions of jobs $\{n_v + 1, n_v + 2, \ldots, n_{v'}\}$

Machine 1	$D_1(n_v)$	p_{1,n_v+1}	p_{1,n_v+2}	$\cdots$	$p_{1,n_{v'}-1}$	$p_{1,n_{v'}}$
Machine 2	$D_2(n_v)$	p_{2,n_v+1}	p_{2,n_v+2}	$\cdots$	$p_{2,n_{v'}-1}$	$p_{2,n_{v'}}$

In this case $(D_1(n_v) + p_{1,n_v+1} \le D_2(n_v) + p_{2,n_v+1})$, we first give a upper bound on $D_1(n_v) + p_{1,n_v+1}$ prepared for the following proof. Since

$$D_1(n_v) + p_{1,n_v+1} \le D_2(n_v) + p_{2,n_v+1} \le \max\{D_1(n_v),\ D_2(n_v)\} + p_{2,n_v+1}$$

and

$$D_1(n_v) + p_{1,n_v+1} \le \max\{D_1(n_v),\ D_2(n_v)\} + p_{1,n_v+1},$$

we obtain that

$$D_1(n_v) + p_{1,n_v+1} \le \max\{D_1(n_v),\ D_2(n_v)\} + \min\{p_{1,n_v+1},\ p_{2,n_v+1}\}$$
$$= \|\mathbf{D}(n_v)\|_\infty + p_{n_v+1}. \tag{3}$$

We then analyze properties that holds for the subgame. According to the decisions of players, we know that for any $n' \in \{n_v + 1, n_v + 2, \ldots, n_{v'} - 1\}$, the reason why player n' choose machine 2 is that he/she believes player $n' + 1$ will choose machine 1 if he/she choose machine 1, i.e.,

$$D_1(n_v) + p_{1,n'} + p_{1,n'+1} \le D_2(n_v) + \sum_{j=n_v+1}^{n'-1} p_{2,j} + p_{2,n'+1} \tag{4}$$

Thus, machine 2 is a better choice for player n', i.e.,

$$D_2(n_v) + \sum_{j=n_v+1}^{n'} p_{2,j} \le D_1(n_v) + p_{1,n'} + p_{1,n'+1}. \tag{5}$$

Define a function

$$\Phi(n') = \max\left\{ D_1(n_v) + p_{1,n'+1}, \; D_2(n_v) + \sum_{j=n_v+1}^{n'} p_{2,j} \right\}.$$

Due to (5), we have

$$\Phi(n') \leq \max\left\{ D_1(n_v) + p_{1,n'+1}, \; D_1(n_v) + p_{1,n'} + p_{1,n'+1} \right\}$$
$$= D_1(n_v) + p_{1,n'} + p_{1,n'+1} \tag{6}$$

$$\leq \max\left\{ D_1(n_v) + p_{1,n'}, \; D_2(n_v) + \sum_{j=n_v+1}^{n'-1} p_{2,j} \right\} + p_{1,n'+1}. \tag{7}$$

Substituting (4) into (6) yields

$$\Phi(n') \leq D_2(n_v) + \sum_{j=n_v+1}^{n'-1} p_{2,j} + p_{2,n'+1}$$

$$\leq \max\left\{ D_1(n_v) + p_{1,n'}, \; D_2(n_v) + \sum_{j=n_v+1}^{n'-1} p_{2,j} \right\} + p_{2,n'+1}. \tag{8}$$

According to (7) and (8), we get a critical inequality of $\Phi(n')$:

$$\Phi(n') \leq \max\left\{ D_1(n_v) + p_{1,n'}, \; D_2(n_v) + \sum_{j=n_v+1}^{n'-1} p_{2,j} \right\} + \min\left\{ p_{1,n'+1}, \; p_{2,n'+1} \right\}$$
$$\tag{9}$$

$$= \Phi(n'-1) + p_{n'+1}.$$

Therefore, we obtain that

$$\Phi(n_{v'}-1) \leq \Phi(n_{v'}-2) + p_{n_{v'}} \leq \ldots \leq \Phi(n_v+1) + \sum_{j=n_v+3}^{n_{v'}} p_j$$

where

$$\Phi(n_v+1) \leq \max\left\{ D_1(n_v) + p_{1,n_v+1}, \; D_2(n_v) \right\} + p_{n_v+2} \quad \text{by inequality (9)}$$
$$\leq \max\left\{ \|\mathbf{D}(n_v)\|_\infty + p_{n_v+1}, \; D_2(n_v) \right\} + p_{n_v+2} \quad \text{by inequality (3)}$$
$$= \|\mathbf{D}(n_v)\|_\infty + p_{n_v+1} + p_{n_v+2}.$$

Therefore, it holds that

$$\Phi(n_{v'}-1) \leq \|\mathbf{D}(n_v)\|_\infty + \sum_{j=n_v+1}^{n_{v'}} p_j.$$

Since (2), we have

$$\|\mathbf{D}(n_{v'})\|_\infty = \Phi(n_{v'} - 1) \le \|\mathbf{D}(n_v)\|_\infty + \sum_{j=n_v+1}^{n_{v'}} p_j \,,$$

which concludes the proof of Claim 1, and therefore the lemma is proved. □

Theorem 1. *For the sequential scheduling game on two unrelated machines where players have 1-lookahead, SPoA = 2.*

Proof. According to Lemma 1 and an obvious lower bound on the optimal cost, namely $OPT(N) \ge \sum_{j \in N} p_j/2$, we obtain

$$\text{SPoA} = \frac{L_{\max}(\mathbf{0}, N)}{OPT(N)} \le \frac{\sum_{j \in N} p_j}{\sum_{j \in N} p_j/2} = 2 \,.$$

We then introduce a game that shows SPoA ≥ 2. There are only two jobs in this game (as shown in Table 4). The first job has processing times $1 + \epsilon$ and 1 on machines 1 and 2, respectively, and the second job has processing times 2 and $1 + \epsilon$ on machines 1 and 2, respectively.

Table 4. A game of two players

	Job 1	Job 2
Machine 1	$1 + \epsilon$	2
Machine 2	1	$1 + \epsilon$

In this sequential game job 1 will choose machine 2, and thus job 2 will choose machine 1. The resulting makespan is 2. However, the optimal makespan is $1 + \epsilon$, where job 1 chooses machine 1 and job 2 chooses machine 2. Therefore, we have SPoA $\ge \frac{2}{1+\epsilon}$. By taking $\epsilon \to 0$, we obtain SPoA ≥ 2. □

4 Players with k-Lookahead

This section focuses on the general case where players have k-lookahead. We first prove a key lemma showing that each job can only contribute a certain amount to the makespan:

Lemma 2. $\Delta L([\ell : n]) \le \Delta L([\ell + 1 : n]) + p_\ell + \Delta L(K_\ell)$ *for* $\ell = 1, 2, \ldots, n$.

Proof. For $\ell \in [1 : n]$, given a job set $[\ell : n]$ and an initial load vector $\mathbf{D}$. We define two notations regarding the decision of job ℓ. One is the new initial load after job ℓ chooses machine $i \in M$:

$$\tilde{\mathbf{D}}^{\to i} = \mathbf{D} + (\underbrace{0, \ldots, 0}_{i-1}, \ p_{i,\ell}, \ \underbrace{0, \ldots, 0}_{m-i}) \,.$$

The other one is the anticipated cost of job ℓ with a lookahead set K_ℓ if he/she chooses machine $i \in M$:

$$\widetilde{L}_i = L_i(\widetilde{\mathbf{D}}^{\to i}, K_\ell) \,.$$

Without loss of generality, we suppose job ℓ chooses machine i^*. Thus, the makespan for the game of the set $[\ell : n]$ of players and the initial load $\mathbf{D}$ is

$$L_{\max}(\mathbf{D}, [\ell : n]) = L_{\max}(\widetilde{\mathbf{D}}^{\to i^*}, [\ell + 1 : n])$$
$$\leq \|\widetilde{\mathbf{D}}^{\to i^*}\|_\infty + \Delta L([\ell + 1 : n]) \,.$$

We first discuss a trivial case, where $\|\widetilde{\mathbf{D}}^{\to i^*}\|_\infty = \|\mathbf{D}\|_\infty$, that is, $\|\mathbf{D}\|_\infty$ will not increase after job ℓ chooses machine i^*. This case indicates that

$$L_{\max}(\mathbf{D}, [\ell : n]) \leq \|\mathbf{D}\|_\infty + \Delta L([\ell + 1 : n]) \,.$$

The lemma is proved, since the inequality holds for any $\mathbf{D}$:

$$\Delta L([\ell : n]) = \sup \left\{ L_{\max}(\mathbf{D}, [\ell : n]) - \|\mathbf{D}\|_\infty : \mathbf{D} \in \mathbb{R}_+^M \right\}$$
$$\leq \Delta L([\ell + 1 : n]) \,.$$

Then we discuss the case $\|\widetilde{\mathbf{D}}^{\to i^*}\|_\infty > \|\mathbf{D}\|_\infty$. Because the increment of $\|\mathbf{D}\|_\infty$ is due to job ℓ chooses machine i^*, we know that $\|\widetilde{\mathbf{D}}^{\to i^*}\|_\infty = D_{i^*} + p_{i^*, \ell}$. This indicates that the anticipated cost of job ℓ is at least $\|\widetilde{\mathbf{D}}^{\to i^*}\|_\infty$, i.e.,

$$\widetilde{L}_{i^*} \geq \|\widetilde{\mathbf{D}}^{\to i^*}\|_\infty \,.$$

Let's focus on the moment when job ℓ makes decision. Job ℓ knows the initial load $\mathbf{D}$ and the lookahead set K_ℓ. Thus, the anticipated cost of job ℓ for choosing any machine $i \in M$ is

$$\widetilde{L}_i = L_i(\widetilde{\mathbf{D}}^{\to i}, K_\ell) = \|\widetilde{\mathbf{D}}^{\to i}\|_\infty + \Delta L_i(\widetilde{\mathbf{D}}^{\to i}, K_\ell) \,.$$

Since job ℓ chooses machine i^*, it holds that

$$\widetilde{L}_{i^*} \leq \min_{i \in M} \left\{ \widetilde{L}_i \right\} = \min_{i \in M} \left\{ \|\widetilde{\mathbf{D}}^{\to i}\|_\infty + \Delta L_i(\widetilde{\mathbf{D}}^{\to i}, K_\ell) \right\} \leq \min_{i \in M} \left\{ \|\widetilde{\mathbf{D}}^{\to i}\|_\infty \right\} + \Delta L(K_\ell) \,.$$

According to the definition of $\widetilde{\mathbf{D}}^{\to i}$, we know that

$$\|\widetilde{\mathbf{D}}^{\to i}\|_\infty \leq \|\mathbf{D}\|_\infty + p_{i, \ell} \,.$$

Thus it holds that

$$\widetilde{L}_{i^*} \leq \|\mathbf{D}\|_\infty + \min_{i \in M}\{p_{i, \ell}\} + \Delta L(K_\ell) = \|\mathbf{D}\|_\infty + p_\ell + \Delta L(K_\ell) \,.$$

Since $\widetilde{L}_{i^*} \geq \|\widetilde{\mathbf{D}}^{\to i^*}\|_\infty$, it follows that

$$\|\widetilde{\mathbf{D}}^{\to i^*}\|_\infty \leq \|\mathbf{D}\|_\infty + p_\ell + \Delta L(K_\ell)$$

Therefore we have

$$L_{\max}(\mathbf{D}, [\ell : n]) \leq \|\widetilde{\mathbf{D}}^{-i^*}\|_\infty + \Delta L([\ell + 1 : n])$$
$$\leq \|\mathbf{D}\|_\infty + p_\ell + \Delta L(K_\ell) + \Delta L([\ell + 1 : n]).$$

Since the inequality holds for any $\mathbf{D}$, we obtain

$$\Delta L([\ell : n]) = \sup\left\{L_{\max}(\mathbf{D}, [\ell : n]) - \|\mathbf{D}\|_\infty : \mathbf{D} \in \mathbb{R}_+^M\right\}$$
$$\leq p_\ell + \Delta L(K_\ell) + \Delta L([\ell + 1 : n]),$$

which completes the proof. $\qquad\square$

According to Lemma 2, we obtain the following theorem (see the full version [5] for the detailed proof):

Theorem 2. *For the sequential scheduling game where players have k-lookahead, the SPoA is at most $O(k^2)$ for the two unrelated machines case, and at most $O(2^k \cdot \min\{mk, n\})$ for the m unrelated machines case.*

5 Simple-Minded Players

A simple-minded player makes decision only via simple calculations. When a simple-minded player j makes decision, job j will select a machine with minimum anticipated load assuming that all the follow-up players will simply choose machines with minimum processing time. We show in this section that the SPoA is exactly m, the number of machines. The proofs are in the full version.

Theorem 3. *For the sequential scheduling game on m unrelated machines where players are simple-minded, SPoA $= m$.*

6 Conclusion

One of our main contributions to the area of algorithmic game theory is the reconsideration of "perfect rationality" assumption for the players. This work helps, in some degree, to understand why some games in reality perform much better than the theoretical prediction. As an example, the inefficiency of the subgame-perfect equilibrium for scheduling game on two unrelated machines is unbounded (for unbounded number of players). However it might not be so bad in realty, since the real world players might only have bounded rationality. Our results just explain this phenomenon in a theoretical way. We believe this work takes a promising step in further understanding the role that bounded rationality plays in algorithmic game theory.

References

1. Aspnes, J., Azar, Y., Fiat, A., Plotkin, S.A., Waarts, O.: On-line routing of virtual circuits with applications to load balancing and machine scheduling. J. ACM **44**(3), 486–504 (1997). https://doi.org/10.1145/258128.258201

2. Bilò, V., Fanelli, A., Moscardelli, L.: On lookahead equilibria in congestion games. Math. Struct. Comput. Sci. **27**(2), 197–214 (2017). https://doi.org/10.1017/S0960129515000079

3. Bilò, V., Flammini, M., Monaco, G., Moscardelli, L.: Some anomalies of farsighted strategic behavior. Theory Comput. Syst. **56**(1), 156–180 (2013). https://doi.org/10.1007/s00224-013-9529-1

4. Chen, C., Giessler, P., Mamageishvili, A., Mihalák, M., Penna, P.: Sequential solutions in machine scheduling games. CoRR abs/1611.04159 (2016), http://arxiv.org/abs/1611.04159

5. Chen, C., Xu, Y.: The curse of rationality in sequential scheduling games. CoRR abs/2009.03634 (2020). https://arxiv.org/abs/2009.03634

6. Di, X., Liu, H.X.: Boundedly rational route choice behavior: a review of models and methodologies. Transp. Res. Part B Methodol. **85**, 142–179 (2016)

7. Groenland, C., Schäfer, G.: The curse of ties in congestion games with limited lookahead. In: André, E., Koenig, S., Dastani, M., Sukthankar, G. (eds.) Proceedings of the 17th International Conference on Autonomous Agents and MultiAgent Systems, AAMAS 2018, Stockholm, Sweden, 10–15 July 2018, pp. 1941–1943. ACM (2018). http://dl.acm.org/citation.cfm?id=3238031

8. Koutsoupias, E., Papadimitriou, C.H.: Worst-case equilibria. Comput. Sci. Rev. **3**(2), 65–69 (2009). https://doi.org/10.1016/j.cosrev.2009.04.003

9. Kroer, C., Sandholm, T.: Limited lookahead in imperfect-information games. Artif. Intell. **283**, 103218 (2020). https://doi.org/10.1016/j.artint.2019.103218

10. Lee, C.: Bounded rationality and the emergence of simplicity amidst complexity. J. Econ. Surv. **25**(3), 507–526 (2011)

11. Leme, R.P., Syrgkanis, V., Tardos, É.: The curse of simultaneity. In: Goldwasser, S. (ed.) Innovations in Theoretical Computer Science 2012, Cambridge, MA, USA, 8–10 January 2012, pp. 60–67. ACM (2012). https://doi.org/10.1145/2090236.2090242

12. Mirrokni, V., Thain, N., Vetta, A.: A theoretical examination of practical game playing: lookahead search. In: Serna, M. (ed.) SAGT 2012. LNCS, pp. 251–262. Springer, Heidelberg (2012). https://doi.org/10.1007/978-3-642-33996-7_22

13. Shannon, C.: Programming a computer for playing chess. Philos. Mag. **41**(4), 256–275 (1950)

14. Simon, H.A.: A behavioral model of rational choice. Q. J. Econ. **69**(1), 99–118 (1955)

15. Velupillai, K.V.: Foundations of boundedly rational choice and satisficing decisions. Adv. Decis. Sci. **2010**, 16 (2010)

Sequential Solutions in Machine Scheduling Games

Cong Chen[1], Paul Giessler[2], Akaki Mamageishvili[3(✉)], Matúš Mihalák[2], and Paolo Penna[4]

[1] School of Business Administration, South China University of Technology, Guangzhou, China
[2] Department of Data Science and Knowledge Engineering, Maastricht University, Maastricht, The Netherlands
[3] Department of Management, Technology and Economics, ETH Zurich, Zurich, Switzerland
amamageishvili@ethz.ch
[4] Department of Computer Science, ETH Zurich, Zurich, Switzerland

Abstract. We consider the classical machine scheduling, where n jobs need to be scheduled on m machines, and where job j scheduled on machine i contributes $p_{i,j} \in \mathbb{R}$ to the load of machine i, with the goal of minimizing the makespan, i.e., the maximum load of any machine in the schedule. We study inefficiency of schedules that are obtained when jobs arrive sequentially one by one, and the jobs choose themselves the machine on which they will be scheduled, aiming at being scheduled on a machine with small load. We measure the inefficiency of a schedule as the ratio of the makespan obtained in the worst-case equilibrium schedule, and of the optimum makespan. This ratio is known as the *sequential price of anarchy (SPoA)*. We also introduce two alternative inefficiency measures, which allow for a favorable choice of the order in which the jobs make their decisions. As our first result, we disprove the conjecture of [22] claiming that the sequential price of anarchy for $m = 2$ machines is at most 3. We show that the sequential price of anarchy grows at least linearly with the number n of players, assuming arbitrary tie-breaking rules. That is, we show **SPoA** $\in \Omega(n)$. Complementing this result, we show that **SPoA** $\in O(n)$, reducing previously known exponential bound for 2 machines. Furthermore, we show that there exists an order of the jobs, resulting in makespan that is at most linearly larger than the optimum makespan. To the end, we show that if an authority can change the order of the jobs adaptively to the decisions made by the jobs so far (but cannot influence the decisions of the jobs), then there exists an adaptive ordering in which the jobs end up in an optimum schedule.

Keywords: Machine scheduling · Price of anarchy · Price of stability

1 Introduction

We consider the classical optimization problem of scheduling n jobs on m *unrelated* machines. In this problem, each job has a (possibly different) processing

© Springer Nature Switzerland AG 2020
X. Chen et al. (Eds.): WINE 2020, LNCS 12495, pp. 309–322, 2020.
https://doi.org/10.1007/978-3-030-64946-3_22

time on each of the m machines, and a schedule is simply an assignment of jobs to machines. For any such schedule, the load of a machine is the sum of all processing times of the jobs assigned to that machine. In this optimization problem, the objective is to find a schedule minimizing the *makespan*, that is, the maximum load among the machines.

In the *game-theoretic* version of this scheduling problem, also known as the *load balancing game*, jobs correspond to players who *selfishly* choose the machine to which the job is assigned. The cost of a player is the *load* of the machine to which the player assigned its own job. Such a setting models, for example, the situation where the machines correspond to servers, and the communication with a server has a latency that depends on the total traffic to the server.

The decisions of the players lead to some *equilibrium* in which no player has an incentive to deviate, though the resulting schedule may not necessarily be optimal in terms of makespan. Such an equilibrium might have a rather high *social cost*, that is, the makespan of the corresponding schedule[1] is not guaranteed to be the optimal one, as in Example 1 below.

Example 1 (two jobs on two unrelated machines [5]). Consider two jobs and two unrelated machines, where the processing times are given by the following table:

	job 1	job 2
machine 1	1	ℓ
machine 2	ℓ	1

The allocation represented by the gray box is a pure Nash equilibrium in the load balancing game (if a job moves to the other machine, its own cost increases from ℓ to $\ell + 1$), and has makespan ℓ. The optimal makespan is 1 (swap the allocations). This example shows that the makespan of an equilibrium can be arbitrarily larger than the optimum.

The inefficiency of equilibria is a central concept in algorithmic game theory. Typically, one aims to quantify the *efficiency loss* resulting from a *selfish behavior* of the players, where the loss is measured in terms of the social cost. Arguably, the two most popular measures of inefficiency of equilibria are the *price of anarchy* (**PoA**) [27] and the *price of stability* (**PoS**) [4], which, intuitively, consider the *most pessimistic* and the *most optimistic* scenario:

- The *price of anarchy* is the ratio of the cost of the *worst* equilibrium over the optimal social cost;
- The *price of stability* is the ratio of the cost of the *best* equilibrium over the optimal social cost.

---

[1] When each player chooses deterministically one machine, this definition is obvious. When equilibria are *mixed* or randomized, each player chooses one machine according to some probability distribution, and the social cost is the expected makespan of the resulting schedule.

The price of anarchy corresponds to the situation (anarchy) in which there is no authority, and players converge to some equilibrium by themselves. In the price of stability, one envisions that there are means to suggest the players how to play, and if that is an equilibrium, then they will indeed follow the suggestion, as no unilateral deviation can improve a player's individual cost. Furthermore, the price of stability provides a lower bound on the efficiency loss of an equilibrium outcome, if, for example, no equilibrium is actually a social optimum.

Example 1 thus shows that the **price of anarchy** of load balancing games is **unbounded even for two jobs and two machines**. Interestingly, the price of stability instead is one (**PoS** = 1), for any number of jobs and any number of machines. This is because there is always an optimal solution that is also a pure Nash equilibrium [17] (see Sect. 1.3 for details). In a pure Nash equilibrium, players choose their strategies deterministically, as opposed to *mixed* Nash equilibria. In this work, we will also focus on the case in which players act deterministically, though in a sequential fashion (see below).

As the price of anarchy for unrelated machines is very high (unbounded in general), one may ask whether Nash equilibria are really what happens as an outcome in the game, or whether a central authority, which cannot influence the choices of the players (jobs), may alter some aspects of the scheduling setting, and as a result, improve the performance of the resulting equilibria.

Motivated by these issues, in [28] the authors consider the variant in which players, instead of choosing their strategies simultaneously, play sequentially taking their decisions based on the previous choices and also knowing the order of players that will make play. Formally, this corresponds to an *extensive-form game*, and the corresponding equilibrium concept is called a *subgame-perfect equilibrium*. Players always choose their strategy deterministically. The resulting inefficiency measure is called the *sequential price of anarchy (SPoA)*.

There are two main motivations to study a sequential variant of the load balancing game. First, assuming that all players decide simultaneously to choose the machine to process their jobs is a too strong and unnatural modeling assumption in many situations; furthermore, expecting that all players choose the worst-case machine, as was the case in Example 1, is unnatural as well. Second, one may have the power to explicitly ask the players to make sequential decisions, and make this the policy, which the players are aware of, with the view of lowering the loss of efficiency of the resulting equilibrium schedules. In a sense, such an approach of adjusting the way the players access the machines resembles *coordination mechanisms* [11], which are scheduling policies aiming to achieve a small price of anarchy (see Sect. 1.3 for more details).

1.1 Prior Results (SPoA for Unrelated Machines)

The first bounds on the **SPoA** for unrelated machines have been obtained in [28], showing that

$$n \leq \textbf{SPoA} \leq m \cdot 2^n.$$

Therefore, **SPoA** is *constant* for a constant number of machines and jobs, while **PoA** is *unbounded* even for two jobs and two machines (recall Example 1).

The large gap in the previous bound naturally suggests the question of what happens for *many jobs* and *many machines*. This was addressed by [7] which improved significantly the prior bounds by showing that

$$2^{\Omega(\sqrt{n})} \leq \mathbf{SPoA} \leq 2^n.$$

At this point, one should note that these lower bounds use a *non-constant* number of machines. In other words, it still might be possible that for a *constant number of machines* the **SPoA** is constant. For *two machines*, [22] proved a lower bound **SPoA** ≥ 3, and in the same work the authors made the following conjecture:

Conjecture 1 [22]. For two unrelated machines, $\mathbf{SPoA} = 3$ for any number of jobs.

1.2   Our Contributions

In this paper, we disprove Conjecture 1 by showing that in fact, **SPoA** on two machines is *not even constant*. Indeed, it must grow linearly and the conjecture fails already for few jobs:

- For *five jobs* we have **SPoA** ≥ 4 (Theorem 2);
- In general, with arbitrary tie-breaking rules, it holds that **SPoA** $\geq \Omega(n)$ (Theorem 3).

Note that the result of Theorem 3 uses suitable player-specific tie-breaking rules (see Definition 1). We discuss the implications of using tie-breaking rules more in detail at the end of this subsection.

While Theorem 2 settles the conjecture, the result of Theorem 3 says that **SPoA** is non-constant already for two machines (as the number of jobs grows) for generic tie-breaking rules. We actually conjecture that there exist instances for which the **SPoA** is unbounded without having ties. Moreover, it implies a *strong separation* with the case of *identical* machines, where **SPoA** $\leq 2 - \frac{1}{m}$, for any number m of machines [22]. In Theorem 4 we show that **SPoA** is upper bounded by $2(n - 1)$, reducing the exponential upper bound obtained in [7] for arbitrarily many machines to linear bound for 2 machines.

The original idea behind the notion of price of stability (**PoS**) is that an authority can suggest to the players how to play:

> *[...] The best Nash equilibrium solution has a natural meaning of stability in this context – it is the optimal solution that can be proposed from which no user will defect. [...] As a result, the global performance of the system may not be as good as in a case where a central authority can simply dictate a solution; rather, we need to understand the quality of solutions that are consistent with self-interested behavior [4].*

We borrow this idea of an authority suggesting desirable equilibria. Specifically for our setting, the authority suggests the order in which players make their decisions, so to induce a good equilibrium. This can be viewed as the price of stability (**PoS**) for these sequential games. We introduce this notion in two variants (a weaker and a stronger):

- *Sequential Price of Stability (SPoS)*. The authority can choose the order of the players' moves. This order determines the tree structure of the corresponding game.
- *Adaptive Sequential Price of Stability (adaptive SPoS)*. The authority decides the order of the players' moves *adaptively* according to the choices made at each step.

The study of these two notions for two unrelated machines is also motivated by our lower bound, and by the lack of any good upper bound on this problem. We prove the following upper bounds for two unrelated machines (Theorems 5 and 6):

$$\textbf{SPoS} \leq \frac{n}{2} + 1 \ , \qquad\qquad \textbf{adaptive SPoS} = 1 \ .$$

The next natural question is to consider *three* or more machines. Here we show an impossibility result, namely **adaptive SPoS** $\geq 3/2$ already for three machines (Theorem 7). That is, even with the strongest type of adaptive authority, it is not possible to achieve the optimum. This shows a possible disadvantage of having players capable of complex reasoning, like in extensive-form games. In the classical strategic-games setting, where we consider pure Nash equilibrium, here is an optimum which *is* an equilibrium, that is, **PoS** $= 1$ for any number of machines and jobs. This result follows from [17] (see Sect. 1.3 for details).

As mentioned above, some of our results rely on the use of a suitable tie-breaking rules. Using tie-breaking rules to prove lower bounds on the **SPoA** is not new: in [25] the authors showed that, in *routing games*, the sequential price of anarchy is *unbounded*. Their proof is based on carefully chosen tie-breaking rules. This way of using tie-breaking rules is not part of the players' strategy interactions. In contrast, some works consider settings where among equivalent choices, each player i can use the one that hurts prior agents who chose a strategy that player i would prefer they had not chosen (see [30]).

1.3 Further Related Work

The load balancing games considered in this work are one of the most studied models in algorithmic game theory (see, e.g., [2,15,16,18,19,26,27]). In all these works, players correspond to jobs, their cost is the load of the machine they choose, and the social cost is defined as the makespan of the jobs allocation. In particular, the seminal paper [27] which introduced the concept of the price of anarchy, considers the case of *identical* and *related* machines, two simpler versions of unrelated machines (related machines is the setting where each machine has a speed, each job has a certain size, and the processing time equals the job size divided by the machine speed; the case of identical machines is the restriction in which all speeds are the same).

Interestingly, the price of anarchy for *related* or *identical* machines is much better than in the case of unrelated machines (where the price of anarchy is unbounded). Indeed, for related and identical machines, the price of anarchy is *bounded* for any *constant number of machines* [15,16,18–20,26,27] (some of these results give bounds also for *mixed* Nash equilibria). Specifically, for pure Nash equilibria, $\mathbf{PoA} = (2 - \frac{2}{m+1})$ for identical machines as implied by the analysis of [20], while $\mathbf{PoA} = O(\frac{\log m}{\log \log m})$ for related machines [15].

As already mentioned above, the **PoS** for *unrelated* machines is 1. This is due to the work [17] which shows that, starting from any schedule, an iterative process of applying unilateral improving-strategy changes of players leads to a pure Nash equilibrium (the same property has been observed earlier in [21] for related machines). This condition implies the existence of a pure Nash equilibrium.

Requiring that players make their decisions sequentially, according to a given and known order can be seen as a mean of a central authority that can control access to the resources (machines), but not the choices of the players (jobs). In this sense, changing the access from simultaneous to sequential can be seen as a kind of control mechanism like a *coordination mechanism* [11]. In load balancing games where the cost of a player (job) is the completion time of the job (and not the total load of the machine on which the job is scheduled), a coordination mechanism is a scheduling policy, one for every machine, which determines the order of the jobs in which they will be scheduled on the machine. The scheduling policy needs to be fixed and (publicly) known to the players. For load balancing games in normal form (i.e., where players make simultaneous decisions, as opposed to the sequential decisions, which we consider in this paper), coordination mechanisms have been studied both for the version where the social cost is the makespan (see, e.g., [6,8,9,24] and the references therein), or the total (weighted) completion time (see, e.g., [1,12,14,23,31] and the references therein).

As already discussed above, the concept of a sequential price of anarchy is not new. In addition to the results for unrelated machines discussed in Sect. 1.1, the sequential price of anarchy has been studied also for other games. These include congestion games with affine delay functions [25], isolation games [3], and network congestion games [13]. Interestingly, the latter work shows that the sequential price of anarchy for these games is *unbounded*, as opposed to the price of anarchy which was known to be 5/2.

Naturally, there is a huge literature on the classical algorithm-theoretic research on machine scheduling, see, e.g., the textbook [29] and the survey [10] for fundamental results and further references.

2   Preliminaries

In unrelated machine scheduling there are n jobs and m machines, and the processing time of job j on machine i is denoted by p_{ij}. A solution (or schedule) consists of an assignment of each job to one of the machines, that is, a vector $s = (s_1, \ldots, s_n)$ where s_j is the machine to which job j is assigned to. The *load*

$l_i(s)$ of a machine i in schedule s is the sum of the processing times of all jobs allocated to it, that is, $l_i(s) = \sum_{j:s_j=i} p_{ij}$. The social cost of a solution s is the *makespan*, that is, the maximum load among all machines.

Each job j is a *player* who attempts to minimize her own cost $cost_j(s)$, that is, the load of the machine she chooses: $cost_j(s) = l_{s_j}$. Every player j decides s_j, the assignment of job j to a machine. The combination of all players strategies gives a schedule $s = (s_1, \ldots, s_n)$.

In the extensive-form version of these games, players play sequentially; they decide their strategies based on the choices of the previous players and knowing that the remaining players will play rationally. We consider a *full information* game. As players enter the game sequentially, they can compute their optimal moves by the so-called *backward induction*: the last player makes her move greedily, the player before the last makes the move also greedily (taking into account what the last player will do), and so on. Any game of this type can be modeled by a *decision tree*, which is a rooted tree where the non-leaf vertices correspond to the players in certain states, while edges correspond to the strategies available to the players in a given state.

Each leaf corresponds to a solution (schedule), which is simply the strategies on the unique leaf-to-root path. Given the processing times $P = (p_{ij})$, the players can compute the loads on the machines in each of the leaves. In case of ties, all players know the deterministic tie-breaking rules of all the other players. A player can calculate what the final outcome would be for each of her strategies, and choose the strategy that minimizes her cost. This method is called backward induction. Strategies obtained in this way for each internal node constitute what is called the *subgame-perfect equilibrium*: for each subtree, we know what is the outcome achieved by the players in this subtree if they play rationally. We usually represent the strategies (edges) that are chosen by players in the **subgame perfect equilibrium** in **bold**, and the other strategies as *dashed* edges.

It is easy to see that a subgame-perfect equilibrium always exists and it is unique, for given tie-breaking rules. On the other hand, its computation is difficult, as proved in [28]:

Theorem 1 [28]. *Computing the outcome of a subgame perfect equilibrium in Unrelated Machine Scheduling is PSPACE-complete.*

Notation and Formal Definitions. We consider n jobs and m machines, denoted by $J = (J_1, J_2, \ldots, J_n)$ and $M = (M_1, M_2, \ldots, M_m)$ respectively. The processing times are given by a matrix $P = (p_{ij})$, with p_{ij} being the processing time of job J_j on machine M_i. The set of all such nonnegative $n \times m$ matrices is denoted by $\mathcal{P}_{n,m}$ and it represents the possible instances of the game. For any $P \in \mathcal{P}_{n,m}$ as above, we denote by $\mathcal{T}_{n,m}$ the set of all possible depth-n, complete m-ary decision trees where each path from the root to a leaf contains every job (player) exactly once. The whole game (and the resulting subgame perfect equilibrium) is fully specified by P, T, and the *tie-breaking rule* used by the players. The most general – worst case – scenario is that ties are arbitrary (see Definition 1). In the following, we do not specify the dependency on the ties, and simply denote by

$SPE(P, T)$ the cost (makespan) of the subgame perfect equilibrium of the game. One type of worst-case analysis is to assume the players' order to be adversarial, and the tree T being chosen accordingly. This is the same as saying that players arrive in a fixed order (say $J_1, J_2, \ldots, J_n$) and their costs P is chosen in an adversarial fashion. In this case, we simply write $SPE(P)$ as the tree structure is fixed. For a fixed order σ (a permutation) of the players, and costs P, we also write $SPE(P, \sigma)$ to denote the quantity $SPE(P, T)$ where T is the tree resulting from this order σ of the players. The optimal social cost (makespan) is denoted by $OPT(P)$.

We next introduce formal definitions to quantify the inefficiency of subgame perfect equilibria in various scenarios (from the most pessimistic to the most optimistic). The *sequential price of anarchy (SPoA)* compares the worst subgame perfect equilibrium with the optimal social cost,

$$\textbf{SPoA} = \sup_{P \in \mathcal{P}_{n,m}} \frac{SPE(P)}{OPT(P)}.$$

In the *sequential price of stability (SPoS)*, we can choose the order σ in which players play depending on the instance P. The resulting subgame perfect equilibrium has cost $SPE(P, \sigma)$, which is then compared to the optimum,

$$\textbf{SPoS} = \sup_{P \in \mathcal{P}_{n,m}} \min_{\sigma \in \mathcal{S}_n} \frac{SPE(P, \sigma)}{OPT(P)},$$

where σ ranges over all permutations $\mathcal{S}_n$ of the n players. In *adaptive sequential price of stability (adaptive SPoS)*, we can choose the whole structure of the tree, meaning that for each choice of a player, we can adaptively choose which player will play next. This means that every path from any leaf to the root corresponds to a permutation of the players. The adaptive price of stability is then defined as

$$\textbf{adaptive SPoS} = \sup_{P \in \mathcal{P}_{n,m}} \min_{T \in \mathcal{T}_{n,m}} \frac{SPE(P, T)}{OPT(P)}.$$

Note that by definition **adaptive SPoS** $\leq$ **SPoS** $\leq$ **SPoA**.

3   Linear Lower Bound for SPoA

In this section, we consider the sequential price of anarchy for *two* unrelated machines. In [22] the authors proved a lower bound **SPoA** ≥ 3 for this case, and they conjectured that this was also a tight bound. We show that unfortunately this is not the case: Already for five jobs, **SPoA** ≥ 4, and with more jobs the lower bound grows linearly, i.e., **SPoA** $= \Omega(n)$.

3.1   A Lower Bound for $n = 5$ Players

Theorem 2. *For two machines and at least five jobs, the **SPoA** is at least 4.*

3.2   Linear Lower Bound

Extending the construction for $n = 5$ players is non-trivial as this seems to require rather involved constants that multiply the ε terms. However, we notice that these terms only help to induce more involved tie-breaking rules of the following form:

Definition 1 (arbitrary tie-breaking rule). *We say that the tie-breaking rule is arbitrary if each player uses a tie-breaking rule between machines which possibly depends on the allocation of all players.*

The following theorem gives our general lower bound:

Theorem 3. *Even for two machines, the **SPoA** is at least linear in the number n of jobs, in the case of arbitrary tie-breaking rule.*

Note that it is important to have seemingly equivalent jobs J_2 and J_3. They use different tie-breaking rules, which creates the asymmetry between them and increases the **SPoA**.

We solved linear programs with strict inequalities obtained from the subgame perfect equilibria tree structure given in the example from the proof of Theorem 3, by introducing small ε for strict inequalities. We found solutions for $n = 8$ and $n = 11$, that is linear programs are feasible. Therefore, at least for small n's we can drop the assumption about tie-breaking rules. As the solutions replace the ε terms by rather more complicated coefficients, we do not present them here. For the general case, we conjecture that the statement of Theorem 3 holds without the assumption on the tie-breaking rules, and that the latter are merely used to make the analysis easier:

Conjecture 2. For two machines, the **SPoA** is at least linear in n.

4   Linear Upper Bound for SPoA

Additional Notation. To prove the upper bound for **SPoA**, we introduce some additional notation. We define a vector $D = (d_1, d_2)$ of initial load on the machines before the jobs play the game. Consequentially, the load of each machine i becomes

$$l_i(D, s) = d_i + \sum_{j:s_j=i} p_{ij} \,,$$

where $s = (s_1, s_2, \ldots, s_n)$ is the schedule (SPE) achieved by the jobs playing the game with initial load D on the machines; the cost of each job j is

$$cost_j(D, s) = l_{s_j}(D, s) \,.$$

The notation for the makespan is renewed as $SPE_D(P)$ for the SPE with initial load D. Additionally, we define $\varDelta SPE(P)$ as the maximum possible increase of the makespan due to the players, with processing time P, for any initial load D:

$$\varDelta SPE(P) = \sup_D \{SPE_D(P) - ||D||_\infty\} \,.$$

Moreover, for a given P, we use $P_{[u:v]}$ to represent the processing times only for jobs $(J_u, J_{u+1}, \ldots, J_v)$, that is, $P_{[u:v]} = (p_{ij})$ where $j = u, u+1, \ldots, v$.

We first show a key lemma showing that each job can only contribute a certain amount (bounded by the total minimum processing time) to the makespan:

Lemma 1. $\Delta SPE\left(P_{[\ell:n]}\right) - \Delta SPE\left(P_{[\ell+1:n]}\right) \leq \sum_{j=\ell}^{n} \min_i p_{ij}$ for $\ell = 1, 2, \ldots, n-1$.

Theorem 4. *For two machines, the **SPoA** is at most $2(n-1)$.*

Proof. Applying Lemma 1, we have

$$\Delta SPE\left(P_{[1:n]}\right) \leq \Delta SPE\left(P_{[2:n]}\right) + \sum_{j=1}^{n} \min_i p_{ij}$$

$$\leq \Delta SPE\left(P_{[3:n]}\right) + 2\sum_{j=1}^{n} \min_i p_{ij}$$

$$\leq \cdots$$

$$\leq (n-1)\sum_{j=1}^{n} \min_i p_{ij}.$$

Since the optimal cost is at least $OPT \geq \sum_{j=1}^{n} \min_i p_{ij}/2$ (for 2 machines), it follows that

$$\mathbf{SPoA} \leq \frac{\Delta SPE\left(P_{[1:n]}\right)}{OPT} \leq 2(n-1),$$

which completes the proof.   □

5   Linear Upper Bound on the SPoS

In this section, we give a *linear upper bound* on the sequential price of stability for two machines (Theorem 5 below). Unlike in the case of the sequential price of anarchy, here we have the freedom to choose the order of the players. Each player can choose *any* tie-breaking rule. Since we consider a full information setting, the tie-breaking rules are also public knowledge.

Though finding the best order can be difficult, we found that a large set of permutations already gives a linear upper bound on **SPoS**. In particular, it is enough that the authority divides the players into *two groups* and puts players in the first group first, followed by the players from the second group. Inside each group players can form *any order*. The main result of this section is the following theorem:

Theorem 5. *For two machines, the **SPoS** is at most $\frac{n}{2} + 1$.*

This result cannot be extended to *three* or more machines, because the third machine changes the logic of the proof. In particular, we can no longer assume that the players on the second machine in the optimal assignment can guarantee low costs for themselves by simply staying on that machine. For two machines, we conjecture that actually there is always an order which leads to the optimum:

Conjecture 3. For two machines, the **SPoS** is 1.

Though we are not able to prove this conjecture, in the next section, we introduce a more restricted solution concept, and show that in that case the optimum can be achieved.

6   Achieving the Optimum: The Adaptive SPoS

In this section, we study the adaptive sequential price of stability. Unlike the previous models, here we assume that there is some authority, which has full control over the order of the players' arrival in the game. It does not only fix the initial complete order, but can also change the order of arrivals depending on the decision that previous players made. On the other hand, the players still have the freedom to choose any action in a given state, each of them aiming at minimizing her own final cost. The players also know the whole decision tree, and thus the way the authority chooses the order. As in the previous section, each player can use *any* tie-breaking rule, and the tie-breaking rules are also known to all players.

This model is the closest instantiation of a general extensive form game compared to the previously studied models in this paper. In this way, the authority has an option to punish players for deviating from the optimal path (path leading to a social optimum) by placing different players after the deviating decisions of the deviating player. As a result, rational players may achieve much better solutions in the end. The following theorem shows that achieving the optimum solution is possible for 2 machines:

Theorem 6. *For two machines, the **adaptive SPoS** is 1.*

The previous result cannot be extended to more than 2 machines:

Theorem 7. *For three or more machines, the **adaptive SPoS** is at least $\frac{3}{2}$.*

Proof. Consider the following instance with three machines and three jobs, where the optimum is shown as gray boxes:

	J_1	J_2	J_3
M_1	$4-\varepsilon$	2	2
M_2	4	3	3
M_3	6	$6-\varepsilon$	$6-\varepsilon$

We distinguish two cases for the first player to move (the root of the tree), and show that in neither case the players will implement the optimum:

1. *The First to Move is J_1.* This player will choose the cheapest machine M_1, because none will join this machine. Indeed, the second player to move will choose M_2 knowing that the last one will then choose M_3.

2. *The First to Move is J_2 or J_3.* This player will choose M_2 and *not* M_1. Indeed, if the first player to move, say J_2, chooses M_1, then either (I) the other two follow also the optimum (which costs 4 to J_2) or (II) they choose another solution, whose cost is at least $6 - \varepsilon$. In the latter case, we have the lower bound. In case (I), we argue that choosing M_2 is better for J_2, because no other player will join: for the following players, being both on machine M_1 is already cheaper than being on M_2 with J_2.

In the first case, given that J_1 is allocated to M_1, the cheapest solution costs $6 - \varepsilon$. In the second case, one among J_2 or J_3 is allocated to M_2. The best solution, in this case, costs again $6 - \varepsilon$. This completes the proof.   □

Remark 1. The following example shows that the analysis of Theorem 6 cannot be extended to 3 machines even in the case of identical machines. Assume that we have $m = 3$ machines, the initial loads on these machines are $(0, 2, 6)$ and there are 3 jobs left to be assigned with processing times $7, 5$ and 5. Note that the constrained optimum here is $(10, 9, 6)$, that is the first job with processing time 7 gets assigned to the second machine M_2, while both jobs with processing times 5 and 5 get assigned to machine M_1. On the other hand, if any of these players chooses different machine their cost is strictly decreasing in the subgame perfect equilibrium solution. We did not find any example showing that **adaptive SPoS** > 1 for more than 2 identical machines, unlike the case of unrelated machines.

7   Conclusions

In this paper, we disprove a conjecture from [22] and give a linear lower bound construction for the sequential price of anarchy. On the other hand, we show linear upper bound. For the best sequence of players, we prove a linear upper bound, that is 4 times lower than the upper bound for sequential price of anarchy. Moreover, we prove the existence of a sequential extensive game which gives an optimum solution. One possible direction for future research is to investigate whether the sequential price of stability is 1 for any number of *identical* machines. In this work, we give some evidence that the case of three (or more) machines is different from the case of two machines (see Theorem 7 and Remark 1).

Our linear lower bound on the sequential price of anarchy (Theorem 3) suggests that subgame perfect equilibria do not guarantee in the worst case a price of anarchy independent of the number of jobs, even for two machines. Though our lower bound is based on a suitable tie-breaking rule, we believe it holds without any tie being involved (Conjecture 2).

Acknowledgment. We are grateful to Thomas Erlebach for spotting a mistake in an earlier proof of Theorem 6 and for suggesting a fix of the proof. We thank Paul Dütting for valuable discussions. We also thank anonymous reviewers and seminar participants of OR 2016 for suggestions that improved the paper.

References

1. Abed, F., Correa, J.R., Huang, C.-C.: Optimal coordination mechanisms for multi-job scheduling games. In: Schulz, A.S., Wagner, D. (eds.) ESA 2014. LNCS, vol. 8737, pp. 13–24. Springer, Heidelberg (2014). https://doi.org/10.1007/978-3-662-44777-2_2
2. Andelman, N., Feldman, M., Mansour, Y.: Strong price of anarchy. Games Econ. Behav. 2(65), 289–317 (2009)
3. Angelucci, A., Bilò, V., Flammini, M., Moscardelli, L.: On the sequential price of anarchy of isolation games. J. Comb. Optim. 29(1), 165–181 (2013). https://doi.org/10.1007/s10878-013-9694-9
4. Anshelevich, E., Dasgupta, A., Kleinberg, J.M., Tardos, É., Wexler, T., Roughgarden, T.: The price of stability for network design with fair cost allocation. SIAM J. Comput. 38(4), 1602–1623 (2008)
5. Awerbuch, B., Azar, Y., Richter, Y., Tsur, D.: Tradeoffs in worst-case equilibria. Theoret. Comput. Sci. 361(2), 200–209 (2006)
6. Azar, Y., Fleischer, L., Jain, K., Mirrokni, V., Svitkina, Z.: Optimal coordination mechanisms for unrelated machine scheduling. Oper. Res. 63(3), 489–500 (2015)
7. Bilò, V., Flammini, M., Monaco, G., Moscardelli, L.: Some anomalies of farsighted strategic behavior. Theory Comput. Syst. 56(1), 156–180 (2015). https://doi.org/10.1007/978-3-642-38016-7_19
8. Caragiannis, I.: Efficient coordination mechanisms for unrelated machine scheduling. Algorithmica 66(3), 512–540 (2013)
9. Caragiannis, I., Fanelli, A.: An almost ideal coordination mechanism for unrelated machine scheduling. Theory Comput. Syst. 63(1), 114–127 (2018). https://doi.org/10.1007/s00224-018-9857-2
10. Chen, B., Potts, C.N., Woeginger, G.J.: A review of machine scheduling: complexity, algorithms and approximability. In: Du, D.Z., Pardalos, P.M. (eds.) Handbook of Combinatorial Optimization. Springer, Boston (1998). https://doi.org/10.1007/978-1-4613-0303-9_25
11. Christodoulou, G., Koutsoupias, E., Nanavati, A.: Coordination mechanisms. Theor. Comput. Sci. 410(36), 3327–3336 (2009). Graphs, Games and Computation: Dedicated to Professor Burkhard Monien on the Occasion of his 65th Birthday
12. Cole, R., Correa, J.R., Gkatzelis, V., Mirrokni, V., Olver, N.: Decentralized utilitarian mechanisms for scheduling games. Games Econ. Behav. 92, 306–326 (2015)
13. Correa, J.R., de Jong, J., de Keijzer, B., Uetz, M.: The inefficiency of Nash and subgame perfect equilibria for network routing. Math. Oper. Res. 44(4), 1286–1303 (2019)
14. Correa, J.R., Queyranne, M.: Efficiency of equilibria in restricted uniform machine scheduling with total weighted completion time as social cost. Naval Res. Logist. (NRL) 59(5), 384–395 (2012)
15. Czumaj, A., Vöcking, B.: Tight bounds for worst-case equilibria. ACM Trans. Algorithms 3(1), 4:1–4:17 (2007)
16. Epstein, L.: Equilibria for two parallel links: the strong price of anarchy versus the price of anarchy. Acta Informatica 47(7), 375–389 (2010)
17. Even-Dar, E., Kesselman, A., Mansour, Y.: Convergence time to Nash equilibria. In: Baeten, J.C.M., Lenstra, J.K., Parrow, J., Woeginger, G.J. (eds.) ICALP 2003. LNCS, vol. 2719, pp. 502–513. Springer, Heidelberg (2003). https://doi.org/10.1007/3-540-45061-0_41

18. Feldmann, R., Gairing, M., Lücking, T., Monien, B., Rode, M.: Nashification and the coordination ratio for a selfish routing game. In: Baeten, J.C.M., Lenstra, J.K., Parrow, J., Woeginger, G.J. (eds.) ICALP 2003. LNCS, vol. 2719, pp. 514–526. Springer, Heidelberg (2003). https://doi.org/10.1007/3-540-45061-0_42

19. Fiat, A., Kaplan, H., Levy, M., Olonetsky, S.: Strong price of anarchy for machine load balancing. In: Arge, L., Cachin, C., Jurdziński, T., Tarlecki, A. (eds.) ICALP 2007. LNCS, vol. 4596, pp. 583–594. Springer, Heidelberg (2007). https://doi.org/10.1007/978-3-540-73420-8_51

20. Finn, G., Horowitz, E.: A linear time approximation algorithm for multiprocessor scheduling. BIT Numer. Math. **19**(3), 312–320 (1979). https://doi.org/10.1007/BF01930985

21. Fotakis, D., Kontogiannis, S., Koutsoupias, E., Mavronicolas, M., Spirakis, P.: The structure and complexity of Nash equilibria for a selfish routing game. In: Widmayer, P., Eidenbenz, S., Triguero, F., Morales, R., Conejo, R., Hennessy, M. (eds.) ICALP 2002. LNCS, vol. 2380, pp. 123–134. Springer, Heidelberg (2002). https://doi.org/10.1007/3-540-45465-9_12

22. Hassin, R., Yovel, U.: Sequential scheduling on identical machines. Oper. Res. Lett. **43**(5), 530–533 (2015)

23. Hoeksma, R., Uetz, M.: The price of anarchy for Minsum related machine scheduling. In: Solis-Oba, R., Persiano, G. (eds.) WAOA 2011. LNCS, vol. 7164, pp. 261–273. Springer, Heidelberg (2012). https://doi.org/10.1007/978-3-642-29116-6_22

24. Immorlica, N., Li, L.E., Mirrokni, V.S., Schulz, A.S.: Coordination mechanisms for selfish scheduling. Theoret. Comput. Sci. **410**(17), 1589–1598 (2009)

25. de Jong, J., Uetz, M.: The sequential price of anarchy for atomic congestion games. In: Liu, T.-Y., Qi, Q., Ye, Y. (eds.) WINE 2014. LNCS, vol. 8877, pp. 429–434. Springer, Cham (2014). https://doi.org/10.1007/978-3-319-13129-0_35

26. Koutsoupias, E., Mavronicolas, M., Spirakis, P.: Approximate equilibria and ball fusion. Theory Comput. Syst. **36**(6), 683–693 (2003). https://doi.org/10.1007/s00224-003-1131-5

27. Koutsoupias, E., Papadimitriou, C.: Worst-case equilibria. In: Meinel, C., Tison, S. (eds.) STACS 1999. LNCS, vol. 1563, pp. 404–413. Springer, Heidelberg (1999). https://doi.org/10.1007/3-540-49116-3_38

28. Leme, R.P., Syrgkanis, V., Tardos, É.: The curse of simultaneity. In: Proceedings of Innovations in Theoretical Computer Science (ITCS), pp. 60–67 (2012)

29. Pinedo, M., Hadavi, K.: Scheduling: theory, algorithms and systems development. In: Gaul, W., Bachem, A., Habenicht, W., Runge, W., Stahl, W.W. (eds.) Operations Research Proceedings 1991. Operations Research Proceedings 1991, vol 1991. Springer, Heidelberg (2012). https://doi.org/10.1007/978-3-642-46773-8_5

30. Tranæs, T.: Tie-breaking in games of perfect information. Games Econ. Behav. **22**(1), 148–161 (1998)

31. Zhang, L., Zhang, Y., Du, D., Bai, Q.: Improved price of anarchy for machine scheduling games with coordination mechanisms. Optim. Lett. **13**(4), 949–959 (2018). https://doi.org/10.1007/s11590-018-1285-3

Nash Social Welfare in Selfish and Online Load Balancing

Vittorio Bilò[1], Gianpiero Monaco[2], Luca Moscardelli[3],
and Cosimo Vinci[4(✉)]

[1] University of Salento, Lecce, Italy
vittorio.bilo@unisalento.it
[2] University of L'Aquila, L'Aquila, Italy
gianpiero.monaco@univaq.it
[3] University of Chieti-Pescara, Chieti, Italy
luca.moscardelli@unich.it
[4] Gran Sasso Science Institute, L'Aquila, Italy
cosimo.vinci@gssi.it

Abstract. In load balancing problems there is a set of clients, each wishing to select a resource from a set of permissible ones, in order to execute a certain task. Each resource has a latency function, which depends on its workload, and a client's cost is the completion time of her chosen resource. Two fundamental variants of load balancing problems are *selfish load balancing* (aka. *load balancing games*), where clients are non-cooperative selfish players aimed at minimizing their own cost solely, and *online load balancing*, where clients appear online and have to be irrevocably assigned to a resource without any knowledge about future requests. We revisit both selfish and online load balancing under the objective of minimizing the *Nash Social Welfare*, i.e., the geometric mean of the clients' costs. To the best of our knowledge, despite being a celebrated welfare estimator in many social contexts, the Nash Social Welfare has not been considered so far as a benchmarking quality measure in load balancing problems. We provide tight bounds on the price of anarchy of pure Nash equilibria and on the competitive ratio of the greedy algorithm under very general latency functions, including polynomial ones. For this particular class, we also prove that the greedy strategy is optimal as it matches the performance of any possible online algorithm.

1 Introduction

In load balancing problems there is a set of clients, each wishing to select a resource from a set of permissible ones, in order to execute a certain task. Each resource has a latency function, which depends on its workload, and a client's cost is the completion time of her chosen resource. These problems stand at the

This work was partially supported by the Italian MIUR PRIN 2017 Project ALGADIMAR "Algorithms, Games, and Digital Markets".

X. Chen et al. (Eds.): WINE 2020, LNCS 12495, pp. 323–337, 2020.
https://doi.org/10.1007/978-3-030-64946-3_23

foundations of the Theory of Computing and have been studied under a variety of objective functions, such as the maximum client's cost (aka. the makespan) [24–26,30] and the average weighted client's cost (see [18] for an excellent survey).

Two extensively studied variants of load balancing problems are *selfish load balancing* [40] (aka. *load balancing games*) and *online load balancing* [24]. Selfish load balancing, where clients are non-cooperative selfish players aimed at minimizing their own cost solely, constitutes a notable subclass of *weighted congestion games* [34] and, as such, enjoys some nice theoretical properties. For instance, they always admit pure Nash Equilibria [27]. In online load balancing, instead, clients appear online and have to be irrevocably assigned to a resource without any knowledge about future requests. Interpreting the set of clients of a load balancing problem as a society and adopting the terminology of welfare economics, the makespan and the average weighted client's cost objective functions get called, respectively, the *egalitarian* and the *utilitarian* social function. In the case of unweighted tasks, the egalitarian function is defined as $\max_i x_i$, and the utilitarian one is defined as $\frac{1}{n} \sum_i x_i$, where n is the number of clients and $x = (x_1, x_2, ...)$ is the vector encoding the clients' costs. Another interesting social function is the *Nash Social Welfare* (NSW) [32], which is defined as $(\prod_i x_i)^{\frac{1}{n}}$, i.e., as the geometric mean of the clients' costs. These definitions naturally extend to the more general case of weighted tasks (see Sect. 2).

The NSW is a celebrated welfare measure in many settings, such as Fisher markets [6,13] and fair division [16,20], as it satisfies a set of interesting properties and achieves a balanced compromise between the equity of the egalitarian social welfare function and the efficiency of the utilitarian one. We notice that when $x_i > 0$, for any $i = 1, \ldots, n$, this balance holds regardless of whether the objective is maximizing or minimizing the NSW. It is easy to see that an outcome that minimizes the NSW is Pareto optimal. Another interesting motivation for considering the NSW in load balancing comes from the following observation. An alternative reasonable way to define a client's cost can come by taking the ratio between the completion time of her chosen resource and the completion time she could obtain when being the only client in the system (i.e., when she is the unique user of the fastest resource). This definition avoids situations where the cost of a specific client determines almost completely the value of the social welfare. This happens, for instance, when there is a client i owing a highly time-consuming task. Here, both the utilitarian and the egalitarian social welfare end up depending on the cost of i, thus almost neglecting the other clients' costs. In this setting, the NSW is the proper metric to use. More generally, the NSW is the only correct mean to use when averaging normalized results, that is, results that are presented as ratios to reference values [22]. It is important to emphasize the scale-freeness of the NSW in load balancing problems, that is, the NSW is a robust social welfare function as its analysis is not affected by this change in the definition of a client's cost.

1.1   Related Work

Selfish Load Balancing. The literature concerning the efficiency of Nash equilibria in selfish load balancing is highly tied with that of its superclass of congestion games. In the following, we first focus on results for the mostly studied case of the *utilitarian social welfare*. In this setting, it is assumed that all clients selecting the same resource experience the same cost.

Exact bounds for both weighted and unweighted congestion games with polynomial latency functions have been given in [1], and in [7,23] it is proved that they hold even for unweighted load balancing games and symmetric weighted load balancing games, respectively. These results have been further generalized in [10], where it is shown that, under general latency functions encompassing polynomial ones, the worst-case price of anarchy of both symmetric weighted congestion games and unweighted congestion games is attained by load balancing instances. For the class of non-atomic congestion games, bounds on the price of anarchy under general latency functions are given in [35–37], where it is also proved that they are tight even for a two-node network with two parallel links. The price of anarchy for the *egalitarian social welfare* of load balancing has been studied in [21,29].

Online Load Balancing. The performance of greedy load balancing with respect to the utilitarian social welfare and under affine latency functions has been studied in [3,15,38]. A more general model where each client has a load vector denoting her impact on each resource (i.e., how much her assignment to a resource will increase its load) and the objective is to minimize the L_p norm of the load of the resources is considered in [3,14]. A logarithmic tight bound on the competitiveness of the greedy algorithm under the egalitarian social welfare is given in [2,4]. A different online algorithm (usually termed one-round walk starting from the empty state) for load balancing under affine latency functions has been analysed in [9,19]. Bounds for the case of polynomial latencies are given in [8,11,28], while more general latency functions are addressed in [10,39], with respect to atomic and non-atomic congestion games, respectively.

1.2   Our Contribution

We revisit both selfish and online load balancing under the objective of minimizing the NSW. To the best of our knowledge, this is the first work adopting the NSW as a benchmarking quality measure in load balancing problems. We analyze the price of anarchy [29] of pure Nash equilibria (the loss in optimality due to selfish behavior) and the competitive ratio of online algorithms (the loss in optimality due to lack of information) under very general latency functions. These questions have been widely addressed under the utilitarian and egalitarian functions, but never under the NSW.

We notice that, by adopting the NSW as new metric, we are not going to modify the set of Nash equilibria but only the social values. The main difference between the NSW and the classical notion of utilitarian social welfare consists in the fact that, while in the latter the players' costs are summed, in the former they are multiplied. This may lead to think that, by turning the costs into their logarithms, a classical utilitarian analysis can be easily adapted to deal with the NSW, but this is not the case.[1] Thus, the analysis of the NSW requires different proof arguments. Furthermore, while the simpler combinatorial structure of load balancing games does not improve the price of anarchy of general congestion games for the utilitarian social welfare (see [10,15]), the price of anarchy drops from n to 2 for the NSW and linear latency functions (the details are deferred to the full version of this paper).

All upper bounds shown in this paper are quite general, given that they hold for any non-decreasing and positive latency function. Moreover, the provided matching lower bounds hold for latency functions verifying mild assumptions; it is worth to remark that they are satisfied by the well studied class of polynomial latency functions and by many other ones. In particular, in Subsects. 3.1, 3.2, and 3.3, we provide tight bounds to the price of anarchy of weighted, unweighted, and non-atomic games, respectively, and we apply such results to the case of polynomial latency functions. For the online setting, we analyze the greedy algorithm that assigns every client to a resource minimizing the total cost of the instance revealed up to the time of its appearance. We provide a tight analysis of the competitive ratio of the greedy algorithm, and we show that, when considering polynomial latency functions, there exists no online algorithm achieving a competitive ratio better than the one of the greedy algorithm (see Sect. 4). In Table 1, we summarize the results obtained for polynomial latency

Table 1. Tight bounds on the performance of load balancing with polynomial latency functions of maximum degree p, under the NSW and the utilitarian social welfare (USW). Φ_p denotes the unique solution of equation $x^{p+1} = (x+1)^p$, and $k := \lfloor \Phi_p \rfloor$. We observe that the performance for the NSW is definitely better (even asymptotically) than that for the USW, except for the non-atomic setting.

	NSW	USW
Weighted	2^p	$(\Phi_p)^{p+1} \sim \Theta\left(\frac{p}{\log(p)}\right)^{p+1}$, [1]
Unweighted	2^p	$\frac{(k+1)^{2p+1} - k^{p+1}(k+2)^p}{(k+1)^{p+1} - (k+2)^p + (k+1)^p - k^{p+1}} \sim \Theta\left(\frac{p}{\log(p)}\right)^{p+1}$, [1]
Non-atomic	$\left(e^{\frac{1}{e}}\right)^p$	$\left(1 - p(p+1)^{-(p+1)/p}\right)^{-1} \sim \Theta\left(\frac{p}{\log(p)}\right)$, [35]
Online	4^p	$\left(2^{1/(p+1)} - 1\right)^{-(p+1)} \sim \Theta(p)^{p+1}$, [14]

---

[1] In fact, on the one hand, using this idea for bounding a performance ratio (e.g., the price of anarchy or the competitive ratio), one obtains a bound on the ratio between two logarithms (each one having the product of the players' costs as argument). On the other hand, we are interested in bounding the ratio between the argument of these logarithms, and there is no direct correlation between these two ratios (notice that logarithm of the latter ratio is equal to the difference between the corresponding utilitarian social costs, and therefore it is not related to the former one).

functions, and we compare them with the ones holding for the utilitarian social welfare studied in some previous works.

Due to lack of space, some proofs are either sketched or omitted, and are left to the full version of the paper.

2 Model

Given $k \in \mathbb{N}$, let $[k] := \{1, 2, \ldots, k\}$. A class $\mathcal{C}$ of functions is called *ordinate-scaling* if, for any $f \in \mathcal{C}$ and $\alpha \geq 0$, the function g such that $g(x) = \alpha f(x)$ for any $x \geq 0$, belongs to $\mathcal{C}$; *abscissa-scaling* if, for any $f \in \mathcal{C}$ and $\alpha \geq 0$, the function g such that $g(x) = f(\alpha x)$ for any $x \geq 0$, belongs to $\mathcal{C}$; *all-constant-including* if it contains all the constant functions (i.e., all functions f such that $f(x) = c$ for some $c > 0$); *unbounded-including* if all the latency functions f, except for the constant ones, verify $\lim_{x \to \infty} f(x) = \infty$. Let $\mathcal{P}(p)$ denote the class of polynomial latencies of maximum degree p, i.e., the class of functions $f(x) = \sum_{d=0}^{p} \alpha_d x^d$, with $\alpha_d \geq 0$ for any $d \in [p] \cup \{0\}$ and $\alpha_d > 0$ for some $d \in [p] \cup \{0\}$. A function f is *quasi-log-convex* if $x \ln(f(x))$ is convex. We first deal with *selfish load balancing*, and then we turn our attention to the online setting.

2.1 Selfish Load Balancing

(Atomic) Load Balancing Games. A *weighted (atomic) load balancing game*, or *load balancing game* for brevity, is a tuple $\mathsf{LB} = (N, R, (\ell_j)_{j \in R}, (w_i)_{i \in N}, (\Sigma_i)_{i \in N})$, where N is a set of $n \geq 1$ players (corresponding to clients), R is a finite set of resources, $\ell_j : \mathbb{R}_{>0} \to \mathbb{R}_{>0}$ is the (non-decreasing and positive) latency function of resource $j \in R$, and, for each $i \in N$, $w_i > 0$ is the weight of player i and $\Sigma_i \subseteq R$ (with $\Sigma_i \neq \emptyset$) is her set of strategies (or admissible resources). For notational simplicity, we assume that each latency function ℓ verifies $\ell(0) = 0$.

An *unweighted load balancing game* is a weighted load balancing game with unitary weights. A *symmetric weighted load balancing game* is a load balancing game in which each player can select all the resources, i.e., $\Sigma_i = R$ for any $i \in N$.

Given a class $\mathcal{C}$ of latency functions, let $\mathsf{ULB}(\mathcal{C})$ be the class of unweighted load balancing games, $\mathsf{WLB}(\mathcal{C})$ be the class of weighted load balancing games, and $\mathsf{SWLB}(\mathcal{C})$ be the class of weighted symmetric load balancing games, all having latency functions in the class $\mathcal{C}$. We say that resources are *identical* if all of them have the same latency function.

Non-atomic Load Balancing Games. The counterpart of the class of atomic load balancing games is that of *non-atomic load balancing games* [5,33,41]: these games are a good approximation for atomic ones when players become infinitely many and the contribution of each player to social welfare becomes infinitesimally small. A *non-atomic load balancing game* is a tuple $\mathsf{NLB} = (N, R, (\ell_j)_{j \in R}, (r_i)_{i \in N}, (\Sigma_i)_{i \in N})$, where N is a set of $n \geq 1$ *types* of players,

R is a finite set of resources, $\ell_j : \mathbb{R}_{>0} \to \mathbb{R}_{>0}$ is the (non-decreasing and positive) latency function of resource $j \in R$; moreover, given $i \in N$, $r_i \in \mathbb{R}_{\geq 0}$ is the amount of players of type i and $\Sigma_i \subseteq R$ is the set of strategies of every player of type i.

Given a class $\mathcal{C}$ of latency functions, let $\mathsf{NLB}(\mathcal{C})$ be the class of non-atomic load balancing games, and $\mathsf{SNLB}(\mathcal{C})$ be the class of symmetric non-atomic load balancing games, all having latency functions in the class $\mathcal{C}$.

Strategy Profiles and Cost Functions. In atomic load balancing games, a *strategy profile* is an n-tuple $\boldsymbol{\sigma} = (\sigma_1, \ldots, \sigma_n)$, where $\sigma_i \in \Sigma_i$ is the resource chosen by each player $i \in N$ in $\boldsymbol{\sigma}$. Given a strategy profile $\boldsymbol{\sigma}$, let $k_j(\boldsymbol{\sigma}) := \sum_{i \in N : \sigma_i = j} w_i$ be the *congestion* of resource $j \in R$ in $\boldsymbol{\sigma}$, and let $cost_i(\boldsymbol{\sigma}) := \ell_{\sigma_i}(k_{\sigma_i}(\boldsymbol{\sigma}))$ be the *cost* of player $i \in N$ in $\boldsymbol{\sigma}$.

In non-atomic load balancing games, a *strategy profile* is an n-tuple $\boldsymbol{\Delta} = (\Delta_1, \ldots, \Delta_n)$, where $\Delta_i : \Sigma_i \to \mathbb{R}_{\geq 0}$ is a function denoting, for each resource $j \in \Sigma_i$, the amount $\Delta_i(j)$ of players of type i selecting resource j, so that $\sum_{j \in \Sigma_i} \Delta_i(j) = r_i$. Observe that $\Delta_i(j) = 0$ if $j \notin \Sigma_i$. For a strategy profile $\boldsymbol{\Delta}$, the congestion of resource $j \in R$ in $\boldsymbol{\Delta}$, denoted as $k_j(\boldsymbol{\Delta}) := \sum_{i \in N} \Delta_i(j)$, is the total amount of players using resource j in $\boldsymbol{\Delta}$ and its cost is given by $cost_j(\boldsymbol{\Delta}) = \ell_j(k_j(\boldsymbol{\Delta}))$. The cost of a player of type i selecting a resource $j \in \Sigma_i$ is equal to $cost_j(\boldsymbol{\Delta})$ and each player aims at minimizing it.

Nash Social Welfare. In atomic load balancing games, the *Nash Social Welfare (NSW)* of a strategy profile $\boldsymbol{\sigma}$ is defined as:

$$\mathsf{NSW}(\boldsymbol{\sigma}) := \left(\prod_{i \in N} cost_i(\boldsymbol{\sigma})^{w_i} \right)^{\frac{1}{\sum_{i \in N} w_i}}.$$

Using the previous definition, for unweighted games we get $\mathsf{NSW}(\boldsymbol{\sigma}) = \left(\prod_{i \in N} cost_i(\boldsymbol{\sigma}) \right)^{\frac{1}{n}}$. Given a strategy profile $\boldsymbol{\sigma}$, let $R(\boldsymbol{\sigma}) := \{j \in R : k_j(\boldsymbol{\sigma}) > 0\}$. For weighted load balancing games we get:

$$\mathsf{NSW}(\boldsymbol{\sigma}) = \left(\prod_{i \in N} cost_i(\boldsymbol{\sigma})^{w_i} \right)^{\frac{1}{\sum_{i \in N} w_i}} = \left(\prod_{j \in R(\boldsymbol{\sigma})} \ell_j(k_j(\boldsymbol{\sigma}))^{k_j(\boldsymbol{\sigma})} \right)^{\frac{1}{\sum_{i \in N} w_i}}$$

$$= \left(\prod_{j \in R(\boldsymbol{\sigma})} \ell_j(k_j(\boldsymbol{\sigma}))^{k_j(\boldsymbol{\sigma})} \right)^{\frac{1}{\sum_{j \in R(\boldsymbol{\sigma})} k_j(\boldsymbol{\sigma})}}.$$

Let $\mathsf{SP(LB)}$ be the set of strategy profiles of an atomic load balancing game LB. An optimal strategy profile $\boldsymbol{\sigma}^*(\mathsf{LB})$ of a load balancing game LB is a strategy profile $\boldsymbol{\sigma}^* \in \arg\min_{\boldsymbol{\sigma} \in \mathsf{SP(LB)}} \mathsf{NSW}(\boldsymbol{\sigma})$, i.e., a strategy profile minimizing the NSW. Analogously, for the non-atomic setting, we have

$$\mathsf{NSW}(\boldsymbol{\Delta}) = \left(\prod_{j \in R(\boldsymbol{\Delta})} cost_j(\boldsymbol{\Delta})^{k_j(\boldsymbol{\Delta})} \right)^{\frac{1}{\sum_{j \in R(\boldsymbol{\Delta})} k_j(\boldsymbol{\Delta})}},$$

where $R(\boldsymbol{\Delta}) := \{j \in R : k_j(\boldsymbol{\Delta}) > 0\}$. Let $\mathsf{SP(NLB)}$ be the set of strategy profiles of a non-atomic load balancing game NLB. An optimal strategy profile $\boldsymbol{\Delta}^*(\mathsf{NLB})$ of a load balancing game NLB is a strategy profile $\boldsymbol{\Delta}^* \in \arg\min_{\boldsymbol{\Delta} \in \mathsf{SP(NLB)}} \mathsf{NSW}(\boldsymbol{\Delta})$, i.e., a strategy profile minimizing the NSW.

Pure Nash Equilibria and their Efficiency. In the atomic setting, for a given strategy profile $\boldsymbol{\sigma}$, let $(\boldsymbol{\sigma}_{-i}, \sigma_i') := (\sigma_1, \sigma_2, \ldots, \sigma_{i-1}, \sigma_i', \sigma_{i+1}, \ldots, \sigma_n)$, i.e., a strategy profile equal to $\boldsymbol{\sigma}$, except for strategy σ_i'. A *pure Nash equilibrium* is a strategy profile $\boldsymbol{\sigma}$ such that $cost_i(\boldsymbol{\sigma}) \leq cost_i(\boldsymbol{\sigma}_{-i}, \sigma_i')$ for any $\sigma_i' \in \Sigma_i$ and $i \in N$, i.e., a strategy profile in which no player can improve her cost by unilateral deviations. Let $\mathsf{PNE(LB)}$ be the set of pure Nash equilibria of a load balancing game LB. The *Nash price of anarchy* of LB is defined as: $\mathsf{NPoA(LB)} = \sup_{\boldsymbol{\sigma} \in \mathsf{PNE(LB)}} \frac{\mathsf{NSW}(\boldsymbol{\sigma})}{\mathsf{NSW}(\boldsymbol{\sigma}^*(\mathsf{LB}))}$ Given a class $\mathcal{G}$ of load balancing games, the *Nash price of anarchy* of $\mathcal{G}$ is defined as $\mathsf{NPoA}(\mathcal{G}) = \sup_{\mathsf{LB} \in \mathcal{G}} \mathsf{NPoA(LB)}$. In the non-atomic setting, a *pure Nash equilibrium* is a strategy profile $\boldsymbol{\Delta}$ such that, for any player type $i \in N$, resources $j, j' \in \Sigma_i$ such that $\Delta_i(j) > 0$, $cost_j(\boldsymbol{\Delta}) \leq cost_{j'}(\boldsymbol{\Delta})$ holds, that is, an outcome of the game in which no player can improve her situation by unilaterally deviating to another strategy. The *Nash price of anarchy* of a non-atomic game NLB (denoted as $\mathsf{NPoA(NLB)}$) is defined as in the atomic setting, and again, given a class $\mathcal{G}$ of non-atomic load balancing games, the *Nash price of anarchy* of $\mathcal{G}$ is defined as $\mathsf{NPoA}(\mathcal{G}) = \sup_{\mathsf{NLB} \in \mathcal{G}} \mathsf{NPoA(NLB)}$.

2.2 Online Load Balancing

We now introduce online load balancing. There is a natural correspondence between a load balancing game and an instance of the online load balancing problem. When dealing with the online setting, as usual in the literature, we adopt a different nomenclature. In particular, an instance I of the online load balancing problem is a tuple $\mathsf{I} = (N, R, (\ell_j)_{j \in R}, (w_i)_{i \in N}, (\Sigma_i)_{i \in N})$, where $N = [n]$ is a set of $n \geq 1$ *clients*, R is a finite set of resources, $\ell_j : \mathbb{R}_{>0} \to \mathbb{R}_{>0}$ is the (non-decreasing and positive) latency function of resource $j \in R$, and, for each $i \in N$, $w_i > 0$ is the weight of client i and $\Sigma_i \subseteq R$ (with $\Sigma_i \neq \emptyset$) is her set of *admissible resources*. Furthermore, in the online setting an assignment of clients to resources is called state: A *state* is an n-tuple $\boldsymbol{\sigma} = (\sigma_1, \ldots, \sigma_n)$, where $\sigma_i \in \Sigma_i \subseteq R$ is the resource assigned to player $i \in N$ in $\boldsymbol{\sigma}$. As in load balancing games, given a class of latency functions $\mathcal{C}$, let $\mathsf{WLB}(\mathcal{C})$ denote class of load balancing instances with latency functions in $\mathcal{C}$.

The NSW of a state and the optimal state are defined analogously to the selfish load balancing setting.

The Online Setting. In *online load balancing*, clients appear in online fashion, in consecutive *steps*; when a client appears, an irrevocable decision has to be taken in order to assign it to a resource. We assume w.l.o.g. that clients appear in increasing order, i.e., client $i \in [n]$ appears before client $j \in [n]$ if and only if $i < j$. More formally, for any $i \in [n]$, an online algorithm has to assign client i to a resource being admissible for it without the knowledge of the future clients $i + 1, i + 2, \ldots$; the assignment of client i decided by the algorithm at step i cannot be modified at later steps.

Notice that at each step $i > 1$ a new instance is obtained by adding client i to the instance of step $i - 1$.

Competitive Ratio. Following the standard performance measure in competitive analysis, we evaluate the performance of an online algorithm in terms of its *competitiveness* (or *competitive ratio*).

An online algorithm A is *c-competitive* on instance I if the following holds: Let σ and σ^* be the state computed by algorithm A and the optimal state for I, respectively. Then, $\mathsf{NSW}(\sigma) \leq c \cdot \mathsf{NSW}(\sigma^*)$. The competitive ratio $\mathsf{CR_A}(\mathsf{I})$ of algorithm A on instance I is the smallest c such that A is c-competitive on I [12].

Given a class $\mathcal{I}$ of load balancing instances, the competitive ratio $\mathsf{CR_A}(\mathcal{I})$ of Algorithm A on $\mathcal{I}$ is simply given by the supremum competitive ratio of A over all instances $\mathsf{I} \in \mathcal{I}$, i.e., $\mathsf{CR_A}(\mathcal{I}) = \sup_{\mathsf{I} \in \mathcal{I}} \mathsf{CR_A}(\mathsf{I})$.

Greedy Algorithm. A natural algorithm proposed in [3] for this problem is to assign each client to the resource yielding the minimum increase to the social welfare (ties are broken arbitrarily). This results to *greedy assignments*. Therefore, given an instance of online load balancing, an assignment of clients to resources is called a greedy assignment if the assignment of a client to a resource minimizes the total cost of the instance revealed up to the time of its appearance.

3   Selfish Load Balancing

In this section we focus on selfish load balancing. In particular, in Subsect. 3.1 we deal with the analysis of the price of anarchy in weighted load balancing games, in Subsect. 3.2 we consider the subclass of unweighted load balancing games, while in Subsect. 3.3 we analyze the price of anarchy of non-atomic load balancing games.

3.1   The NPoA for Weighted Load Balancing Games

We first provide an upper bound to the Nash price of anarchy of weighted load balancing games. Given a class of latency function $\mathcal{C}$, define $\psi(\mathcal{C}) :=$
$$\sup_{f_1, f_2 \in \mathcal{C}, k_1, k_2, o_1, o_2 \in \mathbb{R}: k_1 \geq o_1 > 0, o_2 > k_2 \geq 0} \left(\frac{f_1(k_1 + o_1)}{f_1(o_1)} \right)^{\frac{(o_2 - k_2)o_1}{k_1 o_2 - k_2 o_1}} \left(\frac{f_2(k_2 + o_2)}{f_2(o_2)} \right)^{\frac{(k_1 - o_1)o_2}{k_1 o_2 - k_2 o_1}}.$$

Theorem 1. *Let $\mathcal{C}$ be a class of latency functions. The Nash price of anarchy of weighted load balancing games with latency functions in $\mathcal{C}$ is $\mathsf{NPoA}(\mathsf{WLB}(\mathcal{C})) \leq \psi(\mathcal{C})$.*

Proof. Let $\mathsf{LB} \in \mathsf{WLB}(\mathcal{C})$ be a weighted load balancing game with latency functions in $\mathcal{C}$, and let $\boldsymbol{\sigma}$ and $\boldsymbol{\sigma}^*$ be a worst case pure Nash equilibrium and an optimal strategy profile of LB, respectively. Let k_j denote $k_j(\boldsymbol{\sigma})$ and o_j denote $k_j(\boldsymbol{\sigma}^*)$. Since $\boldsymbol{\sigma}$ is a pure Nash equilibrium, we have that $cost_i(\boldsymbol{\sigma}) \le cost_i(\boldsymbol{\sigma}_{-i}, \sigma_i^*)$. Thus, we get $\prod_{i \in N} cost_i(\boldsymbol{\sigma})^{w_i} \le \prod_{i \in N} cost_i(\boldsymbol{\sigma}_{-i}, \sigma_i^*)^{w_i}$.

Since $cost_i(\boldsymbol{\sigma}) = \ell_{\sigma_i}(k_{\sigma_i})$ and $cost_i(\boldsymbol{\sigma}_{-i}, \sigma_i^*) \le \ell_{\sigma_i^*}(k_{\sigma_i^*} + w_i)$, it holds that $\prod_{i \in N} cost_i(\boldsymbol{\sigma})^{w_i} = \prod_{i \in N} \ell_{\sigma_i}(k_{\sigma_i})^{w_i} = \prod_{j \in R(\sigma)} \ell_j(k_j)^{\sum_{i:j=\sigma_i} w_i} = \prod_{j \in R(\sigma)} \ell_j(k_j)^{k_j}$ and $\prod_{i \in N} cost_i(\boldsymbol{\sigma}_{-i}, \sigma_i^*)^{w_i} \le \prod_{i \in N} \ell_{\sigma_i^*}(k_{\sigma_i^*} + w_i)^{w_i} \le \prod_{i \in N} \ell_{\sigma_i^*}(k_{\sigma_i^*} + o_{\sigma_i^*})^{w_i} = \prod_{j \in R(\sigma^*)} \ell_j(k_j + o_j)^{\sum_{i:j=\sigma_i^*} w_i} = \prod_{j \in R(\sigma^*)} \ell_j(k_j + o_j)^{o_j}$. By putting together the above inequalities we get

$$\prod_{j \in R(\sigma)} \ell_j(k_j)^{k_j} = \prod_{i \in N} cost_i(\boldsymbol{\sigma})^{w_i} \le \prod_{i \in N} cost_i(\boldsymbol{\sigma}_{-i}, \sigma_i^*)^{w_i} \le \prod_{j \in R(\sigma^*)} \ell_j(k_j + o_j)^{o_j}. \tag{1}$$

By exploiting the properties of the logarithmic function and by using (1), we obtain

$$\ln\left(\mathsf{NPoA}(\mathsf{LB})\right) = \ln\left(\frac{\left(\prod_{j \in R(\sigma)} \ell_j(k_j)^{k_j}\right)^{\frac{1}{\sum_{i \in N} w_i}}}{\left(\prod_{j \in R(\sigma^*)} \ell_j(o_j)^{o_j}\right)^{\frac{1}{\sum_{i \in N} w_i}}}\right)$$

$$\le \ln\left(\frac{\left(\prod_{j \in R(\sigma^*)} \ell_j(k_j + o_j)^{o_j}\right)^{\frac{1}{\sum_{i \in N} w_i}}}{\left(\prod_{j \in R(\sigma^*)} \ell_j(o_j)^{o_j}\right)^{\frac{1}{\sum_{i \in N} w_i}}}\right)$$

$$= \frac{\sum_{j \in R(\sigma^*)} o_j \left(\ln(\ell_j(k_j + o_j)) - \ln(\ell_j(o_j))\right)}{\sum_{i \in N} w_i}. \tag{2}$$

Since $\sum_{i \in N} w_i = \sum_{j \in R} k_j = \sum_{j \in R} o_j$, we have that (2) is upper bounded by the optimal solution of the following optimization problem on some new linear variables $(\alpha_j)_{j \in R}$ (as (2) is the solution obtained by setting $\alpha = 1$ for each $j \in R$):

$$\max \quad \frac{\sum_{j \in R(\sigma^*)} \alpha_j o_j \left(\ln(\ell_j(k_j + o_j)) - \ln(\ell_j(o_j))\right)}{\sum_{j \in R} \alpha_j k_j}$$

$$\text{s.t.} \quad \sum_{j \in R} \alpha_j k_j = \sum_{j \in R} \alpha_j o_j, \quad \alpha_j \ge 0 \ \forall j \in R. \tag{3}$$

Fact 1. *The value of the optimal solution of (3) is at most* $\sup_{\substack{k_1 \ge o_1 > 0, \\ o_2 > k_2 \ge 0, \\ f_1, f_2 \in \mathcal{C}}}$

$$\frac{(o_2 - k_2) o_1 \left(\ln(f_1(k_1 + o_1)) - \ln(f_1(o_1))\right) + (k_1 - o_1) o_2 \left(\ln(f_2(k_2 + o_2)) - \ln(f_2(o_2))\right)}{k_1 o_2 - k_2 o_1}.$$

By Fact 1, and by continuing from (2), we have that the upper bound provided in Fact 1 is higher or equal than $\ln(\mathsf{NPoA}(\mathsf{LB}))$. Thus, by exponentiating this inequality, we get $\mathsf{NPoA}(\mathsf{LB}) \le \psi(\mathcal{C})$. Hence, by the arbitrariness of $\mathsf{LB} \in \mathsf{WLB}(\mathcal{C})$, the claim follows. □

In the following theorem we show that the upper bound derived in Theorem 1 is tight under mild assumptions on the latency functions.

Theorem 2. *Let $\mathcal{C}$ be a class of latency functions. (i) If $\mathcal{C}$ is abscissa-scaling and ordinate-scaling, then $\mathsf{NPoA}(\mathsf{WLB}(\mathcal{C})) \geq \psi(\mathcal{C})$. (ii) If $\mathcal{C}$ is abscissa-scaling, ordinate-scaling, and unbounded-including, the previous inequality holds even for symmetric weighted load balancing games.*

Proof (Sketch of the proof). We show part (ii) of the claim only, as the proof of part (i) resorts to similar arguments. Let us assume that $\mathcal{C}$ is abscissa-scaling, ordinate-scaling, and unbounded-including. In order to prove part (ii), we equivalently show that for any $M < \psi(\mathcal{C})$ there exists a game $\mathsf{LB} \in \mathsf{WLB}(\mathcal{C})$ such that $\mathsf{NPoA}(\mathsf{LB}) > M$.

Let $f_1, f_2 \in \mathcal{C}$, $k_1, k_2, o_1, o_2 \geq 0$ such that $k_1 \geq o_1 > 0, o_2 > k_2 \geq 0$, and a sufficiently small $\epsilon > 0$ such that $\left(\frac{f_1(k_1+o_1)}{f_1(o_1)}\right)^{\frac{(o_2-k_2)o_1}{k_1 o_2 - k_2 o_1}} \left(\frac{f_2(k_2+o_2)}{f_2(o_2)}\right)^{\frac{(k_1-o_1)o_2}{k_1 o_2 - k_2 o_1}} > M + \epsilon$. Let $f, g \in \mathcal{C}$ be such that $f(x) := f_1(o_1 x)$ and $g(x) := f_2(o_2 x)$, and let $k := k_1/o_1$ and $h := k_2/o_2$. Since $\left(\frac{f_1(k_1+o_1)}{f_1(o_1)}\right)^{\frac{(o_2-k_2)o_1}{k_1 o_2 - k_2 o_1}} \left(\frac{f_2(k_2+o_2)}{f_2(o_2)}\right)^{\frac{(k_1-o_1)o_2}{k_1 o_2 - k_2 o_1}} = \left(\frac{f(k+1)}{f(1)}\right)^{\frac{1-h}{k-h}} \left(\frac{g(h+1)}{g(1)}\right)^{\frac{k-1}{k-h}}$ we have that, for some $f, g \in \mathcal{C}$, $k \geq 1$, and $h < 1$,

$$\left(\frac{f(k+1)}{f(1)}\right)^{\frac{1-h}{k-h}} \left(\frac{g(h+1)}{g(1)}\right)^{\frac{k-1}{k-h}} > M + \epsilon. \tag{4}$$

Observe that f and g can be chosen in such a way that they are non-constant functions. Indeed, if one of them is constant, it is sufficient replacing it with an arbitrary non-constant function, so that (4) holds as well. As $\mathcal{C}$ is unbounded-including and functions f, g are non-constant, we have that $\lim_{x\to\infty} f(x) = \lim_{x\to\infty} g(x) = \infty$.

We consider the case $h > 0$ only (the case $h = 0$ is analogue and is omitted). Given two integers $m \geq 3$ and $s \geq 1$, let $\mathsf{LB}(m, s)$ be a symmetric weighted load balancing game where the resources are partitioned into $2m$ groups $R_1, R_2, R_3 \ldots, R_{2m}$. Each group R_j has s^{j-1} resources and the latency function of each resource $r \in R_j$ is defined as $\ell_r(x) := \alpha_j \hat{f}_j (\beta_j x)$ with

$$\hat{f}_j := \begin{cases} f & \text{if } j \leq m-1 \\ g & \text{if } j \geq m \end{cases}, \quad \beta_j := \begin{cases} \left(\frac{s}{k}\right)^{j-1} & \text{if } j \leq m-1 \\ \left(\frac{s}{h}\right)^{j-m} \left(\frac{s}{k}\right)^{m-1} & \text{if } m \leq j \leq 2m \end{cases}, \tag{5}$$

$$\alpha_j := \begin{cases} \left(\frac{f(k)}{f(k+1)}\right)^{j-1} & \text{if } j \leq m-1 \\ \left(\frac{g(h)}{g(h+1)}\right)^{j-m} \left(\frac{f(k)}{g(h+1)}\right) \left(\frac{f(k)}{f(k+1)}\right)^{m-2} & \text{if } m \leq j \leq 2m-1 \\ \frac{g(h)}{g(1)} \left(\frac{g(h)}{g(h+1)}\right)^{m-1} \left(\frac{f(k)}{g(h+1)}\right) \left(\frac{f(k)}{f(k+1)}\right)^{m-2} & \text{if } j = 2m \end{cases}. \tag{6}$$

The set of players N is partitioned into $2m - 1$ sets $N_1, N_2, \ldots, N_{2m-1}$, and each group N_j has s^j players having weight $w_j := 1/\beta_{j+1}$. Let σ be the strategy profile in which, for any $j \in [2m-1]$, each resource of group R_j is selected by exactly s players of group N_j (see Fig. 1a). One can show that, for any integer $m \geq 3$, there exists a sufficiently large s_m such that σ is a pure Nash equilibrium of the game $\mathsf{LB}(m, s_m)$.

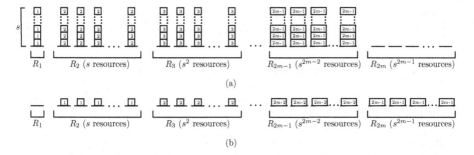

Fig. 1. The LB used in the proof of Theorem 2. Columns represent resources and squares represent players (number j inside a square means that the player belongs to group N_j). (a): a Nash equilibrium σ; (b): the strategy profile σ^*.

Now, let σ^* be the strategy profile of $\mathsf{LB}(m, s_m)$ in which, for any $j \in [2m-1]$, each resource of group R_{j+1} is selected by exactly one player of group N_j (see Fig. 1b). By exploiting the definitions of $\alpha_j, \beta_j, \hat{f}_j, w_j$, and N_j, and by choosing a sufficiently large m, one can show that the following inequalities hold: $\frac{\mathsf{NSW}(\sigma)}{\mathsf{NSW}(\sigma^*)} \geq \lim_{m \to \infty} \left(\frac{\prod_{j=1}^{2m-1} \left(\alpha_j \hat{f}_j (\beta_j s_m w_j) \right)^{|N_j| w_j}}{\prod_{j=2}^{2m} \left(\alpha_j \hat{f}_j (\beta_j w_{j-1}) \right)^{|N_{j-1}| w_{j-1}}} \right)^{\frac{1}{\sum_{j=1}^{2m-1} |N_j| w_j}} - \epsilon = \left(\frac{f(k+1)}{f(1)} \right)^{\frac{1-h}{k-h}} \left(\frac{g(h+1)}{g(1)} \right)^{\frac{k-1}{k-h}} - \epsilon > M + \epsilon - \epsilon = M$, thus showing part (ii) of the claim. $\qquad\square$

As the class of polynomial latency functions is ordinate-scaling, abscissa-scaling, and unbounded-including, the following corollary of Theorems 1 and 2 establishes the exact Nash price of anarchy for polynomial latency functions.

Corollary 1. *The Nash price of anarchy of weighted load balancing games with polynomial latency functions (even for symmetric games) of maximum degree p is* $\mathsf{NPoA}(\mathsf{WLB}(\mathcal{C})) = 2^p$.

When considering identical resources with polynomial latency functions, the price of anarchy does not decrease (the proof is deferred to the full version).

3.2 The NPoA for Unweighted Load Balancing Games

We first provide an upper bound to the Nash price of anarchy of unweighted load balancing games.

Theorem 3. *Let $\mathcal{C}$ be a class of latency functions. The Nash price of anarchy of unweighted load balancing games with latency functions in $\mathcal{C}$ is* $\mathsf{NPoA}(\mathsf{ULB}(\mathcal{C})) \leq \sup_{f \in \mathcal{C}, k \in \mathbb{N}, o \in [k]} \left(\frac{f(k+1)}{f(o)} \right)^{\frac{o}{k}}$.

We show that the upper bound derived in Theorem 3 is tight if the considered latency functions are ordinate-scaling (the proof is deferred to the full version). The following result for polynomial latency functions holds.

Corollary 2. *The Nash price of anarchy of unweighted load balancing games with polynomial latency functions of maximum degree p is* $\mathsf{NPoA}(\mathsf{ULB}(\mathcal{C})) = 2^p$.

3.3   The NPoA for Non-atomic Load Balancing Games

We first provide an upper bound to the Nash price of anarchy of non-atomic load balancing games.

Theorem 4. *Let $\mathcal{C}$ be a class of latency functions. The Nash price of anarchy of non-atomic load balancing games with latency functions in $\mathcal{C}$ is* $\mathsf{NPoA}(\mathsf{NLB}(\mathcal{C})) \leq$
$$\sup\nolimits_{f \in \mathcal{C}, k, o \in \mathbb{R}: k \geq o > 0} \left(\frac{f(k)}{f(o)} \right)^{\frac{o}{k}}.$$

We show that the upper bound derived in Theorem 4 is tight the considered latency functions are all-constant-including (the proof is deferred to the full version). The following result for polynomial latency functions holds.

Corollary 3. *The Nash price of anarchy of non-atomic load balancing games with polynomial latency functions of maximum degree p (even for symmetric games) is* $\mathsf{NPoA}(\mathsf{NLB}(\mathcal{P}(p))) = \mathsf{NPoA}(\mathsf{SNLB}(\mathcal{P}(p))) = \left(e^{\frac{1}{e}} \right)^p \simeq (1.44)^p$.

4   Online Load Balancing

We first provide an upper bound on the competitive ratio of the greedy algorithm.

Theorem 5. *Let $\mathcal{C}$ be a class of quasi-log-convex functions. The competitive ratio of the greedy algorithm G applied to load balancing instances with latency functions in $\mathcal{C}$ is* $\mathsf{CR}_\mathsf{G}(\mathsf{WLB}(\mathcal{C})) \leq \sup\limits_{\substack{f_1, f_2 \in \mathcal{C}, \\ k_1, k_2, o_1, o_2 \in \mathbb{R}: \\ k_1 \geq o_1 > 0, o_2 > k_2 \geq 0}} \left(\frac{f_1(k_1 + o_1)^{k_1 + o_1}}{f_1(k_1)^{k_1} f_1(o_1)^{o_1}} \right)^{\frac{o_2 - k_2}{o_2 k_1 - o_1 k_2}}$
$\left(\frac{f_2(k_2 + o_2)^{k_2 + o_2}}{f_2(k_2)^{k_2} f_2(o_2)^{o_2}} \right)^{\frac{k_1 - o_1}{o_2 k_1 - o_1 k_2}}$, *where we set* $f_2(0)^0 := 1$.

We show that, when considering the greedy algorithm, the upper bound derived in Theorem 5 is tight if the considered latency functions are abscissa-scaling and ordinate-scaling (the proof is deferred to the full version). The following result for polynomial latency functions holds.

Corollary 4. *The competitive ratio of the greedy algorithm applied to weighted load balancing instances with polynomial latency functions of maximum degree p is* $\mathsf{CR}_\mathsf{G}(\mathsf{WLB}(\mathcal{C})) = 4^p$.

We show that, when considering polynomial latency functions, the upper bound of Corollary 4 is tight for any online algorithm, i.e., we are able to provide a matching lower bound to the online load balancing problem (the proof is deferred to the full version).

5   Concluding Remarks and Open Problems

To the best of our knowledge, this is the first work that adopts the NSW as a benchmarking quality measure in load balancing problems. Several open problems deserve further investigation. Our paper mostly focuses on evaluating the performance of selfish and online load balancing. Concerning complexity issues, it is worth noticing that, on the one hand, when considering unweighted players, an optimal configuration with respect to the NSW can be trivially computed in polynomial time by exploiting the same techniques developed in [17,31] for the utilitarian social welfare; on the other hand, when considering weighted players, a simple reduction from the NP-complete problem PARTITION shows that the problem becomes NP-hard. Therefore, an interesting open problem is that of providing better polynomial time approximation algorithms for the weighted case and polynomial latency functions (we notice that, as shown in Corollary 4, the greedy algorithm provides a constant approximation factor).

References

1. Aland, S., Dumrauf, D., Gairing, M., Monien, B., Schoppmann, F.: Exact price of anarchy for polynomial congestion games. SIAM J. Comput. **40**(5), 1211–1233 (2011)
2. Aspnes, J., Azar, Y., Fiat, A., Plotkin, S.A., Waarts, O.: On-line routing of virtual circuits with applications to load balancing and machine scheduling. J. ACM **44**(3), 486–504 (1997)
3. Awerbuch, B., Yossi, A., Grove, E.F., Kao, M., Krishnan, P., Vitter, J.S.: Load balancing in the l_p norm. In: Proceedings of the 36th Annual Symposium on Foundations of Computer Science (FOCS), pp. 383–391 (1995)
4. Azar, Y., Naor, J., Rom, R.: The competitiveness of on-line assignments. In: Proceedings of the Third Annual ACM/SIGACT-SIAM Symposium on Discrete Algorithms (SODA), pp. 203–210 (1992)
5. Beckmann, M.J., McGuire, C.B., Winsten, C.B.: Studies in the Economics of Transportation. Yale University Press, New Haven (1956)
6. Bei, X., Garg, J., Hoefer, M., Mehlhorn, K.: Earning and utility limits in fisher markets. ACM Trans. Econ. Comput. **7**(2), 10:1–10:35 (2019)
7. Bhawalkar, K., Gairing, M., Roughgarden, T.: Weighted congestion games: price of anarchy, universal worst-case examples, and tightness. ACM Trans. Econ. Comput. **2**(4), 1–23 (2014)
8. Bilò, V.: A unifying tool for bounding the quality of non-cooperative solutions in weighted congestion games. Theory Comput. Syst. **62**(5), 1288–1317 (2018). https://doi.org/10.1007/s00224-017-9826-1
9. Bilò, V., Fanelli, A., Flammini, M., Moscardelli, L.: Performances of one-round walks in linear congestion games. Theory Comput. Syst. **49**(1), 24–45 (2011). https://doi.org/10.1007/s00224-010-9309-0
10. Bilò, V., Vinci, C.: On the impact of singleton strategies in congestion games. In: Proceedings of the 25th Annual European Symposium on Algorithms, (ESA), pp. 17:1–17:14 (2017)
11. Bilò, V., Vinci, C.: Dynamic taxes for polynomial congestion games. ACM Trans. Econ. Comput. **7**(3), 15:1–15:36 (2019)

12. Borodin, A., El-Yaniv, R.: Online Computation and Competitive Analysis. Cambridge University Press, Cambridge (1998)
13. Brainard, W.C., Scarf, H.E.: How to compute equilibrium prices in 1891. Cowles-Foundation Discussion Paper 1270 (2000)
14. Caragiannis, I.: Better bounds for online load balancing on unrelated machines. In: Proceedings of the ACM-SIAM Symposium on Discrete Algorithms (SODA), pp. 972–981 (2008)
15. Caragiannis, I., Flammini, M., Kaklamanis, C., Kanellopoulos, P., Moscardelli, L.: Tight bounds for selfish and greedy load balancing. Algorithmica 61(3), 606–637 (2011). https://doi.org/10.1007/s00453-010-9427-8
16. Caragiannis, I., Kurokawa, D., Moulin, H., Procaccia, A.D., Shah, N., Wang, J.: The unreasonable fairness of maximum Nash welfare. In: Proceedings of the 2016 ACM Conference on Economics and Computation (EC), pp. 305–322 (2016)
17. Chakrabarty, D., Mehta, A., Nagarajan, V., Vazirani, V.: Fairness and optimality in congestion games. In: Proceedings of the 6th ACM Conference on Electronic Commerce (EC), pp. 52–57 (2005)
18. Chekuri, C., Khanna, S.: Handbook of Scheduling: Algorithms, Models, and Performance Analysis, Chap. Approximation Algorithms for Minimizing Average Weighted Completion Time. Chapman & Hall/CRC, London (2004)
19. Christodoulou, G., Mirrokni, V.S., Sidiropoulos, A.: Convergence and approximation in potential games. Theor. Comput. Sci. 438, 13–27 (2012)
20. Cole, R., Gkatzelis, V.: Approximating the Nash social welfare with indivisible items. SIAM J. Comput. 47(3), 1211–1236 (2018)
21. Czumaj, A., Vöcking, B.: Tight bounds for worst-case equilibria. ACM Trans. Algorithms 3(1), 4:1–4:17 (2007)
22. Fleming, P.J., Wallace, J.: How not to lie with statistics: the correct way to summarize benchmark results. Commun. ACM 29(3), 218–221 (1986)
23. Gairing, M., Schoppmann, F.: Total latency in singleton congestion games. In: Deng, X., Graham, F.C. (eds.) WINE 2007. LNCS, vol. 4858, pp. 381–387. Springer, Heidelberg (2007). https://doi.org/10.1007/978-3-540-77105-0_42
24. Graham, R.L.: Bounds for certain multiprocessing anomalies. Bell Syst. Tech. J. 45(9), 1563–1581 (1966)
25. Hochbaum, D.S., Shmoys, D.B.: Using dual approximation algorithms for scheduling problems: theoretical and practical results. J. ACM 34, 144–162 (1987)
26. Horowitz, E., Sahni, S.K.: Exact and approximate algorithms for scheduling nonidentical processors. J. ACM 23, 317–327 (1976)
27. Ieong, S., McGrew, R., Nudelman, E., Shoham, Y., Sun, Q.: Fast and compact: a simple class of congestion games. In: Proceedings of the 20th AAAI Conference on Artificial Intelligence (AAAI), pp. 489–494 (2005)
28. Klimm, M., Schmand, D., Tönnis, A.: The online best reply algorithm for resource allocation problems. In: Fotakis, D., Markakis, E. (eds.) SAGT 2019. LNCS, vol. 11801, pp. 200–215. Springer, Cham (2019). https://doi.org/10.1007/978-3-030-30473-7_14
29. Koutsoupias, E., Papadimitriou, C.: Worst-case equilibria. In: Meinel, C., Tison, S. (eds.) STACS 1999. LNCS, vol. 1563, pp. 404–413. Springer, Heidelberg (1999). https://doi.org/10.1007/3-540-49116-3_38
30. Lenstra, J.K., Shmoys, D.B., Tardos, E.: Approximation algorithms for scheduling unrelated parallel machines. Math. Program. 46, 259–271 (1990). https://doi.org/10.1007/BF01585745
31. Meyers, C.A., Schulz, A.S.: The complexity of welfare maximization in congestion games. Networks 59(2), 252–260 (2012)

32. Nash, J.: The bargaining problem. Econometrica **18**(2), 155–162 (1950)
33. Pigou, A.C.: The Economics of Welfare. Macmillan and Co., London (1938)
34. Rosenthal, R.W.: A class of games possessing pure-strategy Nash equilibria. Int. J. Game Theory **2**, 65–67 (1973). https://doi.org/10.1007/BF01737559
35. Roughgarden, T.: The price of anarchy is independent of the network topology. J. Comput. Syst. Sci. **67**(2), 341–364 (2003)
36. Roughgarden, T., Tardos, E.: How bad is selfish routing? J. ACM **49**(2), 236–259 (2002)
37. Roughgarden, T., Tardos, E.: Bounding the inefficiency of equilibria in nonatomic congestion games. Games Econ. Behav. **47**(2), 389–403 (2004)
38. Suri, S., Tóth, C., Zhou, Y.: Selfish load balancing and atomic congestion games. Algorithmica **47**(1), 79–96 (2007). https://doi.org/10.1007/s00453-006-1211-4
39. Vinci, C.: Non-atomic one-round walks in congestion games. Theor. Comput. Sci. **764**, 61–79 (2019)
40. Vöcking, B.: Algorithmic Game Theory, chap. Selfish Load Balancing, Cambridge (2007)
41. Wardrop, J.G.: Some theoretical aspects of road traffic research. Proc. Inst. Civ. Eng. Part II **1**(36), 352–362 (1952)

Fairness

Simultaneously Achieving Ex-ante and Ex-post Fairness

Haris Aziz[✉]

UNSW Sydney and Data61 CSIRO, Sydney, Australia
haziz@cse.unsw.edu.au

Abstract. We present a polynomial-time algorithm that computes an ex-ante envy-free lottery over envy-free up to one item (EF1) deterministic allocations. It has the following advantages over a recently proposed algorithm: it does not rely on the linear programming machinery including separation oracles; it is SD-efficient (both ex-ante and ex-post); and the ex-ante outcome is equivalent to the outcome returned by the well-known probabilistic serial rule. As a result, we answer a question raised by Freeman, Shah, and Vaish (2020) whether the outcome of the probabilistic serial rule can be implemented by ex-post EF1 allocations. In the light of a couple of impossibility results that we prove, our algorithm can be viewed as satisfying a maximal set of properties. Under binary utilities, our algorithm is also ex-ante group-strategyproof and ex-ante Pareto optimal. Finally, we also show that checking whether a given random allocation can be implemented by a lottery over EF1 and Pareto optimal allocations is NP-hard.

1 Introduction

Who gets what is a significant and ubiquitous issue. When making any kind of allocation among self-interested agents, fairness is an important concern. Does a fair allocation exist? Is there an efficient algorithm to compute such an allocation? These are important questions that have been studied in fair division for decades. In this paper, we consider the issue of finding probabilistic allocations that are ex-ante and ex-post fair.

Suppose there are two agents who have additive utilities over three items a, b, c. Both agents have the highest value for items a, then b, and then c. From an ex-ante perspective, envy-freeness can be achieved by giving each item to each agent with probability half. However, there are many ways to achieve this expected probability, some perhaps not too fair. For example, the uniform lottery over the following two deterministic allocations: $(\{a, b, c\}, \emptyset)$ and $(\emptyset, \{a, b, c\})$. It may be desirable to achieve both ex-ante envy-freeness and some weaker form of ex-post envy-freeness. For example a uniform lottery over the following allocations is fairer ex-post: $(\{a\}, \{b, c\})$ and $(\{b, c\}, \{a\})$.

As seen from the example above, achieving target fairness properties is easy when we consider fractional outcomes or view outcomes from an ex-ante perspective. Implementing such desirable ex-ante outcomes by randomizing over

© Springer Nature Switzerland AG 2020
X. Chen et al. (Eds.): WINE 2020, LNCS 12495, pp. 341–355, 2020.
https://doi.org/10.1007/978-3-030-64946-3_24

desirable deterministic outcomes can pose interesting challenges (see, e.g. [1, 11]). This issue was explored by Freeman et al. [15]. They focussed on ex-ante envy-freeness and ex-post envy-freeness up to one item as the target fairness requirements. Both of the properties are known to be individually achievable. An ex-ante envy-free random allocation always exists (for example the outcome of the probabilistic serial rule [8] achieves ex-ante envy-freeness). Similarly, a deterministic envy-free up to one item (EF1) allocation always exists [10]. For example, running the round robin sequential algorithm obtains an EF1 allocation [12]. Freeman et al. [15] explore the question of achieving ex-ante envy-freeness and ex-post EF1 *simultaneously*. They showed that there exists a polynomial-time algorithm to compute a lottery over envy-free up to one item allocations that is also ex-ante envy-free.[1]

The inventive polynomial-time algorithm of Freeman et al. [15] has a couple of possible limitations. Firstly, it requires using the machinery of linear programming separation oracles. It may be desirable to get similar results by simpler combinatorial algorithms. Secondly, the algorithm of Freeman et al. is not ex-post weakly SD (stochastic dominance)-efficient and hence not ex-ante weakly SD-efficient. This is evident from Example 2 of Freeman et al. where they note that their algorithm does not satisfy ordinal efficiency.[2] The fact that an algorithm is not ex-post weakly SD-efficient implies that it can return a deterministic allocation such that there exists another deterministic allocation that gives each agent strictly more utility for all utility functions consistent with the underlying ordinal preferences. Another implication of violating ex-post weak SD-efficiency is that all the agents can trade one of their items for another item to get more utility. Such unamiguous compromise on welfare can be undesirable. For example, the random serial dictatorship rule (which is ex-post SD-efficient) has received criticism that it is not ex-ante SD-efficient [8].

We overcome the two limitations discussed above and show that the algorithmic result of Freeman et al. [15] can be achieved in a relatively simpler and faster way while additionally satisfying SD-efficiency. To the best of our knowledge, our is the first algorithm to simultaneously satisfy weak SD-efficiency, ex-ante EF, and ex-post EF1. The latter two guarantees even hold for all additive utilities consistent with the agents' underlying ordinal preferences. In other words, our algorithm satisfies ex-ante SD-envy-freeness and ex-post SD-EF1. We also show how the algorithm can be further modified by using parametric network flows to additionally achieve both ex-ante and ex-post SD-efficiency. Our results can be viewed as being optimal in the view of the following two impossibility results that we prove. Firstly, ex-ante SD-envy-freeness, ex-post EF1, and

---

[1] Freeman et al. [15] also presented several other results charting the landscape of possibility and impossibility results when considering fairness and efficiency properties ex post and ex-ante. In particular, they study in detail the rule that maximizes ex-ante Nash welfare. However, they show that the rule cannot be implemented by EF1 allocations.

[2] SD-efficiency is also referred to as ordinal efficiency in the literature [8].

ex-post Pareto optimality are incompatible. Secondly, ex-ante Pareto optimality and ex-ante SD-envy-freeness are incompatible.

Our algorithm calls the probabilistic serial algorithm as well as the Birkhoff's decomposition algorithm as subroutines. Freeman et al. raised the question whether the outcome of the probabilistic serial algorithm can be implemented using ex-post EF1 randomized allocations: *"we were not able to determine whether the fractional allocation produced by probabilistic serial can always be implemented using an ex-post EF1 randomized allocation."* We answer the question in the affirmative: our algorithm's outcome is ex-ante equivalent to the outcome of the probabilistic serial rule. In particular, it can be viewed as a desirable way to instantiate the probabilistic serial outcome. Under binary utilities, our algorithm is group-strategyproof, ex-ante efficient, ex-ante envy-free, and ex-post EF1. Finally, we also show that checking whether a given random allocation can be represented over a lottery over EF1 and Pareto optimal allocations is NP-hard.

2   Preliminaries

An allocation problem is a triple (N, O, u) such that $N = \{1, \ldots, n\}$ is the set of agents, $O = \{o_1, \ldots, o_m\}$ is the set of objects, and u specifies an additive utility function $u_i : O \to \mathbb{R}^+$. The utility function profile u induces the preference profile $\succsim = (\succsim_1, \ldots, \succsim_n)$ which specifies for each agent i his preferences $\succsim_i$ over objects in O such that $o \succsim_i o'$ if and only if $u_i(o) \geq u_i(o')$. We use $\succ_i$ for the strict part of $\succsim_i$, i.e., $o \succ_i o'$ iff $o \succsim_i o'$ but not $o' \succsim_i o$. A random allocation p is a $(n \times m)$ matrix $[p_{i,o_j}]$ such that $p_{i,o_j} \in [0, 1]$ for all $i \in N$, and $o_j \in O$; and $\sum_{i \in N} p_{i,o_j} = 1$ for all $o_j \in O$. For a given set $S \subset N$, we will refer by $\succsim_S$ the preference profile restricted to agents in S.

The value p_{i,o_j} represents the probability of object o_j being allocated to agent i. Each row $p_i = (p_{i,o_1}, \ldots, p_{i,o_m})$ represents the allocation of agent i. The set of columns correspond to the objects $o_1, \ldots, o_m$. A feasible random allocation is *deterministic* if $p_{i,o} \in \{0, 1\}$ for all $i \in N$ and $o \in O$. When we say 'an allocation', we will mean random allocation unless we specially specify it is deterministic.

For any agent $i, j \in N$ and an allocation p, the utility of agent i for a bundle p_j is $u_i(p_j) = \sum_{o \in O} p_{j,o} u_i(o)$. Given two random allocations p and q, $p_i \succsim_i^{SD} q_i$ that is, an agent i *SD prefers* allocation p_i to allocation q_i if $\sum_{o_j \in \{o_k : o_k \succsim_i o\}} p_{i,o_j} \geq \sum_{o_j \in \{o_k : o_k \succsim_i o\}} q_{i,o_j}$ for all $o \in O$. We write $p_i \succ_i^{SD} q_i$ if $p_i \succsim_i^{SD} q_i$ and not $q_i \succsim_i^{SD} p_i$.

Fairness Properties. A random allocation p is *SD-envy-free* if for all $i, j \in N$, $p_i \succsim_i^{SD} p_j$. An random allocation p is *envy-free (EF)* if $u_i(p_i) \geq u_i(p_j)$ for all $i, j \in N$. For an agent's allocation p_j, we will denote by p_j^{-o} the allocation p_j in which $p_{j,o}$ is set to 0. For an agent's allocation p_j and $S \subseteq O$, we will denote by p_j^{-S} the allocation p_j in which $p_{j,o}$ is set to 0 for all $o \in S$. A random allocation p is *SD-EF1* if for all $i, j \in N$, either $p_i \succsim_i^{SD} p_j$ or $p_i \succsim_i^{SD} p_j^{-o}$ for some o. o. A random allocation p is *envy-free up to k items (EFk)* if there exist some $S \subset O$

such that $|S| \leq k$ such that $u_i(p_i^{-S}) \geq u_i(p_j^{-S})$. Note that SD-envy-freeness implies envy-freeness which implies EFk. And SD-EF implies SD-EFk.

A given random allocation can be implemented by a lottery over deterministic allocations.[3] We call the latter an implementation of the given random allocation. We say that random allocation p satisfies a property X *ex-ante* if the fractional allocation representing p satisfies property X. When we discuss the ex post properties of a random allocation p, we will also need to consider the lottery implementation over deterministic allocations which achieves the random allocation p. In that case we say that random assignment with a lottery implementation deterministic allocations over $M_1, \ldots, M_K$ satisfies property X *ex-post* if $M_1, \ldots, M_K$ satisfy property X. Therefore for any given property for allocations, we consider it ex-ante as well as ex-post. Figure 1 shows the key fairness concepts that are appropriate from ex-ante and ex-post perspectives. Note that we do not focus ex-post envy-freeness since a deterministic envy-free allocation is not guaranteed to exist. Furthermore, checking whether a deterministic envy-free allocation exists is NP-complete even for 1-0 utilities [2].

Fig. 1. Logical relations between fairness concepts.

Example 1. Consider the example in which $N = \{1, 2\}$, $O = \{a, b, c, d\}$ and the agents have the following utilities over four items.

	a	b	c	d
1	4	3	2	1
2	4	2	3	1

Then, the following is one possible random allocation.

$$p = \begin{array}{c} 1 \\ 2 \end{array} \begin{pmatrix} \begin{array}{cccc} a & b & c & d \\ 1/2 & 1 & 0 & 1/2 \\ 1/2 & 0 & 1 & 1/2 \end{array} \end{pmatrix}$$

In the allocation, $u_1(p_1) = \frac{1}{2}(4) + 1(3) + \frac{1}{2}(1) = 5.5$ and $u_1(p_2) = \frac{1}{2}(4) + 1(2) + \frac{1}{2}(1) = 4.5$. Hence agent 1 is not envious of agent 2.

Allocation p can be implemented by the following uniform lottery over two deterministic allocations as follows.

---

[3] The statement follows from the well-known Carathéodory's Theorem.

$$
p \;=\; \tfrac{1}{2} \begin{array}{c} \\ 1 \\ 2 \end{array}\!\!\begin{array}{c} a\ b\ c\ d \\ \left(\begin{array}{cccc} 1 & 1 & 0 & 0 \\ 0 & 0 & 1 & 1 \end{array}\right) \end{array} + \tfrac{1}{2} \begin{array}{c} \\ 1 \\ 2 \end{array}\!\!\begin{array}{c} a\ b\ c\ d \\ \left(\begin{array}{cccc} 0 & 1 & 0 & 1 \\ 1 & 0 & 1 & 0 \end{array}\right) \end{array}
$$

We say that a deterministic allocation q is *consistent* with a random allocation p if for each $q_{i,o} = 1$, we have that $p_{i,o} > 0$. For $n = m$, a deterministic allocation can be represented by a permutation matrix in which an entry of one denotes the row agent getting the column object. A *decomposition* of a random allocation p is a sum $\sum_{i=1}^{k} \lambda_i P_i$ such that $\lambda_i \in (0,1]$ for $i \in \{1, \ldots, k\}$, $\sum_{i=1}^{k} \lambda_i = 1$, and each P_i is a permutation matrix (consistent with p).

3   The PS-Lottery Algorithm

In this section, we present our main algorithm that we refer to as the PS-Lottery Algorithm. Before we proceed, we summarize two well-known algorithms that we will use as building blocks for our algorithm to simultaneously achieve ex-ante EF and ex-post EF1.

Probabilistic Serial (PS) Algorithm. The PS rule [8] takes as input the strict ordinal preferences of agents over items as well as the available amounts of each of the items. Agents start eating their most preferred item at unit speed until the item is consumed. They continue eating their most preferred items until all the items are consumed. The outcome is a random allocation in which each agent's probability of getting an item is the fraction of the item that she ate. Initially, only presented for the case of single-unit demands, the rule extends seamlessly for the case where agents want to get multiple items [21]. Although described as a continuous rule where agents eat infinitesimal amounts, the PS outcome can be computed by a discrete algorithm in polynomial time $O(nm)$ (see the appendix).

Birkhoff's Algorithm. Consider any random allocation with n agents and n items in which each agent gets one unit of items. Birkhoff's algorithm can decompose such a random allocation (which can be represented by a bistochastic matrix) into a convex combination of at most $n^2 - n + 1$ deterministic allocations (represented by permutation matrices) [7,22]. The following is a description of Birkhoff's algorithm. We initialize i to 1. For a bistochastic matrix M, a permutation matrix P_i consistent with M is guaranteed to exist. Such a permutation matrix corresponds to a perfect matching in a bipartite graph $(N \cup O, E)$ where $(i, o) \in E$ iff $M_{i,o} > 0$. Such a perfect matching and hence the permutation matrix can be computed via the Hopcroft-Karp-Karzanov algorithm which takes time $O(n^{2.5})$ [18,19]. We initialize index i to 1. M is set to $M - \lambda_i P_i$ where $\lambda_i \in (0,1]$ is the smallest non-zero entry in P_i. Index i is incremented by one. The updated M is again bistochastic. The process is repeated (say $k-1$ times) until M is the zero matrix. Then $M = \sum_{i=1}^{k} \lambda_i P_i$.

Now that we have defined the two algorithms, we are in a position to present Algorithm 1. The high-level description of the algorithm is as follows. We first add some dummy items to ensure that there are nc items. The expanded set of items is called O'. We then simulate PS. We track information about how much of each item has been eaten at time steps $1, \ldots, c$. We use this information to form an allocation q' of items in O' to agents in $N' = \{i_1, \ldots, i_c : i \in N\}$. The agents $i_1, \ldots, i_c$ are called the representative agents of each agent i. An agent i_j's allocation is what agent i ate in time interval $[j-1, j]$. Allocation q' can be represented by a bistochastic matrix. We decompose q' into a convex combination of permutation matrices via Birkhoff's algorithm. The permutation matrices are suitably modified to remove the dummy items and also give the allocation of all representatives to the agent they represent. The convex combination over the modified permutation matrices gives us the desired solution, which is both ex-ante EF and ex-post EF1.

Algorithm 1. PS-Lottery Algorithm

Input: $I = (N, O, \succsim)$ where $|N| = n$, $|O| = m$ and $c = \lceil m/n \rceil$.

Output: EF fractional allocation $q = \sum_{j=1}^{K} \lambda_j P_i$ where each P_j represents a deterministic EF1 allocation and $K \leq (cn)^2 - 2cn + 2$.

1: If m is a multiple of n, $D = \emptyset$. Else, $D = \{d_1, \ldots, d_{nc-m}\}$.
2: $O' \leftarrow O \cup D$ so that $|O'| = cn$.
3: $N' = \{i_1, \ldots, i_c : i \in N\}$. The agents $i_1, \ldots i_c$ are termed as the representatives of agent i.
4: Set preference profile $\succsim'$ of agents in $N' \cup N$ as follows: for all $o, o' \in O$ and for all i_j for $j \in \{1, \ldots, c\}$, $o \succsim'_{i_j} o'$ iff $o \succsim_i o'$. For all $o \in O$ and $d \in D$, $o \succ'_{i_j} d$. All the ties in $\succsim'$ are broken lexicographically.
5: Run PS on instance $(N, O', \succsim'_N)$ to get a random outcome r.
6: For each bundle r_i, let agent i re-eat her bundle at unit-speed according to preferences of her representative agents $\succsim'_{i_k}$ with each representative agent i_j eating on behalf of agent i in time interval $[j-1, j]$. Let the result of this eating be allocation q' which is an allocation of items O' to agent representatives in N'.
7: For the (bistochastic) matrix corresponding to q', compute a Birkhoff decomposition $q' = \sum_{j=1}^{K} \lambda_j P'_j$ where $K \leq (cn)^2 - 2cn + 2$.
8: Convert $q' = \sum_{j=1}^{K} \lambda_j P'_j$ into $q = \sum_{j=1}^{K} \lambda_j P_j$ where all the dummy items are ignored and each agent gets the allocation of its representatives.
9: **return** Allocation q for instance I and its decomposition $\sum_{j=1}^{K} \lambda_j P_j$.

Before we prove the main properties of the PS-Lottery Algorithm, we recall a class of deterministic allocation algorithms. The *sequential allocation* algorithm takes as input a sequence π of turns of the agents and returns a deterministic allocation which is a result of agents picking a most preferred unallocated item in their turn. A sequence of turns is called *recursively balanced (RB)* if at each prefix, all agents have the same number of turns, or differ by one [5]. An RB sequence can be viewed as agents coming in c rounds. Note that $cn \leq (m + n)$. In each round except the last one, each agent gets exactly one turn. Since each agent weakly prefers her picked item over all items picked in later rounds, it can easily be proved that the outcome of sequential allocation with an RB sequence is EF1 [3].[4] Since sequential allocation with an RB sequence only uses ordinal preferences of the agents, it is EF1 with respect to all positive utilities consistent with the ordinal preferences [3] and hence SD-EF. An allocation is called an *RB-allocation* if it is an outcome of sequential allocation with respect to some RB-sequence. We will use the perspective of RB-allocations to establish that our algorithm returns a lottery over EF1 allocations.

Theorem 1. *Let $c = \lceil m/n \rceil$. Algorithm 1 is polynomial-time algorithm that takes time $O((cn)^4)$ that computes a lottery over at most $(cn)^2$ deterministic EF1 allocations that is equivalent to the outcome of the probabilistic serial algorithm.*

Proof. Algorithm 1 works as follows. If $m < n$, we set $D = \{d_1, \ldots, d_{n-m}\}$. If $m > n$, we set $D = \{d_1, \ldots, d_{cn-m}\}$. We are now in a position to fix a new allocation instance $I' = (N', O', \succsim')$ that only uses ordinal preferences. The item set O' is $O \cup D$ where $|O'| = cn$. The 'representative' set N' is $\{i_1, \ldots, i_c : i \in N\}$. Note that the number of representatives $|N'|$ is equal to the number of items $|O'|$. The preferences are consistent with the underlying preference profile. The preferences $\succsim'$ of the representatives are set as follows: for all $o, o' \in O$ and for all i_j for $j \in \{1, \ldots, c\}$ $o \succsim'_{i_j} o'$ iff $o \succsim_i o'$. For all $o \in O$ and $d \in D$, $o \succ'_{i_j} d$. All the ties in $\succsim'$ are broken lexicographically.

Note that for the modified allocation problem instance I', an allocation has a corresponding allocation in the original instance I: an agent i gets all the allocations of its representatives $i_1, \ldots i_c$. The allocation of dummy items is ignored.

Let q' be the allocation as a result of applying PS with agent set N and item set O', but for each $j = 0$ to $c - 1$, we change the name of each agent i to i_{j+1} in time interval $[j, j + 1]$. Note that computing r and q' takes time $(cn)^2$. The allocation has a corresponding bistochastic matrix in which the rows correspond to the representatives and the columns correspond to the items. Each entry in the matrix represents the amount of the corresponding item eaten by the corresponding representative.

Note that since q' is bistochastic, a permutation matrix P'_k consistent with q' exists by Birkhoff's theorem. We want to show that any such matrix P'_k must correspond to an RB-allocation of items in O' to agents in N. The RB-allocation is viewed as proceeding in rounds. In each round, each of the representatives representing the n agents pick a most preferred available item. In the j-th round, the representatives involved are $1_j, \ldots, n_j$. In any P'_k, each item is allocated to an agent representative and each agent representative gets one item. In order to

---
[4] In fact an RB allocation satisfies a stronger properly called strong EF1. Stronger EF1 requires that upon removing the same item from agent i's bundle, no other agent j envies i, for all i and j. The property was proposed by Conitzer et al. [13].

establish that P'_k is an RB-allocation of N, it is sufficient to prove two claims: (1) no representative agent strictly prefers any item picked in a later round; and (2) within each round, the items allocated to the representative agents are as a result of sequential allocation.

Claim (1) follows from the fact that no representative i_j strictly prefers any item allocated in a later round. The reason is that when it stopped eating in its turn, it was always eating an item at least as preferred as in later rounds.

Next, we prove Claim (2). Consider any round in which each representative receives one item. We claim that no set of representatives want to reallocate the items given in that round to get an improvement for all representatives in the set. Suppose for contradiction there is a trading cycle in which every agent in the cycle improves: $o_1, 1, o_2, 2, \ldots, o_j, j$. Representative 1 prefers item o_2 over o_1 which means that it started eating o_1 after o_2 was finished. Since 1 ate a strictly positive fraction of o_1, it implies that o_1 finishes strictly after o_2. By a similar argument each $i \in \{1, \ldots j - 1\}$ wants to get o_{i+1} which means that it started eating o_i after o_{i+1} was finished. Agent j prefers item o_1 over o_j which means that it started eating o_j after o_1 was finished which means that o_j finishes strictly after o_1. But then the order of the items according to the finishing times is: $o_1, o_j, o_{j-1}, \ldots, o_3, o_2, o_1$. We have shown that o_1 has two different finishing times which is a contradiction. Since there exists no trading cycle for representatives in the same round, we know that the items in the round can be allocated as a result of sequential allocation.

From the two claims above, the allocation P'_k is an RB-allocation for agents in N if each agent gets the allocations of its representatives. Since any permutation matrix consistent with q' also corresponds to an RB-allocation, we can use P'_k as one of the permutation matrices in which q' is decomposed during Birkhoff's decomposition. We can continue decomposing q' into permutation matrices until we can represent q' by a convex combination of at most $K \leq (cn)^2$ permutation matrices $P'_1, \ldots, P'_K$. Each permutation matrix in the decomposition can be computed by computing a perfect matching in a corresponding bipartite graph via the Hopcroft-Karp-Karzanov algorithm which takes time $O((cn)^{2.5})$.

Finally, note that we can convert allocations $(q', P'_1, \ldots, P'_K)$ for instance I' into the corresponding allocations $(q, P_1, \ldots, P_K)$ for instance I. We do so by removing the dummy items and for each $i \in N$, giving the allocations of all the representatives $i_1, \ldots, i_c$ to agent i. Note that q is the outcome of running PS on instance I. Also, $P_1, \ldots, P_K$ are RB-allocations for instance I and hence EF1 for instance I. □

Remark 1. Algorithm 1 is combinatorial algorithm that computes a lottery over at most $(cn)^2 \leq (m + n)^2$ deterministic allocations. By Carathéodory's Theorem, any $n \times m$ random allocation that is represented by a convex combination of a given K deterministic allocations, can be represented by at most $nm + 1$ deterministic allocations among the K deterministic allocations. We can reduce the support of the lottery returned by Algorithm 1 to one involving at most $nm + 1$ deterministic EF1 and SD-efficient allocations as follows. By using Gaussian elimination, we compute the subset of the set of matrices $\{P_1, \ldots, P_k\}$ that forms the basis of $P_1, \ldots, P_k$. We can compute a convex combination of the matrices in the basis to achieve the same outcome q.

We note that whereas our algorithm provides a way to implement PS by EF1 allocations, not every implementation of the PS outcome may satisfy ex-post EF1. For example, consider the case of two agents with identical preferences over two items. In that case, tossing a coin and then giving both items to one agent is ex-ante equivalent to the PS outcome. However, it is not EF1 if agents have strictly positive utilities for both items.

Algorithm 1 bears similarities to the exponential-time Algorithm 1 (Recursive PS) of Freeman et al. [15]. Just like their algorithm, we make agents successively eat one unit of items. Unlike the algorithm of Freeman et al., we derive the lottery decomposition only after the PS outcome has been computed. In contrast, Freeman et al. probabilistically generate a partial deterministic allocation after each unit time. Their algorithm "branches out into a polynomial number of subinstances" a polynomial number of times which makes it an exponential-time algorithm. In order to ensure polynomial-time computability, they resort to a result about convex polytopes and separation oracles [16].

4   Additionally Achieving Efficiency

In this section, we consider the additional issue of efficiency. Before, we proceed, we present some definitions.

Efficiency Properties. A random allocation p is *fractional Pareto optimal (fPO)* if there exists no other random allocation q such that $u_i(q_i) \geq u_i(p_i)$ for all $i \in N$ and $u_i(q_i) > u_i(p_i)$ for some $i \in N$. A deterministic allocation p is *Pareto optimal (PO)* if there exists no other deterministic allocation q such that $u_i(q_i) \geq u_i(p_i)$ for all $i \in N$ and $u_i(q_i) > u_i(p_i)$ for some $i \in N$. A random allocation p is *SD-efficient* is there exists no random allocation q such that $q_i \succsim_i^{SD} p_i$ for all $i \in N$ and $q_i \succ_i^{SD} p_i$ for some $i \in N$. An allocation p is *weakly SD-efficient* is there exists no allocation q such that $q_i \succ_i^{SD} p_i$ for all $i \in N$. Note that fPO implies PO which implies SD-efficiency which in turn implies weak SD-efficiency. Just as in the case of fairness, we will consider efficiency of both the ex-ante random allocation as well as efficiency properties of the ex-post deterministic allocations that are involved in the lottery.

We note that the random allocation maximizing the Nash social welfare is well-known to be equivalent to the competitive equilibrium with equal incomes solution (see e.g., [14,23]) and satisfies fPO as well as ex-ante envy-freeness. However, due to Theorem 3 of Freeman et al. [15], a rule that is fPO and ex-ante envy-free cannot be ex-post EF1.

Since the outcome returned by Algorithm 1 is a lottery implementation of the PS rule outcome, our algorithm also inherits all the desirable ex-ante properties that the PS rule and its outcome are known to satisfy. Note that Algorithm 1 first breaks ties in the ordinal preferences before running the PS algorithm.

This results in the outcome satisfying weak SD-efficiency rather than SD-efficiency if there are indeed ties in the original preferences. If we care about SD-efficiency, then we do not artificially break any ties and can run the extended probabilistic serial (EPS) algorithm [20]. The EPS algorithm makes coordinated choices for agents to eat one of their most preferred items and uses parametric network flows to compute the outcome. For number of items $m \geq n$, the algorithm takes time $O(m^3 \log m)$.[5]

The exact specification of our *EPS-Lottery algorithm* is to take the PS-Lottery algorithm and replace Step 5 with the following step: Run EPS on instance $(N, O', \succsim_N'')$ to get a random outcome r. Here, the preference profile $\succsim''$ is the same as $\succsim'$ except that only ties within D are broken lexicographically and ties are within O are not broken. Therefore the returned outcome r and hence q' is SD-efficient rather than just weak SD-efficient. The argument of implementing the outcome with EF1 deterministic allocations remains unchanged. The running time is unchanged as well as the bottleneck step is to compute a Birkhoff decomposition which takes time $O((cn)^4)$.

Note that if a random allocation q is SD-efficient, then in any decomposition of q, each of the deterministic allocations is SD-efficient as well. The reason is that if one of the deterministic allocations is not SD-efficient, then q is not SD-efficient. Hence, our algorithm additionally achieves SD-efficiency both ex-ante and ex-post.

Theorem 2. *Let $c = \lceil m/n \rceil$. The EPS-Lottery Algorithm runs takes time $O((cn)^4)$ and computes a lottery over at most $(cn)^2 \leq (m + n)^2$ deterministic EF1 allocations that is equivalent to the outcome of the extended probabilistic serial algorithm (which is SD-envy-free and SD-efficient).*

We note that our algorithm does not achieve ex-post Pareto optimality. One approach to achieving ex-post PO and ex-post EF1 is to check certain random allocations for these properties. Next, we show for an arbitrary random allocation, checking whether it is ex-post EF1 and ex-post Pareto optimal is NP-hard.

Theorem 3. *For n agents and n items, checking whether a given random allocation can be implemented by a lottery over EF1 and Pareto optimal allocations is NP-hard. For n agents and n items, checking whether a given random allocation can be implemented by a lottery over SD-EF1 and Pareto optimal allocations is NP-hard.*

Proof. It was proved that for n agents and n items, checking whether a given random allocation can be implemented by a lottery over balanced Pareto optimal allocations is NP-hard [4]. Their setting assumed ordinal preferences but it works as well for any cardinal preferences consistent with the ordinal preferences.

---

[5] The original EPS algorithm [20] is presented for the case of single-unit demands. However, it can easily be extended to the case of multiple items (see e.g., the Controlled Cake Eating Algorithm (CCEA) algorithm [6]). CCEA is described in the context of cake cutting with piecewise constant valuations. It also applies to allocation of items: each cake segment can be treated as a separate item.

We consider utility functions u_i consistent with ordinal preference $\succ_i$ and assume that $u_i(o) > 0$ for all $o \in O$. Since $u_i(o) > 0$ for all $o \in O$, we know that in any unbalanced deterministic allocation one agent $i \in N$ gets zero items and another agent j gets at least two items. Even if one of j's items is removed, i will be envious of j. Hence, an unbalanced allocation is not EF1. In the other direction, a balanced allocation gives one item to each agent. Even if an agent $i \in N$ is envious of agent j, agent i will not be envious if j's item is removed. We have established that for n agents and n items, the set of deterministic EF1 allocations is equal to the set of deterministic balanced allocations. Therefore, the set of deterministic EF1 and Pareto optimal allocations is equivalent to the set of deterministic balanced and Pareto optimal allocations. It follows that checking whether a given random allocation can be implemented by a lottery over EF1 and Pareto optimal allocation is NP-hard.

The same argument also works for the problem of checking whether a given random allocation can be implemented by a lottery over *SD-EF1* and Pareto optimal allocations. □

5   Impossibility Results

We first recall that Freeman et al. [15] proved that even for two agents, ex-ante fPO, ex-ante envy-freeness, and ex-post EF1 are incompatible. In this section, we present a couple of more impossibility results. The results are logically incomparable to the main impossibility result of Freeman et al. [15]. Our first impossibility is the following one.

Theorem 4. *Ex-ante SD-EF, ex-post EF1, and ex-post PO are incompatible even for 2 agents.*

Proof. Consider the example in which $N = \{1, 2\}$, $O = \{a, b_1, b_2, b_3\}$ and the agents have the following utilities over four items.

	a	b_1	b_2	b_3
1	7	1	1	1
2	4	2	2	2

The three items b_1, b_2, b_3 are identical items that we refer to as b items. Ex-ante SD-EF implies that each agent in expectation gets $1/2$ of a and 1.5 units of type b items. Our first claim is that in any lottery implementing such an ex-ante SD-EF allocation, there is at least one ex-post allocation in which agent 2 must get item a. This follows from the fact that agent 2 gets $1/2$ of a in expectation.

Our second claim is that in any deterministic ex-post EF1 and ex-post PO allocation, agent 2 cannot get item a. Suppose for contradiction that agent 2 gets a. Then, EF1 requires that agent 1 gets at least 2 items of type b. But then, agent 1 can exchange these two items for a to obtain a Pareto improvement.

From the two claims above, it follows that for the problem instance, there exists no lottery over ex-post EF1 and ex-post PO outcomes that implements the SD-EF random outcome. □

Next, we point out that ex-ante fPO and ex-ante SD-EF are incompatible even for 2 agents. The theorem follows directly from Theorem 5 [6] but we re-prove it in our context for the sake of completeness.

Theorem 5. *Ex-ante fPO and ex-ante SD-EF are incompatible even for 2 agents.*

Proof. Consider the following two-agent profile.

	a	b
1	$u_1(a)$	$u_1(b)$
2	$u_2(a)$	$u_2(b)$

Consider an SD-EF and ex-ante PO allocation p. Suppose $u_1(a), v_b^1$, $u_2(a), u_2(b) > 0$ in such a way that $u_1(a) > u_1(b)$ and $u_2(a) > u_2(b)$ and $\frac{u_1(a)}{u_1(b)} > \frac{u_2(a)}{u_2(b)}$. Due to SD-EF, the outcome should be

$$p = \begin{array}{c} \\ 1 \\ 2 \end{array}\begin{array}{c} a \quad b \\ \left(\begin{array}{cc} 1/2 & 1/2 \\ 1/2 & 1/2 \end{array} \right) \end{array}$$

On the other hand, in order for the mechanism to be ex-ante fPO, $p_{1,b} = 0$ or $p_{2,a} = 1$. □

6   Binary Utilities

We assumed that the agents have additive utilities. If we consider the case in which agents have 1-0 utilities, we can achieve stronger results. We show that our EPS-lottery algorithm satisfies very strong properties when agents have 1-0 utilities. In order to ensure ex-ante efficiency of the EPS-lottery algorithm under 1-0 utilities, we can assume that agents do not consume zero utility items and leave them for the consumption by other agents as is done by the Controlled Cake Eating Algorithm (CCEA) algorithm [6]. In case this leads to unbalanced allocations, we can make the allocation balanced by adding appropriate number of *extra* dummy items so that we can implement our lottery decomposition algorithm for a balanced allocation.

Before we proceed, let us recall the definition of leximin optimality. For an allocation π we denote by $\boldsymbol{u}(\pi) \in \mathbb{R}^n$ the vector of the utilities in π sorted in increasing order. For two vectors $\boldsymbol{u}, \boldsymbol{v} \in \mathbb{R}^k$, we say that $\boldsymbol{u}$ leximin-dominates $\boldsymbol{v}$, written $\boldsymbol{u} \succ_{lex} \boldsymbol{v}$, if there exists an $i \leq k$ such that $\boldsymbol{u}_j = \boldsymbol{v}_j, \forall j < i$, and $\boldsymbol{u}_i > \boldsymbol{v}_i$. Finally, π is leximin-optimal if there is no π' such that $\boldsymbol{u}(\pi') \succ_{lex} \boldsymbol{u}(\pi)$.

Under 1-0 utilities, it is known that the following rules are equivalent and polynomial-time computable: (1) leximin rule (2) maximum Nash welfare (MNW) rule (3) competitive equilibirum with equal incomes (CEEI) [23] and (4) Controlled Cake Eating Algorithm (CCEA) rule [6] (which can be viewed as an extension for EPS for multi-unit demands that is also careful about zero utilities). For example, CEEI and MNW are well-known to be equivalent even for general additive utilities. Under binary utilities, leximin, CEEI, and CCEA are equivalent [6]. CCEA satisfies envy-freeness. The conclusion about envy-freeness is also derived from the fact that CEEI outcomes are envy-free (see, e.g. [24]). It is well-known that under additive utilities, the utility profile of the agents is unique (see, e.g., [24]).

For 1-0 utilities, the rules above are known to be ex-ante group-strategyproof (no group of agents can misreport their preferences so that all agents get at least as much utility and at least one agent gets strictly more utility). This fact has been known before as well (see, e.g., [9,20] and [6]). Since the rules are equivalent to the leximin rule, the outcome is by definition leximin optimal and hence ex-ante fPO.

We have already shown that an outcome of the EPS rule can be implemented by a lottery over EF1 allocations. Also, every deterministic allocation consistent with the SD-efficient random outcome is SD-efficient (follows from Lemma 2 [20]) and hence ex-post Pareto optimal for binary utilities. Therefore, we achieve ex-post EF1 and ex-post Pareto optimality.

Theorem 6. *For binary utilities, the EPS-Lottery Algorithm is group-strategyproof, ex-ante fPO, ex-post fPO, ex-ante envy-free, and ex-post EF1. Its outcome is ex-ante equivalent to the leximin random allocation as well as the maximum Nash welfare allocation.*

The theorem above recovers some results that have been proved by Halpern et al. [17] including their Theorem 4 and Corollary 1.

7   Conclusion

We studied the problem of simultaneously achieving desirable fairness properties ex-post and ex-ante. Our main contribution is an algorithm to find a lottery over EF1 allocations that is ex-ante equivalent to the outcome of the (E)PS rule. We noted that we actually compute a lottery over RB-allocations that satisfy strong EF1.

Figure 2 depicts the logical relations between various properties. It also shows some sets of properties that are possible or not possible to satisfy simultaneously. We noted that under 1-0 utilities, all meaningful ex-ante and ex-post fairness and efficiency properties are simultaneously satisfied. Coming back to general additive utilities, we recall that our algorithm achieves ex-ante SD-efficiency and ex-ante SD-EF. If we wish to replace ex-ante SD-efficiency with ex-ante fPO, then such an algorithm does not exist in view of Theorem 5. Again, note that our algorithm achieves ex-post SD-efficiency, ex-ante SD-EF, and ex-post SD-EF1. Even if we weaken ex-post SD-EF1 to ex-post EF1 but strengthen ex-post SD-efficiency to ex-post PO, we again get an impossibility (Theorem 4).

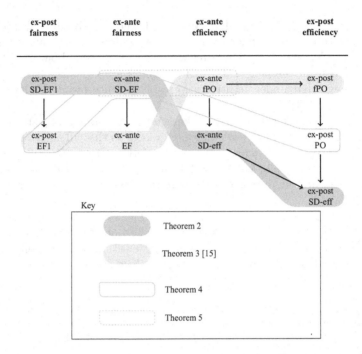

Fig. 2. Logical relations between fairness and efficiency concepts. An arrow from (A) to (B) denotes that (A) implies (B). The properties in green are simultaneously satisfied by our algorithm. The combined properties in the pink shapes (dotted, dashed, or shaded) are impossible to simultaneously satisfy. (Color figure online)

Acknowledgement. Aziz is supported the Defence Science and Technology (DST) under the project "Auctioning for distributed multi vehicle planning" (DST 9190). He thanks Ethan Brown and Dominik Peters for helpful comments.

References

1. Aziz, H.: A probabilistic approach to voting, allocation, matching, and coalition formation. In: Laslier, J.-F., Moulin, H., Sanver, M.R., Zwicker, W.S. (eds.) The Future of Economic Design. SED, pp. 45–50. Springer, Cham (2019). https://doi.org/10.1007/978-3-030-18050-8_8
2. Aziz, H., Gaspers, S., Mackenzie, S., Walsh, T.: Fair assignment of indivisible objects under ordinal preferences. Artif. Intell. **227**, 71–92 (2015)
3. Aziz, H., Huang, X., Mattei, N., Segal-Halevi, E.: The constrained round robin algorithm for fair and efficient allocation. CoRR abs/1908.00161 (2019), http://arxiv.org/abs/1908.00161
4. Aziz, H., Mackenzie, S., Xia, L., Ye, C.: Ex post efficiency of random assignments. In: Proceedings of 14th AAMAS Conference, pp. 1639–1640 (2015)
5. Aziz, H., Walsh, T., Xia, L.: Possible and necessary allocations via sequential mechanisms. In: Proceedings of 24th IJCAI, pp. 468–474 (2015)

6. Aziz, H., Ye, C.: Cake cutting algorithms for piecewise constant and piecewise uniform valuations. In: Liu, T.-Y., Qi, Q., Ye, Y. (eds.) WINE 2014. LNCS, vol. 8877, pp. 1–14. Springer, Cham (2014). https://doi.org/10.1007/978-3-319-13129-0_1

7. Birkhoff, G.: Three observations on linear algebra. Univ. Nac. Tacuman Rev. Ser. A **5**, 147–151 (1946)

8. Bogomolnaia, A., Moulin, H.: A new solution to the random assignment problem. J. Econ. Theory **100**(2), 295–328 (2001)

9. Bogomolnaia, A., Moulin, H.: Random matching under dichotomous preferences. Econometrica **72**(1), 257–279 (2004)

10. Budish, E.: The combinatorial assignment problem: approximate competitive equilibrium from equal incomes. J. Polit. Econ. **119**(6), 1061–1103 (2011)

11. Budish, E., Che, Y.K., Kojima, F., Milgrom, P.: Designing random allocation mechanisms: theory and applications. Am. Econ. Rev. **103**(2), 585–623 (2013)

12. Caragiannis, I., Kurokawa, D., Moulin, H., Procaccia, A.D., Shah, N., Wang, J.: The unreasonable fairness of maximum Nash welfare. In: Proceedings of 17th ACM-EC Conference, pp. 305–322 (2016)

13. Conitzer, V., Freeman, R., Shah, N., Vaughan, J.W.: Group fairness for the allocation of indivisible goods. In: Proceedings of 33rd AAAI Conference (2019)

14. Devanur, N., Papadimitriou, C.H., Saberi, A., Vazirani, V.: Market equilibrium via a primal-dual algorithm for a convex program. J. ACM **55**(5), 1–8 (2008)

15. Freeman, R., Shah, N., Vaish, R.: Best of both worlds: ex-ante and ex-post fairness in resource allocation. Technical report (2020)

16. Grötschel, M., Lovász, L., Schrijver, A.: The ellipsoid method and its consequences in combinatorial optimization. Combinatorica **1**(2), 169–197 (1981). https://doi.org/10.1007/BF02579273

17. Halpern, D., Procaccia, A.D., Psomas, A., Shah, N.: Fair division with binary valuations: one rule to rule them all. Technical report (2020)

18. Hopcroft, J.E., Karp, R.M.: An $n^{5/2}$ algorithm for maximum matchings in bipartite graphs. SIAM J. Comput. **2**(4), 225–231 (1973)

19. Karzanov, A.V.: An exact estimate of an algorithm for finding a maximum flow, applied to the problem on representatives. Probl. Cybern. **5**, 66–70 (1973)

20. Katta, A.K., Sethuraman, J.: A solution to the random assignment problem on the full preference domain. J. Econ. Theory **131**(1), 231–250 (2006)

21. Kojima, F.: Random assignment of multiple indivisible objects. Math. Soc. Sci. **57**(1), 134–142 (2009)

22. Lovász, L., Plummer, M.D.: Matching Theory. AMS Chelsea Publishing, Providence (2009)

23. Varian, H.R.: Equity, envy, and efficiency. J. Econ. Theory **9**, 63–91 (1974)

24. Vazirani, V.V.: Combinatorial algorithms for market equilibria. In: Nisan, N., Roughgarden, T., Tardos, É., Vazirani, V. (eds.) Algorithmic Game Theory, chap. 5, pp. 103–134. Cambridge University Press, Cambridge (2007)

Optimal Bounds on the Price of Fairness for Indivisible Goods

Siddharth Barman[1(✉)], Umang Bhaskar[2], and Nisarg Shah[3]

[1] Indian Institute of Science, Bangalore, India
barman@iisc.ac.in
[2] Tata Institute of Fundamental Research, Mumbai, India
umang@tifr.res.in
[3] University of Toronto, Toronto, Canada
nisarg@cs.toronto.edu

Abstract. In the allocation of resources to a set of agents, how do fairness guarantees impact social welfare? A quantitative measure of this impact is the price of fairness, which measures the worst-case loss of social welfare due to fairness constraints. While initially studied for divisible goods, recent work on the price of fairness also studies the setting of indivisible goods.

In this paper, we resolve the price of two well-studied fairness notions in the context of indivisible goods: envy-freeness up to one good (EF1) and approximate maximin share (MMS). For both EF1 and $1/2$-MMS we show, via different techniques, that the price of fairness is $O(\sqrt{n})$, where n is the number of agents. From previous work, it follows that these guarantees are tight. We, in fact, obtain the price-of-fairness results via efficient algorithms. For $1/2$-MMS our bound holds for additive valuations, whereas for EF1, it holds for the more general class of subadditive valuations. This resolves an open problem posed by Bei et al. (2019).

1 Introduction

What does it mean for an allocation of resources among a set of agents to be fair? The most compelling notion of fairness advocated in prior work is *envy-freeness* (EF) [15], which demands that no agent envy any other (i.e., value the resources allocated to any other agent more than those allocated to herself). When the resources to be allocated contain *indivisible* goods, guaranteeing envy-freeness is impossible.[1] Hence, researchers have sought relaxations such as *envy-freeness up to one good* (EF1) [8,10], which states that it should be possible to eliminate any envy one agent has toward another by removal of at most one good from the latter's allocation.

A different notion advocated in the context of indivisible goods is the *maximin share guarantee* (MMS) [8]. When there are n agents, the maximin share

---

[1] The canonical example is that of a single indivisible good and two agents—the agent that does not receive the good will inevitably envy the other.

© Springer Nature Switzerland AG 2020
X. Chen et al. (Eds.): WINE 2020, LNCS 12495, pp. 356–369, 2020.
https://doi.org/10.1007/978-3-030-64946-3_25

of an agent a is defined as the maximum value a could obtain if she were to divide the goods into n bundles and then receive the least-valued (according to her) bundle. An MMS allocation is an allocation where each agent receives at least her maximin share. This generalizes the classical cut-and-choose protocol for dividing a cake between two agents, where one agent cuts the cake into two pieces, the other agent chooses a piece, and the first agent then receives the remaining piece. Even for agents with additive valuations over the goods,[2] MMS allocations may not exist [18,23]. However, under additive valuations, an allocation where each agent receives at least $3/4$-th of her maximin share—i.e., a $3/4$-MMS allocation—always exists [16,17].

While fairness is important, it is clearly not the only objective of interest. Another central criterion in resource allocation is the aggregate value of the agents from the resources they receive, or the *social welfare* of the allocation. The tradeoff between fairness and social welfare is quantitatively measured by the *price of fairness*, the supremum over all instances of the ratio between the maximum welfare of any allocation and the maximum welfare of any allocation satisfying the desired fairness notion. Intuitively, this quantity measures the factor by which welfare may be lost to achieve desired fairness.

Caragiannis et al. [9] initiated the study of the price of fairness in the canonical setting of cake-cutting, in which a heterogeneous *divisible* good is to be allocated (hence, envy-freeness can be guaranteed) and agents have additive valuations. They proved that the price of envy-freeness is between $\Omega(\sqrt{n})$ and $O(n)$, where n is the number of agents. Later, Bertsimas et al. [6] closed the gap by proving that the correct bound is $\Theta(\sqrt{n})$, and that the matching upper bound can be achieved by maximizing the Nash welfare [6].

For *indivisible* goods and additive valuations, Bei et al. [5] studied the price of fairness for various notions of fairness. They showed that the price of envy-freeness up to one good (EF1) is between $\Omega(\sqrt{n})$ and $O(n)$. One might immediately wonder if maximizing the Nash welfare (which is known to satisfy EF1 in the case of indivisible goods and additive valuations [10]) can be used to derive a matching $O(\sqrt{n})$ upper bound, as in cake-cutting. Unfortunately, Bei et al. also showed that maximizing the Nash welfare can result in an $\Omega(n)$-factor loss with respect to social welfare, and posed settling the price of EF1 as a significant open question. For approximate MMS allocations (since exact MMS allocations may not exist), the price of fairness has not been studied earlier, though a lower bound of $\Omega(\sqrt{n})$ can be obtained from previous constructions [9].

Our Contributions. We consider the allocation of m indivisible goods among n agents. An allocation $\mathcal{A} = (A_1, \dots, A_n)$ partitions the goods into n bundles, where A_i is the bundle assigned to agent i. The preferences of each agent i are specified via a valuation function v_i, which assigns a non-negative value to every subset of goods. Then, $v_i(A_i)$ is the value to agent i under $\mathcal{A}$ and $\sum_{i=1}^{n} v_i(A_i)$ is the social welfare of $\mathcal{A}$. The price of a fairness notion, as defined above, is the

---

[2] A valuation is additive iff the value of a bundle of goods is equal to the sum of the values of the individual goods in the bundle.

supremum of the ratio between the maximum social welfare obtainable, and the maximum social welfare subject to the fairness notion.

Our main contribution is to comprehensively settle the price of EF1 and $1/2$-MMSfairness notions. First, we show that the price of EF1 is $O(\sqrt{n})$. This matches the $\Omega(\sqrt{n})$ lower bound due to Bei et al. [5]. The lower bound is for additive valuations, whereas our upper bound holds for the more general class of subadditive valuations. Hence, our work settles this open question for all valuation classes between additive and subadditive. Computationally, we obtain this upper bound via a polynomial-time algorithm. For subadditive valuations, given the absence of succinct representation, we assume access to a *demand-query oracle*.[3] As a consequence of this result, we also settle the price of a weaker fairness notion—proportionality up to one good (Prop1)—as $\Theta(\sqrt{n})$ for additive valuations.

For the $1/2$-MMS fairness notion and additive valuations, we similarly establish, via a different algorithm, that the price of fairness is $\Theta(\sqrt{n})$. We show that for a fixed $\varepsilon > 0$, a $(1/2 - \varepsilon)$-MMS allocation with welfare within $O(\sqrt{n})$ factor of the optimal can be computed in polynomial time.

Related Work. For resource allocation, the price of fairness was first studied by Caragiannis et al. [9] and Bertsimas et al. [6]. Caragiannis et al. [9] left open the question of the price of envy-freeness in cake-cutting, later settled by Bertsimas et al. [6] as $\Theta(\sqrt{n})$. Bertsimas et al. also showed that the price of proportionality is $\Theta(\sqrt{n})$ and the price of equitability is $\Theta(n)$. In addition, they extended their analysis to the case where agents *dislike* the cake (i.e., a divisible *chore* is being allocated), and the case with indivisible goods or chores. However, in case of indivisible goods, notions such as envy-freeness, proportionality, and equitability cannot be guaranteed. The analysis of Caragiannis et al. [9] simply excluded instances which do not admit allocations satisfying these criteria.

Bei et al. [5] instead focused on notions that can be guaranteed with indivisible goods and chores, such as envy-freeness up to one good (EF1). While they did not settle the price of EF1 (which is the focus of our work), they showed that the price of popular allocation rules such as the maximum Nash welfare rule [10], the egalitarian rule [24], and the leximin rule [7,19] is $\Theta(n)$. They also considered allocations that are balanced, i.e., give all agents an approximately equal number of goods, and settled the price of this guarantee as $\Theta(\sqrt{n})$. To the best of our knowledge, our work is the first to consider the price of approximate maximin share guarantee.

2   Preliminaries

For $k \in \mathbb{N}$, define $[k] := \{1, \ldots, k\}$. We study discrete fair division problems, wherein a set $[m]$ of indivisible goods need to be partitioned in a fair manner among a set $[n]$ of agents.

---

[3] Section 2 provides a formal description of the valuation classes and the query models.

Agent Valuations. The cardinal preference of each agent $i \in [n]$ (over the goods) is specified via the valuation function $v_i : 2^{[m]} \mapsto \mathbb{R}_{\geq 0}$, where $v_i(S) \in \mathbb{R}_{\geq 0}$ is the value that agent i has for the subset of goods $S \subseteq [m]$. We assume valuations are normalized $(v_i(\emptyset) = 0)$, nonnegative $(v_i(S) \geq 0$ for all $S \subseteq [m])$, and monotone $(v_i(A) \leq v_i(B)$ for $A \subseteq B \subseteq [m])$. A fair-division instance is given by a tuple $\langle [n], [m], \{v_i\}_{i \in [n]} \rangle$. We primarily consider two valuation classes:

- Additive: $v_i(S) = \sum_{g \in S} v_i(g)$ for each agent $i \in [n]$ and subset of goods $S \subseteq [m]$. Here, $v_i(g)$ denotes the value that agent i has for good $g \in [m]$.
- Subadditive: $v_i(S \cup T) \leq v_i(S) + v_i(T)$ for each agent $i \in [n]$ and subsets $S, T \subseteq [m]$. Note that the family of subadditive valuations encompasses additive valuations.

Oracle Access. Since describing subadditive valuations may require size exponential in the number of goods, to design efficient algorithms, we assume oracle access to the valuation functions. The literature focuses on two query models.

- Value queries: Given an agent $i \in [n]$ and a subset of goods $S \subseteq [m]$, the oracle returns $v_i(S)$.
- Demand queries: Given an agent $i \in [n]$ and a price $p_g \in \mathbb{R}_{\geq 0}$ for each good $g \in [m]$, the oracle returns a "profit-maximizing" set $S^* \in \arg \max_{S \subseteq [m]} v_i(S) - \sum_{g \in S} p_g$.

Demand queries are strictly more powerful than value queries [22, Section 11.5].

Allocations. Write $\Pi_n([m])$ to denote the set of all n-partitions of the set of goods $[m]$. An allocation $\mathcal{A} = (A_1, A_2, \ldots, A_n) \in \Pi_n([m])$ corresponds to an n-partition wherein the subset $A_i \subseteq [m]$ is assigned to agent $i \in [n]$; such a subset is called a bundle. The term partial allocation denotes an n-partition $(P_1, P_2, \ldots, P_n) \in \Pi_n(S)$ of a subset of goods $S \subseteq [m]$. Here, as before, subset P_i is assigned to agent $i \in [n]$.

Fairness. The notions of fairness considered in this work are defined next.

Definition 1 (Prop1). *An allocation $\mathcal{A}$ is called proportional up to one good (Prop1) if for each agent $i \in [n]$, there exists a good $g \in [m]$, such that $v_i(A_i \cup \{g\}) \geq v_i([m])/n$.*

Definition 2 (EF1). *An allocation $\mathcal{A}$ is called envy-free up to one good (EF1) iff for all agents $i, j \in [n]$ with $A_j \neq \emptyset$, there exists a good $g \in A_j$ such that $v_i(A_i) \geq v_i(A_j \setminus \{g\})$.*

It is easy to check that EF1 implies Prop1 for additive valuations. In a fair-division instance $\mathcal{I} = \langle [n], [m], \{v_i\}_{i \in [n]} \rangle$, the maximin share of agent $i \in [n]$ is defined as

$$\mathrm{MMS}_i := \max_{(P_1, \ldots, P_n) \in \Pi_n([m])} \min_{j \in [n]} v_i(P_j)$$

Definition 3 (α-MMS). *For $\alpha \in [0,1]$, an allocation $\mathcal{A}$ is called α-approximate maximin share fair (α-MMS) if $v_i(A_i) \geq \alpha \cdot \text{MMS}_i$ for each agent $i \in [n]$.*

Social Welfare. The social welfare of an allocation $\mathcal{A}$, denoted $\text{SW}(\mathcal{A})$, is defined as the sum of the values that $\mathcal{A}$ generates among the agents: $\text{SW}(\mathcal{A}) = \sum_{i=1}^{n} v_i(A_i)$. We will use $\mathcal{W}^* = (W_1^*, W_2^*, \ldots, W_n^*)$ to denote a social welfare maximizing allocation, i.e., $\mathcal{W}^* \in \arg\max_{\mathcal{A} \in \Pi_n([m])} \text{SW}(\mathcal{A})$, and OPT to denote the optimal social welfare, $\text{OPT} = \text{SW}(\mathcal{W}^*)$.

Price of Fairness. Given a fairness property X, the price of X is the supremum, over all fair division instances, of the ratio between the maximum social welfare of any allocation and the maximum social welfare of any allocation satisfying property X.

Scaling. To ensure that valuations are on the same scale, much of the literature on fair division assumes that agents' valuations are *scaled*, i.e., $v_i([m]) = 1$ for all $i \in [n]$. Noting that unscaled valuations are common in other areas of social choice (e.g., [13]), we consider both scaled and unscaled valuations.

All missing proofs appear in the full version of the paper [4].

3   Price of Envy-Freeness Up to One Good (EF1)

We begin by studying the price of fairness for EF1 allocations for agents with subadditive valuations. For scaled additive valuations, Bei et al. [5] show that the price of EF1 is between $\Omega(\sqrt{n})$ and $O(n)$. We tighten their upper bound to $O(\sqrt{n})$ (thus matching their lower bound) even when the valuations are subadditive. For unscaled valuations, we show that the bound is $\Theta(n)$. Our main result in this section is as follows.

Theorem 1. *theorem   The price of EF1 is $O(\sqrt{n})$ for scaled subadditive valuations and $O(n)$ for unscaled subadditive valuations. Both bounds are tight even when the valuations are additive.*

We begin by proving the upper bounds for EF1, using Algorithms 1 and 2.

3.1   An Absolute Welfare Guarantee

First, we show (via Algorithm 1) that when agents have subadditive valuations $\{v_i\}_{i \in [n]}$ (not necessarily scaled), there always exists an EF1 allocation $\mathcal{A}$ with social welfare $\text{SW}(\mathcal{A}) \geq \frac{1}{2n} \sum_{i=1}^{n} v_i([m])$.

This absolute welfare guarantee has two implications. First, since $\sum_{i=1}^{n} v_i([m])$ is a trivial upper bound on the optimal social welfare, OPT, the result establishes an $O(n)$ upper bound on the price of EF1. For unscaled valuations, this is exactly the bound we need. For scaled valuations, we need to improve this to $O(\sqrt{n})$. Since $\sum_{i=1}^{n} v_i([m]) = n$ under scaled valuations, the result gives $\text{SW}(\mathcal{A}) \geq 1/2$. Hence, if $\text{OPT} = O(\sqrt{n})$, then we have the desired $O(\sqrt{n})$ upper bound. We analyse the case when $\text{OPT} = \Omega(\sqrt{n})$ in Sect. 3.2.

Algorithm 1. ALG-EF1-ABS

Input: Fair-division instance $\mathcal{I} = \langle [n], [m], \{v_i\}_{i \in [n]} \rangle$ with value-query oracle access to the subadditive valuations v_is.

Output: An EF1 allocation $\mathcal{B}$ with social welfare $\mathrm{SW}(\mathcal{B}) \geq \frac{1}{2n} \sum_{i \in [n]} v_i([m])$.

1: Consider the weighted bipartite graph $G = ([n] \cup [m], [n] \times [m])$ with weight of each edge $(i, g) \in [n] \times [m]$ set as $v_i(g)$. Let π be a maximum-weight matching in G that matches all nodes in $[n]$.

2: Construct the partial allocation $\mathcal{B}'$ such that $B_i' = \{\pi(i)\}$ for each $i \in [n]$. {Note that $\mathcal{B}'$ is trivially EF1 because each agent is assigned a single good.}

3: Use the algorithm of Lipton et al. [20] to extend the partial EF1 allocation $\mathcal{B}'$ into a complete EF1 allocation $\mathcal{B}$ such that $v_i(B_i) \geq v_i(B_i')$ for each agent $i \in [n]$.

4: **return** Allocation $\mathcal{B}$

Lemma 1. *Let $\mathcal{I} = \langle [n], [m], \{v_i\}_{i \in [n]} \rangle$ be a fair-division instance in which agent valuations are subadditive. Then, given value-query oracle access to the valuations, ALG-EF1-ABS (Algorithm 1) efficiently computes an EF1 allocation $\mathcal{B}$ with social welfare $\mathrm{SW}(\mathcal{B}) \geq \frac{1}{2n} \sum_{i \in [n]} v_i([m])$.*

3.2 The Case of High Optimal Welfare

As noted in Sect. 3.1, Lemma 1 allows us to focus on fair division instances with scaled subadditive valuations in which the optimal social welfare is $\mathrm{OPT} = \Omega(\sqrt{n})$. This allows us to sacrifice $O(\sqrt{n})$ of the welfare in OPT, obtain $O(\sqrt{n})$ approximation to the *remaining* welfare through an EF1 allocation, and yet achieve $O(\sqrt{n})$ approximation to OPT. In particular, we present an algorithm that efficiently finds an EF1 allocation $\mathcal{A}$ with social welfare $\mathrm{SW}(\mathcal{A}) \geq \frac{\mathrm{OPT} - 2\sqrt{n}}{12\sqrt{n}}$.

Ideally, we would like to use as reference an allocation $\mathcal{W}^*$ with the optimal social welfare OPT. However, for subadditive valuations, computing such an allocation is NP-hard under both value queries and demand queries [12]. For values queries, $\Theta(\sqrt{m})$ is the best possible approximation to OPT with a polynomial number of queries [12,21]. Instead, we turn to demand queries, for which a 2-approximation algorithm is given by Feige [14]. In particular, this algorithm efficiently computes an allocation $\mathcal{W}$ with social welfare at least $\frac{1}{2}$OPT.[4] Outside of the black-box use of this algorithm, the rest of our algorithm uses value queries (which are a special case of demand queries). We emphasize that our use of value or demand queries is only for computation. Our main result—the price of EF1—is existential and independent of any query model.

Starting with the high-welfare allocation $\mathcal{W}$ returned by Feige's algorithm, our algorithm works as follows. It first indexes the m goods as $g_1, g_2, \ldots, g_m$ such that the goods in each W_i receive consecutive indices.[5] Alternatively,

---

[4] This allocation serves as a reference in our algorithm, and may not be EF1 itself.

[5] For example, we can index the goods such that $W_i = \left\{ g_k : 1 + \sum_{j=1}^{i-1} |W_j| \leq k \leq \sum_{j=1}^{i} |W_i| \right\}$ for each agent $i \in [n]$.

consider a line graph $L = ([m], E)$ over the set of goods with edges $E = \{(g_k, g_{k+1}) : k \in [m-1]\}$. Then, each W_i induces a connected subgraph of L.

Definition 4. *Let $L = ([m], E)$ be a line graph over the goods. We say that $S \subseteq [m]$ is a* connected bundle *in L if S induces a connected subgraph of L. Given a partial allocation $\mathcal{P}$, define $\mathcal{U}(\mathcal{P})$ as the set of connected components of L that remain after removing the allocated goods $\cup_{i \in [n]} P_i$. We refer to $U \in \mathcal{U}(\mathcal{P})$ as an* unassigned connected bundle.

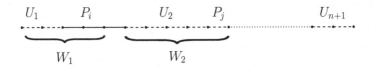

Fig. 1. Line graph over the goods and unassigned components.

In this terminology, each W_i is a connected bundle in L (see Fig. 1). ALG-EF1-HIGH builds a partial allocation $\mathcal{P}$ by giving each agent i her most valuable good from W_i. This allocation trivially satisfies two properties: it is EF1, and each P_i is a connected bundle in L. The algorithm then iteratively updates $\mathcal{P}$ to improve its social welfare while maintaining both these properties. This iterative process is inspired by a similar algorithm for (divisible) cake-cutting (Algorithm 1, Arunachaleswaran et al. [3]).

In particular, at every iteration, our algorithm computes the set of unassigned connected bundles $\mathcal{U}(\mathcal{P})$; note that removing n connected bundles from $\mathcal{P}$ can create at most $n+1$ unassigned connected bundles, as shown in Fig. 1. If there is an unassigned connected bundle $U \in \mathcal{U}(\mathcal{P})$ that some agent envies, then the algorithm finds an *inclusion-wise minimal* subset of U that is envied and allocates it to an envious agent. While this preserves exact envy-freeness in the cake-cutting setting of Arunachaleswaran et al. [3], in our setting we argue that inclusion-wise minimality preserves the EF1 property of $\mathcal{P}$. We also argue that this iterative process terminates at a partial allocation $\mathcal{P}$ that satisfies the desired social welfare guarantee. Finally, we use the algorithm of Lipton et al. [20] (see also [2]) to extend this partial EF1 allocation into a complete EF1 allocation without losing social welfare. The detailed algorithm is presented as Algorithm 2.

We start by proving some relevant properties of ALG-EF1-HIGH.

Lemma 2. *When ALG-EF1-HIGH is run on an instance $\mathcal{I} = \langle [n], [m], \{v_i\}_{i \in [n]} \rangle$ with subadditive valuations, the following hold regarding the partial allocation $\mathcal{P}^t$ constructed after t iterations of the while loop.*

1. *If $t \geq 1$, then for each agent $i \in [n]$, either $P_i^t = P_i^{t-1}$ or $v_i(P_i^t) > v_i(P_i^{t-1})$.*
2. *For each agent $i \in [n]$, P_i is a connected bundle under the line graph L constructed in Line 6.*
3. *$\mathcal{P}^t$ is EF1.*

Algorithm 2. ALG-EF1-HIGH

Input: A fair division instance $\mathcal{I} = \langle [n], [m], \{v_i\}_{i \in [n]} \rangle$ with demand-query oracle access to the subadditive valuations v_is.

Output: An EF1 allocation $\mathcal{A}$ with social welfare $\mathrm{SW}(\mathcal{A}) \geq \frac{\mathrm{OPT}}{12\sqrt{n}} - \frac{1}{6}$.

1: Use Feige's algorithm [14] to compute an allocation $\mathcal{W}$ with social welfare $\mathrm{SW}(\mathcal{W}) \geq 1/2 \cdot \mathrm{OPT}$

2: Re-index the m goods as $g_1, g_2, \ldots, g_m$ such that in the line graph L over the goods containing edges (g_k, g_{k+1}) for $k \in [m-1]$, each W_i forms a connected subgraph

3: Initialize $t = 0$

4: For each agent $i \in [n]$ with $W_i \neq \emptyset$, pick $g_i^* \in \arg\max_{g \in W_i} v_i(g)$ and set $P_i^t = \{g_i^*\}$

5: For each agent $i \in [n]$ with $W_i = \emptyset$, set $P_i^t = \emptyset$
  {For a partial allocation $\mathcal{P}^t$, let $\mathcal{U}(\mathcal{P}^t)$ denote the collection of connected components in the line graph L that remain after the removal of $\cup_{i \in [n]} P_i^t$}

6: **while** $\exists$ agent $i \in [n]$ and connected component $U \in \mathcal{U}(\mathcal{P}^t)$ with $v_i(P_i^t) < v_i(U)$ **do**

7:   Let U consist of goods $\{g_a, g_{a+1}, \ldots, g_b\}$

8:   Let $c \in [a, b]$ be the smallest index such that $v_k(P_k^t) < v_k(\{g_a, g_{a+1}, \ldots, g_c\})$ for some $k \in [n]$
    {The choice of c ensures that no agent k values $\{g_a, \ldots, g_{c-1}\}$ more than her current bundle, i.e., $v_k(P_k^t) \geq v_k(\{g_a, \ldots, g_{c-1}\})$ for every agent k.}

9:   Pick an arbitrary agent k for which $v_k(P_k^t) < v_k(\{g_a, g_{a+1}, \ldots, g_c\})$

10:   Set $P_k^{t+1} = \{g_a, \ldots, g_c\}$ and $P_j^{t+1} = P_j^t$ for all $j \neq k$

11:   Update $t \leftarrow t + 1$

12: **end while**
   {At this point, $v_i(P_i^t) \geq v_i(U)$ for all $i \in [n]$ and $U \in \mathcal{U}(\mathcal{P}^t)$. We will show that $\mathcal{P}^t$ is a partial EF1 allocation.}

13: Use the algorithm of Lipton et al. [20] to extend the partial EF1 allocation $\mathcal{P}^t$ into a complete EF1 allocation $\mathcal{A}$ such that $v_i(A_i) \geq v_i(P_i^t)$ for each $i \in [n]$

14: **return** Allocation $\mathcal{A}$

Lemma 3. *When* ALG-EF1-HIGH *is run on an instance* $\mathcal{I} = \langle [n], [m], \{v_i\}_{i \in [n]} \rangle$ *with subadditive valuations, the following hold.*

1. *The while loop terminates after* $T = O(nm^2)$ *iterations.*
2. *The partial allocation* $\mathcal{P}^T$ *constructed at the end of the while loop satisfies* $v_i(P_i^T) \geq v_i(U)$ *for every agent* $i \in [n]$ *and unassigned connected bundle* $U \in \mathcal{U}(\mathcal{P}^T)$.

Using Lemmas 2 and 3, we can derive the key technical result of this section.

Lemma 4. *Given a fair division instance* $\mathcal{I} = \langle [n], [m], \{v_i\}_{i \in [n]} \rangle$ *with scaled subadditive valuations,* ALG-EF1-HIGH *terminates in polynomial time and returns an EF1 allocation* $\mathcal{A}$ *satisfying*

$$\mathrm{SW}(\mathcal{A}) \geq \frac{\mathrm{OPT}}{12\sqrt{n}} - \frac{1}{6},$$

where OPT *is the optimal social welfare achievable in instance* $\mathcal{I}$.

We now prove the upper bounds in Theorem 1, using Lemmas 1 and 4. As mentioned earlier, the lower bound for scaled valuations is already obtained by Bei et al. [5]. The lower bound for unscaled valuations is shown in the full version [4].

Proof (of Theorem 1). For unscaled valuations, Lemma 1 shows that there exists an EF1 allocation $\mathcal{B}$ with $\mathrm{SW}(\mathcal{B}) \geq \frac{1}{2n} \sum_{i \in [n]} v_i([m]) \geq \frac{1}{2n} \mathrm{OPT}$, which yields the desired $O(n)$ bound.

For an instance $\mathcal{I}$ with scaled valuations, we consider two cases: either $\mathrm{OPT} \leq 8\sqrt{n}$ or $\mathrm{OPT} > 8\sqrt{n}$.

Case 1: Suppose $\mathrm{OPT} \leq 8\sqrt{n}$. Because valuations are scaled (i.e., $v_i([m]) = 1$ for each agent $i \in [n]$), Lemma 1 implies that the EF1 allocation $\mathcal{B}$ returned by ALG-EF1-ABS satisfies $\mathrm{SW}(\mathcal{B}) \geq \frac{1}{2n} \sum_{i \in [n]} v_i([m]) = \frac{1}{2}$. Hence, $\mathrm{SW}(\mathcal{B}) \geq \frac{1}{16\sqrt{n}} \mathrm{OPT}$.

Case 2: Suppose $\mathrm{OPT} > 8\sqrt{n}$. Then, $\frac{1}{6} < \frac{\mathrm{OPT}}{48\sqrt{n}}$. Now, Lemma 4 implies that the EF1 allocation $\mathcal{A}$ returned by ALG-EF1-HIGH satisfies

$$\mathrm{SW}(\mathcal{A}) \geq \frac{\mathrm{OPT}}{12\sqrt{n}} - \frac{1}{6} \geq \frac{\mathrm{OPT}}{12\sqrt{n}} - \frac{\mathrm{OPT}}{48\sqrt{n}} = \frac{\mathrm{OPT}}{16\sqrt{n}}.$$

Thus, in either case, there exists an EF1 allocation with social welfare at least $\frac{1}{16\sqrt{n}} \mathrm{OPT}$, which yields the desired $O(\sqrt{n})$ bound. To obtain the required EF1 allocation, we simply run both algorithms and take the allocation with higher social welfare.

Before concluding this section, we recall that for additive valuations, EF1 implies proportionality up to one good (Prop1). Hence, our upper bounds of $O(\sqrt{n})$ and $O(n)$ on the price of EF1 under scaled and unscaled additive valuations, respectively, carry over to the price of Prop1 as well. These bounds are tight: Our lower bound construction from the proof of Theorem 1 for unscaled valuations and the construction due to Bei et al. [5] for scaled valuations can be modified slightly for Prop1 as well.

Corollary 1. *The price of Prop1 is $\Theta(\sqrt{n})$ for scaled additive valuations and $\Theta(n)$ for unscaled additive valuations.*

4   Price of 1/2-Approximate Maximin Share Guarantee

We now study the price of approximate MMS for additive valuations. Our main result settles the price of 1/2-MMS for scaled and unscaled additive valuations.

Theorem 2. *The price of 1/2-MMS is $\Theta(\sqrt{n})$ for scaled additive valuations and $\Theta(n)$ for unscaled additive valuations.*

We sketch the proof of the upper bound, based on Algorithms 3 and 4. Recall that $\mathcal{W}^* = (W_1^*, \ldots, W_n^*) \in \arg\max_{\mathcal{A} \in \Pi_n([m])} \mathrm{SW}(\mathcal{A})$ is a social welfare maximizing allocation, and $\mathrm{OPT} = \mathrm{SW}(\mathcal{W}^*)$ is the maximum social welfare.

4.1   An Absolute Welfare Guarantee

First, we show that when agents have additive valuations $\{v_i\}_{i \in [n]}$ (not necessarily scaled), there always exists a $1/2$-MMS allocation $\mathcal{A}$ with social welfare $SW(\mathcal{A}) \geq \frac{1}{3n} \sum_{i=1}^{n} v_i([m])$. Algorithm 3 computes such an allocation efficiently.

As for EF1 allocations, there are two implications of this. First, for both scaled and unscaled additive valuations, this establishes that the price of $1/2$-MMS is $O(n)$. For unscaled valuations, this is the bound we seek. For scaled valuations, since $v_i([m]) = 1$ for each agent $i \in [n]$, so $SW(\mathcal{A}) \geq 1/3 = \Omega(1)$. Thus, if $OPT = O(\sqrt{n})$, this gives the desired upper bound of $O(\sqrt{n})$. In Sect. 4.2, we thus limit our attention to instances with $OPT = \Omega(\sqrt{n})$.

Algorithm 3. ALG-MMS-ABS

Input: A fair division instance $\mathcal{I} = \langle [n], [m], \{v_i\}_i \rangle$ with additive valuations $\{v_i\}_{i \in [n]}$.
Output: A $1/2$-MMS   allocation $\mathcal{B}$ with $SW(\mathcal{B})$ $\geq$ $\frac{1}{3n} \sum_{i=1}^{n} v_i([m])$.

1: Initialize set of agents $A = [n]$, set of goods $G = [m]$, and bundles $B_i = \emptyset$, for all $i \in [n]$
2: **while** there exists agent $i \in A$ and good $g \in G$ such that $v_i(g) \geq \frac{1}{2|A|} v_i(G)$ **do**
3:     Set $(i', g') \in \arg\max_{\{(i,g) \in A \times G \,:\, v_i(g) \geq \frac{1}{2|A|} v_i(G)\}} v_i(g)$
4:     Set $B_{i'} = \{g'\}$ and update $A \leftarrow A \setminus \{i'\}$ along with $G \leftarrow G \setminus \{g'\}$
5: **end while**
6: Efficiently compute a Prop1 allocation $(B_i)_{i \in A}$ of the fair division instance $\langle A, G, \{v_i\}_{i \in A} \rangle$
7: **return** allocation $\mathcal{B} = (B_1, B_2, \ldots, B_n)$

Algorithm 3 is a refinement of the algorithm of Amanatidis et al. [1] for computing a $1/2$-MMS allocation: in Line 3, we use an $\arg\max$ to break ties, whereas they use an arbitrary pair (i, g). Since Amanatidis et al. [1] prove that their algorithm always returns a $1/2$-MMS allocation, regardless of any tie-breaking, it follows that our refinement, Algorithm 3, also always returns a $1/2$-MMS allocation. It remains to prove that it also provides the desired welfare guarantee, which is shown in the following lemma.

Lemma 5. *Given any fair division instance* $\mathcal{I} = \langle [n], [m], \{v_i\}_{i \in [n]} \rangle$ *with additive valuations,* ALG-MMS-ABS *(Algorithm 3) efficiently computes a $1/2$-MMS allocation* $\mathcal{B}$ *with social welfare* $SW(\mathcal{B}) \geq \frac{1}{3n} \sum_{i=1}^{n} v_i([m])$.

4.2   The Case of High Optimal Welfare

As argued in Sect. 4.1, Lemma 5 allows us to restrict our attention to scaled additive valuations in which the optimal social welfare $OPT = \Omega(\sqrt{n})$. Similar to the case of EF1, we can now safely sacrifice $O(\sqrt{n})$ welfare, and simply achieve

$O(\sqrt{n})$ approximation of the *remaining* welfare. This is achieved by ALG-MMS-HIGH (Algorithm 4).

However, ALG-MMS-HIGH requires knowledge of the maximin share MMS_i of each agent i. While computing this quantity is known to be strongly NP-hard, there exists a polynomial-time approximation scheme (PTAS) for it [25]. For a fixed $\epsilon \in (0,1)$, this PTAS can compute an estimate $Z_i \in [(1-\epsilon)\text{MMS}_i, \text{MMS}_i]$ for each agent i in polynomial time. We pass these estimates as input to ALG-MMS-HIGH, which runs in polynomial time and yields a $(\frac{1}{2}-\epsilon)$-MMS allocation with the desired welfare guarantee.

We emphasize that the approximation here is solely for computational purposes. To derive our main existential result about the price of 1/2-MMS, we can simply pass $Z_i = \text{MMS}_i$ to ALG-MMS-HIGH, and it returns an exact 1/2-MMS allocation with the desired welfare guarantee.

The intuition behind the algorithm is as follows. Our goal is to assign each agent i a bundle of value at least $\frac{1}{2} \cdot Z_i \geq \left(\frac{1}{2}-\epsilon\right) \cdot \text{MMS}_i$, and ensure that most (all but $\sqrt{n}$) agents i achieve a value at least $\Omega\left(\frac{1}{\sqrt{n}}v_i(W_i^*)\right)$; here, $\mathcal{W} = (W_1^*, \ldots, W_n^*)$ denotes a social welfare maximizing allocation. Therefore, throughout the algorithm, we keep track of two sets of agents, T (temporary) and P (permanent). Each agent $i \in T \cup P$ must have received a bundle B_i worth $v_i(B_i) \geq \frac{1}{2} \cdot Z_i$, and agent $i \in P$ further has $v_i(B_i) \geq \frac{1}{3\sqrt{n}} \cdot v_i(W_i^*)$. The algorithm ensures that an agent is never removed after being added to $P \cup T$. Specifically, once she is added to T, she can only be moved to P. Additionally, once an agent is included in the set P, her assignment is never updated and she remains in P.

Lines 5 and 9 handle easy cases, when an agent i either has $\text{MMS}_i = 0$, or can be added directly to P by giving her a single good from W_i^*. Line 13 addresses agents to whom giving a single good (not necessarily from W_i^*) is sufficient to add them to $P \cup T$. These steps leverage the fact that the maximin share is maintained while assigning away singleton bundles.

Finally, Line 17 leverages an idea similar to what we utilized for EF1. This step slowly grows a bundle by iteratively adding goods ordered according to $\mathcal{W}^*$, and assigns the bundle as soon as its value for some agent is at least half of her maximin share. Line 24 plays a key role in bookkeeping, as we show in our proofs. The following lemma states the main result for Algorithm 4.

Lemma 6. *Given a fair division instance* $\mathcal{I} = \left\langle [n], [m], \{v_i\}_{i \in [n]} \right\rangle$ *with scaled additive valuations, and, for a fixed* $\epsilon \in [0,1)$, *an estimate* $Z_i \in [(1-\epsilon)\text{MMS}_i, \text{MMS}_i]$ *for each agent* i, ALG-MMS-HIGH *(Algorithm 4) efficiently computes a* $(\frac{1}{2}-\epsilon)$-MMS *allocation* $\mathcal{B}$ *with the property that* $3\sqrt{n} \cdot \text{SW}(\mathcal{B}) + 4\sqrt{n} \geq \text{OPT}$; *here,* OPT *denotes the optimal social welfare in* $\mathcal{I}$.

Using the properties of ALG-MMS-ABS and ALG-MMS-HIGH from Sect. 4.1 and 4.2, we can directly prove the upper bounds on the price of 1/2-MMS in Theorem 2. For the lower bounds, we use constructions that appeared in the work of Caragiannis et al. [11]. The complete proofs appear in the full version [4].

Algorithm 4. ALG-MMS-HIGH

Input: A fair division instance $\mathcal{I} = \langle [m], [n], \{v_i\}_i \rangle$ with scaled additive valuations, and for a fixed $\epsilon \in [0, 1)$, an estimate $Z_i \in [(1 - \epsilon)\mathrm{MMS}_i, \mathrm{MMS}_i]$ for each agent i.

Output: A $\left(\frac{1}{2} - \epsilon\right)$-MMS allocation $\mathcal{B}$ with $\mathrm{SW}(\mathcal{B}) \geq \frac{1}{3\sqrt{n}} \mathrm{OPT} - \frac{4}{3}$.

1: Compute a social welfare maximizing allocation $\mathcal{W}^* \in \arg\max_{\mathcal{A} \in \Pi_n([m])} \mathrm{SW}(\mathcal{A})$
2: Index the goods as $g_1, \ldots, g_m$ so that, for each $i \in [n]$, the goods in W_i^* receive consecutive indices
3: Initialize $\mathcal{B}$ with $B_i = \emptyset$ for each $i \in [n]$
4: Initialize $P = T = \emptyset$
5: For each $i \in [n]$ with $\mathrm{MMS}_i = 0$, update $P \leftarrow P \cup \{i\}$ if $v_i(W_i^*) = 0$, and $T \leftarrow T \cup \{i\}$ otherwise. {$\mathrm{MMS}_i = 0$ iff agent i has positive value for less than n goods, which can be checked efficiently.}
6: Let $\Gamma_{\mathrm{single}} = \left\{ i \in [n] \ : \ Z_i < \frac{2}{3\sqrt{n}} v_i(W_i^*) \text{ and } \exists g \in W_i^* \text{ s.t. } v_i(g) \geq \frac{1}{3\sqrt{n}} v_i(W_i^*) \right\}$
7: **for** each $i \in \Gamma_{\mathrm{single}}$ **do**
8:     Pick $g_i \in \arg\max_{g \in W_i^*} v_i(g)$, and set $B_i = \{g_i\}$
9:     Update $P \leftarrow P \cup \{i\}$, and if $i \in T$, update $T \leftarrow T \setminus \{i\}$
10: **end for**
11: **while** there exists an agent $a \in [n] \setminus (P \cup T)$ and a good $h \in [m] \setminus \cup_{b \in [n]} B_b$ such that $v_a(h) \geq \frac{1}{2} \cdot Z_a$ **do**
12:     Set $B_a = \{h\}$.
13:     If $v_a(B_a) \geq \frac{1}{3\sqrt{n}} v_a(W_a^*)$, update $P \leftarrow P \cup \{a\}$, else update $T \leftarrow T \cup \{a\}$
14: **end while**
15: Let $R \leftarrow [m] \setminus \cup_{a \in [n]} B_a$ be the set of remaining goods
16: Initialize $K = \emptyset$ and index $t = 1$
17: **for** $t = 1, \ldots, m$ **do**
18:     **if** $g_t \notin R$ **then**
19:         **continue**
20:     **end if**
21:     Update $K \leftarrow K \cup \{g_t\}$
22:     **if** there exists an agent $i \in T$ such that $g_t \in W_i^*$ and $v_i(K) \geq \frac{1}{3\sqrt{n}} v_i(W_i^*)$ **then**
23:         Set $(B_i, K) \leftarrow (K, B_i)$ {Swap B_i and K}
24:         Update $P \leftarrow P \cup \{i\}$ and $T \leftarrow T \setminus \{i\}$
25:     **end if**
26:     **if** there exists an agent $a \in [n] \setminus (P \cup T)$ such that $v_a(K) \geq \frac{1}{2} \cdot Z_a$ **then**
27:         Set $B_a = K$ and update $K = \emptyset$
28:         If $v_a(B_a) \geq \frac{1}{3\sqrt{n}} v_a(W_a^*)$, update $P \leftarrow P \cup \{a\}$, else update $T \leftarrow T \cup \{a\}$
29:     **end if**
30: **end for**
31: Let $X = [m] \setminus \cup_{a \in [n]} B_a$ be the set of unassigned goods. Assign each $g \in X$ to agent i such that $g \in W_i^*$, i.e., $B_i \leftarrow B_i \cup (W_i^* \cap X)$.
32: **return** allocation $(B_1, B_2, \ldots, B_n)$

Acknowledgements. SB gratefully acknowledges the support of a Ramanujan Fellowship (SERB - SB/S2/RJN-128/2015) and a Pratiksha Trust Young Investigator Award. UB's research is generously supported the Department of Atomic Energy, Government of India (project no. RTI4001), a Ramanujan Fellowship (SERB - SB/S2/RJN-

055/2015), and an Early Career Research Award (SERB - ECR/2018/002766). NS was partially supported by an NSERC Discovery Grant.

References

1. Amanatidis, G., Markakis, E., Nikzad, A., Saberi, A.: Approximation algorithms for computing maximin share allocations. ACM Trans. Algorithms (TALG) **13**(4), 1–28 (2017)
2. Amanatidis, G., Markakis, E., Ntokos, A.: Multiple birds with one stone: beating 1/2 for EFX and GMMS via envy cycle elimination. In: AAAI 2020, pp. 1790–1797. AAAI Press (2020)
3. Arunachaleswaran, E.R., Barman, S., Kumar, R., Rathi, N.: Fair and efficient cake division with connected pieces. In: Caragiannis, I., Mirrokni, V., Nikolova, E. (eds.) WINE 2019. LNCS, vol. 11920, pp. 57–70. Springer, Cham (2019). https://doi.org/10.1007/978-3-030-35389-6_5
4. Barman, S., Bhaskar, U., Shah, N.: Optimal bounds on the price of fairness for indivisible goods. CoRR abs/2007.06242 (2020)
5. Bei, X., Lu, X., Manurangsi, P., Suksompong, W.: The price of fairness for indivisible goods. In: Kraus, S. (ed.) Proceedings of the Twenty-Eighth International Joint Conference on Artificial Intelligence, IJCAI 2019, Macao, China, 10–16 August 2019, pp. 81–87 (2019)
6. Bertsimas, D., Farias, V.F., Trichakis, N.: The price of fairness. Oper. Res. **59**(1), 17–31 (2011)
7. Bogomolnaia, A., Moulin, H.: Random matching under dichotomous preferences. Econometrica **72**, 257–279 (2004)
8. Budish, E.: The combinatorial assignment problem: approximate competitive equilibrium from equal incomes. J. Polit. Econ. **119**(6), 1061–1103 (2011)
9. Caragiannis, I., Kaklamanis, C., Kanellopoulos, P., Kyropoulou, M.: The efficiency of fair division. In: Proceedings of the 5th Conference on Web and Internet Economics (WINE), pp. 475–482 (2009)
10. Caragiannis, I., Kurokawa, D., Moulin, H., Procaccia, A.D., Shah, N., Wang, J.: The unreasonable fairness of maximum Nash welfare. ACM Trans. Econ. Comput. (TEAC) **7**(3), 1–32 (2019)
11. Caragiannis, I., Kaklamanis, C., Kanellopoulos, P., Kyropoulou, M.: The efficiency of fair division. Theory Comput. Syst. **50**(4), 589–610 (2012)
12. Dobzinski, S., Nisan, N., Schapira, M.: Approximation algorithms for combinatorial auctions with complement-free bidders. Math. Oper. Res. **35**(1), 1–13 (2010)
13. Dutta, B., Peters, H., Sen, A.: Strategy-proof cardinal decision schemes. Soc. Choice Welfare **28**(1), 163–179 (2007)
14. Feige, U.: On maximizing welfare when utility functions are subadditive. SIAM J. Comput. **39**(1), 122–142 (2009)
15. Foley, D.: Resource allocation and the public sector. Yale Economics Essays, vol. 7, pp. 45–98 (1967)
16. Garg, J., Taki, S.: An improved approximation algorithm for maximin shares. In: EC 2020, pp. 379–380. ACM (2020)
17. Ghodsi, M., Hajiaghayi, M., Seddighin, M., Seddighin, S., Yami, H.: Fair allocation of indivisible goods: improvements and generalizations. In: Proceedings of the 2018 ACM Conference on Economics and Computation, pp. 539–556 (2018)

18. Kurokawa, D., Procaccia, A.D., Wang, J.: When can the maximin share guarantee be guaranteed? In: Proceedings of the 30th AAAI Conference on Artificial Intelligence (AAAI), pp. 523–529 (2016)
19. Kurokawa, D., Procaccia, A.D., Shah, N.: Leximin allocations in the real world. ACM Trans. Econ. Comput. (TEAC) 6(3–4), 1–24 (2018)
20. Lipton, R.J., Markakis, E., Mossel, E., Saberi, A.: On approximately fair allocations of indivisible goods. In: Proceedings of the 5th ACM Conference on Electronic Commerce, pp. 125–131 (2004)
21. Mirrokni, V., Schapira, M., Vondrák, J.: Tight information-theoretic lower bounds for welfare maximization in combinatorial auctions. In: Proceedings of the 9th ACM Conference on Electronic Commerce, pp. 70–77 (2008)
22. Suzuki, M., Vetta, A.: How many freemasons are there? The consensus voting mechanism in metric spaces. In: Harks, T., Klimm, M. (eds.) SAGT 2020. LNCS, vol. 12283, pp. 322–336. Springer, Cham (2020). https://doi.org/10.1007/978-3-030-57980-7_21
23. Procaccia, A.D., Wang, J.: Fair enough: guaranteeing approximate maximin shares. In: Proceedings of the 14th ACM Conference on Economics and Computation (EC), pp. 675–692 (2014)
24. Rawls, J.: A Theory of Justice. Harvard University Press, Cambridge (1971)
25. Woeginger, G.J.: A polynomial-time approximation scheme for maximizing the minimum machine completion time. Oper. Res. Lett. 20(4), 149–154 (1997)

Fair Division with Binary Valuations: One Rule to Rule Them All

Daniel Halpern[1], Ariel D. Procaccia[1], Alexandros Psomas[2(✉)], and Nisarg Shah[3]

[1] Harvard University, Cambridge, USA
dhalpern@g.harvard.edu, arielpro@seas.harvard.edu
[2] Purdue University, West Lafayette, USA
apsomas@cs.purdue.edu
[3] University of Toronto, Toronto, Canada
nisarg@cs.toronto.edu

Abstract. We study fair allocation of indivisible goods among agents. Prior research focuses on additive agent preferences, which leads to an impossibility when seeking truthfulness, fairness, and efficiency. We show that when agents have binary additive preferences, a compelling rule—maximum Nash welfare (MNW)—provides all three guarantees. Specifically, we show that deterministic MNW with lexicographic tie-breaking is group strategyproof in addition to being envy-free up to one good and Pareto optimal. We also prove that fractional MNW—known to be group strategyproof, envy-free, and Pareto optimal—can be implemented as a distribution over deterministic MNW allocations, which are envy-free up to one good. Our work establishes maximum Nash welfare as the ultimate allocation rule in the realm of binary additive preferences.

Keywords: Fair division · Mechanism design

1 Introduction

Fair division [13,28] is a sprawling field that cuts across scientific disciplines. Among its many challenges, the division of indivisible goods—an ostensible oxymoron—is arguably the most popular in recent years. The goods are "indivisible" in the sense that each must be allocated in its entirety to a single agent (think of pieces of jewelry or tickets to different football games in a season). Each agent has her own *valuation function*, which represents the benefit the agent derives from bundles of goods.

A fully expressive model of valuation functions would have to account for combinatorial preferences. Classic examples include a right shoe that is worthless without its matching left shoe (complementarities), and two identical refrigerators (substitutes). However, rich preferences can be difficult to elicit. It is often assumed, therefore, that the valuation functions are *additive*, that is, that each agent's value for a bundle of goods is the sum of her values for individual goods

© Springer Nature Switzerland AG 2020
X. Chen et al. (Eds.): WINE 2020, LNCS 12495, pp. 370–383, 2020.
https://doi.org/10.1007/978-3-030-64946-3_26

in the bundle. Additive valuations strike a balance between expressiveness and ease of elicitation; in particular, each agent need only report her value for each good separately.

Another advantage of additive valuations is that they admit a practical rule that is both (economically) efficient and fair. Specifically, the Maximum Nash Welfare (MNW) solution—which maximizes the product of valuations and, therefore, is obviously Pareto optimal (PO)—is envy-free up to one good (EF1): for any two agents i and j, it is always the case that i prefers her own bundle to that of j, possibly after removing a single good from the latter bundle [16].

The MNW solution, however, is not *strategyproof*, that is, agents can benefit by misreporting their preferences. In fact, under additive valuations, the only Pareto optimal and strategyproof rule is *serial dictatorship*, which is patently unfair [24]. This profound clash between efficiency and truthfulness holds true even when agents can only have three possible values for goods!

The only hope for reconciling efficiency, fairness and truthfulness, therefore, is to assume that agents' values for goods are *binary*. This assumption is not just a theoretical curiosity: while it obviously comes at a significant cost to expressiveness, it leads to extremely simple elicitation. In this sense, it arguably represents another natural point on the conceptual expressiveness-elicitation Pareto frontier. The same bold tradeoff has long been considered sensible in the literature on voting, where binary values are implicitly represented as *approval* votes [12]; in fact, the assumption underlying some of the recent work on approval-based multi-winner elections [17,26] is nothing but that of binary additive valuations. Thus, it is not surprising that many works in fair division pay special attention to the case of binary additive valuations [1,6,11,20,23].

With this rather detailed justification for binary additive valuations in mind, our primary research question is this: *do binary additive valuations admit rules that are efficient, fair, and truthful?*

1.1 Our Contribution

We provide a positive answer— and then some. Specifically, Theorem 1 asserts that, under binary additive valuations, a particular form of the MNW solution is Pareto optimal, EF1, *group* strategyproof (even a coalition of agents cannot misreport its members' preferences in a way that benefits them all) and polynomial-time computable.

Furthermore, we show that by randomizing over MNW allocations, we can achieve ex ante envy-freeness (each agent's expected value for their random allocation is at least as high as for any other agent's), ex ante Pareto optimality, ex ante group strategyproofness, and ex post EF1 simultaneously in polynomial time. In other words, randomization allows us to circumvent the mild unfairness that is inherent in deterministic allocations of indivisible goods without losing the other guarantees. In our view, these results are essentially the final word on how to divide indivisible goods under binary additive valuations.

1.2 Related Work

There is an extensive body of work on fair division, much too large to survey here. Instead, we focus on the most closely related work on fair division with *binary* valuations.

The most closely related work is that of Babaioff et al. [5], who, independently and in parallel to our work, also discovered some of the results that we present for the deterministic MNW rule. Specifically, their *prioritized egalitarian* mechanism is identical to our deterministic MNW^{tie} mechanism presented in Sect. 3. They show that this rule is strategyproof, EFX,[1] PO, Lorenz-dominating, and polynomial-time computable. This is very similar to our Theorem 1. The difference is that we strengthen strategyproofness to group strategyproofness, but only establish EF1 (weaker than EFX) and do not establish Lorenz-dominance. We note that the EFX property is also established by Amanatidis et al. [3]. We view these results as complementary to ours. Together, they establish that MNW^{tie} is group strategyproof, EFX, PO, Lorenz-dominating, and polynomial-time computable, making it even more compelling. We note that Babaioff et al. [5] do not study randomized allocation rules, which we focus on in Sect. 4.

Ortega [31] studies a slightly more general problem where there may be multiple copies of each good, but each agent can receive at most one copy of any good. His *egalitarian solution* is identical to our fractional MNW rule in terms of the probability of each good going to each agent, but he does not discuss how to implement these fractional allocations as a distribution over integral allocations with good properties. He shows that this rule is ex ante envy-free, ex ante PO, and ex ante group strategyproof. However, he uses a weaker notion of strategyproofness, where agents are only allowed to report a good that they like as one that they do not like, but not vice-versa. As we note in Sect. 4, in our (standard) setting with a single copy of each good, these guarantees (including the stronger strategyproofness notion, or even group strategyproofness) follow directly from prior work [25]. Hence, our main focus in Sect. 4 is to prove an *ex post* EF1 guarantee, which Ortega [31] does not provide.

Two central concepts in our work are maximum Nash welfare (MNW) and leximin allocations. Aziz and Rey [4] show that under binary additive valuations, all leximin allocations are also MNW allocations. As we observe in Sect. 3, this, together with known properties of the two solutions, immediately implies that the sets of MNW and leximin allocations are identical. Benabbou et al. [7] extend this equivalence to a more general valuation class.

On the computation front, our polynomial-time computability result for the deterministic MNW^{tie} rule builds upon on efficient algorithms by Darmann and Schauer [20] and Barman et al. [6] for finding an MNW allocation under binary additive valuations; specifically, our algorithm starts from an arbitrary MNW allocation computed by either of these algorithms, and then iteratively finds a *special* MNW allocation that MNW^{tie} outputs. Benabbou et al. [7] also show

---

[1] There are two popular definitions of EFX [3]; this result holds for the stronger one: an allocation is EFX if the envy that one agent has toward another can be eliminated by removing *any* good from the envied agent's bundle.

that an MNW allocation can be computed efficiently under their more general valuation class.

2 Preliminaries

For $k \in \mathbb{N}$, let $[k] = \{1, \ldots, k\}$. Let $\mathcal{N} = [n]$ denote a set of *agents*, and $\mathcal{M}$ denote a set of m indivisible *goods*. Each agent i has a *valuation* function $v_i : 2^{\mathcal{M}} \to \mathbb{R}_{\geqslant 0}$ such that $v_i(\emptyset) = 0$. It is assumed that valuations are additive: $\forall T \subseteq \mathcal{M}$, $v_i(T) = \sum_{g \in T} v_i(\{g\})$. To simplify notation, we write $v_i(g)$ instead of $v_i(\{g\})$.

We focus on a subclass of additive valuations known as binary additive valuations, under which $v_i(g) \in \{0, 1\}$ for all $i \in \mathcal{N}$ and $g \in \mathcal{M}$. We say that agent i *likes* good g if $v_i(g) = 1$. Sometimes it is easier to think of the valuation function of agent i as the set of goods that agent i likes, denoted $V_i = \{g \in \mathcal{M} : v_i(g) = 1\}$. Note that $v_i(T) = |V_i \cap T|$ for all $T \subseteq \mathcal{M}$. For a set of agents $S \subseteq \mathcal{N}$, let $V_S = \bigcup_{i \in S} V_i$ be the set of goods that at least one agent in S likes. The vector of agent valuations $\mathbf{v} = (v_1, \ldots, v_n)$ is called the *valuation profile*. A problem instance is given by the tuple $(\mathcal{N}, \mathcal{M}, \mathbf{v})$.

For a set of goods $T \subseteq \mathcal{M}$ and $k \in \mathbb{N}$, let $\Pi_k(T)$ denote the set of partitions of T into k bundles. We say that $\mathbf{A} = (A_1, \ldots, A_n)$ is an allocation if $\mathbf{A} \in \Pi_n(T)$ for some $T \subseteq \mathcal{M}$. Here, A_i is the bundle of goods allocated to agent i, and $v_i(A_i)$ is the *utility* to agent i. Let us denote $A_S = \bigcup_{i \in S} A_i$ for $S \subseteq \mathcal{N}$. Let $\mathbb{A} = \bigcup_{T \subseteq \mathcal{M}} \Pi_n(T)$ denote the set of all allocations.

We say that good g is *non-valued* if $v_i(g) = 0$ for all agents i; all the remaining goods are called *valued*. Let $\mathcal{Z}$ denote the set of non-valued goods. We say that an allocation $\mathbf{A}$ is *complete* if it allocates every valued good, i.e., if $A_{\mathcal{N}} \supseteq \mathcal{M} \setminus \mathcal{Z}$; we say that it is *minimally complete* if it is complete and does not allocate any non-valued goods, i.e., if $A_{\mathcal{N}} = \mathcal{M} \setminus \mathcal{Z}$.

We are interested in *fair* allocations. One of the most prominent notions of fairness is envy-freeness [21].

Definition 1 (Envy-freeness). *An allocation* $\mathbf{A}$ *is called* envy-free *(EF) if, for all agents* $i, j \in \mathcal{N}$, $v_i(A_i) \geqslant v_i(A_j)$.

Envy-freeness requires that no agent prefer another agent's bundle over her own. This cannot be guaranteed (imagine two agents liking a single good). Prior literature focuses on its relaxations, such as envy-freeness up to one good [14,27], which can be guaranteed.

Definition 2 (Envy-freeness up to one good). *An allocation* $\mathbf{A}$ *is called* envy-free up to one good *(EF1) if, for all agents* $i, j \in \mathcal{N}$ *such that* $A_j \neq \emptyset$, *there exists* $g \in A_j$ *such that* $v_i(A_i) \geqslant v_i(A_j \setminus \{g\})$.

EF1 requires that it should be possible to remove envy between any two agents by removing at most one good from the envied agent's bundle. We remark that there is a stronger fairness notion called envy-freeness up to the least positively valued good (EFX) [16], which coincides with EF1 under binary additive valuations.[2] Finally, another classic desideratum in resource allocation is Pareto optimality, which is a notion of economic efficiency.

Definition 3 (Pareto optimality). *An allocation* $\mathbf{A}$ *is called* Pareto optimal *(PO) if there does not exist an allocation* $\mathbf{A}'$ *such that for all agents* $i \in \mathcal{N}$, $v_i(A_i') \geqslant v_i(A_i)$, *and at least one inequality is strict.*

It is easy to see that with binary additive valuations, Pareto optimality is equivalent to ensuring that each valued good is allocated to one of the agents who likes it, i.e., that the utilitarian social welfare (sum of utilities) is maximized and is equal to the number of valued goods.

3   Deterministic Setting

In this section, our main goal is to establish the existence of a deterministic allocation rule that is fair, efficient, and truthful under binary additive valuations. Our rule builds upon the concept of maximum Nash welfare allocations [16], which we define below. All missing proofs can be found in the full version of this paper.

Definition 4 (Maximum Nash welfare allocation). *We say that* $\mathbf{A}$ *is a* maximum Nash welfare *(MNW) allocation if, among the set of allocations* $\mathbb{A}$, *it maximizes the number of agents receiving positive utility and, subject to that, maximizes the product of positive utilities. Formally, let* $W(\mathbf{A}) = \{i \in \mathcal{N} : v_i(A_i) > 0\}$ *and* $\mathbb{A}_M = argmax_{\mathbf{A} \in \mathbb{A}} |W(\mathbf{A})|$. *Then,* $argmax_{\mathbf{A} \in \mathbb{A}_M} \prod_{i \in W(\mathbf{A})} v_i(A_i)$ *is the set of MNW allocations.*

Even under general additive valuations, all maximum Nash welfare allocations satisfy EF1 and PO [16]. Our work uses a connection between MNW allocations and the classic concept of leximin allocations, that holds under binary additive valuations.

Definition 5 (Leximin comparison). *For an allocation* $\mathbf{A}$, *let its* utility vector *be* $(v_1(A_1), \ldots, v_n(A_n))$, *and its* utility profile *be the utility vector sorted in a non-descending order. Given two utility profiles* $\mathbf{s} = (s_1, \ldots, s_n)$ *and* $\mathbf{s}' = (s_1', \ldots, s_n')$, *we say that* $\mathbf{s}$ *leximin-dominates* $\mathbf{s}'$, *denoted* $\mathbf{s} \succ_{lex} \mathbf{s}'$, *if there exists* $k \in [n]$ *such that* $u_k > u_k'$ *and* $u_r = u_r'$ *for all* $r < k$. *We say that* $\mathbf{s}$ *weakly leximin-dominates* $\mathbf{s}'$, *denoted* $\mathbf{s} \succcurlyeq_{lex} \mathbf{s}'$, *if* $\mathbf{s} \succ_{lex} \mathbf{s}'$ *or* $\mathbf{s} = \mathbf{s}'$. *Note that this is a total order among utility profiles. We extend these comparisons to utility vectors by applying them to the utility profiles they induce, and call two utility vectors* leximin-equivalent *if they induce the same utility profile.*

---

[2] There are two popular definitions of EFX [3]. The original definition by Caragiannis et al. [16] asks that agent i not envy agent j after removal of any good from agent j's bundle that has *positive* value for agent i, whereas a latter definition omits the requirement of "positive value". Under binary additive valuations, the former definition is equivalent to EF1 whereas the latter definition is stronger than EF1.

Definition 6 (Leximin allocations). *We say that an allocation* **A** *is a leximin allocation if, among all allocations, it lexicographically maximizes the utility profile, i.e., maximizes the minimum utility, subject to that maximizes the second minimum, and so on. Thus, leximin allocations are those whose utility profile is the greatest element of the total order* $\succ_{\text{lex}}$*. We also extend the notions of leximin-dominance and weak leximin-dominance to allocations by comparing their utility vectors.*

Leximin is a refinement of the traditional Rawlsian fairness, which requires maximization of the minimum utility. Plaut and Roughgarden [32] and Freeman et al. [23] study leximin allocations (and variants of this definition), and show that they have related fairness properties as well.

Important to our work is the observation that for binary additive valuations, the sets of leximin and MNW allocations coincide. This is established under a more general valuation class by the contemporary work of Benabbou et al. [7], but for binary additive valuations, this can also be inferred easily from the following observations, which we will use in our work.

Lemma 1. *All leximin allocations have the same utility profile. Further, any allocation with this utility profile is a leximin allocation.*

Lemma 2 (Lemma 21 of Freeman et al. [23]). *Under binary additive valuations, all maximum Nash welfare allocations have the same utility profile. Further, any allocation with this utility profile is a maximum Nash welfare allocation.*

Under binary additive valuations, given the observations above, the sets of MNW and leximin allocations can be either identical or disjoint. Aziz and Rey [4] shows that all leximin allocations are also MNW allocations, which implies that the two sets are identical.

Lemma 3. *Under binary additive valuations, the set of maximum Nash welfare allocations coincides with the set of leximin allocations.*

Henceforth, we will use the terms "MNW allocation" and "leximin allocation" interchangeably. Before we define our deterministic rule, let us define this concept formally. Fix the set of agents $\mathcal{N}$ and the set of goods $\mathcal{M}$. A *deterministic rule* f takes a valuation profile **v** as input and returns an allocation **A**. Note that f is not allowed to return ties. We say that f is EF1 (resp. PO) if it always outputs an allocation that is EF1 (resp. PO). The game-theoretic literature offers the following strong desideratum to prevent strategic manipulations by agents.

Definition 7 (Group strategyproofness). *A deterministic rule* f *is called group strategyproof (GSP) if there do not exist valuation profiles* **v** *and* **v**′*, and a group of agents* $C \subseteq \mathcal{N}$*, such that* $v'_k = v_k$ *for all* $k \in \mathcal{N} \setminus C$ *and* $v_j(A'_j) > v_j(A_j)$ *for all* $j \in C$*, where* $\mathbf{A} = f(\mathbf{v})$ *and* $\mathbf{A}' = f(\mathbf{v}')$*.*

A weaker requirement, which only imposes the above property for group C of size 1 (i.e. prevents manipulations by a single agent) is commonly known as strategyproofness (SP). We are now ready to define our rule, which chooses a special MNW allocation.

Definition 8 (MNW$^{\mathbf{tie}}$). *The deterministic rule* MNW^{tie} *returns an allocation* **A** *such that:*

1. **A** *is an MNW allocation with lexicographically greatest utility vector among all MNW allocations (i.e., among all MNW allocations, it maximizes $v_1(A_1)$, subject to that maximizes $v_2(A_2)$, and so on);[3] and*
2. **A** *is minimally complete (i.e. $A_\mathcal{N} = \mathcal{M} \setminus \mathcal{Z}$).*

If there are several allocations satisfying both conditions, MNW^{tie} *arbitrarily picks one.*

First, observe that MNW$^{\mathbf{tie}}$ is well-defined, i.e., that the set of allocations satisfying both conditions is non-empty. Indeed, the set of allocations satisfying the first condition is trivially non-empty. And for any allocation in this set, there is a corresponding minimally complete allocation—obtained by throwing away all non-valued goods—which has the same utility vector, and therefore still satisfies the first condition.

The following result establishes the compelling properties of MNW$^{\mathbf{tie}}$. The key idea for polynomial-time computability is as follows. Darmann and Schauer [20] and Barman et al. [6] show that under binary additive valuations, *an* MNW allocation can be computed efficiently. Starting from this MNW allocation, we keep moving to lexicographically better MNW allocations, as in the definition of MNW$^{\mathbf{tie}}$. The algorithm and proof are formally presented in the full version of this paper.

Theorem 1. *Under binary additive valuations,* MNW^{tie} *is envy-free up to one good, Pareto optimal, group strategyproof, and polynomial-time computable.*

4   Randomized Setting

In the previous section, we established the existence of a deterministic rule which is EF1, PO, and GSP. For deterministic rules, it is necessary to relax EF to EF1. For example, in case of a single good that is liked by two agents, giving it to either agent would be EF1 but not EF. However, if one is willing to randomize, the natural solution of assigning the good to an agent chosen at random would be "ex ante EF" in addition to being "ex post EF1". This is because each deterministic allocation in the support is EF1, but in expectation, no agent envies the other. This leads to a natural question. *Can randomness help achieve ex ante EF and ex post EF1, in addition to PO and GSP?*

In this section, we answer this question affirmatively for binary additive valuations. In parallel to our work, Freeman et al. [22] show that ex ante EF and ex post EF1 can be achieved simultaneously even under general additive valuations, but they show an impossibility when ex ante PO is added to the combination.

---

[3] We note that tie-breaking by agent index is without loss of generality. One can break ties according to any given ordering of the agents, and the corresponding rule will still satisfy all the desiderata.

Our positive result circumvents this impossibility for binary additive valuations. Additionally, it satisfies GSP, which Freeman et al. [22] do not consider. Missing proofs can be found in the full version of this paper.

Let us first formally extend our framework to include randomness.

Definition 9 (Fractional and randomized allocations). *A fractional allocation* $\mathbf{A} = (A_1, \ldots, A_n)$ *is such that* $A_i(g) \in [0,1]$ *denotes the fraction of good* g *allocated to agent* i *and* $\sum_{i \in \mathcal{N}} A_i(g) \le 1$ *for each good* g. *A randomized allocation* $\overline{\mathbf{A}}$ *is a probability distribution over deterministic allocations.*

There is a natural fractional allocation $\mathbf{A}$ associated with each randomized allocation $\overline{\mathbf{A}}$, where $A_i(g)$ is the probability of good g being allocated to agent i under $\overline{\mathbf{A}}$. In this case, we say that randomized allocation $\overline{\mathbf{A}}$ *implements* fractional allocation $\mathbf{A}$. There may be several randomized allocations implementing a given fractional allocation.

We refer to the expected utility of agent i under a randomized allocation $\overline{\mathbf{A}}$ as simply the utility of agent i under $\overline{\mathbf{A}}$. Note that this is equal to the utility of agent i from the corresponding fractional allocation $\mathbf{A}$, defined as $v_i(A_i) = \sum_{g \in \mathcal{M}} A_i(g) \cdot v_i(g)$. With this notation, the definitions of envy-freeness and Pareto optimality extend naturally to fractional allocations.[4] We say that a randomized allocation $\overline{\mathbf{A}}$ is ex ante envy-free (resp. ex ante Pareto optimal) if the corresponding fractional allocation $\mathbf{A}$ is envy-free (resp. Pareto optimal).

With a fixed set of agents $\mathcal{N}$ and a fixed set of goods $\mathcal{M}$, a *randomized rule* f takes a valuation profile $\mathbf{v}$ as input and returns a randomized allocation $\overline{\mathbf{A}}$. We say that f is *ex ante envy-free* (resp. *ex ante Pareto optimal*) if it always returns a randomized allocation that is ex ante envy free (resp. ex ante Pareto optimal). We say that f is *ex ante group strategyproof* if no group of agents can misreport their preferences so that each agent in the group receives strictly greater expected utility. Note that these ex ante guarantees depend only on the fractional allocation corresponding to the randomized allocation returned by f. Hence, when talking about ex ante guarantees, we will think of the randomized rule f as directly returning a fractional allocation. However, when talking about ex post guarantees, we would need to specify which randomized allocation f returns.

Definition 10 (Ex post EF1). *We say that a randomized allocation* $\overline{\mathbf{A}}$ *is ex post envy-free up to one good if each deterministic allocation in its support is EF1. A randomized rule is ex post EF1 if it always returns a randomized allocation that is ex post EF1.*

Fractional leximin allocations, like their deterministic counterpart, lexicographically maximize the utility profile among all fractional allocations. The same can be said about fractional MNW allocations; however, we can skip the first step of maximizing the number of agents who receive positive utility because

---

[4] In case of Pareto optimality of a fractional allocation, we require that no other *fractional* allocation Pareto-dominate it.

in the fractional case we can simultaneously give positive utility to every agent who likes at least one good (and thus can possibly get positive utility).

Definition 11 (Fractional MNW allocations). *We say that a fractional allocation is a fractional maximum Nash welfare allocation if it maximizes the product of utilities of agents who do not have zero value for every good.*

Bogomolnaia and Moulin [9], Bogomolnaia et al. [10], and Kurokawa et al. [25] study fractional leximin allocations under an assignment setting, and establish several desirable properties. In addition, fractional MNW allocations, also known as competitive equilibria with equal incomes (CEEI), are widely studied in fair division with additive valuations [18,19,30,33]. Our first result shows that under binary additive valuations, these two concepts coincide.

Theorem 2. *Under binary additive valuations, the set of fractional leximin allocations coincides with the set of fractional maximum Nash welfare allocations. All such allocations have identical utility vectors.*

Note that the identical utility vector guarantee in Theorem 2 is much stronger than the identical utility profile guarantee in the deterministic case.

Even under general additive valuations, it is known that every fractional MNW allocation is ex ante EF and ex ante PO [33], and one such allocation can be computed in strongly polynomial time [30,34]. Hence, these properties carry over to our binary additive valuations domain, and due to Theorem 2, also apply to fractional leximin allocations.

For ex ante GSP, we build on the literature on fractional leximin allocations. Kurokawa et al. [25] show that returning a fractional leximin allocation satisfies ex ante EF, ex ante PO, and ex ante GSP whenever four key requirements are satisfied. We describe them in the full version, and show that they are easily satisfied under binary additive valuations, if we return a minimally complete leximin allocation. Hence, we define our fractional leximin/MNW rule to always return a minimally complete fractional leximin/MNW allocation (like our deterministic rule MNW^{tie}).

Definition 12 (Fractional maximum Nash welfare rule). *The fractional maximum Nash welfare rule returns a minimally complete fractional maximum Nash welfare allocation.*

Theorem 3. *Under binary additive valuations, every fractional maximum Nash welfare (equivalently, leximin) allocation is ex ante envy-free and ex ante Pareto optimal. Further, the fractional maximum Nash welfare rule is ex ante group strategyproof.*

The only missing property at this point is ex post EF1. Therefore, the main question we seek to answer in this section is the following: *Can every fractional MNW allocation be implemented as a distribution over deterministic EF1 allocations?* We go one step further and show that it can in fact be implemented as a distribution over deterministic MNW allocations, which are in turn EF1.

Our main tool is the bihierarchy framework introduced by Budish et al. [15], which is a generalization of the classic Birkhoff-von Neumann theorem [8,29]. At a high level, the framework allows implementing any fractional allocation $\mathbf{A}$ using deterministic allocations which satisfy a set of constraints, as long as the set of constraints forms a bihierarchy structure and the fractional allocation itself satisfies those constraints.

In our case, we start with a minimally complete fractional MNW allocation $\mathbf{A}^*$. Let u_i^* denote the utility to agent i under this allocation. We want to implement this as a randomized allocation. We impose the following constraints on a deterministic allocation $\mathbf{A}$ in the support, where $\mathbf{A}$ is represented as a matrix in which $A_i(g) \in \{0,1\}$ indicates whether good g is allocated to agent i.

$$\begin{aligned} \mathcal{H}_1 &: \textstyle\sum_{i \in \mathcal{N}} A_i(g) = \sum_{i \in \mathcal{N}} A_i^*(g), \forall g \in \mathcal{M}, \\ \mathcal{H}_2 &: \lfloor u_i^* \rfloor \leq \textstyle\sum_{g \in \mathcal{M}} A_i(g) \cdot v_i(g) \leq \lceil u_i^* \rceil, \forall i \in \mathcal{N}. \end{aligned} \tag{1}$$

The first family of constraints ensures that under each deterministic allocation $\mathbf{A}$, the set of goods allocated matches that under $\mathbf{A}^*$. Since $\mathbf{A}^*$ is minimally complete, this implies that $\mathbf{A}$ must be minimally complete as well. Crucially, the second family of constraints ensures that each agent has utility that is either the floor or the ceiling of her utility under $\mathbf{A}^*$. That is, $\mathbf{A}$ is not allowed to stray far from $\mathbf{A}^*$.

It can be checked that these constraints form a bihierarchy (each of $\mathcal{H}_1$ and $\mathcal{H}_2$ is a hierarchy); for a formal definition of a hierarchy, we refer the reader to the work of Budish et al. [15]. Importantly, they also provide a polynomial-time algorithm that computes a random allocation such that (a) it implements the fractional allocation $\mathbf{A}^*$, and (b) each deterministic allocation $\mathbf{A}$ in its support satisfies the constraints in 1. We show that in this case, every deterministic allocation in the support must be a deterministic MNW allocation, yielding the desired result.

Theorem 4. *Under binary additive valuations, given any fractional maximum Nash welfare allocation, one can compute, in polynomial time, a randomized allocation which implements it and has only deterministic maximum Nash welfare allocations in its support.*

Proof. Let $\mathbf{A}^*$ be a given fractional MNW allocation with utility vector $\mathbf{u}^*$. Let $\bar{\mathbf{A}}$ be the randomized allocation implementing $\mathbf{A}^*$ that is returned by the polynomial-time algorithm of Budish et al. [15] with the bihierarchy constraints in Eq. 1. Let $\mathcal{A}$ denote the set of deterministic allocations in the support of $\bar{\mathbf{A}}$. Our goal is to show that every allocation in $\mathcal{A}$ is an MNW allocation.

First, let us partition the set of agents $\mathcal{N}$ into sets $S_1, \dots, S_t$ such that any two agents i and j are in the same set if and only if $\lfloor u_i^* \rfloor = \lfloor u_j^* \rfloor$. For $k \in [t]$, let L_k denote the common floor of utilities of agents in S_k under $\mathbf{A}^*$, and $U_k = L_k + 1$. Hence, for $k \in [t]$ and each agent $i \in S_k$, $u_i^* \in [L_k, U_k)$. Further, order the sets so that $U_k \leq L_{k+1}$ for each $k \in [t-1]$. This ensures that if $i \in S_r$, $j \in S_{r'}$, and $r' > r$, then $u_j^* > u_i^*$.

We argue that for each $k \in [t]$, the agents in $\cup_{r \in [k]} S_r$ must be fully allocated all of the goods that they like (i.e. all the goods in $V_{\cup_{r \in [k]} S_r}$) under $\mathbf{A}^*$, resulting in $\sum_{r \in [k]} \sum_{i \in S_r} u_i^* = |V_{\cup_{r \in [k]} S_r}|$. If this is not true, then a positive fraction of some good $g \in V_{\cup_{r \in [k]} S_r}$ must be allocated to an agent $j \in S_{r'}$ for $r' > k$. Let $i \in \cup_{r \in [k]} S_r$ be an agent such that $g \in V_i$. Let $r \in [k]$ be such that $i \in S_r$. Then, by the above argument, we know that $u_j^* > u_i^*$. However, then, transferring a sufficiently small fraction of g from agent j to agent i in $\mathbf{A}^*$ will improve the Nash welfare, which contradicts the fact that $\mathbf{A}^*$ is a fractional MNW allocation.

Note that in any deterministic allocation $\mathbf{A}$, $|V_{\cup_{r \in [k]} S_r}|$ is the highest utility that agents in $\cup_{r \in [k]} S_r$ can collectively have; hence, in any feasible utility vector $\mathbf{u}$,

$$\sum_{r \in [k]} \sum_{i \in S_r} u_i \leq \sum_{r \in [k]} \sum_{i \in S_r} u_i^*, \forall k \in [t]. \tag{2}$$

Because a convex combination of allocations in $\mathcal{A}$ yields the allocation $\mathbf{A}^*$, and utilities are additive, a convex combination of their utility vectors yields the utility vector $\mathbf{u}^*$. Hence, for the utility vector $\mathbf{u}$ of any allocation in $\mathcal{A}$, Eq. 2 must hold with equality. Further, by subtracting each equation from the next, we get that it must further satisfy the following. Here, $\mathcal{H}_2$ is from the bihierarchy constraints (Eq. 1).

$$\begin{aligned} \mathcal{H}_2 &: \lfloor u_i^* \rfloor \leq u_i \leq \lceil u_i^* \rceil, \forall i \in \mathcal{N}, \\ \mathcal{H}_3 &: \sum_{i \in S_k} u_i = \sum_{i \in S_k} u_i^*, \forall k \in [t]. \end{aligned} \tag{3}$$

We say that a utility vector is a *rounded* if it satisfies the constraints in Eq. (3), and say that a deterministic allocation is *rounded* if it has a rounded utility vector. We have already established that every allocation in $\mathcal{A}$ is a rounded allocation. The following lemma completes the proof of Theorem 4.

Lemma 4. *The set of rounded allocations coincides with the set of maximum Nash welfare allocations.*

Let us amend the definition of the fractional MNW rule so that it uses Theorem 4 to implement a minimally complete fractional MNW allocation. Then, we have the following.

Corollary 1. *Under binary additive valuations, the fractional maximum Nash welfare rule is ex ante envy-free, ex ante Pareto optimal, ex ante group strategyproof, ex post envy-free up to one good, and polynomial-time computable.*

5   Discussion

To recap, we showed that under binary additive valuations a deterministic variant of the maximum Nash welfare rule is envy-free up to one good (EF1), Pareto optimal (PO), and group strategyproof (GSP). We also demonstrated that its randomized variant is ex ante EF, ex ante PO, ex ante GSP, and ex post EF1. All our rules are polynomial-time computable.

Amanatidis et al. [2] show that under general additive valuations, there is no deterministic rule that is envy-free up to one good (EF1) and strategyproof, even with two agents and $m \geq 5$ goods. At first glance, Theorem 1, which establishes MNW^{tie} as both GSP and EF1, seems to show that this impossibility result does not hold for the special case of binary additive valuations. However, the impossibility result of Amanatidis et al. [2] only applies to rules that allocate all the goods; by contrast, MNW^{tie} does not allocate non-valued goods. This begs the following question: *Under binary additive valuations, is there a deterministic rule that allocates all the goods and achieves EF1, PO, and GSP?* In the full version, we show that this cannot be achieved by any variant of MNW.

Another open question is whether the ex ante GSP guarantee of Corollary 1 can be strengthened to ex post GSP, which would require the randomized rule to be implementable as a probability distribution over deterministic GSP rules.

Modulo these minor caveats, though, our results are the strongest one could possibly hope for in the domain of binary additive valuations.

References

1. Aleksandrov, M., Aziz, H., Gaspers, S., Walsh, T.: Online fair division: analysing a food bank problem. In: Proceedings of the 24th International Joint Conference on Artificial Intelligence (IJCAI), pp. 2540–2546 (2015)
2. Amanatidis, G., Birmpas, G., Christodoulou, G., Markakis, E.: Truthful allocation mechanisms without payments: characterization and implications on fairness. In: Proceedings of the 18th ACM Conference on Economics and Computation (EC), pp. 545–562 (2017)
3. Amanatidis, G., Birmpas, G., Filos-Ratsikas, A., Hollender, A., Voudouris, A.A.: Maximum Nash welfare and other stories about EFX. In: Proceedings of the 29th International Joint Conference on Artificial Intelligence (IJCAI) (2020, forthcoming)
4. Aziz, H., Rey, S.: Almost group envy-free allocation of indivisible goods and chores. In: Proceedings of the 29th International Joint Conference on Artificial Intelligence (IJCAI) (2020)
5. Babaioff, M., Ezra, T., Feige, U.: Fair and truthful mechanisms for dichotomous valuations. arXiv preprint arXiv:2002.10704 (2020)
6. Barman, S., Krishnamurthy, S.K., Vaish, R.: Greedy algorithms for maximizing Nash social welfare. In: Proceedings of the 17th International Conference on Autonomous Agents and Multi-Agent Systems (AAMAS), pp. 7–13 (2018)
7. Benabbou, N., Chakraborty, M., Igarashi, A., Zick, Y.: Finding fair and efficient allocations when valuations don't add up. arXiv preprint arXiv:2003.07060 (2020)
8. Birkhoff, G.: Three observations on linear algebra. Universidad Nacional de Tucumán, Revista A **5**, 147–151 (1946)
9. Bogomolnaia, A., Moulin, H.: Random matching under dichotomous preferences. Econometrica **72**, 257–279 (2004)
10. Bogomolnaia, A., Moulin, H., Stong, R.: Collective choice under dichotomous preferences. J. Econ. Theory **122**(2), 165–184 (2005)
11. Bouveret, S., Lemaître, M.: Characterizing conflicts in fair division of indivisible goods using a scale of criteria. Auton. Agents Multi-Agent Syst. **30**(2), 259–290 (2016)

12. Brams, S.J., Fishburn, P.C.: Approval Voting, 2nd edn. Springer, New York (2007). https://doi.org/10.1007/978-0-387-49896-6
13. Brams, S.J., Taylor, A.D.: Fair Division: From Cake-Cutting to Dispute Resolution. Cambridge University Press, Cambridge (1996)
14. Budish, E.: The combinatorial assignment problem: approximate competitive equilibrium from equal incomes. J. Polit. Econ. **119**(6), 1061–1103 (2011)
15. Budish, E., Che, Y.K., Kojima, F., Milgrom, P.: Designing random allocation mechanisms: theory and applications. Am. Econ. Rev. **103**(2), 585–623 (2013)
16. Caragiannis, I., Kurokawa, D., Moulin, H., Procaccia, A.D., Shah, N., Wang, J.: The unreasonable fairness of maximum Nash welfare. ACM Trans. Econ. Comput. **7**(3), article 12 (2019)
17. Cheng, Y., Jiang, Z., Munagala, K., Wang, K.: Group fairness in committee selection. In: Proceedings of the 20th ACM Conference on Economics and Computation (EC), pp. 263–279 (2019)
18. Cole, R., Gkatzelis, V.: Approximating the Nash social welfare with indivisible items. SIAM J. Comput. **47**(3), 1211–1236 (2018)
19. Cole, R., Gkatzelis, V., Goel, G.: Mechanism design for fair division: allocating divisible items without payments. In: Proceedings of the 14th ACM Conference on Economics and Computation (EC), pp. 251–268 (2013)
20. Darmann, A., Schauer, J.: Maximizing Nash product social welfare in allocating indivisible goods. Eur. J. Oper. Res. **247**(2), 548–559 (2015)
21. Foley, D.K.: Resource allocation and the public sector. Yale Economics Essays, vol. 7, pp. 45–98 (1967)
22. Freeman, R., Shah, N., Vaish, R.: Best of both worlds: ex-ante and ex-post fairness in resource allocation. In: Proceedings of the 21st ACM Conference on Economics and Computation (EC) (2020, forthcoming)
23. Freeman, R., Sikdar, S., Vaish, R., Xia, L.: Equitable allocations of indivisible goods. In: Proceedings of the 28th International Joint Conference on Artificial Intelligence (IJCAI), pp. 280–286 (2019)
24. Klaus, B., Miyagawa, E.: Strategy-proofness, solidarity, and consistency for multiple assignment problems. Int. J. Game Theory **30**, 421–435 (2001)
25. Kurokawa, D., Procaccia, A.D., Shah, N.: Leximin allocations in the real world. ACM Trans. Econ. Comput. **6**(3–4), article 11 (2018)
26. Lackner, M., Skowron, P.: A quantitative analysis of multi-winner rules. In: Proceedings of the 28th International Joint Conference on Artificial Intelligence (IJCAI), pp. 407–413 (2019)
27. Lipton, R.J., Markakis, E., Mossel, E., Saberi, A.: On approximately fair allocations of indivisible goods. In: Proceedings of the 6th ACM Conference on Economics and Computation (EC), pp. 125–131 (2004)
28. Moulin, H.: Fair Division and Collective Welfare. MIT Press, Cambridge (2003)
29. von Neumann, J.: A certain zero-sum two-person game equivalent to the optimal assignment problem. In: Kuhn, W., Tucker, A.W. (eds.) Contributions to the Theory of Games, vol. 2, pp. 5–12. Princeton University Press (1953)
30. Orlin, J.B.: Improved algorithms for computing fisher's market clearing prices: computing fisher's market clearing prices. In: Proceedings of the 42nd Annual ACM Symposium on Theory of Computing (STOC), pp. 291–300 (2010)
31. Ortega, J.: Multi-unit assignment under dichotomous preferences. Math. Soc. Sci. **103**, 15–24 (2020)

32. Plaut, B., Roughgarden, T.: Almost envy-freeness with general valuations. In: Proceedings of the 29th Annual ACM-SIAM Symposium on Discrete Algorithms (SODA), pp. 2584–2603 (2018)

33. Varian, H.: Equity, envy and efficiency. J. Econ. Theory **9**, 63–91 (1974)

34. Végh, L.A.: Concave generalized flows with applications to market equilibria. Math. Oper. Res. **39**(2), 573–596 (2013)

Consensus Halving for Sets of Items

Paul W. Goldberg[1], Alexandros Hollender[1], Ayumi Igarashi[2],
Pasin Manurangsi[3], and Warut Suksompong[4(✉)]

[1] University of Oxford, Oxford, UK
{paul.goldberg,alexandros.hollender}@cs.ox.ac.uk
[2] National Institute of Informatics, Tokyo, Japan
ayumi_igarashi@nii.ac.jp
[3] Google Research, Mountain View, USA
pasin@google.com
[4] National University of Singapore, Singapore, Singapore
warut@comp.nus.edu.sg

Abstract. Consensus halving refers to the problem of dividing a
resource into two parts so that every agent values both parts equally.
Prior work has shown that when the resource is represented by an interval, a consensus halving with at most n cuts always exists, but is hard to
compute even for agents with simple valuation functions. In this paper,
we study consensus halving in a natural setting where the resource consists of a set of items without a linear ordering. When agents have additive utilities, we present a polynomial-time algorithm that computes a
consensus halving with at most n cuts, and show that n cuts are almost
surely necessary when the agents' utilities are drawn from probabilistic distributions. On the other hand, we show that for a simple class of
monotonic utilities, the problem already becomes PPAD-hard. Furthermore, we compare and contrast consensus halving with the more general
problem of consensus k-splitting, where we wish to divide the resource
into k parts in possibly unequal ratios, and provide some consequences
of our results on the problem of computing small agreeable sets.

Keywords: Consensus halving · PPAD-hardness · Resource allocation

1 Introduction

Given a set of resources, how can we divide it between two families in such a way
that every member of both families believes that the two resulting parts have the
same value? This is an important problem in resource allocation and has been
addressed several times under different names [1,15,20], with *consensus halving*
being the name by which it is best known today [26].

In prior studies of consensus halving, the resource is represented by an interval, and the goal is to find an equal division into two parts that makes a small
number of cuts in the interval.[1] Using the Borsuk-Ulam theorem from topology,

---

[1] Simmons and Su [26] assume that the resource is a two- or three-dimensional object
but only consider cuts by parallel planes; their model is therefore equivalent to that
of a one-dimensional object.

© Springer Nature Switzerland AG 2020
X. Chen et al. (Eds.): WINE 2020, LNCS 12495, pp. 384–397, 2020.
https://doi.org/10.1007/978-3-030-64946-3_27

Simmons and Su [26] established that for any continuous preferences of the n agents involved, there is always a consensus halving that uses no more than n cuts—this also matches the smallest number of cuts in the worst case. In addition, the same authors developed an algorithm that computes an ε-approximate solution for any given $\varepsilon > 0$, meaning that the values of the two parts differ by at most ε for every agent. Although the algorithm is more efficient than a brute-force approach, its running time is exponential in the parameters of the problem. This is in fact not a coincidence: Filos-Ratsikas and Goldberg [9] recently showed that ε-approximate consensus halving is PPA-complete, implying that the problem is unlikely to admit a polynomial-time algorithm. Filos-Ratsikas et al. [11] strengthened this result by proving that the problem remains hard even when the agents have simple valuations over the interval. In particular, the PPA-completeness result holds for agents with "two-block uniform" valuations, i.e., valuation functions that are piecewise uniform over the interval and assign non-zero value to at most two separate pieces.

While these hardness results stand in contrast to the positive existence result, they rely crucially on the resource being in the form of an interval. Most practical division problems do not fall under this assumption, including when we divide assets such as houses, cars, stocks, business ownership, or facility usage. When each item is homogeneous, a consensus halving can be easily obtained by splitting every item in half. However, since splitting individual assets typically involves an overhead, for example in managing a joint business or sharing the use of a house, we want to achieve a consensus halving while splitting only a small number of assets. Fortunately, a consensus halving that splits at most n items is guaranteed to exist regardless of the number of items—this can be seen by arranging the items on a line in arbitrary order and applying the aforementioned existence theorem of Simmons and Su [26]. The bound n is also tight: if each agent only values a single item and the n valued items are distinct, all of them clearly need to be split. Nevertheless, given that the items do not inherently lie on a line, the hardness results from previous work do not carry over. Could it be that computing a consensus halving efficiently is possible when the resource consists of a set of items?

1.1 Overview of Results

We assume throughout the paper that the resource is composed of m items. Each item is homogeneous, so the utility of an agent for a (possibly fractional) set of items depends only on the fractions of the m items in that set. For this overview we focus on the more interesting case where $n \leq m$, but all of our results can be extended to arbitrary n and m.

We begin in Sect. 2 by considering agents with *additive* utilities, i.e., the utility of each agent is additive across items and linear in the fraction of each item. Under this assumption, we present a polynomial-time algorithm that computes a consensus halving with at most n cuts by finding a vertex of the polytope defined by the relevant constraints. This positive result stands in stark contrast with the PPA-hardness when the items lie on a line, which we obtain by discretizing an analogous hardness result of Filos-Ratsikas et al. [11]. We then show that improving the number of cuts beyond n is difficult: even computing a consensus halving that uses at most $n - 1$ cuts more than the minimum possible for a given instance is NP-hard. Nevertheless, we establish that instances admitting a solution with fewer than n cuts are rare. In particular, if the agents' utilities for items are drawn independently from non-atomic distributions, it is almost surely the case that every consensus halving requires no fewer than n cuts.

Next, in Sect. 3, we address the broader class of *monotonic* utilities, wherein an agent's utility for a set does not decrease when any fraction of an item is added to the set. For such utilities, we show that the problem of computing a consensus halving with at most n cuts becomes PPAD-hard, thereby providing strong evidence of its computational hardness.[2] Perhaps surprisingly, this hardness result holds even for the class of utility functions that we call "symmetric-threshold utilities", which are very close to being additive. Indeed, such utility functions are additive across items; for each item, having a sufficiently small fraction of the item is the same as not having the item at all, having a sufficiently large fraction of it is the same as having the whole item, and the utility increases linearly in between. On the other hand, we present a number of positive results for monotonic utilities when the number of agents is constant in the full version of our paper [13].

In Sect. 4, we provide some implications of our results on the "agreeable sets" problem studied by Manurangsi and Suksompong [18]. A set is said to be *agreeable* to an agent if the agent likes it at least as much as the complement set. Manurangsi and Suksompong proved that a set of size at most $\lfloor \frac{m+n}{2} \rfloor$ that is agreeable to all agents always exists, and this bound is tight. They then gave polynomial-time algorithms that compute an agreeable set matching the tight bound for two and three agents. We significantly generalize this result by exhibiting efficient algorithms for any number of agents with additive utilities, as well as any *constant* number of agents with monotonic utilities. In addition, we present a short alternative proof for the bound $\lfloor \frac{m+n}{2} \rfloor$ via consensus halving.

Finally, in Sect. 5, we study the more general problem of *consensus k-splitting* for agents with additive utilities. Our aim in this problem is to split the items into k parts so that all agents agree that the parts are split according to some given ratios $\alpha_1, \ldots, \alpha_k$; consensus halving corresponds to the special case where $k = 2$ and $\alpha_1 = \alpha_2 = 1/2$. Unlike for consensus halving, however, in consensus k-splitting we may want to cut the same item more than once when $k > 2$, so we cannot assume without loss of generality that the number of cuts is equal to the number of items cut. For any k and any ratios $\alpha_1, \ldots, \alpha_k$, we show that there exists an instance in which cutting $(k-1)n$ items is necessary. On the other hand, a generalization of our consensus halving algorithm from Sect. 2 computes a consensus k-splitting with at most $(k-1)n$ cuts in polynomial time, thereby implying that the bound $(k-1)n$ is tight for both benchmarks. We also illustrate

---

[2] We refer to [22, Chapter 20] for a discussion of the complexity class PPAD.

further differences between consensus k-splitting and consensus halving, both with respect to item ordering and from the probabilistic perspective.

1.2 Related Work

Consensus halving falls under the broad area of *fair division*, which studies how to allocate resources among interested agents in a fair manner [4,5,19]. Common fairness notions include *envy-freeness*—no agent envies another agent in view of the bundles they receive—and *equitability*—all agents have the same utility for their own bundle. The fair division literature typically assumes that each recipient of a bundle is either a single agent or a group of agents represented by a single preference. However, a number of recent papers have considered an extension of the traditional setting to groups, thereby allowing us to capture the differing preferences within the same group as in our introductory example with families [16,17,25]. Note that a consensus halving is envy-free for all members of the two groups; moreover, it is equitable provided that the utilities of the agents are additive and normalized so that every agent has the same value for the entire set of items.

A classical fair division algorithm that dates back over two decades is the *adjusted winner procedure*, which computes an envy-free and equitable division between two agents [4].[3] The procedure has been suggested for resolving divorce settlements and international border disputes, with one of its advantages being the fact that it always splits at most one item. Sandomirskiy and Segal-Halevi [24] investigated the problem of attaining fairness while minimizing the number of shared items, and gave algorithms and hardness results for several variants of the problem. Like in our work, both the adjusted winner procedure and the work of Sandomirskiy and Segal-Halevi [24] assume that items are homogeneous and, as in Sect. 2, that the agents' utilities are linear in the fraction of each item and additive across items. Moreover, both of them require the assumption that all items can be shared—if some items are indivisible, then an envy-free or equitable allocation cannot necessarily be obtained.[4]

Besides consensus halving, another problem that also involves dividing items into equal parts is *necklace splitting*, which can be seen as a discrete analog of consensus halving [1,12]. In a basic version of necklace splitting, there is a necklace with beads of n colors, with each color having an even number of beads. Our task is to split the necklace using at most n cuts and arrange the resulting pieces into two parts so that the beads of each color are evenly distributed between both parts. Observe that the difficulty of this problem lies in the spatial

---

[3] See http://www.nyu.edu/projects/adjustedwinner for a demonstration and implementation of the procedure.

[4] This motivates relaxations such as *envy-freeness up to one item (EF1)* and *envy-freeness up to any item (EFX)*, which have been extensively studied in the last few years (e.g., [6,21]). However, as Sandomirskiy and Segal-Halevi [24] noted, when a divorcing couple decides how to split their children or two siblings try to divide three houses between them, it is unlikely that anyone will agree to a bundle that is envy-free up to one child or house.

ordering of the beads—the problem would be trivial if the beads were unordered items as in our setting. While consensus halving and necklace splitting have long been studied by mathematicians, they recently gained significant interest among computer scientists thanks in large part to new computational complexity results [9–11]. In particular, the PPA-completeness result of Filos-Ratsikas and Goldberg [9] for approximate consensus halving was the first such result for a problem that is "natural" in the sense that its description does not involve a polynomial-sized circuit.

2   Additive Utilities

We first formally define the problem of consensus halving for a set of items. There is a set $N = [n]$ of n agents and a set $M = [m]$ of m items, where $[r] := \{1, 2, \ldots, r\}$ for any positive integer r. A *fractional set of items* contains a fraction $x_j \in [0, 1]$ of each item j. We will mostly be interested in fractional sets of items in which only a small number of items are fractional—that is, most items have $x_j = 0$ or 1. Agent i has a utility function u_i that describes her nonnegative utility for any fractional set of items; for an item $j \in M$, we sometimes write $u_i(j)$ to denote $u_i(\{j\})$. A *partition of M into fractional sets of items* $M_1, \ldots, M_k$ has the property that for every item $j \in M$, the fractions of item j in the k fractional sets sum up to exactly 1.

Definition 1. *A consensus halving is a partition of M into two fractional sets of items M_1 and M_2 such that $u_i(M_1) = u_i(M_2)$ for all $i \in N$. An item is said to be* cut *if there is a positive fraction of it in both parts of the partition.*

In this section, we assume that the agents' utility functions are *additive*. This means that for a set M' containing a fraction x_j of item j, the utility of agent i is given by $u_i(M') = \sum_{j \in M} x_j \cdot u_i(j)$. Observe that under additivity, M' forms one part of a consensus halving exactly when

$$\sum_{j \in M} x_j \cdot u_i(j) = \frac{1}{2} \sum_{j \in M} u_i(j) \qquad \forall i \in N. \tag{1}$$

As we mentioned in the introduction, a consensus halving with no more than n cuts is guaranteed to exist regardless of the number of items. Our first result shows that such a division can be found efficiently for additive utilities.

Theorem 1. *For n agents with additive utilities, there exists a polynomial-time algorithm that computes a consensus halving with at most $\min\{n, m\}$ cuts.*

Proof. If $n \geq m$, a partition that divides every item in half is clearly a consensus halving and makes $m = \min\{n, m\}$ cuts. We therefore assume from now on that $n \leq m$ and describe a polynomial-time algorithm that computes a consensus halving using no more than n cuts.

The main idea of our algorithm is to start with the trivial consensus halving where $x_1 = x_2 = \cdots = x_m = 1/2$, and then gradually reduce the number of cuts.

We stop when the process cannot be continued, at which point we show that the consensus halving must contain at most n cuts. Our algorithm is presented below.

1. Let $x_1 = x_2 = \cdots = x_m = 1/2$.
2. Let S denote the set of n equations $\sum_{j \in M} \left(y_j - \frac{1}{2}\right) \cdot u_i(j) = 0$ for $i \in N$, and let $T = \emptyset$.
3. While there exists a solution $(y_1, \ldots, y_m) \neq (x_1, \ldots, x_m)$ to $S \cup T$, do the following:
   (a) For every $j \in M$ such that $y_j \neq x_j$, compute

$$
\gamma_j := \begin{cases} \frac{1-x_j}{y_j - x_j} & \text{if } y_j > x_j; \\ \frac{x_j}{x_j - y_j} & \text{if } y_j < x_j. \end{cases}
$$

   (b) Let $j^* = \operatorname{argmin}_{j \in M, y_j \neq x_j} \gamma_j$.
   (c) For every $j \in M$, let $s_j := (1 - \gamma_{j^*}) \cdot x_j + \gamma_{j^*} \cdot y_j$, and update the value of x_j to s_j.
   (d) Add the equation $y_{j^*} = x_{j^*}$ to T.
4. Output $(x_1, \ldots, x_m)$.

Finding a solution $(y_1, \ldots, y_m)$ to $S \cup T$ that is not equal to $(x_1, \ldots, x_m)$ or determining that such a solution does not exist (Step 3) can be done in polynomial time via Gaussian elimination.[5] Moreover, it is obvious that the other steps of the algorithm run in polynomial time.

We next prove the correctness of our algorithm, starting with arguing that $(x_1, \ldots, x_m)$ forms a consensus halving. Since we start with a consensus halving $x_1 = \cdots = x_m = 1/2$, it suffices to show that each execution of the loop in Step 3 preserves the validity of the solution. Observe that, since both $(x_1, \ldots, x_m)$ and $(y_1, \ldots, y_m)$ are solutions to the Eqs. (1), their convex combination (in Step 3c) also satisfies the Eqs. (1). Furthermore, for each j such that $y_j \neq x_j$, the value γ_j is chosen so that if we replace γ_{j^*} by γ_j in the formula for s_j, we would have $s_j = 1$ for the case $y_j > x_j$, and $s_j = 0$ for the case $y_j < x_j$. Since $\gamma_{j^*} \leq \gamma_j$, we have that $s_j \in [0, 1]$ for all j such that $y_j \neq x_j$. In addition, the value of x_j does not change for j such that $y_j = x_j$. Thus, $(x_1, \ldots, x_m)$ remains a consensus halving throughout the algorithm.

Finally, we are left to show that at most n items are cut in the output $(x_1, \ldots, x_m)$. As noted above, our definition of γ_j ensures that $x_{j^*} \in \{0, 1\}$ after the execution of Step 3c. Furthermore, as the constraint $y_{j^*} = x_{j^*}$ is then immediately added to T, the value of x_{j^*} does not change for the rest of the algorithm. As a result, every item $j \in T$ is uncut. Thus, it suffices to show that $|T| \geq m - n$ at the end of the execution.

---

[5] Specifically, if the linear equations in $S \cup T$ lead to a unique solution $(x_1, \ldots, x_m)$, then Gaussian elimination immediately results in this solution. Otherwise, Gaussian elimination will yield a row echelon form; by setting one of the non-pivots y_j to be an arbitrary number not equal to x_j, we obtain a solution that is not equal to $(x_1, \ldots, x_m)$.

When the while loop in Step 3 terminates, $(x_1, \ldots, x_m)$ must be the unique solution to $S \cup T$. Recall that a system of linear equations with m variables can only have a unique solution when the number of constraints is at least m. This means that $|S \cup T| \geq m$ at the end of the algorithm. Since $|S| = n$, we must have $|T| \geq m - n$, as desired.   □

Note that the above algorithm can be viewed as finding a vertex of the polytope defined by the constraints (1) and $0 \leq x_j \leq 1$ for all $j \in M$. In fact, it suffices to use a generic algorithm for this task; however, to the best of our knowledge, such algorithms often involve solving a linear program, whereas the algorithm presented above is conceptually simple and can be implemented directly. We also remark that our algorithm works even when some utilities $u_i(j)$ are negative, i.e., some of the items are goods while others are chores. Allocating a combination of goods and chores has received increasing attention in the fair division community [2,3].

As we discussed in the introduction, an important reason behind the positive result in Theorem 1 is the lack of linear order among the items. Indeed, as we show next, if the items lie on a line and we are only allowed to cut the line using n cuts, finding a consensus halving becomes computationally hard. This follows from discretizing the hardness result of Filos-Ratsikas et al. [11] and holds even if we allow the consensus halving to be approximate instead of exact. Formally, when the items lie on a line, we may place a number of cuts, with each cut lying either between two adjacent items or at some position within an item. All (fractional or whole) items between any two adjacent cuts must belong to the same fractional set of items in a partition, where the left and right ends of the line also serve as "cuts" in this requirement (see Fig. 1 for an example). We say that a partition into fractional sets of items (M_1, M_2) is an ε-approximate consensus halving if $|u_i(M_1) - u_i(M_2)| \leq \varepsilon \cdot u_i(M)$ for every agent i.

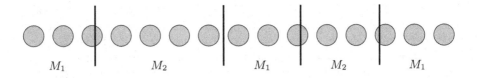

M_1 M_2 M_1 M_2 M_1

Fig. 1. Consensus halving for items on a line: in this example there are 15 items (represented by gray balls) that lie on a line and we have used 4 cuts to obtain a partition into fractional sets of items (M_1, M_2). The labels M_1 and M_2 indicate the set to which each segment belongs.

Theorem 2. *Suppose that the items lie on a line. There exists a polynomial p such that finding a $1/p(n)$-approximate consensus halving for n agents with at most n cuts on the line is PPA-hard, even if the valuations are binary and every agent values at most two contiguous blocks of items.*

The proof of Theorem 2, along with all other omitted proofs, can be found in the full version of our paper [13].

Although Theorem 1 allows us to efficiently compute a consensus halving with no more than n cuts in any instance, for some instances there exists a solution using fewer cuts. An extreme example is when all agents have the same utility function, in which case a single cut already suffices. This raises the question of determining the least number of cuts required for a given instance. Unfortunately, when there is a single agent, deciding whether there is a consensus halving that leaves all items uncut is already equivalent to the well-known NP-hard problem PARTITION. For general n, even computing a division that uses at most $n-1$ cuts more than the optimal solution is still computationally hard, as the following theorem shows.

Theorem 3. *For n agents with additive utilities, it is NP-hard to compute a consensus halving that uses at most $n - 1$ cuts more than the minimum number of cuts for the same instance.*

Theorem 3 implies that there is no hope of finding a consensus halving with the minimum number of cuts or even a non-trivial approximation thereof in polynomial time, provided that P $\neq$ NP. Nevertheless, we show that instances that admit a consensus halving with fewer than n cuts are rare: if the utilities are drawn independently at random from probability distributions, then it is almost surely the case that any consensus halving needs at least n cuts. We say that a distribution is *non-atomic* if it does not put positive probability on any single point.

Theorem 4. *Suppose that for each $i \in N$ and $j \in M$, the utility $u_i(j)$ is drawn independently from a non-atomic distribution $\mathcal{D}_{i,j}$. Then, with probability 1, every consensus halving uses at least $\min\{n, m\}$ cuts.*

As our final remark of this section, consider utility functions that are again additive across items, but for which the utility of each item scales *quadratically* as opposed to linearly in the fraction of the item. That is, for a set M' containing a fraction x_j of item j, the utility of agent i is given by $u_i(M') = \sum_{j \in M} x_j^2 \cdot u_i(j)$. Even though these utility functions appear different from the ones we have considered so far, it turns out that the set of consensus halvings remains exactly the same. Indeed, a partition (M_1, M_2) is a consensus halving under the quadratic functions if and only if

$$\sum_{j \in M} x_j^2 \cdot u_i(j) = \sum_{j \in M} (1 - x_j)^2 \cdot u_i(j) \qquad \forall i \in N.$$

Since $x_j^2 - (1 - x_j)^2 = x_j - (1 - x_j) = 2x_j - 1$, the above condition is equivalent to (1), so all of our results in this section apply to the quadratic functions as well.

3   Monotonic Utilities

Next, we turn our attention to utility functions that are no longer additive as in Sect. 2. We assume that the utilities are *monotonic*, meaning that the utility of an agent for a set of items cannot decrease upon adding any fraction of an item to the set. Our main result is that finding a consensus halving is computationally hard for such valuations; in fact, the hardness holds even when the utilities take on a specific structure that we call *symmetric-threshold*. Symmetric-threshold utilities are additive over items, and linear with symmetric thresholds within every item. Formally, the utility of agent i for a fractional set of items M' containing a fraction $x_j \in [0,1]$ of each item j can be written as $u_i(M') = \sum_{j \in M} f_{ij}(x_j) \cdot u_i(j)$, where

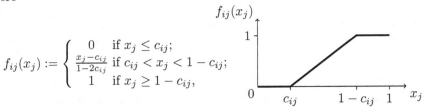

$$f_{ij}(x_j) := \begin{cases} 0 & \text{if } x_j \le c_{ij}; \\ \frac{x_j - c_{ij}}{1 - 2c_{ij}} & \text{if } c_{ij} < x_j < 1 - c_{ij}; \\ 1 & \text{if } x_j \ge 1 - c_{ij}, \end{cases}$$

where $c_{ij} \in [0, 1/2)$ is the *threshold* or *cap* of agent i for item j. Intuitively, symmetric-threshold utilities model settings where having a small fraction of an item is the same as not having the item at all, while having a large fraction of the item is the same as having the whole item. The point where this threshold behavior occurs is controlled by the cap c_{ij}, which can be different for every pair $(i,j) \in N \times M$. It is easy to see that the resulting utility functions are indeed monotonic. Note that although general monotonic utility functions do not necessarily admit a concise representation (see the discussion preceding Theorem 7), symmetric-threshold utility functions can be described succinctly.

Even though symmetric-threshold utility functions are very close to being additive, we show that finding a consensus halving for such utilities is computationally hard. Recall that a partition (M_1, M_2) is an ε-approximate consensus halving if $|u_i(M_1) - u_i(M_2)| \le \varepsilon \cdot u_i(M)$ for every agent i.

Theorem 5. *There exists a constant $\varepsilon > 0$ such that finding an ε-approximate consensus halving for n agents with monotonic utilities that uses at most n cuts is PPAD-hard, even if all agents have symmetric-threshold utilities.*

At a high level, we prove this result by reducing from a modified version of the *generalized circuit* problem. The generalized circuit problem is the main tool that has been used (implicitly or explicitly) to prove hardness of computing Nash equilibria in various settings [7,8,23]. A generalized circuit is a generalization of an arithmetic circuit, because it allows *cycles*, which means that instead of a simple computation, the circuit now represents a constraint satisfaction problem. The version of the problem we use is different from the standard one in two aspects. First, instead of the domain $[0,1]$, we use $[-1,1]$, which is more adapted to the consensus halving problem. Second, we will only allow the circuit to use three types of arithmetic gates. We show that these modifications do not change the complexity of the problem.

4   Connections to Agreeable Sets

We now present some implications of results from consensus halving on the setting of computing agreeable sets. Let us first formally define the agreeable set problem, introduced by Manurangsi and Suksompong [18].[6] As in consensus halving, there is a set N of n agents and a set M of m items. Agent i has a monotonic utility function u_i over *non-fractional* sets of items, where we assume the normalization $u_i(\emptyset) = 0$; this corresponds to a set function.

Definition 2. *A subset of items $M' \subseteq M$ is said to be* agreeable *to agent i if $u_i(M') \geq u_i(M \setminus M')$.*

As one of their main results, Manurangsi and Suksompong [18] showed that for any n and m, there exists a set of at most $\min\left\{\lfloor \frac{m+n}{2} \rfloor, m\right\}$ items that is agreeable to all agents, and this bound is tight. Their proof relies on a graph-theoretic statement often referred to as "Kneser's conjecture", which specifies the chromatic number for a particular class of graphs called Kneser graphs. Here we present a short alternative proof that works by arranging the items on a line in arbitrary order, applying consensus halving, and rounding the resulting fractional partition. As a bonus, our proof yields an agreeable set that is composed of at most $\lfloor n/2 \rfloor + 1$ blocks on the line.

Theorem 6 ([18]). *For n agents with monotonic utilities, there exists a subset $M' \subseteq M$ such that*

$$|M'| \leq \min\left\{\left\lfloor \frac{m+n}{2} \right\rfloor, m\right\}$$

and M' is agreeable to all agents.

Proof. Let $s = \lfloor \frac{m+n}{2} \rfloor$. If $s \geq m$, the entire set of items M has size $m = \min\{s, m\}$ and is agreeable to all agents due to monotonicity, so we may assume that $s \leq m$. Arrange the items on a line in arbitrary order, and extend the utility functions of the agents to fractional sets of items in a continuous and monotonic fashion.[7] Consider a consensus halving with respect to the extended utilities that uses at most n cuts on the line; some of the cuts may cut through items, whereas the remaining cuts are between adjacent items. Let $r \leq n$ be the number of items that are cut by at least one cut. Without loss of generality, assume that the first part M' contains no more full items than the second part M'', so M' contains at most $\lfloor \frac{m-r}{2} \rfloor$ full items. By moving all cut items from

---

[6] The notion of agreeability was introduced in an earlier conference version of the paper [27]. Gourvès [14] considered an extension of the problem that takes into account matroidal constraints.

[7] For example, one can use the *Lovász extension* or the *multilinear extension* (see the full version of our paper [13]). .

M'' to M' in their entirety, M' contains at most $\left\lfloor \frac{m-r}{2} \right\rfloor + r = \left\lfloor \frac{m+r}{2} \right\rfloor \leq s$ items. Since we start with a consensus halving and only move fractional items from M'' to M', we have that M' is agreeable to all agents. Moreover, one can check that M' is composed of at most $\left\lceil \frac{n+1}{2} \right\rceil = \left\lfloor \frac{n}{2} \right\rfloor + 1$ blocks on the line.

In light of Theorem 6, an important question is how efficiently we can compute an agreeable set whose size matches the worst-case bound. Manurangsi and Suksompong [18] addressed this question by providing a polynomial-time algorithm for two agents with monotonic utilities and three agents with "responsive" utilities, a class that lies between additive and monotonic utilities. They left the complexity for higher numbers of agents as an open question, and conjectured that the problem is hard even when the number of agents is a larger constant. We show that this is in fact not the case: the problem can be solved efficiently for any number of agents with additive utilities, as well as for any *constant* number of agents with monotonic utilities. Note that since the input of the problem for monotonic utilities can involve an exponential number of values (even for constant n), and consequently may not admit a succinct representation, we assume a "utility oracle model" in which the algorithm is allowed to query the utility $u_i(M')$ for any $i \in N$ and $M' \subseteq M$.

Theorem 7. *There exists a polynomial-time algorithm that computes a set of at most $\min\left\{\left\lfloor \frac{m+n}{2} \right\rfloor, m\right\}$ items that is agreeable to all agents, for each of the following two cases:*

(i) All agents have additive utilities.

(ii) All agents have monotonic utilities and the number of agents is constant (assuming access to a utility oracle).

5   Consensus k-Splitting

In this section, we address two important generalizations of consensus halving, both of which were mentioned by Simmons and Su [26]. In *consensus splitting*, instead of dividing the items into two equal parts, we want to divide them into two parts so that all agents agree that the split satisfies some given ratio, say two-to-one. In *consensus $1/k$-division*, we want to divide the items into k parts that all agents agree are equal. We consider a problem that generalizes both of these problems at once.

Definition 3. *Let $\alpha_1, \ldots, \alpha_k > 0$ be real numbers such that $\alpha_1 + \cdots + \alpha_k = 1$. A consensus k-splitting with ratios $\alpha_1, \ldots, \alpha_k$ is a partition of M into k fractional sets of items $M_1, \ldots, M_k$ such that*

$$\frac{u_i(M_1)}{\alpha_1} = \frac{u_i(M_2)}{\alpha_2} = \cdots = \frac{u_i(M_k)}{\alpha_k} \qquad \forall i \in N.$$

When the ratios are clear from context, we will simply refer to such a partition as a consensus k-splitting.

As in Sect. 2, we will assume that the utility functions are additive, in which case our desired condition is equivalent to $u_i(M_\ell) = \alpha_\ell \cdot u_i(M)$ for all $i \in N$ and $\ell \in [k]$.

While there is no reason to cut an item more than once in consensus halving, one may sometimes wish to cut the same item multiple times in consensus k-splitting in order to split the item across three or more parts. Hence, even though the number of cuts made is always at least the number of items cut, the two quantities are not necessarily the same in consensus k-splitting. If there are n items and each agent only values a single distinct item, then it is clear that we already need to make $(k-1)n$ cuts for any ratios $\alpha_1, \ldots, \alpha_k$, in particular $k-1$ cuts for each item. Nevertheless, it could still be that for some ratios, it is always possible to achieve a consensus k-splitting by cutting fewer than $(k-1)n$ items. We show that this is not the case: for any set of ratios, cutting $(k-1)n$ items is necessary in the worst case.

Theorem 8. *For any ratios $\alpha_1, \ldots, \alpha_k > 0$, there exists an instance with additive utilities in which any consensus k-splitting with these ratios cuts at least $(k-1)n$ items.*

Next, we show that computing a consensus k-splitting with at most $(k-1)n$ cuts can be done efficiently using a generalization of our algorithm for consensus halving (Theorem 1). Note that such a splitting also cuts at most $(k-1)n$ items.

Theorem 9. *For n agents with additive utilities and ratios $\alpha_1, \ldots, \alpha_k$, there is a polynomial-time algorithm that computes a consensus k-splitting with these ratios using at most $(k-1) \cdot \min\{n, m\}$ cuts.*

As in Theorem 1, our algorithm does not require the nonnegativity assumption on the utilities and therefore works for combinations of goods and chores.

When the items lie on a line, there is always a consensus halving that makes at most n cuts on the line and therefore cuts at most n items—this matches the upper bound on the number of items cut in the absence of a linear order. Theorem 9 shows that the bound n continues to hold for consensus splitting into two parts with any ratios. As we show next, however, this bound is no longer achievable for some ratios with ordered items, thereby demonstrating another difference that the lack of linear order makes.[8]

Theorem 10. *Let $n \geq 2$, $k = 2$ and $(\alpha_1, \alpha_2) = (\frac{1}{n}, \frac{n-1}{n})$. There exists an instance such that the n agents have additive utilities, the items lie on a line, and any consensus k-splitting with ratios α_1 and α_2 makes at least $2n - 4$ cuts on the line.*

For consensus halving, Theorem 4 shows that in a random instance, any solution almost surely uses at least the worst-case number of cuts $\min\{n, m\}$. One might consequently expect that an analogous statement holds for consensus k-splitting, with $(k-1) \cdot \min\{n, m\}$ cuts almost always being required. However,

---

[8] See the definition of the consensus halving problem on a line before Theorem 2.

we show that this is not true: even in the simple case where $n = 1$ and the agent's utilities are drawn from the uniform distribution over $[0, 1]$, it is likely that we only need to make one cut (instead of $k - 1$) for large m.

Theorem 11. *Let $n = 1$, and suppose that the agent's utility for each item is drawn independently from the uniform distribution on $[0, 1]$. For any ratios $\alpha_1, \ldots, \alpha_k > 0$, with probability approaching 1 as $m \to \infty$, there exists a consensus k-splitting with these ratios using at most one cut. Moreover, there is a polynomial-time algorithm that computes such a solution.*

6   Conclusion

In this paper, we studied a natural version of the consensus halving problem where, in contrast to prior work, the items do not have a linear structure. We showed that computing a consensus halving with at most n cuts in our version can be done in polynomial time for additive utilities, but already becomes PPAD-hard for a class of monotonic utilities that are very close to additive. We also demonstrated several extensions and connections to the problems of consensus k-splitting and agreeable sets.

While our PPAD-hardness result serves as strong evidence that consensus halving for a set of items is computationally hard for non-additive utilities, it remains open whether the result can be strengthened to PPA-completeness—indeed, the membership of the problem in PPA follows from a reduction to consensus halving on a line, as explained in the introduction. Obtaining a PPA-hardness result will most likely require new ideas and perhaps even new insights into PPA, since all existing PPA-hardness results for consensus halving heavily rely on the linear structure. Of course, it is also possible that the problem is in fact PPAD-complete. In addition to consensus halving, settling the computational complexity of the agreeable sets problem for a non-constant number of agents with monotonic utilities would also be of interest.

Acknowledgments. This work was partially supported by the European Research Council (ERC) under grant number 639945 (ACCORD), by an EPSRC doctoral studentship (Reference 1892947), and by JST, ACT-X.

References

1. Alon, N.: Splitting necklaces. Adv. Math. **63**(3), 247–253 (1987)
2. Aziz, H., Caragiannis, I., Igarashi, A., Walsh, T.: Fair allocation of indivisible goods and chores. In: Proceedings of the 28th International Joint Conference on Artificial Intelligence (IJCAI), pp. 53–59 (2019)
3. Bogomolnaia, A., Moulin, H., Sandomirskiy, F., Yanovskaya, E.: Competitive division of a mixed manna. Econometrica **85**(6), 1847–1871 (2017)
4. Brams, S.J., Taylor, A.D.: Fair Division: From Cake-Cutting to Dispute Resolution. Cambridge University Press, Cambridge (1996)

5. Brams, S.J., Taylor, A.D.: The Win-Win Solution: Guaranteeing Fair Shares to Everybody. W. W. Norton & Company, New York (1999)
6. Caragiannis, I., Kurokawa, D., Moulin, H., Procaccia, A.D., Shah, N., Wang, J.: The unreasonable fairness of maximum Nash welfare. ACM Trans. Econ. Comput. **7**(3), 12:1–12:2 (2019)
7. Chen, X., Deng, X., Teng, S.H.: Settling the complexity of computing two-player Nash equilibria. J. ACM **56**(3), 14:1–14:57 (2009)
8. Daskalakis, C., Goldberg, P.W., Papadimitriou, C.H.: The complexity of computing a Nash equilibrium. SIAM J. Comput. **39**(1), 195–259 (2009)
9. Filos-Ratsikas, A., Goldberg, P.W.: Consensus halving is PPA-complete. In: Proceedings of the 50th Annual ACM SIGACT Symposium on Theory of Computing (STOC), pp. 51–64 (2018)
10. Filos-Ratsikas, A., Goldberg, P.W.: The complexity of splitting necklaces and bisecting ham sandwiches. In: Proceedings of the 51st Annual ACM SIGACT Symposium on Theory of Computing (STOC), pp. 638–649 (2019)
11. Filos-Ratsikas, A., Hollender, A., Sotiraki, K., Zampetakis, M.: Consensus-halving: does it ever get easier? In: Proceedings of the 21st ACM Conference on Economics and Computation (EC), pp. 381–399 (2020)
12. Goldberg, C.H., West, D.B.: Bisection of circle colorings. SIAM J. Algebraic Discrete Methods **6**(1), 93–106 (1985)
13. Goldberg, P.W., Hollender, A., Igarashi, A., Manurangsi, P., Suksompong, W.: Consensus halving for sets of items. CoRR abs/2007.06754 (2020)
14. Gourvès, L.: Agreeable sets with matroidal constraints. J. Comb. Optim. **37**(3), 866–888 (2018). https://doi.org/10.1007/s10878-018-0327-1
15. Hobby, C.R., Rice, J.R.: A moment problem in L1 approximation. Proc. Am. Math. Soc. **16**(4), 665–670 (1965)
16. Kyropoulou, M., Suksompong, W., Voudouris, A.A.: Almost envy-freeness in group resource allocation. In: Proceedings of the 28th International Joint Conference on Artificial Intelligence (IJCAI), pp. 400–406 (2019)
17. Manurangsi, P., Suksompong, W.: Asymptotic existence of fair divisions for groups. Math. Soc. Sci. **89**, 100–108 (2017)
18. Manurangsi, P., Suksompong, W.: Computing a small agreeable set of indivisible items. Artif. Intell. **268**, 96–114 (2019)
19. Moulin, H.: Fair Division and Collective Welfare. MIT Press, Cambridge (2003)
20. Onicescu, O.: Un théorème d'existence. Annali di Matematica Pura ed Applicata **103**(1), 1–2 (1974). https://doi.org/10.1007/BF02414140
21. Plaut, B., Roughgarden, T.: Almost envy-freeness with general valuations. SIAM J. Discrete Math. **34**(2), 1039–1068 (2020)
22. Roughgarden, T.: Twenty Lectures on Algorithmic Game Theory. Cambridge University Press, Cambridge (2016)
23. Rubinstein, A.: Inapproximability of Nash equilibrium. SIAM J. Comput. **47**(3), 917–959 (2018)
24. Sandomirskiy, F., Segal-Halevi, E.: Fair division with minimal sharing. CoRR abs/1908.01669 (2019)
25. Segal-Halevi, E., Nitzan, S.: Fair cake-cutting among families. Soc. Choice Welf. **53**(4), 709–740 (2019). https://doi.org/10.1007/s00355-019-01210-9
26. Simmons, F.W., Su, F.E.: Consensus-halving via theorems of Borsuk-Ulam and Tucker. Math. Soc. Sci. **45**(1), 15–25 (2003)
27. Suksompong, W.: Assigning a small agreeable set of indivisible items to multiple players. In: Proceedings of the 25th International Joint Conference on Artificial Intelligence (IJCAI), pp. 489–495 (2016)

Learning

Learning Strong Substitutes Demand via Queries

Paul W. Goldberg⬤, Edwin Lock$^{(\boxtimes)}$⬤, and Francisco Marmolejo-Cossío⬤

Department of Computer Science, University of Oxford, Oxford, UK
{paul.goldberg,edwin.lock,francisco.marmolejocossio}@cs.ox.ac.uk

Abstract. This paper addresses the computational challenges of learning strong substitutes demand when given access to a demand (or valuation) oracle. Strong substitutes demand generalises the well-studied gross substitutes demand to a multi-unit setting. Recent work by Baldwin and Klemperer shows that any such demand can be expressed in a natural way as a finite list of weighted bid vectors. A simplified version of this bidding language has been used by the Bank of England. Assuming access to a demand oracle, we provide an algorithm that computes the unique list of weighted bid vectors corresponding to a bidder's demand preferences. In the special case where their demand can be expressed using positive bids only, we have an efficient algorithm that learns this list in linear time. We also show super-polynomial lower bounds on the query complexity of computing the list of bids in the general case where bids may be positive and negative. Our algorithms constitute the first systematic approach for bidders to construct a bid list corresponding to non-trivial demand, allowing them to participate in 'product-mix' auctions.

Keywords: Learning demand · Preference elicitation · Bidding language · Query protocol · Product-mix auction · Strong substitutes

1 Introduction

The Product-Mix Auction [10–12] was devised by Klemperer as a means of providing liquidity to commercial banks and has been used regularly by the Bank of England since 2011. In it, there are a number of distinct *goods* available in multiple discrete units, and a set of buyers who express *strong substitutes* demands amongst these goods.[1] Given strong substitutes constraints on the total quantity of goods available, it is possible to compute market-clearing prices and allocations, in the sense that all buyers receive an allocation that they demand at

---

[1] In the banking context, the goods correspond to liquidity secured against alternative kinds of collateral. Commercial banks pay for liquidity 'products' by committing to interest rates. The values of the bids submitted by the commercial banks correspond to the interest rates they are willing to pay.

© Springer Nature Switzerland AG 2020
X. Chen et al. (Eds.): WINE 2020, LNCS 12495, pp. 401–415, 2020.
https://doi.org/10.1007/978-3-030-64946-3_28

those prices, and all goods are sold. The strong substitutes property guarantees the existence of a competitive equilibrium.

Importantly for the present paper, the auction introduces a novel bidding language in which buyers express their demands in terms of lists of bids, where each bid consists of a price vector (one price for each good) and a weight. Any bid b is understood as a willingness to buy some quantity of goods (the weight of b), and for each good i a price b_i is offered. A bid is rejected if all prices offered are lower than the market-clearing prices of the corresponding goods, otherwise it is accepted on some good that maximises the price offered minus the market-clearing price. The auction currently run by the Bank of England only permits bidders to submit bids with one non-zero vector entry and positive weights, and any such list of such positive bids has the strong substitutes property. It has subsequently been shown that *any* strong-substitutes demand function can be uniquely represented as a list of bids with positive *and* negative weights [2].

While this gives the buyer a general-purpose means of communicating any strong substitutes demand, the buyer faces the problem of expressing her demand in this language. It may be easier for a buyer to answer queries of the form "what bundle would you demand, given the following per-unit prices of goods?". In this paper, we develop query protocols that assist a buyer in constructing her demand function based on a sequence of queries. Given an unknown demand function, the algorithm is assumed to have access to a demand oracle: for any given prices for goods, the algorithm can learn a bundle of goods demanded at those prices. We are interested in minimising the number of queries to the demand oracle.

1.1   Our Contributions

This paper addresses the computational challenges of learning strong substitutes demand, given access to a demand oracle. Under the mild assumption that bidders are able to answer questions of the form "What bundle do you demand at the following per-unit prices?", our algorithms constitute the first systematic approach for bidders to generate a bid list corresponding to their demand, allowing them to participate in Product-Mix Auctions with non-trivial demand preferences. We provide upper and lower bounds on the query complexity of learning demand preferences and expressing these in the bidding language of the Product-Mix Auction, which encodes any strong substitutes demand in a conceptually simple and natural fashion. Full proofs for all the results that are omitted from this paper are given in our full paper [8].

Section 2 outlines three complementary characterisations of the strong substitutes property and introduces the bidding language algebraically and geometrically. A first result of this paper, given in Sect. 3, is to show that demand oracles are not unreasonably powerful: when given access instead to a valuation oracle, it is possible to simulate a demand oracle with $O(n^3 \log(W/n))$ valuation queries, where n is the number of goods and W is the maximum weight of a bid vector. In Sects. 4 and 5, we consider algorithms that learn the unique bid list corresponding to a bidder's demand. The algorithm in Sect. 4 learns demands that can be represented by lists of positive bids, and has linear query complexity.

In the setting where demand may require positive and negative bids to express, we provide an exponential-cost algorithm that proceeds by learning all hyperplanes that contain facets of the Locus of Indifference Prices (LIP), a geometric object introduced by Baldwin and Klemperer [3] to characterise demand.

In the full version of this paper [8] we identify lower bounds on the query complexity of learning bid lists. We note briefly that $\Omega(B \log M)$ queries are required to learn a list of B positive bids, where M is the magnitude of the bid vectors w.r.t. the L_∞ norm. In order to identify the dependence on the number of goods n, we construct an adversarial game using a novel 'island gadget' consisting of bids with weight ± 1. Crucially, the island gadget only changes demand in a local region. For fixed n, we identify the overall query complexity of learning bid lists corresponding to strong substitutes demand as $\Theta(B \log M + B^n)$.

1.2 Related Work

Our work relates to the theory of preference elicitation. In this setting, a centralised agent, such as an auctioneer, wishes to identify an optimal allocation of goods via queries to participants' preferences. Queries typically take the form of value queries, where an agent reports a valuation for a given bundle of goods, or demand queries, where an agent reports a bundle that is demanded at given prices. This paper focuses on using demand queries to learn the bid list representation of strong substitutes demand preferences. This representation can then be used to compute an optimal allocation of goods to agents via the methods of [1].

Much early work in preference elicitation highlights the deep connections to exact learning via membership and equivalence queries from computational learning theory, and our results can also be viewed through this lens. Some notable examples include [4,21]. The authors of [5] explore the use of ranking oracles to exploit the topological structure of bidder preferences to learn optimal allocations. This approach is extended in [6,7], and verified empirically in [9]. The authors of [16] explore the communication complexity of preference elicitation in combinatorial auctions, where they show that for general valuations, finding a value-maximising allocation requires an exponential communication cost in the number of items. In [13], the authors explore connections between preference elicitation and exact learning, but they demonstrate that the representation length of the valuation is an important parameter in the query complexity of computing optimal allocations. This dependence on the representation length provides a way of side-stepping lower bounds from [16], and further justifies the need for succinct yet expressive bidding languages, as explored further in [15].

Our problem is conceptually similar to a problem studied recently in [20], in which the authors also consider algorithms with access to demand queries, and attempt to learn the underlying valuation that gives rise to the demand correspondence. The main difference between their work and ours however is that they consider a different class of value functions. In [20], there are n goods, each in unit supply (whereas we allow multiple copies of goods), and the buyer wants at most k goods, and has additive valuations (whereas our strong substitutes valuations are more general).

2   Preliminaries

We denote $[n] := \{1, \ldots, n\}$ and $[n]_0 := \{0, \ldots, n\}$. In our auction model, there are n distinct goods numbered from 1 to n; a single copy of a good is an *item*. A *bundle* of goods, typically denoted by $\boldsymbol{x}$ or $\boldsymbol{y}$ in this paper, is a vector in $\mathbb{Z}_+^n$ whose i-th entry denotes the number of items of good i. Vectors $\boldsymbol{p}, \boldsymbol{q} \in \mathbb{R}^n$ typically denote vectors of prices, with a price entry for each of the n goods. We write $\boldsymbol{p} \leq \boldsymbol{q}$ when the inequality holds component-wise. Occasionally, it is convenient to work with a notional *reject good* 0 for which prices are always zero; the set of goods is then $[n]_0$ and we identify bundles and prices with the $n+1$-dimensional vectors obtained by adding a 0-th entry of value 0. For any subset $X \subseteq [n]$, $\boldsymbol{e}^X$ denotes the characteristic vector of X, i.e. an n-dimensional vector whose i-th entry is 1 if $i \in X$, and 0 otherwise. Furthermore, $\boldsymbol{e}^i$ denotes the vector whose i-th entry is 1 and other entries are 0.

For any vector $\boldsymbol{v} \in \mathbb{R}^n$, the L_1 and L_∞ norms are defined as $\|\boldsymbol{v}\|_1 = \sum_{i \in [n]} |v_i|$ and $\|\boldsymbol{v}\|_\infty = \max_{i \in [n]} |v_i|$. The L_∞ ball $B_{\boldsymbol{p}}^\varepsilon$ of radius ε at $\boldsymbol{p}$ consists of all points $\boldsymbol{q} \in \mathbb{R}^n$ that satisfy $\|\boldsymbol{p} - \boldsymbol{q}\|_\infty \leq \varepsilon$; note that this a hypercube with edge length 2ε. Any hypercube centred at $\boldsymbol{p}$ can be partitioned into 2^n *orthants*, where every orthant $O_{\boldsymbol{a}}$ is described by some vector $\boldsymbol{a} \in \{-1, 1\}^n$ and consists of the set of points $O_{\boldsymbol{a}} = \boldsymbol{p} + \{\boldsymbol{x} \in \mathbb{R}^n \mid a_i x_i \geq 0, \forall i \in [n]\}$.[2] Every such orthant can be triangulated into $n!$ simplices as follows. For every ordering $[i_1, \ldots, i_n]$ of the indices $[n]$, we define a simplex as the set of points in the orthant that satisfy $a_{i_1} x_{i_1} \leq a_{i_2} x_{i_2} \leq \ldots \leq a_{i_n} x_{i_n}$.

2.1   Strong-Substitutes Demand Preferences

Throughout, we assume that bidders have quasi-linear *strong substitutes* (SS) demand. The SS property is appealing because it is a generalisation of *gross substitutes* (GS) from the single-unit setting that guarantees the existence of a competitive equilibrium in multi-unit auction markets. We first present a characterisation of SS by Shioura and Tamura [18] that elucidates the relationship between GS and SS before introducing the two equivalent characterisations that underpin our algorithmic results and draw from tropical geometry and discrete convex analysis, respectively. For a detailed survey on the relationship between GS and SS, we refer to Shioura and Tamura [18].

Bidders have an implicit *valuation* $v : A \to \mathbb{R}$ for bundles of goods, where $A \subset \mathbb{Z}_+^n$ is a finite set. This is equivalent to defining the valuation as $v : \mathbb{Z}^n \to \overline{\mathbb{R}}$, where $\overline{\mathbb{R}} := \mathbb{R} \cup \{-\infty\}$ denotes the partially extended reals, and we assume that the *effective domain* $\operatorname{dom} v = \{\boldsymbol{x} \in \mathbb{Z}^n \mid v(x) > -\infty\}$ of v is finite and non-negative in the sense that $\boldsymbol{x} \geq \boldsymbol{0}$ for all $\boldsymbol{x} \in \operatorname{dom} v$. Moreover, bidders have quasi-linear utilities, i.e. the utility they derive from bundle $\boldsymbol{x}$ at prices $\boldsymbol{p}$ is $u(\boldsymbol{x}; \boldsymbol{p}) := v(\boldsymbol{x}) - \boldsymbol{p} \cdot \boldsymbol{x}$. A bidder's *demand correspondence* D_v maps prices $\boldsymbol{p}$ to the set of bundles $\boldsymbol{x}$ that maximise $u(\boldsymbol{x}; \boldsymbol{p})$ for this $\boldsymbol{p}$.

---

[2] Orthants in n-dimensional space generalise the notion of quadrants and octants in two- and three-dimensional space, respectively.

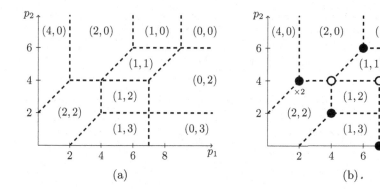

Fig. 1. Left: An illustration of a strong-substitutes demand correspondence with two goods, partitioning price space into piecewise-linear convex regions. Each region is labelled with the bundle demanded at prices in the region. The dashed lines comprise the Locus of Indifference Prices (LIP). Right: Six positive (solid) and two negative (hollow) bids of unit weight are required to express this demand.

Definition 1 captures how GS and SS demand changes when we (weakly) increase prices. Intuitively, the GS property states that the bidder's demand for those goods with unchanged prices does not decrease, while the law of aggregate demand (LAD) guarantees that the overall number of items that are demanded does not increase. The SS property combines the GS property with LAD.

Definition 1 (cf. [18]). *A demand correspondence D_v is gross substitutes (GS) if, for any prices $p' \geq p$ with $D_v(p) = \{x\}$ and $D_v(p') = \{x'\}$, we have $x'_k \geq x_k$ for all k such that $p_k = p'_k$. D_v is strong substitutes (SS) if x and x' additionally satisfy $\|x'\|_1 \leq \|x\|_1$ (the law of aggregate demand).*

Geometric Approach. We give some geometric intuition for strong substitutes demand correspondences that underpins the algorithmic ideas in this paper. It is well-known that any quasi-linear demand divides price space into piecewise-linear convex regions corresponding to bundles. When demand is SS, each such region is a convex lattice [14]. Figure 1 illustrates this.

Recently, Baldwin and Klemperer [3] proposed a new way of characterising demand types. Borrowing from the tropical geometry literature, they introduce the *Locus of Indifference Prices* (LIP), a piecewise-linear geometric object consisting of the set of all prices at which the bidder is indifferent between two or more bundles. They show that the LIP corresponds in a natural way to a polyhedral complex with $n-1$-dimensional facets. In Fig. 1, the LIP is drawn using dashed lines. Noting that the orientation of the separating facet between two adjacent demand regions characterises how demand changes when moving from one region to the other, Baldwin and Klemperer [3] propose a new way of defining demand types by the set of facet-normal vectors of the LIP. In this new paradigm, the strong substitutes demand type is defined as the family of demand correspondences whose LIP facets are normal to e^i or $e^i - e^j$ for some $i, j \in [n]$. In two dimensions, facets of SS LIPs are either horizontal, vertical or normal to $(1, -1)$. Hence it follows directly from this definition that the demand correspondence in Fig. 1 enjoys the strong substitutes property.

Discrete Convex Analysis. A 'price-free' characterisation of the strong substitutes property using the language of discrete convex optimisation is given by Shioura and Tamura [18]. A function $f : \mathbb{Z}^n \to \mathbb{R}$ is called $M^\natural$-*concave* if it satisfies the following *exchange property*: for any $\boldsymbol{x}, \boldsymbol{y} \in \mathrm{dom} f$ and $i \in \mathrm{supp}^+(\boldsymbol{x} - \boldsymbol{y})$, there exists $j \in \mathrm{supp}^-(\boldsymbol{x} - \boldsymbol{y}) \cup \{0\}$ such that $f(\boldsymbol{x}) + f(\boldsymbol{y}) \leq f(\boldsymbol{x} - e^i + e^j) + f(\boldsymbol{y} + e^i - e^j)$. Here we define the positive and negative support of a vector $\boldsymbol{z} \in \mathbb{Z}^n$ as $\mathrm{supp}^+(\boldsymbol{z}) = \{i \in [n] \mid z_i > 0\}$ and $\mathrm{supp}^-(\boldsymbol{z}) = \{i \in [n] \mid z_i < 0\}$, and let $e^0 = \boldsymbol{0}$.

Theorem 1 ([18, Theorem 4.1]). *A quasi-linear demand correspondence D_u is strong substitutes if and only if its valuation u is $M^\natural$-concave.*

$M^\natural$-concave functions are closely related to M-concave functions, which satisfy the above exchange property for some *non-zero* $j \in \mathrm{supp}^-(\boldsymbol{x} - \boldsymbol{y})$. Every n-dimensional $M^\natural$-concave function can be obtained as the projection of an $n+1$-dimensional M-concave function onto an n-dimensional hyperplane. Conversely, the corresponding M-concave function $\hat{f}$ of an $M^\natural$-concave function f is given by

$$\hat{f}(x_0, \boldsymbol{x}) = \begin{cases} f(\boldsymbol{x}) & \text{if } x_0 = -\sum_{i \in [n]} x_i, \\ -\infty & \text{otherwise,} \end{cases} \tag{1}$$

where $(x_0, \boldsymbol{x}) \in \mathbb{Z}^{n+1}$. For further details on $M^\natural$- and M-concave functions we refer to Murota [14].

2.2   The Bidding Language

The Product-Mix Auction introduces a novel bidding language that allows us to express every strong substitutes demand with a finite list $\mathcal{B}$ of positive and negative bids. A *bid* consists of an n-dimensional integral vector $\boldsymbol{b} \in \mathbb{Z}^n$ and a weight $w(\boldsymbol{b}) \in \mathbb{Z}$. When working with the notional reject good 0 introduced above, we identify a bid vector $\boldsymbol{b}$ with the $n + 1$-dimensional vector obtained by adding a 0-th entry of value 0. We note that any bid with a weight of $w(\boldsymbol{b}) \in \mathbb{Z}$ is equivalent to $w(\boldsymbol{b})$ unit bids with the same vector and sign. This allows us to normalise bid lists to their most succinct form, where no two bids share the same vector. In this paper, we wish to learn the unique normalised bid list that represents the bidder's demand correspondence.

For each bid $\boldsymbol{b}$, we can understand b_i as the amount that $\boldsymbol{b}$ is willing to spend on good i. Suppose the auctioneer sets prices $\boldsymbol{p}$. The bid is *rejected* at $\boldsymbol{p}$ if $b_i < p_i$ for all goods i. Otherwise, the bid *demands a good* $i \in [n]$ that maximises $b_i - p_i$ at price $\boldsymbol{p}$. The notational 'reject' good 0 simplifies notation: recalling that we defined $b_0 = 0 = p_0$, we say that $\boldsymbol{b}$ demands good $i \in [n]_0$ if

$i \in \arg\max_{i \in [n]_0}(b_i - p_i)$, and receiving the 'reject' good is equivalent to the bid being rejected. If the set of demanded goods $\arg\max_{i \in [n]_0}(b_i - p_i)$ at $\boldsymbol{p}$ contains more than one good, we say that $\boldsymbol{b}$ is *indifferent* between these goods at $\boldsymbol{p}$. (In particular, a bid may be indifferent between demanding goods and being rejected when $\max_{i \in [n]_0}(b_i - p_i) = 0$). A price $\boldsymbol{p}$ is *marginal* if there are bids indifferent between goods at $\boldsymbol{p}$, and non-marginal otherwise.

We can now introduce the *demand correspondence* $D_{\mathcal{B}}(\boldsymbol{p})$ for a bid list $\mathcal{B}$ as follows. If $\boldsymbol{p}$ is non-marginal, the unique bundle demanded at $\boldsymbol{p}$ is obtained by adding $w(\boldsymbol{b})$ items of $i(\boldsymbol{b})$ to the bundle for each $\boldsymbol{b} \in \mathcal{B}$, where $i(\boldsymbol{b})$ is the unique good that $\boldsymbol{b}$ demands at $\boldsymbol{p}$. If $\boldsymbol{p}$ is marginal, $D_{\mathcal{B}}(\boldsymbol{p})$ consists of the discrete convex hull of the bundles demanded at non-marginal prices arbitrarily close to $\boldsymbol{p}$, where the discrete convex hull of a set of bundles X is defined as $\mathrm{conv}(X) \cap \mathbb{Z}$. In general, this implies that we cannot independently allocate to each bid one of the goods it demand, as this may result in bundles that are not in $D_{\mathcal{B}}(\boldsymbol{p})$.

Baldwin and Klemperer [2] show that any strong substitutes demand correspondence D_v can be represented as a finite list $\mathcal{B}$ of positive and negative bids such that $D_v(\boldsymbol{p}) = D_{\mathcal{B}}(\boldsymbol{p})$ for all prices $\boldsymbol{p}$, and this representation is essentially unique (if we restrict ourselves to positive and negative bids of unit weight). The bids in Fig. 1 (right) represent the strong substitutes demand shown in Fig. 1 (left). Conversely, however, not all lists of positive and negative bids induce a strong substitutes demand correspondence; we call a bid list *valid* if it does. Theorem 2, taken from [1], gives a criterion that allows us to check validity. It is known that the problem of deciding the validity of a bid list is coNP-complete [1].

Theorem 2. *A bid list is valid if and only if the weights of the bids indifferent between i and i' at $\boldsymbol{p}$ sum to a non-negative number for all $\boldsymbol{p} \in \mathbb{R}^n$ and $i, i' \in [n]_0$.*

A special subclass of the strong substitutes demand type is the family of demand correspondences that can be expressed using only positive bids. This family is of particular practical interest, as the Bank of England currently runs the Product-Mix Auction with positive bids only. Note that any list of positive bids is valid, as it trivially satisfies Theorem 2.

2.3   The Computational Challenges

Consider a bidder who has an (unknown) strong substitutes demand correspondence D_v on n goods. We study the problem of learning the unique list $\mathcal{B}$ of positive and negative bids of unit weight that represent a bidder's demand correspondence, i.e. such that $D_v = D_{\mathcal{B}}$. We consider algorithms that learn $\mathcal{B}$ by querying the demand correspondence D_v at different price vectors. More specifically, our algorithms have access to an *adversarial demand oracle* $\mathcal{Q}_{\mathcal{B}}$; given any price vector $\boldsymbol{p}$, $\mathcal{Q}_{\mathcal{B}}(\boldsymbol{p})$ returns a bundle from $D_{\mathcal{B}}(\boldsymbol{p})$. A bidder may demand multiple bundles at some price (i.e. when $|D_{\mathcal{B}}(\boldsymbol{p})| > 1$), in which case the adversarial oracle simply returns a single demanded bundle at that price, and we have no control over which such bundle is returned. Another related setting we address in Sect. 3 is the complexity of learning $\mathcal{B}$ given access to a *valuation oracle*, i.e. given a bundle $\boldsymbol{x}$, the bidder reports their valuation $v(\boldsymbol{x})$.

Let $B := |\mathcal{B}|$ be the number of bids we wish to learn. Moreover, let $M := \max_{b \in \mathcal{B}} \|\boldsymbol{b}\|_\infty$ be the *magnitude* of the bids w.r.t to the L_∞ norm and $W := \max_{b \in \mathcal{B}} w(\boldsymbol{b})$ be the maximum bid weight. For any unknown bid list $\mathcal{B}$, we can determine the value of M with $O(\log M)$ demand queries, as M corresponds to the smallest value m such that the bidder demands the empty bundle at price vector $\boldsymbol{p} = m e^{[n]}$, which can be found using binary search. We are interested in the query complexity of learning $\mathcal{B}$, measured in terms of n, B, $\log M$ and $\log W$. Note that $nB \log M + B \log W$ bits are required to store the bid list $\mathcal{B}$, under the natural assumption that bid vectors and weights are encoded in binary.

3   Simulating $\mathcal{Q}_{\mathcal{B}}$ with a Valuation Oracle

In this section we show that demand oracles are not unreasonably powerful, in the sense that we can use a valuation oracle to simulate a demand oracle with polynomial overhead. Consider the setting where we are given query access to a bidder's valuation function v. We show that a single query to $\mathcal{Q}_{\mathcal{B}}$ can be simulated with a polynomial number of queries to a valuation oracle. This result utilises the equivalence of the strong substitutes property and $M^\natural$-convexity from the discrete convex analysis literature.

Recall that the utility of bundle $\boldsymbol{x}$ at prices $\boldsymbol{p}$ is given by $u(\boldsymbol{x}; \boldsymbol{p}) = v(\boldsymbol{x}) - \boldsymbol{p} \cdot \boldsymbol{x}$. We define $u_p := u(\cdot; \boldsymbol{p})$ for convenience. In order to simulate a demand oracle on input $\boldsymbol{p}$, we wish to compute a bundle $\boldsymbol{x} \in D_v$ that maximises $u_p(\boldsymbol{x})$. Note that we can compute $u_p(\boldsymbol{x})$ for any bundle $\boldsymbol{x}$ using a single query to the valuation oracle. In order to compute a maximiser of $u_p(\cdot)$, we draw from the discrete convex analysis literature. Firstly, we see that u_p is $M^\natural$-concave. Indeed, it is well-known [18] that strong substitutes valuations are $M^\natural$-concave and subtracting a linear term preserves this property. Secondly, let $\hat{u}$ be the corresponding M-concave function to u_p as defined in (1). We see that maximising u_p is equivalent to maximising $\hat{u}$. Moreover, we can compute $\hat{u}(x_0, \boldsymbol{x})$ with a single query to the valuation oracle. Thirdly, note that we have $\|x\|_1 \le BW$ for any bundle $\boldsymbol{x}$ that the bidder demands, as every bid $\boldsymbol{b} \in \mathcal{B}$ contributes at most W items to $\boldsymbol{x}$.

Murota [14, Chapter 10] provides multiple algorithms for maximising M-concave functions f with bounded effective domains dom f. The simplest such algorithm, a straightforward steepest descent method, finds a maximiser with $O(n^2 L)$ queries, where $L := \max\{\|x - y\|_1 \mid x, y \in \text{dom } f\}$. In our setting, we have $L = BW$, yielding a query complexity of $O(n^2 BW)$. This query complexity can be improved to $O(n^3 \log(BW/n))$ by applying the more involved algorithms for maximising M-concave functions given in [17] and [19]. We note that this query complexity is polynomial in n, B and $\log W$.

4   Learning Positive-Weighted Bids

In this section we assume that the bidder's demand correspondence can be expressed by a list of positive bids. Our algorithm learns a list of B positive bids using $O(nB \log M)$ demand queries. This is close to our lower bound of $\Omega(B \log M)$. We proceed by repeatedly finding a bid and 'removing' it, thereby reducing the size of the remaining demand correspondence until all bids have been found. Let $\mathcal{L}$ denote the subset of bids from $\mathcal{B}$ that have already been learnt, and let $\mathcal{B}' := \mathcal{B} - \mathcal{L}$ be the list of remaining bids. We can simulate a demand oracle $\mathcal{Q}_{\mathcal{B}'}(p)$ for the demand correspondence associated with $\mathcal{B}'$: at price vector p, first determine a bundle x demanded by all bids in $\mathcal{B}$ with a single query $\mathcal{Q}_{\mathcal{B}}(p)$, and then subtract from x a bundle y demanded at p by the bids in $\mathcal{L}$.[3] In this way, the problem of learning a bid list reduces to repeatedly identifying a single bid. In the next section, we describe a subroutine that learns the location of a single bid in $\mathcal{B}'$ using $O(n \log M)$ queries. As this subroutine is called B times, this yields an overall query complexity of $O(nB \log M)$ for learning all bids in $\mathcal{B}$. Recall that we can compute M with $O(\log M)$ queries.

4.1   Finding a Single Positive Bid

We present an algorithm that performs binary searches using *delta queries* to successively learn the coordinates $x_1, x_2, \ldots$ of a bid's location x together with its weight. We begin by defining delta queries and establishing some fundamental facts about the results returned by these queries.

Definition 2. *A* delta query $\Delta(q)$ *at* $q \in \mathbb{Z}^n$ *consists of two queries* q^+ *and* q^- *defined by* $q^+ := q' + \frac{1}{2n}e^1$ *and* $q^- := q' - \frac{1}{2n}e^1$, *where we define* $q' := q + \sum_{i \in \{2, \ldots, n\}} \frac{1}{2(n-i+1)}e^i$. *The return value of the delta query is* $\Delta(q) := x_1^- - x_1^+$, *where* x^+ *and* x^- *are the bundles of goods uniquely demanded at* q^+ *and* q^-.

Note that $q_1^+ = q_1 + \frac{1}{2n}$ and $q_1^- = q_1 - \frac{1}{2n}$, and the two query points q^+ and q^- agree on all other coordinates $i \geq 2$. Secondly, $q^{\pm}$ is non-marginal by construction, so any bid $b \in \mathbb{Z}^n$ uniquely demands some good i at $q^{\pm}$. The intuition behind delta queries is as follows. Consider the hyperplane normal to e^1 that contains q. In a first step, we carefully perturb q such that the resulting point q' remains on the hyperplane and no bid is indifferent between any two goods in $\{2, \ldots, n\}$. The points q^- and q^+ are then obtained by perturbing q' in directions $\pm e^1$ such that the prices become non-marginal.

In [8] we observe that bids b satisfying $b_1 = q_1$ and $b \leq q$ demand good 1 at q^- and are rejected at q^+, while all other bids demand the same good at both prices $q^{\pm}$. Hence demand changes only in terms of good 1, and $\Delta(q)$ captures the magnitude of this change. In our current setting where all bids have positive

---

[3] Note that $\mathcal{B}'$ is valid, as lists of positive bids are always valid. If $\mathcal{B}$ consisted of positive and negative bids, removing a single positive bid might result in a bid list that is no longer valid, in which case the algorithm described in this section may fail and return points not corresponding to bid locations.

Algorithm 1. Learning Positive Bids

1: Perform binary search to find largest price $p \in \{(k, M, \ldots, M) \mid k \in [M]_0\}$ at which $\Delta(p) > 0$, and fix $x_1 = p_1$.
2: **for** $i = 2 \ldots n$ **do**
3:    Binary search to find smallest price $p \in \{(x_1, \ldots, x_{i-1}, k, M, \ldots, M) \mid k \in [M]_0\}$ at which $\Delta(p) > 0$, and fix $x_i = p_i$.
4: **return** bid vector $x = (x_1, \ldots, x_n)$ and weight $\Delta(x)$.

---

weights, Corollary 1 notes that this is equivalent to summing the weights of the bids b that satisfy $b_1 = q_1$ and $b \leq q(S)$. Our algorithm exploits this fact in order to learn the coordinates of a bid location as well as the bid weight.

Corollary 1. $\Delta(q)$ *is the sum of the weights of all bids* $b \in \mathcal{B}$ *satisfying* $b_1 = q_1$ *and* $b \leq q$.

Algorithm 1 learns the vector x and weight of a single positive bid with $O(n \log M)$ queries. It determines the value of x_i, $i \in [n]$, by performing a binary search on line segment $L_i := \{(x_1, \ldots, x_{i-1}, z, M, \ldots, M) \mid 0 \leq z \leq M\}$, where the values of $x_1, \ldots, x_{i-1}$ have already been determined and are fixed. As L_i is well-ordered, we can define the 'smallest' and 'largest' points on L_i as $s^i := (x_1, \ldots, x_{i-1}, 0, M, \ldots, M)$ and $l^i := (x_1, \ldots, x_{i-1}, M \ldots, M)$.

Algorithm 1 starts by finding the largest point on L_1 at which demand for good 1 is positive. At any $p \in L_1$, no bid demands items of good $i \geq 2$, i.e. every bid demands an item of good 0 or 1 (or is indifferent between the two). Moreover, the function mapping prices p on L_1 to the demand of good 1 at p is monotonically decreasing and changes only at integral points, as the bids are integral. As B items of good 1 are demanded at s^1, there is a largest price $p^* \in L_1$ at which demand is positive. Hence, we can find p^* using binary search on L_1 by querying demand at $O(\log M)$ prices of the form $(k, M, \ldots, M)$ with $k \in [M]_0$.

The second kind of binary search uses delta queries to find the smallest point p^* for each line segment L_i, $i \geq 2$, at which $\Delta(p^*)$ is positive. Suppose $i \geq 2$. Corollary 1 implies that $\Delta(q)$ restricted to the line L_i is monotonically increasing. Theorem 4 establishes the correctness and running time of Algorithm 1. The proof (given in our full paper [8]) proceeds by induction and makes use of Observation 3. Crucially, we show that the invariant $\Delta(l^i) > 0$ holds when we perform binary search on L_i. Moreover, Δ only changes in value at integral points along L_i, so we can perform binary search to find p^* with $O(\log M)$ delta queries at prices $(x_1, \ldots, x_{i-1}, k, M, \ldots, M)$, where $k \in [M]_0$.

Observation 3. *Let* $i \geq 2$. *Suppose Algorithm 1 has successfully determined the first* $i - 1$ *coordinates* $x_1, \ldots, x_{i-1}$ *and binary search (using delta queries) finds the smallest point* $p = (x_1, \ldots, x_i, M, \ldots, M)$ *on* L_i *at which* $\Delta(p) > 0$. *By Corollary 1 (a) none of the bids* $b \in \mathcal{B}$ *satisfy* $b \leq p$ *and* $b_i < p_i$, *and (b) there is at least one bid* b *with* $b \leq p$ *and* $b_i = p_i$.

Theorem 4. *Algorithm 1 finds a bid vector and weight with* $O(n \log M)$ *queries.*

5   Learning Positive and Negative Bids

In this section, we provide an algorithm for learning valid bid lists that may contain both positive and negative bids. Introducing negative bids significantly complicates learning the location of bids, as negative bids are able to 'cancel out' facets. Consider, for instance, a bid b of weight 2 at position $(2, 4)$ in the setting with two goods. Without negative bids, its horizontal and vertical facets extend indefinitely from b in direction e^1 and e^2. In contrast, Fig. 1 demonstrates how two negative bids of weight 1 cancel out b's horizontal facet (from $(7, 4)$ onwards). Similarly, the vertical facet of the bid at $(4, 2)$ in the same figure is cancelled out by the negative bid at $(4, 4)$. As a result, some bids may only be detectable if we query in their local neighbourhood; for more details see our full paper [8], where we exploit this phenomenon to show a super-polynomial lower bound on learning positive and negative bids.

Recall from Sect. 2.1 that the demand correspondence of a SS demand (and hence of a valid bid list) corresponds to a polyhedral complex over price space, the LIP, where the boundaries between unique demand regions are $n - 1$-dimensional facets. Our algorithm learns the collection of all hyperplanes that contain these facets, as well as each vertex arising from the intersection of n such hyperplanes. We note that every bid must lie at a vertex but, conversely, not every such vertex contains a bid. In order to check for existence of a bid at a vertex, we introduce *super queries*. These super queries, applied at integral points p, provide complete information about the demand correspondence in the local neighbourhood of p. This also allows us to perform a principled search for new hyperplanes: at each iteration of the algorithm, either the local information around two vertices points us in the direction of a new hyperplane, or we have succeeded in learning all hyperplanes, and thus all bids.

Super Queries. Suppose $p \in \mathbb{Z}^n$ is an integral price vector. We show that it is possible to obtain complete knowledge of $D_\mathcal{B}(p')$ for all prices p' with $\|p - p'\|_\infty < 1$ using a *super query*, which consists of a specific set of demand queries at non-marginal query points in the vicinity of p. Intuitively, this works because bid vectors are integral and facets of an SS LIP can only have specific orientations. Super queries (Definition 3) are used by our algorithm in two ways: firstly to determine the existence and weight of a bid at a given integral point p, and secondly to provide information that leads to a new separating hyperplane. With a slight abuse of notation, we say that we 'super query' a price vector p if we query all price vectors in $SQ(p)$. Figure 2 illustrates super queries in the case of two goods $(n = 2)$. The following lemma demonstrates the use of super queries. Let $U_1(p), \ldots, U_{2^n}(p)$ denote the 2^n orthants of the unit L_∞-ball around p. Each orthant is a hypercube that can be triangulated into $n!$ simplices (one for each permutation of the coordinates $[n]$), as described in Sect. 2. We denote these simplices for the i-th orthant by $U_i^1(p), \ldots, U_i^{n!}(p)$.

Definition 3. *A super query at $p \in \mathbb{Z}^n$ is a collection $SQ(p)$ of representative prices from the interior of each $U_i^j(p)$, where $i \in [2^n]$ and $j \in [n!]$.*

Lemma 1. *Querying the points in* $\mathrm{SQ}(\boldsymbol{p})$ *once is sufficient to ascertain* $D_{\mathcal{B}}(\boldsymbol{p}')$ *for any* $\boldsymbol{p}'$ *with* $\|\boldsymbol{p} - \boldsymbol{p}'\|_{\infty} < 1$. *This allows us to learn all facets of the LIP containing* $\boldsymbol{p}$, *as well as determining the existence and weight of a bid at* $\boldsymbol{p}$.

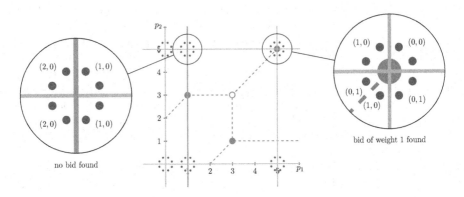

Fig. 2. A snapshot of Algorithm 2 learning the bid list consisting of one negative bid of weight -1 at $(3,3)$ and three positive bids of weight 1 at $(1,3), (3,1)$ and $(5,5)$. The initial axis-aligned hyperplanes are drawn in orange. Moreover, the algorithm has learnt one additional vertical hyperplane ($x = 1$) drawn in purple. The super queries made at the hyperplane intersections are represented by blue query points. Two super queries are highlighted to illustrate how the existence of a bid is determined. (Colour figure available online)

Finding Separating Hyperplanes. Suppose $0 \leq \boldsymbol{q}, \boldsymbol{q}' \leq (M + 1)\boldsymbol{e}^{[n]}$ are distinct price vectors in the interior of different demand regions. Note that we have $\|\boldsymbol{q} - \boldsymbol{q}'\|_{\infty} \leq M + 1$. As demand regions are convex and have piecewise-linear boundaries, there exists some facet F of the LIP separating $\boldsymbol{q}$ and $\boldsymbol{q}'$. In order to find the hyperplane containing F, we perform $O(\log M)$ steps of binary search on $\mathrm{conv}(\boldsymbol{q}, \boldsymbol{q}')$ to obtain a point $\boldsymbol{p}$ that is within $\varepsilon = 1/4$ (w.r.t. the L_{∞} norm) of the closest point to $\boldsymbol{q}$ at which demand differs from demand at $\boldsymbol{q}$. Hence by construction, the L_{∞}-ball $B_{\varepsilon}^{\infty}(\boldsymbol{p})$ of radius ε at $\boldsymbol{p}$ intersects F. Let $\boldsymbol{p}'$ be the point obtained from $\boldsymbol{p}$ by rounding each entry to the nearest integer. Then it follows that F also intersects $B_{\varepsilon + \frac{1}{2}}^{\infty}(\boldsymbol{p}')$. Moreover, the geometry of integral bids implies that any facet intersecting $B_{\varepsilon + \frac{1}{2}}^{\infty}(\boldsymbol{p}')$ must contain $\boldsymbol{p}'$. Hence we can learn F, and the hyperplane containing F, with a single super query at $\boldsymbol{p}'$. In total, we see that finding a separating hyperplane costs $O(\log M + 2^n n!)$ queries.

5.1   The Main Algorithm

Algorithm 2 learns bid lists that may comprise positive and negative bids. The algorithm maintains a set of hyperplanes $\mathcal{H}$ that it has learnt. We initialise $\mathcal{H}$ with the axis-aligned hyperplanes $\boldsymbol{e}^i = 0$ and $\boldsymbol{e}^i = M$ for all $i \in [n]$. The algorithm also keeps track of the corresponding set of vertices $\mathcal{V}$ arising from

---

Algorithm 2. Learning Positive and Negative Bids

Initialisation:

1: Let $\mathcal{H}$ be hyperplanes of the form $e^i \cdot x = 0$ and $e^i \cdot x = M$ for all $i \in [n]$.
2: Update $\mathcal{V}, \mathcal{Q}$ and $\mathcal{P}$ according to $\mathcal{H}$.
3: Super query at each $v \in \mathcal{V}$ to check for bid at v and add each new-found bid to $\hat{\mathcal{B}}$.

Main loop:

4: **while** $\exists$ hyperplane witnesses $q, q' \in \mathcal{Q}$ **do**
5:     Find a hyperplane separating q and q' (cf. Sect. 5) and add it to $\mathcal{H}$.
6:     Update $\mathcal{V}, \mathcal{Q}$ and $\mathcal{P}$ accordingly (cf. Sect. 5).
7:     **for** each new vertex v in $\mathcal{V}$ **do**
8:         Super query at v to check for bid at v and add a newly found bid to $\hat{\mathcal{B}}$.
9: **return** $\hat{\mathcal{B}}$

---

intersections of hyperplanes in $\mathcal{H}$, the set of query points $\mathcal{Q} = \bigcup_{v \in \mathcal{V}} \mathrm{SQ}(v)$, as well as the set of polytopes $\mathcal{P}$ of the subdivision of $\mathbb{R}^n$ by the hyperplanes in $\mathcal{H}$. Finally, $\hat{\mathcal{B}}$ denotes the set of bids that the algorithm has learnt. Two query points $q, q' \in \mathcal{Q}$ are *hyperplane witnesses* if they lie in the same polytope $P \in \mathcal{P}$ but have different demand. Figure 2 shows a snapshot of Algorithm 2 after learning a single hyperplane.

We now argue that Algorithm 2 is well-defined and learns a bid list in $O(Bn^2)$ iterations by identifying all the hyperplanes containing a facet of the LIP. As each bid gives rise to at most $O(n^2)$ facets, the total number of such hyperplanes is $O(Bn^2)$. The algorithm learns a new hyperplane in each iteration, as hyperplane witnesses lie in the same polytope by definition, which implies that Step 5 of the algorithm finds a new hyperplane that is not in $\mathcal{H}$. Moreover, every bid must lie at the intersection of n such hyperplanes, and we perform a super query at each intersection to check for the existence of a bid at that point. We show in our full paper [8] that Algorithm 2 learns all $O(Bn^2)$ hyperplanes containing facets of the LIP. This immediately implies that the algorithm identifies the locations and weights of all bids, leading to Theorem 5.

Theorem 5. *Algorithm 2 requires* $O\left(Bn^2 \log M + 2^n n! \binom{Bn^2}{n}\right)$ *queries to learn a bid list that may consist of positive and negative bids. For n constant, this is* $O\left(B \log M + B^n\right)$.

6 Conclusions

Our algorithms for learning demand are conceptually simple and provide the first systematic approach for bidders to express their preferences in the bidding language used by the Product-Mix Auction. This allows bidders with non-technical backgrounds to participate in these auctions under the mild assumption that they are able to answer demand oracle queries. In the setting where demand can be expressed using positive bids only, our algorithm achieves linear query complexity. When demand may only be expressible using positive *and* negative bids, our hyperplane finding algorithm performs well if the number of goods is not too large. Further work could address extending our positive-bid algorithm to allow a small number of negative bids, approximate learning of the demand function, and dealing with errors in answers to queries.

References

1. Baldwin, E., Goldberg, P.W., Klemperer, P., Lock, E.: Solving strong-substitutes product-mix auctions. ArXiv preprint (2019). http://arxiv.org/abs/1909.07313
2. Baldwin, E., Klemperer, P.: Implementing Walrasian equilibrium - the language of product-mix auctions (2019, in preparation)
3. Baldwin, E., Klemperer, P.: Understanding preferences: "demand types", and the existence of equilibrium with indivisibilities. Econometrica **87**(3), 867–932 (2019)
4. Blum, A., Jackson, J.C., Sandholm, T., Zinkevich, M.: Preference elicitation and query learning. J. Mach. Learn. Res. **5**, 649–667 (2004)
5. Conen, W., Sandholm, T.: Preference elicitation in combinatorial auctions. In: Proceedings of the 3rd ACM-EC Conference, pp. 256–259 (2001)
6. Conen, W., Sandholm, T.: *Differential*-revelation VCG mechanisms for combinatorial auctions. In: Padget, J., Shehory, O., Parkes, D., Sadeh, N., Walsh, W.E. (eds.) AMEC 2002. LNCS (LNAI), vol. 2531, pp. 34–51. Springer, Heidelberg (2002). https://doi.org/10.1007/3-540-36378-5_3
7. Conen, W., Sandholm, T.: Partial-revelation VCG mechanism for combinatorial auctions. In: Proceedings of the 18th National Conference on AI and 14th Conference on Innovative Applications of AI, pp. 367–372. AAAI Press/MIT Press (2002)
8. Goldberg, P.W., Lock, E., Marmolejo-Cossío, F.: Learning strong substitutes demand via queries. ArXiv preprint (2020). https://arxiv.org/abs/2005.01496
9. Hudson, B., Sandholm, T.: Effectiveness of query types and policies for preference elicitation in combinatorial auctions. In: Proceedings of the 3rd AAMAS Conference, vol 1, pp. 386–393. IEEE Computer Society (2004)
10. Klemperer, P.: A new auction for substitutes: central bank liquidity auctions, the U.S. TARP, and variable product-mix auctions (2008). https://www.nuffield.ox.ac.uk/economics/Papers/2008/substsauc.pdf, working paper
11. Klemperer, P.: The product-mix auction: a new auction design for differentiated goods. J. Eur. Econ. Assoc. **8**(2–3), 526–536 (2010)
12. Klemperer, P.: Product-mix auctions, working paper 2018–W07 (2018). https://www.nuffield.ox.ac.uk/economics/Papers/2018/2018W07productmix.pdf
13. Lahaie, S.M., Parkes, D.C.: Applying learning algorithms to preference elicitation. In: Proceedings of the 5th ACM-EC Conference, pp. 180–188 (2004)
14. Murota, K.: Discrete Convex Analysis. SIAM Monographs on Discrete Mathematics and Applications Series, Society for Industrial and Applied Mathematics (2013)
15. Nisan, N.: Bidding and allocation in combinatorial auctions. In: Proceedings of the 2nd ACM Conference on Electronic Commerce, pp. 1–12 (2000)
16. Nisan, N., Segal, I.: The communication requirements of efficient allocations and supporting prices. J. Econ. Theory **129**(1), 192–224 (2006)
17. Shioura, A.: Fast scaling algorithms for M-convex function minimization with application to the resource allocation problem. Discrete Appl. Math. **134**(1), 303–316 (2004)
18. Shioura, A., Tamura, A.: Gross substitutes condition and discrete concavity for multi-unit valuations: a survey. J. Oper. Soc. Japan **58**(1), 61–103 (2015)

19. Tamura, A.: Coordinatewise domain scaling algorithm for M-convex function min-imization. Math. Program. **102**(2), 339 (2004)
20. Zhang, H., Conitzer, V.: Learning the valuations of a k-demand agent (2020). Preprint at https://users.cs.duke.edu/~hrzhang/papers/k-demand.pdf
21. Zinkevich, M.A., Blum, A., Sandholm, T.: On polynomial-time preference elici-tation with value queries. In: Proceedings of the 4th ACM-EC Conference, pp. 176–185 (2003)

A Cardinal Comparison of Experts

Itay Kavaler$^{(\boxtimes)}$ and Rann Smorodinsky

Technion–Israel Institute of Technology, Technion, 3200003 Haifa, Israel
itayk@campus.technion.ac.il, rann@technion.ac.il

Abstract. In various situations, decision makers face experts that may provide conflicting advice. This advice may be in the form of probabilistic forecasts over critical future events. We consider a setting where the two forecasters provide their advice repeatedly and ask whether the decision maker can learn to compare and rank the two forecasters based on past performance. We take an axiomatic approach and propose three natural axioms that a comparison test should comply with. We propose a test that complies with our axioms. Perhaps, not surprisingly, this test is closely related to the likelihood ratio of the two forecasts over the realized sequence of events. More surprisingly, this test is essentially unique. Furthermore, using results on the rate of convergence of supermartingales, we show that whenever the two experts' advice are sufficiently distinct, the proposed test will detect the informed expert in any desired degree of precision in some fixed finite time.

Keywords: Forecasting · Probability · Testing

1 Introduction

Consider an individual who repeatedly consults two weather forecasting websites. It is reasonable to ask what should the individual do when the two forecasts repeatedly contradict. In what way can the individual rank the two? Should the individual trust one site and (eventually) ignore the other?

The weather example above serves as a metaphor for a plethora of settings where a decision maker faces conflicting expert advice. Take for example an elected official who must rely on professional input from civil servants, a patient who receives prognosis from various doctors or, more abstractly, a learning algorithm mechanism that uses input from various sources.

In this paper, we set the stage for defining the notion of a *cardinal comparison test*. The setting we have in mind is a sequential one. At each stage t two forecasters provide a probability over some future event (e.g., the occurrence of rain) and then the event is either realized or its complement is. Before the next day's forecasts the test must rank the two forecasters. We calibrate these ranks so they add up to one. One way to think of the rank is a recommendation for a coin flip to decide which of the two experts' advice should be taken.

We pursue a test that complies with the following set of properties which we consider natural:

© Springer Nature Switzerland AG 2020
X. Chen et al. (Eds.): WINE 2020, LNCS 12495, pp. 416–429, 2020.
https://doi.org/10.1007/978-3-030-64946-3_29

Anonymity - A test is *anonymous* if it does not depend on the identity of the experts but only on their forecasts.

Error-free - A test is *error-free* if from their perspective, each of the experts cannot entertain the thought that the other expert will be overwhelmingly preferred (i.e., he assigns relatively lower probability). Another way to think about a notion of an error-free test is to assume that one of the experts has the correct model. In such a case, the test will probably not point at the second expert as the superior one.

Reasonable - Let us consider an event, A, that has positive probability according to the first expert but relatively lower probability according to the second. Conditional on the occurrence of event A, a *reasonable* test must assign positive probability to the first expert being better informed than the second.

One thing to emphasize about the cardinal comparison test we pursue and the related properties is that they are not designed to evaluate whether either of the two forecasters is correct in some objective sense. They are only designed to compare the two. To make this point, assume that Nature follows a fair coin for deciding on rain and one forecaster insists on forecasting rain with probability 60% while the other insists on 10%. While both are wrong, a cardinal comparison test should somehow gravitate towards the former one as being better.

There is a large body of literature on expert testing that studies the question of whether a self-proclaimed expert is a true expert or a charlatan (see Sect. 1.2 for more details) and many of the results point to the difficulty or impossibility of designing such tests that are immune to strategic forecasters.

A comparison test may often be a more natural question than the one on whether the forecaster is correct. Indeed, when a decision maker must act, then she must choose which of the experts to follow. In the case of a single expert, the dismissal of that expert leaves the decision maker working with her own unsubstantiated beliefs, which may lead to an even worse outcome. In case a decision maker faces two forecasters with conflicting input, she may choose to somehow aggregate the two instead of dismissing one or the other. We discuss this alternative line of research in Sect. 1.2.

Due to space constraints, all omitted proofs and extensions of our results are relegated to the full version of the paper [12].

1.1   Results

Given an ordered pair of forecasters, f and g, at any finite time t, we consider the corresponding likelihood ratio of the actual outcome and calibrate it so that it and its inverse add up to one. We call this the finite derivative test at time t. We prove that this test is anonymous, error-free and reasonable. Furthermore, modulo an equivalence relation, it is unique. In fact, for any test that differs from the aforementioned construction and which is anonymous and reasonable, there exist two forecasters which render the test not error-free.

Moreover, our constructed test perfectly identifies the correct forecaster whenever the two measures induced by the forecasters are mutually singular with respect to each other. Requiring the test to identify the correct expert when the measures are not mutually singular is shown to be impossible.

A test could potentially take a long while until it converges to a verdict on the better expert. We show that the proposed comparison test converges fast and uniformly. In fact, when disregarding the stages at which the two experts provide similar forecasts, then with high probability the correct verdict will emerge in finite time that is independent of the underlying probabilities.

One can ask whether *ideal* tests can exist, that is, tests that always rank the correct forecaster higher regardless of what forecasting strategies other experts might submit. Unfortunately, this turns out to be impossible as we discuss in [12]. Since an ideal test does not exist, it is natural to explore the ideality of a test over a limited class of data-generating processes. We provide a full characterization for the existence of ideal tests over sets by showing that an ideal test with respect to a set A exists if and only if, A is pairwise mutually singular.

1.2   Related Literature

Single expert testing. A substantial part of the literature on expert testing focuses on the single expert setting. This literature dates back to the seminal paper of [5], who proposes the calibration test as a scheme to evaluate the validity of weather forecasters. Dawid asserts that a test must not fail a true expert. [9] show how a charlatan, who has no knowledge of the weather, can produce forecasts which are always calibrated. The basic ingredient that allows the charlatan to fool the test is the use of random forecasts. [13] and [19] extend this observation to a broader class of calibration-like tests. Finally, [18] shows that there exists no error-free test that is immune to such random charlatans (see also extensions of Sandroni's result in [20] and [16]).

To circumvent the negative results, various authors suggest limiting the set of models for which the test must be error-free (e.g., [1] and [17]), or limiting the computational power associated with the charlatan (e.g., [8]) or replacing measure theoretic implausibility with topological implausibility by resorting to the notion of category one sets (e.g., [6]).

Multiple expert testing. Comparing performance of two (or more) experts gained very little attention in the literature. Apart from our previous work, [11], we are only familiar with [2]. That paper proposes a test based on the likelihood ratio for comparing two experts. They show that if one expert knows the true process whereas the other is uninformed, then one of the following must occur: either, the test correctly identifies the informed expert, or the forecasts made by the uninformed expert are close to those made by the informed one. It turns out that the test they propose is anonymous and reasonable but is not error-free (please refer to [12] for the formal definition).

Another approach was suggested by [7], who study an infinite horizon model of testing multiple experts, using a cross-calibration test. In their test, N experts are tested simultaneously; each expert is tested according to a calibration restricted to dates where not only does the expert have a fixed forecast but the other experts also have a fixed forecast, possibly with different values. That is to say, where the calibration test checks the empirical frequency of observed outcomes conditional on each forecast, the cross-calibration test checks the empirical frequency of observed outcomes conditional on each profile of forecasts (please refer to [12] for the formal definition).

They showed that if an expert predicts according to the data-generating process, the expert is guaranteed to pass the cross-calibration test with probability 1, no matter what strategies the other experts use. In addition, they prove that in the presence of an informed expert, the subset of data-generating processes under which an ignorant expert (a charlatan) will pass the cross-calibration test with positive probability, is topologically "small".

In a previous paper, [11], we construct a comparison test over the infinite horizon. In that paper, the test outputs one verdict at the end of all times which is in one of three forms—it points to either one of the forecasters as advantageous or it is indecisive. The main result in that paper was the identification of an essentially unique infinite-horizon, ordinal test that adheres with some natural properties. The properties studied in the current paper (as well as the associated terminology) are inspired by the ones studied in [11]. The test we identify is based on the likelihood ratio. Interestingly, the tests identified in [2] and that identified by [17] for testable paradigms are also based on the likelihood ratio.

An alternative approach to that of comparing and ranking experts is that of aggregating forecasts by a non-Bayesian aggregator. For aggregation schemes that do well in a single stage setting, see [3], as well as [14], and [15]; for schemes that work well in a repeated setting and produce small regret, see the rich literature in machine learning surveyed in [4].

2   Model

At the beginning of each period $t = 1, 2, \ldots$ an outcome, ω_t, drawn randomly by Nature from the set $\Omega = \{0, 1\}$, is realized.[1] A *realization* is an infinite sequence of outcomes, $\omega := \{\omega_1, \omega_2, \ldots\} \in \Omega^\infty$. We denote by $\omega^t := \{\omega_1, \omega_2, \ldots, \omega_t\}$ to be the prefix of length t of ω (sometimes referred to as the partial history of outcomes up to period t) and use the convention that $\omega^0 := \emptyset$. At the risk of abusing notation, we will also use ω^t to denote the cylinder set $\{\hat{\omega} \in \Omega^\infty : \hat{\omega}^t = \omega^t\}$. In other words, ω^t will also denote the set of realizations which share a common prefix of length t. For any t we denote by $\mathcal{G}_t$ the σ-algebra on Ω^∞ generated by the cylinder sets ω^t and let $\mathcal{G}_\infty := \sigma(\bigcup_{t=0}^{\infty} \mathcal{G}_t)$ denote the smallest σ-algebra which consists of all cylinders (also known as the Borel σ-algebra). Let $\Delta(\Omega^\infty)$ be the set of all probability measures defined over the measurable space $(\Omega^\infty, \mathcal{G}_\infty)$.

Before ω_t is realized, two self-proclaimed experts (sometimes referred to as forecasters) simultaneously announce their forecast in the form of a probability distribution over Ω. Let $(\Omega \times \Delta(\Omega) \times \Delta(\Omega))^t$ be the set of all sequences

---

[1] For expository reasons, we restrict attention to a binary set $\Omega = \{0, 1\}$. The results extend to any finite set.

composed of realizations and pairs of forecasts made up to time t and let $\bigcup_{t \geq 0} (\Omega \times \Delta(\Omega) \times \Delta(\Omega))^t$ be the set of all such infinite sequences.

A (pure) forecasting strategy f is a function that maps finite histories to a probability distribution over Ω. Formally, $f : \bigcup_{t \geq 0} (\Omega \times \Delta(\Omega) \times \Delta(\Omega))^t \longrightarrow \Delta(\Omega)$. Note that each forecast provided by one expert may depend, inter alia, on those provided by the other expert in previous stages. Let F denote the set of all forecasting strategies.

A probability measure $P \in \Delta(\Omega^\infty)$ naturally induces a (set of) corresponding forecasting strategy, denoted f_P, that satisfies for any $\omega \in \Omega^\infty$ and any t such that $P(\omega^t) > 0$

$$f_P(\omega^t, \cdot, \cdot)(\omega_{t+1}) = P(\omega_{t+1} | \omega^t).$$

Thus, the forecasting strategy f_P derives its forecasts from the original measure, P, via Bayes rule. Note that this does not restrict the forecast of f_P over cylinders, ω^t, for which $P(\omega^t) = 0$.[2]

In the other direction, a realization ω, and an ordered pair of forecasting strategies, $\boldsymbol{f} := (f, g)$, induce a unique play path, $(\omega, \boldsymbol{f}) \in (\Omega \times \Delta(\Omega) \times \Delta(\Omega))^\infty$, where the corresponding t - history is denoted by $(\omega, \boldsymbol{f})^t \in (\Omega \times \Delta(\Omega) \times \Delta(\Omega))^t$ started at the Null history, $(\omega, \boldsymbol{f})^0 := \emptyset$, which in turn induce a pair of probability measures, denoted for simplicity by (f, g), over Ω^∞, as follows:

$$f(\omega^t) = \prod_{n=1}^{t} f((\omega, \boldsymbol{f})^{n-1})[\omega_n], \quad g(\omega^t) = \prod_{n=1}^{t} g((\omega, \boldsymbol{f})^{n-1})[\omega_n].$$

By Kolomogorov's extension theorem, the above is sufficient in order to derive the whole measure. Observe that a pair of forecasting strategies induces a pair of probability measures, whereas each single forecasting strategy does not induce a single measure due to the dependency between the two forecasters.

2.1   A Cardinal Comparison Test

At each stage t a third party (the 'tester') who observes the forecasts and outcomes compares the performance of both forecasters and decides who she thinks is better. Formally,

Definition 1. *A cardinal comparison test is a sequence* $T := (T_t)_{t>0}$, *where* $T_t : (\Omega \times \Delta(\Omega) \times \Delta(\Omega))^\infty \longrightarrow [0, 1]$ *is* $\mathcal{G}_t$−*measurable for all* $t > 0$.

In other words, for any t and any realization ω and any sequence of forecasts $\boldsymbol{f}$, the tester, conditional on a t - history, announces her level of confidence that the first forecaster (the one using f) is better than the second one (we

---

[2] An expert who uses f_P to derive the correct predictions is referred to as informed, whereas an expert who concocts predictions strategically to pass the test without any knowledge on P is referred to as uninformed.

will interchangeably refer to this as his propensity that f is superior to g).[3].
Note that announcing 0.5 means that both are equally capable (this should not
be confused with the statement that they are both capable or both incapable).
Whenever $T_t(\omega, \boldsymbol{f}) = 1$ (respectively, 0) the tester is confident that f outperforms
g (respectively, g outperforms f).

Definition 2. T *is called* anonymous *if for all* $\omega \in \Omega^\infty, t > 0$ *and for all*
$f, g \in F$,

$$T_t(\omega, f, g) = 1 - T_t(\omega, g, f).$$

In other words, the test's propensity at each period should not depend on the
expert's identity. Note that whenever $f = g$ an anonymous test T must output
a propensity of 0.5 for all $\omega \in \Omega^\infty$, $t > 0$.

For a given test T, an ordered pair of forecasting strategies $\boldsymbol{f} = (f, g)$, and
a realization ω, we denote by $T(\omega, \boldsymbol{f}) = lim T_t(\omega, \boldsymbol{f})$ whenever the limit exists.
For $\epsilon \in (0, 1)$, let $L_{T,\epsilon}^f := \{\omega : T(\omega, \boldsymbol{f}) > \epsilon\}$ be the set of realizations for which
the limit of T exists and from some time on assigns a propensity larger than ϵ
to f (similarly we denote $R_{T,\epsilon}^f := \{\omega : T(\omega, \boldsymbol{f}) < \epsilon\}$). Notice that the following
is a straightforward observation derived from Definition 2. If T is an anonymous
test, then $\omega \in R_{T,\epsilon}^{(f,g)}$ if and only if $\omega \in L_{T,1-\epsilon}^{(g,f)}$; we use the last for some of our
proofs.

When ω is in $L_{T,\epsilon}^f$ and $\epsilon > 0.5$, the test eventually assigns a higher propensity
to f than to g. On the other hand, for $\epsilon < 0.5$, the test assigns a higher propensity
to g whenever ω is in $R_{T,\epsilon}^f$. Thus, we will typically focus on the sets $L_{T,\epsilon}^f$ with
$\epsilon > 0.5$ and on the sets $R_{T,\epsilon}^f$ for $\epsilon < 0.5$.

2.2   Desirable Properties

In this section, we introduce a set of axioms we deem desirable for a cardinal
comparison test. Our first property asserts that any set that is contained in $R_{T,\epsilon}^f$
must not be assigned a high probability according to f in comparison with the
probability assigned by g. In particular, the ratio of these probabilities must be
bounded by $\frac{\epsilon}{1-\epsilon}$.

Definition 3. T *is* error-free *if for all* $\boldsymbol{f} := (f, g) \in F \times F$, *for all* $\epsilon \in (0, \frac{1}{2})$
and for all measurable set A

$$f(A \cap R_{T,\epsilon}^f) \le (\frac{\epsilon}{1-\epsilon}) g(A \cap R_{T,\epsilon}^f) \tag{1}$$

(Similarly, $g(A \cap L_{T,\epsilon}^f) \le (\frac{1-\epsilon}{\epsilon}) f(A \cap L_{T,\epsilon}^f)$ *for* $\epsilon \in (\frac{1}{2}, 1)$*).*

---

[3] It should be emphasized that the results in this paper hold even for the general
case for which Definition 1 is extended such that a tester may condition his one
step ahead decisions on his own past decisions. Formally, whenever T has the form
$T_t : (\Omega \times \Delta(\Omega) \times \Delta(\Omega) \times \{f, g\})^\infty \longrightarrow [0, 1]$..

Note, in particular, as ϵ approaches 0, the set $R^f_{T,\epsilon}$ captures the paths where g is clearly deemed better than f and so the property of error-freeness implies that although g may assign a subset of $R^f_{T,\epsilon}$ a positive probability, it must be the case that f assigns it near-zero probability. On the other hand, whenever ϵ approaches 0.5, the corresponding ratio approaches 1 and so error-freeness requires that f assigns that event a probability no greater than g.

In particular, each forecaster must believe that a test cannot point out the other forecaster as correct. From his perspective, he is either preferred or the test is indecisive.

Consider a set of realizations assigned positive probability by one forecaster whereas his colleague assigns it a relatively lower probability. We shall call a test 'reasonable' if the former forecaster assigns a positive probability to the event that the test will eventually provide a high propensity to her. Formally:

Definition 4. T *is* reasonable *if for all $\boldsymbol{f} \in F \times F$, for all $\epsilon \in (0, \frac{1}{2})$ and for all measurable set A,*

$$g(A) > 0 \text{ and } f(A) < (\frac{\epsilon}{1-\epsilon})g(A) \implies g(A \cap R^f_{T,\epsilon}) > 0. \qquad (2)$$

(Similarly, $f(A) > 0$ and $g(A) < (\frac{1-\epsilon}{\epsilon})f(A) \implies f(A \cap L^f_{T,\epsilon}) > 0$ for $\epsilon \in (\frac{1}{2}, 1)$).

It should be emphasized that reasonableness and error-freeness are not related notions; further analysis and examples that these properties are independent are discussed in [12].

Remark 1. One could propose to replace error-freeness with a stronger and more appealing property in which a test points out the better informed expert with probability one. Informally, we would like to consider tests that have the following property $f(T(\omega, \boldsymbol{f}) = 1) = 1$ whenever $f \neq g$. However, there could be pairs of forecasters that are not equal but induce the same probability distribution. In [12], we formalize this and refer to tests that satisfy this stronger requirement as an *ideal*. We, furthermore show, as the name suggests, that such tests essentially do not exist.

3   An Error-Free and Reasonable Test

We now turn to propose an anonymous cardinal comparison test that is error-free and reasonable. For any pair of forecasters, $\boldsymbol{f} := (f, g) \in F \times F$, $\omega \in \Omega^\infty$, $t \geq 0$, the *finite derivative test*, $\mathcal{D}$, is defined as follows:

$$\mathcal{D}_{t+1}(\omega, \boldsymbol{f}) = \begin{cases} \frac{f(\omega^t)}{f(\omega^t)+g(\omega^t)}, & g(\omega^t) > 0 \text{ or } f(\omega^t) > 0 \\ \frac{1}{2}, & \text{other.} \end{cases}$$

It should be noted that the ratio between $\mathcal{D}_{t+1}(\omega, \boldsymbol{f})$, the rank associated with the forecast f and $1 - \mathcal{D}_{t+1}(\omega, \boldsymbol{f})$, the rank associated with the forecast g, equals the likelihood ratio between the two forecasters. Clearly, $\mathcal{D}$ is anonymous. We turn to show that it is reasonable and error-free. Before doing so, some preliminaries are required.[4]

Lemma 1. Let $\boldsymbol{f} := (f, g)$. Then the limit of $\mathcal{D}_t(\cdot, \boldsymbol{f})$ exists and is finite $f - a.s.$

Proof. For $\omega \in \Omega^\infty$ where $f(\omega^t) > 0$ define the likelihood ratio between the two forecasters at time t as

$$D_f^t g(\omega) = \prod_{n=1}^t \frac{g((\omega, \boldsymbol{f})^{n-1})[\omega_n]}{f((\omega, \boldsymbol{f})^{n-1})[\omega_n]},$$

and observe that $\mathcal{D}_{t+1}(\omega, \boldsymbol{f}) = \frac{1}{1+D_f^t g(\omega)}$.[5] Applying Lemma 2 from [11], we know that the limit of $D_f^t g$, denoted $D_f g$, exists and is finite $f - a.s.$ It readily follows that $\mathcal{D}(\omega, \boldsymbol{f}) := \frac{1}{1+D_f g(\omega)} := \lim \mathcal{D}_t(\omega, \boldsymbol{f})$ exists and is finite $f - a.s.$ $\square$

Now that we have established the existence and the finiteness of the test $\mathcal{D}$, let us contend that it complies with the two central properties for cardinal comparison tests:

Proposition 1. $\mathcal{D}$ is *error-free*.

Proposition 2. $\mathcal{D}$ is *reasonable*.

Propositions 1 and 2 jointly prove our first main theorem:

Theorem 1. $\mathcal{D}$ is an anonymous, reasonable and error-free test.

We now turn to show that the finite derivative test is essentially the unique anonymous cardinal comparison test that is reasonable and error-free.

4   Uniqueness

Although there may be other error-free and reasonable cardinal comparison tests, they are essentially equivalent to the finite derivative test. To motivate this idea, consider the following example.

Example 1. Consider the realization $\tilde{\omega} := (1, 1, 1, , ,)$, and two forecasters $\tilde{f}$ and $\tilde{g}$, both using a coin to make predictions. $\tilde{f}$ uses a fair coin whereas $\tilde{g}$ uses a biased coin with probability one for the outcome to be 1. Let $\overrightarrow{h_1^t}$ be the history of length t induced by $(\tilde{\omega}, \tilde{f}, \tilde{g})$ and let $\overleftarrow{h_1^t}$ be the one induced by $(\tilde{\omega}, \tilde{g}, \tilde{f})$. Let $c > 1$ and consider the following test:

$$T_t(\omega, \boldsymbol{f}) = \begin{cases} \mathcal{D}_t(\omega, \boldsymbol{f}), & other \\ \frac{1}{1+c \cdot D_f^t g(\omega)}, & (\omega, \boldsymbol{f})^t = \overrightarrow{h_1^t} \\ 1 - \frac{1}{1+c \cdot D_f^t g(\omega)}, & (\omega, \boldsymbol{f})^t = \overleftarrow{h_1^t}. \end{cases}$$

---

[4] Notice that $\mathcal{D}$ is unaffected by the so-called "counterfactual" predictions. These predictions are referred to events which may not occur. On the contrary, the outcome of $\mathcal{D}$ depends only on predictions which were made along the realized play path.

[5] If $f((\omega, \boldsymbol{f})^{n-1})[\omega_n] = 0$ for some n, we set $D_f^t g(\omega) = \infty$ for all $t \geq n$.

Hence, the propensities of T differ from those provided by $\mathcal{D}$ only along the play paths $\overrightarrow{h_1}, \overleftarrow{h_1}$, in which case the limit of T converges slower to $1, 0$, respectively, than $\mathcal{D}$.

Proposition 3. T is an anonymous error-free and a reasonable test.

To capture the concept of equivalence, we introduce the following equivalence relation over tests;

Definition 5. Let $\boldsymbol{f} := (f, g) \in F \times F$. We say that $T \sim_{\boldsymbol{f}} \hat{T}$ if

$$f(\{\omega : T(\omega, \boldsymbol{f}) \neq \hat{T}(\omega, \boldsymbol{f})\}) = g(\{\omega : T(\omega, \boldsymbol{f}) \neq \hat{T}(\omega, \boldsymbol{f})\}) = 0.$$

We say that $T \sim \hat{T}$ if and only if $T \sim_{\boldsymbol{f}} \hat{T}$ for all $\boldsymbol{f}$.

That is, two tests are equivalent if and only if, given an ordered pair of forecasting strategies, there is zero probability according to each forecaster that the tests will converge to different propensities.

Proposition 4. The relation $\sim$ is an equivalence relation on $\top := \{T : \ T - cardinal \ comparison \ test\}$.

The next theorem asserts that, up to an equivalence class representative, there exists a unique anonymous reasonable and error-free cardinal comparison test. That is, any anonymous test $T \nsim T_{\mathcal{D}}$ which is reasonable, admits an error. To this end, we will show that any $T \nsim T_{\mathcal{D}}$ can be associated with a pair of forecasting strategies for which the error-free condition fails. More importantly, the power of the theorem stems from the premise that T admits an error at any pair $\boldsymbol{f}$ whenever $T \nsim_{\boldsymbol{f}} \mathcal{D}$.

Before proceeding, we make the observation that Definition 5 can be stated equivalently by the next lemma which is invoked in our adjacent uniqueness theorem proof.

Lemma 2. Let $\boldsymbol{f} := (f, g) \in F \times F$. Then $T \sim_{\boldsymbol{f}} \hat{T}$ if and only if for all $\epsilon \in (0, 1) \cap \mathbb{Q}$

$$f((L_{T,\epsilon}^{f} \cap R_{\hat{T},\epsilon}^{f}) \cup (L_{\hat{T},\epsilon}^{f} \cap R_{T,\epsilon}^{f})) = g((L_{T,\epsilon}^{f} \cap R_{\hat{T},\epsilon}^{f}) \cup (L_{\hat{T},\epsilon}^{f} \cap R_{T,\epsilon}^{f})) = 0.$$

The uniqueness theorem is therefore stated as follows:

Theorem 2. Let T be an anonymous and reasonable cardinal comparison test. If $T \nsim \mathcal{D}$ then T is not error-free.

5   Decisiveness in Finite Time

In this section we provide a natural sufficient condition for which a tester achieves a higher level of confidence in favor of the informed forecaster with any desired degree of precision in some fixed finite time. To this end, we show the existence of a uniform bound on the rate at which a cardinal comparison test converges. Consider expert $f's$ point of view. Not only should he maintain that, whenever expert g's forecasts are different from his, then he should eventually be ranked higher than him, but if expert g's forecasts are relatively far, then this should essentially happen uniformly fast. Indeed, as we show in this section, this holds for our finite derivative test. This observation tightly builds on a theory of active supermartingales due to [10].

To determine whether a test is 'almost' certain about a forecaster requires the two forecasters to provide significantly different forecasts as captured by the following definition:

Definition 6. *A pair of forecasting strategies $\boldsymbol{f} := (f, g)$ is $\epsilon - close$ along ω at period $t > 0$, if*

$$|f((\omega, \boldsymbol{f})^{t-1})[\omega_t] - g((\omega, \boldsymbol{f})^{t-1})[\omega_t]| < \epsilon$$

The next theorem asserts that, given an arbitrarily small $\epsilon > 0$, there exists a finite uniform bound, K, which is independent of any pair of forecasting strategies, such that if the forecasts of the uninformed expert are sufficiently different from those of the informed one in more than K periods, then the finite derivative test, $\mathcal{D}$, will eventually settle on the informed expert with a high level of confidence. In the latter scenario, it furthermore surprisingly asserts that, given any sufficiently large time n, $\mathcal{D}_n$ ranks the informed expert higher than $(1 - \epsilon)$ and up to ϵ - amount of accuracy as it would have ranked had it continued to rank the expert following his test to infinity.

Theorem 3. *For all $0 < \epsilon < 1$ there exists $K = K(\epsilon)$ such that for all $\boldsymbol{f} := (f, g)$, and for all $n > 0$, there is a set of which the probability according to f is at least $(1 - \epsilon)$ such that for any ω in that set:*

1. *Either $\boldsymbol{f}$ is $\epsilon - close$ along ω in all but K periods in $\{1...n\}$ or*
2. *$\omega \in L_{\mathcal{D}, 1-\epsilon}^{f}$. Furthermore, $|\mathcal{D}_t(\omega, \boldsymbol{f}) - \mathcal{D}_n(\omega, \boldsymbol{f})| < \epsilon$ for all $t \geq n$.*

In words, with high probability, given any sufficiently large n and any sufficiently small ϵ, the only reason that the tester is not 'almost' settled on the correct forecaster at time n (and onward) is because the uninformed expert made excellent predictions along the play path. Moreover, Theorem 3 is universal in the following manner: The bound on the number of periods in which the two experts' forecasts must be different, K, for the finite derivative test to rank the informed one higher, depends on the required level of accuracy, but is independent of any pair of forecasting strategies, f or g.

The proof of Theorem 3 is relegated to [12]. Nevertheless let us briefly provide some technical intuition. At the heart of the proof of Theorem 3 lies a theorem due to regarding the rate of decrease of *active* supermartingales. Consider an abstract setting with a probability measure P in $\Delta(\Omega^\infty)$ and a filtration $\{\mathcal{G}_t\}_{t=1}^\infty$.

Definition 7. *A $(\mathcal{G}_t)$ - adapted, real-valued process $\tilde{\mathcal{D}} := \{\tilde{\mathcal{D}}_t\}_{t=0}^\infty$ is called a supermartingale under P if*

1. $E|\tilde{\mathcal{D}}_t| < \infty$ for all $t > 0$;
2. $E[\tilde{\mathcal{D}}_t|\mathcal{G}_s] \leq \tilde{\mathcal{D}}_t$ for all $s \leq t$, $P - a.s.$

Intuitively, a supermartingale is a process that decreases on average. The proof of Theorem 3 implies that the finite derivative test is associated with a supermartingale property with respect to the natural filtration which is defined in Sect. 2. Let us further consider the following class of supermartingales called active supermartingales. This notion was first introduced in [10] who studied reputations in infinitely repeated games:

Definition 8. *A non-negative supermartingale* $\tilde{\mathcal{D}}$ *is active with activity* $\psi \in (0,1)$ *under* P *if*

$$P(\{\omega : |\frac{\tilde{\mathcal{D}}_t(\omega)}{\tilde{\mathcal{D}}_{t-1}(\omega)} - 1| > \psi\}|\tilde{\omega}^{k-1}) > \psi$$

for P *- almost all histories* $\tilde{\omega}^{t-1}$ *such that* $\tilde{\mathcal{D}}_{t-1}(\tilde{\omega}) > 0$.

In other words, a supermartingale has activity ψ if the probability of a jump of size ψ at time t exceeds ψ for almost all histories. Note that $\tilde{\mathcal{D}}$ being a supermartingale, is weakly decreasing in expectations. Showing that it is active implies that $\tilde{\mathcal{D}}_t$ substantially goes up or down relative to $\tilde{\mathcal{D}}_{t-1}$ with probability bounded away from zero in each period. [10], Theorem A.1, showed the following remarkable result

Theorem 4 ([10]). *For every* $\epsilon > 0$, $\psi \in (0,1)$, *and* $0 < \underline{D} < 1$ *there is a time* $K < \infty$ *such that*

$$P(\{\omega : \sup_{t>K}\tilde{\mathcal{D}}_t(\omega) \leq \underline{D}\}) \geq 1 - \epsilon$$

for every active supermartingale $\{\tilde{\mathcal{D}}_t\}$ *with* $\tilde{\mathcal{D}}_0 \equiv 1$ *and activity* ψ.

Theorem 4 asserts that if $\tilde{\mathcal{D}}$ is an active supermartingale with activity ψ, then there is a fixed time K by which, with high probability, $\tilde{\mathcal{D}}_t$ drops below $\underline{D}$ and remains below $\underline{D}$ for all future periods. It should be noted that the power of the theorem stems from the fact that the bound, K, depends solely on the parameters $\epsilon > 0$, ψ and $\underline{D}$, and is otherwise independent of the underlying stochastic process P.

We exploit the active supermartingale property in a different way. In the context of cardinal comparison testing, we consider two strategies, one for each expert, which are updated using Bayes rule. Given sufficiently small $\epsilon > 0$, our comparative test ranks an expert depending on whether the posterior odds ratio is above or below ϵ. The active supermartingale result implies that there is a uniform bound (independent of neither the length of the game nor the true distribution) on the number of periods where the uninformed expert can be substantially wrong, without being detected, such that if this bound is exceeded, the probability that the tester ranks high the uninformed expert is small.

6   Concluding Remarks

The paper proposes a normative approach to the challenge of comparing between two forecasters who repeatedly provide probabilistic forecasts. The paper postulates three basic norms: anonymity, error-freeness and reasonableness and provides a cardinal comparison test, the finite derivative test, that complies with them. It also shows that this test is essentially unique. Finally, it shows that the test converges fast and hence is meaningful in finite time. In the future we hope to extend our results to settings with more than two forecasters and study alternative sets of norms.

6.1   Implications

The axiomatic premise adopted in this paper can be considered as a contribution to the hypothesis testing literature in statistics where a forecaster is associated with a hypothesis. In this context we propose a hypothesis test that complies with a set of fundamental properties which we refer to as axioms. In contrast, a central thrust for the hypothesis testing literature (for two hypotheses) is the pair of notions of significance level and power of a test. In that literature one hypothesis is considered as the null hypothesis while the other serves as an alternative. A test is designed to either reject the null hypothesis, in which case it accepts the alternative, or fail to reject it (a binary outcome). The significance level of a test is the probability of rejecting the null hypothesis whenever it is correct (type-1 error) while the power of the test is the probability of rejecting the null hypothesis assuming the alternative one is correct (the complement of a type-2 error).

In contrast with the aforementioned binary outcome that is prevalent in the hypothesis testing literature we allow, in addition, for an inconclusive outcome. Recall the celebrated Neyman-Pearson lemma which characterizes a test with the maximal power subject to an upper bound on the significance level. The possibility of an inconclusive (ranking) outcome, in our framework, allows us to design a test where both type-1 and type-2 errors have relatively low probability.[6]

Interestingly, the test proposed in the Neyman-Pearson lemma, similar to ours, also hinges on the likelihood ratio.[7] In our approach we, a priori, treat both hypotheses symmetrically. In the statistics literature, however, this is not the case and the null hypothesis is, in some sense, the status quo hypothesis. This asymmetry is manifested, for example, in the Neyman-Pearson lemma.

---

[6] Note that we abuse the statistical terminology. In statistics the notion of rejection is always used in the context of the null hypothesis. In our model, we assume symmetry between the alternatives and so we discuss rejection also in the context of the alternative hypothesis. As a consequence, an error of type-1 is defined as the probability of accepting the alternative hypothesis whenever the null hypothesis is correct, and symmetrically, an error of type-2 is the probability of accepting the null hypothesis whenever the alternative one is correct.

[7] The test proposed in the Neyman-Pearson lemma rejects the null hypothesis whenever the likelihood ratio falls below some positive threshold.

Note that in order to design a test that complies with a given significance level and a given power one must know the full specification of the two hypotheses. This is in contrast with our test which is universal, in the sense that it does not rely on the specifications of the two forecasts. Finally, let us comment that whereas hypothesis testing is primarily discussed in the context of a finite sample, typically from some iid distribution, our framework allows for sequences of forecasts that are dependent on past outcomes as well as past forecasts of the other expert.

Acknowledgments. Smorodinsky gratefully acknowledges the United States-Israel Binational Science Foundation and the National Science Foundation (grant 2016734), the German-Israel Foundation (grant I-1419-118.4/2017), the Ministry of Science and Technology (grant 19400214), the Technion VPR grants, and the Bernard M. Gordon Center for Systems Engineering at the Technion.

References

1. Al-Najjar, N., Sandroni, A., Smorodinsky, R., Weinstein, J.: Testing theories with learnable and predictive representations. J. Econ. Theory **145**(6), 2203–2217 (2010)
2. Al-Najjar, N., Weinstein, J.: Comparative testing of experts. Econometrica **76**(3), 541–559 (2008)
3. Arieli, I., Babichenko, Y., Smorodinsky, R.: Robust forecast aggregation. Proc. Nat. Acad. Sci. **115**(52), E12135–E12143 (2018)
4. Cesa-Bianchi, N., Lugosi, G.: Prediction, Learning, and Games. Cambridge University Press, New York (2006)
5. Dawid, P.: The well-calibrated Bayesian. J. Am. Stat. Assoc. **77**, 605–613 (1982)
6. Dekel, E., Feinberg, Y.: Non-Bayesian testing of a stochastic prediction. Rev. Econ. Stud. **73**, 893–936 (2006)
7. Feinberg, Y., Stewart, C.: Testing multiple forecasters. Econometrica **76**, 561–582 (2008)
8. Fortnow, L., Vohra, R.: The complexity of forecast testing. Econometrica **77**, 93–105 (2009)
9. Foster, D., Vohra, R.: Asymptotic calibration. Biometrika **85**, 379–390 (1998)
10. Fudenberg, D., Levine, D.: Maintaining a reputation when strategies are imperfectly observed. Rev. Econ. Stud. **59**, 561–579 (1992)
11. Kavaler, I., Smorodinsky, R.: On comparison of experts. Games Econ. Behav. **118**, 94–109 (2019)
12. Kavaler, I., Smorodinsky, R.: A cardinal comparison of experts. Full version https://arxiv.org/abs/1911.04752 (2020)
13. Lehrer, E.: Any inspection is manipulable. Econometrica **69**, 1333–1347 (2001)
14. Levy, G., Razin, R.: Combining forecasts in the presence of ambiguity over correlation structures. Unpublished results (2018)
15. Levy, G., Razin, R.: An explanation-based approach to combining forecasts. Unpublished results (2018)
16. Olszewski, W., Sandroni, A.: Manipulability of future-independent tests. Econometrica **76**, 1437–1466 (2008)
17. Pomatto, L.: Testable forecasts. Caltech, Unpublished results (2016)

18. Sandroni, A.: The reproducible properties of correct forecasts. Int. J. Game Theory **32**, 151–159 (2003)
19. Sandroni, A., Smorodinsky, R., Vohra, R.: Calibration with many checking rules. Math. Oper. Res. **28**, 141–153 (2003)
20. Shmaya, E.: Many inspections are manipulable. Theoret. Econ. **3**, 367–382 (2008)

Minimum-Regret Contracts for Principal-Expert Problems

Caspar Oesterheld$^{(\boxtimes)}$ and Vincent Conitzer

Department of Computer Science, Duke University, Durham, NC, USA
{ocaspar,conitzer}@cs.duke.edu

Abstract. We consider a principal-expert problem in which a principal contracts one or more experts to acquire and report decision-relevant information. The principal never finds out what information is available to which expert, at what costs that information is available, or what costs the experts actually end up paying. This makes it challenging for the principal to compensate the experts in a way that incentivizes acquisition of relevant information without overpaying. We determine the payment scheme that minimizes the principal's worst-case regret relative to the first-best solution. In particular, we show that under two different assumptions about the experts' available information, the optimal payment scheme is a set of linear contracts.

1 Introduction

A company has to choose one of a number of different projects, where a project might be to develop a particular product. While the company's personnel is suited to successfully execute any of these projects, the company lacks expertise in market research to decide which of the projects will yield the highest expected profit. To make an informed choice, the company (henceforth, the *principal*) would like to contract faculty members from a nearby business school to give advice on which project to pursue and to make a prediction about the outcome of that project.

While the business school's faculty members (henceforth, the *experts*) have relevant expertise, they need to invest some effort into conducting one relevant research project or another before they can give useful advice. The so-called *first-best solution* is to acquire the information that maximizes expected profit net of the costs of that information. The principal would have to reimburse the experts for those costs, but could keep the rest of the project's profits. However, in general, the principal is unaware of what information can be acquired at what costs and cannot verify the experts' effort or report. The principal can use a payment scheme or *contract* that compensates the experts based on both their final collective report and the outcome of pursuing the recommended project (but not on what would have happened if another project had been chosen). What contract should the principal use?

One way to arrive at a solution would be for the principal to assign some prior probability distribution over configurations of available evidence and select

© Springer Nature Switzerland AG 2020
X. Chen et al. (Eds.): WINE 2020, LNCS 12495, pp. 430–443, 2020.
https://doi.org/10.1007/978-3-030-64946-3_30

the contract that maximizes expected profit net of payment to the experts [2,8,19,25]. However, determining such a prior is often impractical. For many priors, it may also be computationally infeasible to identify the optimal contract. We therefore ask what contract ensures the minimum worst-case regret relative to the first-best solution.

Outline. After describing our setup and goals in more detail (Sects. 2 and 3), we show (in Sects. 4 and 5) how linear contracts – which simply pay each expert some fixed fraction of the company's profits – ensure regret bounds. In Sect. 6, we go on to show that the optimal regret bound is achieved only by a particular linear contract: the one that pays each of the n experts $1/(n + 1)$ of the profit obtained. This ensures a regret bound of $v(\mathbf{E}^*)n/(n + 1)$, where $v(\mathbf{E}^*)$ is the expected profit (prior to subtracting costs) of the first-best solution. Under stronger assumptions, the approach of this paper can be used to derive different linear contracts to achieve better optimal bounds. In Sect. 7, we give an example of this. Section 8 puts our work in the context of the literature.

2 Setup

Principal and Experts. We consider a *principal* ("she") who has to choose one of a finite set of projects or *actions* A, each of which probabilistically gives rise to outcomes from some finite set Ω. The principal would like to maximize the expected value of some utility function $u : \Omega \to \mathbb{R}$. To figure out which action is best, she may interact (in ways specified below) with n *experts*. An important special case is $n = 1$. This case has received the most attention in the literature. Many of the assumptions that we will make later (e.g., about how the experts coordinate) are very weak or even vacuous in the case of $n = 1$, while for $n \geq 2$ they are realistic in some but not all applications.

Each expert $i = 1, ..., n$ can choose to observe the value of a random variable in some set of random variables $\mathbb{H}_i$. We will refer to these variables as *evidence variables*. We also require that these sets of values are finite. To observe $E_i \in \mathbb{H}_i$, expert i must pay a *cost* (or effort) of $c_i(E_i)$, where $c_i : \mathbb{H}_i \to \mathbb{R}_{\geq 0}$ is some cost function. We assume that each $\mathbb{H}_i$ contains the constant (trivial) random variable E^0 and that $c_i(E^0) = 0$ for all i. That is, each expert has the option to acquire no information and expend no cost. The experts, on the other hand, all know what evidence variables the other experts have access to and at what costs. They also have a common prior P which, for any vector of random variables $\mathbf{E} \in \mathbb{H} := \bigtimes_{i=1}^{n} \mathbb{H}_i$ and any vector $\mathbf{e}$ of values of $\mathbf{E}$, assigns a probability $P(\mathbf{e}) := P(\mathbf{E} = \mathbf{e})$, as well as for any outcome $\omega \in \Omega$ and action $a \in A$, the probability $P(\omega \mid a, \mathbf{e})$ of obtaining outcome ω after taking action a if $\mathbf{E} = \mathbf{e}$ was observed. For simplicity, we also assume that every observation of $\mathbf{E} = \mathbf{e}$ is consistent, i.e., that for all $\mathbf{E} \in \mathbb{H}$ and $\mathbf{e}$ in the Cartesian product of the sets of values of $E_1, ..., E_n$, we have $P(\mathbf{e}) > 0$. Some common-knowledge assumptions such as these are necessary to determine the experts' strategies within standard game-theoretic paradigms. Of course, as is usually the case in such models, the common-knowledge assumptions – in particular, exact knowledge of one another's cost of acquisition – are only approximately realistic in practice. Alternatively, one might imagine that they have probabilistic beliefs about each other's costs or perhaps that they can communicate about each other's cost. However, this adds an additional layer of complications in expert coordination, which is beyond the scope of the present paper.

The principal knows little about the experts. In particular, she does not know what the $\mathbb{H}_i$ or c_i are, nor does she know the probability distribution P which specifies the probabilities $P(\mathbf{e})$ and $P(\omega \mid a, \mathbf{e})$.

We require that u is normalized s.t. $\max_{a \in A} \mathbb{E}[u(O) \mid a] = 0$, where O is the random variable distributed according to the (prior) probability distribution $P(\cdot \mid a)$ that arises from conditioning only on null evidence E^0.

Contracts for Information Elicitation. The principal wants the experts to acquire and honestly report useful information. Since acquiring information is costly, the principal has to set some kind of incentive. If she could observe expended costs, then this problem would be easy: simply reimburse costs and pay some small bonus that is positive affine in the utility obtained by the principal net of the overall reimbursements for the experts' acquisition costs. However, we assume that effort is unobservable to the principal. We furthermore assume that the information obtained is unverifiable.

We will consider a simple class of mechanisms in which the experts only submit (potentially dishonest) reports $\hat{\mathbf{e}}$ on what information they obtained. The principal then takes the best action given $\hat{\mathbf{e}}$, i.e., takes $a_{\hat{\mathbf{e}}} := \arg\max_{a \in A} \mathbb{E}[u(O) \mid \hat{\mathbf{e}}, a]$, where ties are broken arbitrarily and O is the random variable distributed according to $P(\cdot \mid \hat{\mathbf{e}}, a)$. Of course, to determine $a_{\hat{\mathbf{e}}}$ based on $\hat{\mathbf{e}}$, one has to know (at least partially) $P(\cdot \mid \cdot, \hat{\mathbf{e}})$, which so far we have assumed the principal not to know. For example, we could imagine that the experts convene to summarize their evidence into a report that the principal can interpret.

Some authors have allowed the principal to randomize between projects – giving the most probability to the best ones – to have some chance of testing the predictions made for suboptimal actions [7, 27, 28]. Of course, randomization comes at the cost of sometimes taking suboptimal actions. Indeed, our negative results (see Sect. 6 and Theorem 5) can be extended to show that to minimize worst-case regret, the principal must always select the best action given the report.

Finally, each expert i is rewarded only based on the probability distribution resulting from the overall report and the observed outcome, i.e., based on $s_i(P(\cdot \mid \hat{\mathbf{e}}, a_{\hat{\mathbf{e}}}), \omega)$, where s_i is some *scoring rule* or *contract*. Again, we have to imagine that the principal somehow learns about $P(\cdot \mid \hat{\mathbf{e}}, a_{\hat{\mathbf{e}}})$, e.g., by having the experts provide that distribution. Note that the payoff depends only on the prediction about the recommended action $a_{\hat{\mathbf{e}}}$. Other predictions are not tested and it is therefore futile to ask for predictions about them, as pointed out by Othman and Sandholm [22, Theorems 1 and 4] and Chen et al. [7, Theorem 4.1]. It is easy to show that the results of this paper generalize to a setting in which the principal's scoring rule can depend on all of $P(\cdot \mid \hat{\mathbf{e}}, \cdot)$.

More importantly, we assume that the principal scores only according to the aggregated expert report. That is, we assume that the principal does not know the experts' information structure and therefore cannot determine the *relative* value of individual experts' contributions. Similarly, we assume that the principal does not ask the experts for the cost of their information. In principle, in the case of multiple experts (i.e., $n \geq 2$), different kinds of mechanisms could also be considered. In particular, the principal could ask the experts to report on the value and cost of each other's information. However, this will often be unrealistic. For instance, consider the members of a team in a firm. The members of the team may have a good understanding of each other's abilities and contributions as well as of how costly these contributions are to the different members, but the firm will generally not ask the team members to report on these things and instead determine salaries based on relatively little information. (Note that none of these considerations are relevant to the single-expert case.)

The Principal's and Experts' Goals. We assume that the principal accounts for her payments to the experts quasilinearly, so that her overall utility after payments is given by $u(\omega) - \sum_{i=1}^{n} s_i(P(\cdot \mid \hat{\mathbf{e}}, a_{\hat{\mathbf{e}}}), \omega)$.

As for the experts, a configuration of available evidence $\mathbb{H}$ with prior P and costs $(c_i)_{i=1,\dots,n}$, and a (multi-expert) scoring rule $\mathbf{s}$ induce an n-player game played by the experts. Each player's strategy σ_i consists of two parts, one determining which evidence he obtains and one determining how observed evidence is mapped onto reports. Throughout this paper, we use $\mathbf{E} \in \mathbb{H}$ to denote the strategy profile in which each player i obtains and honestly reports E_i. A strategy profile $\boldsymbol{\sigma}$ gives rise to an expected payoff $\mathrm{EU}_\mathbf{s}^i(\boldsymbol{\sigma})$ for expert (or player) i and an expected utility net of payments $\mathrm{EU}_\mathbf{s}(\boldsymbol{\sigma})$ for the principal.

Since the experts play a strategic game, we use Nash equilibrium to describe their behavior. We say that $\boldsymbol{\sigma}$ is a *Nash equilibrium* iff for each i and each alternative strategy σ_i' for i, we have $\mathrm{EU}_\mathbf{s}^i(\boldsymbol{\sigma}) \geq \mathrm{EU}_\mathbf{s}^i(\boldsymbol{\sigma}_{-i}, \sigma_i')$. In general, the game resulting from a configuration and scoring rule will have many equilibria. For $n \geq 2$, it is futile to ask for regret bounds that hold for *all* Nash equilibria. For example, imagine that the value for the principal of $\mathbf{E}$ being obtained is high if $\mathbf{E} = \mathbf{E}^*$ and low otherwise. Imagine further that $c(E_i^*)$ is small but positive for all i. Then in the first-best solution, $\mathbf{E}^*$ is acquired. But, if there are multiple experts, everyone obtaining E^0 (no information) is also a Nash equilibrium with (arbitrarily close to) maximum regret. Throughout the rest of this paper, we therefore ask: what is the regret in the Nash equilibrium that is *best* for the principal? (Cf. the notion of *price of stability* [1, 24, Section 1.3], as opposed to the price of anarchy [18, 23].) Our negative results, of course, are made stronger by the fact that they say that *no* Nash equilibrium can exceed a certain bound. Our positive results, on the other hand, are mostly about a particular kind of Nash equilibria (see Lemma 1) which arise from maximizing the experts' profit.

In what follows, we do not require our scoring rules to be proper, i.e., we do not require that they incentivize the experts to report honestly. However, our results will show that the optimal contract is indeed proper. We do require that our scoring rules satisfy an individual rationality constraint. In particular, we require that each expert i receives an expected payoff of at least 0 in the strategy profile $\mathbf{E}^0 = (E^0, ..., E^0)$ where everyone honestly reports the null information, i.e., we require that for all i, $EU_s^i(\mathbf{E}^0) \geq 0$. Note that this is a fairly weak notion of individual rationality. For instance, it does *not* say that the expected payoff for the expert is nonnegative if others truthfully report non-null information. This makes our negative results stronger. The linear contracts of our positive results will in fact satisfy stronger versions of individual rationality. For instance, they do ensure nonnegative ex-ante expected scores whenever all experts submit information honestly.

3   Competitive Analysis

In this paper, we analyze scoring rules in the style of competitive analysis, a technique for analyzing algorithms that combines two ideas. The first is worst-case analysis. To avoid dependence on some prior probability distribution over, in our case, configurations of costs and available evidence, we consider how a scoring rule performs in the worst case. The second idea of competitive analysis is to consider worst-case expected utility *relative to some benchmark* for the problem. Similar approaches have been used in the literature on principal-expert and -agent problems before [4–6,16].

As is common in principal-agent problems, we use the *first-best solution* as a benchmark, i.e., the utility (net of information acquisition costs) that the principal could obtain if she had full control over the experts and knew everything about the information structure that the experts know. Formally, let $v(\mathbf{E}) := \mathbb{E}_{\mathbf{E}}[\mathbb{E}_O[u(O) \mid a_{\mathbf{E}}, \mathbf{E}]]$ be the expected utility obtained from acquiring $\mathbf{E}$ and then taking the best action according to it. Also, let $c(\mathbf{E}) := \sum_{i=1}^n c_i(E_i)$ be the overall cost of acquiring $\mathbf{E}$. Then the expected utility net of costs of the first-best solution is $EU_{OPT} := \max_{\mathbf{E} \in \mathbb{H}} v(\mathbf{E}) - c(\mathbf{E})$. We will use $\mathbf{E}^*$ to denote a first-best solution itself, i.e., a maximizer of $v(\mathbf{E}) - c(\mathbf{E})$.

There are two ways in which the performance of an algorithm is commonly compared against the benchmark: competitive ratios and regret. Unfortunately, we cannot derive any nontrivial competitive ratio. Consider the case where there is just one expert and only one available piece of evidence E with $v(E) = 1$. Then to be competitive (i.e., to get positive utility at all), if the cost of E is $c(E) = 1 - \epsilon$, the principal has to reward the expert with almost 1. To be reasonably competitive at $c(E) = \epsilon$, on the other hand, she cannot give away anything close to 1. Because the rewards cannot depend on the cost function (which the principal does not know), obtaining a non-trivial competitive ratio is generally impossible, even in the single-expert case. That said, we will give two competitive-ratio-like results (Proposition 2 and Theorem 3) in which EU_{OPT} is replaced with a weaker benchmark.

Our primary focus will be on regret, which is the *difference* between the first-best solution's utility (net of costs) and the utility (net of payments to the experts) achieved by using the scoring rule. So, for any strategy profile σ we define the regret for that strategy profile as $\mathrm{REGRET_s}(\sigma) := \mathrm{EU_{OPT}} - \mathrm{EU_s}(\sigma)$. We will also use $\mathrm{REGRET_s}$ to denote the lowest regret achieved in any Nash equilibrium σ for $\mathbf{s}$, i.e., $\mathrm{REGRET_s} = \min_{\sigma \in \mathbf{NE(s)}} \mathrm{REGRET_s}(\sigma)$. Roughly, the regret is what is sometimes called the agency cost in the literature on principal-agent and -expert problems, or the price of stability in mechanism design [1,24, Sect. 1.3].

4 Linear Contracts

In this paper, we study and justify the use of a particular type of scoring rule: *linear contracts*. For any $\alpha \in (0,1]^n$ with $\sum_{i=1}^n \alpha_i \leq 1$, define the linear scoring rule $\mathbf{q}^\alpha$ as scoring according to $q_j^\alpha(\hat{P}, \omega) = \alpha_j u(\omega)$ for all outcomes ω and reported probability distributions over outcomes $\hat{P}$. That is, each expert receives a fixed fraction of the total payoff generated. Requiring $\alpha_i > 0$ for all i is done for simplicity. All the positive results about linear scoring rules can easily be generalized to linear contracts in which $\alpha_i = 0$ for some i.

Before proceeding with our detailed analysis of linear contracts, it is worth pointing out some immediately obvious and appealing properties. Most importantly, by rewarding according to a positive affine transformation of the principal's utility, they align the experts' interests with the principal's. In contrast, if one were to, say, reward one expert in proportion to $\exp(u(\omega))$, then that expert would sometimes want the principal to take a risky (high variance) rather than a safe action, even if the risky action has lower expected utility. When using linear scoring rules, the only misalignment between experts and principal is that the experts only receive a fraction of the utility obtained and therefore do not value information as highly as the principal would in the first-best solution. Many other desirable properties have been pointed out in the literature; see the discussion of related work in Sect. 8.

From the definition of linear contracts, it is immediately clear that, while they reward the choice of a good action, beyond that they do not reward accurate probabilistic forecasts about the outcome. Because the principal may additionally like to know what to expect for the chosen action, this is an undesirable aspect of linear scoring rules. Note, however, that Oesterheld and Conitzer [21, Sect. 2.5.1] show that linear scoring rules are the only ones which incentivize honest reporting of the best action without incentivizing the expert to sometimes prefer acquiring decision-irrelevant over decision-*relevant* evidence variables.

A more substantial issue with linear contracts is that (in some configurations of available evidence) they violate *ex-interim* individual rationality constraints. After acquiring some piece of evidence E_i, an expert i may come to believe that the expected utility of the principal is negative. Expert i may then wish to withdraw from the mechanism. Also, because utilities can end up being negative, linear contracts cannot be used if the experts are protected by limited liability.

However, these concerns do not apply in cases where the principal always has an option to walk away with utility 0, regardless of the evidence.

5   General Regret and Ratio Bounds for Linear Scoring Rules

In this section, we give positive results about what regret (and competitive ratio-like) bounds linear scoring rules achieve. Because linear contracts do not score experts on their reported beliefs, all of these results carry over to generic principal-agent problems. We start with a lemma on which the subsequent results of this section are based.

Lemma 1. *Let* $\mathbf{q}^{\alpha}$ *be a linear contract. Then for all configurations of available evidence, any*

$$\hat{\mathbf{E}} \in \arg\max_{\mathbf{E} \in \mathbb{H}} v(\mathbf{E}) - \sum_{i=1}^{n} \frac{1}{\alpha_i} c_i(E_i) \tag{1}$$

is a Nash equilibrium of the game induced by $\mathbf{q}^{\alpha}$.

Based on Lemma 1 we now give a bound on the regret of using any linear scoring rule. Let $\alpha_{\min} := \min_i \alpha_i$.

Theorem 1. *For all configurations of available evidence, the Nash equilibria* $\hat{\mathbf{E}}$ *of Lemma 1 satisfy*

$$\mathrm{REGRET}_{\mathbf{q}^{\alpha}} (\hat{\mathbf{E}}) \leq \max \left(\sum_{i=1}^{n} \alpha_i, 1 - \alpha_{\min} \right) v(\mathbf{E}^*). \tag{2}$$

In particular, setting $\alpha_j = 1/(n+1)$ *for all* j *achieves a regret bound of* $\mathrm{REGRET}_{\mathbf{q}^{\alpha}} (\hat{\mathbf{E}}) \leq nv(\mathbf{E}^*)/(n+1)$.

The regret bound $\mathrm{REGRET}_{\mathbf{q}^{\alpha}} (\hat{\mathbf{E}}) \leq nv(\mathbf{E}^*)/(n+1)$ is the best bound that a linear contract can achieve without any assumptions about the configuration of available evidence. One might have hoped for a better bound, at least for larger n. Also, it requires the principal to give each expert a share of the proceeds equal to her own, which means that unless a large fraction of the experts pay an amount close to $v(\mathbf{E}^*)/(n+1)$, regret is generally high. However, we will see (in Sect. 6) that the regret bound is tight not only for linear scoring rules but that no scoring rule can achieve a better bound. We will also consider two ways of making assumptions about the configuration of available evidence to achieve better bounds. One is based on a competitive-ratio-type bound from the literature and is discussed in the rest of this section. The other targets regret and will be the subject of Sect. 7.

Theorem 1 gives a regret bound for a specific equilibrium. It is natural to ask whether this equilibrium is a plausible one. If it was a bad equilibrium for the experts, we might not expect that equilibrium to be played. The first thing to note is that in the case of $n = 1$, there is only one Nash equilibrium, anyway, and in this Nash equilibrium the single expert maximizes his expected profit. For the multi-expert case, notice first that the equilibrium of Lemma 1 explicitly maximizes a term that is closely tied to the experts' expected utility. A more formal point is the following.

Proposition 1. *Let* $\mathbf{q}^\alpha$ *be a linear contract and* $\tilde{\mathbf{E}}$ *be a Nash equilibrium of the game induced by* $\mathbf{q}^\alpha$. *If* $\tilde{\mathbf{E}}$ *is not strongly Pareto-dominated (for the experts) by* $\mathbf{E}^*$, *then* $\tilde{\mathbf{E}}$ *satisfies the regret bound of Ineq. 2.*

Intuitively, this means that if some equilibrium does not satisfy Ineq. 2, then the expert dislikes this equilibrium in the sense of it being strictly Pareto dominated by $\mathbf{E}^*$. Unfortunately, $\mathbf{E}^*$ itself may not be a Nash equilibrium. In fact, it may be that all Nash equilibria of the game induced by $\mathbf{q}^\alpha$ are strictly Pareto-dominated by $\mathbf{E}^*$.

Lemma 1 also gives us the following result, which is a generalization to the multi-expert case of a result shown by Chassang [6, Theorem 1.i] and Carroll [4, Sect. 2.3].

Proposition 2. *For all configurations of available evidence, the Nash equilibria* $\hat{\mathbf{E}}$ *of Lemma 1 for the linear scoring rule* $\mathbf{q}^\alpha$ *satisfy*

$$\mathrm{EU}_{\mathbf{q}^\alpha}(\hat{\mathbf{E}}) \geq \left(1 - \sum_{i=1}^n \alpha_i\right) \max_{\mathbf{E}} \left(v(\mathbf{E}) - \sum_{i=1}^n \frac{1}{\alpha_i} c_i(E_i)\right). \tag{3}$$

Proposition 2 is essentially a competitive-ratio-type result, except that the benchmark is lower than the first-best solution. Chassang [6, Theorem 1.ii] shows how in a single-expert version of this result, the principal can optimize α if she knows a bound on the cost-to-value ratio of information. If information is known to be cheap, then α can be small. Chassang's proof only operates on the $n = 1$ special case of Ineq. 3. A similar line of reasoning applies to our multi-expert setting. Such a result is useful for practical purposes. It also shows how the existing results can be used to give better bounds and recommendations that are to some extent tailored to specific settings. Unfortunately, it seems that if the cost-to-value bounds vary between experts, no succinct expression for the optimal contracts can be given.

6   Unique Optimality of Linear Scoring Rules

Having proven bounds on the regret of linear contracts, the natural next question is: can we do any better by using a different scoring rule? In particular, can we do better by eliciting predictions of what outcome will materialize, in addition to recommendations of what action to take? It is easy to come up with examples of particular prior probability distributions over configurations of available evidence under which the answer is yes. But it turns out that in the worst case and without further assumptions, we cannot get any better regret bounds; moreover, linear contracts are in fact the *only* ones that achieve the optimal regret bound in general. This is true even if the principal knows the pre-cost expected utility $v(\mathbf{E}^*)$ of the information acquired in the first-best solution.

Theorem 2. *Let* $0 < H < \max_{\omega \in \Omega} u(\omega)$ *and let* **s** *be a scoring rule. Then if for all configurations with* $v(\mathbf{E}^*) = H$, $\text{REGRET}_\mathbf{s} \leq nH/(n+1)$, *then it must be that for all* $j = 1, ..., m$, $s_j(\hat{P}, \omega) = u(\omega)/(n+1)$, *whenever* $\omega \in \text{supp}(\hat{P})$. *There is no scoring rule* **s** *s.t. for all configurations,* $\text{REGRET}_\mathbf{s} < nH/(n+1)$.

We briefly give a sketch of the proof, which consists of two parts. In the first part, we identify "critical cases" for any **s**, i.e., a small set of classes of configurations on which the bound is tight and which together determine s_j to be the hypothesized linear scoring rule. One critical case is that in which $v(\mathbf{E}^*) = H$ and $\mathbf{E}^*$ is in fact free to acquire. To keep regret low in this case, the principal has to make sure that she does not give away too much. Overall, she can only give away $nH/(n+1)$ in expectation. The other critical case is that in which $v(\mathbf{E}^*) = H$ and in $\mathbf{E}^*$ exactly one expert j acquires information at a price of $H/(n+1) - \epsilon$. To achieve low regret in these cases, the principal must make sure that whenever an expectation of H is achieved, any expert j receives an expected payoff of at least $H/(n+1)$ (or, gets at least $H/(n+1)$ more than it gets for reporting the prior). The critical cases together imply that if information $\mathbf{E}^*$ with value $v(\mathbf{E}^*) = H$ is acquired, each expert receives an expected payoff of $H/(n+1)$ (and that if the prior is reported, each expert receives an expected payoff of 0). The second part of the proof shows that this (across all possible $\mathbf{E}^*$ with $v(\mathbf{E}^*) = H$) implies that s_j is as claimed in the theorem. Roughly, in this part we show that the scoring rule must be linear, using the fact that the expected payoff is constant across different distributions with the same mean.

The different aspects of this result depend on the details of our setup to different extents. The result that worst-case regret is $nH/(n+1)$ generalizes far beyond our setting. In particular, even if the principal knows the experts' information structure, there will still be cases with regret $nH/(n+1)$ if the principal cannot obtain reliable information about the different experts' costs of acquisition. The uniqueness of linear scoring rules in minimizing worst-case regret, on the other hand, does hinge on our assumption that the principal does not know the information structure. With knowledge of the specific information structure, the principal can use very different contracts. As a straightforward example, if it is known that one expert cannot obtain sufficiently useful information, the scoring rule need not pay that expert at all.

A result analogous to Theorem 2 holds true for the competitive ratio-based bound and can be proven with very similar ideas.

Theorem 3. *Let* $\boldsymbol{\alpha} \in (0,1)^n$ *with* $\sum_{j=1}^n \alpha_j < 1$ *and* **s** *be a scoring rule. Then if for all configurations there is Nash equilibrium* $\hat{\mathbf{E}}$

$$\text{EU}_\mathbf{s}(\hat{\mathbf{E}}) \geq \left(1 - \sum_{i=1}^n \alpha_i\right) \max_\mathbf{E} \left(v(\mathbf{E}) - \sum_{i=1}^n \frac{1}{\alpha_i} c_i(E_i)\right), \tag{4}$$

then it must be the case that for all $j = 1, ..., m$, $s_j(\hat{P}, \omega) = \alpha_i u(\omega)$, whenever $\omega \in \text{supp}(\hat{P})$. There is no scoring rule $\mathbf{s}$ s.t. Ineq. 4 is always strict.

7 Restrictions on the Configurations of Available Evidence

In this section we consider a setting in which the principal is assumed to have a particular type of knowledge about the configuration of available evidence (similar to Chassang's [6, Theorem 1.ii] result, mentioned at the end of Sect. 5). With this we would like to show that (as one would expect) under stronger assumptions, substantially better bounds can be derived. Perhaps more importantly, it shows that the strategy in the proof of Theorem 2 of using critical cases to derive linear contracts and their optimality generalizes to settings with additional assumptions.

Arguably, much of the reason why our general bound is not better than it is that we do not know who has access to decision-relevant information. While we use the term "experts", we allow for configurations in which almost all of the "experts" cannot acquire decision-relevant information at a reasonable cost. Indeed, these cases drive the proof of Theorem 2. In many real-world settings, the principal is able to select a set of experts who all can acquire relevant information. We will model this by introducing the assumption that all experts have access to the same set of evidence variables – though note that of this set each expert can still only obtain one element.

Assumption 1. $\mathbb{H}_1 = \mathbb{H}_2 = ... = \mathbb{H}_n$.

Furthermore, we assume that there is some known bound on how much acquisition costs differ.

Assumption 2. There is some known $\Lambda \in (0, 1]$ such that for any two experts i, j and non-trivial evidence variables E_i, E_j we have $c_j(E_j) > 0$ and $\Lambda \leq c_i(E_i)/c_j(E_j)$.

If $\Lambda = 1$, then all experts pay the exact same price for all pieces of information. If Λ is small, then some experts may be able to acquire information much cheaper than others. Note that Assumption 2 not only restricts how costs differ between experts but also between different evidence variables (both across experts and for a single expert).

We add another assumption:

Assumption 3. For all vectors of information $\mathbf{E} \in \mathbb{H}$ and any expert i, we have $v(\mathbf{E}_{-i}) \in \{0, v(\mathbf{E})\}$.

Roughly, this means that any set of evidence variables is either fully complementary (in which case $v(\mathbf{E}_{-i}) = 0$ for all i that acquire non-trivial information) or has some redundant piece of information (in which case $v(\mathbf{E}_{-i}) = v(\mathbf{E})$ for some i). There are some settings in which such an assumption is (at least approximately) natural. For instance, we may imagine that the principal and experts are morally or legally obliged to pay due diligence and cannot pursue projects unless they are fully researched. In the context of this paper, another reason we consider this assumption is that it allows for an equilibrium analysis that is more powerful than that of Lemma 1.

As before (Sects. 5 and 6), we first provide the positive result. That is, we show that a particular linear scoring rule achieves a particular regret bound. We then show (Theorem 5) that this scoring rule is optimal and the only one that achieves the given regret bound. It turns out that in this case the optimal scoring rule is much harder to guess. We hope that the proof sketch of Theorem 5 makes clear where its parameters come from.

Theorem 4. *Let $n \in \mathbb{N}$ be the number of experts. Given Assumptions 1 to 3, define*

$$B_{\Lambda,n} := 1 - \frac{1}{1 + \sum_{i=1}^{n} \frac{1}{1+(i-1)\Lambda}}. \tag{5}$$

and for $j = 1, ..., n$

$$\alpha_j = \frac{1}{(1 + (j-1)\Lambda)\left(1 + \sum_{i=1}^{n} \frac{1}{1+(i-1)\Lambda}\right)}. \tag{6}$$

Then, $\mathrm{REGRET}_{\mathbf{q}^\alpha} \leq B_{\Lambda,n} v(\mathbf{E}^*)$.

We now prove that the scoring rule of Theorem 4 is the only one that achieves its regret bound. Our strategy is the same as the strategy behind the proof of Theorem 2 and the omitted proof of Theorem 3. Very roughly, the idea is as follows. For any given linear contract q^α, we guess the cases where the regret is highest. The first such case is – as in the proof of Theorem 2 – the one in which information is free to the experts and regret is entirely a result of the principal having to give away some fraction of her profits that she can keep in the first-best solution. Second, there is a critical case for each $k = 1, ..., n$, in which k pieces of information are needed and the expert i with the k-th highest α_i cannot quite afford a relevant piece of information. One can then find the given bound and parameters of the linear contract by minimizing worst-case regret across these cases. Using these cases, one can prove as in the proof of Theorem 2 that to obtain the bound, one has to use this linear rule.

Theorem 5. *Let $0 < H < \max_{\omega \in \Omega} u(\omega)$, and $\mathbf{s}$ be a scoring rule. Then, if for all configurations with $v(\mathbf{E}^*) = H$ that satisfy Assumptions 1 to 3, we have $\mathrm{REGRET}_{\mathbf{s}} \leq B_{\Lambda,n} H$, then – up to permutation of the experts – for all $j = 1, ..., m$: $s_j(\hat{P}, \omega) = \alpha_j u(\omega)$ whenever $\omega \in \mathrm{supp}(\hat{P})$, where the α_j are as defined in Eq. 6. There is no scoring rule $\mathbf{s}$ s.t. $\mathrm{REGRET}_{\mathbf{s}} < B_{\Lambda,n} H$ for all configurations.*

If $\Lambda = 0$, then $B_{\Lambda,n} = n/(n+1)$ and $\alpha_j = 1/(n+1)$ for $j = 1, ..., n$. That is, as the restriction on the cost ratios becomes vacuous, the optimal bound and scoring rule approach the optimal *general* bound and scoring rule of Theorems 1 and 2. If $\Lambda = 1$ (i.e., all costs are the same), then $B_{\Lambda,n} = h_n/(h_n + 1)$ and $\alpha_j = 1/((h_n + 1)j)$, where $h_n = \sum_{i=1}^{n} 1/i$ is the n-th harmonic number.

Note that even though – for all the principal knows – the experts are all identical, the minimum-regret contract varies the numbers of shares in the project given to different experts. Theorem 5 therefore provides another (and quite different) demonstration of a point made by Winter [26], who shows that the optimal reward structure for a principal-(multi-)agent problem sometimes has to treat identical agents differently. To understand why in our setting optimal rewards are asymmetric despite symmetry between agents, consider only the cases where $\Lambda = 1$, i.e., where all experts pay exactly the same price for all pieces of information. Consider the question of how many experts we should give enough shares to overcome some given acquisition cost of c. If that number is k, then our worst-case regret at cost c from no information being acquired is $H - (k + 1)c$ and occurs in the case where $k + 1$ pieces of information (all at cost c) are needed. Since this number decreases with k, giving k experts sufficiently many shares to outweigh a cost of a sufficiently large c at some point becomes non-critical for minimizing regret. Given regret considerations in other cases (in particular the one where all information is essentially free), the minimum-regret value of k will therefore be smaller than n but bigger than 0 for many values of c.

8 Related Work

The most closely related strand of literature is that on principal-expert (and more generally principal-agent) problems. Our results merely concern one of many possible variants of and approaches to such problems. For example, much of the literature on principal-expert problems differs from the present work in that they do not let the expert submit (or reveal by selection of a contract from a contract menu) any information apart from a recommendation. We are not the first to approach the problem from a worst-case perspective [4–6,16]; but many others have derived very different kinds of results without the worst-case assumption, for instance by considering specific (types of) distributions or other restrictions [2,8,12,14,19,25,27]. Also, many papers have richer problem representations and specialized foci on issues that do not arise in the present framework. For instance, most authors take into account that the expert is protected by limited liability. With a few exceptions [2,13], existing work only considers settings with a single expert. While, as we have noted, some of our results can be seen as generalizations of corresponding single-expert results (one of which – Proposition 2 – was already given in the literature for the single-expert case), Sect. 7 discusses issues that are very specific to the multi-expert case. To our knowledge, our main optimality arguments (the proofs of Theorems 2, 3 and 5) and most of our results are also unique. At the same time, our results support other work which has aimed to discuss and explain the use of linear contracts [4–6,10,11,16,21,25, Sect. 2.5.1].

In mechanism design, a few authors have worked to characterize scoring rules that incentivize experts to honestly report *existing* (or free) decision-relevant information [7,21,22]. The setups of these papers do not give any objective that allows one to identify particular scoring rules as optimal; they allow for rewards of tiny scale (say, giving the experts a trillionth of the principal's profit).

The introduction of information acquisition costs into the model forces the use of nontrivial rewards, and allows us to ask meaningful questions about what scoring rule is optimal. Overcoming acquisition costs is one way to introduce a target for optimization among scoring rules that gives a reason to give larger-scale scores. The same can be achieved by introducing conflicts of interest that arise if the expert has (contrary to the setup of this paper) an intrinsic interest in the principal's decision. The expert may have an incentive to misreport (or not report anything if information is verifiable) to make the principal take the *expert's* (rather than the principal's) favorite option [3,9,15,20]; cf. the literature on Bayesian persuasion [17].

9   Conclusion

We have shown how competitive analysis can be used to derive the optimality of particular linear contracts in principal-expert problems. We demonstrated that when adding specific assumptions about the structure and cost of available information, the analysis can also provide optimal scoring rules for specific settings. The optimal scoring rules in all of these settings give away a substantial fraction of the principal's profit. The present work therefore motivates the use of more complicated mechanisms when dealing with multiple experts. For instance, the principal may look to save money by asking the experts to reveal each other's costs of acquisition. Can similar arguments as in this paper then still be used to justify the use of linear scoring rules? Further, it is worth asking what the cost of the worst-case simplification is: how much better can we do if the principal formulates a prior over configurations of available evidence and optimizes the expected utility over the set of contracts [2,8,19,25]?

Acknowledgments. We are thankful for comments from our anonymous reviewers and support from NSF under award IIS-1814056.

References

1. Anshelevich, E., Dasgupta, A., Kleinberg, J., Éva Tardos, Wexler, T., Roughgarden, T.: The price of stability for network design with fair cost allocation. SIAM J. Comput. **38**(4), 1602–1623 (2008)
2. Barron, J.M., Waddell, G.R.: Executive rank, pay and project selection. J. Financ. Econ. **67**, 305–349 (2003)
3. Boutilier, C.: Eliciting forecasts from self-interested experts: scoring rules for decision makers. In: Winikoff, C., van der Hoek, P. (eds.) Proceedings of the 11th International Conference on Autonomous Agents and Multiagent Systems, Richland, South Carolina, pp. 737–744 (2012)
4. Carroll, G.: Robustness and linear contracts. Am. Econ. Rev. **105**(2), 536–563 (2015)
5. Carroll, G.: Robust incentives for information acquisition. J. Econ. Theory **181**, 382–420 (2019)
6. Chassang, S.: Calibrated incentive contracts. Econometrica **81**(5), 1935–1971 (2013)

7. Chen, Y., Kash, I.A., Ruberry, M., Shnayder, V.: Eliciting predictions and recommendations for decision making. ACM Trans. Econ. Comput. **2**(2), 6:1–6:27 (2014)
8. Core, J.E., Qian, J.: Project selection, production, uncertainty, and incentives (2002). https://doi.org/10.2139/ssrn.297461
9. Crawford, V.P., Sobel, J.: Strategic information transmission. Econometrica 50(6), 1431–1451 (1982)
10. Diamond, P.: Managerial incentives: on the near linearity of optimal compensation. J. Polit. Econ. **106**(5), 931–957 (1998)
11. Dütting, P., Roughgarden, T., Talgam-Cohen, I.: Simple versus optimal contracts. In: Proceedings of the 2019 ACM Conference on Economics and Computation, New York, pp. 369–387 (2019)
12. Feess, E., Walzl, M.: Delegated expertise - when are good projects bad news? Econ. Lett. **82**(1), 77–82 (2004)
13. Gromb, D., Martimort, D.: Collusion and the organization of delegated expertise. J. Econ. Theory **137**(1), 271–299 (2007)
14. Häfner, S., Taylor, C.R.: On young turks and yes men: Optimal contracting for advice (2019). https://doi.org/10.2139/ssrn.3229927
15. Holmström, B.: On the theory of delegation. Discussion Papers 438, Northwestern University, Center for Mathematical Studies in Economics and Management Science (1980). https://ideas.repec.org/p/nwu/cmsems/438.html
16. Hurwicz, L., Shapiro, L.: Incentive structures maximizing residual gain under incomplete information. Technical report, pp. 77–83 (1977). https://conservancy.umn.edu/bitstream/handle/11299/54918/1977-83.pdf
17. Kamenica, E., Gentzkow, M.: Bayesian persuasion. Am. Econ. Rev. **101**, 2590–2615 (2011)
18. Koutsoupias, E., Papadimitriou, C.: Worst-case equilibria. In: Meinel, C., Tison, S. (eds.) STACS 1999. LNCS, vol. 1563, pp. 404–413. Springer, Heidelberg (1999). https://doi.org/10.1007/3-540-49116-3_38
19. Lambert, R.A.: Executive effort and selection of risky projects. RAND J. Econ. **17**(1), 77–88 (1986)
20. Milgrom, P., Roberts, J.: Relying on the information of interested parties. RAND J. Econ. **17**(1), 18–32 (1986)
21. Oesterheld, C., Conitzer, V.: Eliciting information for decision making from individual and multiple experts (2019). https://users.cs.duke.edu/~ocaspar/DecisionScoringRules.pdf. Short version appeared in WINE 2020
22. Othman, A., Sandholm, T.: Decision rules and decision markets. In: Proceedings of the 9th International Conference on Autonomous Agents and Multiagent Systems, pp. 625–632 (2010)
23. Papadimitriou, C.H.: Algorithms, games, and the internet. In: Talk at STOC 2001, Hersonissos, Crete, Greece, 6-8 July 2001 (2001)
24. Roughgarden, T., Tardos, É.: Introduction to the inefficiency of equilibria. In: Nisan, N., Roughgarden, T., Tardos, É., Vazirani, V.V. (eds.) Algorithmic Game Theory, Chap. 17, pp. 443–459. Cambridge University Press, Cambridge (2007)
25. Stoughton, N.M.: Moral hazard and the portfolio management problem. J. Finance **48**(5), 2009–2028 (1993)
26. Winter, E.: Incentives and discrimination. Am. Econ. Rev. **94**(3), 764–773 (2004)
27. Zermeño, L.: A principal-expert model and the value of menus (2011). http://economics.mit.edu/files/7299
28. Zermeño, L.: The role of authority in a general principal-expert model (2012). http://economics.mit.edu/files/7627

Bayesian Repeated Zero-Sum Games with Persistent State, with Application to Security Games

Vincent Conitzer[1], Yuan Deng[1(✉)], and Shaddin Dughmi[2]

[1] Duke University, Durham, USA
{conitzer,ericdy}@cs.duke.edu
[2] University of Southern California, Los Angeles, USA
shaddin@usc.edu

Abstract. We study infinitely-repeated two-player zero-sum games with one-sided private information and a persistent state. Here, only one of the two players learns the state of the repeated game. We consider two models: either the state is chosen by nature, or by one of the players. For the former, the equilibrium of the repeated game is known to be equivalent to that of a one-shot public signaling game, and we make this equivalence algorithmic. For the latter, we show equivalence to one-shot team max-min games, and also provide an algorithmic reduction. We apply this framework to repeated zero-sum security games with private information on the side of the defender and provide an almost complete characterization of their computational complexity.

Keywords: Bayesian repeated game · Equilibrium characterization · Equilibrium computation · Computational complexity

1 Introduction

Private information can give one a strategic advantage over other players in a game. However, if play is repeated, then taking advantage of one's private information through one's actions risks leaking that information and thereby the advantage. This is nicely illustrated in the movie *The Imitation Game*, in which British intelligence, having cracked the *Enigma* code, strategically decides not to act on some of its information, in order to preserve its informational advantage [12]. Less dramatically, consider a buyer and a seller that interact repeatedly. The seller has a higher-quality and a lower-quality version of the item for sale, and offers these at different prices. The buyer may, at the current prices, prefer the higher-quality version – but worry that choosing this option will reveal her (persistently) high valuation/type, causing the seller to raise prices in the future, and therefore choose the cheaper low-quality version instead.

V. Conitzer—Supported by NSF Award IIS-1814056.
S. Dughmi—Supported by NSF CAREER Award CCF-1350900.

In equilibrium, to what extent should a party with an informational advantage refrain from acting on this information? This is the question we set out to address in this paper. It is, in its most general form, a challenging question to answer. The state of the game may change over time; there may be a multiplicity of equilibria; the discount factor matters; and so on. Thus, answering the question in general would require us to simultaneously resolve a number of fundamental questions in (algorithmic) game theory. In this paper, in order to stay focused on the question at hand, we focus on the following special case:

- The state of the game is *persistent*, i.e., it does not change over time (the game is repeated rather than stochastic).
- Only one player has private information, and it does not change.
- The game is two-player and zero-sum.
- Each agent cares about their long-term average payoff.

Even in this setting, it is easy to see that the optimal answer is in general not one of the two extremes – either exploit information fully, or never use it. Some information may not be actionable for the adversary so that one can simply take advantage of it and not worry about revealing it. On the other hand, for other information, it is possible that the adversary would be able to make even better use of it than the initially better-informed player. In that case, the benefits of getting to use the information for one round, without the adversary being able to use it in that particular round, will be completely wiped out by the infinitely many remaining rounds in which the adversary can use the information better.

The technical and conceptual foundations for the study of repeated games of incomplete information with persistent state were laid by [2]. They consider a persistent state of the game drawn by nature from a common prior, and agents who receive private signals regarding this state. [14] provides an in-depth accounting of the special case of this model with two players and zero-sum payoffs. The aforementioned texts reveal that the even-more-special case we consider, that of repeated two-player zero-sum games with one-sided private information, admits an essentially-unique equilibrium (in the sense of payoff equivalence) with an elegant, simple, and instructive characterization which is robust to modeling assumptions. In particular, the equilibrium of the repeated two-player game is equivalent, in a precise technical sense, to the equilibrium of a one-shot *public signaling game* with three players. Moreover, this characterization is robust to how one chooses to model long-term payoffs; say through using a discount factor, taking the limit of the finite repeated game as the number of stages grows to infinity, or considering the infinite game directly. Even mild generalizations of this special case, for example to more players, non-zero-sum payoffs, or incomplete information on both sides, lead to the collapse of this characterization, and such settings are not yet fully understood to the best of our knowledge. This further cements our model as the timely choice for algorithmic study.

1.1   Our Contributions

We examine repeated two-player zero-sum games with one-sided private information from the perspective of algorithmic game theory, both in general and as exemplified by application to the influential domain of security games [16]. We consider both the case when the state is drawn by nature—this is the classical model in [2,14]—as well as a natural, and to our knowledge novel, variant in which the (typically randomized) state is chosen by one of the players, who is therefore the informed party. We refer to this variant as the *allocation* model.

The domain-agnostic part of the paper is organized as follows. For the classical model, where the game state is drawn by nature, we first provide (a) our own exposition of the previously-described equilibrium characterization in terms of one-shot public signaling games, one that is particularly tailored to an algorithmic game theory audience and makes explicit the connection to recent work on public signaling games (e.g., [6–8]). Then, we turn to our novel contributions. We provide (b) an efficient reduction to equilibrium computation in the related one-shot public signaling game to make the equilibrium characterization constructive. For the allocation model, where one of the players determines the (persistent) state, we provide (a') a characterization of the equilibrium of the repeated game as equivalent, in a precise technical sense, to the equilibrium of a one-shot three-player *team max-min game*, as first studied by [15]; (b') an efficient reduction to computing the equilibrium of the associated team max-min game. We note that, in both (b) and (b'), the uninformed player's strategy is particularly nontrivial, and involves efficiently solving a related instance of *Blackwell's approachability* [1,4]. We also note that the reductions in (b) and (b') are "reversible", since both the repeated game and the associated one-shot game share the same game value. Finally, we (c) show that the allocation model is computationally easier than the classical model by way of a polynomial time reduction. We note that this is not reversible, and the complexity relationship is strict, as evidenced by our results for security games which we describe next.

We then examine repeated zero-sum security games with private information on the side of the defender. In the security games we consider, the state is a deployment of "treasures" to "locations", a defender strategy is a deployment of "defensive resources" to the locations, and the attacker's strategy is a location to attack. Such security games are particularly versatile exemplars for both the classical and allocation models of repeated games with persistent state. The classical model abstracts challenges faced in recent applications to environmental protection [9,17,18], where the locations of environmental assets (the treasures) are determined by nature and slow to change over time. The allocation model can be applied to armed conflict scenarios in which supply-chain assets (the treasures) must be deployed covertly to locations early on in the conflict, and can not be easily moved from stage to stage. We show that the classical model of repeated security games is strongly NP-hard even when treasures, locations, and defensive resources are homogeneous. A more nuanced picture emerges for the allocation model of repeated security games: the fully homogeneous case is tractable, as is the case where only the treasures are heterogeneous. The fully heterogeneous case is strongly NP-hard. Remaining cases are either weakly or strongly NP-hard, and we provide an almost complete accounting of the computational complexity of all combinations.

2   Preliminaries

2.1   One-Shot Games

A one-shot two-player zero-sum game of complete information is described by a utility function $\mathcal{U} : S_1 \times S_2 \to \mathbb{R}$, where S_i is the family of *pure strategies* for player i, and $\mathcal{U}(s_1, s_2)$ is the utility of player 1 when player 1 plays $s_1 \in S_1$ and player 2 plays $s_2 \in S_2$. Implicitly, the utility of player 2 is $-\mathcal{U}(s_1, s_2)$. A *mixed strategy* for player i is $s_i \in \Delta(S_i)$, where $\Delta(S_i)$ is the set of distributions over S_i. A one-shot two-player Bayesian zero-sum game with incomplete information on one side $\left(\Pi, \{\mathcal{U}^\theta\}_{\theta \in \Theta} \right)$ is given by: (1) pure strategy sets S_1 and S_2 for players 1 and 2 respectively; (2) a family Θ of *states of nature*; (3) for each state $\theta \in \Theta$, a one-shot two-player zero-sum game of complete information $\mathcal{U}^\theta$; and (4) a *prior distribution* Π over states of nature Θ.

In such a game, nature draws θ from Θ according to the prior Π and then player 1 learns the state θ while player 2 is uninformed about the state. Both players simultaneously choose their strategies s_i (while s_1 can depend on θ but s_2 cannot), which results in a utility of $\mathcal{U}^\theta(s_1, s_2)$ to player 1 and $-\mathcal{U}^\theta(s_1, s_2)$ to player 2. Moreover, given a distribution Π over Θ, we denote by $\mathcal{U}^\Pi$ the game induced by Π such that player 1's payoff is $\mathcal{U}^\Pi(s_1, s_2) = \sum_{\theta \in \Theta} \Pi(\theta) \cdot \mathcal{U}^\theta(s_1, s_2)$. We restrict attention to games where Θ, S_1, S_2 are finite, or at least compact. All *mixed* Nash equilibria of such a game are payoff equivalent to the Nash equilibrium in which each player employs their maximin mixed strategy [11].

2.2   Bayesian Repeated Games

We now describe the classical model of Bayesian repeated games that we consider, henceforth just *Bayesian repeated games* for convenience. Here, a Bayesian zero-sum game is repeated infinitely many times, with incomplete information on one side. We call the one-shot game the *stage game*, and refer to each iteration as a *stage*. We replicate the standard assumptions made by [2,14], as follows. We assume that the state of nature is *persistent*: it does not change from stage to stage.[1] Moreover, we assume that players observe each others' pure strategies after each stage, but do not observe the payoffs directly. This assumption is necessary for the model to be interesting: If players can observe the payoffs directly, then the uncertainty in the game is superfluous, as players can eventually reconstruct relevant entries of the game matrix and the state of nature. Obscuring

---

[1] If the state of nature is drawn afresh at each stage, then repetition is superfluous for a zero-sum game: the folk theorem and minimax theorem imply that repeating the minimax equilibrium at each stage is the essentially unique equilibrium of the repeated game (up to payoff equivalence).

payoffs in this manner can be viewed as abstracting a situation where payoffs are delayed till the end of the (long, many stage) game. Formally, given a two-player Bayesian zero-sum stage game $G_{\texttt{repeated}} = \left(\Pi, \{\mathcal{U}^\theta\}_{\theta \in \Theta} \right)$ as described above, the Bayesian repeated game proceeds as follows:

1. θ is drawn by nature from Π and player 1 learns θ while player 2 does not;
2. The stage game $\mathcal{U}^\theta$ is repeated infinitely many times. After each stage, each player observes the pure strategy played by the other player, but does not directly observe the utility gained.

A *history* of play with T stages $H_T = \left((s_1^1, s_2^1), (s_2^2, s_2^2), \ldots, (s_1^T, s_2^T) \right)$ is a finite sequence, where s_i^t is player i's pure strategy at stage t. For convenience, we will use the vectorized form without superscript $s_i = (s_i^1, \cdots, s_i^T)$ to represent the strategy of player i. A pure strategy for player 1 in the repeated game is a function which maps the state θ and an observed history H to player 1's strategy in the next stage of the repeated game, while a pure strategy for player 2 simply maps the observed history H to player 2's strategy in the next stage. A mixed strategy is naturally a distribution over such functions.

2.3   Bayesian Allocation Games

In addition to classical Bayesian repeated games, we introduce a novel variant, the *Bayesian allocation game*, in which the distribution Π of the states is determined by player 1 instead of the nature. Formally, given one-shot games $G_{\texttt{alloc}} = \left(\{\mathcal{U}^\theta\}_{\theta \in \Theta} \right)$, the Bayesian allocation game proceeds as follows:

1. Player 1 selects a prior Π over Θ that player 2 cannot observe;
2. θ is drawn by nature from Π and player 1 learns θ while player 2 does not;
3. The stage game $\mathcal{U}^\theta$ is repeated infinitely many times. After each stage, each player observes the pure strategy played by the other player, but does not directly observe the utility gained.

In the Bayesian allocation game, in addition to choosing the actions to play at each stage, player 1's strategy also includes a choice of the prior $\Pi \in \Delta(\Theta)$.

2.4   Utility and Equilibrium Model

We consider the utility/equilibrium models deduced from the infinitely-repeated game perspective for agents that are interested in their long-term payoffs. Each player's expected utility is the limit, as $T \to \infty$, of his average expected utility over the first T stages alone. Though this limit may not exist in general, we can nevertheless define a value and equilibrium as in [2,14]. The max-min value of the game is the supremum over all player 1's mixed strategies, of the infimum over player 2's mixed strategies, of the limit infimum as $T \to \infty$ of player 1's average expected utility. Player 1's max-min strategy is that attaining this supremum. We can similarly define the min-max value of the game and Player 2's min-max strategy. When both the max-min and min-max values are equal we refer to them as the value of the game, and the corresponding max-min and min-max strategies form the equilibrium. For a Bayesian repeated game G_{repeated} and a Bayesian allocation game G_{alloc}, we denote their game value by $\nu_{\text{repeated}}(G_{\text{repeated}})$ and $\nu_{\text{alloc}}(G_{\text{alloc}})$, respectively. Several other natural utility/equilibrium models are equivalent to this one, and we defer the detailed discussions to the full version.

Example 1. Consider a zero-sum security game with 3 identical locations (denoted by ℓ_A, ℓ_B, ℓ_C) and 2 identical treasures, in which the defender can defend 1 location. The defender determines how to allocate the treasures to the locations (once) and how to defend them (every round). The attacker earns one unit of payoff if she attacks an undefended location with a treasure, and zero otherwise. For comparison, in the one-shot Bayesian allocation game (i.e., if there is only a single round), it is straightforward to verify that the optimal strategy for the defender is to allocate two treasures uniformly at random, and for each realization, defend each of the two locations with a treasure with probability $\frac{1}{2}$, leading to an expected payoff $\frac{1}{3}$ for the attacker. However, it turns out that in the infinitely-repeated version, an optimal strategy (unique up to symmetries) to allocate the treasures for the defender is as follows:

- Allocate a treasure to ℓ_A with probability 1;
- Allocate the remaining treasure to ℓ_B with probability $\alpha = \frac{\sqrt{5}-1}{2} \approx 0.618$ and to ℓ_C with probability $1 - \alpha = \frac{3-\sqrt{5}}{2} \approx 0.382$.

In each stage of the repeated game, the defender defends ℓ_A with probability α (so that the attacker's utility of attacking this location is $1 - \alpha$), and defends ℓ_B with probability $1 - \alpha$ (so that the attacker's utility of attacking this location is $\alpha^2 = 1 - \alpha$). The defender never defends ℓ_C (so that the attacker's utility for attacking this target is also $1 - \alpha$).

The above example illustrates a fundamental difference between a one-shot Bayesian allocation game and its infinitely-repeated counterpart. In the one-shot version, the optimal strategy for the defender correlates the allocation and the defensive strategy, and thus, the game is reduced to a two-player zero-sum normal-form game so that the minimax theorem can be applied. However, in the infinitely-repeated version, we will show that in the equilibrium, the allocation of treasures and the defensive strategy are *independent*, as in the example above. In other words, there exists no benefit for the defender to correlate the allocation and the defensive strategy in the infinitely-repeated Bayesian allocation game. Note that the attacker's payoff is larger in the infinitely-repeated version as $1 - \alpha = \frac{3-\sqrt{5}}{2} > \frac{1}{3}$. Intuitively, this is because the attacker can observe the defender's historical defensive actions in the infinitely-repeated game. This is disadvantageous for the defender: either the defensive actions over time give away where the treasures are, or these actions have to be chosen in such a way that they do not, which is a costly constraint. We also emphasize that the game value is an irrational number, demonstrating that the infinitely-repeated Bayesian allocation game cannot be solved by a linear program.

3   Reductions from Repeated Games to One-Shot Games

In this section, we discuss the relationship between one-shot games and both our models of infinitely repeated games, so that one can solve the infinitely repeated game by first solving the corresponding one-shot game. The equivalence between classical Bayesian repeated games and public signaling games has already been shown by [2] and [14]; for completeness, we will fully elaborate on this equivalence first in Sect. 3.1. This will set the stage for our novel results on the equivalence between Bayesian allocation games and team max-min games (Sect. 3.2), and on the computational complexity of both models (Sect. 3.3). The omitted proofs in this paper are deferred to the full version.

3.1   Equivalence Between Bayesian Repeated Games and Public Signaling Games (Reproducing Known Results)

We begin with reproducing the known result relating the classical model of Bayesian repeated games to public signaling games [2,14].

Definition 1 (Public Signaling Game [6–8]). *Consider a one-shot two-player zero-sum game* $G_{signal} = \left(\Pi, \{\mathcal{U}^\theta\}_{\theta \in \Theta}\right)$ *where players a-priori know nothing about* θ *besides its prior* Π*. We consider a credible principal who is privy to the realization of* θ*. The principal designs a* public signaling scheme*: a randomized function* $\varphi : \Theta \to \Delta(\Sigma)$ *mapping states of nature to an abstract set of signals* Σ*. The order of events is as follows:*

- *The principal commits to* φ*;*
- *The nature draws* $\theta \sim \Pi$ *and the principal learns* θ*;*
- *The principal invokes the signaling scheme to obtain a signal* $\sigma \sim \varphi(\theta)$*;*
- *Both players learn* σ*, and update their beliefs about the state* θ*, denoted as* $\Pi_{\varphi,\sigma}$*, according to the Bayes' rule:* $\Pi_{\varphi,\sigma}(\theta) = \frac{\mathbf{Pr}[\varphi(\theta)=\sigma] \cdot \Pi(\theta)}{\sum_{\theta' \in \Theta} \mathbf{Pr}[\varphi(\theta')=\sigma] \cdot \Pi(\theta')}$*.*
- *Players play the equilibrium strategies in the zero-sum game* $\mathcal{U}^{\Pi_{\varphi,\sigma}}$*.*

We assume that the principal designs φ *so as to maximize player 1's expected utility, the maximum value of which, denoted by* $\nu_{signal}(G_{signal})$*, is the game value of the public signaling game.*

It turns out the equilibrium in Bayesian repeated games corresponds to the solution of the above signaling problem in a precise sense, stated below [2,14].

Theorem 1. $\nu_{repeated}(G_{repeated}) = \nu_{signal}(G_{signal})$ *when* $G_{repeated} = G_{signal}$*.*

We will prove Theorem 1 by constructing the equilibrium strategy s_1^*, s_2^* for player 1 and 2, respectively in the Bayesian repeated game $G_{repeated}$ from the solution of the public signaling game G_{signal}. For convenience, in the Bayesian repeated game, we will refer to player 1 (the informed player) as the *leader* and player 2 (the uninformed player) as the *follower*.

In particular, we will show that in the Bayesian repeated game G_{repeated}, if the leader plays strategy s_1^*, then no matter how the follower reacts, the leader can guarantee himself an average utility at least the game value $\nu_{\text{signal}}(G_{\text{signal}})$ in the public signaling game G_{signal} over the first T stages as $T \to \infty$. On the other hand, if the follower plays strategy s_2^*, then no matter how the leader reacts, the follower can guarantee the leader an average utility at most $\nu_{\text{signal}}(G_{\text{signal}})$ over the first T stages as $T \to \infty$.

Lemma 1. *When $G_{\text{repeated}} = G_{\text{signal}}$, in the Bayesian repeated game G_{repeated}, consider the following strategy for the leader:*

- *upon learning the state θ of the nature, the leader invokes the optimal signaling strategy φ of the public signaling game G_{signal} to obtain $\sigma \sim \varphi(\theta)$;*
- *the leader then discards all information other than σ, i.e., behaves as if his belief is $\Pi_{\varphi,\sigma}$, and plays the maximin strategy in the game $\mathcal{U}^{\Pi_{\varphi,\sigma}}$, i.e., $\text{argmax}_{s_1} \min_{s_2} \mathcal{U}^{\Pi_{\varphi,\sigma}}(s_1, s_2)$, repeatedly.*

This strategy can guarantee the leader an average expected utility $\nu_{\text{signal}}(G_{\text{signal}})$.

Although the strategy for the leader is easy to construct from the signaling scheme of the public signaling game, the follower's strategy is not so straightforward. The main difficulty is that there does not exist a credible principal in the repeated game as in the public signaling game, and therefore, the follower is uncertain about whether the leader exactly follows the scheme. In particular, the leader might have incentive to deviate by sending a different signal: conditioned on his type θ, choose σ^* such that $\sigma^* = \text{argmax}_{\sigma \in \Sigma} \mathcal{U}^\theta(s_1^*(\sigma), s_2^*(\sigma))$, where

$$s_1^*(\sigma) = \underset{s_1}{\text{argmax}} \min_{s_2} \mathcal{U}^{\Pi_{\varphi,\sigma}}(s_1, s_2) \quad \text{and} \quad s_2^*(\sigma) = \underset{s_2}{\text{argmin}} \max_{s_1} \mathcal{U}^{\Pi_{\varphi,\sigma}}(s_1, s_2).$$

In other words, the leader can send a signal σ^* that gives himself the maximum utility conditioned on θ. Therefore, the follower's strategy cannot rely on the possibly non-credible signaling scheme.

To circumvent this difficulty, we will construct an adaptive strategy for the follower, which does not depend on the non-credible signal σ but only depends on the prior Π and the history of play. Our approach relies on the solution of the dual program of the public signaling game. For convenience, given a distribution Π over Θ, let $f(\Pi) = \max_{s_1} \min_{s_2} \mathcal{U}^\Pi(s_1, s_2)$ be the game value of the induced game $\mathcal{U}^\Pi$. The problem of computing the optimal public signaling scheme can be formulated as the following linear program with infinitely many variables $x(\Pi')$ for $\Pi' \in \Delta(\Theta)$ [6–8]:

$$\begin{aligned}
\max \ & \textstyle\sum_{\Pi' \in \Delta(\Theta)} x(\Pi') \cdot f(\Pi') \\
\text{s.t.} \ & \textstyle\sum_{\Pi' \in \Delta(\Theta)} x(\Pi') \cdot \Pi'(\theta) = \Pi(\theta) \ \forall \theta \in \Theta \\
& x(\Pi') \geq 0 \hspace{3.5cm} \forall \Pi' \in \Delta(\Theta)
\end{aligned} \tag{1}$$

Intuitively, a signaling scheme can be viewed as a convex decomposition of the prior Π into a collection of posteriors $\{\Pi'\}$ [8,10]. Based on the primal, we can construct its dual with $|\Theta|$ variables $y(\theta)$ for $\theta \in \Theta$ as follows:

$$\begin{aligned}
&\min \sum_{\theta \in \Theta} y(\theta) \cdot \Pi(\theta) \\
&\text{s.t. } \sum_{\theta \in \Theta} y(\theta) \cdot \Pi'(\theta) \geq f(\Pi') \; \forall \Pi' \in \Delta(\Theta)
\end{aligned} \tag{2}$$

Let x^* and y^* be the solution of the primal and the dual, respectively. By strong duality, $\sum_{\Pi' \in \Delta(\Theta)} x^*(\Pi') \cdot f(\Pi') = \sum_{\theta \in \Theta} y^*(\theta) \cdot \Pi(\theta) = \nu_{\texttt{signal}}(G_{\texttt{signal}})$. We will interpret y and Π as vectors such that $\boldsymbol{y} = (y(\theta_1), \cdots, y(\theta_{|\Theta|}))$ and $\boldsymbol{\Pi} = (\Pi(\theta_1), \cdots, \Pi(\theta_{|\Theta|}))$. The inner product $\langle \boldsymbol{y}, \boldsymbol{\Pi} \rangle$ is defined as $\sum_{\theta \in \Theta} y(\theta) \cdot \Pi(\theta)$. The next proposition directly follows the feasibility of $\boldsymbol{y}^*$ and strong duality:

Proposition 1. *For any prior $\boldsymbol{\Pi}$ in the public signaling game, there exists $\boldsymbol{y}^*$ such that $\langle \boldsymbol{y}^*, \boldsymbol{\Pi} \rangle = \nu_{signal}(G_{signal})$ and $\forall \Pi' \in \Delta(\Theta)$, $\langle \boldsymbol{y}^*, \boldsymbol{\Pi}' \rangle \geq f(\Pi')$.*

Hence, if the follower can ensure that for any strategy s_1 deployed by the leader, there exists an adaptive mixed strategy s_2 for the follower such that,

$$\forall \theta \in \Theta, \lim_{T \to \infty} \frac{\sum_{t=1}^{T} \mathcal{U}^\theta(s_1^t, s_2^t)}{T} \leq y^*(\theta), \tag{3}$$

then the average utility of the leader as $T \to \infty$ would be

$$\lim_{T \to \infty} \sum_{\theta \in \Theta} \Pi(\theta) \cdot \frac{\sum_{t=1}^{T} \mathcal{U}^\theta(s_1^t, s_2^t)}{T} \leq \sum_{\theta \in \Theta} \Pi(\theta) \cdot y^*(\theta) = \nu_{\texttt{signal}}(G_{\texttt{signal}}).$$

To prove (3), it is equivalent to show that $\mathcal{R}(\boldsymbol{y}^*) = \{\boldsymbol{v} \mid \boldsymbol{v} \leq \boldsymbol{y}^*\}$ is approachable.

Definition 2 (Blackwell's Approachability [4]). *Given a convex set $\mathcal{R}$ of vectors of utilities, we say $\mathcal{R}$ is approachable from the perspective of the follower, if for any strategy of the leader s_1, there exists an adaptive strategy s_2 for the follower such that $\lim_{T \to \infty} \text{dist}\left(\frac{1}{T} \sum_{t=1}^{T} \mathcal{U}(s_1^t, s_2^t), \mathcal{R}\right) = 0$ almost surely, where $\mathcal{U}(s_1, s_2) = (\mathcal{U}^{\theta_1}(s_1, s_2), \cdots, \mathcal{U}^{\theta_{|\Theta|}}(s_1, s_2))$ and $\text{dist}(\boldsymbol{u}, \mathcal{R}) = \min_{\boldsymbol{v} \in \mathcal{R}} \|\boldsymbol{v} - \boldsymbol{u}\|$.*

Theorem 2 ([2,14]). *$\mathcal{R}(\boldsymbol{y}^*) = \{\boldsymbol{v} \mid \boldsymbol{v} \leq \boldsymbol{y}^*\}$ is approachable.*

To establish the approachability of $\mathcal{R}(\boldsymbol{y}^*)$, we first consider a halfspace $\mathcal{H}(\boldsymbol{\Pi}', b)$ such that $\boldsymbol{v} \in \mathcal{H}(\boldsymbol{\Pi}', b)$ if and only if $\langle \boldsymbol{\Pi}', \boldsymbol{v} \rangle \leq b$.

Lemma 2. *A halfspace $\mathcal{H}(\boldsymbol{\Pi}', b)$ is approachable if $f(\Pi') \leq b$.*

Theorem 3 ([4]). *A convex set $\mathcal{R}$ is approachable if and only if all halfspaces containing $\mathcal{R}$ are approachable.*

All that remains to show is that all halfspaces containing $\mathcal{R}(\boldsymbol{y}^*)$ are approachable.

Lemma 3. *All halfspaces containing $\mathcal{R}(\boldsymbol{y}^*) = \{\boldsymbol{v} \mid \boldsymbol{v} \leq \boldsymbol{y}^*\}$ are approachable.*

Proof. Notice that any minimal halfspace containing $\mathcal{R}(\boldsymbol{y}^*)$ must cross $\boldsymbol{y}^*$ by the construction of $\mathcal{R}(\boldsymbol{y}^*)$. Therefore, such a halfspace can be represented by $\mathcal{H}(\boldsymbol{\Pi}', \langle \boldsymbol{\Pi}', \boldsymbol{y}^* \rangle)$ with $\boldsymbol{\Pi}' \in \Delta(\Theta)$. By Proposition 1, $f(\boldsymbol{\Pi}') \leq \langle \boldsymbol{\Pi}', \boldsymbol{y}^* \rangle$, and therefore, by Lemma 2, $\mathcal{H}(\boldsymbol{\Pi}', \langle \boldsymbol{\Pi}', \boldsymbol{y}^* \rangle)$ is approachable.

Combining Theorem 3 and Lemma 3, we finish the proof of Theorem 2. We can then apply Blackwell's construction [4] to obtain an adaptive strategy for the follower that approaches $R(\boldsymbol{y}^*)$ almost surely.

Intuitively, at stage t, if $\frac{1}{t-1}\sum_{\tau=1}^{t-1}\mathcal{U}(s_1^\tau, s_2^\tau) \notin \mathcal{R}(\boldsymbol{y}^*)$, then the follower first finds a halfspace $\mathcal{H}(\boldsymbol{\Pi}', \langle \boldsymbol{\Pi}', \boldsymbol{y}^* \rangle)$ that separates $\frac{1}{t-1}\sum_{\tau=1}^{t-1}\mathcal{U}(s_1^\tau, s_2^\tau)$ and $\mathcal{R}(\boldsymbol{y}^*)$. Given such a $\boldsymbol{\Pi}'$, the follower plays the minimax strategy of $\mathcal{U}^{\boldsymbol{\Pi}'}$ at stage t, and then the distance between the vector of average utilities and $\mathcal{R}(\boldsymbol{y}^*)$ will become smaller after stage t. Observe that the follower's strategy can be computed from the prior Π, the game $G_{\texttt{repeated}}$, and the history of play. In doing so, it guarantees that the expected average utility of the leader is at most $\nu_{\texttt{signal}}(G_{\texttt{signal}})$ in the limit, and Proposition 2 follows:

Proposition 2. *In a Bayesian repeated game* $G_{\texttt{repeated}} = \left(\Pi, \{\mathcal{U}^\theta\}_{\theta \in \Theta} \right)$, *given* $\boldsymbol{y}^*$ *satisfying Proposition 1 and an oracle to compute the minimax strategy of the zero-sum game* $\mathcal{U}^{\boldsymbol{\Pi}'}$ *for all* $\boldsymbol{\Pi}' \in \Delta(\Theta)$, *there exists an efficient algorithm to construct the follower's optimal strategy.*

We will elaborate the complexity of computing $\boldsymbol{y}^*$ in Sect. 3.3.

3.2   Equivalence Between Bayesian Allocation Games and Team Max-Min Games

Definition 3 (Team Max-Min Game [15]). *In a zero-sum team max-min game* $G_{\texttt{team}} = \left(\{\mathcal{U}^\theta\}_{\theta \in \Theta} \right)$, *in addition to player 1 and 2, there is a player 3 whose set of pure strategies is* Θ. *Player 1 and player 3 form a team and share the same utility such that when player 1 plays* $s_1 \in S_1$, *player 2 plays* $s_2 \in S_2$, *and player 3 plays* $\theta \in \Theta$, *the utility for both player 1 and player 3 is* $\mathcal{U}^\theta(s_1, s_2)$, *while the utility for player 2 is* $-\mathcal{U}^\theta(s_1, s_2)$. *A team max-min equilibrium is a Nash equilibrium that maximizes the team's utility and we denote its game value by* $\nu_{\texttt{team}}(G_{\texttt{team}})$: $\nu_{\texttt{team}}(G_{\texttt{team}}) = \max_{s_1 \in \Delta(S_1), \Pi \in \Delta(\Theta)} \min_{s_2 \in \Delta(S_2)} \mathcal{U}^\Pi(s_1, s_2)$.

We emphasize that player 1's strategy and player 3's strategy are not allowed to be correlated; otherwise, the team max-min game degenerates to a classic two-player zero-sum game in which player 1 and 3 can be treated as a single player. [15] show that a team max-min equilibrium always exists. It turns out the equilibrium in Bayesian allocation games corresponds to the solution of the above team max-min games in a precise sense, stated below.

Theorem 4. $\nu_{\texttt{alloc}}(G_{\texttt{alloc}}) = \nu_{\texttt{team}}(G_{\texttt{team}})$ *when* $G_{\texttt{alloc}} = G_{\texttt{team}}$.

To prove Theorem 4, we will construct strategies for players in the Bayesian allocation game from the equilibrium strategies in the team max-min game.

Lemma 4. *When $G_{alloc} = G_{team}$, let s_1^*, s_2^*, Π^* be the equilibrium strategies for the team max-min game G_{team}. In the Bayesian allocation game G_{alloc}, consider the following strategy for the leader:*

– set the prior Π to be Π^*; then repeatedly play strategy s_1^* for every stage.

This strategy can guarantee the leader an average expected utility $\nu_{team}(G_{team})$.

In comparison to the Bayesian repeated games in which the follower knows the prior, the follower does not even know the prior set by the leader in the Bayesian allocation game. To overcome this obstacle, observe that in the Bayesian repeated game, the approachability of a convex set is a property that only depends on the collection of games $(\{\mathcal{U}^\theta\}_{\theta \in \Theta})$ but independent of the prior. Motivated by this observation, we show that $\mathcal{R}(\nu_{team}(G_{team}) \cdot \mathbf{1}) = \{v \mid v \le \nu_{team}(G_{team}) \cdot \mathbf{1}\}$ is approachable where $\mathbf{1}$ is a vector of all ones.

Lemma 5. $\mathcal{R}(\nu_{team}(G_{team}) \cdot \mathbf{1})$ *is approachable.*

It is straightforward to show that, when $\mathcal{R}(\nu_{team}(G_{team}) \cdot \mathbf{1})$ is approachable, for any prior $\Pi \in \Delta(\Theta)$, the average utility of the leader is at most $\nu_{team}(G_{team})$.

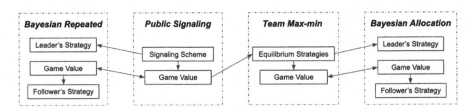

Fig. 1. The relationships of computational problems, assuming the minimax strategy of $\mathcal{U}^\Pi$ can be computed efficiently for all $\Pi \in \Delta(\Theta)$: the arrows point to problems that are computationally easier.

3.3 Computational Complexity of the Follower's Optimal Strategy

As demonstrated before, constructing the follower's optimal strategy in Bayesian repeated games requires a solution to the dual program (2). Hence, it is not immediate that one can efficiently construct the follower's optimal strategy if the public signaling game is efficiently solvable. Here, we say an algorithm is efficient if the running time of the algorithm is polynomial in terms of the number of states $|\Theta|$, and the number of pure strategies $|S_1| + |S_2|$.

We manage to show that, when the minimax strategy of $\mathcal{U}^\Pi$ can be computed efficiently for all $\Pi \in \Delta(\Theta)$, in both Bayesian repeated games and Bayesian allocation games, the follower's optimal strategy can be efficiently constructed if the corresponding game values are given. We further show that team max-min game is computationally easier than the public signaling game, and therefore, Bayesian allocation game is computationally easier than the Bayesian repeated game. Figure 1 summarizes the relationships of the computational problems discussed in this section, while the proofs are deferred to the full version.

4   Bayesian Repeated Security Games

In Sect. 3, we have shown that Bayesian repeated games can be reduced to public signaling games, while Bayesian allocation games can be reduced to team max-min games. However, it has been shown that both public signaling games and team max-min games are computationally intractable for general zero-sum games and even worse, no FPTAS is possible [5,8]. Particularly, public signaling games do not even admit PTAS [3,13].

Motivated by the applications in the domain of repeated security games, we will concern ourselves with repeated games where the stage game is a *security game* of a particularly simple form. The one-shot complete-information security games are described by a set L of *locations*, a set M of *treasures*, and a set R of *defensive resources*. For convenience, we use $\perp$ to denote a *null* treasure or a *null* defensive resource. $v : L \times (M \cup \perp) \to \mathbb{R}_{\geq 0}$ is a *location-treasure importance* function such that $v(\ell, m)$ characterizes the utility loss of the defender if location $\ell \in L$ with treasure $m \in M$ allocated is attacked without defense. In addition, there is a *defense-quality* function $q : L \times (M \cup \perp) \times (R \cup \perp) \to \{0, 1\}$ such that $q(\ell, m, r)$ characterizes the effectiveness of allocating defensive resource $r \in R$ to defend location $\ell \in L$ that hosts treasure m. Note that in our setting, a defensive resource is either 100% effective for a combination of location and treasure or totally useless. For a *null* treasure, we have $v(\ell, \perp) = 0$ for all ℓ, and for a *null* defensive resource, we have $q(\ell, m, \perp) = 0$ for all ℓ and m.

A state of nature is a matching $\theta : L \to M$ that maps the locations to treasures such that for any $i, j \in L$ with $i \neq j$, $\theta(i) \neq \perp$, and $\theta(j) \neq \perp$, we have $\theta(i) \neq \theta(j)$. A pure strategy for the defender is also a matching $D : L \to R$ that maps the locations to the defensive resources such that for any $i, j \in L$ with $i \neq j$, $D(i) \neq \perp$, and $D(j) \neq \perp$, we have $D(i) \neq D(j)$. Finally, a pure strategy for the attacker is a single location $a \in L$ to attack. A mixed strategy is naturally a distribution over such functions. The defender's utility under θ when the defender plays D and the attacker plays a is $\mathcal{U}^\theta(D, a) = -\big(1 - q(a, \theta(a), D(a))\big) \cdot v\big(a, \theta(a)\big)$, while the attacker's utility is simply $-\mathcal{U}^\theta(D, a)$.

We say the treasures are *homogeneous* if for all $m \in M$, $v(\ell, m)$ equals to some constant for all $\ell \in L$; the locations are *homogeneous* if for all $\ell \in L$, $v(\ell, m)$ equals to some constant for all $m \in M$; and the defensive resources are *homogeneous* if $q(\ell, m, r) = 1$ for all $\ell \in L$, $m \in M$, and $r \in R$. If the condition of homogeneity is not satisfied, we say they are *heterogeneous*.

We analyze the complexity of repeated security games under the contexts of both Bayesian repeated games and Bayesian allocation games. In Bayesian repeated games, an algorithm is efficient if its running time is in polynomial of $|\Theta|$, $|L|$, $|M|$, and $|R|$; while in Bayesian allocation games, an algorithm is efficient if its running time is in polynomial of $|L|$, $|M|$, and $|R|$.

Proposition 3. *Given the marginals of Π, the optimal strategies for both the defender and the attacker in the security game $\mathcal{U}^\Pi$ can be computed efficiently.*

However, for our class of security games with a general prior Π, computing the game value of the Bayesian repeated games is computationally intractable.

Theorem 5. *It is strongly NP-hard to compute the game value of the Bayesian repeated games with a security game as the stage game, even when all of treasures, locations, and defensive resources are homogeneous. Moreover, no FPTAS is possible. Consequently, it is strongly NP-hard to compute any representation of the equilibrium which permits computing the game value.*

5 Bayesian Allocation Security Games

We turn to Bayesian allocation games with a security game as the stage game. It turns out that a Bayesian allocation game with a security game as the stage game can be efficiently solved when only the treasures are heterogeneous (Fig. 2).

Theorem 6. *There exists an efficient algorithm to compute the game value and the defender's optimal strategy of a Bayesian allocation game with a security game as the stage game, when only the treasures are heterogeneous.*

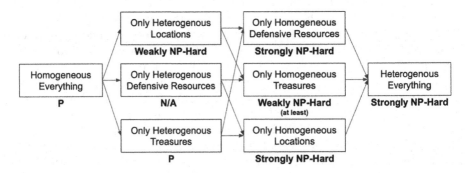

Fig. 2. The computational complexity of Bayesian allocation games with a security game as the stage game: the arrows point to more general versions of the problem.

Moreover, the following lemma illustrates that one can efficiently construct the attacker's strategy when the game value is given.

Lemma 6. *Given the game value of a Bayesian allocation game with a security game as the stage game, there exists an efficient algorithm to compute the attacker's optimal strategy.*

Therefore, one can efficiently construct both the defender's optimal strategy and the attacker's optimal strategy when only the treasures are heterogeneous. However, going beyond, the problem becomes computationally intractable.

Theorem 7. *It is weakly NP-hard to compute the game value of the Bayesian allocation games with a security game as the stage game, when only the locations are heterogeneous. Moreover, there exists a pseudo-polynomial time algorithm that can compute the game value.*

Theorem 8. *It is strongly NP-hard to compute the game value of the Bayesian allocation games with a security game as the stage game, when only the defensive resources are homogeneous, or only the locations are homogeneous.*

There are three other settings that have not been discussed: (1) heterogeneous everything; (2) only treasures are homogeneous; and (3) only defensive resources are heterogeneous. For the setting in which everything is heterogeneous, it is also strongly NP-hard to compute the game value since it is a more general setting than the settings in which only defensive resources are homogeneous or only locations are homogeneous. As for the setting in which only treasures are homogeneous, it is at least weakly NP-hard to compute the game value since it is a more general setting than the case in which only locations are heterogeneous. We leave it as an open question to settle whether it is strongly NP-hard. Finally, for the setting in which only defensive resources are heterogeneous, this setting is not well-defined: since the locations and the treasures are homogeneous, a defensive resource should be either effective or ineffective for any combination of the locations and the treasures. Consequently, the defender can simply eliminate the ineffective defensive resources to focus on effective ones, which reduces the problem to the case in which everything is homogeneous.

References

1. Abernethy, J., Bartlett, P.L., Hazan, E.: Blackwell approachability and no-regret learning are equivalent. In: Proceedings of the 24th Annual Conference on Learning Theory, pp. 27–46 (2011)
2. Aumann, R.J., Maschler, M.: Repeated games with incomplete information. MIT Press, Cambridge (1995)
3. Bhaskar, U., Cheng, Y., Ko, Y.K., Swamy, C.: Hardness results for signaling in Bayesian zero-sum and network routing games. In: Proceedings of the 2016 ACM Conference on Economics and Computation, pp. 479–496 (2016)
4. Blackwell, D.: An analog of the minimax theorem for vector payoffs. Pac. J. Math. **6**(1), 1–8 (1956)
5. Borgs, C., Chayes, J., Immorlica, N., Kalai, A.T., Mirrokni, V., Papadimitriou, C.: The myth of the folk theorem. Games Econ. Behav. **70**(1), 34–43 (2010)
6. Cheng, Y., Cheung, H.Y., Dughmi, S., Emamjomeh-Zadeh, E., Han, L., Teng, S.H.: Mixture selection, mechanism design, and signaling. In: 2015 IEEE 56th Annual Symposium on Foundations of Computer Science. pp. 1426–1445. IEEE (2015)
7. Dughmi, S.: Algorithmic information structure design: a survey. ACM SIGecom Exchanges **15**(2), 2–24 (2017)
8. Dughmi, S.: On the hardness of designing public signals. Games Econ. Behav. **118**, 609–625 (2019)
9. Fang, F., Nguyen, T.H.: Green security games: apply game theory to addressing green security challenges. ACM SIGecom Exchanges **15**(1), 78–83 (2016)
10. Kamenica, E., Gentzkow, M.: Bayesian persuasion. Am. Econ. Rev. **101**(6), 2590–2615 (2011)
11. Neumann, J.V.: Zur theorie der gesellschaftsspiele. Mathematische annalen **100**(1), 295–320 (1928)

12. Rockmore, D.: What's missing from "the imitation game", November 2014. https://www.newyorker.com/tech/annals-of-technology/imitation-game-alan-turing. Accessed 23 Jan 2020

13. Rubinstein, A.: Eth-hardness for signaling in symmetric zero-sum games. CoRR abs/1510.04991 (2015)

14. Sorin, S.: A First Course on Zero-Sum Repeated Games, vol. 37. Springer, Heidelberg (2002)

15. von Stengel, B., Koller, D.: Team-maxmin equilibria. Games Econ. Behav. **21**(1–2), 309–321 (1997)

16. Tambe, M.: Security and Game Theory: Algorithms, Deployed Systems, Lessons Learned. Cambridge University Press, Cambridge (2011)

17. Wang, Y., et al.: Deep reinforcement learning for green security games with real-time information. In: Proceedings of the AAAI Conference on Artificial Intelligence, vol. 33, pp. 1401–1408 (2019)

18. Xu, H., et al.: Optimal patrol planning for green security games with black-box attackers. In: Rass, S., An, B., Kiekintveld, C., Fang, F., Schauer, S. (eds.) International Conference on Decision and Game Theory for Security. GameSec 2017. Lecture Notes in Computer Science, vol. 10575, pp. 458–477. Springer, Cham (2017). https://doi.org/10.1007/978-3-319-68711-7_24

Abstracts

Large Random Matching Markets with Localized Preference Structures Can Exhibit Large Cores

Ross Rheingans-Yoo$^{(\boxtimes)}$ (iD)

Jane Street, New York, NY, USA
ross@r-y.io

Abstract. Prior work considering random matching markets has suggested that, when agents have uniformly-distributed preferences, the fraction of agents with incentives to manipulate core-selecting mechanisms generally tends to vanish as markets become large. Contrasting these results, I present a class of models for non-homogeneous agent preferences (drawn from the computer science literature on network structure) that support significant incentives for agents to manipulate matching outcomes, even as markets become large and unbalanced.

Specifically, I consider agent preference structures that exhibit locality, with focus on a simple model of spatial locality for the main results. In an appendix, I discuss an extension of these results to a broader class of preference-structure models, with a generalized locality condition.

A constructive probabilistic technique, similar to Hassidim *et al.* [1], shows that a non-vanishing fraction of agents can improve their outcomes by misreporting their true preferences, in a market with simple spatial locality. Simulation results demonstrate that the fraction of such agents is substantial in practice under market specifications between 60 and 12,000 agents. These results contrast prior work which assumed homogeneous preferences, finding a vanishing fraction and little scope for manipulation. Furthermore, this scope for manipulation corresponds directly to core size and differences in agents' welfare between core outcomes.

These results suggest that largeness and cross-side imbalance may be insufficient to explain empirical observations of small cores in matching markets; I discuss alternative explanations.

Keywords: Matching · Large markets · Incentives

The a full version of this paper is available at: https://static.rossry.net/papers/ps-core_wine20.pdf.

The author thanks Ravi Jagadeesan, Scott Duke Kominers, Kahn Mason, Duncan Rheingans-Yoo, Ran Shorrer, Terry Yoo, and several anonymous referees for helpful comments, and Chengqi Song for review of simulation code.

This text presents independent work and only the opinions of the named author.

X. Chen et al. (Eds.): WINE 2020, LNCS 12495, pp. 461–462, 2020.
https://doi.org/10.1007/978-3-030-64946-3

Reference

1. Hassidim, A., Romm, A., Shorrer, R.I.: Need vs. Merit: The large Core of College Admissions Markets (2018), Working Paper (https://ssrn.com/abstract=3071873)

The Influence of One Strategic Agent on the Core of Stable Matchings

Ron Kupfer[(⊠)]

The Hebrew University of Jerusalem, Jerusalem, Israel
ron.kupfer@mail.huji.ac.il

Abstract. In this work, we analyze the influence of a single strategic agent on the quality of the other agents' matchings in a matching market. We consider a stable matching problem with n men and n women when preferences are drawn uniformly from the possible $(n!)^{2n}$ full ranking options. We focus on the effect of a single woman who reports a modified preferences list in a way that is optimal from her perspective. We show that in this case, the quality of the matching dramatically improves from the other women's perspective. When running the Gale–Shapley men-proposing algorithm, the expected women-rank is $O(\log^4 n)$ and almost surely the average women-rank is $O(\log^{2+\epsilon} n)$, rather than a rank of $O(\frac{n}{\log n})$ in both cases under a truthful regime. On the other hand, almost surely, the average men's rank is no better than $\Omega\left(\frac{n}{\log^{2+\epsilon} n}\right)$, compared to a rank of $O(\log n)$ under a truthful regime.

All of the results hold for any matching algorithm that guarantees a stable matching, which suggests that the core convergence observed in real markets may be caused by the strategic behavior of the participants.

The full paper can be found at https://arxiv.org/abs/1806.04034.

R. Kupfer—This project has received funding from the European Research Council (ERC) under the European Union's Horizon 2020 research and innovation program (grant agreement No. 740282).

How Many Citizens Have Already Voted? The Effect of (Interim) Turnout Rate Polls in Elections

Akaki Mamageishvili[✉] and Oriol Tejada

CER-ETH – Center of Economic, Research at ETH Zurich, Zürichbergstrasse 18, 8092 Zurich, Switzerland
amamageishvili@ethz.ch

Abstract. We examine the effect of interim turnout rate polls on elections within a costly voting model of a large electorate with private values and two alternatives. We consider that *(i)* one group of citizens votes before the rest and *(ii)* the individuals of the second group know the first group's turnout rate—but not the vote tally—before they vote. The alternative that receives more votes in total is implemented. We show that the probability that each alternative is implemented under this voting procedure is the same as in one-round voting without interim turnout rate polls. An interpretation is that these polls might not be distorting election outcomes. This observation can rationalize why some democracies report the ongoing turnout rate at several points in time during election day.

Keywords: Elections · Poisson games · Polls · Private value · Voting costs · Rational voter

JEL Classification: C72 · D70 · D72

A full draft of the paper is available at https://papers.ssrn.com/sol3/papers.cfm?abstract_id=3545948

We Are Grateful to Hans Gersbach and Mattias Polborn for Insightful Comments. All Errors Are Our Own

X. Chen et al. (Eds.): WINE 2020, LNCS 12495, p. 464, 2020.
https://doi.org/10.1007/978-3-030-64946-3

Online Hypergraph Matching with Delays

Marco Pavone[1], Amin Saberi[2], Maximilian Schiffer[3], and Matthew Tsao[4(✉)]

[1] Department of Aeronautics and Astronautics, Stanford University, Stanford, USA
pavone@stanford.edu
[2] Department of Management Science and Engineering, Stanford University,
Stanford, USA
saberi@stanford.edu
[3] Technical University of Munich School of Management, Munich, Germany
schiffer@tum.de
[4] Department of Electrical Engineering, Stanford University, Stanford, USA
mwtsao@stanford.edu

Abstract. Motivated by high-capacity ridesharing applications where multiple users can be assigned to the same vehicle to share a ride, we study an online hypergraph matching problem with delays. In this model, the problem instance is represented by a hypergraph. Vertices represent users, and hyperedges represent groups of users that can be efficiently served with a single vehicle. Hyperedges can contain at most k vertices, representing the capacity of service vehicles. Users arrive to a ridesharing platform sequentially, and are willing to wait up to d timesteps to be matched, after which they will leave the system in favor of an outside option. A hyperedge is revealed to the platform once all of its vertices have arrived, and can only be included into the matching before any of its vertices leave the system.

We consider both the utility maximization and cost minimization settings in this model. In the utility maximization setting, hyperedge weights represent the utility of serving the associated vertices with a single vehicle. The platform's objective is to construct a matching with large total weight. In the cost minimization setting, hyperedge weights represent the cost of serving the associated vertices with a single vehicle. The platform's objective is to find a matching with low total weight.

We present results for both variants of the problem. In the utility maximization setting, the optimal competitive ratio is $\frac{1}{d}$ whenever $k \geq 3$, and is achievable in polynomial-time for any fixed k. In the cost minimization variation, when $k = 2$, the optimal competitive ratio for deterministic

---

The full paper can be found at http://arxiv.org/abs/2009.12022. This research was supported by the National Science Foundation under CAREER Award CMMI-1454737, and the Toyota Research Institute (TRI).

© Springer Nature Switzerland AG 2020
X. Chen et al. (Eds.): WINE 2020, LNCS 12495, pp. 465–466, 2020.
https://doi.org/10.1007/978-3-030-64946-3

algorithms is $\frac{3}{2}$ and is achieved by a polynomial-time thresholding algorithm. When $k > 2$, we show that a polynomial-time randomized batching algorithm is $(2 - \frac{1}{d}) \log k$-competitive, and it is NP-hard to achieve a competitive ratio better than $\log k - O(\log \log k)$.

Keywords: Online algorithms · Competitive analysis · Ridesharing

Market Equilibrium in Multi-tier Supply Chain Networks

Tao Jiang[1], Young-San Lin[2(✉)] (ID), and Thành Nguyen[1] (ID)

[1] Krannert School of Management, Purdue University, West Lafayette, IN, USA,
taujiang300@gmail.com, nguye161@purdue.edu
[2] Department of Computer Science, Purdue University, West Lafayette, IN, USA
lin532@purdue.edu

Abstract. We consider a sequential decision model over multi-tier supply chain networks and show that in particular, for series parallel networks, there is a unique equilibrium. We provide a linear time algorithm to compute the equilibrium and study the impact and invariant of the network structure to the total trade flow and social welfare. Sequential decision making is a well-observed phenomenon in supply chains. Firms at the top tier typically need to make decisions on the quantity and the price to sell to firms in the next tier, and the buying firms then decide how much to buy from which suppliers, and continue to pass on the goods by determining the quantity and price for firms at the next level. One needs to analyze the subgame perfect equilibria of the market, where each firm internalizes the decisions of all the firms downstream and compete with all the firms of the same tier. The length and the number of trading routes are the two main factors that impact the efficiency of a supply chain network. On one hand, a large variety of options to trade indicates a high degree of competition. On the other hand, a long trading path causes double, triple and higher degree marginalization problems. We study series parallel networks because they are rich enough for investigating the factors described above and simple enough for characterizing the equilibrium outcomes. The unique equilibrium and equilibrium comparative statics are derived from a closed-form expression between the price and quantity, by judiciously using the structure of series parallel networks and the concavity of the firm utilities.

The full version of this paper is available at https://arxiv.org/pdf/2009.13021.pdf.

Young-San Lin is supported by NSF CCF-1910659 and NSF CCF-1910411.
Thành Nguyen is supported by NSF Award 1728165.

X. Chen et al. (Eds.): WINE 2020, LNCS 12495, p. 467, 2020.
https://doi.org/10.1007/978-3-030-64946-3

Decision Scoring Rules

Caspar Oesterheld[✉] and Vincent Conitzer

Department of Computer Science, Duke University, Durham, NC, USA
{ocaspar,conitzer}@cs.duke.edu

Abstract. A *principal* faces a choice from a set A of *actions* that give rise to *outcomes* from a set Ω. An *expert* has, for each action $a \in A$, a probabilistic belief $P(\cdot \mid a) \in \Delta(\Omega)$ about which outcome will occur given that the principal chooses a. The principal would like to select an action from $\arg\max_{a \in A} \mathbb{E}_{O \sim P}[u(O) \mid a]$ that maximizes the expectation of a utility function $u \colon \Omega \to \mathbb{R}$ given the *expert*'s belief. The principal asks the expert for a report consisting of a recommendation $\hat{a}$ and a probabilistic prediction $\hat{P}_{\hat{a}} \in \Delta(\Omega)$ about what outcome will occur if the recommendation is implemented. The principal then follows the recommendation and observes an outcome. Finally, the principal pays the expert based on the prediction and the outcome, according to some decision scoring rule (DSR) $s \colon \Delta(\Omega) \times \Omega \to \mathbb{R}$. We assume that for any given belief P, the expert submits the report that maximizes their expected score. We call a DSR s *proper* if for all possible expert beliefs P, at least one of the maximizers $\hat{a}, \hat{P}_{\hat{a}}$ of the expert's expected score consists of an expected-utility-maximizing action a^* and the expert's true belief P_{a^*}.

Our first result is that (aside from degenerate cases) no proper DSR can strictly incentivize honest reporting on any aspect of the prediction $\hat{P}_{\hat{a}}$ other than the expected utility of taking the recommended action. We can thus limit attention to scoring rules s that are only a function of the reported expected utility $\mathbb{E}_{\hat{P}_{\hat{a}}}[u(O)]$ as opposed to the entire reported distribution. Second, the score can (aside from degenerate cases) only depend on the *utility* of the outcome obtained, i.e., the score must be the same for outcomes with equal utility. We can therefore write scores as $s(\hat{\mu}, y)$, where $\hat{\mu}$ is the reported expected utility and y is the utility obtained.

We characterize proper DSRs as ones that can be written as

$$s(\hat{\mu}, y) = f(\hat{\mu})(y - \hat{\mu}) + \int_0^{\hat{\mu}} f(x)dx + C$$

for some non-negative, non-decreasing f and constant $C \in \mathbb{R}$. We show that the characterization admits the following interpretation: all DSRs can be interpreted as giving and selling to the expert shares in the principal's project. Each share pays, e.g., \$1 per unit of utility obtained by the principal. Owning these shares makes the expert want to maximize the principal's utility by giving the best-possible recommendation. Furthermore, if shares are offered at a continuum of prices, this makes the expert reveal the value of a share and therefore the expected utility of the principal conditional on following the recommendation.

Full paper at https://users.cs.duke.edu/~ocaspar/DSRWINE.pdf

© Springer Nature Switzerland AG 2020
X. Chen et al. (Eds.): WINE 2020, LNCS 12495, p. 468, 2020.
https://doi.org/10.1007/978-3-030-64946-3

Bayesian Learning in Dynamic Nonatomic Routing Games

Emilien Macault[1]([envelope]), Marco Scarsini[2], and Tristan Tomala[1]

[1] HEC Paris, 1 Rue de la Libération, 78350 Jouy-en-Josas, France
emilien.macault@hec.edu
[2] Dipartimento di Economia e Finanza, LUISS,
Viale Romania 32, 00197 Rome, Italy

Abstract. We consider a discrete-time nonatomic routing game with single origin and destination, where the cost function of each edge depends on some uncertain persistent state parameter. At every period, an i.i.d. random traffic demand enters the network and travels from origin to destination according to a Bayes-Wardrop equilibrium, i.e., the Wardrop equilibrium for the expected costs; the realized costs are then publicly observed and the belief about the state parameter is updated according to Bayes' rule. We say that *strong learning* is achieved if beliefs converge to the truth and *weak learning* is achieved if equilibrium flows converge to the flows of a Wardrop equilibrium under complete information. This paper studies the joint dynamics of equilibrium and beliefs and characterizes the conditions required for the two types of learning to occur.

We first prove that the joint dynamics of beliefs and equilibria converge to a stable point where no additional information is acquired. Using a counter-example, we show that this rest point need not belong to the set of full-information equilibria and that it can be arbitrarily inefficient. This counter-example generalizes in the following sense: in any dynamic routing game with incomplete information, in the absence of exogenous randomness, there exists a set of latency functions and states such that neither strong nor weak learning occurs. We then prove that, when both the support of the demand and the cost functions are unbounded, weak learning occurs if and only if the routing network has a series-parallel structure. We provide a constructive proof showing that if the network does not belong to the series-parallel class, then there exist a set of cost functions and a prior belief such that learning will not occur. Finally, we prove that, under the same conditions, strong learning occurs if and only if the demand's support is $\mathbb{R}^+$.

Keywords: Routing games · Incomplete information · Social learning

A full draft of the paper is available at https://arxiv.org/abs/2009.11580.

This Work Was Partially Supported by the COST Action 16228 (GAMENET), PRIN 2017 ALGADIMAR, and the GNAMPA-INdAM Project 2020 "Random Walks on Random Games."

X. Chen et al. (Eds.): WINE 2020, LNCS 12495, p. 469, 2020.
https://doi.org/10.1007/978-3-030-64946-3

Privacy Rights and Data Security: GDPR and Personal Data Driven Markets

T. Tony Ke[1](✉) and K. Sudhir[2]

[1] The Chinese University of Hong Kong, Shatin, N.T., Hong Kong, China
tonyke@cuhk.edu.hk
[2] Yale University, New Haven, CT 06511, USA

Abstract. The paper investigates how the two key features of GDPR (EU's data protection regulation)—privacy rights and data security—impact personal data driven markets. First, GDPR recognizes that individuals own and control their data in perpetuity, leading to three critical *privacy rights*: (i) right to explicit consent (data opt-in), (ii) right to be forgotten (data erasure), and (iii) right to portability (switch data to competitor). Second, GDPR has *data security* mandates protection against privacy breaches through unauthorized access. The right to explicit opt-in allows goods exchange without data exchange. Erasure and portability rights discipline firms to provide ongoing value and reduces consumers' holdup using their own data. Overall, privacy rights restrict *legal* collection and use, while data security protects against *illegal* access and use. We develop a two-period model of forward-looking firms and consumers where consumers exercise data privacy rights balancing the cost (privacy breach, price discrimination) and benefits (product personalization, price subsidies) of sharing data with firms. We find that by reducing expected privacy breach costs, data security mandates increase opt-in, consumer surplus and firm profit. Privacy rights reduce opt-in and mostly increase consumer surplus at the expense of firm profits; interestingly they hurt firms more in competitive than in monopolistic markets. While privacy rights *can* reduce surplus for both firms and consumers, these conditions are unlikely to be realized when breach risk is endogenized. Further, by unbundling data exchange from goods exchange, privacy rights facilitate trade in goods that may otherwise fail to occur due to privacy breach risk.

Keywords: GDPR · Privacy · Data security · Personalization · Price discrimination · Data security · Digital marketing

The full version is available at ssrn.com/abstract=3643979.

© Springer Nature Switzerland AG 2020
X. Chen et al. (Eds.): WINE 2020, LNCS 12495, p. 470, 2020.
https://doi.org/10.1007/978-3-030-64946-3

Closing the Gap: Mitigating Bias in Online Résumé-Filtering

Jad Salem[(✉)][iD] and Swati Gupta[iD]

Georgia Institute of Technology, Atlanta, GA 30332, USA
{jsalem7,swatig}@gatech.edu

Abstract. We consider the problem of online résumé-filtering, in which résumés are presented to an algorithm one-by-one, and the algorithm must give immediate decisions on whether or not to grant the applicants interviews. This model captures the sequential nature of hiring, as decisions must be made with partial knowledge of the applicant pool. We cast this problem as a k-secretary problem, requiring that at most k applicants be granted interviews, and seek to maximize the total quality of selected applicants.

Algorithms which sift through applications typically numerically score applicants, providing a basis for comparison. There is, however, wide prevalence of bias in evaluations of applicants from different demographic groups, and applicants experience disparate access to job and training opportunities. These complex socio-economic issues pose unique modelling challenges, which are further compounded due to the current pandemic. To address these issues, we introduce *poset bias*, which is based on the following idea: due to experiences of applicants, which may be correlated with their demographic makeups, some pairs of applicants cannot be reliably ranked. Mathematically, we assume that the algorithm can only observe rankings of applicants according to a fixed partial order. This allows for a more individualized notion of bias compared to previous models, specifically generalizing the group bias model of Kleinberg and Raghavan [2] and the intersectional model of Celis et al. [1].

When ranking candidates, one goal we attempt to meet is that *similarly qualified individuals be treated similarly*. In the context of poset bias, we interpret this idea as follows: any two applicants who can be swapped by an order isomorphism (with respect to the partial order) should have the same probability of being selected. In other words, we require that any two applicants who are *indistinguishable* in the poset be treated equally by the algorithm. We call this algorithmic property *ranked demographic parity*, as it equalizes treatment by the partial ranking of the candidate. We show that any algorithm for the k-secretary problem under poset bias is $\Omega(\omega)$-competitive, where ω is the width of the poset—in other words, the competitive ratio scales with the maximum number of mutually incomparable applicants. We then show that this bound is tight by providing an $\mathcal{O}(\omega)$-competitive algorithm (which

This work is partially supported by the Thos and Clair Muller Research Fund. The full paper is available at https://tinyurl.com/yypw2mqs.

X. Chen et al. (Eds.): WINE 2020, LNCS 12495, pp. 471–472, 2020.
https://doi.org/10.1007/978-3-030-64946-3

satisfies ranked demographic parity). Our proposed algorithm selects applicants in parallel over randomly generated groups (not demographic groups), and uses the structural information learned about the poset to appropriately make selections within each random group.

Keywords: Secretary problem · Bias · Online selection · Affirmative action · Poset

References

1. Celis, L.E., Mehrotra, A., Vishnoi, N.K.: Interventions for ranking in the presence of implicit bias. In: Proceedings of the 2020 Conference on Fairness, Accountability, and Transparency, pp. 369–380 (2020)
2. Kleinberg, J., Raghavan, M.: Selection problems in the presence of implicit bias. In: 9th Innovations in Theoretical Computer Science Conference (ITCS 2018). Schloss Dagstuhl-Leibniz-Zentrum fuer Informatik (2018)

Catastrophe by Design in Population Games: Destabilizing Wasteful Locked-In Technologies

Stefanos Leonardos[(✉)], Iosif Sakos, Costas Courcoubetis, and Georgios Piliouras

Singapore University of Technology and Design, 8 Somapah Rd, Singapore 487372, Singapore
{stefanos_leonardos,costas,georgios}@sutd.edu.sg, iosif_sakos@mymail.sutd.edu.sg

In multi-agent environments in which coordination is desirable, the history of play often causes lock-in at sub-optimal outcomes. Notoriously, technologies with a significant environmental footprint or high social cost persist despite the successful development of more environmentally friendly and/or socially efficient alternatives. The displacement of the status quo is hindered by entrenched economic interests and network effects. To exacerbate matters, the standard mechanism design approaches based on centralized authorities with the capacity to use preferential subsidies to effectively dictate system outcomes are not always applicable to modern decentralized economies. What other types of mechanisms are feasible?

In this paper, we develop and analyze a mechanism that induces transitions from inefficient lock-ins to superior alternatives. This mechanism does not exogenously favor one option over another – instead, the phase transition emerges endogenously via a standard evolutionary learning model, Q-learning, where agents trade-off exploration and exploitation. Exerting the same transient influence to both the efficient and inefficient technologies encourages exploration and results in irreversible phase transitions and permanent stabilization of the efficient one. On a technical level, our work is based on bifurcation and catastrophe theory, a branch of mathematics that deals with changes in the number and stability properties of equilibria. Critically, our analysis is shown to be structurally robust to significant and even adversarially chosen perturbations to the parameters of both our game and our behavioral model. The full version of the paper can be found at https://arxiv.org/abs/2007.12877.

Stefanos Leonardos—gratefully acknowledgeS MOE AcRF Tier 2 Grant 2016-T2-1-170 and NRF 2018 Fellowship NRF-NRFF2018-07. Georgios Piliouras gratefully acknowledges MOE AcRF Tier 2 Grant 2016-T2-1-170, grant PIE-SGP-AI-2018-01, NRF2019-NRF-ANR095 ALIAS grant and NRF 2018 Fellowship NRF-NRFF2018-07.

X. Chen et al. (Eds.): WINE 2020, LNCS 12495, pp. 473–474, 2020.
https://doi.org/10.1007/978-3-030-64946-3

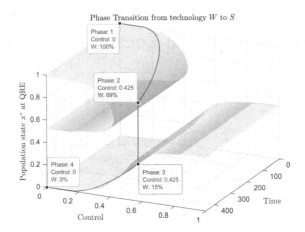

Fig. 1. The Quantal Response Equilibria (QRE) surface projected in time and the transition from the prevailing wasteful technology (*W*) to the efficient technology (*S*) via an induced *catastrophe*. At phase 1, all resources are invested in *W*, and there is no control, i.e., *T*=0. As *T* increases, the population moves along the red line on the QRE surface. At phase 2, *T* reaches the critical value at which the two upper QRE merge into one. At the very next moment, phase 3, when *T* increases slightly above the critical level, the system undergoes an abrupt transition (catastrophe) at which the merged QRE vanish. After this point, *T* is reset to 0, and due to the resulting *hysteresis effect*, the population converges to the new equilibrium at which the (new) technology *S* is adopted.

Assortment Planning for Two-Sided Sequential Matching Markets

Itai Ashlagi[1], Anilesh K. Krishnaswamy[2], Rahul Makhijani[3(✉)],
Daniela Saban[1], and Kirankumar Shiragur[1]

[1] Stanford University, 450 Serra Mall, Stanford, CA 94305, USA
[2] Duke University, Durham, NC 27708, USA
[3] Facebook, 1 Hacker Way, Menlo Park, CA 94025, USA
rahulmakhijani19@gmail.com

Abstract. Two-sided matching platforms provide users with menus of match recommendations. To maximize the number of realized matches between the two sides (referred to as customers and suppliers respectively), the platform must balance the inherent tension between recommending customers more potential suppliers to match with and avoiding potential collisions. We introduce a stylized model to study the above trade-off. The platform offers each customer a menu of suppliers, and customers choose, simultaneously and independently, to either select a supplier from their menu or remain unmatched. Suppliers then see the set of customers that have selected them, and choose to either match with one of these customers or remain unmatched. A match occurs if a customer and a supplier choose each other (in sequence). Agents' choices are probabilistic, and proportional to the public scores of agents in their menu and a score that is associated with the outside option of remaining unmatched. The platform's problem is to construct menus for customers to maximize the number of matches. We show the problem is strongly NP-hard and provide an efficient algorithm that achieves a constant-factor approximation to the optimal expected number of matches. Our algorithm uses bucketing techniques, which group similar suppliers into buckets, together with linear programming based relaxations and rounding. We finally provide simulations to better understand how the algorithm might behave in practice.

The full version of this paper is available at https://arxiv.org/abs/1907.04485.

X. Chen et al. (Eds.): WINE 2020, LNCS 12495, p. 475, 2020.
https://doi.org/10.1007/978-3-030-64946-3

Author Index

Ahunbay, Mete Şeref 147
Arsenis, Makis 191
Ashlagi, Itai 475
Aziz, Haris 341

Barman, Siddharth 356
Bender, Max 220
Benita, Francisco 252
Berger, Ben 206
Bhaskar, Umang 356
Bilò, Vittorio 252, 323
Boehmer, Niclas 31
Bredereck, Robert 59

Chen, Cong 295, 309
Colini-Baldeschi, Riccardo 45
Collina, Natalie 17
Conitzer, Vincent 430, 444, 468
Courcoubetis, Costas 473

Deng, Yuan 444
Drosis, Odysseas 191
Dughmi, Shaddin 444

Eden, Alon 206

Feldman, Michal 206

Giannakopoulos, Yiannis 177
Giessler, Paul 309
Gilbert, Jacob 220
Goel, Ashish 89
Goldberg, Paul W. 384, 401
Gollapudi, Sreenivas 3
Graf, Lukas 237
Gupta, Swati 471

Halpern, Daniel 370
Harks, Tobias 237
Heeger, Klaus 31, 59
Hollender, Alexandros 384

Igarashi, Ayumi 384
Immorlica, Nicole 17

Jalota, Devansh 102
Jiang, Tao 467

Karlin, Anna R. 266
Kavaler, Itay 416
Kleinberg, Robert 191
Knop, Dušan 59
Kollias, Kostas 3
Krishnan, Aditya 220
Krishnaswamy, Anilesh K. 475
Kupfer, Ron 463

Leonardos, Stefanos 473
Leyton-Brown, Kevin 17
Lin, Young-San 467
Lock, Edwin 401
Lucier, Brendan 17

Ma, Will 162
Macault, Emilien 469
Makhijani, Rahul 475
Mamageishvili, Akaki 309, 464
Manurangsi, Pasin 384
Marmolejo-Cossío, Francisco 401
Mestre, Julián 45
Mihalák, Matúš 309
Monaco, Gianpiero 323
Monnot, Barnabé 252
Morgenstern, Jamie 266
Moscardelli, Luca 323

Newman, Neil 17
Nguyen, Thành 467
Niedermeier, Rolf 59

Oesterheld, Caspar 430, 468

Pavone, Marco 102, 465
Penna, Paolo 309
Piliouras, Georgios 252, 473
Plaut, Benjamin 3, 77, 89
Poças, Diogo 177

Procaccia, Ariel D.   370
Pruhs, Kirk   220
Psomas, Alexandros   370

Qi, Qi   102

Ravindran Vijayalakshmi, Vipin   280
Rheingans-Yoo, Ross   461

Saban, Daniela   475
Saberi, Amin   465
Sakos, Iosif   473
Salem, Jad   471
Saraf, Aditya   266
Scarsini, Marco   469
Schiffer, Maximilian   465
Schoenebeck, Grant   119
Schrijvers, Okke   45
Shah, Nisarg   356, 370
Shiragur, Kirankumar   475
Skopalik, Alexander   280

Smorodinsky, Rann   416
Sudhir, K.   470
Suksompong, Warut   384

Tejada, Oriol   464
Tomala, Tristan   469
Tony Ke, T.   470
Tsao, Matthew   465
Tsigonias-Dimitriadis, Alexandros   177

Vetta, Adrian   147
Vinci, Cosimo   252, 323

Wilkens, Christopher A.   45

Xu, Yinfeng   295

Ye, Yinyu   102
Yu, Fang-Yi   119

Zhang, Hanrui   133

Printed in the United States
By Bookmasters